MW01075711

If it's APRIL 2007
and you are still using this Directory,
it's time to order the NEW Edition.

Please visit our website

www.cabells.com

or contact us at

Cabell Publishing Company
Box 5428, Beaumont, Texas 77726-5428
(409) 898-0575
Fax (409) 866-9554

Cabell's Directory
of Publishing Opportunities in

Educational
Curriculum and Methods

VOLUME I A thru J of D
SEVENTH EDITION 2005-2006

David W. E. Cabell, Editor
McNeese State University
Lake Charles, Louisiana

Deborah L. English, Editor
Twyla J. George, Assistant Editor
Lacey E. Earle, Assistant Editor

To order additional copies
visit our web site
www.cabells.com

or contact us at

Box 5428 Beaumont, Texas 77726-5428
(409) 898-0575 Fax (409) 866-9554

$114.95 U.S. for addresses in United States
Price includes shipping and handling for U.S.
Add $50 for surface mail to countries outside U.S.
Add $100 for airmail to countries outside U.S.

ISBN # 0-911753-27-3

ii

iv

vi

viii

Preface

The objective of *Cabell's Directory of Publishing Opportunities in Educational Curriculum and Methods* is to help you publish your ideas.

The *Directory* contains the editor's name(s), address(es), phone and fax number(s), and e-mail and web address(es) for over 360 journals.

To help you in selecting those journals that are most likely to publish your manuscripts the **Index** classifies the journals into twenty-eight different topic areas. In addition, the Index provides information on the journal's type of review process, number of external reviewers and acceptance rate.

To further assist you in organizing and preparing your manuscripts, the *Directory* includes extensive information on the style and format of most journals. If a journal has its own set of manuscript guidelines, a copy of these guidelines is published in the *Directory*. Also, each entry indicates the use of a standard set of publication guidelines by a journal. For example, some journals use the *Chicago Manual of Style* or the *Publication Manual of the American Psychological Association*.

Furthermore, the *Directory* describes the type of review process used by the editor(s) of a journal, type of review, number of reviewers, acceptance rate, time required for review, availability of reviewers comments, fees charged to review or publish the manuscript, copies required and manuscript topics. Information on the journal's circulation, readership and subscription prices are also provided.

Although this *Directory* focuses on journals in the specialized area of **Educational Curriculum and Methods**, the other directory focuses on **Educational Psychology and Administration**. The division of education journals into these two directories more appropriately meets the researcher's need for publishing in his area of specialization.

The decision to place journals in this directory is based on the manuscript topics selected by the editor as well as the journals' guidelines for authors.

Also, the *Directory* includes a section titled **"What is a Refereed Article?"** which tends to emphasize the value of a blind review process and use of external reviewers. However, this section cautions individuals using these criteria to also consider a journal's reputation for quality. Additionally, it indicates that differences in acceptance rates may be the result of different methods used to calculate these percentages and the number of people associated with a particular area of specialization.

How To Use the Directory

TABLE OF CONTENTS
Table of Contents provides over 360 journals to help your locate a publication.

INDEX
Index classifies the journals according to twenty-eight (28) different manuscript topics. It also includes information on the type of review, number of external reviewers, acceptance rate and page number of each journal.

ADDRESS FOR SUBMISSION
Address for Submission provides: the Editor's Name(s), Mailing Address(es), Telephone and Fax numbers(s), and E-mail and Web address(es).

PUBLICATION GUIDELINES
Manuscript Length refers to the length of the manuscript in terms of the number of double-spaced typescript pages.

Copies Required indicates the number of manuscript copies you should submit to the editor.

Computer Submission indicates whether the journal prefers hardcopy (paper) or electronic submissions such as disk, e-mail attachment, or a combination of methods.

Format refers to the type of word processing programs or computer programs the journal requires for reviewing the manuscript. Some examples of these programs are Microsoft Word, WordPerfect, PDF, or RTF.

Fees to Review refers to whether the journal charges a fee to review the manuscript. Knowing this item permits the author to send the required funds with the manuscript.

Manuscript Style refers to the overall style guide the journal uses for text, references within the text and the bibliography. This is usually either the *Chicago Manual of Style* or the *Publication Manual of the American Psychological Association (APA)*.

REVIEW INFORMATION
Type of Review specifies blind, editorial, or optional review methods. A blind review indicates the reviewer(s) does not know who wrote the manuscript. An editorial review indicates the reviewer knows who wrote the manuscript. The term "optional" indicates the author may choose either one of these types of review.

No. of External Reviewers and *No. of In House Reviewers*
These two items refer to the number of reviewers who review the manuscript prior to making a decision regarding the publication of the manuscript. Although the editor attempted to determine whether the reviewers were on the staff of the journal or were outside reviewers, many of the respondents had trouble distinguishing between internal and external reviewers. Thus it may be more accurate to add these two categories and determine the total number of reviewers.

Acceptance Rate refers to the number of manuscripts accepted for publication relative to the number of manuscripts submitted within the last year. The method of calculating acceptance rates varies among journals.

Time to Review indicates the amount of time that passes between the submission of a manuscript and notification to the author regarding the results of the review process.

Reviewer's Comments indicates whether the author can obtain a copy of the reviewer's comments. In some cases, the author needs to request that the editor send these remarks.

Invited Articles indicates the percentage of articles for which the editor requests an individual to write specifically for publication in the journal. The percentage is the number of invited articles relative to the total number of articles that appeared in a journal within the past year.

Fees to Publish refers to whether the journal charges a fee to publish the manuscript. Knowing this item assists the author in his decision to place the manuscript into the review process.

CIRCULATION DATA
Reader indicates the predominant type of reader the publication seeks to attract. These are divided into a group designated as practitioners and professionals, or another group referred to as administrators and counselors in the educational discipline.

Frequency of Issue indicates the number of times a journal will be published in a year.

Copies per Issue indicates the number of copies the journal distributes per issue.

Sponsor/Publisher indicates the journal's affiliation with a professional association, educational institution, governmental agency, and/or publishing company.

Subscribe Price indicates the cost to order a year's subscription unless otherwise indicated.

MANUSCRIPT TOPICS
Manuscript Topics indicates those subjects the journal emphasizes.

MANUSCRIPT GUIDELINES/COMMENTS
Manuscript Guidelines/Comments provides information on the journal's objectives, style and format for references and footnotes that the editor expects the author to follow in preparing his manuscript for submission.

How the Directory Helps You Publish

Although individuals must communicate their ideas in writing, the *Directory* helps the author determine which journal will most likely accept the manuscript. In making this decision, it is important to compare the characteristics of your manuscript and the needs of each journal. The following table provides a framework for making this comparison.

Information Provided by the Directory for Each Journal	Manuscript Characteristics
Topic(s) of Articles Manuscript Guidelines	Theme
Acceptance Rate Percentage of Invited Articles	Significance of Theme
Type of Reader	Methodology and Style
Circulation Review Process	Prestige
Number of Reviewers Availability of Reviewers Comments Time Required for Reviewer	Results of Review

This framework will help the author determine a small number of journals that will be interested in publishing the manuscript. The *Directory* can assist the author in determining these journals, yet a set of unwritten and written laws prevent simultaneous submission of a manuscript to more than one journal. However, a manuscript can be sent to another journal in the event of a rejection by any one publication.

Furthermore, copyright laws and editorial policy of a given publication often require the author to choose only one journal. Consequently, some journals will require the author to sign a statement indicating the manuscript is not presently under review by another publication.

Publication of the manuscript in the proceedings of a professional association does not prevent the author from sending it to a journal, however there usually are some restrictions attached. Most professional associations require that the author acknowledge the presentation of the manuscript at the associate meeting.

Since the author is limited to submission of a manuscript to only one journal and the review process for each journal requires a long period of time, a "query" letter may help the author determine the journal most likely to publish the manuscript.

The query letter contains the following information:

- Topic, major idea or conclusion of the manuscript
- The subject sample, research setting conceptual framework, methodology type of organization or location
- The reasons why the author thinks the journal's readers would be interested in your proposed article
- Asks the editor to make comments or suggestions on the usefulness of this type of article to the journal

While the query letter is helpful in selecting a journal that will be likely to publish the manuscript, the author could use the *Directory* and the framework presented to develop a set of journals which would be likely to publish the manuscript. With this number of possible journals, it makes the sending of a query letter more feasible and tends to achieve the objective of finding the journal most likely to publish the manuscript.

Relating the Theme of the Manuscript to the Topics of Articles Published by Each Journal

To begin the process of choosing the journals to receive the "query" letter and, at some future time, the manuscript, the author needs to examine the similarity between the theme of the manuscript and the editor's needs. The *Directory* describes these needs by listing the topics each publication considers important and the manuscript guidelines. To find those journals that publish manuscripts in any particular area, refer to the topic index.

In attempting to classify the theme, the author should limit his choice to a single discipline. With the increasing specialization in the academic world, it is unlikely that reviewers, editors, or readers will understand an article that requires knowledge of two different disciplines. If these groups do not understand a manuscript, the journal will reject it.

If a manuscript emphasizes an interdisciplinary approach, it is important to decide who will be reading the article. The approach should be to explain the theoretical concepts of one discipline to the specialist in another discipline. The author should not attempt to resolve theoretical issues present in his discipline and explain their implications for specialists in another discipline.

Although the discipline classifications indicate the number of journals interested in your manuscript topic, the manuscript guidelines help the author determine the journals that will most likely have the greatest interest in the manuscript. The manuscript guidelines provide a detailed statement of the criteria for judging manuscripts, the editorial objectives, the readership and the journal's content and approach. This information makes it possible to determine more precisely the congruence between the manuscript and the type of articles the journal publishes. **The *Directory* contains the manuscript guidelines for a large number of journals.**

The Relationship Between the Journal's Acceptance Rate and Significance of the Theme of the Manuscript

In addition to determining the similarity between the topic of the manuscript and the topic of articles published by the journal, an examination of the significance of the theme to the discipline is also an important criterion in selecting a journal. The journals with the lowest acceptance rate will tend to publish those manuscripts that make the most significant contributions to the advancement of the discipline. Since these journals receive a large number of manuscripts, the editors distinguish those manuscripts likely to make a significant contribution to the reader's knowledge.

Defining newness or the contribution of any one study to the understanding of a discipline is difficult. However, it is possible to gain some insights into this definition by asking the following questions:

1. Is the author stating the existence of a variable, trend or problem, not previously recognized by the literature?

2. Is the author testing the interactions of a different set of variables or events?

3. Is the author presenting a new technique to cope with a problem or test an idea not previously presented in the literature?

4. Is the author using a subject sample with different characteristics than previously presented in the literature?

If the manuscript does not satisfy one of the first two categories, it is unlikely that a journal with a low acceptance rate will accept it for publication. Thus, the author should send the manuscript to those journals where the acceptance rate is higher.

Although the *Directory* provides the acceptance rates of manuscripts for many different journals, it is important to examine the data on percentage of invited articles for each journal. A high acceptance rate may result because the editor has asked leaders in the discipline to write articles on a particular subject. These invited articles are usually accepted. Since the author of an unsolicited manuscript competes with the leaders in the discipline, the manuscript will have to make a significant contribution to receive the editor's approval.

The Relationship of the Manuscript's Style and Methodology to the Journal's Readership

Another factor in selecting the journal to receive the manuscript is the journal's readership. The readers of each journal include either, practitioners and professionals, academics, administrators and counselors in educational curriculum and methods, or a combination of these groups.

Since the most important goal for an author is to publish the manuscript, the author should consider the prestige of the journal only after the manuscript has a relatively high probability of being published by more than one journal. This probability is determined by the responses the author received to his query letter and the similarity between the finished manuscript and the needs of the journal.

The method of determining the prestige of a journal varies depending on its readership and the goals of the author. If the readership is primarily administrators or practicing professionals and the goal of the author is to improve the author's image and that of the institution, the journal's circulation would probably be the best indicator of prestige.

In contrast, the author whose goal is to become known among the author's colleagues might consider the type of review process the journal uses as well as its circulation. With a few exceptions, the most prestigious journals with academic readership use a refereed review process.

The Possible Results of the Review Process and the Selection of a Journal to Receive the Manuscript

Despite the fact that a journal with lower prestige would most likely publish the article, the author might be willing to take a chance on a journal with a greater amount of prestige. Since this will decrease the chances of manuscript acceptance, the author should also consider the consequences of rejection. The consequences include the knowledge the author will gain from having his manuscript rejected.

To determine the amount of knowledge the author is likely to gain requires consideration of the number of reviewers the journal uses in the review process, the availability of the reviewer's comments and the time required for the review process. If the journal makes the reviewer's comments available to the author, this provides a great learning opportunity. Also, the more people that review the manuscript, the greater the author's knowledge will be concerning how to improve the present manuscript. Hopefully, the author will transfer the knowledge gained from writing this manuscript to future manuscripts.

Should the review process take a small amount of time relative to a long period of time, the author is provided with a greater opportunity to use this knowledge to revise the manuscript. To assist the author in determining those journals that provide a suitable learning opportunity, each journal in the *Directory* includes information on the number of reviewers, availability of reviewer's comments to the author and time required for review.

Sending the Manuscript

Before sending the manuscript to an editor, the author should write a cover letter, make sure the manuscript is correctly typed, the format conforms to the journal's guidelines and the necessary copies have been included. **The author should always keep a copy of the manuscript.**

The cover letter that is sent with the manuscript makes it easy for the editor to select reviewers and monitor the manuscript while it is in the review process. This letter should include the title of the manuscript, the author name(s), mailing address(es) phone and fax number(s) and e-mail addresses. In addition, this letter should provide a brief description of the manuscript theme, its applicability and significance to the journal's readership. Finally it should request a copy of the reviewer's comments regardless of whether the manuscript is accepted or rejected.

Receipt of the Reviewer's Comments

The reviewers may still reject the article although the author may have followed this procedure and taken every precaution to avoid rejection. When this occurs, the author's attitude should be focused on making those changes that would make the manuscript more understandable to the next editor, and/or reviewer. These changes may include providing additional information and/or presenting the topic in a more concise manner. Also, the author needs to determine whether some error occurred in selecting the journal to receive the manuscript. Regardless of the source of the errors, the author needs to make those changes that will improve the manuscript's chances of being accepted by the next journal to receive it.

Unless the journal specifically requests the author to revise the manuscript for publication, the author should not send the manuscript to the journal that first rejected it. In rejecting the manuscript, the reviewers implied that it could not be revised to meet their standards for publication. Thus, sending it back to them would not improve the likelihood that the manuscript will be accepted.

If your manuscript is accepted, go out and celebrate but write another one very quickly. When you find you're doing something right, keep doing it so you won't forget.

"What is a Refereed Article?"

With some exceptions a refereed article is one that is blind reviewed and has at least two external reviewers. The blind review requirement and the use of external reviewers are consistent with the research criteria of objectivity and of knowledge.

The use of a blind review process means that the author of the manuscript is not made known to the reviewer. With the large number of reviewers and journals, it is also likely that the name of the reviewers for a particular manuscript is not made known to the author. Thus, creating a double blind review process. Since the author and reviewers are frequently unknown, the manuscript is judged on its merits rather than on the reputation of the author and/or the author's influence on the reviewers.

The use of two (2) or more reviewers permits specialists familiar with research similar to that presented in the paper to judge whether the paper makes a contribution to the advancement of knowledge. When two reviewers are used it provides a broader perspective for evaluating the research. This perspective is further widened by the discussion between the editor and reviewers in seeking to reconcile these perspectives.

In contrast to these criteria, some journals that have attained a reputation for quality do not use either a blind review process or external reviewers. The most notable is *Educational Studies in Mathematics* that uses an editorial review process. Its reputation for quality results from its readership whose continual subscription attests to its quality.

In addition to these criteria, some researchers include the journal's acceptance rate in their definition of a refereed journal. However, the method of calculating acceptance rates varies among journals. Some journals use all manuscripts received as a base for computing this rate. Other journals allow the editor to choose which papers are sent to reviewers and calculate the acceptance rate on those that are reviewed that is less than the total manuscripts received. Also, many editors do not maintain accurate records on this data and provide only a rough estimate.

Furthermore, the number of people associated with a particular area of specialization influences the acceptance rate. If only a few people can write papers in an area, it tends to increase the journal's acceptance rate.

Although the type of review process and use of external reviewers is one possible definition of a refereed article, it is not the only criteria. Judging the usefulness of a journal to the advancement of knowledge requires the reader to be familiar with many journals in their specialization and make their own evaluation.

AACE Journal (formerly Educational Technology Review)

ADDRESS FOR SUBMISSION:

Gary Marks, Editor
AACE Journal (formerly Educational
   Technology Review)
   (Electronic)
ONLINE SUBMISSIONS ONLY
AACE
PO Box 3728
Norfolk, VA 23514-3728
USA
Phone: 757-623-7588
Fax: 703-997-8760
E-Mail: pubs@aace.org
Web: www.aace.org/pubs
Address May Change:

PUBLICATION GUIDELINES:

Manuscript Length: Max 30
Copies Required: Online Submission Only
Computer Submission: Yes by Submission
   Form
Format: MS Word, html, or RTF
Fees to Review: 0.00 US$

Manuscript Style:
   American Psychological Association

CIRCULATION DATA:

Reader: Administrators, Professors,
   Reseachers, Developers
Frequency of Issue: Quarterly
Copies per Issue: Online Only
Sponsor/Publisher: (AACE) Assn. for the
   Advancement of Computers in Education
Subscribe Price:
   Free to members

REVIEW INFORMATION:

Type of Review: Blind Review
No. of External Reviewers: 2-4
No. of In House Reviewers: 2
Acceptance Rate: 11-20%
Time to Review: 2-4 Months
Reviewers Comments: Yes
Invited Articles: 0-5%
Fees to Publish: 0.00 US$

MANUSCRIPT TOPICS:
Educational Technology Systems; Higher Education; Secondary/Adolescent Studies

MANUSCRIPT GUIDELINES/COMMENTS:

- Current issues and discussions
- Review papers
- Reports on innovative applications and projects
- Courseware experiences
- Opinions

Note. Research articles should not be submitted to *AACE Journal* but rather are welcome in other AACE journals. For the list of all AACE journals, see: **www.aace.org/pubs**.

2

About the Journal
AACE's member journal is the focal point for AACE members to exchange information between disciplines, educational levels, and information technologies.

The purpose of this exchange should result in the growth of ideas and practical solutions that can contribute toward the improvement of education and learning through information technology. All AACE members receive the *AACE Journal* as a benefit of membership.

Editorial Objectives
AACE publications have the overall objective to advance the knowledge, theory, and quality of teaching and learning at all levels with computing technologies. The international readership of each Journal is multidisciplinary and includes professors, researchers, classroom teachers, developers, teacher educators, and administrators.

Editorial objectives are to:
- Serve as a forum to report the interdisciplinary research, development, integration, and applications of computing in education.
- Contribute toward the professional development of all who seek in-depth yet practical knowledge about the important research results, latest developments and applications of teaching and learning with computers.
- Present articles of interest on educational computing problems.
- Provide creative ideas, practical strategies, and experiences on instruction with computers.
- Offer information on various aspects of computer literacy for educators.
- Provide information on new computer materials, methods of use, and evaluative criteria.

Please read through the guidelines below before submitting your paper.

Journal Content
Contributions for all journals may include research papers, case studies, tutorials, courseware experiences, evaluations, review papers, and viewpoints.

General Guidelines
Material must be original, scientifically accurate, and in good form editorially. The manuscript should be informative, summarizing the basic facts and conclusions, and maintaining a coherence and unity of thought.

Tutorial or how-to-do-it articles should preferably include a section on evaluation. Controversial topics should be treated in a factually sound and reasonably unbiased manner.

The format of headings, tables, figures, citations, references, and other details should follow the (APA) style as described in the *Publication Manual of the American Psychological Association*, 5th edition, available from APA, 750 1st St., NE, Washington, DC 20002 USA.

Preview
Manuscripts sent to the Editor for review are accepted on a voluntary basis from authors. Before submitting an article, please review the following suggestions. Manuscripts received in correct form serve to expedite the processing and prompt reviewing for early publication.

Spelling, punctuation, sentence structure, and the mechanical elements of arrangements, spacing, length, and consistency of usage in form and descriptions should be studied before submission. Due to the academic focus of AACE publications, the use of personal pronoun (I, we, etc.) and present tense is strongly discouraged.

Pre-publication
No manuscript will be considered which has already been published or is being considered by another journal.

Copyright
These journals are copyrighted by the Association for the Advancement of Computing in Education. Material published and so copyrighted may not be published elsewhere without the written permission of AACE.

Author Note(s)
Financial support for work reported or a grant under which a study was made should be noted just prior to the Acknowledgments. Acknowledgments or appreciation to individuals for assistance with the manuscript or with the material reported should be included as a note to appear at the end of the article prior to the References.

Handling of Manuscripts
All manuscripts are acknowledged upon receipt. Review is carried out as promptly as possible. The manuscript will be reviewed by at least two members of the Editorial Review Board, which takes approximately five months. When a decision for publication or rejection is made, the senior author or author designated to receive correspondence is notified. At the time of notification, the author may be asked to make certain revisions in the manuscript, or the Editor may submit suggested revisions to the author for approval.

Presentation
Accepted Submission File Formats - All submissions must be sent in electronic form using the Article Submission Form. **No hard copy submission papers will be accepted**. Do NOT submit compressed files. Do not use any word processing options/tools, such as--strike through, hidden text, comments, merges, and so forth.

Submit your manuscript in either of the following formats:
- **DOC** - Microsoft Word (preferred)
- RTF - Rich Text Format

Manuscripts should be double-spaced and a font size of 12 is preferred.

Length. In general, articles should not exceed 30 double-spaced pages. Long articles or articles containing complex material should be broken up by short, meaningful subheads.

4

Title sheet. Do NOT include a title sheet. Manuscripts are blind reviewed so there should be no indication of the author(s) name on the pages.

Abstract. An informative, comprehensive abstract of 75 to 200 words must accompany the manuscript. This abstract should succinctly summarize the major points of the paper, and the author's summary and/or conclusions.

Tables, Figures & Graphics

All tables and figure graphics must be embedded within the file and of such quality that when printed be in camera-ready form (publication quality). Within the submitted file, number and type captions centered at the top of each table. Figures are labeled at the bottom of the figure, left justified, and numbered in sequence.

Any graphics that go in the article must be submitted as separate files. The highest quality master (e.g. TIF) is preferred. Additionally, the graphics must also be embedded in the correct locations within the document so the copyeditors know the proper placement. Please note that any graphics created in Microsoft Word must also be submitted as separate files.

Graphics, tables, figures, photos, and so forth, must be sized to fit a 6 x 9 publication with margins of: top, 1" inside 1" outside, .75" and bottom, 1" an overall measurement of 4.5 X 6.75 is the absolute limit in size. A table or figure sized on a full size 8.5 by 11 piece of paper does not always reduce and remain legible. Please adhere to the size stipulation or your manuscript will be returned for graphics/figure's or tables to be re-done.

Quotations

Copy all quoted material exactly as it appears in the original, indicating any omissions by three spaced periods. At the close of the quotation, give the complete source including page numbers. A block quote must be a minimum of 40 words or four lines, single spaced.

Terminology and Abbreviations

Define any words or phrases that cannot be found in Webster's Unabridged Dictionary. Define or explain new or highly technical terminology. Write out the first use of a term that you expect to use subsequently in abbreviated form. Abbreviations (i.e., e.g., etc.) are only acceptable in parenthesis, otherwise they must be spelled out, that is, for example, and so forth, respectively. Please avoid other foreign phrases and words such as via.

Program Listings

Program listings will appear with the published article if space permits. Listings should be publication quality. The brand of computer required should be included. Lengthy program listings (more than four 6 x 9 pages) can not be published, but may be made available from the author; a note to that effect should be included in the article.

Citations

Citations should strictly follow *American Psychological Association* (APA) style guide. Examples of references cited within the texts of articles are as follows: (Williams, Allen, & Jones, 1978) or (Moore, 1990; Smith, 1991) or Terrell (1977). In citations, "et al." can only be used after all authors have been cited or referenced with the exception of six or more authors. As per APA all citations must match the reference list and vice versa. Over use of references is discouraged.

References
Authors are responsible for checking the accuracy of all references and that all references cited in the text also appear in the Reference section. All references should be in alphabetical order by author (unnumbered) *American Psychological Association* (APA), 5th edition, style. Citation examples (1) book and (2) periodical:

Knowles, M.S. (1975). *Self-directed learning: A guide for learners and teachers.* New York: Association Press.

Raybould, B. (1995). Performance support engineering: An emerging development methodology for enabling organizational learning. *Performance Improvement Quarterly*, 8(1), 7-22.

Citing Electronic Media
The following forms for citing on-line sources are taken from the *APA* Publication Guidelines, Appendix 3-A, Section I (pp. 218-222). Please see the *APA* manual for additional information on formatting electronic media. A block quote must be a minimum of 40 words or four lines, single spaced (not 20 and double spaced as is presently noted). In citations, et al., can only be used after all authors have been cited or referenced. As per APA all citations must match the reference list and vice versa.

Elements of references to on-line information
Author, I. (date). Title of article. Name of Periodical [On-line], xx. Available: Specify path

Author, I., & Author, I. (date). Title of chapter. In Title of full work [On-line]. Available: Specify path

Author, I., Author, I., & Author, I. (date). Title of full work [On-line]. Available: Specify path

The date element should indicate the year of publication or, if the source undergoes regular revision, the most recent update; if a date cannot be determined, provide an exact date of your search. (p. 219)

An availability statement replaces the location and name of a publisher typically provided for text references. Provide information sufficient to retrieve the material. For example, for material that is widely available on networks, specify the method used to find the material, such as the protocol (Telnet, FTP, Internet, etc.), the directory, and the file name. (p. 219)

Other Electronic Media
Author, I. (Version number) [CD-ROM]. (date). Location of producer/distributor: Name of producer/distributor.

6

Author, I. (date). Title of article [CD-ROM]. Title of Journal, xx, xxx-xxx. Abstract from: Source and retrieval number

Author, I. (date). Name of Software (Version number) [Computer software]. Location of Location of producer/distributor: Name of producer/distributor.

After the title of the work, insert in brackets as part of the title element (i.e., before the period) the type of medium for the material (current examples include CD-ROM, Electronic data tape, cartridge tape, and computer program). (p. 220)

Include the location and name of the producer and distributor if citing an entire bibliographic database. (p. 220)

Please carefully read and adhere to these guidelines. Manuscripts not submitted according to the guidelines will be rejected and returned to the author.

Academic Exchange Quarterly

ADDRESS FOR SUBMISSION:

Melinda Pierson, Michael Lorenzen CoEds
Academic Exchange Quarterly
P O Box 131
Stuyvesant Falls, NY 12174
USA
Phone: 714-278-3573
Fax: 714-278-3110
E-Mail: mpierson@fullerton.edu
Web: http://rapidintellect.com/AEQweb/
Address May Change:

PUBLICATION GUIDELINES:

Manuscript Length: 6-10
Copies Required: Three
Computer Submission: Yes Disk, Email
Format: MS Word doc file type
Fees to Review: 0.00 US$

Manuscript Style:
    See Manuscript Guidelines

CIRCULATION DATA:

Reader: Practicing Teachers, Academics
Frequency of Issue: Quarterly
Copies per Issue: 1,001 - 2,000
Sponsor/Publisher: Rapid Intellect Group
    Inc. URL http://rapidintellect.com/
Subscribe Price: 126.00 US$ Individual
    156.00 US$ Institution

REVIEW INFORMATION:

Type of Review: Blind Review
No. of External Reviewers: 2
No. of In House Reviewers: 2
Acceptance Rate: 21-30%
Time to Review: 1 - 2 Months
Reviewers Comments: Yes
Invited Articles: 0-5%
Fees to Publish: 0.00 US$

MANUSCRIPT TOPICS:
Counseling & Personnel Services; Curriculum Studies; Education
Management/Administration; Educational Psychology; Educational Technology Systems;
English Literature; Health & Physical Education; Higher Education; Library
Science/Information Resources; Reading; Religious Education; ROTC Military Training;
Science Math & Environment; Social Studies/Social Science; Special Education; Teacher
Education; Tests, Measurement & Evaluation

MANUSCRIPT GUIDELINES/COMMENTS:

Call for Manuscripts
Academic Exchange Quarterly, ISSN 1096-1453, independent double-blind-peer-reviewed
print journal, welcomes research, commentary, and other manuscripts that contribute to the
effective instruction and learning regardless of level or subject. See specific Call for
Manuscripts by Keyword.

In addition to faculty submissions, our primary authorship group, we accept articles co-
authored by graduate students and professors. View articles published by your colleagues,
School Index.

8

We encourage <u>doctoral students</u> to position themselves as emerging professionals.

Early submission is encouraged; it facilitates journal's double-blind-peer-reviewed process and offers:

* longer time for revision
* eligibility to have article's abstract posted, greater exposure, on journal's official web portal <u>main page</u>
* early opportunity to be considered for <u>Editors' Choice</u> and/or <u>Monthly Exchange</u>
* often, it is picked up by other publications, e.g., <u>Why Teachers Should Also Write</u>

Procedure, Requirements, Deadline & Editorial Policy
To speed up the process, please read it carefully and observe requirements.

Six simple manuscript submission steps
When your answer is affirmative to all six steps, we guarantee to review your manuscript in 6-9 weeks.

1. I am (we are) college or secondary school teacher(s) or administrator(s)
2. manuscript's length (abstract, text, references) is 2000 - 3000 words; and adheres to the following sample manuscript layout
3. manuscript can be identified by a keyword listed in KEYWORD INDEX
4. there are no tables, figures, charts, mathematical formulas, or foreign script
5. submission is a clean copy - free of metadata, hidden text, and header/footer
6. submission can be made by e-mail as an attachment in MS Word doc file to **academicexchange@yahoo.com**
   * Once you revise properly, we promise to publish it in the next available issue.
   * Submit early and have an opportunity to be considered for Editors' Choice and/or Monthly Exchange

Submission Procedure
Electronic
Send e-mail attachment, MS-Word-doc-file type, to **academicexchange@yahoo.com**. We do not accept zipped or compressed files or over 75 KB in size. Follow <u>sample manuscript layout</u>. **E-mail** will be our way to communicate with you.

Paper
Submit 3 copies to: Academic Exchange Quarterly, P.O. Box 131 Stuyvesant Falls, NY 12174 USA Put on first page: date, author's name, address, title, and 2-3 line academic bio. Pay optional <u>"pm-fee"</u> Switch to ELECTRONIC submission and pay nothing. Submit final version in two formats: one paper copy and one electronic. **Postal mail** will be our way to communicate with you.

1. To ensure rapid quality review, remember that manuscript submission is a step-by-step process. Please adhere to Submission Procedure # 1-12 and Format Requirements # 13-19. See <u>feedback from authors.</u>

2. All articles are accepted with the understanding that they have not been accepted or published elsewhere. We will, however, publish work that has been presented at a conference. Please identify your submission with a proper <u>KEYWORD.</u> Note, we will consider only one-submission-per-author(s)-per-issue.

3. We seek to acknowledge receipt of submissions, Electronic or Paper, within five business days. You will receive <u>manuscript submission number.</u> Use it in all correspondence with this journal. This journal uses several email address, each reserved for a specific function/activity, send one reply to one email address in a timeframe specified by this journal.

4. In general, allow 1-5 months for review and evaluation process, four distinct stages. The timeline depends on author's submission date in relation to publication deadline; plus on reviewers' interest/inclination to read it. Authors can monitor the four stages, by article submission number and title, at <u>track-your-submission.</u> Note, early submission will allow you more time for revision. We welcome your questions.

5. Journal's double-blind-peer-reviewed policy assures that the reviewers do not know the name of the author and vice versa. Authors: to preserve anonymity, before you send your submission, make sure that your name/identity appears only once in the submission, right below paper's title, <u>see sample.</u>

6. In order to receive reviews, you must sign and return by postal mail or e-mail the following <u>Manuscript Authentication & Copyright Agreement.</u> Do not send with your submission. Wait for submission number and then send it promptly. Failure to comply may result in disqualification or penalty fee.

7. Reviewers come from <u>*AEQ* Editorial Staff</u> and may select any manuscript by entry number. Occasionally, *AEQ* may invite a subject specialist outside journal's staff. See <u>Manuscript Reviewing Guidelines.</u> When reviews are completed, you will be notified whether your manuscript was accepted as is, accepted pending revision, or rejected. See journal's <u>acceptance rate.</u> Usually, authors receive all-reviews-in-one: 2-3 reviews are combined into one file/attachment.

8. As you compose your final copy, remember revising and editing is the most important stage in this submission process. Please follow reviewers' notes on how to improve the content and to correct grammar, spelling, and so forth. Your final copy will be read and verified against the reviewers' copy. If there is a conflict between reviewers, use designated review as your guideline.

9. Your final copy must be free of reviewers notes and have all parts: title, 2-3 line author's biography, abstract, text, references... <u>See some lay-out samples,</u> observe Format Requirements.

10. Reviewers have invested time and effort in your manuscript and so should you. Careless or sloppy revision will disqualify your submission from further consideration. You may reapply by paying <u>Redactory Fee</u> and revise again per original instruction. Your article mirrors your scholarship.

11. Authors with papers requiring major revisions are encouraged to take advantage of journal's free of charge <u>Telementor Program.</u>

12. This journal does not offer page proofs, offprints, hard copy of galleys or author's complimentary copy of the issue. Instead, see your library for a free electronic copy or check whether you qualify for <u>FREE</u> paper copy. If you plan to purchase a paper copy, you may want to <u>order it now.</u> Usually, *Academic Exchange Quarterly* is sold out the month it is printed.

Published articles have the following audience:
- print edition, 25, 000+ readers.
- electronic version, hundreds of thousand potential readers, available
  - o world-wide from Gale Group 2-3 months after print edition,
  - o access via three databases:
    - Expanded Academic ASAP
    - Expanded Academic ASAP International
    - Infotrac OneFile
      See your library.

Format Requirements

Because of the interdisciplinary nature of Academic Exchange, no single format of manuscript style is required. Authors are free to use whatever style they see appropriate for their work: APA, CBE, MLA, or Chicago. For a quick review see The Ohio State University Libraries Citation Style Guides. The editors reserve the right to make changes, in accepted manuscripts, for clarity and space considerations.

13. Observe 2000-3000 word article limit (title, authors, academic bio, abstract, text, notes, references). Excess-Page fee is charged for exceeding the set limit.

14. Avoid:
    a. author's information at the end of the article
    b. double spacing (in electronic submission)
    c. metadata, hidden text, and header/footer like footnotes at the end of each page; footnotes should be endnotes visible in normal layout; any special formatting such as Word or WordPerfect footnote functions, special margins or tabs or control characters; hard carriage-returns for line breaks - instead use the automatic word-processing wraparound feature; tracking marks on the side; "Printout Layout" under "View." All text should be left-aligned, unjustified, in uniform font, tracking changes turned off. See sample manuscript layout.
    d. quotation marks if you are using a direct quotation which is longer than two sentences, the quote should be indented five spaces and quotation marks omitted
    e. indention (instead use one line space between consecutive paragraphs)
    f. listing any references not cited in the text
    g. pagination (number pages with pencil on a hard copy if supplied); running head; period, colons, quotation marks, etc... after References, manuscript's title or any subtitle, e.g., References. Subtitle: "Title"
    h. superscripts and subscript (instead use bracketed numbers); in dates and editions write, e.g. 5th or 3rd ed.
    i. word underline and UPPERCASE (use of bold-face or italics is acceptable)
    j. When using bulleted lists, follow journal style a hollow bullet.
    k. Make your title and abstract meaningful as they include important keywords. When researchers search for articles to cite, they search for keywords. If the keywords are missing from the title/abstract, the article will not "pop up" in a literature search. For title and/or abstract length see sample manuscript layout. Avoid citing references in abstract.

15. Avoid tables, figures, charts, appendixes etc... When used, usually, table etc... is published on journal's webpage instead of the print copy. See example, Spring 2002 or Summer 2002. Your table should be able to stand alone: define all abbreviations, make headings descriptive and easily understood. Put it in a separate attachment as TXT file or GIF file type, file size no more than 60 KB. If over 60KB, send a hard copy. In the manuscript, indicate where each table is to be placed as follows: [Figure ONE] To be accepted, you must comply with Table-Figure-Chart-Appendix charge.

16. Types of personal communications: personal interviews, letters, memos, emails, messages from discussion groups and bulletin boards, telephone conversations etc... This journal assumes that any personal communication used by the author has interviewee's knowledge/permission. It should be listed parenthetically within the text and not cited in the list of References. Example: (A. Smith, personal communication: telephone, May 17, 2003).

17. Use English letters only as all other letters and diacritic characters are deleted automatically. If you must have some, like mathematical formula or foreign script, the most economical option is to rewrite mathematical notation; other option is to put in the Appendix as a webpage. See entry #15 above. However, if you insist to be published in journal's print/paper edition then be prepared to comply with camera-ready-page fee. See Table-Figure-Chart-Appendix-charge in entry #15 above.

18. Whilst all care is taken, it is the author's responsibility to ensure that any factual, stylistic and grammatical errors are corrected prior to publication.

Deadline

Academic Exchange Quarterly is published four times a year: Spring, Summer, Fall, Winter. There are **two submission deadlines: regular and short**. All accepted submissions which meet the regular deadline will appear in the given issue. All accepted submissions which fall into the short deadline will appear in the given issue or in later issues.

Issue	regular deadline	publication date
Spring	any time until the end of November	March
Summer	any time until the end of February	June
Fall	any time until the end of May	September
Winter	any time until the end of August	December

Issue	short deadline	publication date
Spring	December and January	March
Summer	March and April	June
Fall	June and July	September
Winter	September and October	December

- Short deadline submissions, to be eligible for publication, must comply with journal's Short Deadline Redactory Fee.
- Authors are encouraged to suggest issue of publication for their manuscripts.

12

Editorial Policy
19. *Academic Exchange Quarterly* retains <u>copyright</u> of anything published in the print journal and/or uploaded to journal's website. For the latter, this journal will not seek copyright agreement.
20. This quarterly does not guarantee that the information on our website, e-mail communication, or journal itself will be accurate, complete, continuously available, or error-free. All information is provided "as is."
21. This journal is not responsible for lost, late, damaged postal mail or e-mail and any resulting publishing consequences.
22. Corrections & Clarifications, any errors of consequence and factual matter will be published in Errata. Please compose 3-5 line text and send to the editor ASAP.
23. This journal does not keep, store or archive submitted paper copies or disks. Submissions are not returned.
24. In a virtual organization environment, it is author's responsibility to monitor manuscript submission process.
25. Finally, remember that journal's associates answering your e-mail or postal mail are not reviewers or editors. They can not pass any judgment or wave any submission requirements.
26. We do not reveal reasons for our publication decisions beyond the one stated in blind reviews. The Copy Editor's decision is final.
27. We reserve the right to remove from publication any submission at any time for any reason.
28. We welcome comments and suggestions: **AEQ@rapidintellect.com**
29.
- Checklist for **submitting your manuscript**: have you
  - read Submission Procedure
  - prepared your manuscript according to Format Requirements
  - noticed that there are NO article processing charges or any other publication fees
  - observed <u>Optional Charges</u> apply when you do not follow Format Requirements; often your department, school or university will cover the expense; we will give you proper <u>Paid-in-full invoice</u>
- Checklist for **submitting your final copy**: have you read entries # 7, 8, 9, 10 in Submission Procedure.
- Observance of the aforesaid Procedure, Requirements, Deadline & Editorial Policy is a material condition for publishing your submission. Failure to comply may result in a redactory fee.
- Payment of Optional Fees (redactory fees) or subscription to the journal etc... has no influence on the blind review process and does not guarantee publication.
- Thanks for selecting *Academic Exchange Quarterly* for your professional needs.

Academic Exchange Quarterly
P.O. Box 131 Stuyvesant Falls, NY 12174 USA
Article submission e-mail: <u>academicexchange@yahoo.com</u>

Action in Teacher Education

ADDRESS FOR SUBMISSION:

John Chiodo & Priscilla Griffith, Eds
Action in Teacher Education
University of Oklahoma
College of Education
114 Collings Hall
Norman, OK 73019-0260
USA
Phone: 405-325-1498
Fax: 405-325-4061
E-Mail: jjchiodo@ou.edu
Web: See Guidelines
Address May Change:

PUBLICATION GUIDELINES:

Manuscript Length: 12-20
Copies Required: Five
Computer Submission: No
Format: N/A
Fees to Review: 0.00 US$

Manuscript Style:
    American Psychological Association

CIRCULATION DATA:

Reader: Academics
Frequency of Issue: Quarterly
Copies per Issue: 4,001 - 5,000
Sponsor/Publisher: Association of Teacher
    Educators
Subscribe Price: 75.00 US$ With Member

REVIEW INFORMATION:

Type of Review: Blind Review
No. of External Reviewers: 3
No. of In House Reviewers: 0
Acceptance Rate: 20-25%
Time to Review: 6 Months
Reviewers Comments: Yes
Invited Articles: 0-5%
Fees to Publish: 0.00 US$

MANUSCRIPT TOPICS:
Teacher Education

MANUSCRIPT GUIDELINES/COMMENTS:

Website is **www.siu.edu/departments/coe/ate/media/ate_jrn2l.htm**

Content
Most journal issues will have thematic and nonthematic sections. The journal provides a forum for the exchange of information and ideas concerning the improvement of teacher education. Manuscripts submitted should reflect this purpose. Manuscripts should concern concepts, practices, or research studies that have implications and applicability for practitioners involved with teacher education.

Style
Manuscripts must adhere strictly to guidelines set in the most current *Publication Manual of the American Psychological Association.*

Length
The manuscript, including all references, charts, figures, and tables, generally should not exceed 20 pages.

Typing
Double-space all text, with 1½ inch margins all round. Please place tables, charts, figures, or illustrations at the end of the manuscript on separate pages.

Cover Page
Include the following information on a separate sheet.
1. Title of the manuscript.
2. Thematic or nonthematic topic.
3. Date of submission.
4. Author's name, complete mailing address, business and home phone numbers, institutional affiliation, and address.
5. Bibliographical information about each author, which may not exceed 30 words per author.

Abstract
Describe the essence of the manuscript in 100-150 words on a separate sheet of paper at the beginning of the manuscript. Do not include your name or any other identifying information on the abstract or the manuscript.

Form
Send the following to the editors.
1. Hard copy: Send five copies of the manuscript and abstract, along with one cover page.
2. Computer disk: Please do not send a computer disk with your initial Submission. If your manuscript is accepted, we will then require a disk to accompany your revised manuscript.

Mailing Address
Manuscripts, editorial correspondence, and any questions should be sent to *Action in Teacher Education*, John Chiodo and Priscilla Griffith, Editors.

Authors will be notified of the receipt of the manuscript via email. After an initial review by the editors, those manuscripts that meet specifications will be sent to reviewers. Those that do not will be returned to the authors. Manuscripts are subject to review by members of the Professional Journal Committee, editorial reviewers, and editors. Points of view and opinions are those of the individual authors and are not necessarily those of the Association. Permission to reproduce articles must be requested from the editors. The journal editors reserve the right to make final editorial changes.

ADE Bulletin

ADDRESS FOR SUBMISSION:

David Laurence, Editor
ADE Bulletin
Association of Deaprtments of English
26 Broadway 3rd Floor
New York, NY 10004-1789
USA
Phone: 646-576-5137
Fax: 646-835-4056
E-Mail: dsteward@mla.org
Web: www.ade.org
Address May Change:

PUBLICATION GUIDELINES:

Manuscript Length: 16-20
Copies Required: No Paper Copy Required
Computer Submission: Yes email
Format: MS Word
Fees to Review: 0.00 US$

Manuscript Style:
, MLA

CIRCULATION DATA:

Reader: Academics, Administrators
Frequency of Issue: 3 Times/Year
Copies per Issue: 3,001 - 4,000
Sponsor/Publisher: Modern Language
   Association
Subscribe Price: 27.00 US$ Individual
   30.00 US$ Institution

REVIEW INFORMATION:

Type of Review: Editorial Review
No. of External Reviewers: 0
No. of In House Reviewers: 2
Acceptance Rate: 21-30%
Time to Review: 1 - 2 Months
Reviewers Comments: Yes
Invited Articles: 80-90%
Fees to Publish: 0.00 US$

MANUSCRIPT TOPICS:
Adult Career & Vocational; Education Management/Administration; English Literature;
Higher Education; Languages & Linguistics; Reading; Teacher Education

MANUSCRIPT GUIDELINES/COMMENTS:

The *ADE Bulletin* is published three times a year by the Association of Departments of
English, a subsidiary of the Modern Language Association. The *Bulletin* prints articles and
surveys dealing with professional, pedagogical, curricular, and departmental issues.
Manuscripts should be prepared according to the *MLA Style Manual* and submitted as a Word
attachment to **dsteward@mla.org** or in two copies to the editor at the address above.

ADFL Bulletin

ADDRESS FOR SUBMISSION:

Nelly Furman, Editor
ADFL Bulletin
ELECTRONIC SUBMISSION
  ENCOURAGED
(adfl@mla.org)
26 Broadway, 3rd Floor
New York, NY 10004-1789
USA
Phone: 646-576-5134
Fax: 646-458-0030
E-Mail: adfl@mla.org
Web: www.adlf.org
Address May Change:

PUBLICATION GUIDELINES:

Manuscript Length: 10-20
Copies Required: Two
Computer Submission: Yes Encouraged
Format: N/A
Fees to Review: 0.00 US$

Manuscript Style:
   , MLA

CIRCULATION DATA:

Reader: Academics, Administrators
Frequency of Issue: 3 Times/Year
Copies per Issue: 1,001 - 2,000
Sponsor/Publisher: Association of
   Departments of Foreign Languages
Subscribe Price: 21.00 US$

REVIEW INFORMATION:

Type of Review: Blind Review
No. of External Reviewers: 2
No. of In House Reviewers: 2
Acceptance Rate: 50%
Time to Review: 2 - 3 Months
Reviewers Comments: Yes
Invited Articles: 50% +
Fees to Publish: 0.00 US$

MANUSCRIPT TOPICS:
Education Management/Administration; Foreign Language; Languages & Linguistics;
Management & Pedagogy

MANUSCRIPT GUIDELINES/COMMENTS:

About the Journal
The *ADFL Bulletin* is a refereed journal published three times a year by the Association of
Departments of Foreign Languages, a subsidiary of the Modern Language Association. The
ADFL Bulletin prints essays dealing with professional, pedagogical, curricular, and
departmental matters.

Adolescence

ADDRESS FOR SUBMISSION:

Editor
Adolescence
Libra Publishers, Inc.
3089C Clairmont Drive, PMB 383
San Diego, CA 92117
USA
Phone: 858-571-1414
Fax: 858-571-1414
E-Mail:
Web:
Address May Change:

PUBLICATION GUIDELINES:

Manuscript Length: Any up to 40
Copies Required: Two
Computer Submission: No
Format: N/A
Fees to Review: 0.00 US$

Manuscript Style:
        American Psychological Association

CIRCULATION DATA:

Reader: Academics
Frequency of Issue: Quarterly
Copies per Issue: 2,001 - 3,000
Sponsor/Publisher: Libra Publishers, Inc.
Subscribe Price: 100.00 US$ Individual
        143.00 US$ Institution

REVIEW INFORMATION:

Type of Review: Blind Review
No. of External Reviewers: 2
No. of In House Reviewers: 2
Acceptance Rate: 11-20%
Time to Review: 2 - 3 Months
Reviewers Comments: No
Invited Articles: 0-5%
Fees to Publish: 1.00 US$
        18.00 US$ Opt/Early Publication

MANUSCRIPT TOPICS:
Counseling & Personnel Services; Curriculum Studies; Educational Psychology;
Secondary/Adolescent Studies; Tests, Measurement & Evaluation

MANUSCRIPT GUIDELINES/COMMENTS:

General Policy
Adolescence is not dominated by a single point of view and wishes to present as many views as possible. It relies for its contents mainly on solicited material, but ideas and suggestions will be welcomed by the editor. Authors should not submit manuscripts; they should write to us about them and furnish short abstracts first. Material submitted should be accompanied by a stamped, self-addressed envelope to insure safe return.

Manuscripts, References, and Reprints
Manuscripts must be typewritten, double-spaced, on one side of the page, and in duplicate. Footnotes, charts, tables, graphs, etc. should be kept to a minimum and submitted in the original, camera-ready copy. (We prefer that when practical, the information contained in the material be incorporated into the text instead.) References to books and articles should follow the *APA* style.

Authors will be furnished galley proofs, which must be returned to the editor within two days. Corrections should be kept to a minimum. A schedule of reprint costs and order blanks for reprints will be sent with galley proofs.

Book Reviews

Adolescence contains a substantial book review section. In each issue, a large number of books will be described in abstract form. More space may be devoted to some books deemed to warrant extensive review, but this will not be done at the expense of the larger number of brief reviews.

Publishers are invited to send copies of books they would like us to review. Naturally, we cannot promise that all books submitted will be reviewed. Book reviews appear in alphabetical order by means of authors.

Adult Basic Education: An Interdisciplinary Journal for Adult Literacy Educators

ADDRESS FOR SUBMISSION:

Ken Melichar, Editor
Adult Basic Education: An Interdisciplinary
    Journal for Adult Literacy Educators
Piedmont College
Department of Social Sciences
P O Box 10
Demorest, GA 30535
USA
Phone: 706-778-3000
Fax: 706-776-2811
E-Mail: kmelichar@piedmont.edu
Web: www.coabe.org/journal/abe_journal
Address May Change: 12/31/2005

PUBLICATION GUIDELINES:

Manuscript Length: 21-25
Copies Required: Four
Computer Submission: Yes Disk, Email
Format: N/A
Fees to Review: 0.00 US$

Manuscript Style:
        American Psychological Association

CIRCULATION DATA:

Reader: Practicing Teachers
Frequency of Issue: 3 Times/Year
Copies per Issue: 1,001 - 2,000
Sponsor/Publisher: Commission on Adult
    Basic Education
Subscribe Price: 30.00 US$

REVIEW INFORMATION:

Type of Review: Blind Review
No. of External Reviewers: 3
No. of In House Reviewers: 1
Acceptance Rate: 40%
Time to Review: 1 - 2 Months
Reviewers Comments: Yes
Invited Articles: 0-5%
Fees to Publish: 0.00 US$

MANUSCRIPT TOPICS:
Adult Career & Vocational; Adult Literacy

MANUSCRIPT GUIDELINES/COMMENTS:

Types of Manuscripts
Critical essays, research of all types, philosophical and theoretical pieces, and other scholarly work of relevance to those working in adult literacy education.

Review Criteria
1.   Practical relevance to adult literacy education.
2.   Importance of the topic or problem.
3.   Soundness of the approach.
4.   Soundness of inferences and conclusions.
5.   Organization, writing quality, and readability.

Manuscript Specifications

1. All manuscripts must conform to the guidelines set forth in the *Publication Manual of the American Psychological Association* (5th edition). Authors are asked to keep in mind that the readership for this journal consists primarily of adult literacy practitioners.
2. All manuscripts must be double-spaced with 1.5-inch margins at the top, bottom, and sides.
3. Most manuscripts should not exceed 5,000 words.
4. A removable cover page must be attached to each manuscript. This cover page should include:
    a) the title of the manuscript;
    b) the name, complete address and phone number, title, and institutional affiliation of each author;
    c) any necessary notes identifying the contributions of colleagues of or any oral presentation of contents of the manuscript;
    d) a typed, dated, and signed statement reading as follows:

    I hereby confirm the assignment of first publication rights to the manuscript named above in all forms to the Commission on Adult Basic Education, effective if and when it is accepted for publication in the ADULT BASIC EDUCATION: AN INTERDISCIPLINARY JOURNAL FOR ADULT LITERACY EDUCATORS. I warrant that my manuscript is original work and has not been accepted for publication by another periodical. I further warrant that my work does not infringe upon any copyright or statutory rights of others, does not contain libelous statements, and that editorial board members, staff, and other officers of the Commission on Adult Basic Education are indemnified against all costs, expenses, and damages arising from any breach of the fore going in regard to this manuscript. Finally, I acknowledge that the Commission on Adult Basic Education is relying on this statement in any publishing of the manuscript's information.

5. The first page of the manuscript must repeat the title (but not the authors' names) and include a clearly written abstract of approximately 100 words.

6. Tables should be used sparingly, if at all, and must be explained in the text.

7. Figures should be used only when absolutely necessary. If figures are used, the authors must be prepared to submit camera-ready copy at time of acceptance.

Number of Copies

Four complete copies of the manuscript must be submitted on standard bond or copy paper. Authors should retain a copy of the manuscript; no copies will be returned.

Adult Education Quarterly

ADDRESS FOR SUBMISSION:

B. Courtenay & R. Hill, Co-Editors
Adult Education Quarterly
University of Georgia
Department of Adult Education
River's Crossing, Room 422
850 College Station Road
Athens, GA 30602
USA
Phone: 706-542-2214
Fax: 706-542-4024
E-Mail: bcourt@coe.uga.edu
Web: http://www.uga.edu/aeq/
Address May Change:

PUBLICATION GUIDELINES:

Manuscript Length: Max 7,500 words
Copies Required: One
Computer Submission: Yes Email, Disk
Format: MS Word
Fees to Review: 0.00 US$

Manuscript Style:
American Psychological Association

CIRCULATION DATA:

Reader: , Scholars & Practitioners
Frequency of Issue: Quarterly
Copies per Issue: 2,001 - 3,000
Sponsor/Publisher: American Association
of Adult & Continuing Education
(AAACE) / Sage Publications
Subscribe Price: See Website
67.00 US$ Individual Print Only
229.00 US$ Institution Print+ E-access

REVIEW INFORMATION:

Type of Review: Blind Review
No. of External Reviewers: 3
No. of In House Reviewers: 0
Acceptance Rate: 11-30%
Time to Review: 2 - 3 Months
Reviewers Comments: Yes
Invited Articles: No Reply
Fees to Publish: 0.00 US$

MANUSCRIPT TOPICS:
Adult Career & Vocational

MANUSCRIPT GUIDELINES/COMMENTS:

AEQ Mission Statement
The *Adult Education Quarterly (AEQ)* is a scholarly refereed journal committed to advancing the understanding and practice of adult and continuing education. The journal strives to be inclusive in scope, addressing topics and issues of significance to scholars and practitioners concerned with diverse aspects of adult and continuing education. *AEQ* publishes research employing a variety of methods and approaches, including (but not limited to) survey research, experimental designs, case studies, ethnographic observations and interviews, grounded theory, phenomenology, historical investigations, and narrative inquiry as well as articles that address theoretical and philosophical issues pertinent to adult and continuing education. Innovative and provocative scholarship informed by diverse orientations is encouraged, including (but not limited to) positivism, post-positivism, constructivism, critical theory, feminism, race-based/Africentric, gay/lesbian, and poststructural/postmodern theories.

22

AEQ aims to stimulate a problem-oriented, critical approach to research and practice, with an increasing emphasis on inter-disciplinary and international perspectives. The audience includes researchers, students, and adult and continuing education practitioners of many orientations including teachers, trainers, facilitators, resource persons, organizational developers, community organizers, and policy designers.

Guidelines for Contributors
The *Adult Education Quarterly* is committed to the dissemination of knowledge produced by disciplined inquiry in the field of adult and continuing education. Three criteria are used in the review and selection process. First, articles must significantly advance knowledge and practice. Second, all material must be accurate and technically correct. Finally, articles must be well-crafted and well-written. To facilitate the preparation and submission of manuscripts, we offer the following information, guidelines, and procedures.

General Information
Journal Address:
University of Georgia
Department of Adult Education
River's Crossing, Room 422
850 College Station Road
Athens, GA 30602, USA
Phone: (706) 542-2214; Fax: (706) 542-4024
E-Mail: **bcourt@coe.uga.edu**; Web: **http://www.coe.uga.edu/aeq/**

Editorial Staff:
Editors
Bradley Courtenay, University of Georgia
Robert Hill, University of Georgia

Book Review Editors
Mary Alfred, University of Wisconsin-Milwaukee
Barbara J. Daley, University of Wisconsin-Milwaukee

Editorial Associate
Elisabeth Bennett, University of Georgia

Organizational Sponsorship
American Association for Adult and Continuing Education (AAACE)
Commission of Professors of Adult Education (CPAE)
4380 Forbes Blvd.
Lanham, MD 20706 USA
Phone: 301-918-1913; Fax: 301-918-1846

Scope
AEQ is a blind-review scholarly journal committed to the dissemination of research and theory that advances the understanding and practice of adult and continuing education.

Types of Articles Published
- Research approaches including (but not limited to): survey research, experimental designs, case studies, ethnographic observations and interviews, grounded theory, phenomenology, historical investigations, and narrative inquiry
- Inquiry orientations including (but not limited to): positivism, post-positivism, constructivism, critical theory, feminism, race-based/Africentric, gay/lesbian, and poststructural/postmodern theories
- Theory building and philosophical analysis
- Critical integrative reviews of adult and continuing education literature
- Forum (position statements or reasoned critiques of articles previously printed in *AEQ*)
- Essay reviews (commissioned by the editors)
- Book reviews (contact the book review editor; see the book review section)
- "To the Editor" comments and contributions

Editorial Style
Publication Manual of the American Psychological Association (fourth edition).

Preparation for Submission
Prospective authors might consider the following strategies in preparing manuscripts for *AEQ:*
- Study the Editorial Policy and its sections on guidelines to ensure that your manuscript falls within the scope of the journal and will meet stylistic requirements.
- Consider the "Review Criteria" (see that section of the Editorial Policy) in developing and crafting your manuscript.
- Study back issues of *AEQ* and its predecessor, *Adult Education*, focusing especially on articles of purpose and form similar to your manuscript.
- Ask at least two colleagues who are insightful and constructive in their appraisals to critically review the manuscript before submitting it to *AEQ*.

Technical and Stylistic Requirements
For the editorial process to begin, all submissions must meet the following technical and stylistic requirements:

Typed Copy
Submit typed, **double-spaced** copy with numbered pages, using one inch margins on all sides.

Number of Copies
Submit one paper copy and one electronic (on either PC or Mac platform by either a disk or by email attachment). We would prefer that the manuscript be in MS Word. Be sure to label the disk or email message with the platform and word processing software you are using. Authors should retain a copy of their manuscripts. The editors are not responsible for returning copies to authors.

Article Length
Articles generally should not exceed 7500 words, including charts, tables, and bibliography.

24

Title Page
On the title page, indicate the following: title of paper; full name(s) of author(s), author titles and institutional affiliations, postal addresses, phone numbers, fax numbers, and email addresses; brief acknowledgement of the contribution of colleagues or students, if warranted; statement of place and date of previous oral presentation, if any; and date of submission.

Abstract
In 150 words or less, summarize the purpose, approach, and conclusions of the paper in an abstract immediately following the title page. Include only the title of the paper on   this   and subsequent pages.

Text
Repeat a shortened version of the title of the manuscript (a running head) on the top of each page of the text. The name of the author(s) must not appear on any page, other than through standard reference usage.

Stylistic Requirements
Manuscripts submitted to *AEQ* must be grammatically correct and stylistically consistent. *AEQ* uses the *Publication Manual of the American Psychological Association*, fourth edition. Consult this publication for rules governing references and citations as well as other elements of grammar and style.

Warrant Statement
Any submission must include a typed, dated, and signed warrant statement assigning first publication rights to AAACE effective if and when it is accepted for publication by the editors. Manuscripts cannot be processed for publication until the editors of *AEQ* have received this signed statement, worded as follows:

> I hereby confirm the assignment of first publication rights only in and to the manuscript named above in all forms and media to AAACE effective if and when it is accepted for publication by the *AEQ* editorial board. I warrant that my manuscript is original work and has not bee accepted for publication by another periodical. I further warrant that my work (including tables, figures, photographs, and other illustrative material) does not infringe on the copyright or statutory rights of others, does not contain libelous statements, and that the editorial board members, staff, and officers of AAACE are indemnified against costs, expenses, and damages arising from any breach of the foregoing in regard to the manuscript. Finally, I acknowledge that *AEQ* is relying on this statement in any publishing of this manuscript's information.

Manuscripts submitted to *AEQ* should not be under consideration for publication by any other journals, nor should they have been published previously in any form. A paper may, however, have been presented at a meeting or conference. In such cases, the author should state where and when such a paper was presented. After acceptance, a paper may not be published elsewhere without written permission from AAACE and/or CPAE.

Letter of Transmittal
Attach a letter addressed to the editors indicating the title of the manuscript, date of submission, and all authors with their institutional affiliations.

Editorial Procedure
AEQ editorial staff initially reviews all manuscript submissions for compliance with *AEQ* editorial policy. If the manuscript fails to fall within the scope and stylistic guidelines of the journal, it is returned to the authors. If a manuscript is in accord with the scope of the journal and meets submission guidelines, all references to the author name and institution are removed from the manuscript, and it is submitted for blind reviews to three *AEQ* consulting editors. Each consulting editor is a professional scholar judged competent to appraise such manuscripts.

In compliance with advice of consulting editors, the editors make one of four decisions: *accept*; conditional accept, contingent upon major revisions; reject and encourage revision; or reject. In the case of conditional acceptance, the editors will specify necessary revisions in writing to the author. When revisions are completed and the editors accept a manuscript, the editors will then notify and inform the author(s) about the next steps in the publication process.

Review Criteria
In seeking to advance the understanding and practice of adult and continuing education, the journal strives to be inclusive in scope and aims to stimulate a problem-oriented, critical approach to research and practice, with an increasing emphasis on inter-disciplinary and international perspectives. The following are used to review scholarly papers submitted to *AEQ*:

Importance of the Problem
A problem or subject addressed by a manuscript should contribute to knowledge or theory pertinent to adult and continuing education. Importance is enhanced when a paper promotes understanding or improvement of practice.

Background
Through the abstract and a brief introduction, readers should be provided with sufficient background information to understand the problem being addressed.

Problem/Purpose
The purpose of the paper should be clearly and unambiguously stated. This typically requires a clearly described research problem.

Literature Review
Research and scholarship should be linked to relevant empirical and theoretical literature. The applicability of the research and the quality of the discussion are more important than the length of the literature review.

Methodology
The approach and procedures must be appropriate for addressing the stated research problem(s) and purpose(s).

Findings
Findings must be presented and documented to show clear relationships to the purpose(s) and research question(s). Evidence needed to support conclusions must be clearly identified and amply arrayed, including (but not limited to) the presentation of statistics, charts, and graphs; use of quotations; observational data; references; and citations.

Conclusions
Conclusions and logical inferences should be pertinent, clearly drawn, and convincingly supported by evidence.

Readability
All manuscripts must be well organized, well written, and readable.

Book Reviews
The book review editor solicits, edits, and manages the book review process. Suggestions for books to be reviewed or nominations to review books should be submitted to:

Book Review Editors
Mary Alfred and Barbara J. Daley
University of Wisconsin-Milwaukee
Adult & Continuing Education
Administrative Leadership, Enderis Hall
P.O. Box 413
Milwaukee, WI 53201-0413
Phone: 414-229-4311 or 414-229-5495; Fax: 414-229-5300

Subscription Prices
Individual (Print Only) $67.00 US / £45.00 GBP
Institution: Combined (Print & E-access) $229.00 US / £153.00 GBP
Electronic only & Print only subscriptions are available at a discounted rate.

ALAN Review (The)

ADDRESS FOR SUBMISSION:

James Blasingame, Lori A. Goodson, Eds
ALAN Review (The)
Arizona State University
Attn: Dr. Blasingame
Dept of English / English Education
P O Box 870302
Tempe, AZ 85287-0302
USA
Phone:
Fax:
E-Mail: james.blasingame@asu.edu
Web:
Address May Change:

PUBLICATION GUIDELINES:

Manuscript Length: 11-15
Copies Required: Three
Computer Submission: Yes Disk, Email
Format: MS Word
Fees to Review: 0.00 US$

Manuscript Style:
, MLA

CIRCULATION DATA:

Reader: Academics
Frequency of Issue: 3 Times/Year
Copies per Issue: 2,001 - 3,000
Sponsor/Publisher: NCTE
Subscribe Price: 20.00 US$

REVIEW INFORMATION:

Type of Review: Blind Review
No. of External Reviewers: 2-3
No. of In House Reviewers:
Acceptance Rate: 35%
Time to Review: 2 - 3 Months
Reviewers Comments: Yes
Invited Articles: 11-20%
Fees to Publish: 0.00 US$

MANUSCRIPT TOPICS:
Adolescent Literature; English Literature

MANUSCRIPT GUIDELINES/COMMENTS:

The *Assembly* publishes The ALAN Review three times each year (fall, winter, and spring) with a current circulation of 2,500. The journal contains articles on YA literature and its teaching, interviews with authors, reports on publishing trends, current research on YA literature, a section of reviews of new books, and ALAN membership news. An Electronic Archive of Past Issues is available. The ALAN Review co-editors are James Blasingame (**James.Blasingame@asu.edu**), and Lori Atkins Goodson (**lagoodson@cox.net**). Correspondence may also be sent to: James Blasingame, The ALAN Review, ASU English Dept., P.O. Box 870302, Tempe, AZ 85287-0302.

Submitting the Manuscript. Send three clear copies and a disk of the manuscript to: James Blasingame. Articles submitted only by facsimile or e-mail cannot be considered, except when sent from overseas.

Deadlines. Please follow these deadlines if you wish to have your article considered for a particular issue of The ALAN Review: FALL ISSUE Deadline: MAY 15; WINTER ISSUE Deadline: OCTOBER 15; SPRING ISSUE Deadline: FEBRUARY 15. Please note that the journal will be organized to reflect the following themes in each issue, but that all manuscript/article submissions do not have to focus on one of the themes to receive equal consideration for publication: Winter 2005 Issue: The Art of Young Adult Literature. These themes are intended to be flexible and YA enthusiasts submitting manuscripts are encouraged to interpret these themes in a variety of ways.

Alternatives Journal

ADDRESS FOR SUBMISSION:

Tara Flynn, Executive Editor
Alternatives Journal
University of Waterloo
Faculty of Environmental Studies
Waterloo, ON N2L 3G1
Canada
Phone: 519-888-4442
Fax: 519-746-0292
E-Mail: editor@alternativesjournal.ca
Web: www.alternativesjournal.ca
Address May Change:

PUBLICATION GUIDELINES:

Manuscript Length: 500-2,500 words
Copies Required: Three
Computer Submission: Yes Email
Format: MS Word
Fees to Review: 0.00 US$

Manuscript Style:
    See Manuscript Guidelines

CIRCULATION DATA:

Reader: Academics, Practicing Teachers,
    Administrators, Students, Policy Makers
Frequency of Issue: Bi-Monthly
Copies per Issue: 4,700 - 5,000
Sponsor/Publisher: Non Profit Corp. &
    University
Subscribe Price: 37.45 CAN$ Individual
    80.25 CAN$ Institution
    64.00 CAN$ Individual - 2 year subsc.

REVIEW INFORMATION:

Type of Review: Blind Review
No. of External Reviewers: 2
No. of In House Reviewers: 1
Acceptance Rate: 21-30%
Time to Review: 2 - 3 Months
Reviewers Comments: Yes
Invited Articles: 0-5%
Fees to Publish: 0.00 US$

MANUSCRIPT TOPICS:
Ecology; Environmental and Social Justice; Environmental Issues/Development;
Environmental Thought; Policy & Action; Science Math & Environment

MANUSCRIPT GUIDELINES/COMMENTS:

Manuscript topics cover a broad range of environmental issues: international development, sense of place/community, corporate power, market/individual rights vs. common goods, tourism and environment, energy, transportation, urban planning, culture, desire, good work, activism, climate change, food, health and eco-restoration.

Alternatives is a bi-monthly journal dedicated to in-depth analysis of environmental issues, including ecological, social and economic dimensions. It combines the learned rigour of an academic journal with the accessible style and format of a general-audience magazine. This unique hybrid has proved itself by its staying power: the journal has been publishing continuously in Canada since 1971, making it the oldest environmental policy journal in the country. *Alternatives* is published by Alternatives Inc., a non-profit charitable corporation. *Alternatives* aims to publish the best environmental writing in the country -- writing that is engaging to read and that provides a deeper level of analysis and insight than can be gained from the mainstream press. We invite feature articles, shorter reports, notes, interviews, resource guides, visual images related to article themes, cultural commentary and humour.

Features are of about 2000-4000 words and cover a topic in-depth. Features may be written in an essay style where the author ruminates on a topic, an investigative style, where the author tells a story based on interviews with stakeholders and published material, or an academic style that sets out a logical framework and systematically explores an issue based on the author's previous work and that of others in the field. Endnotes are acceptable for a feature article. Feature articles must meet the highest standards in terms of the analytical rigour and reliability of the information presented. However, they must also be lively, well written and accessible to a non-expert readership. Authors are encouraged to use illustrative cases for theoretical or general points and to avoid using specialized language (i.e., jargon). If possible, authors should supply contact names and addresses for readers to find further information about the topic. Manuscripts are subject to review by experts in the field. Acceptance of a manuscript, or the assignment of a commission, does not guarantee publication.

Reports (up to 1500 words) are less analytical than features and are usually written to convey a story or inform the reader of new initiatives or recent developments in policy, thought, technology or action. They are usually written in a balanced, news style approach with some analytical content, but other styles will be considered: e.g., case study, research report, recounting a personal experience, etc. Shorter reports normally do not have endnotes.

Notes (up to 500 words) are intended to inform busy readers about interesting topics that can be summarized quickly. They are written in a to-the-point news style.

Themes
Each issue of *Alternatives* contains both theme and non-theme material. Recent themes have included Industrial Redesign, Green Energy, Community Redesign, Biodiversity, Urban Transportation, and Food. Upcoming themes are listed on our web site. Theme-related submissions should clearly identify which theme is being submitted for.

Readers
Alternatives has built a subscriber base that is exceptionally large by Canadian journal standards. The journal has about 2300 subscribers and typically sells another 1000 to 2000 copies of each issue, mostly on news stands or for course texts. It can be found in most university and college libraries. Readers include educators and students, consultants, activists, and policy makers.

Procedure for Submission
Although we do consider completed manuscripts, we prefer to work with authors from the proposal stage to a finished manuscript. Proposals should explain what you plan to cover and how you will proceed with the writing. The proposal should convey your approach, tone, and style; and should answer the following: What are your specific qualifications to write on this topic? What sources do you plan to use? What is your essential argument? How long do you anticipate the article being?

If you have not published with *Alternatives* before, please include samples of past published material in your proposal submission. Keep in mind that our lead time is several months and submissions should not be so time-bound that they will appear dated once published.

Both proposals and finished manuscripts should be submitted electronically, either as an e-mail attachment or a posted disk. While we do not normally accept material that has already appeared in other major publications, we will consider articles that have already received a very limited or regional audience.

Revisions

Initial acceptance of a proposal or a manuscript does not guarantee publication. After initial acceptance, authors are expected to work closely with an *Alternatives* editor to revise the manuscript. Two to four iterations are usually necessary before a manuscript is finalized. Revisions or additions to articles accepted for publication must be sent within two weeks after they are requested. Final copy is sent to authors for approval. Although the author's views are taken into account, the title to be used on the article is chosen by *Alternatives'* editors.

Payment

Honouraria are negotiated with the author. Payment is made upon publication. Full time academics are not paid.

Copyright

Alternatives purchases first North American serial rights. We distribute some articles for not-for-profit research and educational purposes. These include some ongoing arrangements with library and research databases that make our articles available as reference materials. We also promote the copying of articles for use as university course texts.

Style Guidelines

Alternatives requires all submissions to be written in a non-sexist manner. Quotes that include sexist terms should be avoided. If a sexist term is unavoidable, it should be followed by "[sic]". For reference see Bobbye D. Sorres, *The Nonsexist Communicator* (New Jersey: Prentice-Hall, 1983).

Alternatives follows the *Oxford Canadian Dictionary* for spelling and the *Globe and Mail* and Canadian Press Style Guides for style.

At the end of feature articles, under the subheading Notes, authors should provide explanatory notes and references. A literary style of documentation should be used, presented as follows:

For a Journal
A.B. Author, "Article Title," Journal Name, 2:3 (1982), pp. 123-25.

For a Book
A.B. Author, Book Title (Place of publication: Publisher, 1982), p. 101.

Figures and tables should appear on separate pages, be numbered and have appropriate titles. One original copy of tables and graphics should be submitted with the manuscript. These may

32

be black ink drawings or high contrast black and white photos. Photocopies are not suitable for publication purposes but may be included in copies of the manuscript submitted for refereeing.

Accepted submissions will be illustrated with photographs, drawings or other graphics. If possible, please submit illustrative graphic material, or suggest sources of appropriate photos. All original artwork supplied will be returned.

All manuscripts should be submitted to:
Tara Flynn, Executive Editor
Alternatives Journal
Faculty of Environmental Studies
University of Waterloo
Waterloo, Ontario, Canada N2L 3G1
Tel: (519) 888-4442, Fax: (519) 746-0292,
E-mail: **altsed@fes.uwaterloo.ca**
Web: **www.alternativesjournal.ca**

For more editorial information contact:
Tara Flynn, Executive Editor
Tel: (519) 888-4442
E-mail: **editor@alternativesjournal.ca**

American Annals of the Deaf

ADDRESS FOR SUBMISSION:

Donald Moores, Editor
American Annals of the Deaf
Fowler Hall, Rm. 409
800 Florida Avenue, N.E.
Washington, DC 20002-3695
USA
Phone: 202-651-5530
Fax: 202-651-5860
E-Mail: donald.moores@gallaudet.edu
Web: gupress.gallaudet.edu/annals
Address May Change:

CIRCULATION DATA:

Reader: Academics
Frequency of Issue: 5 Times/Year
Copies per Issue: 2,000
Sponsor/Publisher: CEASD - CAID Joint
    Committee
Subscribe Price: 50.00 US$ Individual
    90.00 US$ Institution
    50.00 US$ Canada / $70 US Foreign

PUBLICATION GUIDELINES:

Manuscript Length: Avg. 16-20
Copies Required: Three
Computer Submission: Yes
Format: Required - PC
Fees to Review: 0.00 US$

Manuscript Style:
    American Psychological Association

REVIEW INFORMATION:

Type of Review: Blind Review
No. of External Reviewers: 3+
No. of In House Reviewers: 1
Acceptance Rate: 40%
Time to Review: 2 - 3 Months
Reviewers Comments: Yes
Invited Articles: 0-5%
Fees to Publish: 0.00 US$

MANUSCRIPT TOPICS:

Audiology/Speech Pathology; Bilingual/E.S.L.; Counseling & Personnel Services; Curriculum Studies; Deaf Education; Education Management/Administration; Educational Psychology; Educational Technology Systems; Elementary/Early Childhood; Health & Physical Education; Languages & Linguistics; Psychology; Rural Education & Small Schools; Science Math & Environment; Secondary/Adolescent Studies; Social Studies/Social Science; Special Education; Teacher Education; Technology; Tests, Measurement & Evaluation

MANUSCRIPT GUIDELINES/COMMENTS:

Terms of Acceptance

Original articles will be accepted for review with the understanding that they are not being considered by another publication. The author is responsible for all statements made in the submitted manuscript, including changes made by the copy editor, unless the author challenges the changes at the time the manuscript is reviewed. Although rejected manuscripts are usually returned to the author, the *Annals* is not responsible for loss.

Accepted manuscripts become the property of the *Annals* and may not be published elsewhere without written permission. Accepted manuscripts are subject to quality review concerning acceptability of illustrations, reference accuracy, and completeness.

Manuscript style should be consistent with the *Publication Manual of the American Psychological Association* (Fifth Edition). General style requirements are indicated below. Manuscripts not meeting the submission criteria will still be reviewed by the Editorial Board. If accepted, the author must agree to correct any deficiencies.

Typing Requirements
All manuscripts must be typed double spaced on 8.5 x 11 paper, with one-inch margins all around.

Elements of the Manuscript
Each element of the manuscript including the title page (include the author's title, institution, address, E-mail address, phone number, and fax number), first page of text, synopsis abstract, references, and legends for illustration should begin on a new page.

Synopsis Abstract
The synopsis abstract replaces the summary. It differs in that it should not exceed 135 words in length and it is placed at the beginning of the article rather than at the end. Include only essential features of the report. Emphasize data and avoid generalizations. Do not repeat the title of the manuscript.

Illustrations
Illustrations consist of all material that cannot be set in type, such as photographs, line drawings, graphs, charts, and tracings. Omit all illustrations that fail to increase understanding of the text. Drawings and graphs should be black and white and camera ready.

Illustrations should be numbered and cited in the text. Legends must accompany each and should be placed together on a separate sheet of paper (type double spaced).

Tables
Tables should be typed on separate sheets of paper. Tables will be set in type for publication.

Reference Bibliography
The reference bibliography will be critically examined at the time of review for acceptance. Referencing and other matters of bibliographic style should follow the form set by the *APA Publication Manual.*

Order of Publication
Articles are generally published in order of acceptance. Authors seeking early publication of accepted articles may expedite publication by payments of page charges. Authors of exceptionally long articles who prefer not to condense them may pay charges for excess pages. Charges are made because both arrangements result in added pages in the regular issue. Of course, these manuscripts must pass through the same Editorial Board review process as all other manuscripts.

Manuscript Submission
Send a good original and two copies by first-class mail. Articles may also be submitted electronically. Designate one author as correspondent. Send manuscripts to: Donald Moores, Editor, at the address above. If a manuscript is accepted for publication, the author will be asked to submit a PC-compatible floppy disk. Do not send disks with the original submission.

American Biology Teacher

ADDRESS FOR SUBMISSION:

Ann Haley MacKenzie, Interim Editor
American Biology Teacher
Miami University
Department of Teacher Education
McGuffey Hall
Oxford, OH 45056
USA
Phone: 513-529-1688
Fax: 513-529-4931
E-Mail: mackenah@muohio.edu
Web: www.nabt.org
Address May Change:

PUBLICATION GUIDELINES:

Manuscript Length: 11-15
Copies Required: Three
Computer Submission: Yes
Format: MS Word, WordPerfect
Fees to Review: 0.00 US$

Manuscript Style:
American Psychological Association

CIRCULATION DATA:

Reader: Practicing Teachers
Frequency of Issue: 10 Times/Year
Copies per Issue: 10,001 - 25,000
Sponsor/Publisher: National Association of
Biology Teachers
Subscribe Price: 60.00 US$

REVIEW INFORMATION:

Type of Review: Blind Review
No. of External Reviewers: 2
No. of In House Reviewers: 1
Acceptance Rate: 50%
Time to Review: 1 - 2 Months
Reviewers Comments: Yes
Invited Articles: 11-20%
Fees to Publish: 0.00 US$

MANUSCRIPT TOPICS:
Education Management/Administration; Educational Technology Systems; Science Math &
Environment; Teacher Education

MANUSCRIPT GUIDELINES/COMMENTS:

The *American Biology Teacher* is a journal primarily for high school and college biology
teachers, although intended to be of interest to teachers at all levels. Its articles are devoted to
topics of interest and of use to teachers. The following are examples of suitable topics for
articles:

- Results of research on teaching alternatives, including careful evaluation of a new
  methods versus a traditional one; cooperative learning; use of concept maps; learning
  contracts; investigative experiences, use of computers in instruction; simulations and
  games; and articles focusing on values and the process of making value judgments.
- Social and ethical implications of biology and ways to incorporate such concerns into
  instructional programs; aging and death; genetic engineering; energy; pollution;
  agriculture; population; health care; nutrition; sexuality; gender; and drugs.

- Specific how-to-do-it suggestions for laboratory, field activities or interdisciplinary programs.
- Review articles on recent advances in the life sciences that summarize information useful to teachers and provide references to original sources.
- Articles presenting imaginative views of the future and suggestions for coping with changes.

(Articles that fall within the first three categories should include evaluations of the techniques described.)

Manuscript Selection Criteria

We use the following criteria in deciding whether to accept or reject a manuscript. These are listed in their approximate order of importance.

1. Information in the manuscript must be useful to teachers at the high school or introductory college levels.

2. The manuscript must contain material that has not been published recently in our journal.

3. The manuscript should be organized logically and coherently; the writing style should be clear.

4. Illustrations, such as photographs, line drawings, graphs and tables, should be included with any manuscript to which they add clarity or increase reader interest.

5. Manuscripts should be no longer than 4,000 words (or 16 typewritten, double-spaced pages), including references and excluding illustrations. We prefer short, concisely written articles to lengthy elaborations of a topic.

6. Format specifications should be followed carefully.

Format

Your adherence to our format will hasten the publication of your article by lessening the tasks of our editorial staff.

- The title of your manuscript should function primarily as a label; your choice of words also can make it an invitation to readers. Make it descriptive but concise. Please avoid colons and semicolons in your title.
- A good introductory paragraph captures the reader's attention (and that of the manuscript reviewers as well). You need not include an abstract of your article in the first paragraph, but your introduction should highlight the major points you intend to make in subsequent paragraphs.
- Not all articles in *ABT* contain subheads, but it is helpful to include them in any manuscript longer than five pages. Whether or not your subheads are used, they will be helpful to you, to our reviewers and to our editorial staff in evaluating the organization of material. Like titles, subheads act as labels and as invitations to read further.

- Most articles need formal conclusions. The context of this section will depend, of course, on the topic of the article. In many cases, suggestions for implementing ideas are more useful than summaries.
- List references in alphabetical order at the end of your article on a separate page. References must be complete and in *ABT* style. The following examples illustrate *ABT's* style format:

To List a Magazine or Journal Article
Ennis, R.N. (1975). Children's ability to handle Piaget's propositional logic: A Conceptual critique. Review of Educational Research, 45, (1), 5-8.

To List a Book
Lindsay, P.H. & Norman, D.A. (1972). Human information processing. New York: Academic Press.

To List an Article in an Edited Book
Margaria, R. & Cerretelli, P. (1968). The respiratory system and exercise. In H.B. Falls (Ed.), Exercise physiology (pp. 10-12). New York: Academic Press.

In-Text References
"Blue-green algae have the simplest nutritional requirements of any known organism (Keeton 1973). (or) Keeton (1973) has noted that blue green algae have the simplest."

For more guidelines on preparing references, see the *Publication Manual of the American Psychological Association*, 3rd ed. (1983).

Style
On questions, of punctuation, abbreviation and style, ABT follows the *University of Chicago Manual of Style*. Our spellings are those preferred in *Webster's Third New Collegiate Dictionary* and its abridgement, *Webster's New Collegiate Dictionary*. There are excellent articles and books on effective writing styles (e.g. *The Elements of Style*, 3rd ed., by W. Strunk, Jr. and E.B. White).

We feel a variety of styles makes a journal more interesting; thus, we offer the following general guidelines in the interest of reducing the need for editorial changes:

- Use the active voice whenever possible.
- Use concise, concrete words to emphasize your point rather than gimmicks such as capitalization, underlining or italics.
- Speak to your readers in first-person statements.
- Attempt to minimize in-text references. We do not use footnotes. Documentation is necessary in most scientific writing, but it should not distract readers from your ideas.
- Use S1 units (with or without English equivalents) for all measurements.

Editorial Procedures
- We direct communications to the senior author of multiple author articles.

- We acknowledge receipt of articles as they arrive.
- At least two individuals review each article. This is a blind review process in which reviewers are not informed of the names of the author(s).
- We attempt to make decisions on articles within eight weeks after receipt. Articles not accepted are returned to their authors. Whenever possible, we include suggestions for adapting articles to our needs, or names of other journals for which they may be more appropriate. (Be sure to include a self-addressed envelope and return postage with your article).
- The editor submits the accepted manuscripts to the managing editor, who edits them. The managing editor will contact authors by phone or mail when questions arise or clarification is needed. We edit articles for both style and content, but the author is ultimately responsible for scientific and technical accuracy. Check it carefully before submitting your article. Galley proofs are not sent to authors unless requested before the managing editor receives the manuscript.
- If your article is accepted for publication, we will need biographical information and a copyright release from each author.
- Authors receive one complimentary copy of the issue in which their article appears. A price schedule and order form for off prints is sent to authors prior to publication. Reprints also may be ordered any time after publication. (Off prints are substantially less expensive, because they are made at the time of the initial printing).

Before submitting your manuscript, follow this checklist.
To minimize editorial time and expense, please follow the procedures below:

☐ **Type All Copy.** Be sure your typewriter ribbon is new and produces easy to read copy. Do not submit mimeographed or spirit duplicated copy. Manuscripts generated with a dot-matrix printer should be dark enough to photocopy well. Please, no blue or gray ink.

☐ **Double Space All Copy**, including tables, figure captions and references. Put your title on a separate page and do not underline titles or subtitles.

☐ **Use Standard Paper and the Following Page Format**: one side of 8½ x 11" white bond, leaving a 1½ inch margin on all sides. This leaves room for editorial and typesetting marks.

☐ **Be Sure All Figures Are Camera Ready.** Present all tables, graphs and line drawings on separate sheets of paper at the end of the manuscript. Photos should be glossy black and white prints at least 3½ x 5 inches in size. Authors are responsible for all costs of converting slides or color prints to black and white. Illustrations should be drawn using black ink on white paper (no pencil drawings accepted). The goal is for the figures to appear to have been professionally produced. Labeling must be suitable for camera ready reproduction. Key each illustration and photo on the back to its caption, but place all captions on a separate sheet. Include credits. Be sure you have all permissions necessary. Mark the top and bottom of photos and figures. Indicate placement of tables, photographs and figures within the body of the manuscript. All copies of the manuscript must be accompanied by glossy prints of all photographs - photocopies of photographs are not acceptable. It is permissible to include photocopies of line drawings for reviewers. Note: ABT no longer publishes computer programs. See Computer Center, ABT, 49 (6). Figures that do not appear to have been professionally produced will not be included.

☐ **Include Machine Copies of Quotations You Make**. Regardless of their length, you should do this so that we may verify quotes and avoid copyright problems.

☐ **Include a Written and Signed Verification** from you and your coauthor(s) that you manuscript is neither being nor has it been accepted for publication elsewhere.

☐ **Include a Diskette Containing a Copy of Your Manuscript**. We prefer Macintosh diskettes using Microsoft Word software, but can accommodate IBM compatible diskettes using Microsoft Word, Word Perfect or Zywrite software.

☐ **Submit an Original and Three Copies of Your Manuscript**. Include your address(es) and phone number(s) where you can be reached. Mail manuscripts to the Editor.

☐ **Double-check Your Format**. Manuscripts not submitted in the proper form will be returned for preparation. Be sure that any photocopies submitted are fully readable.

In the event that you cannot comply with any of the above requirements, please explain in a letter accompanying your manuscript.

We look forward to seeing your manuscript soon.

American Journal of Education

ADDRESS FOR SUBMISSION:

William Lowe Boyd, Editor
American Journal of Education
University of Chicago
Judd Hall 008
5835 S. Kimbark Avenue
Chicago, IL 60637
USA
Phone: 773-702-1555
Fax:
E-Mail: ajed@psu.edu
Web: www.journals.uchicago.edu/AJE/
Address May Change:

PUBLICATION GUIDELINES:

Manuscript Length: 26-30
Copies Required: Five
Computer Submission: Yes
Format: MS Word
Fees to Review: 0.00 US$

Manuscript Style:
See Manuscript Guidelines

CIRCULATION DATA:

Reader: Academics
Frequency of Issue: Quarterly
Copies per Issue: No Reply
Sponsor/Publisher:
Subscribe Price:

REVIEW INFORMATION:

Type of Review: Blind Review
No. of External Reviewers: 3
No. of In House Reviewers: 1
Acceptance Rate: 6-10%
Time to Review: 4 - 6 Months
Reviewers Comments: Yes
Invited Articles: 0-5%
Fees to Publish: 0.00 US$

MANUSCRIPT TOPICS:
Curriculum Studies; Education Management/Administration; Policy Studies in Education; Research; Teacher Education; Tests, Measurement & Evaluation; Urban Education, Cultural/Non-Traditional

MANUSCRIPT GUIDELINES/COMMENTS:

Founded as *School Review* in 1893, *AJE* acquired its present name in November 1979. The *Journal* seeks to bridge and integrate the intellectual, methodological, and substantive diversity of educational scholarship, and to encourage a vigorous dialogue between educational scholars and practitioners. To achieve that goal, papers are published that present research, theoretical statements, philosophical arguments, critical syntheses of a field of educational inquiry, and integrations of educational scholarship, policy, and practice.

Information for Contributors
Editorial Procedures. The editors review all submissions and those deemed appropriate for *AJE* are sent anonymously to reviewers. The editors rely heavily on reviewers' judgments, although they are not bound by them. Strong efforts are made to ensure prompt decisions

about acceptance. To protect anonymity, only the title should appear on the manuscript. A separate cover page should carry the title, and author's name and author's affiliation. All identifying references and notes should be separated from other references and notes. Citations in text to these references should be to "Identifying Reference" and the publication date.

Manuscript Acceptance Policy. Manuscripts are accepted for publication subject to copyediting. Manuscript submission indicates the author's commitment to publish in *AJE* and to give *AJE* first publication rights. No paper known to be under consideration by another journal will be reviewed. Upon publication, the University of Chicago Press owns all rights, including subsidiary rights. Authors retain the right to use their articles, after they have appeared in the *Journal*, without charge in any book they write or edit. Our policy is to require the assignment of copyright on most articles, but we do not usually ask copyright assignment for other contributions. We understand that, in return for publication, the *Journal* has the nonexclusive right to publish the contribution and the continuing unlimited right to include the contribution as part of any issue and/or volume reprint of the *Journal* in which the contribution first appeared by any means and in any format, including computer-assisted storage and readout, in which the issue and/or volume may be reproduced by the publisher or by its licensed agencies.

Preparation of Copy
1. Type *all* copy double-spaced--including indented matter, footnotes and references-- allowing generous margins at top, bottom, and sides of page.

2. Footnotes are to be used only for substantive observations. Number consecutively and place on a separate page titled "Notes."

3. Tables. Type each double-spaced on a separate page; refer to each in numerical order in the text; do not use vertical lines; place footnotes at bottom of table; mark footnotes with letters.

4. Draw figures on white paper with India ink. High-quality computer graphics are also acceptable. The original or glossy print of each figure will be required if manuscript is accepted.

5. Include an abstract (100 words or less) summarizing paper's chief contribution.

6. On a separate sheet, please provide a two- or three-line biographical description (see recent issues of *AJE* for examples).

7. *Five copies* of the manuscript and abstract, on white paper, must be submitted, addressed to *American Journal of Education,* Penn State University, 200 Rackley Building, University Park, PA 16802. *Manuscripts are not returned to authors.*

8. Also be sure to send an electronic copy of your paper and abstract (in a Microsoft WORD document), as an email attachment to **ajed@psu.edu** or on a floppy disk. To ensure anonymity, be sure to remove your name and any identifying references, etc., from the

electronic version, as well as from the hard copies you submit. *Important: Include your email address as well as your postal address and phone and fax numbers.*

References. *Citations in text.* All references to books, monographs, articles, and statistical sources must be identified at appropriate point in text by author's last name, publication year, and pagination where appropriate, as indicated. When author's name is in text: Rader (1975). When author's name is not in text: (Wills 1976). When citing pagination (for a quote): (Bell 1967, p. 62). With dual authorship, give both names; for three or more, use et al. For institutional authorship, identify from beginning of complete citation: (U.S. Bureau of the Census 1963, p. 117). With more than one reference to an author in one year, distinguish them by use of letters (*a,b*) attached to publication year: (1956*a*). Enclose a series of references within one pair of parentheses, separated by semicolons.

Reference format. List all items alphabetically by author and, within author, by publication year, on a separate page titled "References." Do not use APA style. Examples of common references follow:

Bowles, Samuel, and Herbert Gintis. *Schooling in Capitalist America.* New York: Basic Books, 1976.

Coleman, James S. "Loss of Power." *American Sociological Review* 38 (1973): 1-17. (*a*)
Dorsey, John, ed. *On Mencken.* New York: Knopf, 1980.

Kaiser, Ernest. "The Literature of Harlem." In *Harlem: A Community in Transition,* edited by J. H. Clarke. New York: Citadel, 1964.

Trent, James Williams. "The Development of Intellectual Disposition within Catholic Colleges." Ph.D. dissertation, University of California, Berkeley, 1964.

U.S. Bureau of the Census. *County and City Data Book, 1972.* Washington D.C.: Government Printing Office, 1973.

Editorial Policy
The *American Journal of Education* is devoted to original inquiries in education, to the evaluation and synthesis of educational scholarship, and to scholarly commentary on educational practice. The *Journal* seeks (1) to bridge and integrate the intellectual, methodological, and substantive diversity of educational scholarship, and (2) to encourage a vigorous dialogue between educational scholars and practitioners across a full spectrum of education - from early childhood to adult education - including matters of policy and governance and of the management and conduct of schools, colleges and universities.

Therefore, the *American Journal of Education* is hospitable to scholarly writing on a variety of educational topics, from differing conceptual, methodological, and substantive approaches. Four kinds of papers are especially encouraged: (1) research reports addressing important topics and issues; (2) scholarly writing of other kinds - for example, theoretical statements and philosophical arguments; (3) critical syntheses of a field of educational inquiry; and (4) integrations of educational scholarship, policy, and practice.

Manuscripts will be reviewed for the significance of the problem, the originality of the contribution, the cogency of the method and argument, and the crispness and clarity of prose.

Authors who wish to respond in print to a review are encouraged to submit a brief response of no more than 500 words. Reviewers will be given the opportunity to respond in the same issue.

American Journal of Health Education

ADDRESS FOR SUBMISSION:

Becky Smith, Executive Editor
American Journal of Health Education
American Assoc. of Health Education
1900 Association Drive
Reston, VA 20191
USA
Phone: 703-476-3437
Fax: 703-476-6638
E-Mail: aahe@aahperd.org
Web: www.aahperd.org
Address May Change:

PUBLICATION GUIDELINES:

Manuscript Length: 16-20
Copies Required: Five
Computer Submission: No
Format: N/A
Fees to Review: 0.00 US$

Manuscript Style:
    American Psychological Association

CIRCULATION DATA:

Reader: Academics, Practicing Teachers
Frequency of Issue: 6 Times/Year
Copies per Issue: 5,001 - 10,000
Sponsor/Publisher: American Alliance for
    Health, Physical Education, Recreation,
    and Dance
Subscribe Price:

REVIEW INFORMATION:

Type of Review: Blind Review
No. of External Reviewers: 3
No. of In House Reviewers: 1
Acceptance Rate: 25%
Time to Review: 2 - 3 Months
Reviewers Comments: Yes
Invited Articles: 0-5%
Fees to Publish: 0.00 US$

MANUSCRIPT TOPICS:
Curriculum Studies; Health & Physical Education; Health Education

MANUSCRIPT GUIDELINES/COMMENTS:

The only refereed journal of its kind to cover today's health education and health promotion issues head on with timely, substantive, and thought provoking articles for professionals working in:
- medical care facilities
- professional preparation
- colleges and universities
- community and public health agencies
- public and private schools (K-12)
- business and industry

Features include news from the field, calendar of events, buyers guide, new products and resources, and columns for community and school health educators.

Recent issues featured community health problems, childhood sun exposure, evaluation of cancer prevention strategies, HIV prevention in communities of color, and health information on the world wide web.

Guidelines for Authors

The following guidelines must be observed when submitting manuscripts to the *American Journal of Health Education*. The first section below describes the process that authors need to follow in order to submit manuscripts. Following the description of the process is information pertaining to format, style, commentaries, and column submissions.

Electronic Review

We are now using an on-line journal submission and review process through a company called **JournalSubmit.com**. JournalSubmit.com is a self-explanatory web-based submission and review process. Authors are encourages to go to the website to learn more about how the new process works. This process should expedite the review process by eliminating postal mailing time between the authors, the Journal office, and the reviewers. This process should reduce the time from manuscript submission to disposition to not more than 2 months. Every manuscript submitted to the *American Journal of Health Education* must be submitted through the JournalSubmit.com website.

Begin the process by going to **www.JournalSubmit.com**. From the JournalSubmit.com home page, authors should click on the "Submit a Manuscript" link to login. If this is the first time submitting a manuscript using the on-line JournalSubmit.com service, real #1 below. Otherwise proceed to #2.

1. Click on the "First Time Author" link below the login button. Complete the information on the subsequent screen including the creation of a password and then click the submit button. Follow the on-screen instructions to proceed. Proceed to #2 below.

2. This page should read "Submit a Manuscript."
a. Enter the Journal ID code that corresponds to the type of manuscript you are submitting:

Manuscript Type	Journal ID
Regular Article	AJHE
Teaching Idea Column	AJHE-TI
CLIPs Column	AJHE-CLIPS
Administrative Ideas Column	AJHE-ADMIN

b. Enter the e-mail address that you entered when you originally signed up for the JournalSubmit.com service. This is your user ID.
c. Enter the password you created when you originally signed up to submit manuscripts on-line. If you forgot your password, click on the "forgot your password" link and follow the on-screen instructions.
d. Click the "Login" button.

3. The next screen is where you enter the corresponding author information and the contact information for co-authors. In the appropriate fields, enter the following:"

a. Contact information for corresponding author.

b. Complete title of article.

c. The box below the "title of article" field must be clicked on to indicate that the manuscript has not been previously published and is not currently under review at another journal. If this field is not selected, the process will not continue.

d. Co-author information for each co-author.

e. Select your manuscript to submit. This can be done by clicking the "Browse" button and searching for the manuscript that you wish to submit. Highlight the file you wish to submit then click the "Open" button. The manuscript MUST be submitted to Microsoft Word format. Please not that all identifying information should be removed from the manuscript before the file is selected.

f. Click the "Submit" button. This is the final step. Once this button is clicked, the manuscript is sent to the *American Journal of Health Education* for review. Please make sure that the correct file is selected and that the correct contact information is given before completing this step.

4. Manuscripts may be tracked by going to **www.journalsubmit.com** and selecting the "Track Manuscripts" option. Follow the on-screen options.

Guidelines for Authors

Many types of original manuscripts are suitable-practice, theoretical, technical, historical, or controversial. Use simple, clear writing and stick to the topic. Philosophical justifications or historical backgrounds are usually not necessary. Write for the Journal's readers-health educators in schools and colleges, community and public health agencies, and health care settings in the workplace. The Journal will accept ideas, opinions, research, and professional preparation types of manuscripts having broad general application and implications for health education. Authors are encouraged to submit health education and promotion manuscripts related to these three categories: (1) community development, policy, and awareness strategies, (2) professional and instructional program, and (3) individual health enhancement and maintenance methods.

Research-based manuscripts should include the purpose, significance, methods, principle findings, discussions, and conclusions of the investigation.

Please conform to the following organization for all types of manuscripts.

1. **Type manuscripts, including quoted material and references**, double-spaced on 8 x 11 inch paper, with one-inch margins, using 12-point font size.

2. **Format the manuscript accordingly**:

a. **Title Page**. Authors should no longer include a title page on their manuscripts. All identification will be entered into corresponding fields on the JournalSubmit.com website.

b. **Abstract**. An abstract of 200 words or less must accompany all submissions. The abstract should include up to five keywords or descriptive terms that summarize the article. Use keywords that are found in two professional publications: Thesaurus of ERIC Descriptors (Educational Resources Information Center of the U.S. Department of Education, 195). The former thesaurus is found in any public or academic library.

The second thesaurus, the Health Promotion and Education Thesaurus, can be obtained from the Technical Information and Editorial Services Branch, National Center for Chronic Disease Prevention and Health Promotion, Centers for Disease Control and Prevention, 4770 Buford Highway NE, Mail Stop K-13, Atlanta, GA 30341-3724, (770) 488-5080.

Note: Manuscripts without abstracts or keywords will be returned.

c. **The Text**. Keep length to 15 typewritten pages for regular manuscripts, and three to five pages for column manuscripts, not including title page, abstract, tables, figures, illustrations, and a maximum of 35 references. Follow *American Psychological Association* (APA) 5th edition style manual for the narrative portion and for the references in both text and listing. Use the Electronic Reference Formats Recommended by the *American Psychological Association*.

Reference examples:
Roberts, M.M., French, K., & Duffy, J. (1984). Breast Cancer and breast self-examination: What do Scottish Women know? *Social Science and Medicine*, 18, 791-797.

Fynn, A. (1981). Cigarette advertising and health education: Use and abuse of media. In D.S. Leathar, G.B. Hastings, & J.K. Davies (Eds.), *Health education and the media* (29-36). Oxford, U.K.: Permagon Press.

Bergler, R. (1981). Advertising and cigarette smoking: A psychological study. Bern, Switzerland: Hans Huber.

Prevalence of Overweight and Obesity Among Adults: United States, 1999. (2000). [Online] Available: www.cdc.gov/nchs. Hyattsville, MD: National Center for Health Statistics [Producer and Distributor].

Note: Manuscripts in which references are not in this format will be returned without review.

d. **Tables**. Tables should be numbered in sequence throughout the article; however, each should be on a separate sheet at the end of the manuscript. A note should be inserted in the test to indicate placement, e.g., "Table 1 about here". Include descriptive title and headings for any columns or rows with no abbreviations. General footnotes to tables should be collected as "Note:" or "Notes:" Sequenced letters -- a, b, c, etc.-- should be used in footnotes. Use asterisks * and/or ** to indicate .05 and .01 levels of significance, respectively. Do not photo-reduce tables.

e.   **Figures and illustrations; drawings and photos**. These should be numbered in sequence with each one having a caption. Insert a notation indicating approximate placement of each. Those submitted with your final draft must be "camera-ready" in black ink on white paper, lettered in pen and ink…and legible. Submit clear, sharp, well-composed photos and line drawings with manuscripts, if available and applicable. Original artwork may be submitted. No additional artwork, redrawing, or typesetting will be done to submitted work.

Note: If you wish materials returned, indicate with name and address on the back of each piece submitted.

3. **Submit manuscripts through the JournalSubmit.com website**. Instructions for this are located at the beginning of the Guidelines for Authors.

4. **Commentary**. Periodically the editor will solicit a commentary to a manuscript accepted for publication. It will be in response to a controversial or unique contribution to the Journal. The intent is to spark discussion in the Journal by authors who may respond with Letters to the Editor.

5. **Letters to the Editor** are considered for publication (subject to editing and abridgement) providing they do not contain material that has been submitted or published elsewhere. Please not the following: (a) Your letter must be typewritten and double spaced; (b) its text, not including references, must not exceed 400 words – please include the actual word count; (c) it must have no more than five references and on figure or table; (d) letters referring to a recent article in the Journal must be received within 4 weeks of publication of the article; and (e) please include your full mailing address, telephone number, E-mail address, and fax number (if appropriate). You may send us your letter via postal, fax, or electronic mail. Please not that we cannot acknowledge receipt of your letter, but we will notify you when we have made a decision about planned publication.

General Information

- The *American Journal of Health Education* cannot consider any manuscript simultaneously considered for publication elsewhere. All authors listed must have made a significant contribution to the manuscript. It is expected that all authors will adhere to ethical guidelines included in the Code of Ethics for health educators. This includes disclosure of potential financial conflicts of interest.
- All manuscripts except editorials and Personal Perspectives are blindly reviewed by three reviewers. The evaluative disposition may be: accept, accept with revision, revise and resubmit, or reject.
- Articles in the *American Journal of Health Education* are a contribution to the profession and no remuneration can be made. Authors receive two complimentary copies of the issue containing their manuscript. Page charges are not levied against authors. Authors may purchase reprints of their articles.
- The *American Journal of Health Education* is published by the American Alliance for Health, Physical Education, Recreation, and Dance.

American Journal of Public Health

ADDRESS FOR SUBMISSION:

Mary Northridge, Editor-in-Chief
American Journal of Public Health
Nancy Johnson, Managing Editor
American Public Health Association
ELECTRONIC SUBMISSIONS ONLY
800 I Street N.W.
Washington, DC 20001
USA
Phone:
Fax:
E-Mail:
Web: www.ajph.org / submit.ajph.org
Address May Change:

PUBLICATION GUIDELINES:

Manuscript Length: 1,500-5,500 words
Copies Required: Electronic only
Computer Submission: Yes Submit
    electronic
Format: MSWord, English, New Times
    Roman
Fees to Review: 0.00 US$

Manuscript Style:
    Chicago Manual of Style, , AMA

CIRCULATION DATA:

Reader: Academics, Public Health
    Administration & Practitioners
Frequency of Issue: Monthly
Copies per Issue: More than 25,000
Sponsor/Publisher: American Public Health
    Association
Subscribe Price: 180.00 US$ Indv. Print
    250.00 US$ Institutional Print
    170.00 US$ Online Only-Indv/$435 Inst

REVIEW INFORMATION:

Type of Review: Blind Review
No. of External Reviewers: 3
No. of In House Reviewers: 0
Acceptance Rate: 11-20%
Time to Review: 2 - 3 Months
Reviewers Comments: Yes
Invited Articles: 0-5%
Fees to Publish: 0.00 US$

MANUSCRIPT TOPICS:
Education; Health & Physical Education; Policy; Practice; Public Health

MANUSCRIPT GUIDELINES/COMMENTS:

"What *AJPH* Authors Should Know"
The foremost mission of the *American Journal of Public Health* (the *Journal*) is to promote public health research, policy, practice, and education. We aim to embrace all of public health, from global policies to the local needs of public health practitioners. Contributions of original unpublished research, social science analyses, scholarly essays, critical commentaries, departments, and letters to the editor are welcome. The *Journal* adheres to the criteria of the International Committee of Medical Journal Editors.

Deciding What to Submit
Informal Inquiries. The editors cannot respond to individual queries regarding the appropriateness of planned contributions. Therefore, if a planned contribution is close to completion, please consult the guidelines detailed here in order to better judge a paper's

appropriateness for our readership. It is also helpful to consult recent issues of the *Journal* regarding our scope of coverage of public health issues. On our web site, **http://www.ajph.org**, you can search for and view abstracts in specific subject areas at no charge. If you are a subscriber or member, you have access to full text as well. Alternatively, you may purchase access from your personal computer to individual articles for 1 day at a cost of US $7 and to all articles for 2 days at a cost of US $20. Simply find the article you wish to view, click on full text, and follow the prompts.

Authors desiring special guidance on writing or reviewing for scholarly publication are encouraged to attend the seminar offered each year by the Editorial Board of the *Journal* at the Annual Meeting of the American Public Health Association.

Authors wishing to discuss groundbreaking public health initiatives with the Editor-in-Chief, Dr. Mary Northridge, may e-mail her at **men11@columbia.edu**, or contact Editorial Assistant Cynthia Dunbar at 212-305-1744 or **cd254@columbia.edu**. Organizations wishing to discuss publication of special supplements should contact the APHA Director of Publications, Ellen Meyer, at **ellen.meyer@apha.org**.

Appropriate Format. A variety of *Journal* formats are available in order to reach diverse audiences and fill varied needs within public health. Scholarly essays, critical analyses, and policy papers may be submitted as **Commentaries** (up to 2500 words in main text, 2 tables/figures, and an unstructured abstract of 120 words). **Analytic Essays** (up to 3500 words in main text, 4 tables/figures, and an unstructured abstract of 120 words) provide a forum for critical analyses of public health issues from disciplines other than the biomedical sciences, including (but not limited to) the social sciences, human rights, and ethics. Papers that report the results of original quantitative or qualitative public health research are published as **Research and Practice articles** (up to 3500 words in main text, 4 tables/figures, and a structured abstract of 180 words). Preliminary or novel findings may be reported as **Briefs** (up to 800 words in main text, 2 tables/figures, and an abstract of up to 80 words).

Essays in the **Health Policy and Ethics Forum** present critical views on public health policy and ethics controversies (up to 3500 words in main text, 4 tables/figures, and an unstructured abstract of 120 words). **Government, Politics, and Law** encourages both new and familiar voices to sound off on essential public health topics, with arguments grounded in critical analysis (up to 3500 words in main text, 4 tables/figures, and an unstructured abstract of 120 words). **Public Health Matters** features social science scholarship (both research reports and general analytical articles), the work of new disciplines within public health, and applications of frameworks to or critical perspectives of public health problems (up to 6500 words in main text, 4 tables/figures, and an unstructured abstract of 120 words). **Public Health Then and Now** is devoted to history that bears on contemporary public health (up to 5500 words in main text, 4 images, and an unstructured abstract of 150 words). **Voices From the Past** presents brief historical extracts from the works of public health pioneers that are republished with an accompanying biographical sketch (up to 2500 words in main text, no abstract). **Field Action Reports** feature practice-based programs and initiatives that have the potential to advance the public's health, both locally and more broadly (up to 1000 words in main text, 3 tables/figures/images, and a summary). **Letters** comment briefly on findings of *Journal* articles or other noteworthy public health advances (up to 400 words in main text, no abstract,

52

limited to 10 references). Please note that word counts refer exclusively to the main text and do not include abstract, references, or acknowledgments.

You may see other formats in the *Journal*. **Editorials, Images of Health, Going Public,** and **Faces of Public Health** are typically commissioned by the *Journal's* editors. If you wish to submit in one of these categories, please contact **ajph.submissions@apha.org** for referral to the appropriate editor.

On-line Submission

The *Journal* uses a web-based submissions system. All authors wishing to submit their mansucripts must do so online, as we can no longer accept hardcopy versions of papers. We hope authors will enjoy their experience with the *Journal's* new on-line submission, review, and production tracking system. Advantages include instantaneous file access; reference checking via links to MEDLINE; manuscript status information; automated record keeping; deadline reminders for authors, editors, and reviewers; faster peer review and publication; savings on postage;and enhanced archival capability. Staff are available during the day to answer questions.

If you have not done so previously, you must first register at **http://submit.ajph.org** to access the Author Area. Please make certain that the email address you use allows for the receipt of automated emails, as the *Journal's* online system will email updates to you as your paper moves through submission/production processes. Be aware that certain email addresses (such as those associated with EarthLink spamBlocker) WILL block the *Journal's* automated emails to authors. If you know that your email address has spam protection that deflects automated emails, you may want to register using a different email address with lowered spam protection. Also check your spam/bulk mail folder from time to time to ensure that none of the *Journal's* email updates concerning your paper have been misdirected as spam. If you have questions, contact the submissions staff at **ajph.submissions@apha.org** for guidance.

At the beginning of the submission process, you will be asked to enter some basic manuscript, keyword, and author information. Then you will upload relevant electronic files. The system subsequently converts your manuscript file to a PDF and appends other figure files for the anticipated review process. If you encounter any difficulties, technical assistance is available during normal business hours. Simply click the FEEDBACK button located at the top of each page.

The following instructions apply specifically to electronic submission of new manuscripts. Instructions for preparing revised manuscripts are provided through correspondence at later stages of review. Instructions for preparing final version production files are available at **http://www.ajph.org/misc/production.shtml**.

Providing Manuscript, Keyword, and Author Information

In the Manuscript Information section, you will be prompted to fill in a series of required information fields. Explanations of the content of some fields are given below. These fields will remain a part of your manuscript record and will be viewed on a confidential basis by editors and staff as needed. Reviewers will see only the abstract information. (Please be sure to keep a personal copy of your statements of contribution, acknowledgments, and Human

Participant Protection, as you will not be able to access it online after submission.) Information that you will need to complete in this section includes

- Author contributions;
- Article type and category;
- Special theme, conference, or companion paper designation;
- Abstract;
- Cover letter;
- Acknowledgments;
- Human participant protection statement;
- Submission agreement signature; and
- Names and email addresses of suggested reviewers.

Authorship and Contributorship. Individual contributions of each author must be specified in a single brief statement. Listing more than 6 authors requires justification.

Example: E.C. Frampton conceived of the study and supervised all aspects of its implementation. S. Hampton assisted with the study and completed the analyses. R.E. Lewison synthesized analyses and led the writing. N.C. Smithson assisted with the study and analyses. All authors helped to conceptualize ideas, interpret findings, and review drafts of the manuscript.

Authors must confirm that the content has not been published elsewhere and does not overlap or duplicate their published work. Exceptions are made for abstracts and reports from scientific meetings. Upon acceptance, all authors must certify that they will take public responsibility for the content and provide any relevant data upon request. All authors must also certify that they have contributed substantially to conception and design or analysis and interpretation of the data, drafting or revision of content, and approval of the final version. Copyright is transferred to the American Public Health Association upon acceptance.

Cover Letter. Disclose all possible conflicts of interest (e.g., funding sources for consultancies or studies of products). A brief indication of the importance of the paper to the field of public health is helpful in gaining peer review. Do not include this cover letter in the manuscript file that you later will upload for review.

Abstract. Good abstracts are paramount. Use complete sentences, and spell out acronyms at first mention. Abstracts for most articles should be 120 words or less (not including headings); abstracts for Public Health Then and Now, should not exceed 150 words, and for Research and Practice articles and briefs should not exceed 180 and 80 words, respectively. Research and Practice articles have structured abstracts with four headings: Objectives, Methods, Results, and Conclusions. Article types/departments that have unstructured (without headings) abstracts are as follows: Analytic Essays, Briefs; Commentaries; Field Action Reports; Government, Politics, and Law; Health Policy and Ethics Forum; Public Health Matters; and Public Health Then and Now. Departments that do not have abstracts include Editorials; Letters; and Voices From the Past.

You will need to copy and paste your abstract into the text box provided on the first page of the online submission form. We use this version of your abstract to solicit referees to review your manuscript. Potential reviewers may view it before they accept or decline the assignment.

We ask that the authors of Editorials, which are not published with abstracts, copy the first few paragraphs (Introduction) of their paper into the abstract text box located on the first page of the submission form.

Acknowledgments. Disclosure of all financial and material support is required. Upon acceptance, the first author will be asked to certify that all persons who have contributed substantially to the work but who do not fulfill authorship criteria have been listed, and that written permission for listing them has been obtained.

Your acknowledgments should be copied and pasted into the space provided on the first page of the submission form.

Human Participant Protection. If human participants are involved, a statement of approval by an institutional review board (IRB) and the participants' informed consent is required. The *Journal* adheres to the Declaration of Helsinki of the World Medical Association (http://www.wma.net). If IRB approval was not obtained, an explanation is required.

Next, you will be asked to select Keywords and to list Author Information. Then you will be ready to upload your files.

Uploading Your Files
After completing Manuscript, Author, and Keyword information, you will answer a few questions about word counts and the number of tables and figures. You will then upload files for review purposes. Contained within the main Manuscript File should be your title page, abstract, text, references, tables, and figures. This file will be converted to a PDF file that reviewers can print and read. You also may upload figure files separately from your manuscript file for review; these will be appended to the PDF version of your manuscript. In addition, supplementary and image files may be uploaded within the system.

Please submit only a Word .DOC manuscript file. (If you prefer, you may submit in PDF format, but for review purposes only; a Word .DOC file will later be required as a final version for production if the article is accepted.) The *Journal* follows the guidelines of the International Committee and the *American Medical Association Manual of Style* (9th ed) for all quantitative research articles.

Title Page (page 1 of the Manuscript File). All that is necessary on the title page is the title itself. **Authorship information must not appear on the title *page*** (nor anywhere else in the Manuscript File). *AJPH's* review process is double-blind--to ensure an impartial evaluation, reviewers' identities will not be divulged to authors, and author's identities will not be available to reviewers until after an editorial decision is made. If you would like to include information such as the word counts for your abstract, main text, and references, as well as the number of tables/figures on the title page, please do so. This easily accessible information can be very useful to editors and reviewers.

Abstract (page 2 of the Manuscript File). Copy and paste your abstract as provided in the Manuscript Information section previously.

Text (begins on page 3 of the Manuscript File). Add subheads for clearer presentation and informed reading (at least 1 subhead for every 2 pages). Text heads should be brief. Editorial staff reserve the right to shorten heads to fit. Use acronyms sparingly, if at all.

We recommend that you use only certain fonts: Times, Times Roman, Arial, and the Symbol font for special characters. Using other fonts could make the PDF more difficult to read.

References (within the Manuscript File). Format your references according to the *AMA Manual of Style* (or see *JAMA*. 1998;279:68). The *Journal* lists up to 6 authors; for more, list the first 3 and add "et al." Number references in the order cited in text, tables, and figures (assume tables and figures fall at first call-out). If you have used an automatic footnote or endnote system, please remove all automatic links between citation numbers and the references. (Note that some bibliographic software offer one-step removal of linking codes specifically for submitting manuscripts to publishers.) Verify all references using MEDLINE. For secondary sources, direct quotations, and citations from books or reports, give specific page numbers. Cite personal (written or oral) communications in the text only, giving source, degrees, type, and date [Example: (H.R. Smith, PhD, MPH, oral communication, May 1996.).] For *Public Health Then and Now* and *Public Health Matters* only, authors may follow endnote style (Documentation 1) in the *Chicago Manual of Style* (14th ed. 1993:487-635). Note that *Letters* and *Responses* are limited to 10 references.

References should appear after the main text (and before tables and figures) in the manuscript file that you will upload. They will become both a part of the PDF and a separate HTML file with links to the MEDLINE database and to journals hosted by HighWire Press. These links will allow editors and reviewers immediate access to works cited.

Tables and Figures (within the Manuscript File). Please note the following guidelines for the number of tables, figures, and images: *Analytic Essays* (4 tables/figures), *Articles* (4 tables/figures), *Briefs* (2 tables/figures), *Commentaries* (2 tables/figures), *Field Action Reports* (3 tables/figures/images), *Public Health Matters* (4 tables/figures), and *Public Health Then and Now* (4 images).

Each table and figure should have a self-contained title that is fully comprehensible without reference to the text. Lettering in figures should be large enough to read once reduced to print. Figures should include legends and should be professionally drawn or created using a computer program. All figures and tables must be in black and white. Click here for a more in-depth explanation of our graphics requirements.

Tables should each be placed on a separate page at the end of the manuscript file you will upload. Figures in Excel format should appear directly after tables, each on a separate page.

Figures in other than Excel format can either (1) be pasted onto the end of the Manuscript File, each on a separate page, or (2) be uploaded as figure files (see Other Figure Files below).

Note: Excel tables are preferred. Only simple or text-heavy tables should be created in Word. Do not upload Excel files as figure files. Instead, you must submit Excel-based figures by cutting and pasting them into the end of your manuscript file. If you try to upload them as figure files, they will not appear with the PDF and may prevent conversion altogether.

Other Figure Files. Upload non-Excel black-and-white (no color) charts and graphs as Figure Files. Formats not supported include the following: Bitmap (.bmp), Canvas (.cnv), CorelDRAW (.cdr), Excel (.xls), PhotoShop (.psd), PICT (.pict), and locked or encrypted PDFs. Multi-page PowerPoint files (.ppt) are not supported; however, one slide per file is acceptable. Your figures will be converted and appended to the PDF of your manuscript.

Supplementary/Image Files. Upload relevant prior publications in-press or in-process if they contain related or potentially duplicative findings. These are files that will not appear with the print article, though they might accompany the final version of the paper on-line at the Editor-in-Chief's discretion. Supplementary files are not converted to PDF for review but will be available to editors and staff exactly as you upload them.

Images. *AJPH* uses photography and graphics to illustrate the issues raised in our published articles. We are particularly interested in finding images for these departments: *Commentaries, Editorials, Field Action Reports, Going Public,* and *Public Health Then and Now.*

High-quality digital photos and other images should be uploaded as "Supplementary/Image Files." These files are not converted to PDF for review but will be available to editors and staff exactly as you upload them. Image formats accepted are TIFF, PSD, EPS, WMF, PDF, and JPEG files of minimum 300 dpi resolution at 4 by 6 inches. TIFF files are preferred. Do not submit low-resolution images such as GIFs saved from your Web browser as image files.

Any images uploaded as "Figure Files" will appear in the PDF, and thus will be seen by reviewers. You may upload a small, low-resolution image as a Figure File, IF you also upload a high-quality version as a supplementary/image file, or plan to send one by mail or e-mail upon acceptance. For further guidance on images, we recommend you carefully read our graphics requirements.

Appendixes and Extensive Tables. Appendixes are not published in print but may accompany the final version of the paper on-line at the Editor-in-Chief's discretion. A text note can indicate availability either from the author or (at moderate cost) from the National Auxiliary Publication Service. For more information, consult the Production Editor at **ajph.production@apha.org**.

Submission Checklist
- Cover letter with conflict of interest disclosure
- Justification for more than 6 authors
- Explanation of authors' contributions

- Abstract (correct format and word limit)
- Text (manuscript file in Word format)
- References (accuracy, style, and numbering)
- Acknowledgments (funding sources, contributors who didn't fulfill authorship requirements)
- Human Participant Protection (IRB approval, consent)
- Tables (numbered, with title and footnotes)
- Figures (numbered, black-and-white, EPS, WMF, PPT, or PDF)
- Related supplementary material, including images (TIFF, PSD, EPS, WMF, PDF, or JPEG of more than 300 dpi, 4" x 6")

Review, Editing, and Production

We acknowledge new, revised, and resubmitted manuscripts upon receipt. About 60% of submissions are rejected upon initial screening by the editors, usually within 1-2 weeks of receipt. Peer review of the remainder takes 2 months from submission to initial decision. The review process is double blind, with authors unaware of the identities of reviewers and reviewers unaware of the identities of authors until acceptance. Upon acceptance, authors will be asked to submit final version source files for editing and production. Please visit our **Production Page** for information regarding the production process. The *Journal* publishes about 20% of initial submissions. Publication of uncommissioned manuscripts currently occurs within 10 to 12 months of acceptance.

Questions? Send an e-mail to **ajph.submissions@apha.org**.

American Psychologist

ADDRESS FOR SUBMISSION:

Norman B Anderson, Editor-in-Chief
American Psychologist
750 First Street, N.E.
Washington, DC 20002-4242
USA
Phone: 202-336-5500
Fax:
E-Mail: Apeditor@apa.org
Web: www.apa.org
Address May Change:

PUBLICATION GUIDELINES:

Manuscript Length: 21-25 Max, double-
spaced
Copies Required:
Computer Submission: Yes See website
Format:
Fees to Review: 0.00 US$

Manuscript Style:
American Psychological Association

CIRCULATION DATA:

Reader: Academics
Frequency of Issue: Monthly
Copies per Issue: Over 113,000
Sponsor/Publisher: American Psychological
Association
Subscribe Price: 198.00 US$ Individual
449.00 US$ Institution

REVIEW INFORMATION:

Type of Review: Blind Review
No. of External Reviewers: 3
No. of In House Reviewers: 0
Acceptance Rate: 12%
Time to Review: 6 Months
Reviewers Comments: Yes
Invited Articles: 31-50%
Fees to Publish: 0.00 US$

MANUSCRIPT TOPICS:
Educational Psychology; Psychology

MANUSCRIPT GUIDELINES/COMMENTS:

Topics Include
Current issues, empirical, theoretical, and practical articles on broad aspects of psychology.

Manuscript Preparation. Authors should prepare manuscripts according to the *Publication Manual of the American Psychological Association* (5th ed.). Manuscripts should be no more than 25 double-spaced pages, including references. All manuscripts must include an abstract containing a maximum of 120 words. Formatting instructions, including instructions on preparing tables, figures, references, metrics, and abstracts, appear in the *Manual.* All manuscripts are copyedited for bias-free language. Comments should be submitted no later than two months from the date of the issue containing the article to which they respond. (Comments on comments are rarely considered.) Comments on matters of APA policy are also considered. Comments must be limited to 1,000 words (about five pages) and should contain no more than nine references. As in all manuscripts, authors should include page numbers and references for quotes. *APA* can now place supplementary materials online, which will be available via the journal's Web page as noted above. To submit such materials, please see **www.apa.org/journals/supplementalmaterial.html** for details.

Publication Policy. APA policy prohibits an author from submitting the same manuscript for concurrent consideration by two or more publications. APA policy prohibits as well publication of any manuscript that has already been published in whole or substantial part elsewhere. Authors have an obligation to consult journal editors if there is any question concerning prior publication of part or all of their submitted manuscripts. Authors are required to obtain and provide to APA prior to production all necessary permissions to reproduce in print and electronic form any copyrighted work, including, for example, test materials (or portions thereof) and photographs of people. Also, authors of research reports submitted to APA journals are expected to have their data available throughout the editorial review process and for at least five years after the date of publication. Of course, APA expects authors submitting to this journal to adhere to the APA ethical standards regarding previous publication of data (Standard 8.13) and making research data available (Standard 8.14). Authors of research reports will be required to state in writing that they have complied with APA ethical standards in the treatment of their sample, human or animal, or to describe the details of treatment. A copy of the APA Ethical Principles may be obtained at www.apa.org/ethics/ or by writing the APA Ethics Office, 750 First Street, NE, Washington, DC 20002-4242. APA requires authors to reveal any possible conflict of interest in the conduct and reporting of research (e.g., financial interests in a test or procedure, funding by pharmaceutical companies for drug research).

Review Policy. The first step in the *AP* editorial review process is performed by the *AP* Editor-in-Chief/APA, CEO. Approximately 70% of author-submitted manuscripts are returned without review within 30 days for a host of reasons: Empirical manuscripts are more appropriate for one of the APA primary journals; topic of the manuscript or style of the writing is too specialized for the broad *AP* readership; the same topic was recently covered in the journal; inappropriate content or style; or other, more typical reasons such as the paper does not offer a major contribution to the field or is simply not written well enough. As a matter of policy, the identities of authors and reviewers are masked. Manuscripts that are peer reviewed are circulated without their title pages to mask the identity of the authors. Each copy of a manuscript should include a separate title page with authors' names and affiliations, and these should not appear anywhere else on the manuscript. Footnotes that identify the authors should be typed on a separate page. Authors should make every effort to see that the manuscript itself contains no clue to their identity.

Manuscript Submission. Submit manuscripts electronically via the Manuscript Submission Portal at **www.apa.org/journals/amp**. In addition to addresses and phone numbers, authors should supply electronic mail addresses and fax numbers, if available. Authors should keep a copy of the manuscript to guard against loss. General correspondence may be directed to Norman B. Anderson, Editor-in-Chief, *American Psychologist*, 750 First Street, NE, Washington, DC 20002-4242

E-Mail Address. To contact the editorial office of the *American Psychologist* via electronic mail (Internet), contact **APeditor@apa.org**.

American Secondary Education

ADDRESS FOR SUBMISSION:

James A. Rycik, Editor
American Secondary Education
Ashland University
Weltmer Center
401 College Avenue
Ashland, OH 44805
USA
Phone: 419-289-5273
Fax: 419-207-6264
E-Mail: jrycik@ashland.edu
Web: www.ashland.edu/ase
Address May Change:

PUBLICATION GUIDELINES:

Manuscript Length: 20-25 pgs. Articles
Copies Required: Three
Computer Submission: Yes
Format: 3.5 Disk/IBM
Fees to Review: 0.00 US$

Manuscript Style:
American Psychological Association

CIRCULATION DATA:

Reader: Academics, Practicing Teachers,
Administrators
Frequency of Issue: 3 Times/Year
Copies per Issue: Less than 500
Sponsor/Publisher: Ashland University
Subscribe Price: 30.00 US$
40.00 US$ International

REVIEW INFORMATION:

Type of Review: Blind Review
No. of External Reviewers: 2
No. of In House Reviewers: 1
Acceptance Rate: 45%
Time to Review: 2 - 3 Months
Reviewers Comments: Yes
Invited Articles: 0-5%
Fees to Publish: 0.00 US$

MANUSCRIPT TOPICS:
Adult Career & Vocational; Counseling & Personnel Services; Curriculum Studies; Education Management/Administration; School Law; Secondary/Adolescent Studies; Teacher Education; Tests, Measurement & Evaluation; Urban Education, Cultural/Non-Traditional

MANUSCRIPT GUIDELINES/COMMENTS:

American Secondary Education is a distinctive journal because it is one of the few scholarly journals that is focused solely on issues of concern to administrators, teachers, and researches in middle and high school education. Articles submitted to the journal should address current theory research, and practice that has a clear relevance to secondary education. The journal features two kinds of articles. Research reports and reviews of literature should be unbiased and scholarly in nature. Such articles may be 20-25 pages in length. Informed commentary articles argue for a particular action agenda by citing relevant literature. Articles in the category should be limited to 10-15 manuscript pages. The Editor welcomes articles about innovative school and district programs, effective classroom practices at the high school and middle school levels and issues relating to the achievement, lifestyle, attitudes, and culture of adolescents. Manuscripts submitted for publication should be sent in triplicate to:

Dr. James A. Rycik, Editor
American Secondary Education
Ashland University/Weltmer Center
401 College Avenue
Ashland, OH 44805-3702

Instructions for Submissions

Three copies of the original manuscript must be submitted for publication in *American Secondary Education*. Each must be typed on one side of the paper, double spaced, with margins of at least one inch. When employed, heading and subheadings should be consistent. Indentations or other special arrangements of the text should be clearly indicated. It is essential that the entire manuscript be double spaced, including footnotes, references, and tables. Manuscripts should be approximately 10 - 30 pages in length, including a 100-word abstract. The *Publication Manual of the American Psychological Association* (APA) 5th Edition is to be used to guide the preparation of the manuscript. Electronic copy in Microsoft Word will be requested at the time of acceptance.

When submitting a manuscript, please include your educational affiliation, academic title, terminal degree, and/or other qualifications or experiences pertinent to your article. It is assumed that the author of the article will include written permission for any quoted materials that require it. All manuscripts are submitted blind to two reviewers for evaluation. The Editor reserves the right to make any editorial changes in manuscripts to achieve greater clarity. Manuscripts will not be returned unless specifically requested, and a stamped envelope is forwarded to the editors. Authors must not submit any manuscript which is under consideration by another publisher.

Annals of Dyslexia

ADDRESS FOR SUBMISSION:

C.K. Leong, Editor
Annals of Dyslexia
c/o International Dyslexia Association
382 Chester Building
8600 LaSalle Road
Baltimore, MD 21286-2044
USA
Phone: 410-296-0232
Fax: 410-321-5069
E-Mail: leong@sask.usask.ca
Web: www.interdys.org
Address May Change:

PUBLICATION GUIDELINES:

Manuscript Length: 21-25 (Text)
Copies Required: One + 3 hard copies
Computer Submission: Yes + 3 hard copies
Format: Double space using 12-point type
Fees to Review: 0.00 US$

Manuscript Style:
    American Psychological Association,
    (5th Edition)

CIRCULATION DATA:

Reader: Academics, Practicing Teachers,
    Administrators, Counselors
Frequency of Issue: 2 Times/Year
Copies per Issue: 10,001 - 25,000
Sponsor/Publisher: The International
    Dyslexia Association
Subscribe Price: 30.00 US$ Individual
    60.00 US$ Individual - yearly
        Free to members

REVIEW INFORMATION:

Type of Review: Blind Review
No. of External Reviewers: 2+
No. of In House Reviewers: 1+
Acceptance Rate: No Reply
Time to Review: 1-3 Months
Reviewers Comments: Yes , sent to author
Invited Articles: No Reply
Fees to Publish: 0.00 US$

MANUSCRIPT TOPICS:

Bilingual/E.S.L.; Educational Psychology; Educational Technology Systems;
Elementary/Early Childhood; Gifted Children; Languages & Linguistics; Reading; Scientific
Study of Dyslexia; Teacher Education

MANUSCRIPT GUIDELINES/COMMENTS:

The Annals of Dyslexia is an interdisciplinary peer-reviewed journal dedicated to the scientific study of dyslexia, its comorbid conditions; and theory-based practices on remediation, and intervention of dyslexia and related areas of written language disorders including spelling, composing, and mathematics. Primary consideration for publication is given to original empirical studies, significant reviews and well documented reports of evidence-based effective practices. Manuscripts are peer-reviewed according to the following criteria: 1) general significance in dyslexia research and practice and for the *Annals* readership; 2) specific contribution within the paradigm adopted; 3) soundness of research methods and interpretation of results; and 4) clarity and organization of writing. Manuscripts should not be submitted simultaneously to other journals and only original papers are considered for publication.

Manuscripts may be submitted throughout the year, and are reviewed by the Editor and at least two other reviewers. The initial review process seldom requires more than three months. The editorial decision letter will communicate suggestions to the author(s) that should facilitate the preparation of the revision and the final version. *Annals* is published twice per year, in June and November.

The 2001 5th edition of the *Publication Manual of the American Psychological Association (APA)* is the primary reference for journal style, format, and related aspects. Authors should follow this *Manual* in preparation of their manuscripts. Some examples are provided in these guidelines. Other examples can be found in such journals as *The Journal of Learning Disabilities,* and the *Journal of Educational Psychology* and others.

Submit one electronic copy (MS WORD) of the manuscript directly to the Editor (**leong@sask.usask.ca**), and three hard copies simultaneously to IDA (address above). An abstract of the paper not exceeding 200 words must be included. The title page should contain the full names, affiliations, postal addresses, phone and fax numbers, and e-mails of **all authors**, along with mailing addresses. All acknowledgement by the authors should be listed on this title page and not at the end of the text, which will be detached when the manuscript is sent for masked review. The manuscript title (without the names and affiliations of the authors) should be repeated on the second or abstract page. If the final version of the paper is accepted, a computer disk containing this final version (Microsoft Word) and two hard copies are required.

PREPARATION OF MANUSCRIPT
Spacing, Formatting, Headings
Manuscript length should be proportional to contribution to research and practice, and normally should not exceed 25 text pages, double-spaced throughout, using 12- point type, plus references, a judicious number of statistical tables and figures. Microsoft Word should be used for word processing. Please put an extra space between each reference. All margins--, left, right, top and bottom -- should be at least one inch wide. Each page should have the abbreviated title at the top left-hand corner of the page (but no author identification). The title of the article should be concise and specific.

"A" and "B" headings should be typed on separate lines with double space in between each heading. Do not italicize or underscore the headings. "A" headings should be centered, and "B" headings should be placed at the left margin. "C" headings should begin at the appropriate paragraph, using capitals and lower case, followed by one space that runs into the text; "D" heads should be underlined. No heads, A, B, C, or D, should be typed in all capital letters.

Page Numbering
All manuscript pages should be numbered consecutively, beginning with the title page. Footnotes should be numbered consecutively in the text, indicated by superscript numbers and typed on a separate page labeled Footnotes. This page should be placed after the text and before references.

64

References in Text
References cited in the text should be followed, in parentheses, by the author's surname (unless it is given in the text of the sentence, as in *a* and *c* below) and years of publication. If there are two or more references cited for the same author with the same year of publication, they are designated by the use of lowercase letters after the year such as 2002a, 2002b.

Examples:
a. The group is receiving the Auditory Discrimination in Depth Program as outlined by Lindamood and Lindamood (1984).
b. The brain, of the rat has been altered as a result of hormone treatments (Diamond, Dowling, and Johnson, 1981).
c. Orton (1928c, 1928d) provided several case studies which support this position.
d. Kamhi and his colleagues indicated that extensive exposure might be necessary to retain accurate representation of a new lexical item if the phonological form of the word is imprecise or unstable (Kamhi, Catts, & Mauer, 1990).

Note: When a work has six or more authors, cite in the text only the surname of the first author followed by et al. and the year for the first and subsequent citations. In the reference list, however, provide the surnames and initials of **all authors**.

Reference List (Samples Only)
The reference list should include only those references cited in the text. Entries in the reference list should be alphabetical by the authors' surnames. Do not number the references. If there is more than one publication by a given author in the same year, add the letters a, b, and so on after the date. Double-space all entries and follow the style of the examples given below. See 2001 *Publication Manual of APA* or journals that use APA style for other examples.

Book
Adams, M.J. (1990). *Beginning to read: Thinking and learning about print.* Cambridge, MA: The MIT Press.

Editored Book and Chapter in Edited Book
Brady, S., & Shankweiler, D. (Eds.). (1991) *Phonological processes in literacy: A tribute to Isabelle Y. Liberman.* Hillsdale, NJ: Lawrence Erlbaum Associates.
Lyon, G. R., Fletcher, J. M., & Barnes, M. C. (2003). Learning disabilities. In E.J. Mash & R. A. Barkley (Eds.), *Child psychopathology* (2nd ed., pp. 520-586). New York: Guilford Press.

Journal Article
Lyon, G. R., Shaywitz, S.E., & Shaywitz, B. A. (2003). A definition of dyslexia. *Annals of Dyslexia, 53,* 1-14.
Rack, J. P., Snowling, M. J., & Olson, R. K. (1992). The nonword reading deficit in developmental dyslexia: A review. *Reading Research Quarterly, 27,* 29-53.

Dissertation or Thesis
Jones, A.J. (1947). *Laterality and dominance in preschool deaf children.* Unpublished doctoral dissertation, Northeastern University, Boston.

Unpublished Paper Read at a Meeting
Snow, C. (1999, November). *Preventing reading difficulties in young children.* Paper presented at the 50th Annual Conference of The International Dyslexia Association, Chicago, IL

Illustrations, Tables and Figures
Illustrations should be original inked drawings in a form suitable for reduction without retouching or redrawing. Suggested size is 8½ x 11 inches. Lettering, numerals and symbols should be large enough so that they will be completely legible after reduction. Photographs should be the original and on glossy paper. Place overlays on all photographs to avoid damage. Permission must be obtained for any illustrative material previously published in a book or journal. Legends for illustrations should not be attached, but typed double-spaced on a separate page and clearly keyed to the illustrations. Electronic artwork should be submitted in EPS or TIFF format only. Minimum resolution for all electronic artwork should be 300 dpi. For color photographs showing fine-grained fMRI, ERP, and other neuroscience findings, a partial fee may be levied to defray the high cost of printing such color diagrams.

In the text, number the tables with Roman numerals in the order in which the tables are first mentioned. Citations in the text to the tables should also be in Roman numerals. Place the citation at the end of the paragraph in which that table is mentioned (for example, Insert Table I about here). Place the actual tables and figures at the end of the article after the references. Type a brief title directly above each table. Place explanatory material for the table in a footnote. Double-space the table, title and explanatory material.

In the text, number the figures in sequence with Arabic numerals and in the order of their mention in the text. Their citations should be in Arabic numerals in the text. Place the citation at the end of the paragraph in which that figure is mentioned (for example, *Insert Figure 1 about here).* Place the actual figure at the end of the article after the references and before each table. Type the legend in double-space and in sequence on a separate page of the manuscript labeled figure 1, 2, 3 etc.; do not type the legend on the figure.

Send Manuscript to the editor.
Reminder: Manuscripts may be sent throughout the year. One electronic copy of the manuscript should be sent to the Editor, Che Kan Leong, Ph.D., D. Litt.; **leong@sask.usask.ca** and three hard copies to Diane Nies of IDA. The International Dyslexia Association, 8600 LaSalle Road, 382 Chester Building, Baltimore, MD 21286-2044, USA

Anthropology & Education Quarterly

ADDRESS FOR SUBMISSION:

Teresa McCarty, Editor
Anthropology & Education Quarterly
Arizona State University
College of Education
Div of Edu Leadership & Policy Studies
Farmer Bldg. 120 / P O Box 852411
Tempe, AZ 85287-2411
USA
Phone: 480-965-6357
Fax: 480-965-1800
E-Mail: aequart@asu.edu
Web: www.aaanet.org/cae/aeq/index.htm
Address May Change:

PUBLICATION GUIDELINES:

Manuscript Length: 30-35
Copies Required: Four + 1 Electronic
Computer Submission: Yes w/hard copies
Format: MS Word
Fees to Review: 0.00 US$

Manuscript Style:
    Chicago Manual of Style, American
    Anthropological Assn. Guidelines

CIRCULATION DATA:

Reader: Academics,
    Researcher/Practitioner/Policy-maker &
    Prg Dvlpr/Gov & NGO
Frequency of Issue: Quarterly
Copies per Issue: 1,400-2,000
Sponsor/Publisher: American
    Anthropological Association, Council on
    Anthropology & Education
Subscribe Price: 89.00 US$ Non-Member
    89.00 US$ Institution
    42.00 US$ CAE Member/part of dues

REVIEW INFORMATION:

Type of Review: Blind Review
No. of External Reviewers: 3-4
No. of In House Reviewers: 1-2
Acceptance Rate: 11-15%
Time to Review: 4 - 6 Months
Reviewers Comments: Yes
Invited Articles: 0-5%
Fees to Publish: 0.00 US$

MANUSCRIPT TOPICS:
Bilingual/E.S.L.; Cultural Foundations of Education; Cultural Studies, Pedagogy; Curriculum Studies; Edu. Technology Applications and Research; Educational Anthropology; Ethnography of Schooling; Elementary/Early Childhood; Foreign Language; Higher Education; Home-School-Community Relations; Immigrant/Refugee Education; Languages & Linguistics; Literacy(ies) Inside and Outside of Schools; Minority Education; Race/Class/Gender sexuality; Identity & Schooling; Reading; Rural Education & Small Schools; Science Math & Environment; Secondary/Adolescent Studies; Social Studies/Social Science; Social/Emotional Issues; Teacher Education; Urban Education, Cultural/Non-Traditional

MANUSCRIPT GUIDELINES/COMMENTS:

Anthropology & Education Quarterly is a peer-reviewed journal that publishes scholarship on schooling in diverse social and cultural contexts and on human learning both inside and outside of schools. Articles rely primarily on ethnographic research to address immediate problems of practice as well as broad theoretical questions. *AEQ* also publishes on educational-ethnographic fieldwork and the teaching of anthropology. *Anthropology & Education Quarterly* is the journal of the Council on Anthropology and Education, a professional association of anthropologists and educational researchers and a section of the American Anthropological Association that meets at the annual meeting of the association. The journal is published by the University of California Press for the American Anthropological Association.

Information for Authors
Send manuscripts to Editor at the above address.

Manuscripts are accepted for review under the following conditions:
1. The manuscript (4 hard copies and 1 electronic copy) should be no more than 35 pages in length (or, for *Reflections from the Field* and *Reflections on the Field*, 10-15 pages), typed, with one-inch margins on all sides, and written in English. *Page length and spacing include endnotes, references, and any tables or figures;* all text should be in 12-point Times New Roman font. *All elements of the manuscript (abstracts, block quotes, dialogue excerpts, endnotes, references, etc.) must be double-spaced.* The right margin should not be justified. Pages should be numbered consecutively, including endnotes, references cited, tables, and figures. Authors of papers chosen for publication should be prepared to submit a copy of their paper's final version electronically or on diskette.

2. The same work has not been and will not be published elsewhere nor is presently submitted elsewhere. *AEQ will consider only 1 manuscript by the same author(s) at a time.* All persons listed as authors have given their approval for the submission of the paper. Copies of letters granting permission to reproduce illustrations, tables, or lengthy quoted passages should be included with the manuscript.

3. All author-identifying information in the body of the text, endnotes, and references must be removed.

4. Each manuscript submitted should include, on a separate page, an abstract of 50 to 75 words.

5. The first page should contain the article title, author(s), affiliation(s), a short form of the title as a suggested running head (less than 45 characters including spaces and letters), and the name, phone number, email address, and complete mailing address of the author to whom correspondence should be sent.

6. Ordinarily the past tense rather than the "ethnographic present" is more appropriate for describing past fieldwork. It is perfectly acceptable to use first-person pronouns.

7. References cited should begin on a separate page following the endnotes. All references must be cited in text or notes. References cited must follow AAA style, as exemplified in this journal and listed in the *AAA Style Guide.*

8. The manuscript should be written according to AAA style guidelines. For punctuation, abbreviations, grammar, compounding, and other matters of style, consult the *Chicago Manual of Style* (14th ed., University of Chicago Press, 1993); for spelling and hyphenation, consult *Webster's Third New International Dictionary* (1981) or its latest abridgment, *Merriam-Webster's Collegiate Dictionary* (10th ed., 2000).

9. Tables and figures should be completely understandable independent of the text. Each table and figure must be cited in the text, given a title or caption, and consecutively numbered with Arabic numerals. Authors must provide good quality originals of all figures to be directly reproduced for publication; photocopies are not acceptable. Tables and figures should be attached to the end of the manuscript following the references cited.

Because *AEQ* is a refereed journal, manuscripts appropriate for *AEQ* are sent to outside reviewers. This process takes 4-5 months.

If the manuscript is accepted for publication, copyright of the article will be assigned exclusively to the publisher, and it is understood that the publisher will not refuse any reasonable request by the author for permission to reproduce any of his or her contributions to *AEQ*.

Appraisal: Science Books for Young People

ADDRESS FOR SUBMISSION:

Diane Holzheimer, Editor
Appraisal: Science Books for Young People
Notheastern University
5 Holmes Hall
Boston, MA 02115
USA
Phone: 617-373-7539
Fax: 508-655-5145
E-Mail: appraisal@lynx.neu.edu
Web: www.appraisal.neu.edu
Address May Change:

PUBLICATION GUIDELINES:

Manuscript Length: Any
Copies Required: Two
Computer Submission: Yes
Format: N/A
Fees to Review: 0.00 US$

Manuscript Style:
    See Manuscript Guidelines

CIRCULATION DATA:

Reader: , Librarians, Science Educators
Frequency of Issue: Quarterly
Copies per Issue: 2,001 - 3,000
Sponsor/Publisher: Edu. Dept. of
    Northeastern University & The New
    England Roundtable of Children's
    Librarians
Subscribe Price:

REVIEW INFORMATION:

Type of Review: Editorial Review
No. of External Reviewers: 0
No. of In House Reviewers: 2
Acceptance Rate: No Reply
Time to Review: 4 - 6 Months
Reviewers Comments: No Reply
Invited Articles: No Reply
Fees to Publish: 0.00 US$

MANUSCRIPT TOPICS:
Educational Psychology; Educational Technology Systems; Elementary/Early Childhood;
Gifted Children; Health & Physical Education; Library Science/Information Resources;
Reading; Science Math & Environment; Teacher Education

MANUSCRIPT GUIDELINES/COMMENTS:

Appraisal is a nonprofit quarterly publication that reviews current science books for children
and teenagers. Our quarterly publications review individual books, series, science activities
and experiments, reference books, photographic essays, picture books, science biographies
and educational software.

Now in its 33rd year of publication, *Appraisal* is a well respected advocate for excellence in
educational science materials for children and teenagers.

For the past 33 years *Appraisal: Science Books for Young People* has been dedicated to the
rigorous evaluation of science materials for children and teenagers. Each book is reviewed by
a practicing children's librarian as well as a scientist in the relevant field.

Appraisal reviews individual books, series, science activities and experiments, reference books, photographic essays, picture books, science biographies and educational software.

Educators find useful reviews in the "Teacher Resources" section – in addition, each issue of *Appraisal* includes a timely article or essay on trends in science education.

Argumentation & Advocacy

ADDRESS FOR SUBMISSION:

Randall Lake, Editor
Argumentation & Advocacy
University of Southern California
Annenberg School for Communication
3502 Watt Way
Los Angeles, CA 90089-0281
USA
Phone:
Fax:
E-Mail: jafa@usc.edu
Web: See Guidelines
Address May Change:

PUBLICATION GUIDELINES:

Manuscript Length: 21-25
Copies Required: Four
Computer Submission: No
Format: N/A
Fees to Review: 0.00 US$

Manuscript Style:
American Psychological Association, &
MLA

CIRCULATION DATA:

Reader: Academics
Frequency of Issue: Quarterly
Copies per Issue: 1,001 - 2,000
Sponsor/Publisher: American Forensic
Association
Subscribe Price: 60.00 US$

REVIEW INFORMATION:

Type of Review: Blind Review
No. of External Reviewers: 3
No. of In House Reviewers: 0
Acceptance Rate: 11-20%
Time to Review: 2 - 3 Months
Reviewers Comments: Yes
Invited Articles: 0-5%
Fees to Publish: 0.00 US$

MANUSCRIPT TOPICS:
Argumentation & Debate; Political and Legal Communication; Teacher Education

MANUSCRIPT GUIDELINES/COMMENTS:

Call for Submissions

Argumentation and Advocacy, the flagship publication of the American Forensic Association, invites scholarly submissions concerning any dimension of argumentation studies, contemporary or historical, including but not limited to argumentation theory, culture and argument, public and political argument, legal argument, and forensics and pedagogy. Studies employing any appropriate research methodology are welcome. Manuscripts conforming to the guidelines for submissions may be directed to:

Randall A. Lake, Editor, *Argumentation and Advocacy*
Annenberg School for Communication
University of Southern California
3502 Watt Way, Los Angeles, CA 90089-0281
Website: **www.americanforensics.org/AA/aa_info.html**

72

Call for Book Reviews

Argumentation & Advocacy invites reviews of scholarly books relevant to the interdisciplinary study of argumentation, including but not limited to argumentation theory, historical and contemporary studies of public argument, legal argumentation, and forensics. Reviews should be no longer than 1500 words; single reviews of more than one book may vary accordingly. Reviews should include relevant data about the book, the text of the review, reviewer's name and affiliation, and references, if necessary. Reviews should be submitted in hard copy format as well as on disk. Questions and submission may be directed to:

Karla Leeper, Book Review Editor
Argumentation & Advocacy
One Bear Place #97368
Baylor University
Waco, TX 76798

Submission Guidelines

Argumentation and Advocacy seeks to publish the best in studies of argumentation in all its forms and from diverse theoretical and methodological perspectives. It seeks to address a broad intellectual audience interested in argumentation studies but not necessarily conversant with a specialized vocabulary.

The journal follows a policy of blind peer review. Manuscripts for regular issues ordinarily will be read by two or three reviewers selected from among the Editorial Board and invited referees; manuscripts for special issues will be read by a guest Editor and invited referees.

To ensure blind review, a detachable title page should contain the author's name, current academic title and affiliation, mailing address, telephone number, fax number, and e-mail address, and post-secondary institutions attended and degrees earned; any material that would identify the author should be stripped from the text. Include a history of the manuscript: whether it is derived from a graduate thesis (if so, identify the advisor), any previous public presentation or publication of any portion, or other relevant information.

Manuscripts should be double-spaced throughout, including long quotations, notes and references. On a separate page, include an abstract of no more than 100 words with a list of five suggested key words. Notes, lists of works cited, tables and figures should appear on separate pages following the text. The title of the essay (without the author's name) should repeat on the first page of the manuscript. Text should be left-justified only.

Manuscripts should be prepared using WordPerfect (preferred) or Microsoft Word for Windows, and conform to either the *MLA Handbook for Writers of Research Papers*, 6th ed., 2003 (preferred; use the reference system described in Chapters 5-6), or the *Publication Manual of the American Psychological Association*, 5th ed., 2001. Content notes may be used with either style, but should be kept to a minimum. Upon acceptance of the manuscript for publication, authors should be prepared to furnish photocopies of all quotations for verification purposes, and to provide a final version of the essay in both hard and digital form, including camera-ready copy for artwork and figures.

Manuscripts submitted to *Argumentation and Advocacy* obligate the author to grant exclusive right of review to this journal until such time as s/he receives the results of our review. Essays that have been published previously in their entirety in other sources should not be submitted; essays that have been published previously in part should be substantially revised before submission. Upon acceptance, copyright should be assigned to the American Forensic Association.

Submit three hard and one digital copy of the manuscript to: Randall A. Lake Annenberg School for Communication, University of Southern California, 3502 Watt Way, Los Angeles, CA 90089-0281. The digital copy may be e-mailed as an attachment to **jafa@usc.edu**, with the title in the subject line. Manuscripts will not be processed for review until both hard and digital copies have been received.

Copyright and Photocopy Policy
Photocopies of all material published by the American Forensic Association including *Argumentation and Advocacy* and its predecessor the *Journal of the American Forensic Association* may be made for classroom use free of charge if all of the following criteria are fulfilled: (1) no fees above the actual duplication costs are charged, (2) the materials are photocopies and not reprints or republications, (3) a single notice of use is mailed to the Executive Secretary of the Association, and (4) the material includes a full bibliographic citation and the following statement: "Copyrighted by the American Forensic Association. Photocopied by permission of the publisher." A photocopy of this statement serves as the American Forensic Association's official permission for using materials in this way. This free permission is *not applicable,* under any of the following circumstances: when an additional fee is charged for the material; when the material is retained electronically for nonprint access; when the material is reprinted in a commercial publication. The American Forensic Association encourages the availability of material from its publications in such sources, but the Association may charge an additional fee, and the explicit permission from the Executive Secretary of AFA is required. Address such requests and reports of photocopying to:

James W. Pratt
Executive Secretary, American Forensic Association
Box 256
River Falls, WI 54022

Art Education

ADDRESS FOR SUBMISSION:

B. Stephen Carpenter, Editor
Art Education
Virginia Communwealth University
Department of Art Education
PO Box 843084
Richmond, VI 23284
USA
Phone: 804-828-3592
Fax: 804-827-0255
E-Mail: bscarpenter@vcu.edu
Web: http://www.naea-reston.org
Address May Change: 3/26/2006

CIRCULATION DATA:

Reader: Practicing Teachers, Academics,
    Administrators & Counselors
Frequency of Issue: 6 Times/Year
Copies per Issue: 10,001 - 25,000
Sponsor/Publisher: The National Art
    Education Association
Subscribe Price: 25.00 US$ NAEA
    Member
      50.00 US$ Non-Member
      75.00 US$ Canada & Other Non-
      Member

PUBLICATION GUIDELINES:

Manuscript Length: 11-15
Copies Required: Three
Computer Submission: Yes Email
Format: MS Word, RTF
Fees to Review: 0.00 US$

Manuscript Style:
    American Psychological Association

REVIEW INFORMATION:

Type of Review: Blind Review
No. of External Reviewers: 2
No. of In House Reviewers: 1
Acceptance Rate: 35%
Time to Review: 2 - 3 Months
Reviewers Comments: Yes
Invited Articles: 0-5%
Fees to Publish: 0.00 US$

MANUSCRIPT TOPICS:

Art Museum Education; Art/Music; Curriculum Studies; Educational Technology Systems; Elementary/Early Childhood; Gifted Children; Higher Education; Higher Education; Secondary/Adolescent Studies; Special Education; Teacher Education; Tests, Measurement & Evaluation; Urban Education, Cultural/Non-Traditional

MANUSCRIPT GUIDELINES/COMMENTS:

What kinds of manuscripts may be submitted to *Art Education*?
Manuscripts should deal with topics of professional interest to a diverse audience of art educators. Research reports should be submitted to journals such as *Studies in Art Education*. How-to ideas should be submitted to other appropriate journals.

How should a manuscript be prepared?
In general, manuscripts should be prepared in accordance with the guidelines in the *Publication Manual of the American Psychological Association*, 5th edition:

- All textual materials must be typed double-spaced with ample margins and numbered pages.
- Type text flush left with quadruple spacing between paragraphs. Do not indent.
- Do not use hyphens to break a word at the end of a line; let the word wrap to the next line.
- Underline all type that should be in italics.
- **Bold** all copy that should be emphasized.
- Text for footnotes should be placed at end of the article, following the References section.
- Text for illustration captions should follow the References and Footnotes sections.

The title should appear on the first page of the text. Include a page with the author's name, position or title, address, e-mail address, telephone numbers, and a word count for the text of the manuscript. Page numbers and a running header are helpful. If possible, also include photocopies of photographs for review purposes. Submit three copies of the manuscript. Also include a cover letter stating that the manuscript is neither currently under review nor previously published in other journals.

How long should a manuscript be?
Manuscripts for articles should be close to 3,000 words. Manuscripts for the Instructional Resources section should be approximately 2,750 words. Submissions that vary significantly from these limits will be returned without review.

When should manuscripts be submitted?
Manuscripts are welcome at any time. The review process begins shortly after a submission is received. Manuscripts sent to *Art Education* must be neither published in nor under review for other journals.

What writing style should authors use?
Write in a precise and straightforward manner. Avoid passive constructions. A conversational tone is conducive for reading.

What about quotations and references?
Avoid excessive use of quotations. Use quotations only when paraphrasing fails to convey another author's meaning. Be sure that all quotations and citations in your manuscript are correctly referenced in the References section. If you wish to include a list of publications not cited in your article, list them in a Resources section at the end of the article.

What about pictures?
Photographs that enhance the text are welcome. Other than Polaroid pictures, almost any type of photograph or slide is acceptable. Disks for digital images should be labeled with the appropriate application and author's name. Include fonts with Encapsulated Postscript (EPS) files. Provide a laser print for each digital image.

Digital images for article manuscripts must be the equivalent of 300 dpi (color or b/w) and should measure about 4"x6". Digital images for Instructional Resource must be 300 dpi and about 8"x10". Preferably, images for Instructional Resources should be submitted to NAEA for scanning by the magazine's printer.

Only one set of photographs is necessary. (Include photocopies of the images with each of the three manuscripts for review.) Release forms must accompany each photograph. Use a standard form, as provided by schools or museums, or contact the editorial assistant or publications office at NAEA.

Photographs relating to art education topics may be submitted without accompanying text for possible use in Association publications. Send them to the *Art Education* production assistant, National Art Education Association, 1916 Association Drive, Reston, VA 22091. Credit will be given for any photographs used. Images used for publication are not returned unless specifically requested.

Where should the manuscript be sent?
Send manuscripts, cover letter, and images to: B. Stephen Carpenter, II, Department of Art Education, Virginia Commonwealth University, Department of Art Education, P.O. Box 843084, Richmond, Virginia 23284, USA.

What happens next?
The editorial assistant inspects all submissions. Manuscripts of appropriate length are then sent for review to members of the editorial board or review panel. At that point, the author receives notification that the review process has begun. Because *Art Education* receives hundreds of manuscripts each year, the review process may take 12 weeks or longer. After the reviews have been returned, the editor contacts the author. (Only one co-author is notified and is responsible for conveying the information to all other authors of the manuscript.) Virtually every manuscript considered for publication requires revisions and further editing. Some manuscripts must undergo a second review.

How will the manuscript be edited?
The editor and reviewers edit the manuscript. Suggested modifications may be required for publication such as condensing the article, deleting paragraphs, adding material, making stylistic changes, or changing the title. The intent of this process is to publish articles that convey ideas in the clearest, most effective manner.

Why is a manuscript rejected?
More manuscripts are submitted to *Art Education* than can be published in the journal. Some rejected manuscripts are poorly written, or they address topics that are dated or of limited interest. Manuscripts that are commercial or self-promotional are also rejected. Other manuscripts may be rejected because their topics have received adequate coverage or they fail to complement the editorial agenda of the Association. Position papers and articles written in a scholarly style about pedagogy should be submitted to *Studies in Art Education*. Manuscripts that are not accepted for publication will be returned upon request.

If accepted, when will a manuscript be published?

It may be many months before an accepted manuscript appears in print. The publication process typically takes four months, and the editor holds manuscripts for appropriate topical groupings in issues. Authors receive notification when their manuscripts are sent to Reston for publication.

What about galley proofs?

Galley proofs are sent to the author for proofreading. The only changes that can be accommodated at this stage are corrections to typographical errors or the insertion of missing text. The author, editor, and editorial staff all read the galley proofs to ensure accurate publication.

What about copyright?

The National Art Education Association (NAEA) copyrights the journal. Unless other arrangements are made in advance of publication, NAEA controls future rights to each article. It is NAEA policy not to grant permission for commercial use without author consent. Generally, authors may reprint their articles in other publications after a formal request is made through the NAEA office.

What about other requests?

Send questions about the content and form of manuscripts, the editorial review process, or other editorial matters to the editor.

INSTRUCTIONAL RESOURCES GUIDELINES
What are Instructional Resources?

Instructional Resources, published in each issue of *Art Education*, consist of full-color reproductions of museum art objects and artworks with appropriate information for classroom use.

Who can submit Instructional Resources?

Anyone with access to museum objects and artworks, and curriculum-writing expertise is welcome to submit. In the past, instructional resources have come from individuals or teams of teachers and museum educators.

How should I begin?

First, read the general author guidelines for *Art Education*. Next, you might start by looking at recent Instructional Resources to study their format and see what topics have been covered. Then, contact a co-author, if desired; establish a topic or theme; and identify related art artworks.1 Determine a grade range and begin drafting text (no longer than 2,750 words) in compliance with the guidelines.

What else should I take into consideration?

- Instructional Resources should state an objective and have immediate and practical classroom applications for teachers.
- Content must be derived from the artworks and must relate the works to each other and to the objective.

- The material must include information about the artworks or artists or provide cultural or historical context.
- More than one approach to studying art should be used within the lesson plan.
- There must be an identified, specific grade range. (K-12 is too broad).
- There must be an evaluation component to determine achievement of the objectives.
- The writer(s) must have firsthand knowledge of the artworks used.
- Submissions should not be promotional in nature.
- Appropriate national or other standards may be listed briefly.
- The reference list must cite your sources of information about the artworks or artists, and these citations must appear within the text. Do not submit alternate listings, such as bibliographies or reference lists.

The Instructional Resources coordinator and the editor of *Art Education* also attend to the following:
- How well a submission relates to any designated theme without replicating other Instructional Resources.
- The degree to which the submission complements the range and diversity of artworks presented in multiple issues of the journal.
- Whether the submission contributes to an annual balance of content areas (aesthetic, critical, historical, art production).

How should I submit images and what format should I use?
Submitted images may be prints, transparencies, or negatives. If digital images are submitted, they should be the highest quality scan available, and sized to 8x10 inches at 300 dpi. When digital images, transparencies, or scans are sent, they should be accompanied by color proofs for the printer to reference, or else the color proofs will be sent to the author (or gallery, museum, etc.) for approval before printing. Please specify the person who will assume this responsibility.

Where should I send my submission?
Send one copy only with reproductions (or photocopies) to the Instructional Resources coordinator at the address listed below. Retain a copy for your files.

What if I have other questions?
Refer to the general author guidelines for *Art Education*, or contact the Instructional Resources coordinator.

[1] Authors are responsible for securing permission to reproduce the artworks included in Instructional Resources.

Arts Education Policy Review (Design for Arts in Education)

ADDRESS FOR SUBMISSION:

Thomas O'Brien, Managing Editor
Arts Education Policy Review (Design for
    Arts in Education)
Heldref Publications, Inc.
1319 18th Street, N.W.
Washington, DC 20036
USA
Phone: 202-296-6267 ext. 256
Fax: 202-296-5149
E-Mail: aepr@heldref.org
Web: www.heldref.org
Address May Change:

PUBLICATION GUIDELINES:

Manuscript Length: 3500 - 4500 Words
Copies Required: Two
Computer Submission: Yes
Format: MS Word
Fees to Review: 0.00 US$

Manuscript Style:
    Chicago Manual of Style

CIRCULATION DATA:

Reader: Academics, Administrators
Frequency of Issue: Bi-Monthly
Copies per Issue: 1,000-2,000
Sponsor/Publisher: Heldref Publications,
  Inc.
Subscribe Price: 54.00 US$ Individual
    108.00 US$ Institutional
    16.00 US$ Add'l for Outside U.S.

REVIEW INFORMATION:

Type of Review: Editorial Review
No. of External Reviewers: 2
No. of In House Reviewers: 0
Acceptance Rate: No Reply
Time to Review: 1 - 2 Months
Reviewers Comments: No
Invited Articles: 50% +
Fees to Publish: 0.00 US$

MANUSCRIPT TOPICS:

Adult Career & Vocational; Art/Music; Curriculum Studies; Education
Management/Administration; Higher Education; Policy Studies in Art Education; Teacher
Education; Tests, Measurement & Evaluation

MANUSCRIPT GUIDELINES/COMMENTS:

Arts Education Policy Review asks that contributors learn about the journal before submitting
articles. Ask us for indexes of articles and topics covered. The following guidelines are
intended to suggest the *kind* of treatment that any topic should receive.

Contributors should make sure that any submission is a policy article, complete with policy
recommendations about arts education from prekindergarten through twelfth grade. Articles
about college education should focus on teacher preparation for these grades or teacher
retention in arts education.

AEPR intends to provide a unique service by bringing fresh analytical vigor to both perennial and new policy issues in arts education. *AEPR* presents analyses and recommendations focused on policy. The goal of any article should not be description or celebration (although reports of successful programs could be part of a policy article). Any article focused on a program (or programs) should address why something works or doesn't work, how it works, how it could work better, and most important, what various policymakers (from teachers to legislators) can do about it. *Many articles are rejected because they lack this element.*

Because its subject matter is ideas, *AEPR* does not promote individuals, institutions, methods, or products. It does not aim to repeat commonplace ideas. Editors want articles that show originality, probe deeply, and take discussion beyond common wisdom and familiar rhetoric. Articles that merely restate the importance of arts education, call attention to the existence of issues long since addressed, or repeat standard solutions cannot be considered.

AEPR is an open forum in the sense that it has no editorial bias regarding particular approaches to arts education. Rather, its purpose is to present and explore many points of view; it contains articles for and against all sorts of ideas, policies, and proposals for arts education. Its overall purpose is to help readers think for themselves, rather than to tell them how they should think.

Policy Orientations

AEPR respects scholarship and research, but these alone do not constitute policy content. Policy analysis often involves educated opinion about the meanings of ideas, events, decisions, decision-making frameworks, and educational content, such as the following:

- gathering and interpreting information about simple or complex issues in order to suggest what should be done;
- looking at decisions of the past and suggesting what went right or wrong and why;
- taking a body of research or scholarship and exploring its ramifications;
- focusing on decisions in process or decisions already made, perhaps explaining agreement or disagreement or developing a list of potential promises and pitfalls.

These orientations can be applied to many issues—from the structure and results of psychometric research to the values climate that would support the arts as an educational basic. They can deal with the relationships of teacher preparation to cultural development, the problems of curriculum building in the midst of an information and data explosion, the particular challenges of teaching specific art forms, and the impact of political, economic, cultural, artistic, and other climates on decision making for arts instruction. The list is endless; the permutations cover a rich and vast territory for intellectually based work. *AEPR* seeks to cover as much of that territory as possible.

When starting an article, readers not only expect to learn more about an issue, but they also expect to have their horizons expanded. Even if they disagree with the author's conclusions, they want to feel that the insights gained were worth the time expended. They expect an intellectually rich, thorough, and logical analysis of real or projected consequences as the basis for recommendations about next steps.

Writing

AEPR seeks writing that is clear, cogent, incisive, and illuminating, irrespective of its specific style. Neither simplicity nor complexity, brevity nor length is considered a virtue itself. Articles must exhibit compositional craft; they must have internal integrity and flow logically. Titles and subtitles should be consistent with each other and the text. Texts must be primarily the author's own work; quotations from others strung together by scraps of original text cannot be published. Any accounts of personal experience must be tied to policy analyses or recommendations. *AEPR* editors work diligently with each author to ensure the best possible text. However, they will not turn rough drafts into finished articles. At the time of submission, the writing—by its content, organization, and professional finish—should reflect the importance of the ideas being presented.

Preparation of Articles

When preparing an article, make sure that its subject matter and approach are consistent with the requirements of a policy-oriented journal. Question the extent to which the text meets the guidelines and criteria outlined above. Think of important individuals you would like to reach with your ideas. Edit and polish until you are sure that even the most knowledgeable and intellectually exacting of your readers will be impressed with what you have to say and how you say it.

Most of all, question the extent to which statements and conclusions will withstand careful scrutiny and analysis. Remember that the policy arena is about resolving disagreements over what should be done. Targets are always moving. It is not the author's obligation to develop the perfect solution or an unanswerable argument, but facts must be accurate. Conclusions or proposals must flow from analyses and be defensible. The reader should be able to enjoy the pleasure of fine work, even when the subject matter is serious, the analyses profound, or the conclusions difficult.

Submission Guidelines

AEPR uses *The Chicago Manual of Style*, 15th edition, for all matters of style, including references in author/date format (authors may use Humanities style capitalization; see *CMS* 16.7) Authors are responsible for checking that all quotations are accurate and obtaining permission to reprint, where necessary. Include full bibliographical information, including page numbers for all quotations.

E-mail. You may submit an article electronically as a double-spaced Word file with minimal formatting in Times or Times, New Roman. PLEASE do not use style sheets, forced section or page breaks, or automatic footnotes. E-mail tables in one separate file and figures in another separate file. Send a hard-copy version of text, tables, and figures as backup. E-mail address: **aepr@heldref.org**.

Regular mail. Submit two copies, double-spaced, of each article to the managing editor, with generous margins to allow for editing. Enclose a letter that includes your name, address, and telephone and fax numbers and states that the manuscript has not been submitted elsewhere or previously published. If you have questions or need assistance, call the managing editor at 202-296-6267, ext. 256, or e-mail; **aepr@heldref.org**.

82

Reminders

1. Do your homework before submitting articles; check our indexes; read guidelines carefully.
2. Make sure any submission is a policy article, focused on pre-k–12 arts education.
3. Articles should not be merely descriptions or celebrations of programs; why something works or how it could work better is key.
4. Do not promote individuals, institutions, methods, or products or repeat commonplace ideas. We know arts education is important. We know it could use more funding. What should we do if we get it, and why?
5. Always include policy recommendations in your article.

Send manuscripts to: Managing Editor, *Arts Education Policy Review*, Heldref Publications, 1319 Eighteenth Street NW, Washington DC 20036-1802; e-mail, **aepr@heldref.org**.

Asia-Pacific Journal of Teacher Education

ADDRESS FOR SUBMISSION:

Editors
Asia-Pacific Journal of Teacher Education
Australian Centre - Educational Studies
Macquarie University
Building X5B
New South Wales, 2109
Australia
Phone: +61 2 9850 9864
Fax:
E-Mail: APJTE@aces1.aces.mq.edu.au
Web: www.tandf.co.uk/journals
Address May Change:

PUBLICATION GUIDELINES:

Manuscript Length: 21-25
Copies Required: Three Electronic
    preferred
Computer Submission: Yes
Format: Word or RTF formates
Fees to Review: 0.00 US$

Manuscript Style:
    See Manuscript Guidelines

CIRCULATION DATA:

Reader: Academics
Frequency of Issue: 3 Times/Year
Copies per Issue:
Sponsor/Publisher: Australian Teacher
    Education Association / Taylor & Francis
Subscribe Price: 291.00 US$ Individual
    812.00 US$ Institution

REVIEW INFORMATION:

Type of Review: Blind Review
No. of External Reviewers: 2
No. of In House Reviewers: No Reply
Acceptance Rate: 6-10%
Time to Review: 4 - 6 Months
Reviewers Comments: Yes
Invited Articles: 0-5%
Fees to Publish: 0.00 US$

MANUSCRIPT TOPICS:
Teacher Education

MANUSCRIPT GUIDELINES/COMMENTS:

Aims and Scope
This journal promotes critical analysis of pedagogy across early childhood, primary, secondary and post compulsory education, focusing on:
- The pre-service and continuing education of teachers
- New ideas and innovative practices
- The professional development of teachers
- Teaching as work
- Social and policy contexts of teacher education
- New Technology

This international, peer-reviewed journal is published on behalf of the Australian Teacher Education Association (ATEA).

84

Instructions for Authors
Note to Authors: please make sure your contact address information is clearly visible on the **outside** of all packages you are sending to Editors.

The Editor invites submission of papers covering all aspects of teacher education. Papers will not be considered if they have been published previously or are being considered for publication elsewhere.

Manuscripts for submission, and all editorial correspondence, should be sent to: The Editors, Asia Pacific Journal of Teacher Education, Building X5B, Macquarie University, NSW 2109, Australia. Email: **APJTE@aces1.aces.mq.edu.au**.

Manuscripts
1. Manuscripts should be typed double-spaced on one side of the paper, with generous margins all round. Single-spaced manuscripts will not be considered for publication.

2. For anonymity in the reviewing process, authors' names, affiliations, postal addresses and telephone numbers should appear on a separate covering page.

3. An abstract of approximately 150 words should accompany each manuscript.

4. Manuscripts should conform to the style of papers published in the *Asia-Pacific Journal of Teacher Education*.

5. References should be indicated in the manuscript by giving the author's name, with the year of publication in parentheses. If several papers by the same author and from the same year are cited, a, b, etc. should be placed after the year of publication. References should be listed in full at the end of the paper in the following standard form:

For books
Everitt, B. (1980) Cluster analysis (2nd edn) (London, Heinemann).

For articles
Toomey, R. (1989) Caution: classroom under observation, Asia-Pacific Journal of Teacher Education, 28(3), 47-56.

For chapters within books
Clark, C. M. & Peterson, P. S. (1986) Teachers' thought processes, in: M. C. Wittrock (Ed.) Handbook of research on teaching (3rd edn) (New York, Macmillan), 223-254.

For conference proceedings
McKinnon, D. H. & Sinclair, K. E. (1986) Teachers teaching teachers, paper presented at the Annual Conference of the Australian Association for Research in Education, Melbourne, 1-3 November.

6. All figures must be in camera-ready form.

7. Three good quality copies of the manuscript should be submitted.

8. Once a manuscript has been accepted (usually after revisions), it must be submitted on a microcomputer disk as well as in hard copy. The required format is:

   IBM compatible 5.25 inch 360k disk (Double Sided Double Density)
   IBM compatible 3.50 inch 720k disk (Double Sided High Density)
   The preferred data formats are: MS DOS using Word V.5 or ASCII.
   Machintosh MS Word V5.0 or V6: also acceptable.

9. Manuscripts not conforming to the above guidelines will not be considered for publication.

Electronic Submission. Authors should send the final, revised version of their articles in both hard copy paper and electronic disk forms. It is essential that the hard copy (paper) version **exactly** matches the material on disk. Please print out the hard copy from the disk you are sending. Submit three printed copies of the final version with the disk to the journal's editorial office. Save all files on a standard 3.5 inch high-density disk. We prefer to receive disks in Microsoft Word in a PC format, but can translate from most other common word processing programs as well as Macs. Please specify which program you have used. Do not save your files as "text only" or "read only".

Book Reviews
1. Books relevant to teacher education may be sent to the Editor, who will consider soliciting a review for inclusion in the Journal.

2. Book reviews must be typed double-spaced, and should be prepared in the style of reviews published in the Journal. One copy only of book reviews is required.

Proofs
Proofs will be sent to the authors if there is sufficient time to do so. They should be corrected and returned to the Editor within **three days**. Major alterations to the text cannot be accepted.

Early Electronic Offprints. Corresponding authors can now receive their article by e-mail as a complete PDF. This allows the author to print up to 50 copies, free of charge, and disseminate them to colleagues. In many cases this facility will be available up to two weeks prior to publication. Or, alternatively, corresponding authors will receive the traditional 50 offprints. A copy of the journal will be sent by post to all corresponding authors after publication. Additional copies of the journal can be purchased at the author's preferential rate of £15.00/$25.00 per copy.

Copyright. It is a condition of publication that authors vest or license copyright in their articles, including abstracts, in the Australian Teacher Education Association. This enables us to ensure full copyright protection and to disseminate the article, and the journal, to the widest possible readership in print and electronic formats as appropriate.

86

Authors may, of course, use the article elsewhere **after** publication without prior permission from Carfax, provided that acknowledgement is given to the Journal as the original source of publication, and that Carfax is notified so that our records show that its use is properly authorised. Authors are themselves responsible for obtaining permission to reproduce copyright material from other sources.

Australasian Journal of Educational Technology

ADDRESS FOR SUBMISSION:

Catherine McLoughlin, Editor
Australasian Journal of Educational
  Technology
ELECTRONIC SUBMISSION ONLY
  (via email)
Western Australia
Phone: +61 8 9367 1133
Fax:
E-Mail: ajet-editor@ascilite.org.au
Web: www.ascilite.org.au/ajet/
Address May Change:

PUBLICATION GUIDELINES:

Manuscript Length: 7,500 words
Copies Required: One No Hardcopy
Computer Submission: Yes Email
Format: MS Word, other formats
Fees to Review: 0.00 US$

Manuscript Style:
    American Psychological Association,
    See Guidelines

CIRCULATION DATA:

Reader: Practicing Teachers, Academics
Frequency of Issue: 3 Times/Year
Copies per Issue: Less than 1,000
Sponsor/Publisher: ASCILITE, ASET
Subscribe Price: 30.00 US$ Individual
    30.00 US$ Institution/Library

REVIEW INFORMATION:

Type of Review: Blind Review
No. of External Reviewers: 2
No. of In House Reviewers: 1
Acceptance Rate: 25-35%
Time to Review: 1 - 2 Months
Reviewers Comments: Yes
Invited Articles: 10%
Fees to Publish: 0.00 US$

MANUSCRIPT TOPICS:

Computers; Education Management/Administration; Educational Technology Systems;
Higher Education; Instructional Design; Technology; Telecommunications

MANUSCRIPT GUIDELINES/COMMENTS:

Topics also include: educational applications of computer technologies, educational
telecommunications, educational media, multimedia, online courses, e-learning, in all sectors
of education.

The Australian Journal of Educational Technology is a refereed journal publishing research
and review articles in educational technology, instructional design, educational applications of
computer technologies, educational telecommunications and related areas. AJET's principal
supporting societies are:
    Australasian Society for Computers in Learning in Tertiary Education (ASCILITE)
    Australian Society for Educational Technology (ASET)
    International Society for Performance Improvement, Melbourne Chapter

AJET invites submissions of short features (up to 1000 words) and articles (up to 7500 words). Original contributions are welcome from writers in any organisation in any country, and membership of a supporting society is not a requirement for submissions. Articles are subjected to peer review on a double blind, confidential basis by at least two referees from the Board's Panel of Reviewers. *AJET* is a recognised peer reviewed journal listed in Ulrich's Periodicals Directory. Australian authors may note that articles published in *AJET* earn the classification "Journal Article" (previously known as "C1" category) for the purposes of DEST's Higher Education Research Data Collection. Articles should be previously unpublished and if accepted will be published in *AJET* and the Journal's world wide web site **http://www.ascilite.org.au/ajet/.**

Editor
Associate Professor Catherine McLoughlin
School of Education (ACT), Australian Catholic University
PO Box 256, Dickson ACT 2602, Australia
Tel: +61 2 6209 1100 Fax +61 2 6209 1185
Email: **c.mcloughlin@signadou.acu.edu.au**

Production Editor and Business Manager
Dr. Roger Atkinson
Unit 5, 202 Coode Street, Como WA 6152, Australia
Tel: +61 8 9367 1133 Email: rjatkinson@bigpond.com
Email communications preferred please

Australian Journal of Early Childhood

ADDRESS FOR SUBMISSION:

Sue Wales, Publication Officer
Australian Journal of Early Childhood
Early Childhood Australian
P.O. Box 7105
Watson ACT, 2602
Australia
Phone: +61 2 6242 1800
Fax: +61 2 6242 1818
E-Mail: publishing@earlychildhood.org.au
Web: See Guidelines
Address May Change:

PUBLICATION GUIDELINES:

Manuscript Length: 11-15 or 25-28 pg dbl
    sp
Copies Required: Three
Computer Submission: Yes disk or email
Format: MS Word
Fees to Review: 0.00 US$

Manuscript Style:
    See Manuscript Guidelines

CIRCULATION DATA:

Reader: Administrators, Practicing
    Teachers, Childcare Workers, Academics
Frequency of Issue: Quarterly
Copies per Issue: 3,000
Sponsor/Publisher: Early Childhood
    Australia
Subscribe Price: 60.00 AUS$

REVIEW INFORMATION:

Type of Review: Blind Review
No. of External Reviewers: 2-3
No. of In House Reviewers: 0
Acceptance Rate: 75%
Time to Review: 2-6 Months
Reviewers Comments: Yes
Invited Articles: 31-50%
Fees to Publish: 0.00 US$

MANUSCRIPT TOPICS:
Adult Career & Vocational; Art/Music; Audiology/Speech Pathology; Bilingual/E.S.L.;
Cultural Studies, Pedagogy; Curriculum Studies; Education Management/Administration;
Educational Psychology; Educational Technology Systems; Elementary/Early Childhood;
Gifted Children; Health & Physical Education; Languages & Linguistics; Reading; Rural
Education & Small Schools; Science Math & Environment; Social Studies/Social Science;
Special Education; Teacher Education; Urban Education, Cultural/Non-Traditional

MANUSCRIPT GUIDELINES/COMMENTS:

The *Australian Journal of Early Childhood* is sponsored by Early Childhood Australia. It
features up-to-date articles designed to impart new information and encourage the critical
exchange of ideas among practitioners in the early childhood field. The *AJEC* committee
invites contributions on all aspects of the education and care of young children. The journal is
controlled by an editorial board and all papers submitted to the journal are peer-reviewed.

Original work expressing an authoritative viewpoint, profiles of associations and organisations
dealing with young children, and short reports and letters commenting on earlier published
articles will also be considered.

- In preparing manuscripts for publication, contributors should consider the audience of parents and policy makers; academics; and professional, paraprofessional and volunteer workers in the early childhood field. Manuscripts should be written in a language and style, and with content appropriate for this audience.
- Non-sexist language should be used. Articles should avoid the arbitrary use of titles which stereotype males and females, i.e. 'fireman' should be 'firefighter', and authors should avoid pronouns such as 'he', 'him' and 'his' in reference to a hypothetical person.
- Contributions should be typed on one side of A4 paper, double-spaced, with page numbers and headers/footers. A 150-word abstract should be included. Three copies of each manuscript, including tables and illustrations should be submitted, together with a copy on disk or supplied by email.
- Graphs and charts should be supplied in original format as well within Word.
- Manuscripts should not include footnotes.
- The cover sheet should contain the author's name and contact details. This information should NOT appear anywhere else in the manuscript.
- Tables should be numbered with Arabic numerals. All tables and figures should be referred to in the text and their approximate position marked in the text margin.
- Acknowledgement of receipt of manuscripts will be sent to contributing authors prior to consideration by the Editorial Committee. Authors will then be advised within six months if the manuscript will be published in a forthcoming issue of the Journal. Contributions should be sent to the Publications Officer.
- Harvard academic referencing is to be used.

The major aim of these guidelines is to assist authors to submit their work to ECA in a form which can be efficiently transformed into timely and attractive publications via our in-house production process. If manuscripts do not conform to the guidelines they will be sent back far revision.

1. Length of manuscripts
Manuscripts should contain 3000 words (and no more than 3500 words) OR 6000 words (and no more than 6500 words). This includes a 150-word abstract, charts, tables, illustrations, references etc. The manuscript will be fitted on to approximately six OR twelve printed journal-sized pages. A maximum of 50% of articles at 6000 words will be included in any edition of A4C. Articles for themed editions may appear in two parts over two issues. The author must specify their intention to the edition editor and the publications section and submit both parts together.

2. Form of submission
Material should be submitted to ECA on disk together with three hard copies. Please use Microsoft Word and put lists of figures into tables using Word. Graphs or illustrations may be re-created by our Graphic Designer. Call the Publications Section first if you have questions.

The following are publication prerequisites:
- Cover Sheet. Showing author's name, affiliations and contact details ONLY on cover sheet for blind review purposes.

- 150-word Abstract (on a separate page).
- Double line spacing.
- Pace numbering and a running heading.
- Copies of all charts, tables, illustration, etc.
- Document word count must be included.

Please mark headings, subheadings and paragraphs clearly. For example,

This is a Page or Article Heading (Bold, first letter of each word is a capital).
This is a subheading or side heading (italics, only the initial letter is a capital).

3. Style

The current *Australian Government Publishing Service Style Manual* is used as the basis for ECA's house style. *The Macquarie Dictionary* is the accepted dictionary of ECA publications. ECA requests all manuscripts conform with these styles. ECA prefers to use non-stereotypical language in its publications, i.e., authors should avoid the use of sexist, ageist, or racist terminology. For example, don't use 'fireman' when you could use 'firefighter'.

4. Using numbers in figures

The use of metric measurement is preferred. As a general rule, figures rather than words should be used for:

sums of money	$5.08 or 25¢, $2000 (no commas or space in thousands)
times of day	10.30 a.m., 50 min., 11 o'clock
dates	14 September 1994 (day month year)
mass	250t, 120kg, 50g
measures	56 litres, 25mL, 26km, 16mm, 25cm
temperature	35°C
percentages	nine per cent (if appearing infrequently) or 9% (if appearing frequently or in tables)
age	60 years old; an eight-year-old
numbers in text	(0-9) should generally be expressed as words but (10 onwards) should be written as figures, e.g. there are 23 children in the room; but, five people saw them. Variations such as Year 1 students, Table 1, etc., may be used.

5. References (please keep to minimum)

Academic referencing (Harvard, see *American Psychological Association* website: www.wisc.edu/writing/Handbook/DocAPAReferences.html) is preferred. In the body of the article, reference; should be made only to the author/s and the year of publication (Johnson & Johnson, 1992), or, Johnson and Johnson (1992)... If a direct quote is cited, a page number is added (Johnson & Johnson, 1992, p.139), or, Johnson and Johnson (1992, p.139)... Please include your reference list at the end of the article in the following formats:

From a book
Dom, L R, & Ryrerson, D. (1984). Elements of a healthy childhood (2nd ed.). New York: Macmillan

Article or chapter from an edited book
Makin, L. (1996). Play and the language profiles and scales. In M. Fleer (Ed.) *Play through the profiles, Profiles through play* (pp. 67-69). Canberra, ACT: Australian Early Childhood Association. (One editor=Ed. More than one=Eds).

From a journal
Scott, I. (1992). Home injury to children. *Australian Journal of Early Childhood*, 17(3),18-24.

From a series
Parker, J. (1996). *Understanding, separation and divorce*. AECA Resource Book Series, 3 (1). Canberra, ACT: Australian Early Childhood Association.

From a newspaper/periodical
Bantick, C. (1999, October 27). The duty of care amplifies a loss, The Canberra Times, p, 16,

The duty of care amplifies a loss. (1999, October 27). The Canberra Tomes, p. 16. (if author unknown).

From the internet
Heinrichs, J. (1997). *Stolen lives*. The Age. Retrieved 01/09/03 from <http//theage.com.au/news/agenews/phstole.htm>

From proceedings
Martino, W. (1995). Gendered learning practices. Exploring the costs of hegemonic masculinity for girls and boys in school. *Proceedings of the Promoting Gender Equity Conference*. Department of Education, Canberra, pp. 343-364.

> Please ensure all publication/paper titles, dates etc. are correct and don't forget page numbers for journal articles or articles in books.

6. Footnotes and Endnotes
ECA does not include footnotes in this journal. Endnotes are restricted to references as above.

7. General
- Avoid underlining, bold and caps in the body of text (we will assume underlining means italic), Refer to names of publications in the text only in italics, Please do not place commas or other punctuation marks in dates, i.e., the 1990s.
- Avoid using two spaces after full stops before a new sentence.
- Avoid (if you can) using double paragraph returns as the extra ones will be removed before final layout.
- Never use hard spaces to spread text across a page.
- Avoid over-formatting your document. Formatting must be removed before final layout can occur.

8. Author Licence Agreement form

Author Licence Agreement forms will be sent to authors on acceptance of final manuscript and illustrations, photographs, etc. (if used) prior to publishing. This acceptance will occur following the blind review process and incorporate the conditions laid out in the agreement form.

9. Publication process and timelines

All manuscripts received by ECA are required to undergo an external blind review process. Authors will be promptly notified of receipt of their work and advised of reviewers' comments within at least three months.

Reviewers' comments are intended to assist authors in revising their work for publication, and are forwarded to the author (together with disk or manuscript) for updating. Authors should return the updated disk and reprinted manuscript within twenty one (21) days to the Publications Section.

Should any significant changes be required after they have approved earlier changes, authors will be approached prior to publication.

Please call the ECA publications staff at the earliest possible stage if you would like to discuss anything regarding the publication of your work.

All material and queries should be directed to:

The Publications Section
Early Childhood Australia
PO Box 7105
Watson ACT 2602
Phone: +61 2 6242 1800
Fax: +61 2 6242 1818
Email: **publishing@earlychildhood.org.au**

Sue Wales	Publications Officer
David Kingwell	Publications Assistant (In-house Editor of AJEC)
Claire Connelly	Graphic Design
Ben Galdys	Communications Coordinator
Marilyn Fleer	*AJEC* Editor (Professor of Early Childhood Education at Monash University)

Website: **www.earlychildhoodaustralia.org.au**

Australian Journal of Outdoor Education

ADDRESS FOR SUBMISSION:

Glyn Thomas, Editor
Australian Journal of Outdoor Education
  ELECTRONIC SUBMISSIONS ONLY
Australia
Phone: +61 3 5444 7285
Fax: +61 3 5444 7848
E-Mail: ajoe@latrobe.edu.au
Web:
Address May Change:

CIRCULATION DATA:

Reader: Practicing Teachers, Academics,
  Administrators
Frequency of Issue: 2 Times/Year
Copies per Issue:
Sponsor/Publisher:
Subscribe Price: 0.00 US$

PUBLICATION GUIDELINES:

Manuscript Length: 8,000 words max
Copies Required: Electronic submission
Computer Submission: Yes Email preferred
Format:
Fees to Review: 0.00 US$

Manuscript Style:
  American Psychological Association,
  (5th Edition)

REVIEW INFORMATION:

Type of Review: Blind Review
No. of External Reviewers: 2
No. of In House Reviewers: 0
Acceptance Rate: 80%
Time to Review: 1 Month or Less
Reviewers Comments: Yes
Invited Articles: 0-5%
Fees to Publish: 0.00 US$

MANUSCRIPT TOPICS:
Adult Career & Vocational; Curriculum Studies; Education Management/Administration;
Educational Psychology; Health & Physical Education; Higher Education; Outdoor Education;
Social Studies/Social Science; Special Education; Teacher Education; Urban Education,
Cultural/Non-Traditional

MANUSCRIPT GUIDELINES/COMMENTS:

Audience of the Journal. The *Australian Journal of Outdoor Education* (*AJOE*) is a refereed journal devoted to the scholarly examination of issues in the field of outdoor education. It speaks to teachers, practitioners and researchers, both in Australia and overseas. *AJOE* is published twice a year (March/April and September/ October) and sent to members of organizations affiliated with the Outdoor Council of Australia, and institutional and individual subscribers. Approximately 800 copies are produced per issue.

Goals of *AJOE*. The uniqueness of *AJOE* is its ability to meet the needs of a wide cross-section of readers, be they classroom teachers, academics, or practitioners in the field. *AJOE* attempts to provide clear links between theory, research and practice. *AJOE* **aims to:**
a.   Provide balanced and in-depth investigation of outdoor education practices and theories in a variety of educational contexts.

b.   Enhance understanding of outdoor education issues in relation to their wider educational and social contexts.

c.   Help readers keep abreast of current outdoor education research.

d.   Examine and present research with a view as to how it might be implemented by classroom teachers and practitioners as researchers.

e.   Provide a forum in which outdoor education professionals from all settings can exchange and discuss ideas and practices relevant to their work.

Review process. Manuscripts submitted to *AJOE* are peer-reviewed by two anonymous reviewers. The usual timeframe for the review process is three (3) months and every effort is made to complete the process promptly. Presentation of the manuscript in the required format enhances the speed with which a review can be completed.

Manuscript presentation. Manuscripts are to be submitted electronically via e-mail attachment (in Microsoft Word format) to sure your submission conforms to the requirements of the *APA 5th* referencing system.

Articles should range from 500-8000 words in length. Please do not send hard copies unless requested. Appropriate photographs and/or artwork should also be submitted electronically. As a guide, 15 double-spaced 12 point A4 pages are approximately equivalent to 10 final journal pages. Manuscripts which greatly exceed the word limit will not be reviewed as they would not be considered publishable without considerable revision.

A separate cover page which contains the author's name, address, phone, fax and e-mail contacts should be included with the submission. A biographical statement, About the Author, detailing the author's current position or professional affiliation, research interests, and a contact address for correspondence is to accompany the manuscript.

It is the author's responsibility to ensure that articles contain original work and do not breach copyright. Further, the author is responsible for obtaining permission to reproduce all copyright material (for example, newspaper articles or cartoons).

Themes. *AJOE* does not produce special theme issues. Articles on any topic related to the scholarly advancement of outdoor education will be considered, as will as articles of particular relevance to outdoor education in Australia. Examples of possible topic areas include:

- Relationships between outdoor recreation and outdoor education
- Outdoor education curriculum in schools and institutions
- Creative programming in outdoor education
- Gender issues in outdoor education
- Environmental perspectives
- Research studies, design and/or methodology
- Corporate adventure programs
- Adventure therapy

Bilingual Review Press

ADDRESS FOR SUBMISSION:

Gary D. Keller, Editor
Bilingual Review Press
Arizona State University
Hispanic Research Center
Box 872702
Tempe, AZ 85287-2702
USA
Phone: 480-965-3867
Fax: 480-965-8309
E-Mail: brp@asu.edu
Web: www.asu.edu/brp
Address May Change:

CIRCULATION DATA:

Reader: Academics
Frequency of Issue: 3 Times/Year
Copies per Issue: 1,001 - 2,000
Sponsor/Publisher:
Subscribe Price: 25.00 US$ Individual
        40.00 US$ Institution

PUBLICATION GUIDELINES:

Manuscript Length: 11-30
Copies Required: Two
Computer Submission: No
Format: N/A
Fees to Review: 0.00 US$

Manuscript Style:
    Chicago Manual of Style, Any Standard
    Style

REVIEW INFORMATION:

Type of Review: Editorial Review
No. of External Reviewers: 1
No. of In House Reviewers: 1
Acceptance Rate: 6-10%
Time to Review: 2 - 3 Months
Reviewers Comments: No
Invited Articles: 0-5%
Fees to Publish: 0.00 US$

MANUSCRIPT TOPICS:
Art/Music; Bilingual/E.S.L.; Curriculum Studies; Languages & Linguistics; U.S. Hispanic
Literature

MANUSCRIPT GUIDELINES/COMMENTS:

Bilingual Review is a magazine of U.S. Hispanic life: poetry, short stories, other prose and
theater.

Needs
U.S. Hispanic creative literature. "We accept material in English or Spanish. We publish
original work only—no translations." U.S. Hispanic themes only. Receives 50 unsolicited
fiction manuscripts a month. Accepts 2 manuscripts an issue, 6 manuscripts a year. Often
critiques rejected manuscripts. Recently published work by Nash Candelaria, Andrés
Montoya, and Virgil Suárez. Published work of new writers within the last year.

How to Contact
Send 2 copies of complete manuscript with a self-addressed envelope and loose stamps. Simultaneous and high-quality photocopied submissions OK. Authors advised to keep a duplicate copy of their manuscript as well as an electronic copy. Reports in 2-3 months on manuscript. Publishes manuscript an average of 1 year after acceptance. Sample copy $7.

Payment
2 contributor's copies. 30% discount for extras.

Terms
Acquires all rights (50% of reprint permission fee given to author as matter of policy). Publication copyrighted.

Advice
"Write about events reinforced by deep personal experience or knowledge."

Unsolicited manuscripts are welcome. The journal will not consider for publication manuscripts that have been published previously. We will publish manuscripts consistently styled according to either humanities or social sciences formats. Manuscripts should be double-spaced throughout (including notes and references). Reviews novels and short story collections.

British Educational Research Journal

ADDRESS FOR SUBMISSION:

Harry Torrance, Editor
British Educational Research Journal
Manchester Metropolitan University
Institute of Education
799 Wilmslow Road
Manchester, M20 2RR
UK
Phone: +44 1612 475191
Fax: +44 1612 476353
E-Mail: berj@mmu.ac.uk
Web: www.tandf.co.uk/journals
Address May Change:

PUBLICATION GUIDELINES:

Manuscript Length: 21-30
Copies Required: Three
Computer Submission: No
Format: N/A
Fees to Review: 0.00 US$

Manuscript Style:
    See Manuscript Guidelines

CIRCULATION DATA:

Reader: Academics
Frequency of Issue: 6 Times/Year
Copies per Issue:
Sponsor/Publisher: Carfax (Taylor &
    Francis) SSCI Ranking 18/93
Subscribe Price: 209.00 US$ Individual
    1270.00 US$ Institution

REVIEW INFORMATION:

Type of Review: Blind Review
No. of External Reviewers: 2-3
No. of In House Reviewers: 1
Acceptance Rate: 11-20%
Time to Review: 1 - 2 Months
Reviewers Comments: Yes
Invited Articles: 0-5%
Fees to Publish: 0.00 US$

MANUSCRIPT TOPICS:
Curriculum Studies; Education Management/Administration; Educational Psychology;
Educational Technology Systems; Elementary/Early Childhood; Gifted Children; Health &
Physical Education; Higher Education; Interdisciplinary; Languages & Linguistics; Reading;
Religious Education; Rural Education & Small Schools; Science Math & Environment;
Secondary/Adolescent Studies; Special Education; Teacher Education; Tests, Measurement &
Evaluation

MANUSCRIPT GUIDELINES/COMMENTS:

Aims and Scope
The *British Educational Research Journal* is an international medium for the publication of
articles of interest to researchers in education and has rapidly become a major focal point for
the publication of educational research from throughout the world.

For further information on the association please connect to directly to the British Educational
Research Association web site: **www.bera.ac.uk**

The journal is interdisciplinary in approach, and includes reports of experiments and surveys, discussions of conceptual and methodological issues and of underlying assumptions in educational research, accounts of research in progress, and book reviews. The journal is the major publication of the British Educational Research Association, an organisation which aims to promote interest in education and to disseminate findings and discussions of educational research.

Notes for Contributors

Papers accepted become the copyright of the British Educational Research Association, unless otherwise specifically agreed.

Manuscripts should be sent to David Hustler, Institute of Education, Manchester Metropolitan University, 799 Wilmslow Road, Manchester M20 2RR UK. Articles can only be considered if three complete copies of each manuscript are submitted. They should be typed on one side of the paper, double spaced, with ample margins, and bear the title of the contribution, name(s) of the author(s) and the address where the work was carried out. Each article should be accompanied by an abstract/summary of 100-150 words on a separate sheet. The full postal address of the author who will check proofs and receive correspondence and offprints should also be included. All pages should be numbered. Footnotes to the text should be avoided.

Contributors will normally receive a decision on their article within six weeks of its receipt by the Editor. Rejected manuscripts will not normally be returned to contributors unless sufficient stamps/international postal coupons have been sent.

Tables and captions to illustrations. Tables must be typed out on separate sheets and not included as part of the text. The captions to illustrations should be gathered together and also typed out on a separate sheet. Tables should be numbered by Roman numerals, and figures by Arabic numerals. The approximate position of tables and figures should be indicated in the manuscript. Captions should include keys to symbols.

Figures. Please supply one set of artwork in a finished form, suitable for reproduction. Figures will not normally be redrawn by the publisher.

References should be indicated in the typescript by giving the author's name, with the year of publication in parentheses. If several papers by the same author and from the same year are cited, a, b, c, etc. should be put after the year of publication. The references should be listed in full at the end of the paper in the following standard form:

For books: SCOTT, P. (1984) **The Crisis of the University** (London, Croom Helm).

For articles: CREMIN, L.A. (1983) The problematics of education in the 1980s: some reflections on the Oxford workshop, **Oxford Review of Education**, 9, pp. 33-40.

For chapters within books: WILLIS, P. (1983) Cultural production and theories of reproduction, in: L. BARTON & S. WALKER (Eds) **Race, Class and Education** (London, Croom Helm).

Titles of journals should **not** be abbreviated.

Non-discriminatory writing. Please ensure that writing is free from bias, for instance by substituting 'he' or 'his' by 'he or she' or 's/he' or 'his/her' and by using non-racist language. Authors might wish to note the BERA Ethical Guidelines for Educational Research.

Proofs will be sent to authors if there is sufficient time to do so. They should be corrected and returned to the Editor within three days. Major alterations to the text cannot be accepted.

Offprints. Fifty offprints of each paper are supplied free together with a copy of the issue in which the paper appeared. Additional copies may be purchased and should be ordered when the proofs are returned. Offprints are sent about two weeks after publication.

Copyright. It is a condition of publication that authors vest copyright in their articles, including abstracts, in the British Educational Research Association. This enables us to ensure full copyright protection and to disseminate the article, and the journal, to the widest possible readership in print and electronic formats as appropriate. Authors may, of course, use the article elsewhere **after** publication without prior permission from Carfax Publishing, Taylor & Francis Limited is notified so that our records show that its use is properly authorized. Authors are themselves responsible for obtaining permission to reproduce copyright material from other sources.

Notes For Referees
Referees are asked to bear the following in mind when assessing papers for inclusion.

We want *BERJ* to represent the best of educational research and so it is important that referees are rigorous and demanding, taking into account the status of the journal as a premier international publication.

Articles are welcomed on all kinds and aspects of educational research, and addressing any form of education, formal or informal.

It is the policy of the journal that articles should offer original insight in terms of theory, methodology, or interpretation, arid not be restricted to the mere reporting of results. Submitted work should be substantially original, recent in reference, and unpublished.

It is important that referees pay particular attention to the appropriateness, accuracy, consistency and accessibility of tabular data, arid the specified referencing protocols.

We welcome original ways of presenting research findings, and support accessible, well written accounts.

It is important that referees are decisive in their judgments of submissions.

In writing up their comments on articles submitted to the journal, referees are asked, in a minimum of 250 words.or so, to address whatever is relevant in the following:

- offer a brief critical resume of theoretical, methodological, or substantive issues raised by the author;
- assess how adequately the research is located in terms of previous relevant research;
- make a reasoned appraisal of the overall quality of the submission in terms of its excellence, contribution to knowledge, or originality;
- provide feedback useful to the author (a) for resubmission (b) more generally in terms of the further development of the research. It is helpful in the resubmission process if specific numbered points are made by referees and addressed by authors;
- indicate where appropriate any limitations on their ability to comment.

We also expect referees to be able to report on submissions within a three week period. It is important that these deadlines are respected, Articles published in HERJ include information, on. 'date received' / 'date resubmitted' / 'date finally accepted' and we do not wish to exhibit unprofessional delays between receipt and acceptance/resubmission/ rejection.

Journal's Web Address: www.tandf.co.uk/journals/titles/01411926.asp

British Journal of Educational Technology

ADDRESS FOR SUBMISSION:

Nick Rushby, Editor
British Journal of Educational Technology
209 Junction Road
Burgess Hill, West Sussex, RH15 0NX
UK
Phone: +44 (0) 1444 243092
Fax: +44 (0) 1444 243092
E-Mail: nick.rushby@dial.pipex.com
Web: www.blackwellpublishers.co.uk
Address May Change:

CIRCULATION DATA:

Reader: Academics
Frequency of Issue: Bi-Monthly
Copies per Issue: 1,001 - 2,000
Sponsor/Publisher: Blackwell Publishing
Subscribe Price: 146.00 US$ Personal/US
    72.00 Pounds Personal/Europe
    90.00 Pounds Personal/Rest of World

PUBLICATION GUIDELINES:

Manuscript Length: 11-15
Copies Required: Electronic
Computer Submission: Yes Disk/prefer
    Email
Format: MS Word
Fees to Review: 0.00 US$

Manuscript Style:
    See Manuscript Guidelines

REVIEW INFORMATION:

Type of Review: Editorial Review
No. of External Reviewers:
No. of In House Reviewers: 3
Acceptance Rate: 11-20%
Time to Review: 1 - 2 Months
Reviewers Comments: Yes
Invited Articles: 0-5%
Fees to Publish: 0.00 US$

MANUSCRIPT TOPICS:
Educational Technology Systems

MANUSCRIPT GUIDELINES/COMMENTS:

BJET is a primary source for academics and professionals in the expanding fields of educational and training technology throughout the English speaking world. Articles cover the whole range of education and training, concentrating on the theory, applications and development of educational technology and communications. This includes such subjects as:

- The design and production of learning materials;
- The psychology of communication;
- Curriculum development and course design;
- Evaluation and monitoring;
- Priorities in resources, planning and organization;
- The storage, retrieval and dissemination of resources and information;
- The effectiveness and cost-effectiveness of print, electronic and optical media;
- Delivery systems for open and distance learning;
- Support for self study and for learners at a distance;

- Assessment, notably assessment on demand and of learning from experience;
- Problems and potential of new technologies in education and training;
- Educational research and dissemination.

In addition to full length refereed articles and shorter colloquium pieces, it includes book reviews and notes other publications received.

We welcome jargon-free writing: Say it as simply as you can. Remember that your readers are busy people: conciseness is a virtue, whatever the overall length. Avoid parochial references and assumptions: for many *BJET* readers English is not their mother tongue. Spell out all acronyms the first time around. Reports of experimental work should be analytical, not merely descriptive; reviews of developing fields should be critical, not merely informative; theoretical overviews should contain some original contribution or novel perspective.

Web-linked material

Some authors wish to link their contributions to a Web site containing interactive multimedia material, or to refer to large data sets which cannot be accommodated in the printed journal. We have models for publishing such contributions and I will be pleased to discuss this with you.

Originality and Copyright

It is condition that your contribution is original and has neither been published previously nor is currently being considered for publication elsewhere.

Blackwell, like most manor publishers, has arrangements in place with the UK CLA and similar bodies overseas and can relieve authors of the need to protect their copyright and deal with permissions. We ask authors to assign copyright to the National Council for Educational Technology. You will be sent a copy of the form and accompanying notes and we ask you to complete and return it with the final version of your contribution. You will see (in paragraph 4 of the notes) that it specifically allows you to make copies for your own courses without having to seek permission form NCET.

Articles

Articles should not exceed 4000 words including references to any source that readers might wish to trace. However, there is no merit in lengthy lists per se. Wherever possible, the reasons for citing a reference should be clear from the context. Please check very carefully both the accuracy and presentation

Articles are rigorously refereed. The speed of publication of articles depends greatly on the authors' readiness to respond to the referees' comments. It also helps us if your manuscript confirms to the rules below, particularly in the layout of references. These give us the most problems in copy-editing.

1. Use the format of other articles in *BJET* as a guide for laying out your contribution. all articles should have an abstract (100-200 words) at the beginning.

2. Include a short note about current work or experience (not more than 60 words) and an address for correspondence.

3. As word processing software gets more sophisticated it becomes easier to submit your manuscript in a very professional format. Please do not use these advanced features. The typesetting process works best with simple text form, for example Microsoft Word 97 or 2000. In the final stage of copy-editing we have to remove all of these advanced features and this sometimes changes the sense of what you are trying to say. It is very time-consuming and may delay your article so that it has to be held back to a later issue of the journal. If you are submitting an article which you have formatted for internal use, please help us by removing the advanced features before you submit. Like you, we want to se your article in print as quickly as possible: you can help by keeping it simple and following the guidelines for layout of the text and the references.

4. Where possible, provide machine-readable illustrations (as bmp or tif files). If this in not possible then submit camera-ready illustrations on separately numbered sheets, each bearing an explanatory caption. Please avoid using very pale colours since these do not print well (if at all) in black and white. Use dashed and dotted lines to differentiate lines on graphs. It is not possible to redraw artwork. The ideal position should be shown in the manuscript.

5. Footnotes should not be used: if a point is worth making, it should be included in the main text.

6. Acknowledgements, if needed, appear after the text but before references.

7. References are cited in the text by name, date and (if needed) page number thus: (Isaac 1987, 45), supported by an alphabetical listing by author at the end. Please follow this style (note that if you receive this letter by email, the italicisation may not be apparent):

Book: Mathias H *et al* (1988) (eds) *Designing new systems and technologies for learning* Kogan Page, London.
Race P (1988 *The Open Learning Handbook* Kogan Page, London.

Article: Megarry J (1988) Hypertext and compact discs: the challenge of multimedia learning *British Journal of Educational Technology* **19** 3, 172-183.

Paper: Barbour R H (1984) Gordon Pask: a conversation theory of learning *in* Other A N *(ed)* Proceedings of SERU Conference on theories in education, University of Waikato New Zealand.
NB, please cite published proceedings in book form wherever possible.

A hybrid articles is combines a printed contribution, which is refereed in the normal way, with a more substantial item on the World Wide Web. This gives the author(s) the opportunity to present more detailed work (e.g., a research database) and/or use media that cannot be represented in print.

The Colloquium aims at a style akin to a conversation in print, with shorter contributions (400-900 words) that are not normally subject to refereeing and are therefore published much faster than articles. Possible areas include:

- summary of work in progress raising queries or problems
- short think-piece, perhaps questioning received wisdom
- early warning of the potential and problems of new media
- story of an unsuccessful research attempt and the lessons learned
- reaction to a previous *BJET* contribution.

Submission

We now have a policy of requiring authors to provide a machine readable copy of the final version to accompany the hard copy. It will speed up the referring processes if you can send your initial submission in this form - either on disk or preferably via email (no viruses please!) to: **nick.rushby@dial.pipex.com**. My preferred format is MS WORD: other formats (eg Macintosh) are possible - but more difficult. If you have no alternative to submitting in hard copy, then please provide three (3) copies of the manuscript.

Refereeing

BJET referees read articles very carefully and sometimes make quite detailed suggestions. If the recommendation is in favour of publication, there is a further stage and authors vary in how quickly and how positively they respond to referees' comments. We cannot commence copy editing until we have the final manuscript, so if you are likely to be unavailable or at a different address for any significant time in the near future, please let me know. *BJET* is published five times each year in January, March, June, September and November, and articles occasionally have to be carried over at the last minute because of space constraints, so it is normally not possible to say in advance in which issue a specific contribution will appear, even after it has been accepted for publication in a revised form.

British Journal of Music Education

ADDRESS FOR SUBMISSION:

Stephanie Pitts, Editor
British Journal of Music Education
University of Sheffield
Department of Music
38 Taptonville Road
Sheffield, S10 1GU
UK
Phone: +44 (0) 114 222 0481
Fax: +44 (0) 114 222 0469
E-Mail: s.e.pitts@sheffield.ac.uk
Web: journals.cambridge.org/jid_BME
Address May Change: 12/31/2007

PUBLICATION GUIDELINES:

Manuscript Length: 21-25
Copies Required: Four
Computer Submission: Yes Email
Format: PC/Mac
Fees to Review: 0.00 US$

Manuscript Style:
  See Manuscript Guidelines

CIRCULATION DATA:

Reader: Practicing Teachers, Academics
Frequency of Issue: 3 Times/Year
Copies per Issue: Less than 1,000
Sponsor/Publisher: Cambridge University
  Press
Subscribe Price: 57.00 Pounds Individual
  42.00 Pounds Student
  132.00 Pounds Institution

REVIEW INFORMATION:

Type of Review: Blind Review
No. of External Reviewers: 2
No. of In House Reviewers: 2
Acceptance Rate: 40%
Time to Review: 2 - 3 Months
Reviewers Comments: Yes
Invited Articles: 6-10%
Fees to Publish: 0.00 US$

MANUSCRIPT TOPICS:

Art/Music; Curriculum Studies; Educational Psychology; Elementary/Early Childhood; Gifted Children; Higher Education; Secondary/Adolescent Studies; Special Education; Teacher Education; Tests, Measurement & Evaluation; Urban Education, Cultural/Non-Traditional

MANUSCRIPT GUIDELINES/COMMENTS:

Editorial Policy

British Journal of Music Education aims to provide stimulating and readable accounts of current issues in music education worldwide, together with a section containing extended and useful book reviews. It strives to strengthen connections between research and practice, so enhancing professional development within the field of music education. The range of subjects covers classroom music teaching; individual instrumental teaching and vocal teaching; music in higher education; comparative music education; teacher education and music in the community. The journal is fully refereed and contributors include researchers and practitioners from schools, colleges and universities. Audio examples are occasionally supplied on a CD with no extra charge. Recent articles have covered such topics as listening to music at home and at school, the use of information technology in composing projects and learning strategies in instrumental music practice.

1. Submissions

Contributions and correspondence should be sent to Dr. Gordon Cox, Institute of Education, University of Reading, Bulmershe Court, Reading, RG6 1HY, UK (E-mail: **g.s.a.cox@reading.ac.uk**) or Dr. Stephanie Pitts, Department of Music, University of Sheffield, 38 Taptonville Road, Sheffield, S10 5BR, UK (E-mail: **s.e.pitts@sheffield.ac.uk**).

Material for review and review copy should be sent to Dr. Cox.

Submission of an article is taken to imply that it has not previously been published, and has not been submitted for publication elsewhere. Authors of articles published in the journal assign copyright to Cambridge University Press (with certain rights reserved) and you will receive a copyright assignment form for signature on acceptance of your paper.

Contributors are responsible for obtaining permission to reproduce any material in which they do not own copyright, to be used in both print and electronic media, and for ensuring that the appropriate acknowledgements are included in their manuscript.

2. Manuscript Preparation Length

Copies. Four copies of articles and one of reviews should be submitted and one retained for proof-reading.

Length. Normally around 6,000 words; provide a word count at the end of the article.

Format. When an article has been accepted for publication, the author is required to send a copy of the final version on computer disk (Apple Macintosh or IBM compatible PC) together with the hard copy typescript, giving details of the word-processing software used (Microsoft Word or WordPerfect). However, the publisher reserves the right to typeset material by conventional means if an author's disk proves unsatisfactory. All hard copy must be typed double spaced on A4 or equivalent, one side only, with generous margins and consecutively numbered pages. The author's name should be given on a separate sheet (see Biographical note below) to facilitate the anonymous refereeing process.

Abstract. An abstract of about 100 words, summarizing the contents of the article should be typed immediately below the title and above the main text. A note giving details of any acknowledgements should also be included.

A Biographical note of about 75 words giving the author's name, postal address, affiliation, principal publications, etc. should be submitted on a separate cover sheet.

Language. Writing should be clear, and jargon free; subheadings are helpful in long articles.

Stereotyping. All forms of racial and gender stereotyping should be avoided.

Abbreviations, acronyms should be given in full at their first mention, bearing in mind that the readership of the journal is an international one, thus: postgraduate certificate in education (PGCE).

3. Submitted recordings

It is hoped that writers will take the opportunity to present musical examples in the form of recordings. We aim to produce a CD every one to two years, despatched with the third issue of the Journal. It may refer to articles in each of the issues.

Type. Cassette, mini disc, DAT or CD.

Quality. The highest possible to facilitate transfer.

Content in final edited form. Examples should not be numbered on the tape; a written numbered list of items, with timings, should be provided.

4. Quotations and references

Please identify these in the text by author and by date in brackets, e.g. '(Holmes, 1981)', and list all references alphabetically by surname on a separate sheet at the end. They should be typed double-spaced on A4 paper or equivalent.

For books state surname, initials, publication date (in brackets), title in italics, place of publication, publisher.

For articles state surname, initials, publication date (in brackets), full title (not in italics, in quotes), journal title (in italics), volume number, issue number, page number(s).

For articles in books state author's name, publication date (in brackets), title (in quotes) 'in' editor's name, book title (in italics), page numbers, place of publication, publisher.

Other notes only if essential should be number consecutively and in superscript in a list on separate sheet at end.

Please note: 'Eds' without point and '&' for joint authors and in publishers' names for example:

CAMPBELL, P. S. (1988) *Songs in Their Heads: Music and its Meaning in Children's Lives*. Oxford: Oxford University Press.

KNUSSEN, S. (2003) "Educational programmes', in C. Lawson (Ed) *The Cambridge Companion to the Orchestra* (pp. 239-50). Cambridge: Cambridge University Press.

LAMONT, A., HARGREAVES, D. J., MARSHALL, N. A. & TARRANT, M. (2003) "Young people's music in and out of school', *British Journal of Music Education*, 20 (3) 229-41.

5. Illustrations

Captions. List and number consecutively as Figures on a separate sheet at end of article.

Photographs. Use well-contrasted black and white prints, preferably portrait style no smaller than text width (130 mm) with glossy finish; lightly put writer's name and figure number on the back in pencil.

Diagrams and musical examples. Present in a form suitable for direct reproduction bearing in mind the maximum dimension of 130 mm x 220 mm.

6. Proofs

Typographical or factual errors only may be changed at proof stage, within a given deadline. The publisher reserves the right to charge authors for correction of non-typographical errors.

Offprints

Twenty-five free offprints are supplied to writers of published articles, these shared between joint authors. Extra copies may be purchased from the publisher if ordered at proof stage.

British Journal of Religious Education

ADDRESS FOR SUBMISSION:

Robert Jackson, Editor
British Journal of Religious Education
University of Warwick
Institute of Education / Ursula McKenna
Warwick Religions and
  Education Research Unit
Coventry, CV4 7AL
UK
Phone: +44 (0) 24 7652 3190
Fax: +44 (0) 24 7652 4110
E-Mail: r.jackson@warwick.ac.uk
Web: www.tandf.co.uk/journals
Address May Change:

PUBLICATION GUIDELINES:

Manuscript Length: 21-25
Copies Required: Three
Computer Submission: Yes
Format: MS Word
Fees to Review: 0.00 US$

Manuscript Style:
  See Manuscript Guidelines, (In-house
  Style)

CIRCULATION DATA:

Reader: Academics
Frequency of Issue: 3 Times/Year
Copies per Issue:
Sponsor/Publisher: Christian Education;
  Taylor & Francis
Subscribe Price: 227.00 US$ Individual
  227.00 US$ Institution

REVIEW INFORMATION:

Type of Review: Blind Review
No. of External Reviewers: 2
No. of In House Reviewers: 0
Acceptance Rate: 50%
Time to Review: 1 - 2 Months
Reviewers Comments: Yes
Invited Articles: 0-5%
Fees to Publish: 0.00 US$

MANUSCRIPT TOPICS:
Religious Education

MANUSCRIPT GUIDELINES/COMMENTS:

Aims and Scope
The *British Journal of Religious Education* (*BJRE*) has a pedigree stretching back to 1934
when it began life as *Religion in Education*. In 1961 the title was changed to *Learning for
Living*, and the present title was adopted in 1978. It is the leading journal in Britain for the
dissemination of research in religion and education and for the scholarly discussion of issues
concerning religious education.

BJRE is an international peer reviewed journal which aims to promote and report research and
scholarship in religious education and related fields such as values education, spiritual
education and intercultural education insofar as they relate to the discussion of religion or
religious traditions and movements. Contributions relating to the following are especially
welcome:

- research and scholarship on religious education as understood in the UK publicly funded school sector
- international research and scholarship relating to religious education in the schools of plural societies
- religious education in faith based schools
- religious perspectives on education
- childhood and religion in community and school settings

Contributions are welcome from researchers and scholars of any faith or none in all sectors of education (including higher education, schools, educational administration and inspection). Submissions from graduate students are welcome.

INSTRUCTIONS FOR AUTHORS
Manuscripts
Papers should not exceed 6,000 words. 3 copies should be sent to Ursula McKenna, Warwick Religions and Education Research Unit, Institute of Education, University of Warwick, Coventry CV4 7AL, UK. An electronic version should be emailed to
u.mckenna@warwick.ac.uk.

Papers should be typed on one side of A4 (or equivalent) sized paper, double-spaced, with ample margins, and bear the title of the contribution. In order to guarantee anonymous peer review the name(s) of the author(s) and the address where the work was carried out should only appear on a separate first page. Each article should be accompanied by an abstract/summary of 100-500 words, also on a separate sheet. The full postal address of the author who will check proofs and receive correspondence and offprints should also be included. All pages should be numbered. Endnotes to the text should be avoided as far as possible. Authors should send the final, revised version of their articles in both hard copy paper and electronic forms. It is essential that the hard copy (paper) version exactly matches the material sent either on disk or by email attachment. Please print out the hard copy from the disk you are sending. Submit three printed copies of the final version with the disk/email attachment to the journal's editorial office. Save all files on a standard 3.5 inch high-density disk. We prefer to receive disks in Microsoft Word in a PC format. Please specify which program you have used. Do not save your files as "text only" or "read only. If sending by email attachment then please save as Microsoft Word.

Note to Authors. Please make sure your contact address information is clearly visible on the outside of all packages you are sending to Editors.

Rejected manuscripts will not be returned unless sufficient stamps/international postal coupons have been sent.

Tables and captions to illustrations. Tables must be typed out on separate sheets and not included as part of the text. The captions to illustrations should be gathered together and also typed out on a separate sheet. Tables and figures should be numbered by Arabic numerals. The approximate position of tables and figures should be indicated in the manuscript. Captions should include keys to symbols.

112

Figures. Please supply one set of artwork in a finished form, suitable for reproduction. Figures will not normally be redrawn by the publisher.

References should be indicated in the typescript by giving the author's name, with the year of publication in parentheses. If several papers by the same author and from the same year are cited, a, b, c, etc. should be put after the year of publication. The references should be listed in full at the end of the paper in the following standard form:

For books
Jackson, R. (1997) Religious Education: an Interpretive Approach (London, Hodder & Stoughton).

For articles
Ipgrave, J. (1999) Issues in the delivery of religious education to Muslim pupils: perspectives from the classroom, British Journal of Religious Education, 21 (2), 147-58.

For chapters within books
Grimmitt, M. (2000) Constructivist pedagogies of religious education project, in: M. Grimmitt (Ed.) Pedagogies of Religious Education (Great Wakering, McCrimmons), 29-53.

For online documents
Department of Education, Northern Ireland (DENI) (2003) Enrolments at Schools and in Funded Pre-school Education in Northern Ireland 2002/03. Available online at: www.deni.gov.uk/facts_figures/pr/pr20030429.pdf (accessed 20 May 2003).

Titles of journals should not be abbreviated. Acronyms for the names of organisations, examinations, etc. Should be preceded by the title in full.

Further Guidelines
If you have any further questions about the style for this journal, please submit your questions using the Style Queries form.

Non-discriminatory writing. Articles should make no assumptions about the beliefs or commitments of any reader, should contain nothing which might imply that one individual is superior to another on the grounds of race, sex, culture or any other characteristic, and should use inclusive language throughout. Please ensure that writing is free from bias, for instance by replacing 'he' or 'his' by 'he or she' or 's/he' or 'his/her', and by using non-racist language.

Proofs will be emailed to authors with full instructions, if there is sufficient time to do so. Corrections should be returned within 3 days. Major alterations to the text cannot be accepted.

Early Electronic Offprints. Corresponding authors can now receive their article by e-mail as a complete PDF. This allows the author to print up to 50 copies, free of charge, and disseminate them to colleagues. In many cases this facility will be available up to two weeks prior to publication. Or, alternatively, corresponding authors will receive the traditional 50 offprints. A copy of the journal will be sent by post to all corresponding authors after publication. Additional copies of the journal can be purchased at the authors' preferential rate of £15.00 per copy.

CABE Journal

ADDRESS FOR SUBMISSION:

Bonnie B. Carney, Editor
CABE Journal
The Connecticut Association of Boards
of Education
81 Wolcott Hill Road
Wethersfield, CT 06109
USA
Phone: 860-571-7446
Fax: 860-571-7452
E-Mail: admin@cabe.org
Web: www.cabe.org
Address May Change:

PUBLICATION GUIDELINES:

Manuscript Length: 1-3
Copies Required: One
Computer Submission: Yes
Format: MS Word
Fees to Review: 0.00 US$

Manuscript Style:

CIRCULATION DATA:

Reader: Administrators, School Board
Members
Frequency of Issue: Monthly
Copies per Issue: 2,001 - 3,000
Sponsor/Publisher: The Connecticut
Association of Boards of Education
Subscribe Price: 75.00 US$

REVIEW INFORMATION:

Type of Review: Editorial Review
No. of External Reviewers: 0
No. of In House Reviewers: 2
Acceptance Rate: 21-30%
Time to Review: 1 - 2 Months
Reviewers Comments: No
Invited Articles: 50% +
Fees to Publish: 0.00 US$

MANUSCRIPT TOPICS:
Bilingual/E.S.L.; Counseling & Personnel Services; Curriculum Studies; Education
Management/Administration; Educational Psychology; Educational Technology Systems;
Elementary/Early Childhood; Gifted Children; Health & Physical Education; Public Policy;
Rural Education & Small Schools; School Law; Secondary/Adolescent Studies; Teacher
Education; Urban Education, Cultural/Non-Traditional

MANUSCRIPT GUIDELINES/COMMENTS:

The Association. The Connecticut Association of Boards of Education (CABE), is
Connecticut's not-for-profit association of local and regional boards of education dedicated to
serving the needs of local school districts. We are concerned with improving public education
throughout the state and nation.

The Journal. The *CABE Journal* is our major publication. It reaches virtually all board
members, superintendents and business managers in Connecticut. It's the only publication
which does so on a regular basis. It is designed to encompass all material in an easy-to-read

fashion. Readers of the *CABE Journal* find a wide range of topics covered in each issue. All CABE members receive the Journal free with their membership.

CALICO Journal (Computer Assisted Language Instruction Consortium)

ADDRESS FOR SUBMISSION:

Robert Fischer, Editor
CALICO Journal (Computer Assisted
   Language Instruction Consortium)
Texas State University
214 Centennial Hall
601 University Drive
San Marcos, TX 78666-4616
USA
Phone: 512-245-1417
Fax: 512-245-9089
E-Mail: execdir@calico.org
Web: calico.org
Address May Change:

PUBLICATION GUIDELINES:

Manuscript Length: 26-30
Copies Required: One
Computer Submission: Yes
Format: MS Word
Fees to Review: 0.00 US$

Manuscript Style:
   American Psychological Association

CIRCULATION DATA:

Reader: Academics
Frequency of Issue: 3 Times/Year
Copies per Issue: Less than 1,000
Sponsor/Publisher: CALICO (Computer
   Assisted Language Instruction
   Consortium)
Subscribe Price: 35.00 US$ Individual
   70.00 US$ Institution
   120.00 US$ Corporate

REVIEW INFORMATION:

Type of Review: Blind Review
No. of External Reviewers: 3
No. of In House Reviewers: 2
Acceptance Rate: 20%
Time to Review: 2 - 3 Months
Reviewers Comments: Yes
Invited Articles: 6-10%
Fees to Publish: 0.00 US$

MANUSCRIPT TOPICS:
Bilingual/E.S.L.; Educational Technology Systems; Foreign Language; Languages &
Linguistics

MANUSCRIPT GUIDELINES/COMMENTS:

The *CALICO Journal* is devoted to the dissemination of information concerning the
application of technology to language teaching and language learning. It is the primary means
of print information distributed by the Computer Assisted Language Instruction Consortium
(CALICO). The *CALICO Journal* is a fully refereed journal and publishes articles, research
studies, reports, software reviews, and professional news and announcements.

Articles submitted for publication should fall within the guidelines listed above. Articles
previously published or accepted for publication elsewhere will not be considered.

Authors can submit manuscripts on 3.5" diskettes containing their manuscript either in MS-Word or WordPerfect format (Macintosh or IBM-compatible). Authors should follow the *Publication Manual of the American Psychological Association*, 5th ed. (2001).

Manuscripts must:

- be doubled spaced;
- be no more than 30 pages in length (excluding bibliography, tables, notes, etc.);
- have a title page stating the author's name, plus address, telephone number, fax number, and e-mail address;
- include an abstract of no more than 200 words and a keywords section;
- be accompanied by a bio-statement of (each of) the author(s) not to exceed 120 words per author.

Graphs, charts, and figures should be included in hard copy form on separate pages and in electronic form (preferably in .EPS or .PDF format). Figures should exhibit a high degree of contrast.

Acceptance for publication rests with the reviewers and editorial staff of the Journal and is based on the quality of work in the article, space constraints, and current professional needs and interests. Editorial changes may be made to improve the readability of the article and to fit the article within the space constraints of the journal issue. Authors whose articles are published in the *CALICO Journal* will receive two complimentary issues in which their article appears.

Manuscript should be sent to the above address.

Campus Wide Information Systems

ADDRESS FOR SUBMISSION:

Glenn Hardaker, Editor
Campus Wide Information Systems
University of Huddersfield
Head, Learning and Teaching
   Innovation Unit
Queensgate
Huddersfield, HD1 3DH
UK
Phone:
Fax:
E-Mail: g.hardaker@hud.ac.uk
Web: www.emeraldinsight.com/cwis.htm
Address May Change:

PUBLICATION GUIDELINES:

Manuscript Length: 1,000-4,000 words
Copies Required: One
Computer Submission: Yes Disk, Email
Format: Word or Compatible
Fees to Review: 0.00 US$

Manuscript Style:
   See Manuscript Guidelines

CIRCULATION DATA:

Reader: Academics
Frequency of Issue: 5 Times/Year
Copies per Issue:
Sponsor/Publisher: Emerald Group
   Publishing Limited
Subscribe Price: 709.00 Pounds
   1089.00 US$
   1209.00 Euro

REVIEW INFORMATION:

Type of Review: Blind Review
No. of External Reviewers: 2
No. of In House Reviewers: 1
Acceptance Rate: 60%
Time to Review: 1 - 2 Months
Reviewers Comments: Yes
Invited Articles: 21-30%
Fees to Publish: 0.00 US$

MANUSCRIPT TOPICS:
Education Management/Administration; Educational Technology Systems; Higher Education;
Information Systems

MANUSCRIPT GUIDELINES/COMMENTS:

About the journal
Campus-Wide Information Systems provides comprehensive and independent coverage on the
management, use and integration of information resources and learning technologies. It is a
current and practical information tool, providing up-to-date international research, which
informs decision making in the Higher and Further Education sectors.

Coverage
- **Innovations in Teaching and Learning with Technology.** The changing roles of
teacher and student; Technology and student learning; Teaching in new technology
environments; Interactive teaching modules; Standards and assessment

- **New Technologies**. Wireless communication and instruction; Voice recognition; Mobile computing; Advanced networking applications
- **IT Implementation and Support**. Designing and developing computer networks; Technology support services; Managing Web-based resources; Digital libraries; Information repositories
- **Planning and Administration**. Developing and maintaining networks effectively and efficiently; Managing a networked environment Infrastructure; Course management systems; Accreditation of distance learning programmes; Campus portals; Computer security; Intellectual property

Copyright

Articles submitted to the journal should be original contributions and should not be under consideration for any other publication at the same time. Authors submitting articles for publication warrant that the work is not an infringement of any existing copyright and will indemnify the publisher against any breach of such warranty. For ease of dissemination and to ensure proper policing of use, papers and contributions become the legal copyright of the publisher unless otherwise agreed. Submissions should be sent to:

The Editor

Professor Glenn Hardaker, Head, Learning and Teaching Innovation Unit, University of Huddersfield, Queensgate, Huddersfield, HD1 3DH, UK; Email: **g.hardaker@hud.ac.uk**

The reviewing process

All academic articles are double-blind peer-reviewed; case studies and 'Insights from Industry' are reviewed by the Editor and at least one other subject expert in the field.

Manuscript requirements

Three copies of the manuscript should be submitted in double line spacing with wide margins. All authors should be shown and author's details must be printed on a separate sheet and the author should not be identified anywhere else in the article.

As a guide, articles should be between 1,000 and 4,000 words in length. A title of not more than eight words should be provided. A brief **autobiographical note** should be supplied including full name, affiliation, e-mail address and full international contact details. Authors must supply an **abstract** of 100-150 words. Up to six **keywords** should be included which encapsulate the principal subjects covered by the article.

Where there is a **methodology**, it should be clearly described under a separate heading. **Headings** must be short, clearly defined and not numbered. **Notes** or **Endnotes** should be used only if absolutely necessary and must be identified in the text by consecutive numbers, enclosed in square brackets and listed at the end of the article.

Figures, charts and **diagrams** should be kept to a minimum. They must be black and white with minimum shading and numbered consecutively using Arabic numerals with a brief title and labelled axes. In the text, the position of the figure should be shown by typing on a separate line the words "take in Figure 2". Good quality originals must be provided.

120

Tables should be kept to a minimum. They must be numbered consecutively with roman numerals and a brief title. In the text, the position of the table should be shown by typing on a separate line the words "take in Table IV".

Photos and **illustrations** must be supplied as good quality black and white original half tones with captions. Their position should be shown in the text by typing on a separate line the words "take in Plate 2".

References to other publications should be complete and in Harvard style. They should contain full bibliographical details and journal titles should not be abbreviated. For multiple citations in the same year use a, b, c immediately following the year of publication. References should be shown within the text by giving the author's last name followed by a comma and year of publication all in round brackets, e.g. (Fox, 1994). At the end of the article should be a reference list in alphabetical order as follows:

(a) for books
surname, initials and year of publication, title, publisher, place of publication, e.g.Casson, M. (1979), Alternatives to the Multinational Enterprise, Macmillan, London.
(b) for chapter in edited book
surname, initials and year, "title", editor's surname, initials, title, publisher, place, pages, e.g.Bessley, M. and Wilson, P. (1984), "Public policy and small firms in Britain", in Levicki, C. (Ed.), Small Business Theory and Policy, Croom Helm, London, pp.111-26. Please note that the chapter title must be underlined.
(c) for articles
surname, initials, year "title", journal, volume, number, pages, e.g.Fox, S. (1994) "Empowerment as a catalyst for change: an example from the food industry", Supply Chain Management, Vol 2 No 3, pp. 29-33

If there is more than one author list surnames followed by initials. All authors should be shown.

Electronic sources should include the URL of the electronic site at which they may be found, as follows:
Neuman, B.C.(1995), "Security, payment, and privacy for network commerce", IEEE Journal on Selected Areas in Communications, Vol. 13 No.8, October, pp.1523-31. Available (IEEE SEPTEMBER) http://www.research.att.com/jsac/

Notes/Endnotes should be used only if absolutely necessary. They should, however, always be used for citing Web sites. They should be identified in the text by consecutive numbers enclosed in square brackets and listed at the end of the article. Please then provide full Web site addresses in the end list.

Final submission of the article
Once accepted for publication, the final version of the manuscript must be provided, accompanied by a 3.5" **disk** of the same version labelled with: disk format; author name(s); title of article; journal title; file name.

Each article must be accompanied by a completed and signed **Journal Article Record Form** available from the Editor or on http://www.literaticlub.co.uk/

The manuscript will be considered to be the definitive version of the article. The author must ensure that it is complete, grammatically correct and without spelling or typographical errors.

In preparing the disk, please use one of the following formats: Word, Word Perfect, Rich text format or TeX/LaTeX. Figures which are provided electronically must be in tif, gif or pic file extensions. All figures and graphics must also be supplied as good quality originals.

Final submission requirements
Manuscripts must be clean, good quality hard copy and;
- include an abstract and keywords
- have Harvard style references
- include any figures, photos and graphics as good quality originals
- be accompanied by a labelled disk
- be accompanied by a completed Journal Article Record Form

Technical assistance is available from Emerald's Literati Club on www.emeraldinsight.com/literaticlub or contact Mike Massey at Emerald, e-mail mmassey@emeraldinsight.com.

Canadian Journal of Education (Revue canadienne de l'Education)

ADDRESS FOR SUBMISSION:

Samuel Robinson, Editor
Canadian Journal of Education (Revue
  canadienne de l'Education)
University of Saskatchewan
College of Education
28 Campus Drive
Saskatoon, Saskatchewan, S7N 0X1
Canada
Phone: 306-966-7577
Fax: 306-966-7658
E-Mail: csse.cje@usask.ca
Web:
Address May Change: 5/30/2004

PUBLICATION GUIDELINES:

Manuscript Length: 26-30
Copies Required: Five
Computer Submission: No
Format: N/A
Fees to Review: 0.00 US$

Manuscript Style:
    American Psychological Association, &
    Chicago Manual of Style

CIRCULATION DATA:

Reader: Academics
Frequency of Issue: Quarterly
Copies per Issue: 1,001 - 2,000
Sponsor/Publisher: Canadian Society for
  Studies in Education
Subscribe Price: 80.00 US$ CSSE Member
    100.00 US$ +GST Non-member CSSE
    150.00 US$ Institutional Associate

REVIEW INFORMATION:

Type of Review: Blind Review
No. of External Reviewers: 3
No. of In House Reviewers: 1
Acceptance Rate: 11-20%
Time to Review: 2 - 3 Months
Reviewers Comments: Yes
Invited Articles: 0-5%
Fees to Publish: 0.00 US$

MANUSCRIPT TOPICS:
Curriculum Studies; Education Management/Administration; Educational Technology Systems; Health & Physical Education; Reading; Rural Education & Small Schools; School Law; Special Education; Teacher Education; Tests, Measurement & Evaluation; Urban Education, Cultural/Non-Traditional

MANUSCRIPT GUIDELINES/COMMENTS:

Canadian Journal of Education/Revue canadienne de l'Education accepts articles in both English and French. Regarding manuscript topics, it is a general journal.

Editorial Policy
The *Canadian Journal of Education* publishes scholarly articles, review essays, discussions, book reviews, and research notes broadly but not exclusively related to Canadian education and written to be of interest to a wide, well read general readership.

1. Articles represent a variety of research traditions. They must address a question, take the form of an argument, and lead to conclusions. The *Journal* does not publish descriptive texts, teaching materials, or administrative documents.

2. In submitting a manuscript, authors affirm that the research is original and unpublished, is not in press or under consideration elsewhere, and will not be submitted elsewhere while under consideration by the *Journal*. This applies to evidence or data as well as form of argument.

3. Articles should not exceed 7,000 words (including quotations, notes, and references); review essays, 2,000 words; discussions, 1,500 words; book reviews, 1,000 words; and research notes, 1,000 words.

4. Tables, figures, and graphic material are accepted only when necessary for the rigour of the argument.

5. Manuscripts must be entirely double-spaced (including quotations, notes, references) in 12-point type. Five copies with an abstract of not more than 100 words are required.

6. Articles alone are peer-reviewed. To ensure blind review, authors' names must not appear on their manuscript and manuscripts must not otherwise reveal their authors' identities.

7. The *Journal's* style generally follows the most recent edition of the *Publication Manual of the American Psychological Association* or the *Chicago Manual of Style*; English spelling follows the most recent edition of the *Gage Canadian Dictionary*.

8. Authors of accepted manuscripts assign copyright to the Canadian Society for the Study of Education.

Canadian Journal of Higher Education (The)

ADDRESS FOR SUBMISSION:

Linda Rzeszutek, Managing Editor
Canadian Journal of Higher Education (The)
PO Box 34091
RPO Fort Richmond
Winnipeg, MB R3T 5T5
Canada
Phone: 204-474-6211
Fax: 204-474-7607
E-Mail: cjhe@shaw.ca
Web: www.catchword.com
Address May Change:

PUBLICATION GUIDELINES:

Manuscript Length: 16-20
Copies Required: Electronic Files
Computer Submission: Yes
Format: MS Word, RTF
Fees to Review: 0.00 US$

Manuscript Style:
    American Psychological Association

CIRCULATION DATA:

Reader: Academics, Administrators
Frequency of Issue: 3 Times/Year
Copies per Issue: Less than 1,000
Sponsor/Publisher: Canadian Society for the
    Study of Higher Education
Subscribe Price: 85.00 CAN$ Membership
    40.00 CAN$ Student Membership
    USA Add $10, Foreign Add $15

REVIEW INFORMATION:

Type of Review: Blind Review
No. of External Reviewers: 3
No. of In House Reviewers: No Reply
Acceptance Rate: 21-30%
Time to Review: 3-4 Months
Reviewers Comments: Yes
Invited Articles: 0-5%
Fees to Publish: 0.00 US$

MANUSCRIPT TOPICS:
Adult Career & Vocational; Higher Education

MANUSCRIPT GUIDELINES/COMMENTS:

The *Canadian Journal of Higher Education* is a publication of the Canadian Society for the Study of Higher education.

The *Journal* is intended to serve as a medium of communication among persons directly involved in higher education in Canada, or deeply interested in this field. The principal focus will be on Canadian higher education, but not to the exclusion of the developments in other countries which are of concern to the Canadian scene. Articles making a contribution to any aspect of higher education are welcome.

Subscription Information
Members of the Canadian Society for the Study of Higher Education receive the *Journal* as part of the annual membership dues. Membership fees for individuals are $85.00 per annum and $40 for full-time students and retirees. Canadian institutions can subscribe to the *CJHE* for $75 per year ($70.09 + $4.91 GST); USA add $10; elsewhere add $15. Correspondence

regarding memberships and institutional subscriptions (including back issues), and requests for changes of address should be sent to:

The Canadian Society for the Study of Higher Education
La Société canadienne pour l'étude de l'enseignement supérieur
P.O. Box 34091, RPO Fort Richmond
Winnipeg, MB R3T 5T5 Canada

Editorial Correspondence

All editorial correspondence, including submission of articles and book reviews should be addressed to the *CJHE* Managing Editor and emailed to **cijhe@shaw.ca**.

Instructions to Contributors

Submission of a manuscript to *The Canadian Journal of Higher Education* (*CJHE*) implies and is an undertaking on the part of the author(s), that neither the manuscript nor any substantially similar manuscript has been published, is in press, or is under consideration elsewhere. Prior to publication in the *CJHE*, the author(s) will assign their copyright to the *CJHE* by means of a standard form.

Format

Use a standard typeface and size (i.e., Times Roman 12 pt.) and double-space throughout, including block quotations, references, and notes. **Manuscripts are not to exceed 20 pages, excluding graphics, title page, and bibliography**. Please provide an abstract of approximately 100 - 150 words on a separate page and/or file. To ensure anonymity in the review process, the author's name and affiliation, as well as mailing address and e-mail, should appear **only** on the title page.

Style

Language and format (headings, tables, figures, citations, and references) must conform to the Publication Manual of the *American Psychological Association* (5th Ed.). All figures and tables should appear on separate pages from the text. Indicate placement of figures and tables in text (i.e., *insert Table 3 here*). Figures, charts, and diagrams may be submitted electronically in JPEG or GIF formats.

All references and citations must adhere to the APA format. Sources cited within the text appear in parentheses after each citation and must give the author's name, year of publication. Enclose quotes of 40 words or less in double quotations marks in the text; indent quotes longer than 40 words in block format. Page numbers must be given for all direct quotations. Footnotes are not allowed and endnotes should be minimal and be listed after the text and before the Reference section, having been marked within the text by superscript numerals.

Submitting Manuscripts

To help ensure an efficient review process, it is preferred that authors submit their manuscript and abstract electronically, either as e-mail attachments (preferred) or by post as files on a zip disk or CD. The preferred file format is Microsoft Word or Rich Text Format (RFT). If submitting a zip disk or CD, please indicate the title, author(s) name, along with one hard copy of the manuscript.

Canadian Modern Language Review

ADDRESS FOR SUBMISSION:

Larry Vandergrift, Tracey Derwing, CoEds
Canadian Modern Language Review
CMLR/RCLV - Journals Division
5201 Dufferin Street
North York, Ontario, M3H 5T8
Canada
Phone: 416-667-7994
Fax: 416-667-7881
E-Mail: cmlr@utpress.utoronto.ca
Web: www.utpress.utoronto.ca/journal/
Address May Change:

PUBLICATION GUIDELINES:

Manuscript Length: 16-25
Copies Required: Three
Computer Submission: No
Format: N/A
Fees to Review: 0.00 US$

Manuscript Style:
    See Manuscript Guidelines

CIRCULATION DATA:

Reader: Academics, Practicing Teachers,
    Administrators
Frequency of Issue: Quarterly
Copies per Issue: 2,001 - 3,000
Sponsor/Publisher: University of Toronto
    Press
Subscribe Price: 30.00 US$ Individual
    60.00 US$ Institution
    20.00 US$ Overseas Add Postage

REVIEW INFORMATION:

Type of Review: Blind Review
No. of External Reviewers: 3
No. of In House Reviewers: 0
Acceptance Rate: 21-30%
Time to Review: 2 - 3 Months
Reviewers Comments: Yes
Invited Articles: 50% +
Fees to Publish: 0.00 US$

MANUSCRIPT TOPICS:
Bilingual/E.S.L.; Curriculum Studies; Languages & Linguistics; Reading; Teacher Education;
Tests, Measurement & Evaluation

MANUSCRIPT GUIDELINES/COMMENTS:

1. Major Focus, Scope of the Publication
The Canadian Modern Language Review publishes linguistic and pedagogical articles, book reviews, current advertisements, and other material of interest to teachers and researchers of French as a second language, English as a second language, and other foreign languages at all levels of instruction. Authors wishing to submit articles for publication in the *CMLR/RCLV* should consider the following factors. Manuscripts should appeal and be accessible to the broad readership of the *CMLR/RCLV*. They should contribute to bridging the gap between theory and practice: practical articles should be anchored in theory, and theoretical articles and reports should contain a discussion of implications or applications for practice. The manuscript should offer a new, original insight or interpretation and not just a restatement of the ideas and views of others. Finally it should reflect sound scholarship with appropriate, correctly interpreted references to other authors and works. Circulation approx. 1,000.

2. **Submission of Manuscripts**:

a. **Length of Articles**. Manuscripts not exceeding 25 pages or 6,500 words may be submitted in paper form. The office address of the Editors is listed above.

b. Send the **original plus two copies** of the manuscript. The title of the article, without the name of the author(s) should appear at the beginning of the article.

c. Include a separate **title page** listing the title, the author(s) and the institutions. If the paper has been read at a conference, the title of the conference, the location and the date should be provided.

d. Include an **abstract** (approximately 125 words) in English and French.

e. Include a short **biographical note** in either English or French.

f. Authors will be asked to provide their manuscript on 5 1/41, DOS or 3 1/2', Macintosh or **DOS Disk** when it has been accepted for publication. Any complex graphics such as cartoons or charts should be supplied by authors in camera ready form at the time an article is accepted for publication.

g. **Inclusive Style**. The policy of the *CMLR/RCLV* requires that authors use an inclusive style which eliminates regressive terminology and unequal representation of people from different groups. Authors should be particularly careful about sexual stereotyping and should insure that women are represented as active participants in all aspects of life. Disclaimers at the beginning of manuscripts are not considered sufficient to meet the requirements of this policy. Without resorting to convoluted phraseology, authors should strive to produce a manuscript whose style is as inclusive and/or neutral as possible.

h. It is the responsibility of the authors to obtain permission to reproduce copyrighted materials in their articles.

i. Articles submitted simultaneously to other journals will not be accepted.

3. **References**. All submissions to the *CMLR/RCLV* should conform to the requirements of the *Publication Manual of the American Psychological Association* (4th Edition). *The Publication Manual* is available in most libraries and bookstores or can be obtained from The Order Department, American Psychological Association, 1200 Seventeenth St. NW, Washington, D.C., 20036.

4. **Copyright**
Copyright ownership: Editors of the *CMLR*.

5. **Book Reviews**
a. Suggested length for reviews: 600-700 words, maximum.
b. Books for review: Publishers and authors are invited to submit books for review directly to the Book Review Editors.

6. **Advertisements**
Please contact the advertising coordinator, Journals, University of Toronto Press. Telephone 416-667-7766, Fax 416-776-7881, Email agreenwood@utpress.utoronto.ca

7. Subscriptions

Yearly subscriptions are as follows: Individual: $30.00, Institutions: $60.00 U.S.A.: Same rate in U.S. currency. Overseas: Same rate in U.S. currency plus US $20.00 postage. Canadian subscribers only: Please add 7% GST. Make cheque or money order payable to The Canadian Modern Language Review and mail to: University of Toronto Press, Journals, 5201, Dufferin Street, North York, ON M3H 5T8. Telephone 416-667-7810, Fax 416-667-7881.

Email: **journals@utpress.utoronto.ca**
Web: **www.utpress.utoronto.ca/journal/deptname.htm**

Cataloging & Classification Quarterly

ADDRESS FOR SUBMISSION:

Sandra K. Roe, Executive Editor
Cataloging & Classification Quarterly
Haworth Information Press
500 McKinley Street
Normal, IL 61761-1526
USA
Phone:
Fax:
E-Mail: skroe@ilstu.edu
Web: www.haworthpressinc.com
Address May Change:

PUBLICATION GUIDELINES:

Manuscript Length: 10-40
Copies Required: Three
Computer Submission: Yes
Format: N/A
Fees to Review: 0.00 US$

Manuscript Style:
   Chicago Manual of Style

CIRCULATION DATA:

Reader: Academics, Librarians
Frequency of Issue: 6 Times/Year
Copies per Issue: 1,001 - 2,000
Sponsor/Publisher: Haworth Press, Inc.
Subscribe Price: 45.00 US$ Individual
   325.00 US$ Institution

REVIEW INFORMATION:

Type of Review: Blind Review
No. of External Reviewers: 2
No. of In House Reviewers: No Reply
Acceptance Rate: 65%
Time to Review: 2 - 3 Months
Reviewers Comments: Yes
Invited Articles: 21-30%
Fees to Publish: 0.00 US$

MANUSCRIPT TOPICS:
Library Science/Information Resources

MANUSCRIPT GUIDELINES/COMMENTS:

About the Journal
Cataloging & Classification Quarterly provides an effective international forum for information and discussion in the field of bibliographic organization. This highly respected journal considers the full spectrum of creation, content, management, use, and usability of bibliographic records, including the principles, functions, and techniques of descriptive cataloging; the wide range of methods of subjects analysis and classification; provision of access for all formats of materials including electronic resources; the bibliographic record of the information network; provision of access for all formats of materials; and policies, planning, and issues connected to the effective use of bibliographic records in modern society.

The journal deals with the historic setting as well as with the contemporary and with theory and scholarly research as well as with practical applications. In a rapidly changing field, it seeks out and fosters with, new developments in the transition to new forms of bibliographic control and encourages the innovative and the nontraditional. The computer and other modern

130

technology are considered from the point of view of creators and users of bibliographic records rather than from that of technicians.

Cataloging & Classification Quarterly features fact and opinion from a wide range of individuals covering a broad spectrum of points of views. It deals with both general and specific aspects of cataloging and classification for all forms of library materials in all types of collections. This unique journal has something for everyone. For the cataloger, the journal provides both theoretical background and potential solutions to current problems. For the public services librarian, there are discussions of bibliographic records in actual use and of the importance of feedback from the user to the creator of cataloging systems. For the administrator, it explores the complex elements in the library organization. For the library school teacher, it provides an outlet for research publication as well as source materials for students.

Cataloging & Classification Quarterly emphasizes full-length research and review articles, descriptions of new programs and technology relevant to cataloging and classification, considered speculative articles on improved methods of bibliographic control for the future, and solicited book reviews. To assist in achieving the journal's goal of excellence, articles are refereed. Topics include:
* cataloging and preservation
* cataloging for digital resources
* cataloging for special collections and archives
* classification and subject access
* descriptive cataloging
* education and training for cataloging and classification
* the internationalization of cataloging
* management of cataloging and related functions
* maps and other cartographic and spatial materials
* online retrieval
* usability issues related to the catalog
* use of catalog records

Instructions for Authors
1. **Original Articles Only**. Submission of a manuscript to this Journal represents a certification on the pad of the author(s) that it is an original work, and that neither this manuscript nor a version of A has been published elsewhere no, is being considered far publication elsewhere.

2. **Manuscript Length**. Your manuscript may be approximately **10-40 typed pages** double-spaced (including references and abstract). Lengthier manuscripts may be considered, but only al the discretion of the Editor. Sometimes, lengthier scripts may be considered H they can be divided up into sections for publication in successive Journal Issues.

3. **Manuscript Style**. References, citations, and general style of manuscripts for this Journal should follow the Chicago style (as outlined in the latest edition of the Manual of Style of the University of Chicago Press.) References should be double-spaced and placed in alphabetical

order. The use of footnotes within the text is discouraged. Words should be underlined only when It is intended that they be set in Relics.

If an author wishes to submit a paper that has been already prepared in another style, he or she may do so. However, if the paper is accepted (with or without reviewers alterations), the author is fully responsible for retyping the manuscript in the style as indicated above. Neither the Editor no, the Publisher is responsible for re-preparing manuscript copy to adhere to the Journal's style.

4. Manuscript Preparation.

Margins: leave at least a one-inch margin on all four sides
Paper: use clean, white 8-1/2" x 11" bond paper.
Number of copies:

- Initial Submission: 3 (the original plus two photocopies)
- Final Submission for Publication. 3, plus one on diskette, or send as email attachment

Cover page: *Important*--staple a cover page to the manuscript, indicating only the article title (this is used for anonymous refereeing).

Second "title page": enclose a regular title, page but do not staple it to the manuscript. Include the title again, plus:

- Full authorship
- an ABSTRACT of about 100 words. (Below the abstract provide 3-10 key words for index purposes).
- a header or footer on each page with abbreviated title and page number of total (e.g.. pg 2 of 7)
- an introductory footnote with authors' academic degrees, professional titles, affiliations, mailing and e-mail addresses, and any desired acknowledgment of research support or other credit.

Note: Articles may be submitted via the Internet. Please contact the Editor at **skroe@ilstu.edu** for details.

5. Return Envelopes and Contact Information.

When you submit your three manuscript copies, also include:

- a 9" x 12" envelope, self-addressed and stamped (with sufficient postage to ensure return of your manuscript);
- a regular envelope, stamped and self-addressed. This is for the Editor to send you an "acknowledgement of receipt" letter.
- Email address to facilitate communication with you by the editor.

Note: Postage requirements do not pertain to authors outside the United States.

6. Spelling, Grammar, and Punctuation.

You are responsible for preparing manuscript copy which is clearly written in acceptable, scholarly English and which contains no errors of spelling, grammar, or punctuation. Neither the Editor nor the Publisher is responsible for correcting errors of spelling and grammar. The manuscript, after acceptance by the Editor, must be immediately ready for typesetting as it is finally submitted by the author(s). Check your paper for the following common errors:

- dangling modifiers
- misplaced modifiers
- unclear antecedents
- incorrect or inconsistent abbreviations

Also, check the accuracy of all arithmetic calculations, statistics, numerical data, text citations, and references.

7. **Inconsistencies Must Be Avoided**. Be sure you are consistent in your use of abbreviations, terminology, and in citing references, from one part of your paper to another.

8. **Preparation of Tables, Figures, and Illustrations**. Any material that is not textual is considered artwork. This includes tables, figures, diagrams, charts, graphs, illustrations, appendices, screen captures, and photos. Tables and figures (*including* legend, notes, and sources) should be no larger than 4-1/2 x 6-1/2 inches. Type styles should be Helvetica (or Helvetica narrow if necessary) and no smaller than 8 point We request that computer-generated figures be in black and white and/or shades of gray (preferably no color, for it does not reproduce well). Camera-ready art must contain no grammatical, typographical, of format errors and must reproduce sharply and clearly in the dimensions of the final printed page (4-1/2 x 6-1/2 inches). Photos and screen captures must be on disk as TIFF file, or other graphic file format such as JPEG or BMP. For rapid publication we must receive black-and-white glassy or matte positives (white background with black images and/or wording) in addition to files on disk. Tables should be created in the text document file using the software's *Table* feature.

9. **Submitting Art**. Both a printed hard copy and a disk copy of the art must he provided. We request that each piece of art be sent in its own file, on a disk separate from the disk containing the manuscript text file(s), and be clearly labeled. We request that they are included on a separate artwork disk, just for reference in case of an error in conversion. We reserve the right to (if necessary) *request new art, after art*, or if all else has failed in achieving art that is presentable, delete art. If submitted art cannot be used, the Publisher reserves the right to redo the art and to charge the author for a fee of $35.00 per hour for this service. The Haworth Press, Inc. is not responsible for errors incurred in the preparation of new artwork. Camera-ready artwork must be prepared on separate sheets of paper. Always use black ink and professional drawing instruments. On the back of these items, write your article title and the journal title lightly in soft-lead pencil (please do not write on the face of art). In the text file, skip extra lines and indicate where these figures are placed. Photos are considered part of the acceptable manuscript and remain with the Publisher for use in additional printings.

10. **Electronic Media**. Haworth's in-house typesetting unit la able to utilize your final manuscript material as prepared on most personal computers and word processors. This will minimize typographical errors and decrease overall production time. Please send the first draft and final draft copies, or an electronic submission of your manuscript to the journal Editor in print format for his/her final review and approval. After the final version of your manuscript is

accepted by the editor, please submit it in both hard copy format (4 copies) and disk (2 copies). On the outside of the diskette package write:

1. the brand name of your computer or word processor
2. the word processing program and version that you used
3. the title of your article, and
4. the file name.

Note: Disk and hard copy must agree. In case of discrepancies, it is The Haworth Press' policy to follow hard copy. Authors are advised that no revisions of the manuscript can be made after acceptance by the Editor for publication. The benefits of this procedure are many with speed and accuracy being the most obvious. We look forward to working with your electronic submission which will allow us to serve you more efficiently.

11. **Alterations Required By Referees and Reviewers**. Many times a paper is accepted by the Editor contingent upon charges that are mandated by anonymous specialist referees and members of the Editorial Boats. If the Editor returns your manuscript for revisions, you are responsible for retyping any sections of the paper to incorporate these revisions (If applicable, revisions should also be put on disk).

12. **Typesetting**. You will not be receiving galley proofs of your article. Editorial revisions, if any, must therefore be made while your article is still in manuscript. The final version of the manuscript will be the version you see published. Typesetter's errors will be corrected by the production staff of The Haworth Press. Authors are expected to submit manuscripts, disks, and art that are free from error.

13. **Reprints**. The first author will receive two copies of the journal issue and 25 complimentary reprints of his or her article. Additional authors will receive two copies of the journal issue. These are sent several weeks after the journal issue is published and in circulation. An order form for the purchase of additional reprints will also be sent to all authors at this time. (Approximately 4-6 weeks is necessary for the preparation of reprints.) Please do not query the Journal's Editor about reprints. All Such questions should be sent directly to The Haworth Press, Inc., Production Department, 37 West Broad Street, West Hazleton, PA 18202. To order additional reprints (minimum 50 copies), please contact The Haworth Document Delivery Center, 10 Alice Street, Binghamton, NY 13904-15801; 1-800-342-9678 or Fax (607) 722-6362.

14. **Copyright**. Copyright ownership of your manuscript must be transferred officially to The Haworth Press, Inc. before we can begin the peer-review process. The Editors letter acknowledging receipt of the manuscript will be accompanied by a form fully explaining this. All authors must sign the form and return the original to the Editor as soon as possible. Failure to return the copyright form in a timely fashion will result in a delay in review and subsequent publication.

Catholic Library World

ADDRESS FOR SUBMISSION:

Mary E. Gallagher, General Editor
Catholic Library World
Elms College
291 Springfield Street
Chicopee, MA 01013-2839
USA
Phone: 413-265-2354
Fax: 413-594-7418
E-Mail: gallagherm@elms.edu
Web: www.cathla.org
Address May Change:

PUBLICATION GUIDELINES:

Manuscript Length: 6-10
Copies Required: Two
Computer Submission: Yes Disk, Email
Format: MS Word (attachment)
Fees to Review: 0.00 US$

Manuscript Style:
    See Manuscript Guidelines

CIRCULATION DATA:

Reader: Practicing Teachers, Librarians, &
    Administrators
Frequency of Issue: Quarterly
Copies per Issue: 1,000-2,000
Sponsor/Publisher: Catholic Library
    Association
Subscribe Price: 60.00 US$ CLA Member
    60.00 US$ Non Member
    70.00 US$ Non US Address +$10 Post

REVIEW INFORMATION:

Type of Review: Blind Review
No. of External Reviewers: 3+
No. of In House Reviewers: 1
Acceptance Rate: 6-10%
Time to Review: 2 - 3 Months
Reviewers Comments: No
Invited Articles: 6-10%
Fees to Publish: 0.00 US$

MANUSCRIPT TOPICS:
Library Science/Information Resources; Reading

MANUSCRIPT GUIDELINES/COMMENTS:

General Information
Catholic Library World publishes material on all important subject areas and on all methods and techniques for "Putting Knowledge to Work." New and developing areas of librarianship, information science and information technology are sought. Informative papers on the administration, organization and operation of libraries and information centers are solicited. Scholarly reports of research in librarianship, education, and information science and technology are appropriate contributions. Bibliographies and bibliographic essays, discussions and opinions that are intended to be authoritative or that reflect original research are also published. Professional standards, education, and public relations are other representative subjects for inclusion. Controversy is not shunned.

The *CLW* follows a thematic approach to its focus on library/information concerns.

As the official journal of the Association, *CLW* publishes reports of business of the Association and its Chapters, as well as news of its members and for its members.

CLW does not provide a stipend to authors, contributing editors, reporters or reviewers.

Contributions are solicited from both members and non-members. All papers submitted are juried for publication. Papers are accepted with the understanding that they have not been published, submitted, or accepted for publication elsewhere. Authors will be notified of acceptance, rejection, or need for revision of their manuscripts. All accepted and published manuscripts become the property of the Catholic Library Association.

Copyright by Catholic Library Association. Material protected by this copyright may be photocopies for the non-commercial purpose of scholarship or research.

Types of Contributions

Three types of original contributions are considered for publication: full length articles, brief reports or communications, and reviews. New monographs and significant report publications relating specifically to library and information science, books for children, young adults, religious collections, and audiovisual materials are considered for review.

Editing

Manuscripts are edited primarily to improve the effectiveness of communication between the author and the readers. The most important goal is to eliminate ambiguities. In addition, improved sentence structure often permits the readers to absorb salient ideas more readily.

Manuscripts

Organize your material carefully, putting the significance of your paper or a statement of the problem first, and supporting details and arguments second. Make sure that the significance of your paper will be apparent to your readers outside your immediate field of interest. Avoid overly specialized jargon. Readers will skip a paper which they do not understand. For each proposed paper, one original and one copy (in English only) should be mailed to the Editor. Submissions are accepted on computer disc or email transmissions.

Style

See the following notes for in-house style.

Title

Begin the title with a word useful in indexing and information retrieval. The title should be as brief, specific, and descriptive as possible.

Acknowledgments

Credits for financial support, for materials and technical assistance or advice may be cited in a section headed "Acknowledgments," which should appear at the end of the text or as a footnote on the first page.

Illustrations
Finished artwork must be submitted to *CLW*. Follow the style current in style and layout publications.

References and Notes
Number all references to literature and notes in a single sequence in the order in which they are cited in the text. Cite all references and notes but do not insert reference numbers in titles.

Accuracy and adequacy of the references are the responsibility of the author. Therefore literature cited should be checked carefully with the original publications.

References to periodicals should be in the order: authors, articles, title, unabbreviated journal name, volume number, issue number, inclusive pagination, and date of publications.

Smith, John and Virginia Date. "Librarianship in Action." Catholic Library World 45 (no. n) 678-681 (April 1976).

References to books should be in the order: authors, title, publisher, year, pagination.

Brown, Able. Information at Work. Shoe String Press, 1909. 248 p.

Full-Length Articles
Articles may range in length from about 1,200 words on up.

Insert subheads at appropriate places in the text, averaging about one subhead for two manuscript pages. Do not use more than one degree of subhead in an article.

Write a brief author note, and include position, title and address. In the author note, include information concerning meetings, symposia, etc., where the paper may have been presented orally. Also submit a recent glossy black/white photograph of the authors - if available. Photos to illustrate the article are welcome.

Brief Communications
Short reports or communications will usually be less than 1,000 words in length (up to 4 typed double-spaced manuscript pages.) List the authors on the last page of the text in the form of a signature and include a simple mailing address.

The John Brubaker Memorial Award
The Executive Board of the Catholic Library Association established the John Brubaker Memorial Award (plaque and citation) in 1978 to recognize an outstanding work of literary merit considered on the basis of its significant interest to the library profession published in the *Catholic Library World*, the official journal of the Association. The Memorial Award honors John Brubaker who served the Catholic Library Association as advertising representative for the Association's journal *Catholic Library World* for over twenty years until his death in April, 1977.

A panel of judges will select the winning article from the volume of the *Catholic Library World* previous to the year of the annual convention. The first award was presented at the 58th Annual Catholic Library Association Convention in Philadelphia, Pennsylvania, April 18, 1979. The winning article must be precise in its writing, free of ambiguity, orderly in its presentation of ideas, economical in expression, smooth in its presentation, considerate of its readers, original, and stimulating. Any author is eligible for consideration.

CEA Critic

ADDRESS FOR SUBMISSION:

Daniel Robinson, Editor
CEA Critic
Widener University
Humanities Division
One University Place
Chester, PA 19013
USA
Phone: 610-499-4362
Fax: 610-499-4605
E-Mail: daniel.robinson@widener.edu
Web: www.as.ysu.edu/~english/cea/pubs
Address May Change:

PUBLICATION GUIDELINES:

Manuscript Length: 15-20
Copies Required: No Reply
Computer Submission: Yes
Format: Microsoft Word (Windows)
Fees to Review: 0.00 US$

Manuscript Style:
, MLA

CIRCULATION DATA:

Reader: Academics, Practicing Teachers
Frequency of Issue: 3 Times/Year
Copies per Issue: 1,001 - 2,000
Sponsor/Publisher: College English
  Association
Subscribe Price: 35.00 US$ Membership

REVIEW INFORMATION:

Type of Review: Editorial Review
No. of External Reviewers: 2
No. of In House Reviewers: 1
Acceptance Rate: 21-30%
Time to Review: 3-8 Months
Reviewers Comments: Yes
Invited Articles: 0-5%
Fees to Publish: 0.00 US$

MANUSCRIPT TOPICS:
Culture; English Literature; Film; Literature; Reading; Television; Urban Education, Cultural/Non-Traditional

MANUSCRIPT GUIDELINES/COMMENTS:

The Website is www.as.ysu.edu/~english/cea/pubs.htm
Both Journals, The *CEA Critic* and the *CEA Forum*, are included in the cost of membership for the College English Association.

The *CEA Critic* reflects the energy, variety, and discovery of current research in English literature and language, particularly as it applies in the college and university classroom. It aims to provide as complete a picture as possible of the wide range of scholarship now occurring in the discipline.

The manuscript will be edited of sexist language and in-house style. Submit 2 hard copies and **1 computer disk in Word for Windows.**

CEA Forum

ADDRESS FOR SUBMISSION:

Bege Bowers, Editor
CEA Forum
Youngstown State University
College English Association
One University Plaza
Youngstown, OH 44555
USA
Phone: 330-941-1560
Fax: 330-941-7169
E-Mail: bkbowers@ysu.edu
Web: See Guidelines
Address May Change: 7/1/2005

PUBLICATION GUIDELINES:

Manuscript Length: 6-10
Copies Required: Two
Computer Submission: Yes
Format: Word or RTF
Fees to Review: 0.00 US$

Manuscript Style:
 , MLA

CIRCULATION DATA:

Reader: Academics, Administrators,
   Practicing Teachers
Frequency of Issue: 1 or 2 Times/Year
Copies per Issue: Online
Sponsor/Publisher: College English
   Association
Subscribe Price: 40.00 US$ Individual
   Membership
   (includes CEA Critic)

REVIEW INFORMATION:

Type of Review: Editorial Review
No. of External Reviewers: 1
No. of In House Reviewers: 1
Acceptance Rate:
Time to Review: 1 - 2 Months
Reviewers Comments: Yes
Invited Articles: 0-50%
Fees to Publish: 0.00 US$

MANUSCRIPT TOPICS:
Composition; Curriculum Studies; Education Management/Administration; Higher Education;
Literature; Professional Issues Related to Teaching English; Teacher Education

MANUSCRIPT GUIDELINES/COMMENTS:

The Website is **www.as.ysu.edu/~english/cea/forum1.htm**

The *CEA Forum* serves the professional and pedagogical interests of the association through
the publication of information and opinion of the state of the profession, through the airing of
critical problems facing the discipline and the posting of possible problems, and through the
discussion of innovations, changes, and advancements in the teaching of English in the college
and university classroom.

The manuscript will be edited of sexist language and in-house style. Submit 2 hard copies and
electronic copy or disk copy in Word or RTF.

Child Language Teaching and Therapy

ADDRESS FOR SUBMISSION:

Carol Miller & Jannet Wright, Editors
Child Language Teaching and Therapy
The University of Birmingham
School of Education
Edgbaston
Birmingham, B15 2TT
UK
Phone: +44 0121 414 4853
Fax: +44 0121 414 4865
E-Mail: c.j.miller@bham.ac.uk;
Web: www.clttjournal.com
Address May Change:

PUBLICATION GUIDELINES:

Manuscript Length: 6-30
Copies Required: Four
Computer Submission: No
Format: N/A
Fees to Review: 0.00 US$

Manuscript Style:
    See Manuscript Guidelines

CIRCULATION DATA:

Reader: Practicing Teachers,
    Speech/Language Therapist/Pathologist
Frequency of Issue: 3 Times/Year
Copies per Issue: 1,000
Sponsor/Publisher: Arnold Journals
Subscribe Price: 103.00 US$ Individual
    253.00 US$ Institution
    55.00 Pounds & 133.00 Pounds

REVIEW INFORMATION:

Type of Review: Editorial Review
No. of External Reviewers: 2
No. of In House Reviewers: 2
Acceptance Rate: 75%
Time to Review: 1 - 2 Months
Reviewers Comments: Yes
Invited Articles: 0-5%
Fees to Publish: 0.00 US$

MANUSCRIPT TOPICS:
Audiology/Speech Pathology; Bilingual/E.S.L.; Child Language; Educational Psychology; Elementary/Early Childhood; Languages & Linguistics; Reading; Special Education

MANUSCRIPT GUIDELINES/COMMENTS:

Dr Carol Miller, Co-Editor, School of Education, The University of Birmingham, Edgbaston Birmingham, B15 2TT, UK, Tel: 0121 414 4853, Fax: 0121 414 4865, Email: **C.J. Miller@bham.ac.uk**

Dr Jannet A. Wright, Co-Editor, Department of Human Communication Science, University College London, Chandler House, 2 Wakefield Street, London, WC1N 1PG, UK, Tel: 0171 504 4224, Fax: 0171 713 8061, Email: **jannet.wright@ucl.ac.uk**

Editorial Policy
CLTT exists to help those who have to teach children handicapped by an inadequate command of spoken or written language, for any reason, of any age, in any setting. The range of handicap primarily relates to children who have been variously labeled speech or language-

disordered aphasic, dyslexic, with special (language) needs or with language learning disabilities, but we include also children whose communication problems arise from deafness, emotional difficulty, or from any form of physical or mental handicap. We recognize the relevance of the language problems encountered in multilingual education, foreign or second language teaching, the teaching of normal oracy and literacy skills, and remedial education in a broad sense.

The primary focus of *CLTT* is the principles and practice of teaching language-handicapped children, especially in relation to the demands made upon them by the way language is used in the curriculum. Papers may raise questions of diagnosis, screening, assessment or any other recognized area of concern, as long as the issues are related to learning, teaching, therapy or management, and as long as the primary subject matter is Language. Topics such as alternative communication systems, signing, technical aids, specific assessment techniques or remedial programmes are included, as are topics to do with professional roles, educational provision or government policies, in relation to the needs of these children. Case studies, especially written by members of a team, are welcomed.

Because this is an interdisciplinary field which is rapidly growing, and because levels of training in special language skills vary enormously, we welcome expository critical accounts of important theoretical, methodological or technical developments in fields relevant to remedial language teaching. We ask contributors to be aware at all times of the mixed nature of the readership of this journal, and not to assume familiarity with (for example) the specialized terminology of linguistics, medical nomenclature or statistical rationales in such cases, a degree of exposition will be welcomed.

Notes for Contributors
All items for publication, and all associated correspondence, should be sent to the Editors. Papers should be written in English. The average length of papers is five or six printed pages (3000 words approx.), and they should not usually exceed 10 printed pages (5000 words approx.). Letters submitted for publication should not exceed 500 words.

Four copies of a typescript should be submitted, one of which should be the top copy. Contributions should be clearly typed on one side of the paper only, with double spacing and wide margins, and using a conventional size of paper, preferably A4 (or 21.6 by 28 cm.).

All items should be accompanied by a separate title page, giving the author's name and affiliation, together with an address to which proofs and editorial correspondence can be sent. All papers should include a short abstract (maximum 100 words), which should be typed on a separate sheet. All reviews should include a full specification of book details, e.g. language skills, J. Smith. London: Edward Arnold, 1989. xi 164 pp. A separate style sheet for case studies is available from the editors.

The main text of a paper should be broken up into sections through the use of subheadings, such that most printed pages would be seen to contain at least one subheading. Subheadings should not normally exceed a half-line of print.

When discussing child language data, all examples of actual language use should be underlined, to represent italicization in print. Any glosses for a piece of child language should be given in single quotation marks. Emphasis should be marked by typing the whole word or phrase in capitals. If a series of examples is used, each example should be given its own (Roman) number. If phonetic transcription is necessary, the symbols and conventions of the International Phonetics Association should be used. If regular references to the age of a child are made they should be abbreviated thus: 6;3 (= 6 years, 3 months).

All drawings should be in ink, and suitable for photographic reproduction. Tables, figures or other illustrative material should be drawn on separate pages at the end of an article. Each illustration should have a short title, and there should be an indication in the body of the text as to where it should appear. Footnotes should be used only when absolutely necessary, in which case they should be typed on a separate page at the end of an article. A small number of references may accompany articles or reviews. All works referred to should be typed in alphabetical order on a separate page at the end of the paper, using similar spacing to the main text. The following reference style must be used (note especially capitalization and punctuation conventions):

Smith, J.K. 1966: Language development. Journal of Child Tantrums 66, 123-136.

Brown, J. and Davis, K. 1976: Language and the egg. In Fowler, W., editor. Studies in development, London: Edward Arnold.

Robinson, X. 1984: The future of remedial language studies. London: Edward Arnold.

References in the body of the text should be in parentheses, thus: (Smith, 1968). Page references should follow a colon: (Smith, 1968: 11). If the author's name is part of the text, the following form should be used: 'Smith (1969) has said . . .'. When a work written by three or more authors is referred to, all names should be given in the first citation, with and linking the last two: Smith, Brown and Jones, 1967. In subsequent citations, the first name only should be given, with et al. added.

Authors must obtain permission to reproduce copyright materials. Authors will receive 25 free off prints of their contribution; additional off prints can be purchased if ordered at proof stage.

Child Study Journal

ADDRESS FOR SUBMISSION:

Donald E. Carter, Editor
Child Study Journal
Buffalo State College
Bacon Hall Room 306
1300 Elmwood Avenue
Buffalo, NY 14222-1095
USA
Phone: 716-878-5302
Fax: 716-878-5833
E-Mail: leyonmgm@buffalostate.edu
Web:
Address May Change:

PUBLICATION GUIDELINES:

Manuscript Length: 26-30
Copies Required: Two
Computer Submission: Yes
Format: MS Word + Hardcopy
Fees to Review: 0.00 US$

Manuscript Style:
American Psychological Association

CIRCULATION DATA:

Reader: Academics
Frequency of Issue: Quarterly
Copies per Issue: Less than 1,000
Sponsor/Publisher:
Subscribe Price: 47.00 US$ Institution
15.00 US$ Student
52.00 US$ Foreign

REVIEW INFORMATION:

Type of Review: Editorial Review
No. of External Reviewers: 3+
No. of In House Reviewers: 1
Acceptance Rate: 11-20%
Time to Review: 3 Months
Reviewers Comments: Yes
Invited Articles: No Reply
Fees to Publish: 0.00 US$

MANUSCRIPT TOPICS:
Educational Psychology; Elementary/Early Childhood; Secondary/Adolescent Studies

MANUSCRIPT GUIDELINES/COMMENTS:

Articles Preferred are those devoted to educational and psychological aspects of human development (child and adolescent). Statistical analysis of some aspect of development is greatly preferred over literature reviews or case studies. Adequate sampling procedures are expected.

Format and Style should follow the guidelines presented in the *American Psychological Association Publication Manual.* Two copies with an abstract of 100 words should be submitted.

Acceptance Rate is about 20%. Manuscripts are reviewed by at least one consulting editor and the journal staff. Publication Lag is about 18 months. If you need further information, please let us know. We look forward to hearing from you.

Child Welfare

ADDRESS FOR SUBMISSION:

Managing Editor
Child Welfare
Child Welfare League of America
440 First Street, N.W., Third Floor
Washington, DC 20001-2085
USA
Phone: 202-942-0251
Fax: 202-638-4004
E-Mail: journal@cwla.org
Web: http://www.cwla.org
Address May Change:

PUBLICATION GUIDELINES:

Manuscript Length: 15-20
Copies Required: Four
Computer Submission: No
Format: N/A
Fees to Review: 0.00 US$

Manuscript Style:
    American Psychological Association

CIRCULATION DATA:

Reader: Academics, Administrators, &
    Practitioners
Frequency of Issue: Bi-Monthly
Copies per Issue: 4,00-6,000
Sponsor/Publisher: Child Welfare League
    of America
Subscribe Price: 99.00 US$

REVIEW INFORMATION:

Type of Review: Blind Review
No. of External Reviewers: 2
No. of In House Reviewers: 1
Acceptance Rate: 0-5%
Time to Review: 4-6 Months
Reviewers Comments: Yes
Invited Articles: 0-5%
Fees to Publish: 0.00 US$

MANUSCRIPT TOPICS:

Adoption; Child Abuse and Neglect; Child Welfare; Counseling & Personnel Services;
Elementary/Early Childhood; Foster Care; Independent Living; Juvenile Justice;
Secondary/Adolescent Studies; Social Work

MANUSCRIPT GUIDELINES/COMMENTS:

Child Welfare is a bimonthly journal of policy, practice, and program devoted essentially to
the needs and goals of personnel within and associated with the field of child welfare. It
covers all phases of child welfare as they affect the health, education, and psychosocial needs
of children, offering theoretical concepts as well as practical ideas and strategies. It reports on
innovations in practice, agency administration and board functions, staffing designs and staff
education, legislation, research, and community development.

Material submitted for consideration should extend knowledge in any child and family welfare
or related service; on any aspect of administration, supervision, casework, group work,
community organization, teaching, research, or interpretation; on any facet of interdisciplinary
approaches to the field; or on issues of social policy that bear on the welfare of children,
youths, and their families.

Manuscripts accepted for publication in *Child Welfare* demonstrate a high quality of analysis of issues in the field and describe innovative programs or forms of practice. Papers are invited from all fields whose content reflects aspects of work with children, youths, and their families. *Child Welfare* welcomes contributions, controversial or otherwise, that represent a responsible contribution to the literature. Publication does not imply *CWLA* endorsement of the author's opinions.

Child Welfare does not accept manuscripts published elsewhere or under review by other periodicals, or material that has been extracted from previously published articles and is not so identified. *Child Welfare* reserves exclusive rights of first publication. Authors must be the sole owners of their material.

Special Issue

Twice per year, *Child Welfare* publishes special issues, highlighting or closely studying a single subject extending across the broader range of child welfare interests. Those interested in serving as guest editor for such issues should contact the *Child Welfare* offices.

Format for Submission

Manuscripts submitted to *Child Welfare* conform to general standards of literacy and organization. Authors are responsible for submitting titles that are short, clear, and stimulating, and are strongly encouraged to use subheadings in organizing their materials. Authors should resist basing conclusions on one or a few cases, because material should illustrate rather than prove points.

A cover page containing the title; author name, academic degree, title, and affiliation; and a short (100-word) abstract should be attached to each manuscript submitted. The name and/or affiliation of the author should not appear on any other manuscript page, so that the manuscript may be submitted to reviewers anonymously. Any other identifying information will be removed prior to peer review.

All manuscripts submitted for consideration to *Child Welfare* must be typed legibly, double-spaced throughout (including references, notes, illustrations, and quotations), with approximately 1" margins on all sides. Manuscripts should be submitted on plain 8.5" by 11" white paper, one side only. The use of highly glazed, onionskin, or erasable paper is not permitted.

First-level headings should be typed in boldface; second-level headings should be in italics or underlined. Headings should be in upper- and lowercase, not all capitals.

Major manuscripts should be between 3,500 and 5,000 words (approximately 15 to 20 pages of about 250 words each). Some variability in length is permissible, in relation to the nature of the paper's subject.

Each table, illustration, or figure must be submitted on a separate sheet of paper, with placement indicated in the text. Avoid lengthy tables if possible. Several smaller tables are easier to read, analyze, and handle than one large table. All tables and figures used should be necessary to the comprehension of the material, because textual interpretation of data is often sufficient. It is also possible to suggest in a footnote that interested readers may write to the author for copies of tables, detailed statistical methodology, and so forth.

References and notes should be typed, double-spaced, and placed at the end of the manuscript. *Child Welfare* uses the *Publication Manual of the American Psychological Association* (APA) (4th ed.) for its reference format.

The author is responsible for obtaining written permission to use any material in the text (such as tables, charts, drawings, and extracts over 250 words) that has been previously copyrighted. The author must also indicate that permission for publication has been obtained from any agency from which case illustrations or other materials have been drawn. A copy of the permission should be submitted to *Child Welfare* with the manuscript.

Identifying information in case material must be disguised. Nonessential identifying case information-names and addresses of specific persons, organizations, business firms, and so on-should always be changed. It is frequently advisable to change nationalities, diseases, and other details likely to identify individuals, if the exact nature of the details is not of major importance. Substitutions comparable in significance can usually be made.

Submission Procedure
Submit four clean copies of the manuscript, in the format described above, to Managing Editor, Child Welfare, Child Welfare League of America, 440 First Street NW, Third Floor, Washington, DC 20001-2085.

Accompanying each manuscript submitted should be a telephone number where the author can be reached if the editor wishes to discuss the manuscript, as well as a current mailing address and e-mail address. Correspondence will be addressed to the person who signed the cover letter. Manuscript receipt is acknowledged immediately by postcard.

Peer Review Process
All identifying information is removed from manuscripts before they are submitted to *Child Welfare* peer review board. Book Reviews, Book Briefs, and items for the Readers' Forum are not submitted for review.

Three readers review each major manuscript: two peer review board members and the senior editor. A list of review board members is located on the inside front cover of *Child Welfare*.

Child Welfare editors may prescreen manuscripts to eliminate extremely long or short articles, those where plagiarism or libel is suspected, those whose subject has been overdone, those that are overly similar to articles placed elsewhere by the author, and those otherwise unsuitable for *Child Welfare*.

Manuscripts are assigned to reviewers insofar as possible according to their expertise and interest. Reviewers will disqualify themselves if an article's subject or authorship creates any conflict of interest for them.

Reviewers themselves may submit manuscripts without prejudice; their manuscripts remain anonymous during the review process.

Reviewers may make one of the following recommendations on a manuscript: (1) accept for publication, (2) advise/rewrite, (3) rewrite and resubmit for review, (4) reject. The senior editor will make the final decision regarding a manuscript or send it to other readers when a weight of consensus does not emerge from the reviewing process. The senior editor will notify the author regarding the review comments and decisions. Approximately sixteen weeks should be allowed for completion of the review process.

Rejected Manuscripts
If two or more reviewers reject a manuscript, it is rejected for publication. Authors have a right to know in constructive terms why a manuscript is rejected, and will be clearly informed regarding the principal reasons for rejection. Rejected manuscripts are returned only when authors request their return and provide self-addressed, stamped envelopes. Rejected manuscripts are kept on file at *Child Welfare* for one year from date of rejection.

Accepted Procedure
All manuscripts accepted for publication in *Child Welfare* may require some minor revision. Upon acceptance of a manuscript, the author will receive an author agreement, copyright release and biographical information forms. No manuscript will be published until the author has completed and returned all agreement forms, answered all editorial queries, reformatted references as requested, and provided two clean copies of the manuscript.

The Editors of *Child Welfare* do not want to interfere with the author's meaning or the essential flavor of the author's writing style. In reviewing the edited manuscript, authors should proofread carefully, restore meaning that has been unintentionally changed, and answer all queries. Once a manuscript has been approved and returned by the author, further author's alterations will be accepted only in limited circumstances.

Editing and Style
The *Child Welfare* editorial staff conforms punctuation, capitalization, number forms, and other matters of style to *Child Welfare* usage and format; corrects word usage and grammar; and eliminates repetition and unnecessary words. Since *Child Welfare* is read by lay people connected with the field and by members of other disciplines, as well as by social workers, technical jargon should be avoided as much as possible. Readability is the goal.

Child Welfare uses the *Publication Manual of the American Psychological Association* (APA) (4th ed.) for its reference style, and the *Chicago Manual of Style* (14th ed.) and *Webster's Ninth New Collegiate Dictionary* for its editorial style.

Reprints
A reprint request line appears at the end of every published article. *Child Welfare* expects the author to honor requests for single copies. Authors may have reprints prepared themselves; however, should they wish, *Child Welfare* will have them made up and sent (minimum quantity: 100). A price list and order form are sent with acceptance notification. Authors who receive requests for copies in quantity may forward them to the *CWLA* editorial offices.

Requests received by authors for permission to reprint an article in another publication, whatever the purpose, should be sent to *Child Welfare*'s editorial offices.

Indices and Abstracts
Child Welfare has an annual index, listing articles according to topic and author. This index appears in the November/December issue. Book reviews are also compiled here.

Child Welfare is abstracted and indexed in Abstracts for Social Workers, Chicorel Abstracts to Reading and Learning Disabilities, Child Development Abstracts and Bibliography, Education Index, Educational Resources Information Center/Early Childhood Education, Exceptional Child Education Resources, Sage Family Studies Abstracts, Selected References on the Abused and Battered Child, and Poverty and Human Resources.

Publication Schedule
Child Welfare is published six times a year, on the first day of January (January/February issue), March (March/April issue), May (May/June issue), July (July/August issue), September (September/October issue), and November (November/December issue).

CWLA Documentation Style
All materials submitted for possible publication to the *Child Welfare* League of America should conform as closely as possible in format to *CWLA's* documentation style, which is based on that of the *Publication Manual of the American Psychological Association* (APA) (3rd ed.).

Authors are responsible for providing complete and accurate documentation. Inaccurate reference can discredit manuscripts and create difficulties for readers. Absence of documentation makes it difficult for readers to verify statements and determine the author's contribution to the literature; absence of documentation when using material from published sources can leave an author liable to charges of plagiarism.

References are placed at the end of the article and must be double-spaced. List references alphabetically according to the first initial of the surname of the principal author. Avoid footnotes and endnotes if at all possible; if they must be used, keep them brief.

In-Text Citations
CWLA's documentation style is the same as APA style in its treatment of in-text citations. Source references appear in parentheses at the end of the appropriate sentence. They should include the author's last name and the year of publication.
    Example
    (DeWoody, 1993)

If there are two authors, the names should be joined with an ampersand.
    Example
    (Hess & Folaron, 1993)

Multiple in-text references should be separated with semicolons in alphabetical order.
Examples
(Foster, 1988; Posner, 1990; Roles, 1990)

Page numbers of direct quotes should be indicated in the text. The date of the reference is followed by a comma, a space, and the page number(s) of the quoted material.
Example
(Smith, 1981, pp. 23-24)

If the reference lists two or more works by the same author in one year, add letters (a, b, c) after the date in both the text and the reference entry.
Examples
In text-(Roles, 1990a, 1990b)
In references—Roles, P. (I 990a). *Saying goodbye to a baby: A book about loss and grief in adoption*. Washington, DC: *Child Welfare* League of America.

Name of Author(s)

Authors' names in the reference listing should be given last name first, followed by a comma and the author's initials. A comma should separate each author's name from the others. In the case of two or more authors, an ampersand, preceded by a comma, is used before the final author name.
Examples
Schaefer, K. L. (1993). *What only a mother can tell you about child sexual abuse*. Washington, DC: Child welfare League of America.

Finch, S. J., Fanshel, D., & Grundy, J. F. (1991). *Data collection in adoption and foster care*. Washington, DC: Child Welfare League of America.

If there is no author for a publication produced by an agency or other organization, the agency's name should be listed.
Example
Child Welfare League of America. (1994). *Washington workbook for child advocates*. Washington, DC: Author.

Date of Publication

The date of publication should appear in parentheses following the author's name. The closing parenthesis should be followed by a period. Include the month (or other time identifier) and day only for newspapers and popular magazines.
Examples
Hughes, R. C. (1993). Child welfare services for the catastrophically ill newborn: A guiding ethical paradigm. *Child Welfare*, 72, 423-440.

Sullivan, A. (1994). Update: On transracial adoption. *Children's Voice*, 3(3), 4-5.

Journal Article

The article title follows the date of publication. Only the first word and proper nouns in the article title begin with a capital letter. No quotation marks appear around the article title. The article title is followed by a period.

The complete name of the journal follows the article title. The volume of the journal is separated from the journal title with a comma. The journal name and volume number should be set in italics. Do not abbreviate words in the journal title.

Issue numbers need to be given only if each issue in a volume begins with Page 1. If the issue number is given, it should be placed in parentheses, with no space or punctuation separating it from the volume number.

Examples

Hughes, R. C. (1993). Child welfare services for the catastrophically ill newborn: A guiding ethical paradigm. *Child Welfare, 72,* 423-440.

Sullivan, A. (1994). Update: On transracial adoption. *Children's Voice,* 3(3), 4-5.

Book/Book Chapter

The book title follows the date of publication and is set in italics. Only the first word and proper nouns in the book title should begin with a capital letter. No quotation marks should appear around the book title. The book title should be followed by a period.

The city and state of publication follow the book title. The two-letter postal code abbreviation should be used for the state name. The state name is followed by a colon, then by the name of the publisher. The publisher's name is followed by a period.

Example

Warsh, R., Maluccio, A. N., & Pine, B. A. (1994). *Teaching family reunification: A sourcebook.* Washington, DC: Child Welfare League of America.

When referring to a chapter in a book, the chapter title follows the date of publication, but no italics are used. Only the first word and proper nouns in the chapter title begin with a capital letter. Following the chapter title are the word in, the names of the book's editors (initials and last name), and (Ed.) or (Eds.). A comma separates the book title from the editor information. The book title (see above for form) is followed by the pages on which the chapter appears (preceded by pp.), and the rest of the publication information set forth above.

Example

Day, P., Cahn, K., & Johnson, P. (1993). Building court-agency partnerships to reunify families. In B. A. Pine, R. Warsh, & A. N. Maluccio (Eds.), *Together again: Family reunification in foster care* (pp. 21-33). Washington, DC: Child Welfare League of America.

When citing the entire book, use the following format.

Example

Pine, B. A., Warsh, R., & Maluccio, A. N. (Eds.). (1993). *Together again: Family reunification in foster care.* Washington, DC: Child Welfare League of America.

Forth-Coming Works

For books and articles not yet published, list as much information as is available, using the term "in press" in lieu of a date.

    Example

    Leichtman, H. M. (in press). *Helping work environments work.* Washington, DC: Child Welfare League of America.

Additional Formats

The instructions and examples provided above are a guide to the most common reference types cited in CWLA publications. For guidance on other types of reference formats, please consult the *Publications Manual of the American Psychological Association* (4th ed.).

Editorial Style

To maintain consistency in its publications, the Child Welfare League of America has adopted certain rules regarding word usage, punctuation, and grammar. Authors should take these editorial style rules into consideration when preparing manuscripts for publication by *CWLA*.

Identifying Terminology

The following terms should be used when referring to various ethnic/radical groups:

- African American (no hyphen)
- White
- Latino
- Native American (no hyphen)
- Asian (or Pacific Islander)

People-first language should be used as much as possible, even when it results in somewhat wordy constructions, to avoid labeling. For example, use person with AIDS rather than AIDS patient (or worse, AIDS victim), child with a handicap rather than handicapped child, and so forth.

Child Welfare Terminology

    Out-of-home care is used as a generic term for all forms of placement away from the birthfamily. Family foster care and residential care are used for specific settings.

- Adoptions are legalized, not finalized, as some adoptions may disrupt later.
- Caretakers take care of property; caregivers take care of people.
- Parents and children in the birthfamily should be referred to as birthparents rather than natural, biological, or real parents and children.
- A person with HIV (never the HIV virus) or who is HIV positive is not the same as a person with AIDS; a person with AIDS has the set of symptoms defined by the Centers for Disease Control and Prevention.

    Infants whose mothers used drugs during pregnancy are exposed prenatally to drugs (or alcohol); they are not drug babies or crack babies.

- AOD may be used in a second reference as shorthand for alcohol and other drugs.

Grammar and Punctuation

The Child Welfare League of America uses the *Chicago Manual of Style* (14th ed.) and Webster's Tenth Collegiate Dictionary in deciding matters of spelling and editorial style. The list below summarizes some common usage problems.

- A comma should be used before the word and in a list of three or more items. Example
- The young lambs eat oats, peas, beans, and barley.
- The plural of youth is youth.

Examples

- CWLA is dedicated to helping children, youth, and their families.
- The word data is a plural. The singular is datum.
- The Child Welfare League of America uses "in behalf of," not "on behalf of," except in legal contexts.

Examples

- The guardian ad litem spoke in court on behalf of the three children. *CWLA* testified before Congress in behalf of children.
- Nonprofit is set without a hyphen.
- Policymaker is set without a hyphen, as is decision maker.
- When the word "state" follows the name of the state, it begins with a capital letter, i.e., New York State.

Numbers

- Numbers from zero to nine are spelled out. Numbers 10 and above are written with numerals.
- Percentages are expressed with the percent symbol (%). Numbers used as part of a percentage are expressed in numerals.
- Any number that begins a sentence is spelled out.

Childhood Education

ADDRESS FOR SUBMISSION:

Anne Watson Bauer, Editor
Childhood Education
Association for Childhood Educ. Intl.
17904 Georgia Avenue, Suite 215
Olney, MD 20832
USA
Phone: 301-570-2111
Fax: 301-570-2212
E-Mail: aceied@aol.com
Web: www.acei.org
Address May Change:

PUBLICATION GUIDELINES:

Manuscript Length: 16-20
Copies Required: Four
Computer Submission: Yes
Format: MAC/IBM Compatible,
    MSWord/ASCII
Fees to Review: 0.00 US$

Manuscript Style:
    American Psychological Association

CIRCULATION DATA:

Reader: Academics, Practicing Teachers
Frequency of Issue: 6 Times/Year
Copies per Issue: 10,001 - 25,000
Sponsor/Publisher: Association for
    Childhood Education International
Subscribe Price: 45.00 US$
    29.00 US$ Undergraduate Student

REVIEW INFORMATION:

Type of Review: Blind Review
No. of External Reviewers: 3
No. of In House Reviewers: 0
Acceptance Rate: 11-20%
Time to Review: 2 - 3 Months
Reviewers Comments: Yes
Invited Articles: 11-20%
Fees to Publish: 0.00 US$

MANUSCRIPT TOPICS:
Art/Music; Bilingual/E.S.L.; Counseling & Personnel Services; Curriculum Studies; Education Management/Administration; Educational Psychology; Elementary/Early Childhood; Gifted Children; Health & Physical Education; Reading; Special Education; Teacher Education; Tests, Measurement & Evaluation; Urban Education, Cultural/Non-Traditional

MANUSCRIPT GUIDELINES/COMMENTS:

Childhood Education is the voice of the *Association for Childhood Education International* (*ACEI*) and a professional medium for those concerned with the education and well-being of children from infancy through early adolescence: classroom teachers, teachers-in-training, teacher educators, parents, child care workers, librarians, supervisors, administrators and others. The journal seeks to stimulate thinking rather than advocate fixed practice. It explores emerging ideas, probes various points of view, and presents conflicting opinions supported wherever possible with research.

While avoiding the doctrinaire, *Childhood Education* also aims to express the goals, aspirations and convictions of *ACEI* and its Strategic Plan. It raises questions about emerging ideas from the perspective of basic *ACEI* commitments. To represent the voice of *ACEI* accurately, the journal encourages involvement of the Association's membership in communication of needs and contribution to publication planning.

Content
The Editor solicits articles that develop special topics or themes. At the same time flexibility is built into the schedule to permit the use of unsolicited manuscripts. An attempt is made to include accounts of innovative practices in the classroom and other settings; reviews of research; statements by leaders in education and allied fields, including the family; discussion of timely issues; descriptions of programs and practices beyond United States borders; human interest stories; bits of humor or satire.

Form and Length
Style (particularly references) should be consistent with the *Publication Manual 4th of the American Psychological Association*. Manuscripts (including references) should be typewritten, double spaced, on one side of 8½" x 11" non-erasable paper. Authors must submit four copies (with identifying information on only 1 copy) and the Copyright Transfer Agreement below (or a facsimile).

Preferred length is 2 to 4 journal pages (1400-2800 words). Enclose a stamped, self-addressed manuscript envelope. Photographs or camera-ready diagrams are often desirable (glossy prints, 8" x 10" if possible, with complete captions and credit lines). Authors are to obtain releases for use of photographs. Following publication, photographs are returned to authors.

Review
Childhood Education is a refereed journal. Unsolicited manuscripts are referred for anonymous review to at least three readers on the Publications Committee. The final decision rests with the Editor, who is guided by the reviewers' comments and such considerations as space, timeliness and projected plans.

Manuscript processing and review entail approximately 3 months. Rejected manuscripts are returned only to those authors providing a stamped self-addressed manuscript envelope. The Editor cannot consider proposals or outlines. Send completed manuscripts only.

Remuneration
Authors receive no remuneration other than five advance copies of the journal. Articles and illustrations are considered a contribution to the profession.

Publication
Accepted manuscripts will be published according to timeliness of subject matter, space availability and the projected schedule of themes. Alt manuscripts are edited to conform to the journal's editorial standards and space requirements. Prior to publication, authors are furnished with galley proofs.

COPYRIGHT TRANSFER AGREEMENT

I (the author) transfer copyright to the manuscript _____

_____by

(list all authors)_____

to the Association for Childhood Education International in consideration of publication. This transfer shall become effective if and when the manuscript is accepted for publication, thereby granting *ACEI* the right to authorize republication, reproduction and distribution of the original and derivative material. I further certify that the manuscript under consideration has not been published and is not being considered by another publication.

_____   _____   _____

Print Name   Signature of one author required   Date

Children's Literature in Education

ADDRESS FOR SUBMISSION:

Margaret Mackey, Co-Editor
Children's Literature in Education
PO Box 45034
Lansdowne Postal Outlet
Edmonton, Alberta, T6H 5Y1
Canada
Phone: +1 780-492-2605
Fax: +1 780-492-2430
E-Mail: margaret.mackey@ualberta.ca
Web: www.wkap.nl
Address May Change:

CIRCULATION DATA:

Reader: Practicing Teachers, Academics
Frequency of Issue: Quarterly
Copies per Issue: No Reply
Sponsor/Publisher: Kluwer Academic
    Publishers
Subscribe Price: 56.00 US$ Individual
    342.00 US$ Institution

PUBLICATION GUIDELINES:

Manuscript Length: 18-25
Copies Required: Three
Computer Submission: No
Format: N/A
Fees to Review: 0.00 US$

Manuscript Style:
    See Manuscript Guidelines

REVIEW INFORMATION:

Type of Review: Blind Review
No. of External Reviewers: 2
No. of In House Reviewers: 1-2
Acceptance Rate: 50%
Time to Review: 2 - 3 Months
Reviewers Comments: Yes
Invited Articles: 6-10%
Fees to Publish: 0.00 US$

MANUSCRIPT TOPICS:

Children's Literature; Elementary/Early Childhood; English Literature; Library
Science/Information Resources; Reading; Secondary/Adolescent Studies

MANUSCRIPT GUIDELINES/COMMENTS:

Children's Literature in Education is an international forum for the publication of original
peer-reviewed/refereed articles of interest to librarians, teachers, students, writers, and
interested parents. The journal seeks to promote lively discussion of poetry and prose for
children and young adults and to heighten professional awareness and understanding of this
literature and its use. The Editors welcome critical evaluation of individual authors or single
works, analysis or commentary on social issues reflected in books, interviews with or articles
by authors and illustrators, accounts of classroom practice and experience, and examinations
of the reading process and its developmental role in childhood and adolescence.

Manuscripts should be original and not previously published. Manuscripts not accepted for
publication can be returned only if accompanied by a self-addressed, stamped envelope.

Preparation of Manuscripts
Manuscripts, including references and footnotes, should be typed on double-spaced 8 ½ x 11-in. bond paper or equivalent. Two copies should be submitted. The title page should include title, author's name, and address for correspondence and proofs. The author's name should not appear on the other pages of the manuscript. An abstract is to be provided, preferably no longer than 100 words. A list of 3--5 key words is to be provided directly below the abstract. Key words should express the precise content of the manuscript, as they are used for indexing purposes.

References and their citation. Works discussed are identified at first citation by marginal notes prepared by the publisher. To facilitate this task, authors are asked to submit a separate sequentially numbered list (author and title only) of works cited and to suggest placement of the marginal note by penciling the corresponding number in the margin of the text where the note should appear. To provide the reader with complete bibliographical information, works cited should be listed alphabetically by author under "References" at the end of the paper, according to the following style:

Journal Article
Lewis, Claudia, "Searching for the master touch in picture books," *Children's Literature in Education,* 1984, 15, 198-203.

Book
Applebee, A.N., *The Child's Concept of Story,* chap. 3. Chicago: University of Chicago Press, 1978.

Chapter in edited book
Aiken, Joan, "Writing for enjoyment," in *Writers, Critics, and Children,* Geoff Fox et al., eds., pp. 15-26. London: Heinemann Educational Books, 1976. New York: Agathon Press, 1976.

When possible, give date and publisher with location for both North American and U.K. editions of a book, in chronological sequence.

Footnotes containing additional discussion should be listed separately at the end and indicated in the text by superior numbers. These should be kept to a minimum.

After a manuscript has been accepted for publication and after all revisions have been incorporated, manuscripts should be submitted to the Editor's Office as hard copy accompanied by electronic files on disk. Label the disk with identifying information -- software, journal name, and first author's last name. **The disk *must* be the one from which the accompanying manuscript (finalized version) was printed out.** The Editor's Office cannot accept a disk without its accompanying, matching hard-copy manuscript.

Where to Send Manuscripts
In North America, to **Margaret Mackey,** P.O. Box 45034, Lansdowne Postal Outlet, Edmonton, Alberta, Canada T6H 5Y1.

158

In the U.K. and elsewhere outside North America, to **Geoff Fox,** Aller Down Cottage, Coppice Lane, Sandford, Credition EX17 4EG, United Kingdom.

Springer Open Choice. In addition to the normal publication process (whereby an article is submitted to the journal and access to that article is granted to customers who have purchased a subscription), Springer now provides an alternative publishing option: Springer Open Choice. A Springer Open Choice article receives all the benefits of a regular subscription-based article, but in addition is made available publicly through Springer's online platform SpringerLink. To publish via Springer Open Choice, upon acceptance please visit www.springeronline.com/openchoice to complete the relevant order form and provide the required payment information. Payment must be received in full before publication or articles will publish as regular subscription-model articles. We regret that Springer Open Choice cannot be ordered for published articles.

Choral Journal

ADDRESS FOR SUBMISSION:

Ron Granger, Managing Editor
Choral Journal
American Choral Directors Association
PO Box 2720
Lawton, OK 73101-2720
USA
Phone: 405-232-8161
Fax: 405-232-8162
E-Mail: choraljournal@acdaonline.org
Web: acdaonline.org
Address May Change:

PUBLICATION GUIDELINES:

Manuscript Length: 16-20
Copies Required: Seven
Computer Submission: Yes
Format: PDF preferred
Fees to Review: 0.00 US$

Manuscript Style:
    Chicago Manual of Style, D. Kern
    Holman, Writing About Music

CIRCULATION DATA:

Reader: Academics, Practicing Teachers
Frequency of Issue: 10 Times/Year
Copies per Issue: 20,000
Sponsor/Publisher: American Choral
    Directors Association
Subscribe Price: 35.00 US$ Libraries
    75.00 US$ ACDA Membership
    Journal Included

REVIEW INFORMATION:

Type of Review: Editorial Review
No. of External Reviewers: 3+
No. of In House Reviewers: 1
Acceptance Rate: 15%
Time to Review: 9 Months
Reviewers Comments: No
Invited Articles: 6-10%
Fees to Publish: 0.00 US$

MANUSCRIPT TOPICS:
Art/Music; Choral Music & Conducting; Music Education

MANUSCRIPT GUIDELINES/COMMENTS:

Editorial Mission
The editorial purpose of the *Choral Journal* is, first, to provide ACDA members with practical and scholarly information about choral music and its performance. Articles and columns cover a variety of topics such as:
- Choral conducting and rehearsal techniques
- Composers of choral music and their craft
- Forms of choral music (motets, Masses, part songs, etc.)
- History of choral performance, histories of choral organizations, and biographies of conductors
- History and analysis of choral music
- Conductor and composer viewpoints
- Literature on and music for various types of choruses
- Performance practice, style, and interpretation

- Composing, arranging, editing, and publishing choral music
- Educational techniques and philosophies
- Vocal pedagogy
- Professional and artistic philosophies, esthetics
- Research materials.

The second major purpose of the *Choral Journal* is to provide ACDA members with organizational news about the American Choral Directors Association. Such items include letters from the president, executive director, and editor; information about conventions at the national and division levels; officer elections; proposed bylaw and constitutional changes; endowment and archives reports; and repertoire and standards committee reports.

Columns. In addition to review columns, the *Choral Journal* publishes regular columns that address specific areas of interest fn ACDA members.

Hallelujah! Explores the role of choral music in the worship settings of different faith communities.

Research Report explores current research studies in the choral field, examining such sources as dissertations, bibliographies, and monographs.

Compact Disc Reviews examines recent choral CD recordings (as well as reissues from LP) produced by recording companies both large and small.

Book Reviews takes a look at current biographies, textbooks, music histories, and how-to books published in the choral field.

Choral Reviews, one of the most popular sections of the *Choral Journal*, evaluates the full spectrum of printed music made available to choral directors by today's music publishers. Reviewers examine issues such as how well compositions are suited for specific types of choirs, the appropriateness of texts and how well they are set to music, and the overall quality of compositions.

Special Focus Issues. On occasion the *Choral Journal* has published focus issues covering specific topics such as children's choirs, choral music from around the world, Russian and Estonian choral music, choral music of the Renaissance (emphasizing Palestrina), and the choral works of Henry Purcell. Each January, the *Choral Journal* provides ACDA members with full coverage of the events and people of ACDA's exciting national and division conventions.

Choral Journal Writer's Guidelines

The following guidelines are designed to assist those interested in submitting articles for publication in the *Choral Journal*, the official publication of the American Choral Directors Association (ACDA). Articles not conforming to the guidelines may be returned for revision. Articles submitted for review should be concise and contain primarily new or original information or research relevant to the choral art. This is not meant to exclude a fresh and creative approach to standard materials. The length of the manuscript should generally be limited to a maximum of eighteen double-spaced, typewritten pages. The ideal length for short papers is from six to nine typewritten pages. Lengthy articles should be divided into sections separated by subtitles to lead the reader through the article. The author should use a writing style that is direct and easily understood. Extremes of academic stuffiness, research terminology, vague generalities, and overworked educational jargon should be avoided. The final draft should be carefully proofread and free of grammatical errors. The author should be selective and judicious in presenting evidence and documentation in support of research. Quotations should be brief. Referenced material should be indicated by superscript and cited in end notes, which should be double-spaced, numbered consecutively, and formatted in the style of Kate L. Turabian's *A Manual for Writers of Term Papers, Theses, and Dissertations*, 5th ed.

For articles with musical examples, printed or computer-generated reproductions are preferable. They may be included with the text or paced at the end of the article. In either case, placement of musical examples should be indicated within the body of the article itself (i.e., "Figure 1"). Permission of copyright owner should be given underneath each musical example (e.g., copyright year, publisher, and reprint permission statement). The article is not complete until the author has obtained all necessary copyright permissions.

The title page should contain only the title of the article. The author should enclose, on a separate piece of paper, his/her address and telephone number, and a professional identification, one or two sentences in length. Photographs, artwork, or tables may be submitted and, if deemed 'appropriate, may be published.

All articles submitted are subject to a blind review by the editor, associate editor, and three additional members of the editorial board. Articles are accepted for publication when board members determine that the article contains information that pertains directly to the general interests of the national ACDA membership. Some expanded criteria for acceptance are:

1. Topic is of national importance, will interest man, readers. Editors of state or division newsletters welcome articles on topics of local or regional interest.

2. Article offers new knowledge or offers new insight on the topic. Articles that rely heavily on secondary sources are seldom judged to offer new knowledge. For example, extensive citations from New Grove articles are usually rejected. A compilation of widely scattered secondary sources, however, might effectively demonstrate a new hypothesis.

3. Article will challenge readers' thinking.

4. Material is timely. Anniversaries of composers or events offer timely opportunities for articles.

5. Premise is well-defined, supported, and developed. The purpose of the article should be clear. The author should supply convincing evidence to support the thesis, developing the premise so that a reader unfamiliar with the topic will understand the article's arguments.

6. Scope is appropriate, neither too narrow nor too broad. An example of too broad a scope would be an article that introduced a composer, presented biographical information in detail, and then compared all the composer's cantatas point-for-point with the cantatas of Telemann and Bach. Such an article could be made appropriate in scope by reducing the biographical material to a paragraph or two that discussed aspects of the composer's life and works that were important to the present study. Works relevant to the thesis could then be selected for analysis. If the goal is to prove that this composer imitates the text-symbolism or rhythmic techniques of Bach, for example, a selective presentation of works that strengthen this point would be in order. If numerous works are studied as a part of preparation for the article, findings should be summarized rather than set out in detail work by work.

7. Information is precise, accurate, and well-documented. Sometimes writers use vague, subjective adjectives to describe musical elements<e.g., a "wonderful" melody or "beautiful" harmonies or "fine" orchestration. Precise, objective descriptions are more effective at convincing readers that the work is wonderful, beautiful, or fine.

8. Article is well-written; material flows in an easily read, narrative style. This criterion covers a wide range of stylistic issues.
- Clichés: phrases such as "choir and audience alike," "eminently singable," and overused metaphors may give an article a pretentious or thoughtless tone.
- Imprecise generalizations: phrases such as "Many conductors think. . ." or "One of the most . . ." or "Very frequently, choir. . ." indicate that the author is hoping to convince the reader of something without offering any evidence. For example, it is not known how many conductors the author has surveyed, if any, to support the first phrase above.
- Sentences beginning with "It is . . ." or "There are . . ." are weakly constructed and can usually be recast.
- Repeated use of passive voice also weakens an article's style. The goal is to encourage clear, interesting expository prose that is neither verbose nor chatty. Some grammar can be polished as an article is revised for publication. An article is more likely to be rejected if ambiguous grammar obscures its meaning.

9. Most of the ideas seem to be the author's; quotes enhance the article. Secondary source quotes offering analytical descriptions of scores are not as strong as original musical insights, unless the source of the citation has special significance. Analyses that take a "road-map" approach to the score by simply listing all musical events as they occur cause readers to lose interest.

10. Author uses musical examples judiciously (if applicable). As a rule, it is not desirable to print large excerpts. However, enough music needs to be provided to make the author's descriptive comments understandable.

11. Material is not readily available in other publications. If a topic has been covered in a recent book or journal that overlaps *Choral Journal* readership, it is assumed that readers who are interested in that topic will find that material. Material that may be considered common knowledge by some may be new to developing conductors and, if originally presented in a new context, can prove valuable.

12. Article avoids promoting a company, person, product, or performing organization.

13. Title is appropriate. An article is not rejected for it title; instead, attempts are made to devise a better one.

Christian Education Journal

ADDRESS FOR SUBMISSION:

Kevin E. Lawson, Editor
Christian Education Journal
Talbot School of Theology
13800 Biola Avenue
La Mirada, CA 90639
USA
Phone: 562-906-4598
Fax: 562-906-4502
E-Mail: editor.cej@biola.edu
Web: www.biola.edu/cej
Address May Change:

PUBLICATION GUIDELINES:

Manuscript Length: 11-15
Copies Required: No Reply
Computer Submission: Yes Email
Format: MS Word
Fees to Review: 0.00 US$

Manuscript Style:
    American Psychological Association

CIRCULATION DATA:

Reader: Academics
Frequency of Issue: 2 Times/Year
Copies per Issue: Less than 1,000
Sponsor/Publisher: Talbot School of
    Theology and the North American
    Professors of Christian Education
Subscribe Price:
    See Website

REVIEW INFORMATION:

Type of Review: Blind Review
No. of External Reviewers: 2
No. of In House Reviewers: 1
Acceptance Rate: 21-30%
Time to Review: 1 - 2 Months
Reviewers Comments: Yes
Invited Articles: 21-30%
Fees to Publish: 0.00 US$

MANUSCRIPT TOPICS:
Education Management/Administration; Educational Psychology; Higher Education;
Religious Education

MANUSCRIPT GUIDELINES/COMMENTS:

The *Christian Education Journal* exists for specific purposes and reflects a general theological
perspective. Those with an interest in writing or reviewing articles for the journal need to
understand these purposes and theological position and be able to work within this framework.

Purposes for the Journal
The purpose of the *Christian Education Journal* is to strengthen the conception and practice
of Christian education in church and parachurch settings through:
1. Encouraging reflection on the foundations of Christian education and implications for
    ministry practice
2. Exploring the integration and application of social science theory and research to
    educational ministry concerns
3. Fostering improved teaching in the field of Christian education at colleges and
    seminaries, equipping people for leadership in this field

4. Promoting the assessment of our changing cultural context and of contemporary educational ministry needs, models, and trends
5. Providing reviews of new books in the field of Christian education and other related disciplines that impact educational ministry.

NAPCE Statement of Faith

The North American Professors of Christian Education organization has adopted the following statement of faith from the National Association of Evangelicals. Articles submitted for possible publication in the *Christian Education Journal* are expected to reflect these foundational theological commitments.

- We believe the Bible to be the inspired, the only infallible, authoritative Word of God.
- We believe that there is one God, eternally existent in three persons: Father, Son and Holy Spirit.
- We believe in the deity of our Lord Jesus Christ, in His virgin birth, in His sinless life, in His miracles, in His vicarious and atoning death through His shed blood, in His bodily resurrection, in His ascension to the right hand of the Father, and in His personal return in power and glory.
- We believe that for the salvation of lost and sinful people, regeneration by the Holy Spirit is absolutely essential.
- We believe in the present ministry of the Holy Spirit by whose indwelling the Christian is enabled to live a godly life.
- We believe in the resurrection of both the saved and the lost; they that are saved unto the resurrection of life and they that are lost unto the resurrection of damnation.
- We believe in the spiritual unity of believers in our Lord Jesus Christ.

Writing Guidelines for Submissions

We invite submissions of original research/writing on issues in the field of Christian education. Contributors do not need to be members of NAPCE. All manuscripts should not have been published elsewhere unless specifically approved by the editor. Manuscripts should follow APA format with parenthetical references and limited use of endnotes. See the following volume for formatting details: American Psychological Association. (2001). *Publication Manual of the American Psychological Association*, (5th ed.). Washington, D.C.: Author. Samples of APA reference formatting are available at the journal website: **www.biola.edu/cej**

Articles. The preferred length of articles is between 2,500 and 6,000 words. Contributors should send their submissions to the editor (**editor.cej@biola.edu**) as Word documents. The author's name, address, and e-mail address should appear only on a cover sheet for the article. Authors should also include an abstract of the article (100 words or less). Before acceptance, submissions will be "masked" reviewed by appropriate referees. If accepted for publication, we reserve the right to edit for usage and style. Authors of accepted submissions will receive three *gratis* copies of the journal in which the article appears.

Types of articles desired include the following:
- Research articles:
     Theological/Philosophical foundations and issues impacting Christian education

Historical perspectives on Christian education that shed light on current issues
Empirical research that furthers our understanding of sound practice
- Teaching/Preparing people for educational ministry leadership
- Assessment of congregational/parachurch ministry trends and needs
- Cultural analysis with implications for Christian education practice
- Response/Dialogue with issues or ideas in the broader field of religious education
- Reviews of contemporary ministry models in churches and/or parachurch organizations
- Professional reviews of research, with implications for educational ministry or teaching
- Abstracts of recent dissertations in the field of Christian education

In general, the following qualities are what we are looking for in articles we would publish:
1. The content of the article is clearly relevant to the field of Christian education, whether that be in church, parachurch, or higher education settings where we strive to equip our students to serve well in this vocation. Our general editorial policy is that articles present a position/perspective compatible with evangelical Protestant tradition. (See NAPCE Statement of Faith above.) Occasionally we will invite articles by authors outside this perspective to stimulate and challenge our theory and practice.
2. The article demonstrates both a breadth and depth of understanding of the issues it addresses. The person is knowledgeable and communicates this well.
3. The article explores its topic in new ways. It makes a genuine contribution to our understanding, not just reviewing or rehashing things that have been addressed in other publications.
4. The evidence for the positions taken in the article is sound and well organized (if it is a research article, see below).
5. The author develops reasonable implications for educational ministry practice (or for the preparation of others for educational ministry). We want to see how the issues addressed in the article make a difference for those seeking to carry out their ministries well.
6. The writing style of the article communicates well to the journal audience (e.g., Christian education faculty, students, thoughtful ministry practitioners).

Notes. These are brief discussions of focused issues in the field of Christian education of interest to our readers and may be more personal, responsive, or reflective than regular research articles. Responses to previously published articles in *Christian Education Journal* are published in this section. "Notes" should normally not exceed 3,000 words, but style and submission guidelines are the same as for regular articles.

Book Reviews. Our desire is to publish reviews of new books within the field, and "the best" of books from other disciplines that relate to Christian education. Guidelines for developing book reviews are available at the journal website: **www.biola.edu/cej**

Mini-Theme Issues. We are open to proposals for the publication of a group of articles (4-6) focused on a theme as part of an issue of the journal. Proposals for mini-theme issues should be e-mailed to the journal editor for consideration: **editor.cej@biola.edu**

Classical World

ADDRESS FOR SUBMISSION:

Matthew W. Santirocco, Editor
Classical World
New York University
College of Arts & Science
New York, NY 10003-6688
USA
Phone: 212-998-8100
Fax: 212-995-4141
E-Mail: mss1@i4.nyu.edu
Web: www.caas-cw.org/cwhome.html
Address May Change:

PUBLICATION GUIDELINES:

Manuscript Length: 16-20
Copies Required: Two
Computer Submission: Yes
Format: N/A
Fees to Review: 0.00 US$

Manuscript Style:

CIRCULATION DATA:

Reader: Academics, Practicing Teachers
Frequency of Issue: Quarterly
Copies per Issue: 2,001 - 3,000
Sponsor/Publisher: Classical Association of
    the Atlantic States
Subscribe Price: 35.00 US$ Individual
        50.00 US$ Institution
        45.00 US$ Individual foreign

REVIEW INFORMATION:

Type of Review: Blind Review
No. of External Reviewers: 2
No. of In House Reviewers: 1
Acceptance Rate: 21-30%
Time to Review: 4 - 6 Months
Reviewers Comments: Yes
Invited Articles: 0-5%
Fees to Publish: 0.00 US$

MANUSCRIPT TOPICS:

Classical Civilization/Literature; Curriculum Studies; Foreign Language; Languages & Linguistics

MANUSCRIPT GUIDELINES/COMMENTS:

We welcome contributions on all aspects of Greek and Roman literature, history, and society; on the classical tradition; on the history of classical scholarship; and on the teaching of Latin, Greek, and classical civilization. We do not think it is necessary to write in one way for teachers in schools and in another for scholars in colleges and universities. Our ideal reader is a scholarly teacher or a teaching scholar. Our ideal contributor has something to say to this reader. All articles to be considered for publication, including contributions to "Scholia" and "Paedagogus," should be sent to the Editor. Books for review and items for "In the Schools" and "Notes and News" should be sent to the sub-editors of those departments. Authors should submit two copies, double spaced, with return postage. Since submissions are judged anonymously, authorship and affiliation should be revealed only in a cover letter. Authors of accepted articles are expected to format their final versions in accordance with a style sheet which will be sent to them.

Clearing House (The): A Journal of Education Strategies, Issues, and Ideas

ADDRESS FOR SUBMISSION:

Sarah C. Yaussi, Managing Editor
Clearing House (The): A Journal of
    Education Strategies, Issues, and Ideas
Heldref Publications
1319 Eighteenth Street, N.W.
Washington, DC 20036
USA
Phone: 202-296-6267 ext. 1257
Fax: 202-296-5149
E-Mail: tch@heldref.org
Web: www.heldref.org
Address May Change:

PUBLICATION GUIDELINES:

Manuscript Length: 8-15 dble-spaced pgs
Copies Required: Two
Computer Submission: Yes Email
Format: N/A
Fees to Review: 0.00 US$

Manuscript Style:
    Chicago Manual of Style

CIRCULATION DATA:

Reader: Academics, Administrators, &
    Practicing Teachers
Frequency of Issue: Bi-Monthly
Copies per Issue: 2,001 - 3,000
Sponsor/Publisher: Heldref Publications,
    Inc.
Subscribe Price: 48.00 US$ Individual
    96.00 US$ Institution

REVIEW INFORMATION:

Type of Review: Editorial Review
No. of External Reviewers: 2
No. of In House Reviewers: 0
Acceptance Rate: 30%
Time to Review: 2 - 4 Months
Reviewers Comments: Yes
Invited Articles: 5-10%
Fees to Publish: 0.00 US$

MANUSCRIPT TOPICS:
Art/Music; Bilingual/E.S.L.; Curriculum Studies; Education Management/Administration; Educational Psychology; Educational Technology Systems; English Literature; Foreign Language; Gifted Children; Health & Physical Education; Languages & Linguistics; Reading; School Law; Science Math & Environment; Secondary/Adolescent Studies; Social Studies/Social Science; Special Education; Teacher Education; Tests, Measurement & Evaluation; Urban Education, Cultural/Non-Traditional

MANUSCRIPT GUIDELINES/COMMENTS:

The Clearing House publishes material of interest to middle level and high school teachers and administrators, as well as postsecondary education faculty members and their students. Results of research, discussion of educational trends, and first-person accounts are all invited emphasis should be on the "how-to" aspect of a practice or program. We also publish a limited number of articles presenting opinion on controversial issues.

Consideration is given to articles dealing with educational trends and philosophy; preservice and inservice education; effective schools; curriculum; learning styles; discipline; guidance and counseling; community involvement; education of students with disabilities; teaching and learning climates; gifted and talented programs; international education; instructional leadership; instructional techniques; teaching with computers; testing and measurement; and school law.

1. We prefer manuscripts that do not exceed 3,500 words, although we also accept shorter pieces of roughly 600 words.

2. Indicate that your article has not been published or submitted elsewhere. Manuscripts simultaneously submitted to other publications will be returned.

3. Two copies of each manuscript must be submitted. In addition, the author should keep an exact copy so the editors can refer to specific pages and lines if a question arises. The manuscript should be double-spaced.

4. *The Chicago Manual of Style*, 15th Ed., University of Chicago Press, Chicago, 2003, should be used as a style reference in preparation of manuscripts.

5. Avoid explanatory notes whenever possible by incorporating their content in the text. For essential notes, identify them with consecutive superscripts and list them in a section entitled **Notes** at the end of the text.

6. References should be listed alphabetically according to the author's last name at the end of the manuscript. In the text, reference citations should be in parentheses (author date) or (date).

7. Accepted manuscripts normally are published within six months of acceptance. Authors receive two complimentary copies of the issue in which their article appears. Reprints are available through *The Clearing House.*

8. We reserve the right to edit.

Collection Management

ADDRESS FOR SUBMISSION:

Edward Shreeves, Editor
Collection Management
University of Iowa Libraries
Iowa City, IA 52242
USA
Phone: 319-335-5873
Fax: 319-335-5900
E-Mail: edward-shreeves@uiowa.edu
Web: www.haworthpress.com/journals
Address May Change:

CIRCULATION DATA:

Reader: , Librarians
Frequency of Issue: Quarterly
Copies per Issue: No Reply
Sponsor/Publisher: Haworth Press, Inc.
Subscribe Price: 60.00 US$ Individual
    235.00 US$ Institution

PUBLICATION GUIDELINES:

Manuscript Length: 16-30
Copies Required: Three
Computer Submission: Yes Disk or Email
Format: Word
Fees to Review: 0.00 US$

Manuscript Style:
    Chicago Manual of Style

REVIEW INFORMATION:

Type of Review: Blind Review
No. of External Reviewers: 1
No. of In House Reviewers: 2
Acceptance Rate: 70%
Time to Review: 2 Months or less
Reviewers Comments: Yes
Invited Articles: 15-30%
Fees to Publish: 0.00 US$

MANUSCRIPT TOPICS:
Library Science/Information Resources

MANUSCRIPT GUIDELINES/COMMENTS:

About the Journal
Stay up-to-date on the latest research and applications for library collections!

An essential resource for librarians who develop library collections, *Collection Management* examines the latest developments in the field and their implications for college, university, and research libraries. This practical journal will strengthen all aspects of your collection development program, including management, planning, and resource allocation; selection and acquisitions; development of virtual collections; cooperation, consortia, and resource sharing; preservation and conservation; and facilities, space, and storage.

Collection Management addresses issues that collection development librarians and library administrators face everyday, including:
- developing effective acquisition techniques
- factoring user expectations into acquisition plans
- working with vendors to develop affordable services

- acquiring, moving, and managing materials off-site
- collecting and protecting rare books and other artifacts
- preserving historical materials
- using multimedia as a collection tool
- creating unique digital collections
- maintaining a separate identity in consortia agreements
- balancing access and ownership
- preserving fair use of intellectual property
- dealing with personnel challenges

This comprehensive journal presents articles on an extensive range of topics--some pragmatic and topical, others theoretical, and still others state-of-the-art. In addition, *Collection Management* publishes thematic issues that focus on specific areas of concern. Past thematic issues have included Electronic Resources: Implications for Collection Management; Collection Development: Past and Future; and Access Services in Libraries: New Solutions for *Collection Management.*

Instructions for Authors

1. **Original Articles Only**. Submission of a manuscript to this Journal represents a certification on the part of the author(s) that it is an original work, and that neither this manuscript nor a version of it has been published elsewhere note: being considered for publication elsewhere.

2. **Manuscript Length**. Your manuscript may be approximately **10-20 typed pages**, double-spaced (including references and abstract). Lengthier manuscripts may be considered, but only at the discretion of the Editor. Sometimes, lengthier scripts may be considered 6 they can be divided up into sections for publication in successive Journal issues.

3. **Manuscript Style**. General style of manuscripts far this Journal should follow the latest edition of The *Chicago Manual of Style* (University of Chicago Press). References and citations should follow Chapter 16, *Documentation 2: Author-Date Citations and Reference Lists*. Information on this method is also found in the sixth edition of *A Manual for Writers of Term Papers, Theses, and Dissertations* by Kate L. Turabian. Do not use abbreviations for journal titles. Include both volume and issue number, issue data and inclusive pagination of journal articles. The reference section, like the text, should be double-spaced throughout. Spell out numbers one through nine, it they do not represent precise measurements and are not grouped for comparison with numbers 10 above. Use a combination of words and figures to distinguish between groups of numbers placed back to back, eg. "the first 5 books."

If an author wishes to submit a paper that has been already prepared in another style, he or she may do so. However, if the paper is accepted (with or without reviewer's alterations), the author is fully responsible for retyping the manuscript in the correct style as indicated above. Neither the Editor nor the Publisher is responsible for re-preparing manuscript copy to adhere to the Journal's style.

4. Manuscript Preparation.

Margins. leave at least a one-inch margin on all four sides.

Paper. use clean, white B-1/2• x 11" bond paper.

Number of copies. 3 (the original plus two photocopies).

Cover page. *Important*-staple a cover page to the manuscript, indicating only the article title (this is used far anonymous refereeing).

Second – "title page". enclose a regular title page but do not staple it to the manuscript. Include the title again, plus:

- full authorship
- an ABSTRACT of about 100 words. (Below the abstract provide 3-10 key words far index purposes).
- a header or footer an each page with abbreviated title and page number of total (e.g., pg 2 of 7)
- an introductory footnote with authors' academic degrees, professional titles, affiliations, mailing and e-mail addresses, and any desired acknowledgment of research support or other credit.

5. Return Envelopes.

When you submit your three manuscript copies, also include:

- a regular envelope, stamped and self-addressed. This is for the Editor to send you an "acknowledgement of receipt" letter.

6. Spelling, Grammar, and Punctuation.

You are responsible for preparing manuscript copy which is clearly written in acceptable, scholarly English and which contains no errors of spelling, grammar, or punctuation. Neither the Editor nor the Publisher is responsible for correcting errors of spelling and grammar. The manuscript, after acceptance by the Editor, must be immediately ready for typesetting as it is finally submitted by me authors).

Check your paper for the following common errors:

- dangling modifiers
- misplaced modifiers
- unclear antecedents
- incorrect or inconsistent abbreviations

Also, check the accuracy of all arithmetic calculations, statistics, numerical data, text citations, and references.

7. Inconsistencies Must Be Avoided.

Be sure you are consistent in your use abbreviations, terminology, and in citing references, tram one pad of your paper to another.

8. Preparation of Tables, Figures, and Illustrations.

Any material that is not textual is considered artwork. This includes tables, figures, diagrams, charts, graphs, illustrations, appendices, screen captures, and photos. Tables and figures (including legend, notes, and sources) should be no larger than 4 ½ x 6 ½ inches. Type styles should be Helvetica (or Helvetica narrow if necessary) and no smaller than 8 point. We request that computer-generated figure be in black and while and/or shades of gray (preferably no color, far it does not reproduce well). Camera-ready art must contain no grammatical, typographical, or formal errors and must reproduce sharply and clearly in the dimensions of the final printed page (4 ½ x 6 ½ inches). Photos and screen captures must be on disk as a TIFF file, or other graphic file format such as JPEG or BMP. For rapid publication we must receive black-and-while glossy or matte positives (white background with black images and/or wording) in addition to files on disk. Tables should be created in the text document file using the software's *Table* feature.

9. **Submitting Art**. Both a printed hard copy and a disk copy of the art must be provided. We request that each piece of art be sent in its own file, on a disk separate from the disk containing the manuscript text file(s), and be clearly labeled. We reserve the right to (if necessary) *request new art, altar art*, or if all else has failed in achieving art that is presentable, *delete art*. If submitted art cannot be used, the Publisher reserves the right to redo the art and to charge the author for a fee of $35.00 per hour for this service. The Haworth Press, Inc. is not responsible for errors incurred in the preparation of new artwork. Camera-ready artwork must be prepared on separate sheets of paper. Always use black ink and professional drawing instruments. On the back of these items, write your article title and the journal title lightly in soft-lead pencil (please do not write on the face of art). In the text file, skip extra lines and indicate where these figures are placed. Photos are considered part of the acceptable manuscript and remain with the Publisher for use in additional printings.

10. **Electronic Media**. Haworth's in-house typesetting unit is able to utilize your final manuscript material as prepared on most personal computers and word processors. This will minimize typographical errors and decrease overall production time. Please send the first draft and subsequent drafts of your manuscript to the journal Editor in print format via regular mail, and electronic format, preferably as a word processing document attached to electronic mail for his/her final review and approval. After approval of your final manuscript, please submit the final approved version both on printed format ("hard copy") and floppy diskette. On the outside of the diskette package write:
1) the brand name of your computer or word processor
2) the word processing program and version that you used
3) the title of your article, and
4) the file name.

NOTE: Disk and hard copy must agree. In case of discrepancies, it is The Haworth Press' policy to follow hard copy. Authors are advised that no revisions of the manuscript can be made after acceptance by the Editor for publication. The benefits of this procedure are many with speed and accuracy being the most obvious. We look forward to working with your electronic submission which will allow us to serve you more efficiently.

11. **Alterations Required By Referees and Reviewers**. Many times a paper is accepted by the Editor contingent upon charges that are mandated by anonymous specialist referees and members of the Editorial Board. If the Editor returns your manuscript for revisions, you are responsible for retyping any sections of the paper to incorporate these revisions (if applicable, revisions should also be put on disk).

12. **Typesetting**. You will not be receiving galley proofs of your article. Editorial revisions, if any, must therefore be made while your article is still in manuscript. The final version of the manuscript will be the version you see published. Typesetter's errors will be corrected by the

174

production staff of The Haworth Press. Authors are expected to submit manuscripts, disks, and art that are free from error.

13. **Reprints.** The senior author will receive two copies of the journal issue and 25 complimentary reprints of his or her article. The junior author will receive two copies of the journal issue. These are sent several weeks after the journal issue is published and in circulation. An order form for the purchase of additional reprints will also be sent to all authors at this time. (Approximately 4-6 weeks is necessary for the preparation of reprints.) Please do not query the Journal's Editor about reprints. All such questions should be sent directly to The Haworth Press. Inc., Production Department, 37 West Broad Street, West Hazleton, PA 18202. To order additional reprints (minimum: 50 copies), please contact The Haworth Document Delivery Center, 10 Alice Street, Binghamton, NY 13904-1580; 1-800-342-9678 or Fax (607)722-6362.

14. **Copyright.** Copyright ownership of your manuscript must be transferred officially to The Haworth Press, Inc. before we can begin the peer-review process. The Editor's letter acknowledging receipt of the manuscript will be accompanied by a form fully explaining this. All authors must sign the form and return the original to the Editor as soon as possible. Failure to return the copyright form in a timely fashion will result in a delay in review and subsequent publication.

Communication Disorders Quarterly

ADDRESS FOR SUBMISSION:

Kathy L. Coufal, Editor
Communication Disorders Quarterly
University of Nebraska - Omaha
Kayser Hall 115
Omaha, NE 68182-0054
USA
Phone: 402-554-3338
Fax: 402-554-3572
E-Mail: kcoufal@mail.unomaha.edu
Web: www.proedinc.com/
Address May Change:

PUBLICATION GUIDELINES:

Manuscript Length: 11-15
Copies Required: Five
Computer Submission: No
Format: N/A
Fees to Review: 0.00 US$

Manuscript Style:
    American Psychological Association

CIRCULATION DATA:

Reader: , Communication Disorder
   Specialists
Frequency of Issue: Quarterly
Copies per Issue: 1,001 - 2,000
Sponsor/Publisher: Pro-ed, Inc.
Subscribe Price: 43.00 US$ Individual
   109.00 US$ Institution
   71.00 US$ Ind.& $138 Inst. Foreign

REVIEW INFORMATION:

Type of Review: Blind Review
No. of External Reviewers: 3
No. of In House Reviewers: 1
Acceptance Rate: 21-30%
Time to Review: 2 - 3 Months
Reviewers Comments: Yes
Invited Articles: 21-30%
Fees to Publish: 0.00 US$

MANUSCRIPT TOPICS:
Audiology/Speech Pathology; Special Education

MANUSCRIPT GUIDELINES/COMMENTS:

Aims and Scope
Communication Disorders Quarterly (CDQ) is published fall, winter, spring, and summer. Articles are accepted for review on a continual basis. The editor of *CDQ* welcomes submissions of previously unpublished applied and clinical research manuscripts relating to communication disorders, clinical assessment, and/or clinical remediation of communication disorders in infants, school-age children, and adults. *CDQ* uses masked peer review for submissions.

Manuscript Requirements
Authors are expected to prepare submissions according to the style specified in the *Publication Manual of the American Psychological Association* (4th ed., 1994). Authors should pay special attention to APA style regarding tables, figures, and references. All manuscripts should be accompanied by a cover letter requesting that the submission be considered for publication and stating that it has not been published previously and is not

176

currently being submitted elsewhere. The contact author's business address and phone number should also be included. A cover sheet should include the title (not to exceed 15 words), authors (with degrees), and address to whom correspondence should be directed, as well as a running head (not to exceed 35 characters). The running head should appear at the top of each subsequent page, excluding the abstract page. No other manuscript pages should contain author identification. Responsibility for removal of author identification rests with the contact author. Pages should be numbered in the upper right-hand corner of each page, starting with page 1. The following is the appropriate order for the elements of the manuscript:

Title Page. Title of the article, complete names, and affiliations of all authors.

Abstract. Second manuscript page should contain an abstract not to exceed 100 words.

Text. The text begins on page 3 of the manuscript and should be limited in length to 15 pages, excluding tables, figures, and references.

Author Bios. A short paragraph of no more than 50 words should indicate names, degrees, position, place of employment, and research interests.

Author's Notes. Acknowledgements should appear on a separate page after the bios. Citations of grant or contract support of research should appear here.

Endnotes. Use endnotes as sparingly as possible. Number them with Arabic numerals starting with 1 and continuing through the article; for example: "(see Note 1)."

References. All literature, including names of assessment instruments, cited in the text of the manuscript should be included in the reference list, which immediately follows the last page of the text. References should be listed alphabetically, then chronologically, by senior author surname. Journal titles are spelled out in full. The abbreviation "et al." may not be used in the reference list. All author's surnames should be listed the first time a work is cited in the text. The names of multiple-author citations should be connected by "and" when occurring in the text but by an ampersand if within parentheses or in the reference list. Authors should consult the APA style manual for specifics on citing references and preparing the reference list.

Tables and Figures. Copies of tables and figures should be attached to each copy of the manuscript. Each table and figure should be on a separate page, with tables immediately following the reference list and preceding the figures. Please provide a separate page of figure legends/captions. Tables should be double-spaced and numbered consecutively with Arabic numerals. Table titles and figure legends should be concise but explanatory. All figures should be of professional quality, but camera-ready materials should be retained by the author until manuscript acceptance. In the event that figures are not camera-ready, the author will be expected to pay the cost of the required artwork prior to publication.

Copyright Assignment
If a manuscript is accepted for publication, the author(s) will be required to sign a Transfer of Copyright agreement conveying all copyright ownership to PRO-ED.

Manuscript Preparation

As noted previously, authors should prepare manuscripts according to the *Publication Manual of the American Psychological Association* (4th ed., 1994). Copies may be ordered from: APA Order Department, PO Box 2710, Hyattsville, MD 20784.

After the manuscript has been accepted for publication and after all changes have been incorporated, authors are to send the copies of the manuscript and a computer disk containing the manuscript file to the editor. Label the disk with the following information: type of platform (Mac or PC), name of software and version number, and file name of article (please use last name of first author). Because the publisher will use the computer disk for production purposes, the use of certain word-processing programs is preferable. For PC, it is Microsoft Word 97 or 2000. For Macintosh, it is MSWord (up to and including version 98).

When preparing the manuscript on disk, please adhere to the following guidelines:

1. Please type all copy upper and lower case — do not use all capitals or small capitals. You may use boldface and italics, but please use the word-processing software's italic function, not the underline key.

2. Do not put 2 spaces after any element, such as periods (e.g., only 1 space after closing punctuation for a sentence or after a colon, not 2).

3. Do not use an auto-hyphenation (machine-generated) program—allow words to wrap to next line rather than break them.

4. Do not use lowercase "l" (el) in place of the numeral 1 and vice versa. Do not use capital letter "O" (oh) for zero and vice versa.

5. Use 1 hard return at the end of paragraphs and after each element, such as title, author name(s), heads, etc. **No hard returns at the end of lines**. Never use double hard returns.

6. Indicate correct location of tables and figures in text in boldface, enclosed in angle brackets. Example: **<Fig. 1 here>**

7. Please use your tab key and centering functions to do head alignment, paragraph indents, etc. DO NOT USE THE SPACE BAR.

8. Please make manuscript printouts of this word-processing version, single-sided and double-spaced (including references, bios, tables, etc.) to send to the editor.

9. For figure preparation, do not use rules smaller than 1 point in size.

Editing, Proofing, and Author Alterations

Manuscripts that appear for publication may be returned for revision. Following author final submission, papers are edited to improve style, clarity, and consistency. Responsibility for the accuracy of references and data presented in manuscripts accepted for publication rests with the author(s).

Submission of Manuscripts

Five good-quality, typed, double-spaced, unstapled copies of the manuscript and any editorial correspondence should be sent to:

Kathy L. Coufal, PhD
Editor, CDQ
University of Nebraska–Omaha
Kayser Hall 115
Omaha, NE 68182-0054

Communication Education

ADDRESS FOR SUBMISSION:

Donald Rubin, Editor
Communication Education
University of Georgia
Department of Speech Communication
Athens, GA 30602-1725
USA
Phone: 706-542-3247
Fax: 706-542-3245
E-Mail: ComEd@uga.edu
Web: www.tandf.co.uk/journals
Address May Change: 12/31/2005

PUBLICATION GUIDELINES:

Manuscript Length: 26-30
Copies Required: Three
Computer Submission: Yes Disk
Format: MS Word, RTF
Fees to Review: 0.00 US$

Manuscript Style:
    American Psychological Association

CIRCULATION DATA:

Reader: Academics
Frequency of Issue: Quarterly
Copies per Issue:
Sponsor/Publisher: National
    Communication Association
Subscribe Price: 52.00 US$ Individual
    200.00 US$ Institution

REVIEW INFORMATION:

Type of Review: Blind Review
No. of External Reviewers: 2
No. of In House Reviewers: 1
Acceptance Rate: 11-20%
Time to Review: 2 - 3 Months
Reviewers Comments: Yes
Invited Articles: 0-5%
Fees to Publish: 0.00 US$

MANUSCRIPT TOPICS:
Adult Career & Vocational; Classroom Discourse; Communication; Curriculum Studies; Distance Education; Educational Psychology; Educational Technology Systems; Elementary/Early Childhood; Higher Education; Informal Learning; Interperson; Popular Culture; Rhetoric; Secondary/Adolescent Studies; Teacher Education; Teaching and Learning; Urban Education, Cultural/Non-Traditional

MANUSCRIPT GUIDELINES/COMMENTS:

Subscription Price: Varies with type of membership in organization.

Sponsorship: Published in the months of January, April, July, and October by the National Communication Association, formerly Speech Communication Association.

Journal website. www.arches.uga.edu/~comed

Communication Education publishes original scholarship bearing on the intersections of communication, instruction, and human development. Within this broad purview, it welcomes diverse disciplinary, conceptual, and methodological perspectives, especially scholarship in the following areas:

- Classroom discourse
- Life-span development of communication competence
- Mediating instructional communication with technology
- Diverse backgrounds of learners and teachers in instructional interaction
- Interaction in informal education and in varied instructional settings
- Learning outcomes associated with instructional communication practices across disciplines
- Learning outcomes and processes in the discipline of communication studies
- Rhetorical and organizational aspects of communication among educational agencies, among policy-makers, and among their stakeholders

Manuscripts submitted to *Communication Education* must subscribe to the National Communication Association Code of Professional Ethics for Authors. (See http://www.natcom.org/policies/Internal/code_of_professional_ethics.htm or write NCA, 1765 N Street NW, Washington, DC 20036). These guidelines enjoin authors to use inclusive and nondefamatory language. In addition, submissions should be accompanied by a cover letter attesting that the author has met professional standards for any of the following principles as may apply. (1) The manuscript is original work and proper publication credit is accorded to all authors. (2) Simultaneous editorial consideration of the manuscript at another publication venue is prohibited. (3) Any publication history of the manuscript is disclosed, indicating in particular whether the manuscript or another version of it has been presented at a conference, or published electronically, or whether portions of the manuscript have been published previously. (4) Duplicate publication of data is avoided; or if parts of the data have already been reported, then that fact is acknowledged. (5) All legal, institutional, and professional obligations for obtaining informed consent from research participants and for limiting their risk are honored. (6) The scholarship reported is authentic.

Full-length manuscripts of articles reporting empirical research, critical analyses, historical scholarship, or theoretic expositions should conform to the *Style Manual of the American Psychological Association*, 5th edition (2001). Article manuscripts should generally not exceed 30 double-spaced pages, except in cases in which "thick description" of qualitative data may require it. Authors are asked to submit three manuscript copies along with an electronic file on disk. (Rich Text Format is preferred for the electronic copy.) To facilitate masked review, the author's identity should not be discernible in the text, except on the title page. The title page should also state the history of the manuscript (i.e., whether it has been previously presented at a conference or derives from a thesis or dissertation) and any author acknowledgements. Authors should mail these materials to Don Rubin, Editor, Communication Education, 110 Terrell Hall, The University of Georgia, Athens, GA 30602-1725 [e-mail: ComEd@uga.edu].

Communication Education also solicits briefer manuscripts of approximately 2000 words for a section entitled **The Scholarship of Teaching and Learning in Communication (SOTL/Com)**. **SOTL/Com** builds upon the movement in education studies and policy that began with the Carnegie Foundation's 1990 manifesto *Scholarship Reconsidered*.

SOTL/Com recognizes that teaching communication is a form of scholarship, just as is the scholarship of discovery or of critical analysis. Submissions for **SOTL/Com** will explore questions about student learning in relationship to a particular teaching practice or innovation. Typically these questions will be posed by teachers about their own teaching. The work will be driven by questions about how an instructional communication practice influenced the teaching and learning of a particular subject in a particular setting. Subject matter and setting are not limited to communication classes, but may range across disciplines and across types of institutions. The motivation for the inquiry must be well grounded in theory and research. Manuscripts for **SOTL/Com** will report appropriate quantitative or qualitative assessments of student learning outcomes. Results will be discussed in light of the focal question about student learning, and also in a manner that contributes to a growing understanding of the interplay between communication and education. In keeping with the rigorous standards for **SOTL/Com**, all submissions to this section will be subjected to masked peer review. Submit manuscripts for **SOTL/COM** in electronic form (RTF format preferred) to Associate Editor Ann L. Darling, Department of Communication, 255 South Central Campus Drive, University of Utah, Salt Lake City, UT 84112 [e-mail: Ann.darling@m.cc.utah.edu].

In addition, *Communication Education* publishes **reviews of books and nonprint media** on a broad range of topics related to communication and education. Reviews should not exceed 1000 words, although longer essay reviews of several related works may be considered. The journal does not generally print reviews of course textbooks. Submission of both reviews and books to be considered for review are invited. Review manuscripts (2 print copies and one copy on computer disk in RTF format) and materials should be mailed to Nancy Rost Goulden, Department of Speech Communication, Theatre, and Dance, Nichols 101, Kansas State University, Manhattan, KS 66506 [e-mail: nag@ksu.edu].

Proposals for themed issues will be reviewed by members of the Editorial Advisory Board.

182

This permission does not extend to situations in which 1) extensive amounts of material are reproduced or stored in an electronic or similar data retrieval system, 2) a fee above actual duplicating costs is charged or if there exists a reasonable expectation of profit, or 3) the material is reproduced or reprinted for other than scholarly or educational purposes. In such cases, permission must be obtained prior to reproduction.

Requests for permission to reproduce should be addressed to:
NCA Publications Manager
Taylor & Francis, Ltd
4 Park Square
Milton Park, Abington
Oxfordshire OX14 4RN UK

A reasonable fee will generally be assessed for commercial copying or reproducing. Bookstores and copy centers should contact the Copyright Clearance Center for permission and processing.

Communication Studies

ADDRESS FOR SUBMISSION:

Jim L. Query, Jr., Editor
Communication Studies
University of Houston
School of Communication
203G Communications Building
4800 Calhoun Road
Houston, TX 77204
USA
Phone: 713-743-8608
Fax: 713-743-2876
E-Mail: commstudiesj@uh.edu
Web: www.tandf.co.uk/journals
Address May Change:

PUBLICATION GUIDELINES:

Manuscript Length: 25 Maximum
Copies Required: One + One electronic
Computer Submission: Yes
Format: MS Word or rtf format
Fees to Review: 0.00 US$

Manuscript Style:
    American Psychological Association,
    5th Edition

CIRCULATION DATA:

Reader: Academics
Frequency of Issue: Quarterly
Copies per Issue:
Sponsor/Publisher: Central States
    Communication Association (CSCA) /
    Taylor & Francis
Subscribe Price:
    See Website

REVIEW INFORMATION:

Type of Review: Blind Review
No. of External Reviewers: 3
No. of In House Reviewers:
Acceptance Rate: 16%
Time to Review: 3-4 Months
Reviewers Comments: Yes
Invited Articles: 0-5%
Fees to Publish: 0.00 US$

MANUSCRIPT TOPICS:

Curriculum Studies; Media; Oral, Group, Interpersonal Communication; Teacher Education; Tests, Measurement & Evaluation

MANUSCRIPT GUIDELINES/COMMENTS:

Articles published in *Communication Studies* (*CS*) should represent the diversity of scholarship that composes the study of human communication, regardless of philosophical, theoretical, or methodological underpinnings. Published essays and reports of studies should make important and noteworthy contributions to the advancement of human communication scholarship. *CS* supports research and writing free of sexism and other biases.

Email. **commstudiesj@uh.edu;   jquery@uh.edu**
Website. **www.class.uh.edu/comm/commstudies/**

184

Information for Contributors

Communication Studies is committed to publishing high-quality original scholarship centrally focused on human communication processes. Articles published in *Communication Studies* should represent the diversity of scholarship that composes the study of human communication, regardless of philosophical, theoretical, or methodological underpinnings. Published essays and reports of studies should make important and noteworthy contributions to the advancement of human communication scholarship. *Communication Studies* supports research and writing free of sexism and other biases.

The Editor assumes that manuscripts submitted to *Communication Studies* are original, unpublished, and not under consideration by other publication outlets. *Communication Studies* follows a policy of masked peer review. To ensure such a masked review, include no author-identifying information beyond the title page.

Authors should submit one electronic copy and one hard copy of the manuscript to the Editor. Authors should retain a copy as manuscripts will not be returned. Double-space manuscripts on 8½ by 11 inch paper. An abstract of 120 or fewer words should accompany the manuscript. Manuscript preparation, source citations, and reference style should conform to the fifth edition of the *Publication Manual of the American Psychological Association*. Upon acceptance of the manuscript for publication, authors must submit high quality camera-ready copy for all artwork and figures and must assign, copyright to the Central States Communication Association. *Communication Studies* will not publish any material for which the assignment of copyright to the Central States Communication Association is withheld.

A separate title page must accompany each manuscript. In addition to the title and author(s) of the manuscript, the title page should include a short biographical summary of each author, including full name, professional title, address, telephone number, and electronic mail address (if available). If any portion of the manuscript has been presented in other forms (e.g., speech or colloquy) or in other forums (e.g., convention), include details of the occasion on the title page. Finally, indicate on the title page whether the manuscript is drawn, in whole or part, from a thesis or dissertation, with the name of the director of the study identified.

Communication Studies (formerly the Central States Speech Journal) is a quarterly publication (Spring, Summer, Fall, and Winter) of the Central States Communication Association. Annual subscriptions to *Communication Studies* are: 75.00 US$, which includes a regular CSCA membership; 40.00 US$, which includes student membership; 20.00 US$, which includes an emeritus membership; and 100.00 US$, which includes departmental membership. If outside the USA, add 10.00 US$. Library subscriptions are 170.00 US$ for USA libraries and 200.00 US$ for non-USA libraries.

Send questions about membership, subscriptions, orders for back issues, requests for advertising rates, and/or inquiries into reprinting *Communication Studies* or *Central States Speech Journal* articles to the Executive Director, Scott A. Myers, PO Box 6293, West Virginia University, Morgantown, WV, 26506-6293, **CSCA@mail.wvu.edu**.

Communication Studies is printed by Taylor & Francis.

Comparative Education

ADDRESS FOR SUBMISSION:

Michael Crossley, Editor
Comparative Education
University of Bristol
Graduate School of Education
 c/o Brigid Walker
35 Berkeley Square
Bristol, BS8 1JA
UK
Phone: +44 (0) 1179 287039
Fax: +44 (0) 1179 251537
E-Mail: m.crossley@bristol.ac.uk
Web: www.tandf.co.uk/journals
Address May Change:

PUBLICATION GUIDELINES:

Manuscript Length: 26-30
Copies Required: Four
Computer Submission: No
Format: N/A
Fees to Review: 0.00 US$

Manuscript Style:
 See Manuscript Guidelines

CIRCULATION DATA:

Reader: Academics, Administrators
Frequency of Issue: Quarterly
Copies per Issue:
Sponsor/Publisher: Carfax Publishing
 (Taylor & Francis)
Subscribe Price: 338.00 US$ Individual
 1206.00 US$ Institution

REVIEW INFORMATION:

Type of Review: Editorial Review
No. of External Reviewers: 0
No. of In House Reviewers: 3+
Acceptance Rate: 21-30%
Time to Review: 2-6 Months
Reviewers Comments: No
Invited Articles: 31-50%
Fees to Publish: 0.00 US$

MANUSCRIPT TOPICS:

Adult Career & Vocational; Comparitive Education; Education Policy; Curriculum Studies; Education Management/Administration; Elementary/Early Childhood; Higher Education; Rural Education & Small Schools; Secondary/Adolescent Studies; Teacher Education; Urban Education, Cultural/Non-Traditional

MANUSCRIPT GUIDELINES/COMMENTS:

Aims and Scope

This international journal of educational studies presents up-to-date information with analyses of significant problems and trends throughout the world. It especially considers the implications of comparative studies for the formation and implementation of policies - not only in education but in social, national and international development. Thus it welcomes contributions from associated disciplines in the fields of government, management, sociology - and indeed technology and communications - as these affect educational policy decisions.

Articles submitted to the Editorial Board are assessed by all members and are discussed in detail at Board meetings three times a year - an unusual, if not unique, feature. In addition, expert advice is taken on particular papers.

Over 36 years *Comparative Education's* editorial policy and presentation have evolved to match world developments and the changing concerns of those active in education or involved in its finance, management and wider implications. Our readership has evolved too in proportion as comparative studies of education have attracted the attention of statesmen, the commercial/industrial world, and parents and voters.

The Editorial Board invites contributions dealing with **international or analytically comparative aspects** of education, highlighting such themes as: educational reform and practical problems of implementation; implications of demographic change and the distribution of resources; structural and geographical shifts in employment and professional expectations; the changing 'mix' of 'general' and vocational/professional' education; occupational mobility and regional or international co-operation; post-compulsory and 'young adult' education; part-time, recurrent or alternating education/training; new structures and operational patterns in higher education; the management and supply of educational opportunity, and its location or periodicity; the media and new communications or technologies in education; curricular content, and the learner's experience; teacher preparation and reorientation; education for the disadvantaged, or in neglected fields of competence; ideological and religious interventions; new trends and partnerships in comparative research. Suggestions of themes for articles or special issues will be welcomed.

Manuscripts should be sent to Brigid Walker, Co-ordinating Editor, Graduate School of Education, University of Bristol, 35 Berkeley Square, Bristol BS8 1JA, UK. Articles can be considered only if four complete copies of your manuscript and a disk are submitted unless other arrangements have been made with the editorial office. They should be typed on one side of the paper, double spaced, with ample margins and bear the title of the contribution, name(s) of the author(s) and the address where the work was carried out. Each article should be accompanied by a summary of 100-150 words on a separate sheet, and a short note of biographical details for the 'Notes on Contributors' page. The full postal address of the author who will check proofs and receive correspondence and offprints should also be included. All pages should be numbered.

Footnotes to the text should be avoided wherever this is reasonably possible.

Electronic Submission. Authors should send the final, revised version of their articles in both hard copy paper and electronic disk forms. It is essential that the hard copy (paper) version *exactly* matches the material on disk. Please print out the hard copy from the disk you are sending. Submit three printed copies of the final version with the disk to the journal's editorial office. Save all files on a standard 3.5 inch high-density disk. We prefer to receive disks in Microsoft Word in a PC format, but can translate from most other common word processing programs as well as Macs. Please specify which program you have used. Do not save your files as "text only" or "read only".

Rejected manuscripts will not normally be returned to contributors unless sufficient international postal coupons have been sent.

Tables and captions to illustrations. Tables must be typed out on separate sheets and not included as part of the text. The captions to illustrations should be gathered together and also typed out on a separate sheet. Tables and figures should be numbered by Arabic numerals. The approximate position of tables and figures should be indicated in the manuscript. Captions should include keys to symbols.

Figures. Please supply one set of artwork in a finished form, suitable for reproduction. Figures will not normally be redrawn by the publisher.

Citations of other work should be limited to those strictly necessary for the argument. Any quotations should be brief, and accompanied by precise references.

References should be indicated in the typescript by giving the author's name, with the year of publication in parentheses. If several papers by the same author and from the same year are cited, a, b, c, etc. should be put after the year of publication. The references should be listed in full, including pages, at the end of the paper in the following standard form:

For books: Kress, G. (2003) Literacy in the new media age (London, Routledge).

For articles: Cremin, L. A. (1983) The problematics of education in the 1980s: some reflections on the Oxford Workshop, Oxford Review of Education, 9, 33-40.

For chapters within books: Willis, P. (1983) Cultural production and theories of reproduction, in: L. Barton & S. Walker (Eds) Race, class and education (London, Croom Helm), 25-50.

Titles of journals and names of publishers, etc. should not be abbreviated. Acronyms for the names of organisations, examinations, etc. should be preceded by the title in full.

If you have any further questions about the style for this journal, please submit your questions using the **Style Queries** form.

Proofs will be sent to authors if there is sufficient time to do so. They should be corrected and returned to the Editorial Assistant within three days. Major alterations to the text cannot be accepted.

Early Electronic Offprints. Corresponding authors can now receive their article by e-mail as a complete PDF. This allows the author to print up to 50 copies, free of charge, and disseminate them to colleagues. In many cases this facility will be available up to two weeks prior to publication. Or, alternatively, corresponding authors will receive the traditional 50 offprints. A copy of the journal will be sent by post to all corresponding authors after publication. Additional copies of the journal can be purchased at the author's preferential rate of £15.00/$25.00 per copy.

ELECTRONIC SUBMISSION

Note to Authors: please make sure your contact address information is clearly visible on the **outside** of <u>all</u> packages you are sending to Editors.

Carfax strongly encourages authors to send the final, revised version of their articles in both hard copy paper and electronic disk forms. These guidelines do not apply to authors who are submitting an article for consideration and peer review; they apply only to authors whose articles have been reviewed, revised, and accepted for publication.

It is essential that the hard-copy paper version of your article **exactly** matches the material on disk. Please print-out the hard copy from the disk you are sending. Submit three printed copies of the final version with the disk to the journal's editorial office.

Save all files on a standard 3.5 inch high density disk. We prefer to receive disks in Microsoft Word in a PC format, but can translate from **most other common word-processing programs** and Macs. Please specify which program you have used. Do not save your files as "text only" or "read only".

File names. Tables, Figures and Text should each be saved as separate files. Each file should be named clearly and logically (e.g. Smith_txt.doc, Smith_tables.doc, Smith_figs.doc). End notes, footnotes and references should be saved in the Text file, not in separate files. A list of files and a brief explanation of what each file contains should be supplied with your manuscript.

Figures. Figures may be supplied on disk. We prefer figures to be saved in either TIFF (tagged image file format) or EPS (encapsulated postscript) formats. However, we can accept PICT or JPEG formats. High quality reproducible (i.e. high resolution output) hard copy paper print-outs must be supplied for all figures and must be identical to the disk versions, in case the disk is unusable. Figure captions should also be saved in the same file as the figure, not with the Text file. If figure files are very large, they may be saved on a separate disk. If compressing a file is necessary, please use "pkzip". Please ensure this is clearly labelled. Photographs can be sent on disk, but the hard copy (originals) must also be supplied. Save all photographs as high resolution images.

Tables. Save Tables in a separate file, together with the Table heading. Use the table function provided with the word processing package.

Style. Word processed files should be prepared according to **journal style**. Please consult the journal's **Notes for Contributors** for style matters. The following general points should be followed:

1. Do not bookmark your files.
2. All paragraph indents must be done uniformly; all using tab key is preferred.
3. Do not justify right-hand margins, use normal word wrap function. Do not insert "soft" hyphens at the ends of lines, i.e. do not break words. Turn off any automatic hyphenation feature available with your software.
4. Use one hard space for word spacing throughout the document.

5. Global Search and Replace wherever possible, e.g. change all instances of United States to US (consult Notes for Contributors and/or a back issue of the journal for style).

6. All text which should be bold or italic should appear as bold or italic on the electronic version of your article. All headings should be in the correct format, i.e. font (italic, bold or roman), position (flush left or centered), case (uppercase or lowercase).

7. Use the facility in your software for creating numbered or bullet lists.

8. Flag the position of tables and/or figures in the text, e.g. (Fig. 1 here), (Table 1 here).

9. Displayed material (e.g. displayed quotation) should be typed in the style of the journal, e.g. one line space above and below and indented left and right.

10. All non-ASCII characters (mathematical symbols, Greek letters, or any other unusual accents or characters) should be highlighted on the hard copy.

11. References should be typed journal style. If full caps/small caps are used for authors' names, this must be followed. If small caps are not available, type the authors' names uppercase/lowercase, do not type all uppercase.

Sending your File

1. Virus check your disk before sending it to the Editor.

2. Label your disk with the following information:
   a) Journal title;
   b) Name of author;
   c) File names contained on disk;
   d) Hardware used (PC or Mac);
   e) Software used (name and version, e.g. Microsoft Word 95).

3. Package disks so as to avoid damage in the post.

Author support

If you have any further queries, please e-mail:
   Jessica Feinstein at **Jessica.Feinstein@tandf.co.uk**

Compendium of Teaching Resources

ADDRESS FOR SUBMISSION:

Jeanne Butler, Editor
Compendium of Teaching Resources
University of Nebraska Kearney
CTE, FDHL 2113
Kearney, NE 68849
USA
Phone: 308-865-8006
Fax: 308-865-1545
E-Mail: butlerjm2@unk.edu
Web: www.unk.edu/acad/cte/
Address May Change:

PUBLICATION GUIDELINES:

Manuscript Length: 16-20
Copies Required: Three
Computer Submission: Yes Disk, Email
Format: MS Word, RFT
Fees to Review: 0.00 US$

Manuscript Style:
   American Psychological Association

CIRCULATION DATA:

Reader: Academics
Frequency of Issue: 1 Time/Year
Copies per Issue: 1,001 - 2,000
Sponsor/Publisher: UNK Center for
   Teaching Excellence
Subscribe Price:

REVIEW INFORMATION:

Type of Review: Blind Review
No. of External Reviewers: 1
No. of In House Reviewers: 1
Acceptance Rate: 70-75%
Time to Review: 1 - 2 Months
Reviewers Comments: Yes
Invited Articles: 0-5%
Fees to Publish: 0.00 US$

MANUSCRIPT TOPICS:
Curriculum Studies; Teaching Methods and Materials

MANUSCRIPT GUIDELINES/COMMENTS:

Type of Articles that *CTR* Publishes
Compendium of Teaching Resources (*CTR*) invites submissions that contribute to expanding the body of knowledge in teaching practices and resources in higher education. Articles addressing research, theory, and/or practice are welcome.

Reports of empirical research should include an introduction that discusses the theory and previous research that provides a framework for the problem of interest, a methods section that describes the procedures involved in executing the study, a results section that presents evidence relevant to the purpose of the study, and a discussion section that relates to the research and theory presented in the introduction and discusses the implications of the results.

Theoretical articles should clearly indicate why the theory or problem being presented is worthy of attention. It should also discuss how theory and previous research provide a framework for the problem of interest. Finally it should represent an important contribution to the extant literature on the topic thus contributing to the advancement of educational science.

Articles on teaching practice and resources should include a clear description, recommendation for using the resource or practice in teaching, examples of situations in which the practice or resource can be used, and any results the author has noted when implementing the practice or resource.

Preparation of the Manuscript
Submissions must be written in English, with references in American Psychological Association style 5th edition. Documents that are not written in APA style will be returned to the sender for reformatting. The page requirements are 16-20 pages of double-spaced, 12-font content.

Additionally, all submissions must include the following:
- a short abstract (100 words maximum). After the abstract, include a list of up to 10 key words that will be useful for indexing and searching.
- a title page with the author(s) brief biographies, full names, institutions, and the primary contact's email, telephone, fax, and URL address.

Articles may be submitted in various ways:
- Hard copy (3 copies) mailed to the Center for Teaching Excellence, FNDH 2113, University of Nebraska Kearney, Kearney, NE 68849
- Attached to an email. All documents must be in Microsoft Word or they will be returned to the sender unopened. Additionally, if tables are utilized, it is the author(s) responsibility to submit them in Microsoft Word Table Format.
- CD/DVD/Disk

CTR uses a blind review process with reviewers drawn from the greater educational community (1 external to UNK and 1 international). Information that might identify authors should not be included in the document. CTR currently publishes one compendium a year, normally in August.

Submissions may be sent to
UNK Center for Teaching Excellence. **teachingcenter@unk.edu**

Composition Studies

ADDRESS FOR SUBMISSION:

Ann George and Carrie Leverenz, Editors
Composition Studies
Texas Christian University
English Department
TCU Box 297270
Fort Worth, TX 76129
USA
Phone: 812-257-6896
Fax: 817-257-6238
E-Mail: compositionstudies@tcu.edu
Web: www.compositionstudies.tcu.edu
Address May Change:

PUBLICATION GUIDELINES:

Manuscript Length: 8,000 Words
Copies Required: Three
Computer Submission: No
Format: N/A
Fees to Review: 0.00 US$

Manuscript Style:
,   MLA Handbook

CIRCULATION DATA:

Reader: Academics
Frequency of Issue: 2 Times/Year
Copies per Issue: Less than 1,000
Sponsor/Publisher: Independent
Subscribe Price: 15.00 US$ Individual
        30.00 US$ Institution

REVIEW INFORMATION:

Type of Review: Blind Review
No. of External Reviewers: 2
No. of In House Reviewers: 2
Acceptance Rate: 6-10%
Time to Review: 2 - 3 Months
Reviewers Comments: Yes
Invited Articles: 0-5%
Fees to Publish: 0.00 US$

MANUSCRIPT TOPICS:
Composition; Education Management/Administration; Languages & Linguistics; Rhetoric; Teacher Education; Tests, Measurement & Evaluation

MANUSCRIPT GUIDELINES/COMMENTS:

The editors Email address is: **compositionstudies@tcu.edu**

Composition Studies invites the submission of manuscripts on the theory and practice of rhetoric and composition. Particularly welcome are essays concerning:

1. Rhetorical traditions and theories

2. Challenges to rhetorical traditions and theories (such as feminism, Marxism, post-structualism, deconstructionism, reader-response theory, psychoanalytic interpretations of consciousness and the composing process, meta-linguistic analysis, etc.)

3. Personal reflections on the teaching of writing (especially essays that emphasize a strong personal voice and an unusual perspective).

4. Computer-assisted writing of instruction, writing center theory and practice, and theories of supplemental instruction.

5. Reviews of books and software of interest to writing instructors.

Manuscripts should conform to the 1988 *MLA Handbook* (internal citations). Please send manuscripts with a self-addressed stamped envelope (SASE).

Computers in Human Behavior

ADDRESS FOR SUBMISSION:

Robert D. Tennyson, Editor
Computers in Human Behavior
University of Minnesota
Department of Educational Psychology
211A Burton Hall
178 Pillsbury Drive, S.E.
Minneapolis, MN 55455
USA
Phone: 612-626-1618
Fax: 612-624-8241
E-Mail: rtenny@umn.edu
Web:
Address May Change:

PUBLICATION GUIDELINES:

Manuscript Length: 26-30
Copies Required: Three
Computer Submission: Yes
Format: Final ver./text & ASCII file
Fees to Review: 0.00 US$

Manuscript Style:
         American Psychological Association

CIRCULATION DATA:

Reader: Academics
Frequency of Issue: 6 Times/Year
Copies per Issue: 1,001 - 2,000
Sponsor/Publisher: Profit Oriented Corp. &
    Professional Assoc.
Subscribe Price: 45.00 US$ Individual
    388.00 US$ Institution

REVIEW INFORMATION:

Type of Review: Blind Review
No. of External Reviewers: 2
No. of In House Reviewers: 1
Acceptance Rate: 21-30%
Time to Review: 2 - 3 Months
Reviewers Comments: Yes
Invited Articles: 21-30%
Fees to Publish: 0.00 US$

MANUSCRIPT TOPICS:

Adult Career & Vocational; Business Applications; Computers; Counseling & Personnel Services; Educational Psychology; Educational Technology Systems; Human Development & Resource; Library Science/Information Resources

MANUSCRIPT GUIDELINES/COMMENTS:

Aims and Scope

Computers in Human Behavior is a scholarly journal dedicated to examining the use of computers from a psychological perspective. Original theoretical works, research reports, literature reviews, software reviews, book reviews, and announcements are published. The journal addresses both the use of computers in psychology, psychiatry and related disciplines as well as the psychological impact of computer use on individuals, groups and society. The former category includes articles exploring the use of computers for professional practice, training, research and theory development. The latter category includes articles dealing with the psychological effects of computers on phenomena such as human development, learning cognition, personality, and social interactions.

The journal addresses human interactions with computers, not computers per se. The computer is discussed only as a medium through which human behaviors are shaped and expressed. The primary message of most articles involves information about human behavior. Therefore, professionals with an interest in the psychological aspects of computer use, but with limited knowledge of computers, will find this journal of interest.

Manuscript Submission
Authors should submit an electronic copy of the manuscript via email to: Robert D. Tennyson, **rtenny@umn.edu**. The entire manuscript (including abstract, quotations, tabular material and references) must be typed double-spaced, with ample margins. Consult the *Publication Manual of the American Psychological Association* (4th ed., 1994) for guidelines in manuscript preparation.

Submission of Software for Review
All software that is relevant to researchers, educators and practitioners within psychology, psychiatry, and related professions will be considered for review. This includes but is not limited to software addressing mental health, human development, learning cognition, social behaviors, personality, and personnel selection. Reviews will address both the scientific validity and practical utility of computer packages. Authors and publishers wishing to have their software reviewed should submit two copies of both software and all supporting documentation to the editor. Materials submitted for review cannot be returned.

Title Page
The title page should include (a) the article title (b) the author's names and affiliations at the time the work was completed (c) the corresponding author's address, email address, telephone number; (d) a concise running title, and (e) an unnumbered footnote giving address for reprints and any acknowledgements.

Abstract
An abstract of no more than 200 words should accompany each paper, typed on a separate sheet following the title page.

Headings
Major section headings should be centered on the page; secondary headings should be typed flush to the left margin. Use headings to organize and clarify the text.

References and Style
The reference section must be typed double-spaced and prepared following *American Psychological Association* style. All works cited in the text must be listed in the reference section. Avoid abbreviations of journal titles.

Tables and Figures
All tables and figures should be numbered separately using Arabic numerals, and grouped together at the end of the manuscript. Clearly visible notes within the text should indicate their approximate placement.

Figures must be professionally prepared and camera-ready; photocopies, blue ink, or pencil are not acceptable. Type figure legends on a separate sheet. Write the article title and figure number lightly in pencil on the back of each piece of artwork.

Copyright and Originality

It is a condition of publication that manuscripts submitted to this journal have not been published and will not be simultaneously submitted or published elsewhere. All authors must sign the Transfer of Copyright Agreement, available from the editor, before the article can be published.

Page Proofs and Reprints

The corresponding author will receive page proofs for final proofreading and an order form for reprints as well as copies of the issue in which the article appears. Twenty-five free reprints are supplied to the corresponding author of each article. Orders for additional reprints must be received before printing in order to qualify for lower prepublication rates.

Contemporary Issues in Early Childhood

ADDRESS FOR SUBMISSION:

S. Grieshaber & N. Yeliand, Co-Editors
Contemporary Issues in Early Childhood
RMIT University
School of Education
Box 71 Bundoora
Melbourne, Victoria, 3083
Australia
Phone: +617-386-43176
Fax: +617-386-43989
E-Mail: ciec@rmit.edu.au
Web: www.triangle.co.uk/ciec
Address May Change:

PUBLICATION GUIDELINES:

Manuscript Length: No Reply
Copies Required: Online Journal
Computer Submission: Yes Email Only
Format: English- Any Formatting
Fees to Review: 0.00 US$

Manuscript Style:
    See Manuscript Guidelines

CIRCULATION DATA:

Reader: Practicing Teachers, Academics
Frequency of Issue: 3 Times/Year
Copies per Issue: 5,001 - 10,000: 8,000
    Online Library
Sponsor/Publisher: Triangle Journals Ltd.
Subscribe Price: 168.00 US$ Library
    141.00 Pounds Library

REVIEW INFORMATION:

Type of Review: Blind Review
No. of External Reviewers: 2
No. of In House Reviewers: 1-2
Acceptance Rate: No Reply
Time to Review: 2 - 3 Months
Reviewers Comments: Yes
Invited Articles: No Reply
Fees to Publish: 0.00 US$

MANUSCRIPT TOPICS:
Elementary/Early Childhood

MANUSCRIPT GUIDELINES/COMMENTS:

About the Journal

Contemporary Issues in Early Childhood is an online, fully refereed, international research journal. Over 10 000 readers have already registered their subscriptions. The journal provides a forum for researchers and professionals who are exploring new and alternative perspectives in their work with young children (from birth to eight years of age) and their families. It aims to present opportunities for scholars to highlight the ways in which the boundaries of early childhood studies and practice are expanding, and for readers to participate in the discussion of emerging issues, contradictions and possibilities.

Contemporary Issues in Early Childhood incorporates interdisciplinary, cutting edge work which may include the following areas: poststructuralist, postmodern and postcolonial approaches, queer theory, sociology of childhood, alternative viewpoints of child development, and deal with issues such as language and identity, the discourse of difference, new information technologies, stories and voices, curriculum, culture and pedagogy, or any combination of such ideas.

The Editors encourage submission of a variety of high quality manuscripts including: reports of research from a variety of paradigms; articles about research, literature reviews and theoretical discussions; book reviews; colloquia and responses/critiques; invited commentaries.

How to Contribute

Contemporary Issues in Early Childhood is an international, scholarly, fully-refereed, online-only journal. The journal publishes original articles, colloquia, and book reviews. Papers accepted for publication become the copyright of the Journal, unless otherwise specifically agreed upon. All contributions should be original and once submitted manuscripts should not be presently be under consideration for publication elsewhere. Authors should be aware that they are writing for an international audience and should use non-discriminatory language.

Please send submissions by email attachment or on disk to:

Professor Nicola Yelland OR	**Susan J. Grieshaber, Co-Editor**
RMIT University,	Queensland University of Technology
School of Education	Kelvin Grove Campus
P O Box 71	Victoria Park Road
Bundoora	Kelvin Grove, Queensland
Victoria, 3083,Australia	Australia
nicola.yelland@rmit.edu.au	**s.grieshaber@qut.edu.au**
ciec@qut.edu.au	

Books for review should be sent to the editors at the above address.

The Editors welcome manuscripts (4000-6000 words) which include reports and discussion of interdisciplinary, cutting-edge work that may include, for example, the following areas: poststructuralist, postmodern and postcolonial approaches, queer theory, sociology of childhood, alternative viewpoints of child development, and deal with issues such as language and identities, the discourse of difference, new information technologies, stories and voices, curriculum, culture and pedagogy, or any combination of such ideas. The Editors encourage submission of a variety of high quality manuscripts including:

- reports of research from a variety of paradigms
- articles about research, literature reviews and theoretical discussions
- book reviews
- colloquia and responses/critiques
- invited commentaries

Manuscripts should be submitted as files on disk, or as email attachments in RTF (Rich Text Format), but any major word-processor is acceptable. Please do not over-format the manuscript with the word-processor as this impedes the publication process.

The author's name and affiliation should appear at the beginning of the article, together with full postal and email addresses. This should be followed by a short description of their current position and research/teaching interests.

It is *essential* that an Abstract (100-200 words) be provided for each article.

Figures and tables should have their positions marked clearly and be provided on separate pages. Figure numbers should be shown as Arabic numerals, table numbers as Latin numerals.

Headings and sub-headings should be clearly distinguished.

References should be provided in the text with the authors name followed by the year in brackets, for example: Yelland & Grieshaber (1998). If a direct quote is used the page number will need to be added. For example; Yelland & Grieshaber (1998, p. 13).

All material/works cited in the article need to be included in an alphabetical reference list at the end. Please use the following style:

Book

Cannella, G. S. (1997) *Deconstructing Early Childhood Education: social justice and revolution.* New York: Peter Lang.

Article in a journal

Grieshaber, S.J. (1997) Mealtime rituals: power and resistance in the construction of family mealtime rules, *British Journal of Sociology*, 48, pp. 648-666.

Chapter in a book

Yelland, N.J. & Grieshaber, S.J. (1998) Blurring the edges, in N.J. Yelland (Ed.) *Gender in Early Childhood.* London: Routledge.

Footnotes should not be used. Endnotes need to be located in the text by numbers within square brackets ([1], [2] etc) as normal-size numbers/brackets and *not* as superscripts.

Conventional paper proofs will be sent to the author designated to receive them, and should be corrected and returned immediately to the Editors. Contributors will be notified when the article has been published on the Journal's website.

Colloquium

A colloquium is intended to be a shorter piece of writing (900-1200 words) on a topic of interest that may include, for example:

a summary of a work in progress, raising issues, queries, problems

a review of a particular viewpoint or a reaction to a previously published article.

Please contact our publishers **Triangle Journals** (CIECwebinfo@triangle.co.uk) if you have any questions or need further information about the preparation of word-processed documents for publication.

Contemporary Issues in Technology & Teacher Education

ADDRESS FOR SUBMISSION:

Lynn Bell, Managing Editor
Contemporary Issues in Technology &
   Teacher Education
c/o Joe McDonald
ONLINE SUBMISSION ONLY
AACE
P.O. Box 3728
Norfolk, VA 23514-3728
USA
Phone: 757-623-7588
Fax: 703-997-8760
E-Mail: info@aace.org
Web: www.aace.org/pubs
Address May Change:

PUBLICATION GUIDELINES:

Manuscript Length: Varies Appropriately
Copies Required: One
Computer Submission: Yes Online
   Submission
Format: MS Word, html, or RTF
Fees to Review: 0.00 US$

Manuscript Style:
   See Manuscript Guidelines

CIRCULATION DATA:

Reader: Academics
Frequency of Issue: Quarterly
Copies per Issue: No Reply
Sponsor/Publisher: (AACE) Assn. for the
   Advancement of Computers in Education
Subscribe Price: Free

REVIEW INFORMATION:

Type of Review: Blind Review
No. of External Reviewers: 0
No. of In House Reviewers: 2
Acceptance Rate: 15%
Time to Review: 1 - 2 Months
Reviewers Comments: No Reply
Invited Articles: No Reply
Fees to Publish: 0.00 US$

MANUSCRIPT TOPICS:
Educational Technology Systems; English Literature; Science Math & Environment; Social Studies/Social Science; Special Education; Teacher Education

MANUSCRIPT GUIDELINES/COMMENTS:

Contemporary Issues in Technology and Teacher Education (*CITE*) is an electron
publication of the **Society for Information Technology and Teacher Education** (*SITE*
established as a multimedia, interactive counterpart of the **Journal of Technology an
Teacher Education**.

Funded by a U.S. Department of Education Preparing Tomorrow's Teachers to U
Technology (PT3) catalyst grant, CITE makes possible the inclusion of sound, animate
images, and simulation, as well as allowing for ongoing, immediate dialog about theoretic
issues.

Subscriptions are at no cost thanks to a PT3 grant from the U.S. Department of Education.

SUBMISSION GUIDELINES
CITE includes three major categories of articles:

- Current Issues will include more theoretical discussions of technology and teacher preparation.
- Current Practices will provide shorter, up-to-the-minute snapshots of technology in practice.
- Seminal Articles will include previously published "classic" articles that have advanced the discussion of technology and teacher education.

Articles should address technology and teacher education and may address assessment, attitudes, beliefs, curriculum, equity, research, translating research into practice, learning theory, alternative conceptions, socio-cultural issues, special populations, and integration of subjects.

General Guidelines
Material must be original, reflect the integrity expected of scholarly communication, and demonstrate a coherence and unity that makes the paper both understandable and interesting. Before submitting an article, please review the following suggestions. Original manuscripts received in correct form serve to expedite the review process, others will be returned to author. Spelling, punctuation, sentence structure, and the mechanical elements of arrangements, spacing, length, and consistency of usage in form and descriptions should be studied before submission.

Length
Because this is an electronic journal the length of papers may vary. The length of your paper should be appropriate to the topic and focus. We will accept some papers that are only two or three pages long and some that are as long as 40 or 50 pages. The critical issue is whether the length is appropriate.

Originality
All manuscripts must be original. No manuscript will be considered which has already been published or is being considered by another magazine or journal. However, if work described in conference proceedings is substantially revised and extended, it will be considered. Submission of a manuscript represents certification by the author that the article is not being considered nor has been published elsewhere.

The format of headings, tables, figures, citations, references, and other details should follow the (APA) style as described in the *Publication Manual of the American Psychological Association*, 5th edition, available from APA, 750 1st St., NE, Washington, DC 20002 USA.

Preview
Manuscripts sent to the Editor for review are accepted on a voluntary basis from authors. Before submitting an article, please review the following suggestions. Manuscripts received in correct form serve to expedite the processing and prompt reviewing for early publication.

Spelling, punctuation, sentence structure, and the mechanical elements of arrangements, spacing, length, and consistency of usage in form and descriptions should be studied before submission. Due to the academic focus of AACE publications, the use of personal pronoun (I, we, etc.) and present tense is strongly discouraged.

Pre-publication
No manuscript will be considered which has already been published or is being considered by another journal.

Copyright
These journals are copyrighted by the Association for the Advancement of Computing in Education. Material published and so copyrighted may not be published elsewhere without the written permission of AACE.

Author Note(s):
Financial support for work reported or a grant under which a study was made should be noted just prior to the Acknowledgments. Acknowledgments or appreciation to individuals for assistance with the manuscript or with the material reported should be included as a note to appear at the end of the article prior to the References.

Handling of Manuscripts
All manuscripts are acknowledged upon receipt. Review is carried out as promptly as possible. The manuscript will be reviewed by at least two members of the Editorial Review Board, which takes approximately five months. When a decision for publication or rejection is made, the senior author or author designated to receive correspondence is notified. At the time of notification, the author may be asked to make certain revisions in the manuscript, or the Editor may submit suggested revisions to the author for approval.

Presentation
Accepted Submission File Formats - All submissions must be sent in electronic form using the Article Submission Form. **No hard copy submission papers will be accepted**. Do NOT submit compressed files. Do not use any word processing options/tools, such as--strike through, hidden text, comments, merges, and so forth.

Submit your manuscript in either of the following formats:
- DOC - Microsoft Word (preferred)
- RTF- Rich Text Format

Manuscripts should be double-spaced and a font size of 12 is preferred.

Length. In general, articles should not exceed 30 double-spaced pages. Long articles, or articles containing complex material should be broken up by short, meaningful subheads.

Title sheet. Do NOT include a title sheet. Manuscripts are blind reviewed so there should be no indication of the author(s) name on the pages.

Abstract. An informative, comprehensive abstract of 75 to 200 words must accompany the manuscript. This abstract should succinctly summarize the major points of the paper, and the author's summary and/or conclusions.

Tables, Figures & Graphics

Any graphics that go in the article must be submitted as separate files. The highest quality master (e.g. TIF) is preferred. Additionally, the graphics must also be embedded in the correct locations within the document so the copyeditors know the proper placement. Please note that any graphics created in Microsoft Word must also be submitted as separate files.

Tables. All tables (i.e., data displayed in rows and columns) must be embedded in the manuscript near the first reference to the corresponding table. Tables MUST be no wider than 5.25" in the document. Lengthy tables are discouraged as they are difficult to read online.

Figures. Any graphics that go in the article must be submitted as separate files. Figure graphics (e.g., charts, graphs, photographs, and drawings) must be in either .GIF, .PNG, .TIF, or .JPG format. Filenames for figures must be clearly labeled as Figure 1, Figure 2, etc., at the bottom of the figure, left justified, numbered in sequence, and must be referenced within the text of the article.

ALT tags will be applied to all graphics. The default tag will be the figure caption supplied by the author. Authors should provide tag text for any graphics used as links to audio or videos.

Appendices. All supplemental text not falling under the definition of a table or figure will be considered an appendix. Appendices should be placed at the end of the manuscript, after the reference list. If possible, authors should provide a link from the reference to the appendix in the manuscript (e.g., Òsee Appendix AÓ) to the beginning of the actual appendix.

Videos. All videos must be submitted in a web-optimized format as to allow for progressive-download. The preferred formats are Windows Media, Real, or Quicktime. Videos should be identified in the text as ÒVideo 1, Video 2,Ó etc., and video filenames should include the corresponding video numbers. Authors must provide a link to the video within the article. This link could be a text link (e.g., ÒVideo 1Ó) or a still frame from the video (i.e., a .GIF, .PNG or .JPG file). As encoding video for the web may sometimes require specialized skills, the author may contact the projection staff (michael@aace.org) for assistance.

Audio files. Audio files must also be submitted in a web-optimized format in either Windows Media, Real, or Quicktime formats. Audio files should be identified in the text as ÒAudio 1, Audio 2,Ó etc., and audio filenames should include the corresponding audio numbers. Authors must provide a link to the audio within the article. This link could be a text link (e.g., ÒAudio 1Ó) or a related graphic.

Supporting files. Supporting materials must be in format that can be read by the majority of viewers, such as PowerPoint or PDF. Proprietary supporting materials must be converted to a common file format.

Quotations
Copy all quoted material exactly as it appears in the original, indicating any omissions by three spaced periods. At the close of the quotation, give the complete source including page numbers. A block quote must be a minimum of 40 words or four lines, single spaced.

Terminology and Abbreviations
Define any words or phrases that cannot be found in Webster's Unabridged Dictionary. Define or explain new or highly technical terminology. Write out the first use of a term that you expect to use subsequently in abbreviated form. Abbreviations (i.e., e.g., etc.) are only acceptable in parenthesis, otherwise they must be spelled out, that is, for example, and so forth, respectively. Please avoid other foreign phrases and words such as via.

Citations
Citations should strictly follow *American Psychological Association* (APA) style guide. Examples of references cited within the texts of articles are as follows: (Williams, Allen, & Jones, 1978) or (Moore, 1990; Smith, 1991) or Terrell (1977). In citations, "et al." can only be used after all authors have been cited or referenced with the exception of six or more authors. As per APA all citations must match the reference list and vice versa. Over use of references is discouraged.

References
Authors are responsible for checking the accuracy of all references and that all references cited in the text also appear in the Reference section. All references should be in alphabetical order by author (unnumbered) *American Psychological Association* (APA), 5th edition, style. Citation examples (1) book and (2) periodical:

Knowles, M.S. (1975). Self-directed learning: A guide for learners and teachers. New York: Association Press.

Raybould, B. (1995). Performance support engineering: An emerging development methodology for enabling organizational learning. Performance Improvement Quarterly, 8(1), 7-22.

Citing Electronic Media
All publications must be properly cited and referenced, even those found on the World Wide Web. The following forms for citing on-line sources are taken from the *APA Publication Guidelines*, 5th edition, Chapter 4, section I (pp. 268-281). Please see the *APA Manual* for additional information on formatting electronic media.

Elements of references to online periodical or book.
Author, I. (date). Title of article. Name of Periodical. Retrieved [Date] from [Specify path]

Author, 1., Author, 2., & Author, I. (date). Title of full work. Retrieved [Date] from [Specify path]

Author, 1., & Author, 2. (date). Title of chapter. In [name(s) of editor(s)], Title of full work. Retrieved [Date] from [Specify path]

Elements of references to nonperiodical documents on the Internet.
Author, 1., Author, 2., & Author, I. (date). Title of web page. Retrieved [Date] from [Specify path]

When referring to a specific page of a web site, use the URL for that page, not the home page. When referring to multiple pages from a web site, provide the URL for the entry page.

The date element should indicate the year of publication or, if the source undergoes regular revision, the most recent update. Use Ò(n.d.)Ó if the publication date cannot be determined.

The retrieval date and URL replaces the publisher information. Provide information sufficient to retrieve the material. For example, for material that is widely available on networks, specify the method used to find the material, such as the protocol (Telnet, FTP, Internet, etc.), the directory, and the file name.

URLs
Hyperlinks to the Internet may also be included in an article. Hyperlinks must be fully qualified and typed out. Every hyperlink within the main text of the article must follow a format similar to the following: "All unmanned spaceflights are controlled from NASA's Jet Propulsion Laboratory (http://www.jpl.nasa.gov)." Every link must begin with "http://".

URLs for documents cited in the text should be placed in appropriate APA format in the Reference List. However, authors may want to refer readers to websites as illustrations or examples. To avoid cluttering the text with long and distracting URLs, in many cases, they should be placed in alphabetical order in a Resources section at the end of the manuscript. Include the name of each web site referred to in the article, with the URL beside it. Regardless of where there are placed, only URLs that begin with "http://" will be hotlinked in the online article. See the following example of a Resources section.

Resources
Association for the Advancement of Computing in Education http://www.aace.org/

Center for Technology and Teacher Education http://www.teacherlink.org/

Please carefully read and adhere to these guidelines. Manuscripts not submitted according to the guidelines must be returned.

Please only send all submissions electronically via the Article Submissions Form

All correspondence concerning your submission should be directed to the Publications Coordinator at: **pubs@aace.org**

Current Issues in Language Planning

ADDRESS FOR SUBMISSION:

Richard B. Baldauf,Jr., Executive Editor
Current Issues in Language Planning
University of Queensland
School of Education
Brisbane, QLD 4072
Australia
Phone: +61 7 3365-6496
Fax: +61 7 3365 7199
E-Mail: rbaldauf@bigpond.com
Web: http://www.cilp.net/
Address May Change:

PUBLICATION GUIDELINES:

Manuscript Length: See Guidelines
Copies Required: One
Computer Submission: Yes Preferred
Format: Word, RTF, DOC peferred
Fees to Review: 0.00 US$

Manuscript Style:
    American Psychological Association

CIRCULATION DATA:

Reader: Academics, Administrators,
    Applied Linguists
Frequency of Issue: Quarterly
Copies per Issue: Less than 1,000
Sponsor/Publisher: Multilingual Matters
    Ltd.
Subscribe Price: 75.00 US$ Individual
    345.00 US$ Library

REVIEW INFORMATION:

Type of Review: Blind Review
No. of External Reviewers: 1
No. of In House Reviewers: 2
Acceptance Rate: 21-30%
Time to Review: 2 - 3 Months
Reviewers Comments: Yes
Invited Articles: 50% + (All reviewed)
Fees to Publish: 0.00 US$

MANUSCRIPT TOPICS:
Education Management/Administration; Government Language Planners; Languages &
Linguistics

MANUSCRIPT GUIDELINES/COMMENTS:

Editor-in-Chief & Polity Editor
Robert B. Kaplan, Editor-in Chief & Policy Editor
P.O. Box 577
Port Angeles, WA 98362, USA
Email: **rkaplan@olypen.com**

Executive Editor & Polity Editor
Richard B. Baldauf, Jr., Executive Editor & Policy Editor
School of Education
University of Queensland
Brisbane, QLD 4072, Australia
Email: **rbaldauf@bigpond.com**

Aims of the Journal

Current Issues in Language Planning provides major summative and review studies spanning and focusing the disparate language policy and language planning literature related to: 1) polities and 2) major issues in the field.

The journal brings together two types of material: "The Language Situation in...." and "Issues in Language Planning". Full submission details, plus a table of contents and article abstracts for previously published issues are available on the journal's website. Topics for future issues are also listed. As the journal publishes only topical issues or polity studies – there are no singles issues –, only previously unpublished polity studies or articles related to a language planning issue under development should be submitted. Other submissions will be returned. The journal also publishes book reviews. Publishers and potential reviewers should contact the book reviews' editor, Professor Martin Pütz puetz@uni-landau.de with possible books for review.

Authors are strongly advised to consult the web site which can be found at: **http://www.cilp.net/** and/or to discuss their potential submission with one of the editors before submitting an article.

Guidelines

'Polity studies' and 'issues focus papers' are normally between 25 and 35,000 words. Supporting issues articles should not normally exceed 7000 words. Note that it is our policy not to review papers have been previously published or that are currently under consideration by other journals. Papers should be typed, double-spaced on A4 (or similar) paper, with ample left and right-hand margins, and every page should be numbered consecutively. A cover page should contain only the title, thereby facilitating anonymous reviewing by two independent assessors. Authors may also wish to take precautions to avoid textual references which would identify themselves to the referees. In such cases the authors of accepted papers will have the opportunity to include any such omitted material before the paper is published.

Main contact author should also appear in a separate paragraph on the title page.

An abstract should be included. This should not exceed 200 words (longer abstracts are rejected by many abstracting services).

A short version of the title (maximum 45 characters) should also be supplied for the journal's running headline.

To facilitate the production of the annual subject index, a list of keywords (not more than six) should be provided, under which the paper may be indexed.

Unless there are exceptional circumstances which make such submission impossible, electronic submission is required.

Footnotes should not be used. Essential notes should be numbered in the text and grouped together at the end of the article as End Notes. Diagrams and Figures, if they are considered essential, should be clearly related to the section of the text to which they refer – do not use

208

'Insert Table 1 here'. Electronic versions of all materials are preferred, but original diagrams and figures may be required to be submitted if the manuscript is accepted for publication.

References should be set out in alphabetical order of the author's name in a list at the end of the article. They should be given in standard form, as in the Appendix below.

References in the text of an article should be by the author's name and year of publication, as in these examples: Jones (1997) in a paper on ...(commonest version); Jones and Evans (1997c:22) state that ...(where page number is required); Evidence is given by Smith et al. (1994)...(for three or more authors). Further exploration of this aspect may be found in many sources (e.g. Brown & Green, 1992; Jackson, 1993; White, 1991a) (note alphabetical order, use of & and semi-colons).

Refereeing will be done electronically and feedback may include both general and specific in text comments. Once the refereeing procedures are completed, authors should supply a final, carefully formatted, electronic version of their manuscript file(s), normally as an email attachment. To speed up publication procedures, please follow the submission guideleines carefully. Tables and Figures should be saved in separate files. Authors should use one variety of English consistently throughout the text.

The author of an article accepted for publication will receive page proofs for correction – normally electronically as a PDF file, if there is sufficient time to do so. This stage must not be used as an opportunity to revise the paper. Because alterations are extremely costly; extensive changes will be charged to the author and will probably result in the issue being delayed. The editors reserve the right to proof articles for publication if authors' proofs are not returned promptly. Keeping the editors / publisher informed of your current email address is therefore essential.

Contributions and queries should be sent to the Executive Editor <**rbaldauf@bigpond.com**>. A very large majority of authors' proof-corrections are caused by errors in references. Authors are therefore requested to check the following points particularly carefully when submitting manuscripts:

- Are all the references in the reference list cited in the text?
- Do all the citations in the text appear in the reference list?
- Do the dates in the text and the reference list correspond?
- Do the spellings of authors' names in text and reference list correspond, and do all authors have the correct initials?
- Are journal references complete with volume and pages numbers?
- Are references to books complete with place of publication and the name of the publisher?

It is extremely helpful if references are presented as far as possible in accordance with Multilingual Matters' house style. A few more typical examples are shown below. Note, especially, use of upper & lower case in paper titles, use of capital letters and italic (underlining can be used as an alternative if italic is not available) in book and journal titles, punctuation (or lack of it) after dates, journal titles, and book titles. The inclusion of issue numbers of journals, or page numbers in books is optional but if included should be as per the examples below.

Department of Education and Science (DES) (1985) *Education for All* (The Swann Report). London: HMSO.

Evans, N.J. and Ilbery, B.W. (1989) A conceptual framework for investigating farm-based accommodation and tourism in Britain. *Journal of Rural Studies* 5 (3), 257-266.

Evans, N.J. and Ilbery, B.W. (1992) Advertising and farm-based accommodation: A British case-study. *Tourism Management* 13 (4), 415-422.

Laufer, B (2000) Vocabulary acquisition in a second language: The hypothesis of ' synforms'. PhD thesis, University of Edinburgh.

Mackey, W.F. (1998) The ecology of language shift. In P.H. Nelde (ed.) *Languages in Contact and in Conflict* (pp. 35-41). Wiesbaden: Steiner.

Marien, C. and Pizam, A. (1997) Implementing sustainable tourism development through citizen participation in the planning process. In S. Wahab and J. Pigram (eds) *Tourism, Development and Growth* (pp. 164-78). London: Routledge.

Morrison, D. (1999) Small group discussion project questionnaire. University of Hong Kong Language Centre (mimeo).

U.S. Census Bureau (1998) State profile: California. Online document: http/www.census.gov/statab/www/states/ca.txt.

Zahn, C.J. and Hopper, R (2000) The speech evaluation instrument: A user's manual (version 1.0a). Unpublished manuscript, Cleveland State University.

Zigler, E. and Balla, D. (eds) *Mental Retardation: The Developmental-Difference Controversy.* Hillsdale, N.J: Lawrence Erlbaum.

For more details, please see <**http://www.cilp.net/**> or e-mail us on **multi@multilingual-matters com**.

Curriculum Journal

ADDRESS FOR SUBMISSION:

Bob Moon, Bob McCormick, Editors
Curriculum Journal
The Open University
Katie Bell, Sec. - Curriculum Journal
Stuart Hall Building, Level 3
Faculty of Education & Language Studies
Milton Keynes, MK7 6AA
UK
Phone: 01908 652386
Fax: 01452 813131
E-Mail: r.e.moon@open.ac.uk
Web: www.tandf.co.uk/journals/
Address May Change:

PUBLICATION GUIDELINES:

Manuscript Length: 21-25
Copies Required: Three
Computer Submission: Yes Disk, Email
Format: MS Word
Fees to Review: 0.00 US$

Manuscript Style:

CIRCULATION DATA:

Reader: , Professionals
Frequency of Issue: Quarterly
Copies per Issue:
Sponsor/Publisher: The British Curriculum
    Foundation / Taylor & Francis
Subscribe Price: 244.00 US$ Individual
    1248.00 US$ Institution

REVIEW INFORMATION:

Type of Review: Blind Review
No. of External Reviewers: 1
No. of In House Reviewers: 1
Acceptance Rate: 11-20%
Time to Review: 1-3 Months
Reviewers Comments: Yes
Invited Articles: 0-5%
Fees to Publish: 0.00 US$

MANUSCRIPT TOPICS:
Curriculum Studies; Education Services

MANUSCRIPT GUIDELINES/COMMENTS:

Aims and Scope
The *Curriculum Journal* is essential reading for all professionals wishing to make a positive influence on the direction of future education.

The official journal of the British Curriculum Foundation, it provides a much-needed forum for debate, publishing research into curriculum structure, organization and development in primary and secondary schools and further education.

The *Curriculum Journal* is written for teachers and head teachers, advisors, managers and academics. It features articles on the whole curriculum, cross-curricular issues, assessment requirements and new approaches to teaching and learning. It also takes a regular look at curriculum developments in other countries, putting recent events in the UK into an international context.

Note to Authors. Please make sure your contact address information is clearly visible on the outside of all packages you are sending to Editors.

Authors should submit three complete copies of their text, tables and figures, with any original illustrations, to:

> Editors of the Curriculum Journal, Faculty of Education & Language Studies, Open University, Walton Hall, Milton Keynes, MK7 6AA.

1. The submission should include a cover page showing the author's name, the department where the work was done, an address for correspondence, if different, telephone numbers, email addresses and any acknowledgements.

2. Submissions should be in English, typed in double spacing with wide margins, one side only of the paper, preferably of A4 size. The title, but not the author's name, should appear on the first page of the manuscript.

    Articles should normally be as concise as possible and preceded by an abstract of not more than 150-200 words and a list of up to 6 key words for on-line searching purposes.

3. Within the manuscript there may be up to three levels of heading.

4. **Tables and figures** should not be inserted in the pages of the manuscript but should be on separate sheets. They should be numbered consecutively in Arabic numerals with a descriptive caption. The desired position in the text for each table and figure should be indicated in the margin of the manuscript.

5. Use the Harvard system of referencing which gives the name of the author and the date of publication as a key to the full bibliographical details which are set out in the list of references. When the author's name is mentioned in the text, the date is inserted in parentheses immediately after the name, as in 'Ball (1981)'. When a less direct reference is made to one or more authors, both name and date are bracketed, with the references separated by a semi-colon, as in 'several authors have noted this trend (Carr, 1989; Grundy, 1982; Kemmis, 1984)'. When the reference is to a work of dual or multiple authorship, use only surnames of the abbreviated form as in 'Salter and Tapper (1981)' or Broadfoot et al. If an author has two references published in the same year, add lower case letters after the date to distinguish them, as in 'Elliott (1980a, 1980b)'. For direct quotations use the minimum number of figures in page numbers, dates, etc., e.g. 22-4, 105-6 (but 112-13) for teen numbers and 1968-9.

6. Direct quotations of 40 words or more will be printed as prose extracts; page reference numbers will be required.

7. Notes should be used only where necessary to avoid interrupting the continuity of the text. They should be numbered consecutively using superscript Arabic numerals. They should appear at the end of the main text, immediately before the list of references.

8. Submissions should include a reference list, in alphabetical order, at the end of the article. The content and format should conform to the following examples.

Book and chapter: Bowley, J. (1988) *A Secure Base*. London: Routledge.

Alvarez, A. (1992) 'A developmental view of "defence"'. *In Live Company*. London and New York: Tavistock/Routledge.

Multi-authored or multi-edited books: Szur, R. T. and Miller, S. (eds) (1991) *Extending Horizons*. London: Karnac.

Translated text: Anzieu, D. (ed.) (1990) *Psychic Envelopes*, trans. D. Briggs. London: Karnac.

Article in journal: Winnicott, D. W. (1960) 'The theory of the parent-infant relationship'. *International Journal of Psycho-Analysis* 41: 485-95. (Note: please give journal title in full).

9. For any other matters of presentation not covered by the above notes, please refer to the usual custom and practice as indicated by the last few issues of the *Journal*.

If you have any further questions about the style for this journal, please submit your questions using the Style Queries form.

10. **On acceptance for publication,** authors will be requested to provide a copy of their paper in exact accordance with the conventions listed in the preceding notes. If the final version of the paper is not submitted in accordance with these conventions then publication may be delayed by the need to return manuscripts to authors for necessary revisions. Authors should note that, following acceptance for publication, they will be required to provide not only a hard copy of the final version, but also a copy on a virus-free disk, preferably in MS-Word 6 format, if possible. Authors will also be required to complete a Publishing Agreement form assigning copyrights to the Publisher.

11. **Early Electronic Offprints**. Corresponding authors can now receive their article by e-mail as a complete PDF. This allows the author to print up to 50 copies, free of charge, and disseminate them to colleagues. In many cases this facility will be available up to two weeks prior to publication. Or, alternatively, corresponding authors will receive the traditional 50 offprints. A copy of the journal will be sent by post to all corresponding authors after publication. Additional copies of the journal can be purchased at the author's preferential rate of £15.00/$25.00 per copy.

12. **Page proofs** will be sent for correction to a first-named author, unless otherwise requested. The difficulty and expense involved in making amendments at the page proof

stage make it essential for authors to prepare their typescript carefully: any alteration to the original text is strongly discouraged. Authors should correct printers' errors in red; minimal alterations of their own should be in black. Our aim is rapid publication; this will be helped if authors provide good copy, following the above instructions, and return their page proofs to the editor on the date requested.

Die Unterrichtspraxis/Teaching German

ADDRESS FOR SUBMISSION:

Aleidine J. Moeller, Editor
Die Unterrichtspraxis/Teaching German
University of Nebraska-Lincoln
115 Henzlik Hall
Lincoln, NE 68588-0355
USA
Phone: 402-472-2024
Fax: 402-472-2837
E-Mail: amoeller2@unl.edu
Web: See Guidelines
Address May Change:

PUBLICATION GUIDELINES:

Manuscript Length: Approx. 15 pages
Copies Required: One
Computer Submission: Yes , Email or Disk
Format: Mac or PC/ MS Word,
    WordPerfect
Fees to Review: 0.00 US$

Manuscript Style:
    , MLA Handbook for Writers of
    Research Papers

CIRCULATION DATA:

Reader: Academics, German Teachers
Frequency of Issue: 2 Times/Year
Copies per Issue: 5,001 - 10,000
Sponsor/Publisher: American Association
    of Teachers of German
Subscribe Price: 35.00 US$
    5.00 US$ Non-USA Postage

REVIEW INFORMATION:

Type of Review: Blind Review
No. of External Reviewers: 2
No. of In House Reviewers: No Reply
Acceptance Rate: 30%
Time to Review: 4 Months
Reviewers Comments: Yes
Invited Articles: 0-5%
Fees to Publish: 0.00 US$

MANUSCRIPT TOPICS:

Assessment and Testing; Cultural Background in German-Speaking Countries; Exchange Programs; Foreign Language; German for Special Purposes; German Language; Professional and Program Development; Second Language Acquisition; Teaching Literature, Language, and Film; Teaching Methods and Materials; Translation; Using Instructional Technology

MANUSCRIPT GUIDELINES/COMMENTS:

The Journal's website is: **http://web.utk.edu/~germslav/uphome/index.html**

EDITORIAL POLICY

Editorial Focus: Improvement and promotion of German teaching in the United States at all instructional levels.

Types of Submissions: Pedagogical articles, reports, news, discussions, teaching tips.

Manuscript Length: Articles: up to 15 pages (ca. 3,500 words). Shorter manuscripts very much welcomed. *Tipps*: 1 page (ca. 300 words).

Languages of Publication: English or German.

Single Submission: Manuscripts submitted simultaneously for publication elsewhere cannot be considered. Manuscripts that have been submitted, accepted, or published elsewhere, including on the World Wide Web, cannot be published in *Die Unterrichtspraxis*.

Average Time Between Submission and Publication Decision: Four months.

Average Time Between Publication Decision and Actual Publication: Usually less than one year.

Number of Articles Published Per Year: 25-35.

Number of Book, Software, Video Reviews: 40-50.

Average Rate of Acceptance: 30%.

Electronic Publishing Policy: Media reviews and article abstracts will be published on-line shortly following the mailing of the journal to subscribers. Articles will be available on-line or electronically at a later date.

Complimentary Copies (and Offprints) of Articles: Two. Additional copies available at cost. Must be ordered at the time galley proofs are received.

FORMAT AND SUBMISSION GUIDELINES
Style Sheet
Gibaldi, Joseph. *MLA Handbook for Writers of Research Papers*, 5th ed. New York: MLA, 1999.

Special Typing Conventions
- Double-space all text and notes. One-inch (2.5 cm) margin on all sides.
- Italicize book titles, citations of foreign words, etc.
- Underline only material that is to be underlined in the published form.
- Use "smart" quotes, not "dumb" quotes.
- Right margin ragged (unjustified).
- Words at line ends unbroken (no automatic hyphenation).
- Titles and section headings flush left.
- Use embedded footnotes, i.e. footnotes inserted automatically by a word processor.
- German text in reformed orthography.

Tables and Illustrations
UP is not printed in color. Submit tables and illustrations with this limitation in mind. When submitting tables or illustrations, please provide them not only embedded in the manuscript, but also on separate sheets (in stand-alone files) ready for printing or duplicating.

Copyright Permissions
If permission for reproducing copyrighted material is required, the author should submit such permission with the final copy submitted for typesetting. Copyright or permission fees are the responsibility of the author.

Long Quotations
Long citations that will be indented in smaller type in the journal need not be indented in the manuscript if they are marked as quotes in the manuscript.

A Complete Manuscript Submission Includes
1. Contribution (Article, Report, etc.)
    Omit identifying references to oneself and one's institution.
    Refer to one's own publications in the third person.
2. Separate sheet (file) with
    author(s) name(s),
    affiliation, address,
    home, school, fax numbers,
    e-mail address,
    title of the paper.
3. Abstract (max. 100 words) on separate sheet (in separate file).
4. Short bio on separate sheet (in separate file).

PERMISSIBLE FORMAT OF SUBMISSIONS
Paper: Mail a single clean paper original of contribution and separate sheets to the editor.

Electronic (any of the following)
- 3.5" double-sided, double density diskette.
- 100 MB (Mac or PC) ZIP disk.
- E-mail attachment of files in a readable electronic format (see below).

Please send diskettes in a protected diskette mailing envelope.

Preferred Mode of Submission: Both electronic and paper.

Preferred Word Processor Formats: Microsoft Word or WordPerfect.

Many other word processor formats (for both Mac and PC) are acceptable. For such questions, consult the editor (amoeller2@unl.edu) or editorial assistant, Holly Sexton (hsexton1@unl.edu). No manuscript will be rejected solely because a contributor cannot meet these specifications.

Labeling of Diskettes Should Include
- Name of the author(s).
- Titles of the text files on the diskette.
- Word processor (and version) used.
- Date of submission.

Discourse Processes

ADDRESS FOR SUBMISSION:

Michael Schober, Editor
Discourse Processes
  ELECTRONIC SUBMISION
New School for Social Research
Department of Psychology, F330
65 Fifth Avenue
New York, NY 10003
USA
Phone: 212-220-5787
Fax: 212-989-0846
E-Mail: schober@newschool.edu
Web: See Guidelines
Address May Change:

PUBLICATION GUIDELINES:

Manuscript Length: 26-35
Copies Required: Electronic Submission
Computer Submission: Yes
Format: N/A
Fees to Review: 0.00 US$

Manuscript Style:
    American Psychological Association

CIRCULATION DATA:

Reader: Academics
Frequency of Issue: 6 Times/Year
Copies per Issue: 1,001 - 2,000
Sponsor/Publisher: The Society for Text
  and Discourse
Subscribe Price: 100.00 US$ Individual
    405.00 US$ Institution Print Only
      Visit website for details

REVIEW INFORMATION:

Type of Review: Editorial Review
No. of External Reviewers: 3
No. of In House Reviewers: 0
Acceptance Rate: 21-30%
Time to Review: 2 - 3 Months
Reviewers Comments: Yes
Invited Articles: 11-20%
Fees to Publish: 0.00 US$

MANUSCRIPT TOPICS:
Conversation; Discourse; Psycholinguistics and Social Linguistics; Reading; Writing

MANUSCRIPT GUIDELINES/COMMENTS:

Discourse Processes is the official journal of The Society for Text and Discourse.

Discourse Processes is a multidisciplinary journal providing a forum for cross-fertilization of ideas from diverse disciplines sharing a common interest in discourse--prose comprehension and recall, dialogue analysis, text grammar construction, computer simulation of natural language, cross-cultural comparisons of communicative competence, or related topics. The problems posed by multi-sentence contexts and the methods required to investigate them, although not always unique to discourse, are sufficiently distinct so as to require an organized mode of scientific interaction made possible through the journal.

The journal accepts original experimental or theoretical papers that substantially advance understanding of the structure and function of discourse. Scholars working in the discourse area from the perspective of sociolinguistics, psycholinguistics, discourse psychology, text linguistics, ethnomethodology and sociology of language, education, philosophy of language, computer science, and related sub-areas are invited to contribute. Newer methods and technologies for studying discourse processes in their full complexity can require new ways of presenting data and analyses.

Starting with Volume 39, the electronic version of *Discourse Processes* will allow access to multimedia (video and/or audio) content when it appropriately augments the presentation of a particular piece.

Submission

Submitted papers in most cases should not exceed 35 double-spaced pages, including figures and tables. Brief reports and, in rare instances, articles of monographic length will also be considered.

Submit five copies of the manuscript to the electronic submission system.

Manuscript Preparation

Manuscripts should be prepared according to the guidelines of the *Publication Manual of the American Psychological Association* (4th ed.). Double space all material, including title page, abstract, text, quotations, acknowledgments, references, appendixes, tables, figure captions, and footnotes. The title page should include the title of the manuscript; name and affiliations of all authors; name, address, phone and fax numbers, and e-mail address of the corresponding author; and a running head of no more than 48 letters and spaces. The second page should include the manuscript title and an abstract of 100 to 150 words. All figures must be camera ready. Authors should keep a copy of their manuscript to guard against loss.

Peer Review

To facilitate a prompt review of their articles, authors should submit a list of five possible reviewers, at least three of whom should be on the *Discourse Processes* Editorial Board. The address, email address and telephone number should be included for recommended reviewers who are not on the editorial board.

Permissions

Authors are responsible for all statements made in their work and for obtaining permission from copyright owners to use a lengthy quotation (500 words or more) or to reprint or adapt a table or figure published elsewhere. Authors should write to original author(s) and publisher of such material to request nonexclusive world rights in all languages for use in the article and in future editions. Provide copies of all permissions and credit lines obtained.

Production Notes

Accepted manuscripts are copyedited, the authors review copyediting, and the manuscripts are typeset into page proofs. Authors are asked to read proofs for typesetter's errors and other defects. Correction of typographical errors is made without charge; other alterations are to be prepaid by authors. Authors may order reprints of their articles only when they return page proofs.

Distance Education

ADDRESS FOR SUBMISSION:

Som Naidu, Editor
Distance Education
University of Melbourne
Dept of Teaching, Learn. & Res. Support
Victoria, 3010
Australia
Phone: +61 03 8344 7575
Fax: +61 03 8344 4341
E-Mail: s.naidu@uniwelb.edu.au
Web: www.tandf.co.uk/journals
Address May Change:

CIRCULATION DATA:

Reader: Practicing Teachers, Academics
Frequency of Issue: 3 Times/Year
Copies per Issue:
Sponsor/Publisher: Open and Distance
  Learning Assn. of Australia/Carfax
  (Taylor & Francis)
Subscribe Price: 141.00 US$ Individual
  452.00 US$ Institution

PUBLICATION GUIDELINES:

Manuscript Length: 26-30
Copies Required: One
Computer Submission: Yes
Format: MS Word
Fees to Review: 0.00 US$

Manuscript Style:
  American Psychological Association

REVIEW INFORMATION:

Type of Review: Blind Review
No. of External Reviewers: 3
No. of In House Reviewers: 2
Acceptance Rate: 21-30%
Time to Review: 1 Month or Less
Reviewers Comments: Yes
Invited Articles: 6-10%
Fees to Publish: 0.00 US$

MANUSCRIPT TOPICS:

Adult Career & Vocational; Distance Education; Educational Psychology; Educational Technology Systems; E-Learning; On-line Learning; Rural Education & Small Schools

MANUSCRIPT GUIDELINES/COMMENTS:

General Rules
Language. The language of publication is English.

Length. Usually 6,000 words for an article (longer articles are acceptable after agreement is reached with the Executive Editor), 500-1,000 words for a book review.

Abstract. Each article should be summarised in about 100 words. The abstract should be capable of standing alone as a descriptor of the article.

Author. Please provide full name (with surname capitalised), address for correspondence (including electronic mail), telephone/fax number, and a brief description of professional affiliation or role.

220

Submission. Contributions, including the abstract and the reference list, should be typed, double spaced, on A4 paper and submitted as a paper copy. The abstract, list of references, tables and figures should be typed on separate sheets. *To facilitate the refereeing process, an electronic copy must also be supplied (along with the paper copies) as an email attachment in Rich Text Format or as a disk copy (in MSWord for Windows format).*

Style. Papers submitted should be concise and written in readily understandable style. A left-hand margin of four centimetres is required. Non-technical, non-discriminatory language should be used where possible and specialist terms should be explained for a multi-disciplinary readership. Spelling should be consistent within papers. The editors accept national difference in idiomatic English usage.

Acceptance of papers
Submission of a paper to *Distance Education* will be taken to imply that:
- it represents original work not previously published
- it is not being considered for publication elsewhere
- the contributor has obtained all necessary permission and paid any fees for the use of copyright materials.

Contributors therefore undertake to indemnify ODLAA Inc. for any loss occasioned in consequence of any breach of copyright.

Review by editorial board. Papers are reviewed by members of the Editorial Board with expertise in the area(s) represented by a paper, and/or invited reviewers with special competence in the area(s) covered. After completion of the review process, the Executive Editor will inform contributors whether the article is rejected, or accepted for publication with or without amendments. The Executive Editor reserves the right to make minor alterations where necessary, to accepted manuscripts.

Copies. Contributors will receive ten unbound copies of their paper free of charge; further copies will be supplied at cost upon request.

Copyright. ODLAA Inc. holds copyright on all papers accepted for publication in this journal and also the right to publish, distribute and/or store its contents in one or more of the following forms: paper, electronic or any other publication, distribution, storage and retrieval mechanism. Authors of papers published in the journal have the right to use their material for purely educational purposes. All subsequent publications authorised by the Executive Editor, where in whole or part, must acknowledge this journal as the original publisher of the article.

All contributions should be addressed to: Associate Professor Som Naidu, PhD, Executive Editor, Distance Education, Department of Teaching, Learning and Research Support, The University of Melbourne, Victoria, 3010, Australia, Telephone: (03) 8344 7575. Facsimile: (03) 8344 4341, Email: **s.naidu@unimelb.edu.au**.

Books for review. Publishers are invited to submit books on distance education and related fields for review.

Early Childhood Education Journal

ADDRESS FOR SUBMISSION:

Mary Renck Jalongo, Editor
Early Childhood Education Journal
  ELECTRONIC SUBMISSIONS ONLY
654 College Lodge Road
Indiana, PA 15701-4015
USA
Phone:
Fax:
E-Mail: mjalongo@iup.edu
Web: See Guidelines
Address May Change:

PUBLICATION GUIDELINES:

Manuscript Length: 6-14
Copies Required: Electronic submission
Computer Submission: Yes Required
Format: After Acceptance
Fees to Review: 0.00 US$

Manuscript Style:
  American Psychological Association

CIRCULATION DATA:

Reader: Academics, Practicing Teachers,
  Administrators
Frequency of Issue: Bi-Monthly
Copies per Issue: Paper + electronic
Sponsor/Publisher: Springer/Kluwer
  Academic Publishers
Subscribe Price: 85.00 US$ Individual
  626.40 US$ Institution

REVIEW INFORMATION:

Type of Review: Blind Review
No. of External Reviewers: 1
No. of In House Reviewers: 1
Acceptance Rate: 18%
Time to Review: 2 - 3 Months
Reviewers Comments: Yes
Invited Articles: 40%
Fees to Publish: 0.00 US$

MANUSCRIPT TOPICS:
Elementary/Early Childhood; Reading; Special Education

MANUSCRIPT GUIDELINES/COMMENTS:

The Journal's website is **www.wkap.nl/journalhome.htm/1082-3301**

Early Childhood Education Journal is a publication of Springer/Kluwer Academic Publishers. The *Journal* uses anonymous peer-review system to evaluate manuscripts.

1. **Audience.** The masthead, located on the front inside cover, explains the mission and focus of *Early Childhood Education Journal*. Note that our readership is interested in the education and care of **young** children, ages birth through 8.

2. **Address.** Submit all manuscripts electronically at: **http://ecej.edmgr.com/** by following the instructions for authors.

3. **Types of Manuscripts Published.** We seek manuscripts that blend theory and research with practical application. Manuscripts published in *Early Childhood Education Journal* offer

information and insight to professionals who devote their lives to the care and education of the very young. Feature-length articles are accompanied by a bibliography of sources that the author(s) consulted when preparing the manuscript and/or a bibliography of recommended sources for further reading. Manuscripts are no more than 14 doubles-spaced, typewritten in 12 point Courier Print pages, including references. *Early Childhood Education Journal* is a scholarly publication and does not pay authors for the articles published.

Please Note we do not publish new releases or fiction of any type.

Direct all advertising inquires to the New York office.

4. **Manuscript Preparation**. Articles for *Early Childhood Education Journal* have the following requirements:

- A cover sheet that includes the article title, author's name(s), institutional affiliation, address, telephone number, and e-mail address should be provided. This information should appear on the cover sheet **only**. Type a running head or header (an abbreviated version of the article title) in the upper right-hand corner of each page.

- An abstract of the article's content consisting of no more than three or four sentences (a 150-word maximum) should be provided. If your manuscript is accepted for publication, this abstract will be published in the journal as a way of introducing your article. Key words should express the precise content of the manuscript, as they are used for indexing purposes.

- Illustrations (photographs, diagrams, charts, samples of children's work) are encouraged. Authors must obtain releases for use of any photos or drawings of any material that is under copyright. The illustrations should be numbered consecutively and their placement in the text should be indicated in the manuscript in *APA* style. The captions for any illustrations should be typed double-spaced on a separate sheet of paper. Photographs should be large, glossy prints, showing high contrast. Drawings should be rendered in black india ink. Identify any figures with the author's name and the number of the illustration lightly written on the back. For samples of children's work, use high-quality photocopies or have the work photographed in black and white. Send copies, rather than originals, of these items on the first submission. *Early Childhood Education Journal* does not charge authors a page fee for each illustration published.

- Consult the 5th edition of the *American Psychological Association's* style manual as a resource in preparing all aspects of your manuscript, including the bibliography.

- Use 12-point, Courier typeface.

- Type the manuscript **double-spaced** with 1 inch margins on all sides and **left-justified only**. Make sure that all copies are legible and complete. Pages must be numbered.

5. **Copyright**. Submission of a manuscript to *Early Childhood Education Journal* is a representation that the manuscript has not been previously published and is not currently

under consideration for publication elsewhere. A Publication agreement transferring copyright from the authors to Springer/Kluwer Academic Press will be required before the manuscript can be accepted for publication.

6. **Review Process**. There are three types of editorial decisions: accept with minor revisions, accept with major revisions required, or reject. The most common reasons for rejection are that a manuscript has not been carefully crafted, as not been written for the audience, or is too similar to another article on the topic that was recently published or accepted for publication. Usually the review process takes 8-12 weeks and contributors are notified via e-mail of the Editor's decision.

If the manuscript requires major or minor revisions, make the necessary revisions and resubmit to the Editorial Manager® website.

7. **Publication Process**. After the manuscript is accepted, it is edited to conform to the journal's style and content.

Prior to publication, authors are furnished with page proofs (the typeset version of the manuscript) and are given the opportunity to purchase reprints, a PDF version of their article. **The *Journal* makes no page charges.**

Early Childhood Research & Practice

ADDRESS FOR SUBMISSION:

Lilian G. Katz, Editor
Early Childhood Research & Practice
University of Illinois, Urbana-Champaign
Children's Research Center
51 Gerty Drive
Champaign, IL 61820-7469
USA
Phone: 217-333-1386
Fax: 217-333-3767
E-Mail: ecrp@uiuc.edu
Web: ecrp.uiuc.edu
Address May Change:

PUBLICATION GUIDELINES:

Manuscript Length: 16-20
Copies Required: Two
Computer Submission: Yes Disk & Email
Format: Word
Fees to Review: 0.00 US$

Manuscript Style:
    See Manuscript Guidelines

CIRCULATION DATA:

Reader: Practicing Teachers, Academics
Frequency of Issue: 2 Times/Year
Copies per Issue: No Reply
Sponsor/Publisher:
Subscribe Price: 0.00 US$ Free/Online

REVIEW INFORMATION:

Type of Review: Blind Review
No. of External Reviewers: 2-3
No. of In House Reviewers: 1-2
Acceptance Rate: No Reply
Time to Review: 4 - 6 Months
Reviewers Comments: Yes
Invited Articles: 6-10%
Fees to Publish: 0.00 US$

MANUSCRIPT TOPICS:
Elementary/Early Childhood

MANUSCRIPT GUIDELINES/COMMENTS:

Early Childhood Research & Practice (*ECRP*), a peer-reviewed electronic journal, covers topics related to the development, care, and education of children from birth to approximately age 8. *ECRP* emphasizes articles reporting on practice-related research and development, and on issues related to practice, parent participation, and policy. *ECRP* also includes articles and essays that present opinions and reflections, and letters to the editor.

General Instructions
All work submitted to *Early Childhood Research & Practice* (*ECRP*) for electronic publication should be original and not previously published in or submitted to another journal. If previously included in a proceedings, the version submitted to *ECRP* should significantly extend the proceedings version. Work submitted to *ECRP* will undergo blind review, will be returned to the author if revisions are suggested, and will be copyedited and proofread in-

house. A copy of the Reviewer Instructions Form used by peer reviewers is available on this Web site. The author will be sent a final version to review before publication.

Submission Procedures

To submit work, send an email message to **ecrp@uiuc.edu** and include complete contact information, i.e., the principal author's name, affiliation, address, telephone and fax numbers, and email address. Attach the work as either an ascii file, Microsoft Word file, or WordPerfect file (IBM-compatible formats are preferred). Acknowledgment of receipt of the work will be sent to the author. In addition to the electronic submission, authors should mail two paper copies of the manuscript to the following address:

ECRP Editor
University of Illinois at Urbana-Champaign
Children's Research Center
51 Gerty Drive
Champaign, IL 61820-7469

Authors who do not have access to electronic mail should include a copy of their work on disk when they submit paper copies. Please indicate which operating system and word-processing program were used in preparing the disk.

Obtaining Releases

Authors are responsible for obtaining all necessary releases/permissions required for their article (for example, permission from parents to use and electronically disseminate a photograph of a child or a child's drawing). Authors will be asked to sign a form stating that they have obtained all necessary releases. The kinds of manuscripts requiring releases from individuals, teachers, children, schools, principals, school districts, etc. are quite varied. However, case studies, ethnographies, teacher research, and oral/life history usually require a release from participants. Use of vignettes, portraits, or real life examples may also require authors to obtain releases. As a rule of thumb whenever educational researchers conduct their studies, their standard release forms should include a line stating that this material may be used at some future date for publication in paper or electronic form. Contact *ECRP* editors (**ecrp@uiuc.edu**) with questions about releases.

Copyright

Although authors will retain copyright, the journal requests first serial publication rights and requires that authors sign release forms granting the right to publish their articles in *ECRP* (*ECRP* permission form).

STYLE
Length
- Articles should not exceed 5,000 words and should include a 250-word abstract.

Artwork

Artwork (e.g., figures, graphs, and pictures) should be submitted as separate graphics files (e.g., tif, gif, bmp, .jpg). Tables should be prepared with a word-processing program. Please include hard copies of artwork in camera-ready form for possible scanning.

Sound and Video
ECRP will be able to include sound and video clips with articles. Contact the *ECRP* Webmaster for information on recommended file formats. Authors should provide transcripts for audio or video clips in order to accommodate access for individuals with disabilities.

Links
Authors may indicate in their text suggested places for hypertext links; however, journal staff will make a final determination of which links to include. References cited in text will be linked to the full bibliographic citation included in the references section of the article.

References
Using an author-date citation style, authors should list all works cited in the text alphabetically at the end of the article. *Early Childhood Research & Practice* uses a modified editorial style based on the fourth edition of the *Publication Manual of the American Psychological Association*. *ECRP* style differs from the APA style principally in the use of authors' names as they appear in the cited articles, rather than the use of only first initials.

Sample Article Citation
   Prawat, Richard S., & Jennings, Nancy. (1997). Students as context in mathematics reform: The story of two upper-elementary teachers. *Elementary School Journal*, 97(3), 251-270.

Sample Monograph Citation
   Cremmins, Edward T. (1982). *The art of abstracting*. Philadelphia, PA: ISI Press.

Sample Chapter Citation
   Gano-Phillips, Susan, & Fincham, Frank D. (1995). Family conflict, divorce, and children's adjustment. In Mary Anne Fitzpatrick & Anita L. Vangelisti (Eds.), *Explaining family interactions* (pp. 206-231). Thousand Oaks, CA: Sage.

For more information, please contact journal staff by email at **ecrp@uiuc.edu** or call 800-583-4135.

Early Childhood Research Quarterly

ADDRESS FOR SUBMISSION:

Karen E. Diamond, Editor
Early Childhood Research Quarterly
Purdue University
101 Gates Road
W. Lafayette, IN 47907-2020
USA
Phone: 765-494-0942
Fax: 765-496-1144
E-Mail: ecrq@cfs.purdue.edu
Web:
Address May Change:

PUBLICATION GUIDELINES:

Manuscript Length: 30+
Copies Required: Five
Computer Submission: Yes Email
Format: MS Word
Fees to Review: 0.00 US$

Manuscript Style:
    American Psychological Association

CIRCULATION DATA:

Reader: Academics
Frequency of Issue: Quarterly
Copies per Issue: 2,001 - 3,000
Sponsor/Publisher: Elsevier Science
    Publishing Co.
Subscribe Price: 70.00 US$
    40.00 US$ NAEYC Member

REVIEW INFORMATION:

Type of Review: Blind Review
No. of External Reviewers: 3
No. of In House Reviewers: 0
Acceptance Rate: 11-20%
Time to Review: 3-4 Months
Reviewers Comments: Yes
Invited Articles: 0-5%
Fees to Publish: 0.00 US$

MANUSCRIPT TOPICS:
Elementary/Early Childhood; Special Education

MANUSCRIPT GUIDELINES/COMMENTS:

Sponsored by the National Association for the Education of Young Children, *Early Childhood Research Quarterly* includes articles presenting significant research and scholarship on all topics related to the care and education of children from birth through 8 years. Articles reflect the interdisciplinary nature of the field and of the National Association for the Education of Young Children. The *Quarterly* is published by Elsevier Science.

Five copies of manuscripts from 10-35 pages in length should be submitted to the editor. *An electronic copy should be submitted at the same time to **ecrq@purdue.edu**.*

Manuscripts are accepted for review with the understanding that the same work has not been and will not be published nor is presently submitted elsewhere, and that all persons listed as authors have given their approval for the submission of the paper; further, that any person cited as a source of personal communication has approved such citation. Written authorization may be required at the Editor's discretion. Articles and other material published in *Early*

Childhood Research Quarterly represent the opinions of the authors and should not be construed to reflect the opinions of the Editor, the Publisher, or the Sponsor.

Authors submitting a manuscript do so on the understanding that, if it is accepted for publication, copyright in the article, including the right to reproduce the article in all forms and media, shall be assigned exclusively to the Publisher. The Publisher will not refuse any reasonable request by the author for permission to reproduce any of his or her contributions to the *Quarterly*. Responsibility for the accuracy of material in the manuscript, including appropriate reference to related work, lies entirely with the authors.

In submitting a manuscript, please keep in mind the following instructions:

1. **Manuscript Preparation**. Manuscripts should be word processed, double-spaced, with one-inch margins on all sides. Articles should be concise and in English. Page 1 should contain the article title, author(s), affiliation(s), a short form of the title (less than 55 characters including letters and spaces), and the name, telephone number, and complete mailing address of the author to whom correspondence should be sent. Page 2 should contain a short abstract (100-150 words for a report of an empirical study; 70-100 words for a review or theoretical article).

2. **Style**. The style guidelines of the *Publication Manual of the American Psychological Association*, (5th. ed., 2001) should be followed, especially for reference lists and text citation of sources (see **References**, below). American, not British, spelling and punctuation should be used.

3. **Review**. Since manuscripts are submitted for blind review, all identifying information should be removed from the body of the paper.

4. **Tables and Figures**. Tables and figures should be completely understandable independent of the text. Each table and figure must be mentioned in the text, given a title, and consecutively numbered with Arabic numerals. Authors must provide good-quality originals of all figures, to be directly reproduced for publication. Originals must be legible after reduction to a maximum size of 4½ inches wide by 7½ inches high. Graphs and charts must be professionally prepared and may be submitted as original black ink drawings or as sharp black-and-white photographic reproductions. Color originals, which will be published in black and white, are discouraged.

5. **Footnotes**. Footnotes should be used sparingly and indicated by consecutive numbers in the text. Acknowledgments, grant numbers, or other credits should be given as a separate, asterisked footnote.

6. **References**. All sources cited in the text must be included in the reference list, and vice versa. Below are examples of entries for, respectively, a book, a journal article, a chapter in an edited book, and a paper presented at a meeting.

Austin, G.R. (1976). Early childhood education: An international perspective. New York: Academic.

Bruner, J.S. (1972). The nature and uses of immaturity. American Psychologist, 27, 687-708.

Denmark, G., & Nutter, N. (1984). The case for extended programs of initial teacher preparation. In L.G. Katz & J.D. Raths (Eds.), Advances in teacher education (Vol. 1, pp 203-246). Norwood, NJ: Ablex.

Kagan, J., Reznick, S.J., & Snidman, N. (1984, April). Behavorial inhibition in the early years. Paper presented at the International conference on Infant Studies, New York.

Williams, D.L., Jr. (1984). Parent involvement in education: what a survey reveals. Austin, TX: southwest Educational Development laboratory. (ERIC Document Reproduction service No. ED 253 327).

8. **Permissions**. Copies of any letters granting permission to reproduce illustrations, tables, or lengthy quoted passages should be included with the manuscript.

9. **Corrections**. Authors are expected to correct and return page proofs to the Publisher within a week of receipt. Authors are responsible for the cost of changes, additions, or corrections other than printer's or publisher's errors, although the Publisher may waive such charges.

10. **Reprints**. Reprints must be ordered when page proofs are returned to the publisher.

Early Years: An International Journal of Research and Development

ADDRESS FOR SUBMISSION:

Blenkin, Parker-Rees, Whitehead, Co-Eds
Early Years: An International Journal of
    Research and Development
University of Plymouth/Rolle Sch of Educ
Faculty of Arts and Education
Rod Parker-Rees
Douglas Avenue
Exmouth, Devon, EX8 2AT
UK
Phone:
Fax:
E-Mail: r.parker-rees@plymouth.ac.uk
Web: www.tandf.co.uk/journals
Address May Change:

PUBLICATION GUIDELINES:

Manuscript Length: 16-20
Copies Required: Three
Computer Submission: Yes Email
Format: MS Word
Fees to Review: 0.00 US$

Manuscript Style:
    See Manuscript Guidelines

CIRCULATION DATA:

Reader: Academics
Frequency of Issue: 3 Times/Year
Copies per Issue:
Sponsor/Publisher: TACTYC (Training,
    Advancement & Co-operation in
    Teaching Young Children / Taylor &
    Francis
Subscribe Price: 105.00 US$ Individual
    289.00 US$ Institution

REVIEW INFORMATION:

Type of Review: Blind Review
No. of External Reviewers: 0
No. of In House Reviewers: 2
Acceptance Rate: 47%
Time to Review: 1 - 2 Months
Reviewers Comments: Yes
Invited Articles: 21-30%
Fees to Publish: 0.00 US$

MANUSCRIPT TOPICS:
Elementary/Early Childhood; Teacher Education

MANUSCRIPT GUIDELINES/COMMENTS:

Aims and Scope
The importance of early childhood education and care in providing the foundations for lifelong learning is now widely acknowledged. *Early Years: An International Journal of Research and Development* aims to broaden the international debate about the best provision for young children by representing a wide range of perspectives from different countries, different disciplines and different research methodologies.

As the official journal of TACTYC (Training, Advancement and Co-operation in Teaching Young Children), *Early Years* publishes up-to-date papers on all issues associated with early years education.

There is a growing diversity of approaches to training early years practitioners for complex and demanding work within multi professional teams and with families from diverse social and cultural backgrounds. The editors welcome original, rigorous and clearly written contributions, in English, which:

- relate to the training, education and continuing professional development of all early years practitioners including managers, support staff, qualified teachers and higher education academics teaching on early childhood courses and specialisms;
- compare the experiences, development needs and responsibilities of children, parents and practitioners in different kinds of setting and in different contexts;
- report on research projects;
- review work across an area of research;
- present a detailed analysis of the experiences of individuals or small groups;
- explore new approaches to the publication of knowledge about working with young children

TACTYC has sought for nearly 20 years, through its Journal and related activities, to provide a voice for all educators who work with young children. As a professional association with its own membership, TACTYC lobbies for the raising of standards in early years provision and promotes discussion of all issues associated with the training and development of early years practitioners.

Further details are available from:
TACTYC Membership Secretary
Harvington House; 5 Dunstall Court; Croome Estate
Croome D'Abitot; Severn Stoke
Worcs. WR8 9DW; United Kingdom

Abstracting Information
Early Years is covered by the Australian Education Index (AEI), National Database for Research into International Education (NDRI); British Education Index; Contents pages in Education; Educational Research Abstracts online (ERA).

Instructions for Authors
Note to Authors: please make sure your contact address information is clearly visible on the **outside** of <u>all</u> packages you are sending to Editors.

Early Years welcomes articles of up to 5000 words, which should be original and written in clear, straightforward English. Manuscripts must be typed on one side of A4 paper with double spacing and margins of at least 2.5cm. They should be sent to: Rod Parker-Rees, Rolle School of Education, Faculty of Arts and Education, University of Plymouth, Douglas Avenue, Exmouth, Devon EX8 2AT, UK or email Rod Parker-Rees.

Three copies are required. All pages should be numbered and a total word count given at the end of the article. The title, author's name, institution, role and full correspondence address should be supplied on a separate sheet. The title of the article, an abstract of around 150 words and a list of no more than six key words should be supplied on a further separate sheet. In addition, a disk with the final version of the paper will be required, on either PC or Apple, if the paper is accepted for publication.

Articles submitted to *Early Years: an international journal of research and development* should not be under consideration by any other journal, or have been published elsewhere, and the letter accompanying the submission of any manuscript should contain a clear statement to this effect.

Please conform to the house-style of the journal in all respects:

- Tables, figures and artwork should not be included in the text but must be supplied on **separate sheets in a finished form** suitable for reproduction.
- Illustrations should be good contrast, black and white drawings or photographs (preferably gloss finish) or slides. If only colour photographs are available, negatives should be supplied.
- Status and placing of sub-headings should be clear, as should (pencilled) instructions about the position of tables, diagrams, etc.
- No footnotes should be included and endnotes should be used sparingly, numbered in the text and placed at the end of the article just before the list of references.
- Books, articles, etc. should be referred to in the text by the author's name and date of publication in brackets. References should be listed in full at the end of the paper in the following standard form:

  For **books**. Author/s (Year of publication) Title of Book (Place of publication: Name of Publisher).

  For **articles**. Author/s (Year of publication) Title of article. Title of Journals, Volume No., Issue No., page numbers of article.

  For **chapters in books**. Author/s (Year of publication) Title of chapter, in Names of Editor/s, Title of Book (Place of publication: Name of Publisher).

N.B. Titles of journals should not be abbreviated in references list and **all** authors of co authored books or articles must be given.

Final decisions about the inclusion of articles, illustrations, etc. are made in the light of referees' comments and rest with the Editors and the Editorial board, who may be consulted about all matters relating to the journal.

If you have any further questions about the style for this journal, please submit your question using the Style Queries form.

Early Electronic Offprints. Corresponding authors can now receive their article by e-mail a a complete PDF. This allows the author to print up to 50 copies, free of charge, and disseminate them to colleagues. In many cases this facility will be available up to two week prior to publication. Or, alternatively, corresponding authors will receive the traditional 50 offprints. A copy of the journal will be sent by post to all corresponding authors after publication. Additional copies of the journal can be purchased at the author's preferential rate of £15.00/$25.00 per copy.

Education

ADDRESS FOR SUBMISSION:

Editor
Education
P O Box 8508
Spring Hill Station
Mobile, AL 36689-8508
USA
Phone: 251-633-7802
Fax: 251-639-7360
E-Mail: pfeldman@gulftel.com
Web: //journals825.home.mindspring.com
Address May Change:

CIRCULATION DATA:

Reader: Academics
Frequency of Issue: Quarterly
Copies per Issue: 3,001 - 4,000
Sponsor/Publisher: Project Innovation, Inc.
Subscribe Price: 40.00 US$ Institution
   10.00 US$ Additional - Canada/year
   20.00 US$ Add'l for International /yr

PUBLICATION GUIDELINES:

Manuscript Length: 11-15
Copies Required: Two
Computer Submission: Yes
Format: One data diskette & one hardcopy
Fees to Review:
   US$

Manuscript Style:
   American Psychological Association

REVIEW INFORMATION:

Type of Review: Editorial Review
No. of External Reviewers: 2
No. of In House Reviewers: 1
Acceptance Rate: 50%
Time to Review: 1 Month or Less
Reviewers Comments: No
Invited Articles: 31-50%
Fees to Publish:
   30.00 US$ Per double-spaced page

MANUSCRIPT TOPICS:

Adult Career & Vocational; Art/Music; Audiology/Speech Pathology; Counseling & Personnel Services; Curriculum Studies; Education Management/Administration; Educational Psychology; Educational Technology Systems; Elementary/Early Childhood; Gifted Children; Health & Physical Education; Higher Education; Science Math & Environment; Secondary/Adolescent Studies; Social Studies/Social Science; Teacher Education; Tests, Measurement & Evaluation

MANUSCRIPT GUIDELINES/COMMENTS:

Education publishes original investigations and theoretical papers dealing with worthwhile innovations in learning, teaching, and education. Preference is given to innovations in the school, proposed or actual, and theoretical or evaluative. Papers concern all levels and every area of education and learning. *Education* is primarily concerned with teacher education in all of its many aspects.

Manuscript Submission

Manuscripts must be submitted in duplicate and should be prepared to conform to the style and procedures described in the *Publication Manual of the American Psychological*

Association. Manuscripts must be accompanied by an abstract of 100 to 150 words typed on a separate sheet of paper and a computer diskette. The abstract should contain statements of the (a) problem, (b) method, (c) results, and (d) conclusions when appropriate. The abstract should provide the reader with an idea of the theme and scope of the article.

At least one copy of the manuscript and the abstract must be original with clear, clean typing or printing. We prefer disk-based manuscripts in either Macintosh or MS-DOS format. However, at least one printed copy of the manuscript must be included with the disk.

Review Process
Manuscripts are reviewed by at least two reviewers knowledgeable in the field of study. An attempt is made to review manuscripts within two weeks of receipt when possible.

Fees to Publish
This Journal is not supported by either membership or association dues, or advertising. Authors or their institutions share the cost of publication. Except for invited articles, authors will be involved for their share of publication costs at the time the manuscript is accepted for publication. The article will be scheduled for publication after payment or an institutional purchase order is received.

Reprints
Information concerning reprints and reprint policy is disseminated with page proofs/galleys.

Education and Culture

ADDRESS FOR SUBMISSION:

A. G. Rud, Editor
Education and Culture
ELECTRONIC SUBMISSION ONLY
Phone: 765-494-7310
Fax:　765-496-1228
E-Mail: eandc@purdue.edu
Web: http://johndeweysociety.org
Address May Change: 1/1/2008

PUBLICATION GUIDELINES:

Manuscript Length: 16-20
Copies Required: Electronic
Computer Submission: Yes Only
Format: MS Word doc as RTF format
Fees to Review: 0.00 US$

Manuscript Style:
　　American Psychological Association,
　　Chicago Manual of Style

CIRCULATION DATA:

Reader: Academics, Practicing Teachers
Frequency of Issue: 2 Times/Year
Copies per Issue: Less than 1,000
Sponsor/Publisher: The John Dewey
　Society
Subscribe Price: 40.00 US$ Individual
　　80.00 US$ Institution
　　50.00 US$ Indv. / $100 Inst. Foreign

REVIEW INFORMATION:

Type of Review: Blind Review
No. of External Reviewers: 2
No. of In House Reviewers: 1
Acceptance Rate: 21-30%
Time to Review: 4 - 6 Months
Reviewers Comments: Yes
Invited Articles: 6-10%
Fees to Publish: 0.00 US$

MANUSCRIPT TOPICS:
Adult Career & Vocational; Art/Music; Curriculum Studies; Education Management/Administration; Educational Psychology; Elementary/Early Childhood; Higher Education; Rural Education & Small Schools; School Law; Secondary/Adolescent Studies; Social Studies/Social Science; Teacher Education; Urban Education, Cultural/Non-Traditional

MANUSCRIPT GUIDELINES/COMMENTS:

Education and Culture, published twice yearly by Purdue University Press, takes an integrated view of philosophical, historical, and sociological issues in education. Submissions of Dewey scholarship, as well as work inspired by Dewey's many interests, are welcome. JDS members receive the journal as part of their membership in the society.

The journal publishes critical essays, research studies, essay and book reviews, and "rejoinder" essays. Recommended lengths vary for critical essays, research studies, or essay reviews (7500 words); book reviews (1000-2000 words); and commentaries or rejoinders to published pieces (800 words). Alternative or imaginative submissions, such as poetry, creative nonfiction, and narrative, will be considered; please consult the editor prior to submission.

Send submissions electronically to:
A. G. Rud, Editor
Education and Culture
Purdue University
eandc@purdue.edu

Manuscripts should be sent via e-mail attachment, preferably in rich text format (rtf), and should conform to *APA* or *Chicago* style. Please include complete contact information separate from the manuscript. There should be no author identifiers in the manuscript file, as the review process is anonymous. Most editorial decisions will be rendered within 4 months. Prospective authors are encouraged to contact the editor by e-mail with any questions.

Education and Training in Developmental Disabilities

ADDRESS FOR SUBMISSION:

Stanley H. Zucker, Editor
Education and Training in Developmental
Disabilities
Arizona State University
Special Education Program
Box 872011
Tempe, AZ 85287-2011
USA
Phone: 480-965-1449
Fax: 480-965-4942
E-Mail: etdd@asu.edu
Web: www.dddcec.org
Address May Change:

PUBLICATION GUIDELINES:

Manuscript Length: 16-20
Copies Required: Five
Computer Submission: No
Format: N/A
Fees to Review: 0.00 US$

Manuscript Style:
American Psychological Association

CIRCULATION DATA:

Reader: Practicing Teachers
Frequency of Issue: Quarterly
Copies per Issue: 5,001 - 10,000
Sponsor/Publisher: Professional Association
Subscribe Price: 30.00 US$ Individual
75.00 US$ Institution

REVIEW INFORMATION:

Type of Review: Blind Review
No. of External Reviewers: 3
No. of In House Reviewers: 1
Acceptance Rate: 30-40%
Time to Review: 2 - 3 Months
Reviewers Comments: Yes
Invited Articles: 0-5%
Fees to Publish: 0.00 US$

MANUSCRIPT TOPICS:
Special Education

MANUSCRIPT GUIDELINES/COMMENTS:

Education and Training in Developmental Disabilities focuses on the education and welfare of persons with developmental disabilities. *ETDD* invites research and expository manuscripts and critical reviews of the literature. Major emphasis is on identification and assessment, educational programming, characteristics, training of instructional personnel, habilitation, prevention, community understanding and provisions, and legislation.

Each manuscript is evaluated anonymously by three reviewers. Criteria for acceptance include the following: relevance, reader interest, quality, applicability, contribution to the field, and economy and smoothness of expression. The review process requires two to four months. Viewpoints expressed are those of the authors and do not necessarily conform to positions of the editors or of the officers of the Division.

Submission of Manuscripts

1. Manuscript submission is a representation that the manuscript is the author's own work, has not been published, and is not currently under consideration for publication elsewhere.

2. Manuscripts must be prepared according to the recommendations in the *Publication Manual of the American Psychological Association* (Fifth Edition, 2001). Standard typewriter type, laser or microprocessor dot printing are acceptable.

3. Each manuscript must have a cover sheet giving the names and affiliations of all authors and the address of the principal author.

4. Graphs and figures should be originals or sharp, high quality photographic prints suitable, if necessary, for a 50% reduction in size.

5. Five copies of the manuscript along with a transmittal letter should be sent to the Editor: Stanley H. Zucker, Special Education Program, PO Box 872011, Arizona State University, Tempe, A7 85287-2011.

6. Upon receipt, each manuscript will be screened by the editor. Appropriate manuscripts will then be sent to consulting editors. Principal authors will receive notification of receipt of manuscript

7. The Editor reserves the right to make minor editorial changes which do not materially affect the meaning of the text.

8. Manuscripts are the property of *ETDD* for a minimum period of six months. All articles accepted for publication are copyrighted in the name of the Division on Developmental Disabilities.

Education and Treatment of Children

ADDRESS FOR SUBMISSION:

Bernard Fabry, Managing Editor
Education and Treatment of Children
Western Psychiatric Institute & Clinic
4th Floor, Franklin Building
1011 Bingham Street
Pittsburgh, PA 15203
USA
Phone: 412-235-5320
Fax: 412-235-5387
E-Mail: bdfabry@aol.com
Web: See Guidelines
Address May Change:

CIRCULATION DATA:

Reader: , Varied
Frequency of Issue: Quarterly
Copies per Issue: Less than 1,000
Sponsor/Publisher: The Roscoe Ledger in
cooperation w/California Unv. of
Pennsylvania & West Virginia University
Subscribe Price: 40.00 US$ Individual
80.00 US$ Institution

PUBLICATION GUIDELINES:

Manuscript Length: N/A
Copies Required: N/A
Computer Submission: Yes
Format: MS Word or Adobe PDF
Fees to Review: 0.00 US$

Manuscript Style:
American Psychological Association

REVIEW INFORMATION:

Type of Review: Editorial Review
No. of External Reviewers: 2
No. of In House Reviewers: 2
Acceptance Rate: 21-30%
Time to Review: 2 - 3 Months
Reviewers Comments: Yes
Invited Articles: 11-20%
Fees to Publish: 0.00 US$

MANUSCRIPT TOPICS:

Community Psychology; Educational Psychology; Educational Technology Systems;
Elementary/Early Childhood; Mental Health; Reading; Residential/Foster Care;
Secondary/Adolescent Studies; Teacher Education; Tests, Measurement & Evaluation

MANUSCRIPT GUIDELINES/COMMENTS:

Topics continued. Applied Behavior Analysis of educational and treatment topics related to children and adolescents.

Journal's Website: **www.educationandtreatmentofchildren.net**

Education & Treatment of Children (ETC) is a journal devoted to the dissemination of information concerning the development and improvement of services for children and youth. Its primary criterion for publication is that the material be of direct value to educators and other childcare professionals in improving their teaching/training/ therapy effectiveness. Various types of material are appropriate for publication including original experimental research, experimental replications, data-based case studies, adaptations of previously reported research, research reviews, procedure or program descriptions, issue-oriented papers, and brief reader communications and inquiries. All non-experimental papers will concentrate on the manner in which the described procedure, program, issue, etc., may be applied or related to the practical concerns of professionals in the field.

ETC is a participant journal incorporating a broad base of researchers, educators, practitioners, and graduate students in the editorial review process. Experimental studies will be reviewed for the usefulness of the described procedure, the adequacy of the data in showing a functional relationship between the procedures and the observed behavioral changes, and the evidence that the measures taken were reliable. For non-experimental manuscripts the reviewers will base their judgments primarily on the relevance and/or utility of the content.

Manuscripts
Authors should submit electronic copies of their manuscript in either MS Word or Adobe PDF formats to the Managing Editor. Each copy should include a 100-150 word abstract. Figures must be in camera-ready form. Manuscripts should adhere to the format presented in the *American Psychological Association Publication Manual.*

Books for Review
Should be sent to the Managing Editor at the address.

Education & Treatment of Children is abstracted in Psychological Abstracts, Exceptional Child Education Resources, Child Development Abstracts and Bibliography, Clinical behavior Therapy Review, and Current Index to Journals in Education.

ETC is published by The Roscoe Ledger, Roscoe, PA in cooperation with West Virginia University and California University of Pennsylvania.

Education Research and Perspectives

ADDRESS FOR SUBMISSION:

Clive Whitehead & Marnie O'Neill, Editors
Education Research and Perspectives
The University of Western Australia
Graduate School of Education
Nedlands, WA 6907
Australia
Phone: +61 8 6488 2388
Fax: +61 8 6488 1052
E-Mail: clive.whitehead@uwa.edu.au
Web: See Guidelines
Address May Change:

PUBLICATION GUIDELINES:

Manuscript Length: 16-30
Copies Required: Three
Computer Submission: Yes Disk, Email
Format: Macintosh Office 98
Fees to Review: 0.00 US$

Manuscript Style:
    See Manuscript Guidelines

CIRCULATION DATA:

Reader: Academics
Frequency of Issue: 2 Times/Year
Copies per Issue: Less than 1,000
Sponsor/Publisher: Graduate School of
    Education
Subscribe Price: 40.00 AUS$

REVIEW INFORMATION:

Type of Review: Blind Review
No. of External Reviewers: 1
No. of In House Reviewers: 1
Acceptance Rate: 50-60%
Time to Review: 2 - 3 Months
Reviewers Comments: Yes
Invited Articles: 0-5%
Fees to Publish: 0.00 US$

MANUSCRIPT TOPICS:

Adult Career & Vocational; Art/Music; Audiology/Speech Pathology; Bilingual/E.S.L.; Counseling & Personnel Services; Curriculum Studies; Education Management/Administration; Educational Psychology; Educational Technology Systems; Elementary/Early Childhood; English Literature; Foreign Language; Gifted Children; Health & Physical Education; Higher Education; Languages & Linguistics; Library Science/Information Resources; Reading; Religious Education; Rural Education & Small Schools; School Law; Science Math & Environment; Secondary/Adolescent Studies; Social Studies/Social Science; Special Education; Teacher Education; Tests, Measurement & Evaluation; Urban Education, Cultural/Non-Traditional

MANUSCRIPT GUIDELINES/COMMENTS:

General Topics. In recent years subjects have included history and philosophy of education, curriculum history and theory, teaching, school effectiveness, educational mentoring, female academics, participant observation, and education as a university subject. In recent years two post-graduate theses have been published in full as separate issues.

This journal has been published continuously by the Department of Education/Graduate School of Education since December 1950. Initially it was published as *The Educand*.

In 1961 the title was changed to *The Australian journal of Higher Education*. The present title was adopted in 1974. Throughout its history, the journal has been multi-disciplinary in outlook, with a mixture of general issues and issues devoted to special topics. The range of authors is worldwide. The journal includes articles, review essays and book reviews. Since 1991 the journal has been free of charge on the internet at:

http://www.education.uwa.edu.au

The journal is published on a bi-annual basis (in June and December) and all articles are subject to external review and report. The present joint editors and their email addresses are as follows:

A/Prof. Clive Whitehead (**Clive.Whitehead@uwa.edu.au**) and
Dr. Marnie O'Neill (**Marnie.O'Neill@uwa.edu.au**)

For information about subscriptions to the hard copy edition of the journal or contributing articles see the end pages of any issue or contact one of the joint editors by email or by addressing correspondence to:

The Editors
Education Research and Perspectives
Graduate School of Education
The University of Western Australia
35 Stirling Highway, Crawley, WA 6009

Notes for Contributors
1. Each article should be less than 10,000 words in length.

2. Manuscripts should be submitted in both soft and hard copy.
- The soft copy to be submitted preferably in the word processing program Microsoft Word or WordPerfect in IBM or Macintosh version
- The hard copy should be an original printout in double-spaced typescript on one side only of opaque, white paper, leaving ample top and left-hand margins.

3. Tables and/or figures should be presented on separate sheets and only when essential. The position in the text should be clearly indicated.

4. The title of the article, author's name and affiliation should be set on a separate title page.

5. A mini-abstract, of not more than 100 words, should be provided at the head of the article.

6. Please also supply a three to four line autobiography (stating current academic position, institution, previous education and main research interests) for the 'Contributor's to this Issue' page.

7. Referencing: Due to the multi-disciplinary nature of the journal a variety of established forms of annotation are accepted. In each case it is imperative that authors remain *consistent* in their use of a reference style.

8. All articles submitted are subject to review and report.

Contributions should be addressed to
   The Editors, Education Research and Perspectives, Graduate School of Education
   The University of Western Australia, 35 Stirling Highway, Crawley, WA 6009 Australia

Further information on editorial matters will be supplied on application to the Editors.

Education Review

ADDRESS FOR SUBMISSION:

Gene V. Glass, Editor
Education Review
Arizona State University
College of Education
Tempe, AZ 85287-2411
USA
Phone: 480-965-2692
Fax:
E-Mail: glass@asu.edu
Web: http://edrev.asu.edu
Address May Change:

PUBLICATION GUIDELINES:

Manuscript Length: 11-15
Copies Required: No Paper Copies Req.
Computer Submission: Yes Disk, Email
Format: Rich Text Format
Fees to Review: 0.00 US$

Manuscript Style:
    American Psychological Association

CIRCULATION DATA:

Reader: Academics
Frequency of Issue: 50 Times/Year
Copies per Issue: N/A
Sponsor/Publisher: College of Education,
    Arizona State University
Subscribe Price: 0.00 US$

REVIEW INFORMATION:

Type of Review: Blind Review
No. of External Reviewers: 0
No. of In House Reviewers: 2
Acceptance Rate: 95%
Time to Review: 1 Month or Less
Reviewers Comments: Yes
Invited Articles: 50% +
Fees to Publish: 0.00 US$

MANUSCRIPT TOPICS:
Adult Career & Vocational; Art/Music; Audiology/Speech Pathology; Bilingual/E.S.L.;
Counseling & Personnel Services; Curriculum Studies; Education
Management/Administration; Educational Psychology; Educational Technology Systems;
Elementary/Early Childhood; English Literature; Foreign Language; Gifted Children; Health
& Physical Education; Higher Education; Languages & Linguistics; Library
Science/Information Resources; Reading; Religious Education; Rural Education & Small
Schools; School Law; Science Math & Environment; Secondary/Adolescent Studies; Social
Studies/Social Science; Special Education; Teacher Education; Tests, Measurement &
Evaluation; Urban Education, Cultural/Non-Traditional

MANUSCRIPT GUIDELINES/COMMENTS:

Education Review publishes reviews of recent books in education, covering the entire range of
education scholarship and practice. Reviews are archived and their publication announced by
means of a listserv (EDREV). The *Education Review* is made available to the public without
cost as a service of the College of Education at Arizona State University.

Procedures

All review articles must be submitted in electronic format (either on a floppy disk or transmitted over the Internet as an attachment to an email letter to the appropriate Editor:

Long reviews:
Gene V Glass, Editor **glass@asu.edu**

Brief reviews:
Kate Corby, Brief Reviews Editor **corby@msu.edu**

Reviews in Spanish or Portuguese:
Gustavo E. Fischman, Editor for Spanish & Portugese **fischman@asu.edu**

Reviews should be submitted in a standard word-processing format (such as Microsoft Word or WordPerfect) or, preferably, in "Rich Text Format." Long review articles should be between 2,500 and 5,000 words. Reviews outside these limits may be considered at the Editor's discretion. Brief Reviews call attention to current practical books for teachers and administrators. The Brief Reviews section publishes brief evaluative summaries of books from the current and previous year.

Every review article should begin by citing the book or books to be reviewed, with full bibliographic information including authors (please include first names), copyright date, full title including any subtitle, place of publication, publisher, number of pages, ISBN Number, and price if available. For example,

Hunt, Morton. (1997). How Science Takes Stock: The Story of Meta-Analysis. N.Y: Russell Sage Foundation. Pp. xii + 210. ISBN 0-87154-389-3. $38.95

References and all other citations of published work in the review itself should follow the form specified in the *Publication Manual of the American Psychological Association* (4th Edition). See http://www.apa.org/journals/faq.html. For example,

... as argued by Hedges (1982) in his investigation into the reliability of observations in the physical sciences."

And then in the References at the end of the review, the citation of Hedges (1982) would appear as follows:

References

Hedges, L.V. (1982). How hard is hard science, how soft is soft science? The empirical cumulativeness of research. American Psychologist, 42, 443-455.

Footnotes are not permitted; auxiliary information normally included in footnotes should be included in Endnotes that appear directly before any References at the end of the review.

Submitted articles should be accompanied by a paragraph describing the review author's institutional affiliation and areas of interest.

Editorial Policy
All accepted articles are subject to copyediting by the Editor, including editing for length and format consistency, as well as editing for content. All changes will be submitted to authors for final approval before publication.

Copyright Policy
Copyright for all articles published in *ER* will be retained by the authors. Permission to use any copyrighted material in review articles, or permission to republish reviews also being published elsewhere, must be obtained by the author prior to publication in *ER*.

Review Procedures and Criteria
Review articles are either solicited by the Editor, or offered unsolicited by reviewers. In either case, decisions on acceptance for publication are made by the Editor, who may on occasion solicit assistance from other readers in helping them make a decision. However, the articles are not typically refereed by any standard anonymous review process. In making his decision, the Editor will be guided by the following criteria:

- Does the review help readers form a clear idea of the contents of the book under consideration?
- Is the review fair and accurate in its presentation of the evidence, arguments, and methodology of the book?
- Does the review present a reasoned evaluation of the book and its conclusions?
- Is the article written in a manner that will promote understanding and further discussion? Is it respectful in tone?
- Does the article satisfy editorial standards of clarity of presentation, organization of ideas, and quality of writing?
- Does the article fit within the specific format and length requirements of this journal?

If you are interested in writing a review for *ER*, please contact the Editor at **glass@asu.edu**. *Education Review* discourages unsolicited submissions of book reviews conducted by students, advisees, colleagues, spouses, or personal friends of a book's author. Such relations place the reviewer's credibility into question and could, in certain situations, make a reviewer vulnerable to an untenable conflict of interest.

Publication of commissioned articles is presumed, but only when in the Editor's judgment the criteria listed above are satisfied. In addition, *ER* is committed to prompt turnaround times on its reviews, and commissioned articles should be completed by the agreed upon deadline. Failure to meet such deadlines removes any obligation to publish the article, although this decision remains at the Editor's discretion.

Education Technology & Society

ADDRESS FOR SUBMISSION:

Prof. Kinshuk, Editor
Education Technology & Society
Massey University
Information System Department
Private Bag 11-222
Palmerston North,
New Zealand
Phone: +64 6 350 5799 ext. 2090
Fax: +64 6 350 5725
E-Mail: kinshuk@ieee.org
Web: ifets.ieee.org/periodical/
Address May Change:

PUBLICATION GUIDELINES:

Manuscript Length: 4,000-7,000 words
Copies Required: No Paper Copies
Computer Submission: Yes Email
Format: Word, RTF
Fees to Review: 0.00 US$

Manuscript Style:
    American Psychological Association

CIRCULATION DATA:

Reader: Practicing Teachers, Academics,
    Educational System Developers
Frequency of Issue: Quarterly
Copies per Issue: 500+
Sponsor/Publisher: International Forum on
    Educational Technology & Society
Subscribe Price: Free-Online
    89.00 NZ + 12.5% tax Individual
    107.00 NZ + 12.5% tax Institution

REVIEW INFORMATION:

Type of Review: Blind Review
No. of External Reviewers: 3+
No. of In House Reviewers: 0
Acceptance Rate: 11-20%
Time to Review: 1-3 Months
Reviewers Comments: Yes
Invited Articles: 0-5%
Fees to Publish: 0.00 US$

MANUSCRIPT TOPICS:
Educational Technology Systems; Higher Education

MANUSCRIPT GUIDELINES/COMMENTS:

Scope of the Journal
Educational Technology & Society is a quarterly journal (January, April, July and October), but the articles will be published as soon as they are ready for publication (benefit of the electronic medium!), so that the issue will be built up and at any moment, one issue of the journal would be available to accept the articles.

Educational Technology & Society seeks academic articles on the issues affecting the developers of educational systems and educators who implement and manage such systems. The articles should discuss the perspectives of both communities and their relation to each other:

- Educators aim to use technology to enhance individual learning as well as to achieve widespread education and expect the technology to blend with their individual approach to instruction. However, most educators are not fully aware of the benefits that may be obtained by proactively harnessing the available technologies and how they might be able to influence further developments through systematic feedback and suggestions.

- Educational system developers and artificial intelligence (AI) researchers are sometimes unaware of the needs and requirements of typical teachers, with a possible exception of those in the computer science domain. In transferring the notion of a 'user' from the human-computer interaction studies and assigning it to the 'student', the educator's role as the 'implementer/ manager/ user' of the technology has been forgotten.

The aim of the journal is to help them better understand each other's role in the overall process of education and how they may support each other. The articles should be original, unpublished, and not in consideration for publication elsewhere at the time of submission to *Educational Technology & Society* and three months thereafter.

The scope of the journal is very broad as can be seen from the following list of topics considered to be within the scope of the journal:

- Architectures for Educational Technology Systems
- Computer-Mediated Communication
- Cooperative/Collaborative Learning and Environments
- Cultural Issues in Educational System development
- Didactic/Pedagogical Issues and Teaching/Learning Strategies
- Distance Education/Learning
- Distance Learning Systems
- Distributed Learning Environments
- Educational Multimedia
- Evaluation
- Human-Computer Interface (HCI) Issues
- Hypermedia Systems/Applications
- Intelligent Learning/Tutoring Environments
- Interactive Learning Environments
- Learning by Doing
- Methodologies for Development of Educational Technology Systems
- Multimedia Systems/Applications
- Network-Based Learning Environments
- Online Education
- Simulations for Learning
- Web Based Instruction/Training

Peer Review Manuscript Preparation Guidelines
(These guidelines apply to all full length papers, short papers, critiques and case studies)

Word length of submission
- Full paper: 4000 to 7000 words
- Short paper: up to 3000 words
- Critique: up to 3000 words
- Case study: up to 3000 words

General Guidelines

Each article should have at least the following items:

- title (up to 10 words)
- complete communication details of all authors
- an informative abstract (75 to 200 words) presenting the main points of the paper and the author's conclusions
- four - five descriptive keywords
- main body of paper
- conclusion
- references

Submissions should be single spaced.

Footnotes and endnotes are not accepted, all such information should be included in main text.

The paragraphs should not be indented. There should be one line space between consecutive paragraphs.

There should be single space between full stop of previous sentence and first word of next sentence in a paragraph.

The keywords (just after the abstract) should be separated by **comma**, and each keyword phrase should have initial caps (for example, Internet based system, Distance learning).

Do not use 'underline' to highlight text. Use '*italic*' instead.

Headings

Articles should be subdivided into unnumbered sections, using short, meaningful sub-headings. Please use only two level headings as far as possible. Use 'Heading 1' and 'Heading 2' styles of your word processor's template to indicate them. If that is not possible, use 12 point bold for first level headings and 10 point bold for second level heading. If you must use third level headings, use 10 point italic for this purpose.

There should be one blank line after each heading and two blank lines before each heading (except when two headings are consecutive, there should be one blank like between them).

Tables

Tables should be included in the text at appropriate places and centered horizontally. Captions (maximum 6 to 8 words each) must be provided for every table (below the table) and must be referenced in the text.

Figures

Figures should be included in the text at appropriate places and centered horizontally. Captions (maximum 6 to 8 words each) must be provided for every figure (below the figure) and must be referenced in the text. The figures must **NOT** be larger than 500 pixels in width. Please also provide all figures separately (besides embedding them in the text).

References

- All references should be listed in alphabetical order at the end of the article under the heading 'References.'

- All references must be cited in the article using "authors (year)" style e.g. Merrill & Twitchell (1994) or "(authors1, year1; authors2, year2)" style e.g. (Merrill, 1999; Kommers et al., 1997).
- **Do not use numbering style to cite the reference in the text** e.g. "this was done in this way and was found successful [23]."
- It is important to provide complete information in references. Please follow the patterns below:

Journal article
Laszlo, A. & Castro, K. (1995). Technology and values: Interactive learning environments for future generations. *Educational Technology*, 35 (2), 7-13.

Newspaper article
Blunkett, D. (1998). Cash for Competence. *Times Educational Supplement*, July 24, 1998, 15.
or
Clark, E. (1999). There'll never be enough bandwidth. *Personal Computer World*, July 26, 1999, http://www.vnunet.co.uk/News/88174.

Book (authored or edited)
Brown, S. & McIntyre, D. (1993). *Making sense of Teaching*, Buckingham: Open University.

Chapter in book/proceedings
Malone, T. W. (1984). Toward a theory of intrinsically motivating instruction. In Walker, D. F. & Hess, R. D. (Eds.) *Instructional software: principles and perspectives for design and use*, California: Wadsworth Publishing Company, 68-95.

Internet reference
Fulton, J. C. (1996). *Writing assignment as windows, not walls: enlivening unboundedness through boundaries*, http://leahi.kcc.hawaii.edu/org/tcc-conf96/fulton.html.

Educational Foundations

ADDRESS FOR SUBMISSION:

William T. Pink, Editor
Educational Foundations
Marquette University
School of Education
Dept. of Educational Policy & Leadership
P.O. Box 1881
Milwaukee, WI 53201-1811
USA
Phone: 414-288-1421
Fax: 414-288-3945
E-Mail: william.pink@marquette.edu
Web:
Address May Change:

PUBLICATION GUIDELINES:

Manuscript Length: 16-25
Copies Required: Three
Computer Submission: No
Format: N/A
Fees to Review: 0.00 US$

Manuscript Style:
    Chicago Manual of Style

CIRCULATION DATA:

Reader: Academics
Frequency of Issue: Quarterly
Copies per Issue: Less than 1,000
Sponsor/Publisher: American Educational
    Studies Association / Caddo Gap Press
Subscribe Price: 50.00 US$ Individual
    80.00 US$ Institution/ $100 Non U.S.
    30.00 US$ AESA Member

REVIEW INFORMATION:

Type of Review: Blind Review
No. of External Reviewers: 2
No. of In House Reviewers: 1
Acceptance Rate: 35%
Time to Review: 1 - 2 Months
Reviewers Comments: Yes
Invited Articles: 0-5%
Fees to Publish: 0.00 US$

MANUSCRIPT TOPICS:
Curriculum Studies; Education Management/Administration; Educational Foundations;
Educational Psychology; Elementary/Early Childhood; Higher Education; Rural Education &
Small Schools; Secondary/Adolescent Studies; Social Studies/Social Science; Special
Education; Teacher Education; Tests, Measurement & Evaluation; Urban Education,
Cultural/Non-Traditional

MANUSCRIPT GUIDELINES/COMMENTS:

Educational Foundations seeks to help fulfill the stated mission of the American Educational
Studies Association to enhance scholarship in and among the educational foundations
disciplines by providing a vehicle for publication of articles and essays which feature analysis
of the foundations, of foundations methodology, of applications of such methodology to key
issues of the day, and of significant research which evolves from and unifies the foundations
disciplines, all focusing on the interdisciplinary nature of the educational foundations fields.

Educational Foundations seeks articles and essays in four primary areas:

1. Exposition on the nature of the educational foundations – essays exploring the foundations, highlighting definition, interrelationships, strengths, difficulties, and other aspects of the combined fields.

2. Application of the foundations disciplines to an issue of significance – collections of articles and around a specific theme, bringing to bear the nature of the various foundations disciplines on such themes. Information concerning themes for future issues of the journal may be obtained from the co-editors.

3. Methodology – articles exploring methodological issues of the foundations fields, stressing similarities and differences among the disciplines.

4. Research – articles describing or reporting on new research in the foundations fields, with emphasis on interdisciplinary aspects of such research.

Contributions of *Educational Foundations* are solicited from members of the American Education Studies Association as well as from all other scholars in the foundations of education and related fields of study. While the journal is open to submissions from all interested scholars, the standards for review and acceptance of articles and essays are stringent. Submissions should follow the *Chicago Manual of Style*, with a suggested length of 25-30 double-spaced pages, and be sent in triplicate to: William T. Pink, Editor, *Educational Foundations*, Department of Educational Policy and Leadership, School of Education, Marquette University, Post Office. Box 1881, Milwaukee, Wisconsin 53201-1811. When an article is accepted, authors are asked to submit the final version of their article on computer disk.

Educational Horizons

ADDRESS FOR SUBMISSION:

Managing Editor
Educational Horizons
4101 East Third Street
PO Box 6626
Bloomington, IN 47407-6626
USA
Phone: 812-339-3411
Fax: 812-339-3462
E-Mail: publications@pilambda.org
Web: www.pilambda.org
Address May Change:

CIRCULATION DATA:

Reader: , Educators
Frequency of Issue: Quarterly
Copies per Issue: 10,001 - 25,000
Sponsor/Publisher: Pi Lambda Theta
   International Honor Society and
   Professional Association in Education
Subscribe Price: 18.00 US$

PUBLICATION GUIDELINES:

Manuscript Length: Average 3,000 words
Copies Required: One SASE
Computer Submission: Yes Email preferred
Format: N/A
Fees to Review: 0.00 US$

Manuscript Style:
   , N/A. Any consistent, accurate note
   style accepted.

REVIEW INFORMATION:

Type of Review: Optional
No. of External Reviewers: N/A
No. of In House Reviewers: N/A
Acceptance Rate: N/A
Time to Review: 2 - 3 Months
Reviewers Comments: No
Invited Articles: 50% +
Fees to Publish: 0.00 US$

MANUSCRIPT TOPICS:
Curriculum; Curriculum Studies; Educational Psychology; Educational Technology Systems; Elementary/Early Childhood; Ethical Teaching; Reading; Restructuring Textbooks; Rural Education & Small Schools; Schooling for Democracy; Urban Education, Cultural/Non-Traditional

MANUSCRIPT GUIDELINES/COMMENTS:

Educational Horizons is the official publication of Pi Lambda Theta International Honor Society and Professional Association in Education.

Manuscripts for *Educational Horizons* should be double-spaced, not to exceed 4,000 words in length. Do not use running heads that identify author's name. Length of article is not a determiner of publication potential. Include the title on page 1 to facilitate blind reviews.

Note Style
Notes should be accurate and consistent, whatever style the author prefers. Please avoid using auto-generated footnote functions.

Illustrations and Photographs
Illustrations and photographs are seldom used. Credit will be given to the photographer when specified.

Biographical Information
A bibliographical note accompanies each published article. Please include:

1. present professional position of the author;
2. place of employment; and
3. previous professional experience pertinent to the authority of the article.

Note: Include a self-addressed, postpaid, 9" x 12" envelope for return of all manuscripts that may not be accepted for publication.

Educational Perspectives

ADDRESS FOR SUBMISSION:

Hunter McEwan, Editor
Educational Perspectives
University of Hawaii
College of Education
Wist Hall 112
1776 University Avenue
Honolulu, HI 96822
USA
Phone: 808-956-4242
Fax: 808-956-9100
E-Mail: epedit@hawaii.edu
Web: www.hawaii.edu/edper/
Address May Change:

PUBLICATION GUIDELINES:

Manuscript Length: 16-20
Copies Required: One
Computer Submission: Yes Email
Format: Word . RTF
Fees to Review: 0.00 US$

Manuscript Style:
    Chicago Manual of Style

CIRCULATION DATA:

Reader: Practicing Teachers, Academics
Frequency of Issue: 2 Times/Year
Copies per Issue: 1,001 - 2,000
Sponsor/Publisher: College of Education,
    University of Hawaii
Subscribe Price: 10.00 US$

REVIEW INFORMATION:

Type of Review: Editorial Review
No. of External Reviewers: No Reply
No. of In House Reviewers: No Reply
Acceptance Rate: No Reply
Time to Review: 1 - 2 Months
Reviewers Comments: No
Invited Articles: 90%+
Fees to Publish: 0.00 US$

MANUSCRIPT TOPICS:

Curriculum Studies; Education Management/Administration; Educational Technology Systems; General Issues in Education; Health & Physical Education; Reading; School Law; Teacher Education; Tests, Measurement & Evaluation

MANUSCRIPT GUIDELINES/COMMENTS:

Educational Perspectives is a theme-based publication. Information about forthcoming themes can be obtained at the website **http://www.hawaii.edu/edper**.

Educational Perspectives, the Journal of the College of Education, University of Hawaii at Manoa, is now in its 38th year of publication. It is a professional journal of recognized stature, having been cited for Superior Achievement by the Educational Press Association of America (EdPress) on six separate occasions. It is a 32-page, semiannual publication with a circulation of 1,200. In addition to serving a local need in educational publication, *Educational Perspectives* is in the collection of 500 colleges and universities in the United States, including Stanford, Harvard, Yale, Columbia, The University of Michigan, University of California at Berkeley, and the University of California at Los Angeles.

Internationally, it is mailed to 200 educational institutions, including the College of Education (Lagos, Nigeria), Institut Nauchnoi Informatsii (Moscow, Russia) Chinese University (Hong Kiong), Institut Pedagogique National (Paris, France), University College of Dar es Salaam (Tanzania), Shanghai Normal University (Peoples Republic of China), Universita Karlova (Prague, Czech Republic), Universitas Indonesia (Jakarta), Universitetbiblioteket (Oslo, Norway), Universite de Moncton (New Brunswick, Canada), and the University of the South Pacific (Suva, Fiji).

Educational Perspectives is also received by colleges and universities in Japan, Korea, Taiwan, the Philippines, Mexico, Chile, Colombia, Australia, England, Sweden and India.

The major professional educational publication in the State of Hawaii, *Educational Perspectives* provides a forum for the discussion of educational issues in Hawaii and the Pacific, enabling dissemination of these ideas to other parts of the world.

The University of Hawaii Libraries uses *Educational Perspectives* as a one of the publications in its Gifts and Exchange Program with other colleges and universities.

Educational Perspectives is indexed nationally and internationally in the Standard Periodical Dictionary, Ulrich's International Periodicals Directory, EdPress Directory, and Xerox University microfilms (Michigan, Canada and England).

Preparing & Submitting a Manuscript
When preparing a manuscript for submission to *Educational Perspectives,* the following specifications should be followed:
- Length of manuscript 3,000 to 3,500 words.
- Manuscript should be typewritten, double-spaced.
- Manuscript should be submitted using two formats: 1) a computer program which can be converted into a MacIntosh Pagemaker 6.5 application and 2) one Xeroxed copy.
- Manuscript should be documented and *Chicago Manual of Style* should be followed; footnotes and bibliography included where needed.
- Subheads are desirable.
- Suitable visual material (photographs should accompany the manuscript and should be high contrast, black and white, glossy prints, 8"x10" or contact sheets with negatives).
- Colored slides, 2"x2" may be requested for use as front cover).
- A brief biographical sketch of manuscript's author(s).
- Reworked speeches are acceptable. Reprints from other publications are not used.

All material (manuscript, photography and biography) should be submitted to:
The Editor, Educational Perspectives, College of Education, University of Hawaii, Wist Hall, Room 113, 1776 University Avenue, Honolulu HI 96822

Educational Philosophy and Theory

ADDRESS FOR SUBMISSION:

Michael Peters, Editor
Educational Philosophy and Theory
University of Auckland
School of Education
Private Bag 92019
Auckland,
New Zealand
Phone: +64 9 373.7599 ext. 5044
Fax: +64 9 373 7455
E-Mail: ma.peters@educ.gla.ac.nz
Web:
Address May Change:

PUBLICATION GUIDELINES:

Manuscript Length: 26-30
Copies Required: Three
Computer Submission: Yes
Format: Word Document
Fees to Review: 0.00 US$

Manuscript Style:
    See Manuscript Guidelines

CIRCULATION DATA:

Reader: Academics
Frequency of Issue: Quarterly
Copies per Issue: 1,001 - 2,000
Sponsor/Publisher: Australasian Philosophy
    of Education Association (PESA)
Subscribe Price: 97.00 US$ Individual
    264.00 US$ Institution

REVIEW INFORMATION:

Type of Review: Blind Review
No. of External Reviewers: 2
No. of In House Reviewers: 1
Acceptance Rate: 11-20%
Time to Review: 2 - 3 Months
Reviewers Comments: Yes
Invited Articles: 6-10%
Fees to Publish: 0.00 US$

MANUSCRIPT TOPICS:
Curriculum Studies; Education Management/Administration; Educational Theory & Research Studies; Higher Education

MANUSCRIPT GUIDELINES/COMMENTS:

Aims and Scope
Educational Philosophy and Theory publishes articles concerned with all aspects of educational philosophy. It will also consider manuscripts from other areas of pure or applied educational research. In this latter category the journal has published manuscripts concerned with curriculum theory, educational administration, the politics of education, educational history, educational policy, and higher education.

As part of the journal's commitment to extending the dialogues of educational philosophy to the profession and education's several disciplines, it encourages the submission of manuscripts from collateral areas of study in education, the arts, and sciences, as well as from professional educators.

Nevertheless, manuscripts must be germane to the ongoing conversations and dialogues of educational philosophy.

Author Guidelines

All editorial enquiries and manuscripts should be sent to Professor Michael Peters, Executive Editor, EPAT, Room 312, St. Andrew's Building, University of Glasgow, Glasgow G12 8QH. Email: **ma.peters@educ.gla.ac.uk**

Editorial Policy. *Educational Philosophy and Theory* is an international, blind refereed journal that publishes articles concerned with all aspects of educational philosophy. The journal will also consider manuscripts from other areas of pure or applied educational research. In this latter category the journal has published manuscripts concerned with curriculum theory, educational administration, the politics of education, educational history, educational policy, and higher education. As part of the journal's commitment to extending the dialogues of educational philosophy to the profession and education's several disciplines, it encourages the submission of manuscripts from collateral areas of study in education, the arts, and sciences, as well as from professional educators. Nevertheless, manuscripts must be germane to the ongoing conversations and dialogues of educational philosophy.

Manuscript Information. All manuscripts should be prepared on A4 letter or US letter paper. Manuscripts must be typed and double-spaced. Authors must provide *three hard copies* of their manuscript and a copy via email to Michael Peters (address above). Manuscripts cannot be returned.

Articles should be prepared in accordance with the requirements of the author-date system with endnotes and references. The references should be listed in full, including pages, at the end of the paper in the following standard form:

For books: Beck, U. (1992) *Risk Society* (London, Sage).

For articles: Papastaphanou, M. (2002a) Linguistic Archipelago, *Metaphilosophy*, 33:4.

For chapters within books: Coffield, F. (1997) Nine Learning Facilities, in: F. Coffield (ed.) A *National Strategy for Lifelong Learning* (Newcastle, Department of Education).

Further points of style may be found on the PDF document of the style sheet:
http://www.blackwellpublishing.com/pdf/EPAT.pdf

Successful authors are asked to submit final manuscripts on disk.
Preferred format: IBM PC, or compatible.
Preferred application: Word. Other major applications acceptable, but should be saved as text only.

Offprints. A PDF offprint will be sent to each contributor once the issue has been printed.

Educational Studies

ADDRESS FOR SUBMISSION:

Derek Cherrington, Editor
Educational Studies
University of Gloucestershire
Faculty of Education and Social Sciences
Francis Close Hall
Swindon Road
Cheltenham, Glos, GL50 4AZ
UK
Phone: 01452 813 887
Fax:
E-Mail: elsmac2000@yahoo.co.uk
Web: www.tandf.co.uk/journals
Address May Change:

PUBLICATION GUIDELINES:

Manuscript Length: 16-20
Copies Required: Two
Computer Submission: Yes Email
Format: MS Word
Fees to Review: 0.00 US$

Manuscript Style:
　　See Manuscript Guidelines

CIRCULATION DATA:

Reader: Academics
Frequency of Issue: Quarterly
Copies per Issue:
Sponsor/Publisher: Taylor & Francis
Subscribe Price: 147.00 US$ Individual
　　1205.00 US$ Institution/Library

REVIEW INFORMATION:

Type of Review: Editorial Review
No. of External Reviewers: 3+
No. of In House Reviewers: 0
Acceptance Rate: 40%
Time to Review: 1 - 2 Months
Reviewers Comments: No
Invited Articles: 0-5%
Fees to Publish: 0.00 US$

MANUSCRIPT TOPICS:
Social Studies/Social Science

MANUSCRIPT GUIDELINES/COMMENTS:

Aims and Scope
Educational Studies aims to provide a forum for original investigations and theoretical studies in education. Whilst the journal is principally concerned with the social sciences, contributions from a wider field are encouraged. The editorial board intends to publish fully refereed papers which cover applied and theoretical approaches to the study of education and its closely related disciplines. Such papers may take the form of reports of experimental research, review articles, shorter notes and discussions.

Instructions for Authors
Note to Authors: please make sure your contact address information is clearly visible on the **outside** of all packages you are sending to Editors.

262

Papers accepted become the copyright of the Journal.

Manuscripts should be sent to the Editor, Professor Derek Cherrington, Faculty of Education and Social Sciences, University of Gloucestershire, Francis Close Hall, Swindon Road, Cheltenham, Glos. GL50 4AZ, UK. Articles can only be considered if at least **two complete copies of each manuscript** are submitted. They should be typed on one side of the paper, double spaced, with ample margins, and bear the title of the contribution, name(s) of the author(s) and the address where the work was carried out. The editor would be pleased to accept short papers and would not expect any manuscript to exceed 5000 words. Each article should be accompanied by a summary of 100-150 words on a separate sheet. The full postal address of the author who will check proofs and receive correspondence should also be included. All pages should be numbered. It would be a help to the Editor if a duplicate copy is also submitted. Authors may also submit their papers, electronically, in MS Word format via e-mail to the journal. Please send papers to *Educational Studies*.

Footnotes to the text should be avoided.

Tables and captions to illustrations. Tables must be typed out on separate sheets and not included as part of the text. The captions to illustrations should be gathered together and also typed out on a separate sheet. Tables should be numbered by Roman numerals, and figures by Arabic numerals. The approximate position of tables and figures should be indicated in the manuscript. Captions should include keys to symbols.

Figures. Please supply one set of artwork in a finished form, suitable for reproduction. If this is not possible, figures can be redrawn by the publisher.

References should be indicated in the typescript by giving the author's name, with the year of publication in parentheses. If several papers by the same author and from the same year are cited, a, b, c, etc. should be put after the year of publication. The references should be listed in full at the end of the paper in the following standard form:

For books: SCOTT, P. (1984) **The Crisis of the University** (London, Croom Helm).

For articles: CREMIN, L. A. (1983) The problematics of education in the 1980s: some reflections on the Oxford Workshop, **Oxford Review of Education**, 9, pp. 33-40.

For chapters within books: WILLIS, P. (1983) Cultural production and theories of reproduction, in: L. BARTON & S. WALKER (Eds) Race, Class and Education (London, Croom Helm).

Titles of journals should **not** be abbreviated.

If you have any further questions about the style for this journal, please submit your questions using the **Style Queries** form.

Proofs will be sent to authors if there is sufficient time to do so. They should be corrected and returned to the Editor within three days. Major alterations to the text cannot be accepted.

Early Electronic Offprints. Corresponding authors can now receive their article by e-mail as a complete PDF. This allows the author to print up to 50 copies, free of charge, and disseminate them to colleagues. In many cases this facility will be available up to two weeks prior to publication. Or, alternatively, corresponding authors will receive the traditional 50 offprints. A copy of the journal will be sent by post to all corresponding authors after publication. Additional copies of the journal can be purchased at the author's preferential rate of £15.00/$25.00 per copy.

Educational Studies in Mathematics

ADDRESS FOR SUBMISSION:

Anna Sierpinska, Editor
Educational Studies in Mathematics
Concordia University
Department of Mathematics and Statistics
7141 Sherbrooke St. West
Montreal, Quebec, H4B 1R6
Canada
Phone: 514-848-3239
Fax: 514-848-2831
E-Mail: www.editorialmanager.com/educ
Web: www.editorialmanager.com/educ
Address May Change:

PUBLICATION GUIDELINES:

Manuscript Length: 21-25
Copies Required: Four
Computer Submission: Yes
Format:
Fees to Review: 0.00 US$

Manuscript Style:
   See Manuscript Guidelines

CIRCULATION DATA:

Reader: Academics
Frequency of Issue: 9 Times/Year
Copies per Issue: 1,001 - 2,000
Sponsor/Publisher: Kluwer Academic
   Publishers
Subscribe Price: 265.00 US$ Individual
   700.00 US$ Institution
   240.00 Euro Indv. - $700 Euro Inst.

REVIEW INFORMATION:

Type of Review: Editorial Review
No. of External Reviewers: 2
No. of In House Reviewers: 0
Acceptance Rate: 20%
Time to Review: 2 - 3 Months
Reviewers Comments: Yes
Invited Articles: 0-5%
Fees to Publish: 0.00 US$

MANUSCRIPT TOPICS:
Educational Technology Systems; Science Math & Environment; Teacher Education

MANUSCRIPT GUIDELINES/COMMENTS:

Aims & Scope
Educational Studies in Mathematics presents new ideas and developments of major importance to those working in the field of mathematical education. It seeks to reflect both the variety of research concerns within this field and the range of methods used to study them. It deals with didactical, methodological and pedagogical subjects, rather than with specific programmes for teaching mathematics.

All papers are strictly refereed and the emphasis is on high-level articles which are of more than local or national interest. All contributions to this journal are peer reviewed.

Online Manuscript Submission
Kluwer Academic Publishers now offers authors, editors and reviewers of *Educational Studies in Mathematics* the option of using our fully web-enabled online manuscript submission and

review system. To keep the review time as short as possible (no postal delays!) we encourage authors to submit manuscripts online to the journal's editorial office. Our online manuscript submission and review system offers authors the option to track the progress of the review process of manuscripts in real time. Manuscripts should be submitted to:

www.editorialmanager.com/educ

The online manuscript submission and review system for *Educational Studies in Mathematics* offers easy and straightforward log-in and submission procedures. This system supports a wide range of submission file formats: for manuscripts - Word, WordPerfect, RTF, TXT and LaTex; for figures - TIFF, GIF, JPEG, EPS, PPT, and Postscript.

Note. By using the online manuscript submission and review system, it is NOT necessary to submit the manuscript also in printout + disk. In case you encounter any difficulties while submitting your manuscript on line, please get in touch with the responsible Editorial Assistant by clicking on CONTACT US from the tool bar.

LaTex

For submission in LaTeX, *Kluwer Academic Publishers* have developed a Kluwer LaTeX class file, which can be downloaded from: http://www.wkap.nl/authors/jrnlstylefiles/

Use of this class file is highly recommended. Do not use versions downloaded from other sites. Technical support is available at: texhelp@wkap.nl. If you are not familiar with TeX/LaTeX, the class file will be of no use to you. In that case, submit your article in a common word processor format.

Manuscript Presentation

The journal's language is English. British English or American English spelling and terminology may be used, but either one should be followed consistently throughout the article. Manuscripts should be printed or typewritten on A4 or US Letter bond paper, one side only, leaving adequate margins on all sides to allow reviewers' remarks. Please double-space all material, including notes and references. Quotations of more than 40 words should be set off clearly, either by indenting the left-hand margin or by using a smaller typeface. Use double quotation marks for direct quotations and single quotation marks for quotations within quotations and for words or phrases used in a special sense.

Number the pages consecutively with the first page containing:
- running head (shortened title, which should not exceed 43 characters, including spaces)
- title
- author(s)
- affiliation(s)
- full address for correspondence, including telephone and fax number and e-mail address.

Abstract

Please provide a short abstract of 100 to 250 words in English, and also an abstract in the language in which the article is written, if other than English. The abstract should not contain any undefined abbreviations or unspecified references.

Key Words
Please provide 5 to 10 key words or short phrases in alphabetical order.

Symbols and Units
Unusual symbols should be identified in the margin, and an alternative or equivalent symbol or sign should be provided if the one required is rare. Special care should be taken to distinguish between the letter O and zero, the letter l and the number one, kappa and K, mu and u, nu and v, eta and n. Subscripts and superscripts should be marked if not clear. The use of italics is to be indicated by single underlining; bold-face by wavy underlining.

Figures and Tables
Submission of electronic figures
In addition to hard-copy printouts of figures, authors are requested to supply the electronic versions of figures in either Encapsulated PostScript (EPS) or TIFF format. Many other formats, e.g., Proprietary Formats, PiCT (Macintosh) and WMF (Windows), cannot be used and the hard copy will be scanned instead.

Figures should be saved in separate files *without* their captions, which should be included with the text of the article. Files should be named according to DOS conventions, e.g., 'figure1.eps'. For vector graphics, EPS is the preferred format. Lines should not be thinner than 0.25pts and in-fill patterns and screens should have a density of at least 10%. Font-related problems can be avoided by using standard fonts such as Times Roman and Helvetica. For bitmapped graphics, TIFF is the preferred format but EPS is also acceptable. The following resolutions are optimal: black-and-white line figures - 600 - 1200 dpi; line figures with some grey or coloured lines - 600 dpi; photographs - 300 dpi; screen dumps - leave as is. Higher resolutions will not improve output quality but will only increase file size, which may cause problems with printing; lower resolutions may compromise output quality. Please try to provide artwork that approximately fits within the typeset area of the journal. Especially screened originals, i.e. originals with grey areas, may suffer badly from reduction by more than 10-15%.

AVOIDING PROBLEMS WITH EPS GRAPHICS
Please always check whether the figures print correctly to a PostScript printer in a reasonable amount of time. If they do not, simplify your figures or use a different graphics program.

If EPS export does not produce acceptable output, try to create an EPS file with the printer driver (see below). This option is unavailable with the Microsoft driver for Windows NT, so if you run Windows NT, get the Adobe driver from the Adobe site (www.adobe.com).

If EPS export is not an option, e.g., because you rely on OLE and cannot create separate files for your graphics, it may help us if you simply provide a PostScript dump of the entire document.

HOW TO SET UP FOR EPS AND POSTSCRIPT DUMPS UNDER WINDOWS
Create a printer entry specifically for this purpose: install the printer 'Apple LaserWriter Plus' and specify 'FILE': as printer port. Each time you send something to the 'printer' you will be asked for a filename. This file will be the EPS file or PostScript dump that we can use.

The EPS export option can be found under the PostScript tab. EPS export should be used only for single-page documents. For printing a document of several pages, select 'Optimise for portability' instead. The option 'Download header with each job' should be checked.

Submission of hard-copy figures
If no electronic versions of figures are available, submit only high-quality artwork that can be reproduced as is, i.e., without any part having to be redrawn or re-typeset. The letter size of any text in the figures must be large enough to allow for reduction. Photographs should be in black-and-white on glossy paper. If a figure contains colour, make absolutely clear whether it should be printed in black-and-white or in colour. Figures that are to be printed in black-and-white should not be submitted in colour. Authors will be charged for reproducing figures in colour.

Each figure and table should be numbered and mentioned in the text. The approximate position of figures and tables should be indicated in the margin of the manuscript. On the reverse side of each figure, the name of the (first) author and the figure number should be written in pencil; the top of the figure should be clearly indicated. Figures and tables should be placed at the end of the manuscript following the Reference section. Each figure and table should be accompanied by an explanatory legend. The figure legends should be grouped and placed on a separate page. Figures are not returned to the author unless specifically requested.

In tables, footnotes are preferable to long explanatory material in either the heading or body of the table. Such explanatory footnotes, identified by superscript letters, should be placed immediately below the table. Number all tables with Roman numerals. Vertical lines between the columns are to be avoided.

Section Headings
Section headings should be numbered (e.g., 1., 1.1, 1.1.1, 2., 2.1, etc.).

Appendices
Supplementary material should be collected in an Appendix and placed before the Notes and Reference sections.

Notes
Please use endnotes rather than footnotes. Notes should be indicated by consecutive superscript numbers in the text and listed at the end of the article before the References. A source reference note should be indicated by means of an asterisk after the title. This note should be placed at the bottom of the first page.

Cross-Referencing
In the text, a reference identified by means of an author's name should be followed by the date of the reference in parentheses and page number(s) where appropriate. When there are more than two authors, only the first author's name should be mentioned, followed by 'et al.'. In the event that an author cited has had two or more works published during the same year, the reference, both in the text and in the reference list, should be identified by a lower case letter like 'a' and 'b' after the date to distinguish the works.

268

Examples:
Winograd (1986, p. 204)
(Winograd, 1986a, b)
(Winograd, 1986; Flores et al., 1988)
(Bullen and Bennett, 1990)

Acknowledgements
Acknowledgements of people, grants, funds, etc. should be placed in a separate section before the References.

References
References to books, journal articles, articles in collections and conference or workshop proceedings, and technical reports should be listed at the end of the article in **alphabetical** order. Articles in preparation or articles submitted for publication, unpublished observations, personal communications, etc. should not be included in the reference list but should only be mentioned in the article text (e.g., T. Moore, personal communication).

References to books should include the author's name; year of publication; title; page numbers where appropriate; publisher; place of publication, in the order given in the example below.

Freudenthal, H.: 1973, *Mathematics as an Educational Task*, D. Reidel, Dordrecht, p. 69.

Strauss, A. and Corbin, J.: 1990, *Basics of Qualitative Research: Grounded Theory Procedures and Techniques*, Sage, London, pp. 13-51.

References to articles in an edited collection should include the author's name; year of publication; article title; editor's name; title of collection; first and last page numbers; publisher; place of publication, in the order given in the example below.

Brophy, J. and Good, T.: 1986, 'Teacher behavior and student achievement', in M.C. Wittrock (ed.), *Handbook of Research on Teaching*, 3rd ed., MacMillan, New York, pp. 328-375.

Carraher, T.N., Schliemann, A.D. and Cárraher, D.W.: 1988, 'Mathematical concepts in everyday life', in G.B. Saxe and M. Gearhart (eds.), *Children's Mathematics*, Jossey-Bass, San Francisco, pp. 71-87.

References to articles in conference proceedings should include the author's name; year of publication; article title; editor's name (if any); title of proceedings; first and last page numbers; place and date of conference; publisher and/or organization from which the proceedings can be obtained; place of publication, in the order given in the example below.

Harel, G., Post, T.H. and Behr, M.: 1988, 'On the textual and the semantic structure of mapping rule and multiplication compare problems', *Proceedings of the 12th International Conference, Psychology of Mathematics Education*, Vol. 11, Vezprem, Hungary, pp. 372-379.

References to articles in periodicals should include the author's name; year of publication; article title; full title of periodical; volume number (issue number where appropriate); first and last page numbers, in the order given in the example below.

Begle, E.G.: 1969, 'The role of research in the improvement of mathematics education', *Educational Studies in Mathematics* 2, 232-244.

Kagan, D.: 1990, 'Ways of evaluating teacher cognition: Inferences concerning the Goldilocks Principle', *Review of Educational Research* 60 (3), 419-469.

References to technical reports or doctoral dissertations should include the author's name; year of publication; title of report or dissertation; institution, in the order given in the example below.

Mangan, C.: 1986, *Choice of Operation in Multiplication and Division Word Problems*, Doctoral Dissertation, Department of Psychology, Queens University, Belfast.

Daly, M.: 1997, *From the Experiences of Women Mathematicians: A Feminist Epistemology for Mathematics*, Doctoral Dissertation, Massey University, New Zealand.

Proofs
Proofs will be sent to the corresponding author by e-mail (if no e-mail address is available or appears to be out of order, proofs will be sent by regular mail).

Your response, with or without corrections, should be sent within 72 hours. Please do not make any changes to the PDF file. Minor corrections (+/- 10) should be sent as an e-mail attachment to: proofscorrection@wkap.nl. Always quote the four-letter journal code and article number and the PIPS No. from your proof in the subject field of your e-mail. Extensive corrections must be clearly marked on a printout of the PDF file and should be sent by first-class mail (airmail overseas).

Offprints
Twenty-five offprints of each article will be provided free of charge. Additional offprints (both hard copies and PDF files) can be ordered by means of an offprint order form supplied with the proofs.

Page Charges and Colour Figures
No page charges are levied on authors or their institutions. Colour figures are published at the author's expense only.

Copyright
Authors will be asked, upon acceptance of an article, to transfer copyright of the article to the Publisher. This will ensure the widest possible dissemination of information under copyright laws.

Permissions
It is the responsibility of the author to obtain written permission for a quotation from unpublished material, or for all quotations in excess of 250 words in one extract or 500 words in total from any work still in copyright, and for the reprinting of figures, tables or poems from unpublished or copyrighted material.

Springer Open Choice
In addition to the normal publication process (whereby an article is submitted to the journal and access to that article is granted to customers who have purchased a subscription), Springer now provides an alternative publishing option: Springer Open Choice. A Springer Open Choice article receives all the benefits of a regular subscription-based article, but in addition is made available publicly through Springers online platform SpringerLink. To publish via Springer Open Choice, upon acceptance please visit www.springeronline.com/openchoice to complete the relevant order form and provide the required payment information. Payment must be received in full before publication or articles will publish as regular subscription-model articles. We regret that Springer Open Choice cannot be ordered for published articles.

Additional Information
Additional information can be obtained from:

Publishing Editor Educational Studies in Mathematics
Editor Social Sciences Division
Kluwer Academic Publishers
P.O. Box 17
3300 AA Dordrecht
The Netherlands
Phone: +31-(0)78-6576-183; Fax: +31-(0)78-6576-254
KAP home page: http://www.wkap.nl/

Educational Technology

ADDRESS FOR SUBMISSION:

Lawrence Lipsitz, Editor
Educational Technology
700 Palisade Ave.
Englewood Cliffs, NJ 07632-0564
USA
Phone: 201-871-4007
Fax: 201-871-4009
E-Mail: edtecpubs@aol.com
Web: www.bookstoread.com/etp/
Address May Change:

CIRCULATION DATA:

Reader: Academics, Educators, Trainers
Frequency of Issue: Bi-Monthly
Copies per Issue: 2,500 - 3,000
Sponsor/Publisher: Educational Technology
   Publications
Subscribe Price: 139.00 US$
   159.00 US$ Elsewhere

PUBLICATION GUIDELINES:

Manuscript Length: Any
Copies Required: Two
Computer Submission: Yes
Format: MS Word for PC
Fees to Review: 0.00 US$

Manuscript Style:
   See Manuscript Guidelines

REVIEW INFORMATION:

Type of Review: Editorial Review
No. of External Reviewers:
No. of In House Reviewers: 3+
Acceptance Rate: 10-15%
Time to Review: 2 Weeks or less
Reviewers Comments: No
Invited Articles: 30-40%
Fees to Publish: 0.00 US$

MANUSCRIPT TOPICS:

Adult Career & Vocational; Computer Based Instruct.; Education
Management/Administration; Educational Technology Systems; Higher Education;
Instructional Design; Internet; Library Science/Information Resources; Simulations; Teacher
Education; Tests, Measurement & Evaluation; World Wide Web

MANUSCRIPT GUIDELINES/COMMENTS:

No. of In House Reviewers: More than three for essays

In preparing an article for *Educational Technology Magazine* the primary fact to keep in mind
is that this magazine is not a research journal. It is, as the name implies, a magazine. The
editors are looking generally for articles which *interpret* research and/or practical applications
of scientific knowledge in education and training environments.

Thus, your article should not be cast in the form of a traditional research report; for example,
with headings for "related literature," "hypothesis," "methodology," "findings," etc. The facts
of your research, and the research of others, should be stated succinctly. Then you should go
on to explain the implications of this research, how it can be applied in actual practice, what

suggestions can be made to school administrators, trainers, designers, and others based on the research.

The style of writing should be on the informal side--an essay - since once again this is a magazine and not a formal academic journal. Authors are free to state their opinions, as long as the opinions are clearly identified as such. The use of specialized jargon should be kept to the barest minimum, since this magazine has a very wide interdisciplinary audience--and what may be an "in" word, in one sub-field of educational technology will be considered unintelligible to all others.

There are no minimum and maximum length restrictions. Make your article as short as possible to do the job you intend. As a general rule, most articles are under 3,000 words, and one would require more words only in unusual circumstances. Include charts and photographs if you wish.

In regard to bibliographical style, use whatever format is most comfortable. Our editors will re-work your bibliography, if any, into the style of the magazine. The concern of the editors is that you concentrate on getting your ideas across to the reader--and let us worry about style consistency.

Finally, submit two copies of the manuscript, with a stamped, self-addressed envelope if you wish a rejected article to be returned to you. All papers should be typed double-spaced on standard 81/2 x 11-inch sheets of paper. The author should be identified on the manuscript by his or her current job title (for example, Professor of Education at U.S.A. University). If desired, authors may send manuscripts electronically using MS Word for the PC.

You will be notified of acceptance or rejection within two weeks of our receipt of your manuscript. Publication will follow, as a rule, within six months; however, in some circumstances it will take a full year, depending upon our backlog of articles Upon acceptance, you will be asked to sign a form granting copyright to the magazine, and pledging that the article is your original work, containing absolutely nothing plagiarized from the work of another author.

Note too that this magazine is read in more than 110 countries, by persons holding prominent and influential positions. They expect a very high level of discourse and it is our goal to provide articles of excellence.

Educational Technology Research and Development

ADDRESS FOR SUBMISSION:

Steven M. Ross, Editor
Educational Technology Research and
   Development
University of Memphis
Center for Research in
   Educational Policy
225 Browning Hall
Memphis, TN 38152
USA
Phone: 901-678-3413
Fax: 901-678-4257
E-Mail: smross@memphis.edu
Web:
Address May Change:

PUBLICATION GUIDELINES:

Manuscript Length: 26-30
Copies Required: Four
Computer Submission: No
Format: N/A
Fees to Review: 0.00 US$

Manuscript Style:
   American Psychological Association

CIRCULATION DATA:

Reader: Academics
Frequency of Issue: Quarterly
Copies per Issue: 5,001 - 10,000
Sponsor/Publisher: Association for
   Educational Communications and
   Technology
Subscribe Price: 0.00 US$

REVIEW INFORMATION:

Type of Review: Blind Review
No. of External Reviewers: 3
No. of In House Reviewers: No Reply
Acceptance Rate: 11-20%
Time to Review: 1 - 2 Months
Reviewers Comments: Yes
Invited Articles: 0-5%
Fees to Publish: 0.00 US$

MANUSCRIPT TOPICS:
Educational Psychology; Educational Technology Systems

MANUSCRIPT GUIDELINES/COMMENTS:

Directions to Contributors
Submit four paper copies and one e-copy of your manuscript, typed double-spaced on 8½ x 11" paper. Manuscripts should be between 10 and 30 pages in length and must conform to the style of the *Publication Manual of the American Psychological Association* (4th ed.). The name(s), affiliation(s), address(es), and phone and fax number(s) of the author(s) should appear on a separate cover page. To ensure anonymity in the review process, names of author(s) should not appear elsewhere in the manuscript. An abstract of 100-150 words should be typed on a separate page. Manuscripts that do not conform to these specifications will be returned for proper style change.

If available, also supply computer disk, clearly labeled with author name, hardware (PC or high-density MAC), and name of word-processing software (ASCII is preferred). Content of disk must match manuscript precisely.

Manuscripts are sent to three consulting editors for review. The review process usually takes from two to four months.

Manuscripts primarily concerned with research in educational technology should be sent to the Editor of the research section:

Steven M. Ross, Research Editor, ETR&D, Center for Research in Educational Policy, 325 Browning Hall, The University of Memphis, Memphis, TN 38152.
Phone: 901-678-3413; Email: **smross@memphis.edu**

Manuscripts that are primarily concerned with the design and development of learning systems and educational technology applications should be sent to:

James Klein, Development Editor, ETR&D, Division of Psychology in Education, Arizona State University, Box 870611, Tempe, AZ, 85287-0611.
Email: **james.klein@asu.edu**

Permissions
ETR&D is copyrighted by the Association for Educational Communications and Technology (AECT). Nonprofit organizations may quote from *ETR&D* for noncommercial purposes provided full credit acknowledgments are given and permission of the author(s) is obtained. For permission to quote from or reproduce copyrighted material from *ETR&D* for commercial purposes, write to: Permissions, AECT, 1025 Vermont Ave., N.W., Suite 820, Washington, DC 20005.

All copies, whether reproduced under fair use provisions of the copyright law, or with permission as granted here or by letter from AECT, must carry the following notice (which may be copied from this page):

Copyright 1997 Association for Educational Communications and Technology, 1025 Vermont Ave., N.W., Suite 820, Washington, DC 20005. Reprinted from Educational Technology Research and Development.

Other
The annual index to *ETR&D* is published in the final issue of the volume. *ETR&D* is indexed in Education Index and Current Index to journals in Education.

ETR&D may be cited in bibliographies and indexed as *Educational Technology Research and Development*.

Educational Theory

ADDRESS FOR SUBMISSION:

Nicholas C. Burbules, Editor
Educational Theory
University of Illinois, Urbana-Champaign
Education Building
1310 South Sixth Street
Champaign, IL 61820
USA
Phone: 217-244-0919
Fax: 217-244-7064
E-Mail: edtheory@uiuc.edu
Web: www.blackwellpublishing.com
Address May Change:

PUBLICATION GUIDELINES:

Manuscript Length: 30 Pages Max
Copies Required: Four
Computer Submission: Yes Email
Format: Word
Fees to Review: 0.00 US$

Manuscript Style:
    Chicago Manual of Style

CIRCULATION DATA:

Reader: Academics
Frequency of Issue: Quarterly
Copies per Issue: 2,001 - 3,000
Sponsor/Publisher: Professional Association
    & University, Blackwell Publishers, Inc.
Subscribe Price: 50.00 US$ Individual
    110.00 US$ Library Domestic

REVIEW INFORMATION:

Type of Review: Blind Review
No. of External Reviewers: 3
No. of In House Reviewers: 2
Acceptance Rate: 11-20%
Time to Review: 2 - 3 Months
Reviewers Comments: Yes
Invited Articles: 11-20%
Fees to Publish: 0.00 US$

MANUSCRIPT TOPICS:
Educational Psychology; Policy Issues in Education

MANUSCRIPT GUIDELINES/COMMENTS:

Submitting a Manuscript
Manuscripts should be submitted electronically to *Educational Theory*, preferably as an e-mail attachment. We prefer RTF files. The e-mail address for submissions is EdTheory@uiuc.edu.

Review Procedures
No editorial consideration will be given to manuscripts that have been published elsewhere or are under review for publication elsewhere. (Rare exceptions may be warranted by special circumstances, such as the substantial expansion or revision of previously published material.) Manuscripts are sent out for double-blind review (i.e., reviewers do not know the identity of authors, and authors do not know the identity of reviewers). To preserve the advantages of blind reviewing, authors should avoid self-identification in the text as well as in the footnotes of the manuscript.

Format
The manuscript should be double-spaced throughout, including quotations and footnotes. Footnotes should be numbered within the text and listed on separate sheets at the end of the manuscript, in conformance with the *Chicago Manual of Style*, 14th ed., published by the University of Chicago Press. Manuscripts accepted for publication but not in conformance will be returned to the author for revision. Manuscripts should not exceed 7500 words, including footnotes (roughly 25 manuscript pages, using 12 point type size and standard margins).

Author Responsibilities
Authors alone are responsible for securing permission for quotations from copyrighted materials or materials in private collections. (See entries under "Obtaining Permissions" and "Requesting Permissions" in the *Chicago Manual of Style*, 14th ed.) Authors of accepted manuscripts are also expected to submit, or pay for, the preparation of camera-ready copy of figures or illustrations and to bear the cost of any special typography.

Educational Theory is Indexed In
Current Contents, Education
Education Index
The Philosopher's Index
Language and Language Behavior Abstracts
Current Index to Journals in Education (ERIC)

Electronic Journal in Science and Literacy Education

ADDRESS FOR SUBMISSION:

Sharon Parsons, Editor
Electronic Journal in Science and Literacy
    Education
San Jose State University
    SUBMIT BY EMAIL ONLY
One Washington Square
San Jose, CA 95192-0074
USA
Phone: 408-924-3734
Fax: 408-924-3775
E-Mail: sced@jupiter.sjsu.edu
Web: sweeneyhall.sjsu.edu/ejlts
Address May Change:

PUBLICATION GUIDELINES:

Manuscript Length: 16-20
Copies Required: One Electronic Copy
Computer Submission: Email Only
Format: MS Word (only)
Fees to Review: 0.00 US$

Manuscript Style:
    American Psychological Association

CIRCULATION DATA:

Reader: Practicing Teachers, Academics
Frequency of Issue: Posted when accepted
Copies per Issue: Website
Sponsor/Publisher: San Jose State
    University
Subscribe Price: 0.00 US$ Free Now

REVIEW INFORMATION:

Type of Review: Blind Review
No. of External Reviewers: 3+
No. of In House Reviewers: 2
Acceptance Rate: 30%
Time to Review: 2 - 3 Months
Reviewers Comments: Yes
Invited Articles: 0-5%
Fees to Publish: 0.00 US$

MANUSCRIPT TOPICS:
Bilingual/E.S.L.; Languages & Linguistics; Reading; Science Math & Environment

MANUSCRIPT GUIDELINES/COMMENTS:

Topics. Science & Literacy Education with a focus on: Scientific Literacy, Language Development (Reading and Writing) Bilingualism and Multiculturalism.

About the Journal
Since *EJLTS* is a completely electronic venture, only manuscripts submitted to the editor electronically will be accepted for review. Please send the manuscript to the editor in Microsoft Word. Should your manuscript include any data tables, please format the tables via your word processor. Please check with the editor if questions arise.

All inquires concerning manuscript submission should be e-mailed to the Editor of *EJLTS* at: **sced@jupiter.sjsu.edu**.

Types of Submissions

EJLTS will be devoted to addressing science education by focusing on issues related to "Literacy through Science" for a diverse community. *EJLTS* therefore invites for review manuscripts that address the needs of diverse K-16 students in the areas of:

1. Scientific Literacy for All
2. Language Development (Reading and Writing) and Science Education
3. Bilingualism and Science Education

EJLTS will strive to maintain an overall balance between theory and practice. We therefore invite the following types of manuscripts for review:

1. Research Articles (all types, including teacher research)
2. Scholarly Position Papers
3. Lesson Plans which address "literacy through science"
4. Book Reviews (Ranging from academic book reviews to reviews of popular children's books on science.)
5. Software Reviews

If you have any manuscript ideas which address "literacy through science" but falls outside the above list please contact the editor for suitability.

Manuscript Form

The *EJLTS* will accept manuscripts in Microsoft word format only. Manuscripts will be accepted from the author(s) "as is", meaning no major formatting changes will be done to the manuscript. *EJLTS* will make every attempt to assure that the author(s) manuscript format is retained as submitted. The style manual followed for publication in *EJLTS* is the *Publication Manual of the American Psychological Association*. You should also follow APA's electronic publication guidelines for citing electronic publications.

The electronic nature of *EJLTS* requires some minor formatting modifications to the APA style. They are:

a. No running heads are required.
b. Graphics included in your manuscript should be either in .gif or .jpg formats.
c. For any other style problems, match the *APA* style manual as close as possible.

All manuscripts should be e-mailed to the editor of *EJLTS* Sharon Parsons: **sced@jupiter.sjsu.edu**. Please include the following in your e-mail message to the editor:

a. The author(s) complete name, title, and mailing address.
b. E-mail, office phone and FAX number of lead author.
c. A brief biographical sketch of all authors.

The lead author will be notified of the receipt of the manuscript via e-mail. Upon formal acceptance of the manuscript, a copyright transfer agreement will be e-mailed for signatures to be returned to the editor via mail.

The Review Process
All manuscripts submitted to *EJLTS* will be reviewed anonymously by 3 referees. The editor and the field editors will do all tracking of manuscripts and reviewers. *EJLTS* will not review submissions previously published elsewhere, through print or electronic medium. All attempts will be made to ensure submissions will be reviewed within a month of e-mail submission to the editor. Manuscripts will be returned to the lead author when the review process is complete.

Acceptance and Publication
All accepted manuscripts will be posted at our website upon formal acceptance. The *EJLTS* is not bound to a publishing company's requirements; therefore *EJLTS* will allow a more free exchange of ideas to occur. No attempt will be made to limit number of articles published. There are no membership dues or publication fees for the *EJLTS*.

Electronic Journal of Science Education

ADDRESS FOR SUBMISSION:

John R. Cannon, Editor
Electronic Journal of Science Education
University of Nevada, Reno
College of Education
Mailstop 282
Reno, NV 89523
USA
Phone: 775-784-7961 ext. 2001
Fax: 775-327-5220
E-Mail: jcannon@unr.edu
Web: See Manuscript Guidelines
Address May Change:

PUBLICATION GUIDELINES:

Manuscript Length: No Limit
Copies Required: No Paper Copy
Computer Submission: Yes Email
Format: Any Word Processor or html
Fees to Review: 0.00 US$

Manuscript Style:
      American Psychological Association

CIRCULATION DATA:

Reader: Practicing Teachers, Academics
Frequency of Issue: Quarterly
Copies per Issue: 1,001 - 2,000
Sponsor/Publisher:
Subscribe Price: 0.00 US$

REVIEW INFORMATION:

Type of Review: Blind Review
No. of External Reviewers: 3
No. of In House Reviewers: 0
Acceptance Rate: 21-30%
Time to Review: 1 Month or Less
Reviewers Comments: Yes
Invited Articles: 0-5%
Fees to Publish: 0.00 US$

MANUSCRIPT TOPICS:
Educational Technology Systems; Science Math & Environment

MANUSCRIPT GUIDELINES/COMMENTS:

The *Electronic Journal of Science Education* is the first peer reviewed electronic journal of its kind devoted to the timely sharing of science education information via the World Wide Web. Using communications technology, information and research related to science education issues, K-16, are addressed. All reviewing, editing, and publishing is done via e-mail and the Web, allowing for both quality of product and increased speed and availability to all readers free of charge. The long term mission of the *EJSE* is to continue to offer quality information and research to the science education community at no cost and increased global availability to the articles within each issue of the *EJSE*. The editors and review board hope you find the enclosed articles academically and professionally valuable.

The website is **http://unr.edu/homepage/jcannon/ejse/ejse.html**

All Submissions
All inquires and manuscripts will be e-mailed to the editor of *EJSE* – **jcannon@unr.edu**

US mail address is: John R. Cannon, College of Education/282, University of Nevada, Reno, Reno, NV 89557-0214.

Since *EJSE* is a completely electronic venture, only manuscripts submitted to the editor electronically will be accepted for review. The EJSE converts many popular word processing documents into HTML documents (some examples: Word, WordPerfect [PC and Mac], ClarisWorks). Please send the manuscript to the editor, noting what type of word processing program was used so that the appropriate conversion can be done.

If the manuscript includes data tables of some kind, please format the tables in **table format** via your word processor (example: Word). Special table formats (within word processing programs) can often be translated successfully into HTML also. **Please check with the editor if questions arise**.

Types of Submissions
The scope of *EJSE* is limited to science education issues K-16. Manuscripts that address issues such as, but not limited to, science curriculum, curriculum integration, teacher preparation, science education research, or implementation of science curricula would be acceptable for review. *EJSE* is designed to somewhat fluid in scope concerning science education. Therefore, please contact the editor with any manuscript ideas for suitability.

Manuscript Form
The *EJSE* accepts manuscripts in two formats: HTML or word processed files. The *EJSE* **no longer accepts files in ASCII or plain text formats**. HMTL manuscripts are accepted from the author(s) "as is", meaning no major HTML formatting changes will be done to the manuscript. *EJSE* will make every attempt to assure that the author(s) manuscript format is retained as submitted. The style manual followed for publication in EJSE is the fourth edition Publication Manual of the American Psychological Association (APA, 1994). The electronic nature of *EJSE* requires some minor formatting modifications to the APA style. They are:

a. No running heads are required.

b. **Pay close attention on how your word processor formats tables**.

If your word processor does not form tables, use the following as an example:

Table 1
Title of the table

n	Mean	Median	Mode	SD
Group 1	24	3.45	33	.56
Group 2	7	3.2	22	.77

c. In the reference section, use the following formatting for the titles of books, journals, etc.,:
Cannon, J.R.(1996). Comments about how to get published in the EJSE. *Electronic Journal of Science Education, 1,* 1-12.

d. Graphics included in your manuscript should be either in .gif or .jpg formats. **Please check with the editor if you wish to submit any other type of graphic** for conversion suitability.

e. For any other style problems, match the APA style manual as close as possible.

EXEMPLAR LESSON PLANS
Inquiry & The Learning Cycle:
The Learning Cycle originally credited to Karplus and Thier (1967), who authored *A New Look at Elementary School Science,* has been used in science education from its conception. Probably one of the earliest and foremost supporters of the Learning Cycle was the SCIS (Science Curriculum Improvement Study) program which adapted it and included it in its science curriculum. Although there are several "E" versions (e.g. 3-E, 4-E, 5-E, and other modifications) the basic premise is that children have an experience with the phenomena in the learning of the concept / topic. In other words, the Learning Cycle applied the inquiry approach to teaching into a series of planning strategies. Versions of the Learning Cycle are present in the major science curricula today (FOSS, STC, BSCS, etc.) As well as introduced and used as a science lesson planning strategy in most current Science Methods texts. The BSCS approach to the Learning Cycle is credited to Roger Bybee who developed the 5-E model which will be used in the *Applications of Research & Model Inquiry Lessons* section of *EJSE.* Bybee's 5-E model is as follows:

The Lesson Plan Format - 5-E Learning Cycle (BSCS / Bybee)

ENGAGEMENT (INTRODUCING A LESSON)
Whether you begin in a very directed or less directed manner will depend on the complexity of the concept and the background of the children. Sometimes you will want to use a hands-on experience to create interest and arouse questions, then lead children into a exploration to develop a concept for which they have some background knowledge. Sometimes, because you feel that children lack the background knowledge, you will begin in a very guided manner to carefully introduce the concept and later, when children have become familiar, move to a more exploratory activity. The direction that you take should come from the decisions that you make during preplanning.

Regardless of the direction that you take, your introduction should engage children, arouse curiosity, and set a direction for the lesson. The children should, by the end of your introduction have an idea about the focus of the lesson and what they will be doing. The introductory activity should also help you reaffirm your thinking about your student's background knowledge and readiness for the experience.

EXPLORATION
This is the bulk of the lesson where children are immersed in exploration of topics or concepts. This is the primary activity of the lesson. Students work with one another to explore

ideas through hands-on activities. The teacher is the facilitator and observes and listens to students as they interact. The teacher asks probing questions of the students so that they clarify their own understanding of major concepts. Additional questions may be asked to redirect students' investigations when necessary. Adequate time for thorough investigation is critical at this time.

EXPLANATION

This is the meat of the lesson. Here is where you will carefully develop a specific questioning sequence that relates to the new knowledge that you identified as your purpose of the lesson. The sequence of questions in this portion of the lesson is most important. Here is where your knowledge of children development and learning theory really becomes important. This is the place to reflect on stages of learning, moving from concrete to abstract, from the known to the new. You will also want to refer to people who support inquiry and carefully guide children's exploration of a topic or concept while you probe their thinking and provide feedback.

During lesson development you are the one who is responsible for knowing the content well enough that you can flexibly respond to what children do and say during the lesson development. Your knowledge of various ways to teach will be needed to decide if you must revise your lesson plan in midstream. Your knowledge of management will be needed to help you redirect children who do not follow the "group" as you expected, yet need to be engaged for learning. All of these possibilities make teaching complex and often difficult to do well.

ELABORATION

Depending upon the time that you have allocated for the lesson and the manner in which the lesson development proceeds, you will eventually need to bring the lesson to closure. If you completed the lesson development as you planned. then closure is really an elaboration of what was done and learned during the lesson. It is most helpful here if students are the ones who verbalize what was learned. It is also appropriate here to move students toward possible applications for what was learned. If the lesson development did not go as planned, then closure may merely be a temporary stopping point, with less elaboration, until you can resume tomorrow.

Learning theorists tell us that it helps us to retain new knowledge if we can link it to what is already known and can chunk it in related pieces. This is the purpose that closure serves. We must help children make "chunks" out of the new information and relate it to what they already know so that the new knowledge can successfully stored, then retrieved at a later time.

Closure is important to retention of information and concepts. It is important, then, to watch the timing of the lesson so that ample time will be reserved for the closure. Remember, you will always have tomorrow. What you try to stuff into children's heads in the fleeting moments of a lesson probably won't be retained anyway. The time would be better spent in a good closure, saving other new information for another lesson.

EVALUATION

Evaluation should not wait until the lesson is over. You should be evaluating all along. You will have a sense of how the lesson is proceeding. As you gain experience, you should find it easier to watch the responses of children. In the initial stages it may be difficult for you to do this with much accuracy. But still, you will have a sense of the lesson, which is part of evaluation.

If you planned your lesson to carefully reflect your stated purpose or objective, then evaluation should follow naturally. The type of activities that you plan should allow you to answer the question, "What did children learn about my objective and how did they demonstrate that learning?"

The value of evaluation comes in the closeness of match between your purpose and the activities in which you engage children. One of the most frequent problems that inexperienced teachers have is selecting developmentally appropriate activities that match the proposed objective. This again takes us back to careful preplanning and really knowing what is to be taught and how it might be best learned.

Evaluation of the children's learning should also lead you into evaluating your planning and presentation of the lesson. Here is where objectivity on your part is needed. Every lesson that you teach will not be wonderful and you will need to be objective about your inexperience and what you still need to learn and/or practice. It is hard to move what we know in our heads into our behavior, especially teaching behavior that is so new to us.

Initially, it may be hard for you to be critical of yourself. Perhaps you will need to remind yourself that you are a learner, that you are just beginning, and should not expect that after a few lessons that you will reach perfection. What Lucy Calkins says of writers may also be true for evaluating our teaching, that we should be "passion hot and critic cold." We should revel in what we do well, but we should also be our own critics, striving to find a more informed way to work with children. As we gain experience, we also need to be open to the evaluation of others who have more and varied experiences in teaching.

At the close of a lesson, you should take time to step back and look objectively as you reflect upon your lesson. The reflecting that you will do should help you go back and hear yourself as "teacher," to revisit the lesson as you presented it to inform your evaluation of yourself. One of your goals this semester should be to become a more objective evaluator of yourself.

Required Lesson Format:
Introduction
Title and name of designer
Objective and Proficiencies (NSES Standards)
Background knowledge
Teacher
Student
Materials List
Safety procedures

Lesson Body
Engagement
Exploration
Explanation

Elaboration
Evaluation

Closure
Clean-up

Manuscript And Lesson Plan Submissions
All manuscripts and lesson plans should be e-mailed to the editor of *EJSE* --
jcannon@unr.edu

Include the following in your e-mail message to the editor:

a. The author(s) complete name, title, and US mail address.

b. Office phone and FAX number of lead author.

c. Biographical sketch of all authors.

The lead author will be immediately notified of the receipt of the manuscript via e-mail. Upon formal acceptance of the manuscript, a copyright transfer agreement will be e-mailed to you for your signature to be returned to the editor via US mail.

The Review Process
Submitted manuscripts and lesson plans to *EJSE* are reviewed anonymously by 2-3 international referees. All tracking of manuscripts and reviewers is done by the editor and associate editor. *EJSE* will not review submissions previously published elsewhere, through print or electronic medium. All attempts will be made to ensure submissions will be reviewed within **14 days** of e-mail submission to the editor. Manuscripts will be returned to the lead author when each review is complete.

Acceptance and Publication
Accepted manuscripts are electronically published quarterly *at this time*. The *EJSE* is not bound or limited to a publishing company or their requirements, therefore allowing a more free exchange of ideas to occur when ready. Although attempts will be made to round out each issue with an appropriate number of articles, some issues may be somewhat larger or smaller.

Each issue will be announced primarily over the Association of Educators of Teachers in Science (AETS), the National Association for Research in Science Teaching (NARST), and the *EJSE* (ejse@unr.edu) listservs. Other listservs or Web sites such as the National Science Teacher's Association will also be notified for all new issues when deemed appropriate by the editor or members of the review panel.

There are no membership dues or publication fees for the *EJSE*.

Electronic Library (The)

ADDRESS FOR SUBMISSION:

David Raitt, Editor
Electronic Library (The)
EMAIL SUBMISSION ONLY
david.raitt@esa.int
European Space Agency ESTEC
PO Box 299
Noordwijk, 2200 AG
Netherlands
Phone:
Fax: +31 71 5152712
E-Mail: david.raitt@esa.int
Web: www.emeraldinsight.com/el.htm
Address May Change:

PUBLICATION GUIDELINES:

Manuscript Length: 3-6,000 words
Copies Required: None, Email Only
Computer Submission: Yes Email
Format: MS Word - English
Fees to Review: 0.00 US$

Manuscript Style:
, Harvard

CIRCULATION DATA:

Reader: , Library / Information Community
Frequency of Issue: Bi-Monthly
Copies per Issue: No Reply
Sponsor/Publisher: Emerald Group
   Publishing Limited
Subscribe Price: 519.00 US$
    359.00 Pounds + VAT 31.41
    539.00 Euro + VAT 47.16

REVIEW INFORMATION:

Type of Review: Blind Review
No. of External Reviewers: 1-2
No. of In House Reviewers: 0
Acceptance Rate: 90%
Time to Review: 1 - 2 Months
Reviewers Comments: Yes
Invited Articles: 50% +
Fees to Publish: 0.00 US$

MANUSCRIPT TOPICS:
Information Technology; Internet; Library Science/Information Resources

MANUSCRIPT GUIDELINES/COMMENTS:

About the journal
Keeping abreast of the latest developments in digital information resources can be an endless task, that is why The *Electronic Library* aims to be the definitive source of information for the application of technology in information environments. In addition to providing an independent and unbiased assessment of today's automated library and information center, this international journal offers practical advice, useful information and specific application recommendations. All of this supports high quality, peer-reviewed articles by skilled industry experts and users on all aspects of computerization in libraries.

Coverage
• Libraries and the web
• The digital library

- Software and hardware development
- User interfaces
- The applications and implications of new information technology
- Library networking and automation
- Libraries and the changing face of information
- The latest products, trend and services

NOTES FOR CONTRIBUTORS

Copyright

Articles submitted to the journal should be original contributions and should not be under consideration for any other publication at the same time. Authors submitting articles for publication warrant that the work is not an infringement of any existing copyright and will indemnify the publisher against any breach of such warranty. For ease of dissemination and to ensure proper policing of use, papers and contributions become the legal copyright of the publisher unless otherwise agreed. Submissions should be sent to:

The Editor
David Raitt
The Netherlands
Email: **draitt@esa.int**

Editorial objectives

The *Electronic Library* is devoted to the applications and implications of new technology, library automation, user interfaces, and networks on libraries and information centres. Also the development of software and hardware for such applications. The *Electronic Library* serves as a medium for reporting research results, descriptions, news, reviews and information exchange.

The reviewing process

Each paper is reviewed by the editor and may also be sent to one or more reviewers. The editor then decides whether the paper should be accepted as is, revised or rejected.

Manuscript requirements

Manuscripts should be submitted by e-mail (attached Word file preferred). As a guide, articles should be between 3,000 and 6,000 words in length. A title of not more than eight words should be provided. A brief autobiographical note should be supplied including full name, affiliation, e-mail address and full international contact details. Authors must supply an abstract of 100-150 words. Up to six keywords should be included which encapsulate the principal subjects covered by the article.

Where there is a methodology, it should be clearly described under a separate heading.

Headings must be short, clearly defined and not numbered. Notes or Endnotes should be used only if absolutely necessary and must be identified in the text by consecutive numbers, enclosed in square brackets and listed at the end of the article.

Figures, charts and diagrams should be kept to a minimum. They must be black and white with minimum shading and numbered consecutively using Arabic numerals with a brief title and labelled axes. In the text, the position of the figure should be shown by typing on a separate line the words 'take in Figure 2'. Good quality originals must be provided.

Tables should be kept to a minimum. They must be numbered consecutively with roman numerals and a brief title. In the text, the position of the table should be shown by typing on a separate line the words 'take in Table IV'.

Photos and illustrations must be supplied as good quality black and white original half tones with captions. Their position should be shown in the text by typing on a separate line the words 'take in Plate 20'.

References to other publications should be complete and in *Harvard* style. They should contain full bibliographical details and journal titles should not be abbreviated. For multiple citations in the same year use a, b, c immediately following the year of publication. References should be shown within the text by giving the author's last name followed by a comma and year of publication all in round brackets, e.g. (Fox, 1994). At the end of the article should be a reference list in alphabetical order as follows

(a) *for books*
surname, initials and year of publication, title, publisher, place of publication, e.g. Casson, M. (1979), Alternatives to the Multinational Enterprise, Macmillan, London.

(b) *for chapter in edited book*
surname, initials and year, "title", editor's surname, initials, title, publisher, place, pages, e.g. Bessley, M. and Wilson, P. (1984), "Public policy and small firms in Britain", in Levicki, C. (Ed.), Small Business Theory and Policy, Croom Helm, London, pp.111-26. Please note that the chapter title must be underlined.

(c) *for articles*
surname, initials, year "title", journal, volume, number, pages, e.g.Fox, S. (1994) "Empowerment as a catalyst for change: an example from the food industry", Supply Chain Management, Vol 2 No 3, pp. 29-33

If there is more than one author list surnames followed by initials. All authors should be shown.

Electronic sources should include the URL of the electronic site at which they may be found, as follows: Neuman, B.C.(1995), "Security, payment, and privacy for network commerce", IEEE Journal on Selected Areas in Communications, Vol. 13 No.8, October, pp.1523-31. Available (IEEE SEPTEMBER) http://www.research.att.com/jsac/

Notes/Endnotes should be used only if absolutely necessary. They should, however, always be used for citing Web sites. They should be identified in the text by consecutive numbers enclosed in square brackets and listed at the end of the article. Please then provide full Web site addresses in the end list.

Final submission of the article

Once accepted for publication, the final version of the manuscript must be sent to the editor as an e-mail attachment in Word format.

Each article must be accompanied by a completed and signed Journal Article Record Form available from the Editor or on http://www.literaticlub.co.uk/

The final submission will be considered to be the definitive version of the article. The author must ensure that it is complete, grammatically correct and without spelling or typographical errors.

In preparing the e-mail attachment, please use one of the following formats: Word, Word Perfect, Rich text format or TeX/LaTeX. Figures which are provided electronically must be in tif, gif or pic file extensions. All figures and graphics must also be supplied as good quality originals.

Final submission requirements

- Manuscripts must be clean, good quality hard copy and;
- Include an abstract and keywords;
- Have *Harvard* style references;
- Include any figures, photos and graphics as good quality originals;
- Be accompanied by a labeled disk;
- Be accompanied by a completed Journal Article Record Form.

Electronic Magazine of Multicultrual Education

ADDRESS FOR SUBMISSION:

Heewon Chang, Editor-in-Chief
Electronic Magazine of Multicultrual
   Education
ELECTRONIC SUBMISSION ONLY
Phone: 610-341-1597
Fax: 610-341-4393
E-Mail: emme@eastern.edu
Web: www.eastern.edu/publications/emme
Address May Change:

PUBLICATION GUIDELINES:

Manuscript Length: 6-15
Copies Required:
Computer Submission: Yes Email
Format: MS Word
Fees to Review: 0.00 US$

Manuscript Style:
   American Psychological Association

CIRCULATION DATA:

Reader: Practicing Teachers, Academics,
   Publishers
Frequency of Issue: 2 Times/Year
Copies per Issue: 10,001 - 25,000
Sponsor/Publisher: Eastern University
Subscribe Price: 0.00 US$

REVIEW INFORMATION:

Type of Review: Blind Review
No. of External Reviewers: 0-2
No. of In House Reviewers: 1-2
Acceptance Rate: 40%
Time to Review: 1-3 Months
Reviewers Comments: Yes
Invited Articles: 0-5%
Fees to Publish:
   See Guidelines

MANUSCRIPT TOPICS:
Bilingual/E.S.L.; Curriculum Studies; Elementary/Early Childhood; Higher Education; Languages & Linguistics; Reading; Religious Education; Secondary/Adolescent Studies; Social Studies/Social Science; Special Education; Teacher Education; Urban Education, Cultural/Non-Traditional

MANUSCRIPT GUIDELINES/COMMENTS:

Each topic issue covers a different theme, but all topics are addressed from the perspective of multilingual, cross-cultural, global, and multicultural education.

As we are an online publication, we prefer that all manuscripts be submitted via email. Once manuscripts are received, all editorial communication is conducted via email. We accept manuscripts of the following types: scholarly articles, instructional ideas, and occasionally book/multimedia reviews.

General Guidelines for Submitting Manuscripts
As a free-access electronic journal for scholars, practitioners and students of multicultural education, *Electronic Magazine of Multicultural Education* (*EMME*) publishes a variety of writings: (1) original (and occasionally reprint) scholarly articles, (2) practitioner essays, (3) instructional ideas, and (4) reviews of visual arts, professional and juvenile books, and

multimedia resources. Reviews are generally solicited. Since the inception of the publication in 1999 each issue has focused on a particular theme of multicultural education (go to http://www.eastern.edu/publications/emme/previous.html for back issues). Any paper broadly related to multicultural issues will also be published in the Open Forum section. Currently, over 5,000 readers visit the journal site each month from the United States and other countries. Since 1999 readers from over 40 different countries have freely accessed *EMME*.

Please adhere to the following guidelines for submission:

1. Submissions must be consistent with the styles outlined in the most recent edition of *Publication Manual of the American Psychological Association*.

2. The following word limits are recommended for your manuscript: 3,500 (15 pages double spaced including references) for an original scholarly paper and a practitioner essay and 2,000 (8 pages double spaced) for an instructional idea.

3. An abstract of 50-75 words should be included.

4. Provide your author information in the Author Form that can be found at: **http://www.eastern.edu/publications/emme/about/author.html**.

5. All submission materials (your manuscript, abstract, and the Author Form) should be sent to **emme@eastern.edu** as email attachments in MS Word format.

6. To reprint a copyrighted text as an entirety or beyond 500 words (the APA guidelines) the author must secure written permission from *EMME*. *EMME* will publish reprints only pertaining to issue themes. *EMME* will not be responsible for the cost incurred as a result of the reprint permission. Any reprint submission should follow the same guidelines as original manuscripts.

It is common that submitted manuscripts are asked to be revised before appearing on line. All editorial communication is conducted via email, which usually expedites the publication process. It generally takes less than six months before an accepted manuscript is published.

Upcoming Issue Themes

2005 Spring (Vol. 7, No. 1)
Theme: Multicultural Curriculum for Language Arts
Deadline: March 15, 2005

This issue will focus on integrating multicultural concepts and principles into language arts curriculum at the elementary, secondary, and higher education level. Considered for this issue will be articles discussing pedagogical and curricular issues pertaining to the theme or instructional ideas that may be implemented in classroom settings. The issue is scheduled to come out at the end of June 2005.

292

2005 Fall (Vol. 7, No. 2)
Theme: Multicultural Curriculum for Visual and Performing Arts
Deadline: September 15, 2005

This issue will focus on integrating multicultural concepts and principles into visual and performing arts curriculum--fine arts, music, drama, etc.--at the elementary, secondary, and higher education level. Considered for this issue will be articles discussing pedagogical and curricular issues pertaining to the theme or instructional ideas that may be implemented in classroom settings. The issue is scheduled to come out at the end of December 2005.

2006 Spring (Vol. 8, No. 1)
Theme: Multicultural Education and Distance Education
Deadline: March 15, 2006

Computer technology has revolutionized teaching and learning. It redefines where, how, and what teaching and learning take place. A wide range of multicultural topics concerning distance education will be considered for this issue. The issue is scheduled to come out at the end of June 2006.

AUTHOR FORM

Name:

Title & Affiliation:

Email address:

Website address:

Phone number:

Fax number:

Address:

Biographic Sketch of the Author (20-30 words):

Title of your Submission:

Abstract (50-75 words if your submission is an essay or an instructional idea):

Keywords (5-10 words that best represent the ideas in your article):

Type of Software and version you used:

Type of your submission:

_____ Scholarly essay

_____ Practitioner essay

_____ Instructional idea

_____ Review of (_____)

Date of Submission:

For which issue do you want us to consider your work

Spring or Fall Year:

May we consider your submission for another issue if there seems to be a better match?

Yes or No

Elementary School Journal

ADDRESS FOR SUBMISSION:

Gail M. Hinkel, Managing Editor
Elementary School Journal
University of Missouri - Columbia
College of Education
Townsend Hall
Columbia, MO 65211
USA
Phone: 573-882-7889
Fax:
E-Mail: hinkelg@missouri.edu
Web: www.journals.uchicago.edu/ESJ/
Address May Change:

PUBLICATION GUIDELINES:

Manuscript Length: 35-40
Copies Required: Four
Computer Submission: No
Format: N/A
Fees to Review: 0.00 US$

Manuscript Style:
American Psychological Association

CIRCULATION DATA:

Reader: Academics, Practicing Teachers,
Administrators & Researchers
Frequency of Issue: 5 Times/Year
Copies per Issue: 5,001 - 10,000
Sponsor/Publisher: University of Chicago
Press
Subscribe Price: 38.00 US$ Individual
132.00 US$ Institution
25.00 US$ Student

REVIEW INFORMATION:

Type of Review: Blind Review
No. of External Reviewers: 2
No. of In House Reviewers: 2
Acceptance Rate: 6-10%
Time to Review: 2 - 3 Months
Reviewers Comments: Yes
Invited Articles: 31-50%
Fees to Publish: 0.00 US$

MANUSCRIPT TOPICS:

Curriculum Studies; Educational Theory & Research Studies; Elementary/Early Childhood;
Middle School; Teacher Education

MANUSCRIPT GUIDELINES/COMMENTS:

Invited Articles: Less than 50% - only in 2 special issues published each year. These articles
are solicited directly by guest editors of special issues.

The Elementary School Journal prefers to publish original studies that contain data about
school and classroom processes in elementary or middle schools. The *Journal* tries to publish
articles dealing with both educational theory and research and their implications for teaching
practice. We occasionally publish integrative research reviews and in-depth conceptual
analyses of schooling. The *Journal's* primary audience includes researchers, teacher educators,
and practitioners.

Manuscript Acceptance Policy

Submit four copies of manuscript for editorial review to Managing Editor, *Elementary School Journal*, University of Missouri, College of Education, Townsend Hall, Columbia, MO 65211. Authors who wish to have their manuscripts returned should send a stamped, self-addressed envelope. Articles are judged on two main criteria: *(a)* the quality of data on which the article is based, and *(b)* relevance to practice in elementary or middle schools. Manuscripts are accepted subject to editing. *Elementary School Journal* does not reprint articles that have appeared elsewhere and does not consider manuscripts that have been submitted to other journals concurrently. All manuscripts should include an abstract of 100-150 words.

Preparation of Copy

Type *all* copy double-spaced (including quotations, footnotes, references, tables, figure legends) on 8½ x 11-inch paper. Do not use corrasable bond. Margins all around should be at least 1½ inches. A dot matrix or unusual typeface is acceptable only if it is clear and legible. Because manuscripts are reviewed anonymously, authors should include with each copy of the manuscript a cover sheet that shows the manuscript title and authors' names and institutional affiliations. The first page of the manuscript should include the title of the manuscript. Authors should make every effort to see that the manuscript contains no clues to their identities.

Footnotes

Should be numbered consecutively and placed on a separate page(s) titled "Notes" following the text. They should be numbered in order and should correspond with superscript numbers in text. Any general note about the manuscript (acknowledgments, grants, etc.) should be unnumbered and should precede numbered notes. Footnotes should be kept to a minimum; most important information should be presented in the text.

References

The *Journal* uses the reference style of the *American Psychological Association*. Please consult the *Publication Manual of the APA* (4th ed., 1994) (1200 Seventeenth Street, N.W., Washington, DC 20036) for style and format of references. Do not use a separate section of Reference Notes.

Tables

Each table should be on a separate sheet. No vertical rules, no leaders anywhere. Number tables consecutively as they appear in text and place after References. Footnotes to table go at bottom of table and are cited by the symbols a, b, c, etc.

Figures

Must be numbered consecutively according to their appearance in text. Figure legends should be typed on a separate page and placed at the end of the manuscript with figures.

English Education

ADDRESS FOR SUBMISSION:

Dana Fox & Cathy Fleischer, Editors
English Education
Georgia State University
College of Education
Department of Middle/Secondary Education
30 Pryor Street
Atlanta, GA 30303
USA
Phone: 404-651-4050
Fax: 404-651-2546
E-Mail: dfox@gsu.edu
Web: www.ncte.org/pubs/journals/ee
Address May Change: 2/1/2006

PUBLICATION GUIDELINES:

Manuscript Length: 20-35 pages
Copies Required: Six
Computer Submission: No
Format: N/A
Fees to Review: 0.00 US$

Manuscript Style:
    American Psychological Association

CIRCULATION DATA:

Reader: Academics, Administrators
Frequency of Issue: Quarterly
Copies per Issue: 3,001 - 4,000
Sponsor/Publisher: National Council of
    Teachers of English
Subscribe Price: 15.00 US$

REVIEW INFORMATION:

Type of Review: Blind Review
No. of External Reviewers: 3
No. of In House Reviewers: 0
Acceptance Rate: 10%
Time to Review: 2 - 3 Months
Reviewers Comments: Yes
Invited Articles: Occasional
Fees to Publish: 0.00 US$

MANUSCRIPT TOPICS:
Curriculum Studies; Higher Education; Secondary/Adolescent Studies; Teacher Education; Teachers' Professional Development; Urban Education, Cultural/Non-Traditional

MANUSCRIPT GUIDELINES/COMMENTS:

About CEE
The Conference on English Education (CEE) of the National Council of Teachers of English is an organization concerned with the process of educating teachers of English and language arts. That education involves both the preservice and the inservice development of teachers. Recognizing the reciprocity of teaching and learning, the CEE addresses pertinent theory and research as they inform curriculum, methodology, and certification. Included in the constituency of the CEE are college and university teacher-educators; inservice leaders and consultants; supervisors at local, district, regional, and state levels; mentor teachers; teacher consultants curriculum coordinators and developers; teacher-researchers; and classroom teachers who work with student teachers. *English Education*, the official journal of CEE, is

co-edited by Dana L. Fox of Georgia State University and Cathy Fleischer of Eastern Michigan University.

Submissions
English Education seeks articles focusing on issues related to (1) the nature of our discipline, especially as it spans all levels of instruction, and (2) the education and development of teachers of English at all levels. The editors will ordinarily reach a decision about a manuscript within three months. *English Education* typically publishes fewer than 10% of the manuscripts it receives each year.

Guidelines for Manuscripts
1. Manuscripts should be typed, double-spaced, with one-inch margins and should follow the current *APA* style guide and the NCTE *Guidelines for Non-Sexist Use of Language*. Footnotes should be avoided, with documentation given in the text (following *APA* 4th Edition).

2. Manuscripts should contain the title but not the author's name on the first page of text, and subsequently should be free of internal references to the author's identity.

3. To facilitate the manuscript review process, authors should submit six (6) copies along with sufficient first-class postage (clipped, not pasted or metered) for mailing three copies out for review. Send six copies and postage to:

Dana L. Fox, English Education, Georgia State University, Department of Middle/Secondary Education and Instructional Technology, College of Education, 30 Pryor Street, Atlanta, GA 30303

Please include a letter certifying that the work has not been printed elsewhere, and is not being submitted elsewhere. The editors can be reached by e-mail at **dfox@gsu.edu**, **cathy.fleischer@emich.edu**, or **enged@gsu.edu** or by telephone (404-651-0180).

4. For final editing purposes, if a manuscript is accepted, the author will be required to submit an electronic copy of the manuscript on a diskette in Microsoft Word.

English for Specific Purposes

ADDRESS FOR SUBMISSION:

Diane Belcher, Co-Editor
English for Specific Purposes
Georgia State University
PO Box 4099
Atlanta, GA 30302-4099
USA
Phone: 404-654-5839
Fax: 404-651-3652
E-Mail: dbelcher1@gsu.edu
Web: www.elsevier.com/locate/esp
Address May Change:

PUBLICATION GUIDELINES:

Manuscript Length: 21-25
Copies Required: Three
Computer Submission: No Initial
 Submission
Format: N/A
Fees to Review: 0.00 US$

Manuscript Style:
 American Psychological Association

CIRCULATION DATA:

Reader: Practicing Teachers, Academics,
 Administrators
Frequency of Issue: Quarterly
Copies per Issue: N/A- Accessible Online
Sponsor/Publisher: Elsevier Science
 Publishing Co.
Subscribe Price: 83.00 US$ Individual
 422.00 US$ Institution
 Foreign rates in Guidelines

REVIEW INFORMATION:

Type of Review: Blind Review
No. of External Reviewers: 2
No. of In House Reviewers: 0
Acceptance Rate: 21-30%
Time to Review: 2 - 3 Months
Reviewers Comments: Yes
Invited Articles: 6-10%
Fees to Publish: 0.00 US$

MANUSCRIPT TOPICS:
Bilingual/E.S.L.; Foreign Language; Languages & Linguistics; Teacher Education; Tests,
Measurement & Evaluation

MANUSCRIPT GUIDELINES/COMMENTS:

Description
English for Specific Purposes publishes articles and research notes reporting basic research in
the linguistic description of specialized varieties of English and the application of such
research to specific methodological concerns. Topics such as the following may be treated
from the perspective of English for specific purposes: discourse analysis, second language
acquisition in specialized contexts, needs assessment, curriculum development and evaluation,
materials preparation, teaching and testing techniques, the effectiveness of various approaches
to language learning and language teaching, and the training or retraining of teachers for the
teaching of *ESP*. In addition, the journal welcomes articles and discussions that identify the
aspects of *ESP* needing development, the areas into which the practice of *ESP* may be
expanded, the possible means of cooperation between *ESP* programs and the learners'
professional or vocational interests, and the implications that findings from related disciplines

can have for the profession of *ESP*. The journal also carries reviews of textbook materials and scholarly books on topics of general interest to the profession.

Audience

For linguists and for all others interested in *ESP* and the surrounding issues.

Commenced publication 1980
Year 2002
    Volume 21, 4 issues
    ISSN: 0889-4906
    Institutional price: Order form
- USD 422 for all countries except Europe and Japan
- JPY 50,100 for Japan
- EUR 377 for European countries

Personal price: Order form
- USD 83 for all countries except Europe and Japan
- JPY 9,900 for Japan
- EUR 75 for European countries

INSTRUCTIONS FOR AUTHORS

Submission of Papers

Authors are requested to submit their original manuscript and figures with two copies to one of the two editors:

Diane Belcher, Department of Applied Linguistics/ESL, Georgia State University, 34 Peachtree Street, PO Box 4099, Atlanta, GA 30302-4099, USA. Email: **dbelcher1@gsu.edu**

Martin Hewings, English for International Students Unit, The University of Birmingham, Edgbaston, Birmingham, B15 2TT, UK. Phone: +44 (0) 121 414 5706, Fax: +44 (0) 121 414 3600, Email: **m.j.hewings@bham.ac.uk**

Submission of a paper implies that it has not been published previously, that it is not under consideration for publication elsewhere, and that if accepted it will not be published elsewhere in the same form, in English or in any other language, without the written consent of the publisher. Receipt of manuscripts will be acknowledged, but they cannot be returned; therefore, authors should retain a copy of the paper exactly as it was submitted.

Manuscript Preparation

General. Articles must be written in English and should be related to the teaching of English. Grammatical, lexical and orthographic features may conform to either British or American norms. Manuscripts must be typewritten, double-spaced with wide margins on one side of white paper. Good quality printouts with a font size of 12 or 10 pt arc required. The corresponding author should be identified (include a Fax number and E-mail address). Full postal addresses must be given for all co-authors. Manuscript pages should be consecutively numbered in the upper right hand corner along with the first-named author's last name.

300

Authors should consult a recent issue of the journal for style if possible. An electronic copy of the paper should accompany the final version. The Editors reserve the right to adjust style to certain standards of uniformity. Authors should retain a copy of their manuscript since we cannot accept responsibility for damage or loss of papers. Original manuscripts are discarded one month after publication unless the Publisher is asked to return original material after use.

Paper length. Manuscripts should be no longer than 25 double-spaced pages.

Abstracts. All articles should have abstracts which summarize the scope and purpose of the article and, if applicable, the results of the study. The abstracts should be between 100-200 words in length.

Text. Follow this order when typing manuscripts: Title, Authors, Affiliations, Abstract, Keywords, Main text, Acknowledgements, Appendix, References, Vitae, Figure Captions and then Tables. Do not import the Figures or Tables into your text. The corresponding author should be identified with an asterisk and footnote. All other footnotes (except for table footnotes) should be identified with superscript Arabic numbers.

Citations. Citations may be given of lexical material from other than English; however, citations from languages not employing a Roman alphabet must be given in a Romanized translation or in a transcription which uses standard symbols available in the International Phonetic Alphabet.

References. All publications cited in the text should be presented in a list of references following the text of the manuscript. In the text refer to the author's name (without initials) and year of publication (e.g. "Since Peterson (1993) has shown that" or "This is in the agreement with results obtained later (Kramer. 1994)" For 2-6 authors, all authors are to be listed at first citation, with "&" separating last two authors, for more than six authors, use the first six authors followed by et al. Subsequent citations for three or more authors use author et al. in the text, If quotations are cited, these should additionally have page numbers (e.g. Wilkins, 1776: 21 -22). The list of references should be arranged alphabetically by author's names. The manuscript should be carefully checked to ensure that the spelling or authors' names and dates are exactly the same in the text as in the reference list.

References should be given in the following form:

Daoud, S. (1994). Three strategies for developing awareness of global issues in ESP classes. In M. Abousenna, The global age: issues in English language education, *Proceedings of the 13th national symposium on English language teaching* (pp. 121-32), Cairo: CDELT, Ain Shams University.

Lumley, T. (1998). Perceptions of language-trained raters and occupational experts in a test of occupational English language proficiency, *English for Specific Purposes* 17(4), 347-367.

Prior, P. (1995). Redefining the task: an ethnographic examination of writing and response in a graduate seminar. In D. Belcher, & G. Braine, *Academic writing in a second language: essays on research & pedagogy* (pp. 47-82). Norwood, NJ: Ablcx Publishing Corporation.

Swales, J., & Fcak, C.B. (1994). *Writing for graduate students: Essential tasks and skills.* Ann Arbor: University of Michigan.

Illustrations. All illustrations should be provided in camera-ready form, suitable for reproduction (which may include reduction) without retouching. Photographs, charts and diagrams are all to be referred to as "Figure(s)" and should be numbered consecutively in the order to which they are referred. They should accompany the manuscript, but should not be included within the text. All illustrations should be clearly marked on the back with the figure number and the author's name. All figures are to have a caption. Captions should he supplied on a separate sheet.

Line drawings. Good quality printouts on white paper produced in black ink arc required. All lettering, graph lines and points on graphs should be sufficiently large arid bold to permit reproduction when the diagram has been reduced to a size suitable for inclusion in the journal. Dye-line prints or photocopies are not suitable for reproduction. Do not use any type of shading on computer-generated illustrations.

Photographs. Original photographs must be supplied as they are to be reproduced (e.g. black and white or colour). If necessary, a scale should be marked on the photograph. Please note that photocopies of photographs are not acceptable.

Colour. Where colour figures are required the author will be charged at the current colour printing costs.

Tables. Tables should he numbered consecutively and given a suitable caption and each table typed on a separate sheet. Footnotes to tables should be typed below the table and should be referred to by superscript lowercase letters. No vertical rules should be used. Tables should not duplicate results presented elsewhere in the manuscript, (e.g. in graphs).

Vitae. On a separate page following the list of references give a brief biographical sketch of the author(s) (maximum of 50 words per author). Include the professional affiliations, highlights of professional experience, and important publications.

Electronic Submission

Authors should submit an electronic copy of their paper with the final version of the manuscript. The electronic copy should match the hardcopy exactly. Always keep a backup copy of the electronic file for reference and safety. Full details of electronic submission and formats can be obtained from http://www.elsevier.com/locate/disksub or from Author Services at Elsevier Science.

Offprints

Twenty-five offprints will be supplied free of charge. Writers of reviews will receive 10 free offprints Additional offprints and copies of the issue can be ordered at a specially reduced rate

302

using the order form sent to the corresponding author after the manuscript has been accepted. Orders for reprints (produced after publication of an article) will incur a 50% surcharge.

Copyright
All authors must sign the "Transfer of Copyright" agreement before the article can be published. This transfer agreement enables Elsevier Science Ltd to protect the copyrighted material for the authors, without the author relinquishing his/her proprietary rights. The copyright transfer covers the exclusive rights to reproduce and distribute the article, including reprints, photographic reproductions, microfilm or any other reproductions of a similar nature, and translations. It also includes the right to adapt the article for use in conjunction with computer systems and programs, including reproduction or publication in machine-readable form and incorporation in retrieval systems. Authors are responsible for obtaining from the copyright holder permission to reproduce any material for which copyright already exists.

Author Enquiries
For enquiries relating to the submission of articles (including electronic submission), the status of accepted articles through our Online Article Status Information System (OASIS), author Frequently Asked Questions and any other enquiries relating to Elsevier Science please consult http://www.elsevier.com/locate/authors/. For specific enquiries on the preparation of electronic artwork, consult http://www.elsevier.com/locate/authorartwork/. Contact details for questions arising after acceptance of an article, especially those relating to proofs, are provided when an article is accepted for publication.

English Journal

ADDRESS FOR SUBMISSION:

Louann Reid, Editor
English Journal
Colorado State University
English Department
1773 Campus Delivery
Fort Collins, CO 80523-1773
USA
Phone: 970-491-6417
Fax: 970-491-3097
E-Mail: English-Journal@ColoState.edu
Web: www.englishjournal.colostate.edu
Address May Change: 6/1/2007

PUBLICATION GUIDELINES:

Manuscript Length: 10-15
Copies Required: One + disk
Computer Submission: International Only
Format: N/A
Fees to Review: 0.00 US$

Manuscript Style:
, MLA Review

CIRCULATION DATA:

Reader: Practicing Teachers
Frequency of Issue: 6 Times/Year
Copies per Issue: Over 28,000
Sponsor/Publisher: National Council of
   Teachers of English (NCTE)
Subscribe Price:
   40.00 US$ Membership ($26 Sub.)

REVIEW INFORMATION:

Type of Review: Blind Review
No. of External Reviewers: 2-3
No. of In House Reviewers: 1
Acceptance Rate: 10%
Time to Review: 3 Months
Reviewers Comments: Yes
Invited Articles: 0-5%
Fees to Publish: 0.00 US$

MANUSCRIPT TOPICS:

Bilingual/E.S.L.; Curriculum Studies; English Literature; Languages & Linguistics; Reading; Rural Education & Small Schools; Secondary/Adolescent Studies; Teacher Education; Tests, Measurement & Evaluation; Urban Education, Cultural/Non-Traditional

MANUSCRIPT GUIDELINES/COMMENTS:

English Journal, established in 1912, is published bi-monthly by the National Council of Teachers of English (NCTE); 1111 W. Kenyon Road; Urbana, IL 61801-1096. A refereed publication, it is the official journal of the Secondary Section of NCTE. Its readership of approximately 28,000 is composed largely of middle school, junior high school, and high school teachers, supervisors, and teacher educators.

Types of Manuscripts Sought
We seek manuscripts on any aspect of English language arts teaching in secondary schools. Writers may describe new ideas or innovative practices, discuss an issue, or argue for a particular point of view about the teaching of English language arts. We prefer manuscripts with a conversational tone that place classrooms and classroom practices in the foreground

while acknowledging the relationship of relevant theory and research in providing context for action and reflection. We also seek manuscripts that discuss single works of literature or films that may be taught in a middle school, junior high school, or senior high school class. Such manuscripts should address ways that the particular work could be relevant to the students and English language arts instruction.

Reviews of professional books and classroom materials are handled by the appropriate column editors, who accept unsolicited manuscripts. Poetry may be submitted directly to the Poetry Editor. See the current issue of *EJ* or the Web site at www.englishjournal.colostate.edu for the names and addresses of column editors.

Calls for Particular Topics are announced in the front section of each issue. The calls for manuscripts detail topics, list deadlines, and note if inquiries are welcome. Calls for features and articles are also available at the Web site: www.englishjournal.colostate.edu.

Manuscript Guidelines
Submit one clear copy of the manuscript and one electronic copy on a 3.5" disk formatted for PCs. Word 97 or later is preferred. Authors using Macintosh software should save their work as Word for Windows. Manuscripts and disks cannot be returned. Include a cover letter with a statement guaranteeing that the manuscript has not been published or submitted elsewhere. If the article is intended for a themed issue, indicate that. Writers living outside the United States may submit copy via email. Faxed submissions are not accepted.

In general, manuscripts should be no more than ten to fifteen double-spaced, typed pages in length. Longer manuscripts are discouraged.

Elements of Style
Titles of articles should be limited to no more than twelve words and should clearly indicate the manuscript's content. Clever titles that are obscure or even misleading are not helpful to readers; however, using an inventive title, a colon, and a more descriptive subtitle is acceptable.

The introductory paragraph of the article should clearly indicate the direction of the manuscript. Overly discursive or vague openings are not appropriate for the readership of *English Journal*. Beginning paragraphs should clearly indicate what the manuscript addresses, why anyone should care to read it, and why the writer is qualified to speak on the subject.

The use of "I" is appropriate when a manuscript calls for personal observation. Avoid educational jargon and highly specialized language, clichés and catch-phrases, overuse of adjectives, and vague generalities. Writers are expected to follow the conventions of standard edited American English. Care regarding references is extremely important. Double and triple check page numbers, dates, and other citation elements, keeping in mind that any undetected errors could be carried to 28,000 *EJ* readers.

Ensure that your manuscript adheres to the National Council of Teachers of English *Guidelines for Gender-Fair Use of Language*. Deviation from these guidelines should be requested with explanation in the cover letter accompanying the manuscript; otherwise, the editor will revise to assure conformity to the guidelines. We encourage writers to use plural nouns and pronouns ("teachers help their students"), thus avoiding the awkward his/her construction ("the teacher helps his or her students"). Inclusive language that reflects sensitivity to difference is expected. Prospective contributors should obtain a copy of the *Guidelines for Gender-Fair Use of Language* from the NCTE Web site at **http://www.ncte.org/pubs/publish/journals/107647.htm**.

The Review Process

We will acknowledge receipt of all manuscripts by email. *English Journal* is refereed, and virtually all manuscripts are read by two or more outside reviewers. We will attempt to reach a decision on each article within three months. Pieces written in response to a specific call for manuscripts will be decided on after the deadline.

Generally, letters accompanying rejected manuscripts do not provide extensive reaction or suggestions for revision. Because of the large number of manuscripts received in the *English Journal* office, such detailed responses are impractical. Writers may be comforted by the fact that *EJ* receives many more excellent manuscripts than it can publish; an acceptance rate of 10% is the norm.

If your article is accepted, we will notify you and ask you to complete a Consent-to-Publish form and provide a brief biographical statement. The editor may suggest or make major revisions in consultation with the author; however, because of the press of deadlines, the editor maintains the right to make what she perceives to be minor revisions without seeking the writer's approval. *English Journal* does not pay its contributors an honorarium; however, writers receive two complimentary copies of the issue in which their article appears.

Permissions Policy

It is your responsibility to secure permissions for copyrighted work that appears in your article. While short excerpts from copyrighted material may usually be quoted without permission, excerpts from poetry and song lyrics almost always require written permission. Likewise, any student work, text or graphic, requires a signed release from the student and, if the student is under eighteen, the signature of a parent. To protect the student's identity, you must use a pseudonym unless you have written permission from the student and a parent or legal guardian to use the real name. The *English Journal* office will provide forms for permissions and releases. If you are using student work, please request the Student Consent-to-Publish form.

Permissions related to illustrative material are covered in the next section.

Illustrative Material

Tables, graphics, charts, and other figures can enhance the meaning of the text. If you wish to include illustrative material, please read the following information carefully.

The table, figure, or other graphic should be sent either as a separate file or as a separate page at the end of the article file. Do not embed it in the article at the place it is to appear. Insert a note in the text indicating placement (e.g., TABLE 1 GOES HERE).

Tables and other all-text illustrative material should be sent in Word 97 or later. Make sure that you include a clear printout with the article so that we can double check the material on disk against the printout.

If you are sending in a diagram, graph, bar chart, or anything else that needs to be duplicated exactly, send it as a separate file in a standard image format such as .tif, .jpg, or .eps. It must be a high resolution file (300 dpi) to reproduce well.

For photographs, send an electronic file in a standard image format at 300 dpi. The image should be at least as large as it will appear in the journal. To keep the file size small, the image can be in grayscale, rather than color. If you cannot furnish a high-resolution electronic file, please send the original photograph and we will scan it.

Photographs and artwork are accepted with manuscripts; the same strictures mentioned above with regard to permissions apply. Authors must obtain written permission from the photographer and the subjects in the photograph. If the subjects are students under eighteen, you must also obtain signed permission from a parent or legal guardian. Permission forms are available from the *EJ* office. Please note that acceptance of a manuscript does not automatically imply acceptance of accompanying visuals.

Editorial Correspondence
Editorial correspondence and manuscripts should be directed to:

Louann Reid, Editor
English Journal
English Department
Colorado State University
1773 Campus Delivery
Fort Collins, CO 80523-1773

For inquiries, you may also phone 970-491-6417; fax 970-491-3097; or send e-mail to **English-Journal@ColoState.edu**.

Equity and Excellence in Education

ADDRESS FOR SUBMISSION:

Equity and Excellence in Education
University of Massachusetts
Hills South, Room 370
Amherst, MA 01003
USA
Phone: 413-545-4185
Fax: 413-545-1523
E-Mail: equity@educ.umass.edu
Web: www.tandf.co.uk/journals
Address May Change:

PUBLICATION GUIDELINES:

Manuscript Length: 25-30
Copies Required: Three
Computer Submission: Yes Disk
Format: MS Word or Rich Text Format
Fees to Review: 0.00 US$

Manuscript Style:
American Psychological Association

CIRCULATION DATA:

Reader: Practicing Teachers, Academics,
Administrators
Frequency of Issue: Quarterly
Copies per Issue: 2,001 - 3,000
Sponsor/Publisher: School of Education at
UMass-Amherst / Taylor & Francis
Subscribe Price: 60.00 US$ Individual
133.00 US$ Institution

REVIEW INFORMATION:

Type of Review: Masked
No. of External Reviewers: 2
No. of In House Reviewers: 2
Acceptance Rate: 16%
Time to Review: Min. 2 Months
Reviewers Comments: Yes
Invited Articles: 0-5%
Fees to Publish: 0.00 US$

MANUSCRIPT TOPICS:
Desegregation; Education Management/Administration; Educational Psychology; Gifted
Children; Qualitative Studies in All Areas of Education; Quality in Learning and Expanding
Understanding; Rural Education & Small Schools; School Law; Urban Education,
Cultural/Non-Traditional

MANUSCRIPT GUIDELINES/COMMENTS:

Aims and Scope
Equity & Excellence in Education publishes articles based on scholarly research utilizing
qualitative or quantitative methods, as well as essays that describe and assess practical efforts
to achieve educational equity and are contextualized within an appropriate literature review.
We consider manuscripts on a range of topics related to equity, equality and social justice in
K-12 or postsecondary schooling, and that focus upon social justice issues in school systems,
individual schools, classrooms, and/or the social justice factors that contribute to inequality in
learning for students from diverse social group backgrounds. There have been and will
continue to be many social justice efforts to transform educational systems as well as
interpersonal interactions at all levels of schooling. Some are successful while others fall short
of their goals. This journal provides a record of those important experiments and ventures.

INSTRUCTIONS FOR AUTHORS

Statement of Purpose

Equity & Excellence in Education publishes articles based on scholarly research utilizing qualitative or quantitative methods, as well as essays that describe and assess practical efforts to achieve educational equity and are contextualized within an appropriate literature review. We consider manuscripts on a range of topics related to equity, equality and social justice in K-12 or postsecondary schooling, and that focus upon social justice issues in school systems, individual schools, classrooms, and/or the social justice factors that contribute to inequality in learning for students from diverse social group backgrounds. There have been and will continue to be many social justice efforts to transform educational systems as well as interpersonal interactions at all levels of schooling. Some are successful while others fall short of their goals. This journal provides a record of those important experiments and ventures, and we welcome suggestions for special issues or sections.

Specifications for Submissions

To submit a manuscript, please send 3 typed copies and a 3-½" floppy disk with the manuscript saved as a Word document or in Rich Text Format. Include a separate title page with identifying information: your name, address, telephone number, institutional affiliation, fax number, and your e-mail address (by which we will acknowledge receipt of your manuscript). The first page of each copy of your manuscript should include your article's title and abstract, but no personally identifying information that might influence external peer reviewers.

Authors should follow the 5th edition of the *American Psychological Association Publication Manual* guidelines for citations, references, organization, and ethics. Refer to these guidelines to eliminate bias based on gender, sexual orientation, racial or ethnic group, disability, or age. In accordance with standard practice, we expect that manuscripts submitted to *Equity & Excellence in Education* are original, have not been published elsewhere, and are not under review at any other journal.

Social Groups and Language

We recognize that social identities and their accompanying names are constantly evolving and changing within historical and geographical contexts. We also believe that every group has a right to name itself, and accordingly we honor an author's preferred self-identification. We regard the following as acceptable or interchangeable: African American or Black, Indian or Native American, Latino or Hispanic, Asian or Asian American, White or European. We also recognize that certain terms are considered pejorative, and authors should consult the *APA Publications Manual* 5th edition for guidance about language bias and sensitivity.

In manuscript submissions, we prefer that specific ethnicities are capitalized but not hyphenated. Racial designations such as Black and White are capitalized only when used as proper nouns, but not when used as adjectives (e.g. black communities, white teachers).

Review Process

Receipt of submissions is acknowledged by email. After preliminary evaluation by the editorial staff, manuscripts that we consider appropriate for this journal are sent to external peer reviewers. The outside reviews, along with editorial staff reviews, provide the basis for acceptance, although editorial decisions are not bound by external reviews. Revised work is generally reviewed in-house. We make every effort to assist authors in strengthening their work, whether or not it is ultimately published in this journal.

Equity & Excellence in Education, Hills South 370, School of Education, University of Massachusetts Amherst, MA 01003 **equity@educ.umass.edu** We invite you to visit our website at **http://www.taylorandfrancis.com** or **http://www.eee-journal.com**

Essays in Education

ADDRESS FOR SUBMISSION:

Timothy Lintner, Editor
Essays in Education
University of South Carolina, Aiken
471 University Parkway
Aiken, SC 29801
USA
Phone: 803-641-3564
Fax: 803-641-3698
E-Mail: tlintner@usca.edu
Web: www.usca.edu/essays/
Address May Change:

PUBLICATION GUIDELINES:

Manuscript Length: 16-20
Copies Required: Electronic
Computer Submission: Yes Email
Format: MS Word
Fees to Review: 0.00 US$

Manuscript Style:
American Psychological Association

CIRCULATION DATA:

Reader: Academics
Frequency of Issue: Quarterly
Copies per Issue: N/A
Sponsor/Publisher: University of South
   Carolina, Aiken
Subscribe Price: 0.00 US$

REVIEW INFORMATION:

Type of Review: Blind Review
No. of External Reviewers: 2
No. of In House Reviewers: 1
Acceptance Rate: 21-30%
Time to Review: 2 - 3 Months
Reviewers Comments: Yes
Invited Articles: 0-5%
Fees to Publish: 0.00 US$

MANUSCRIPT TOPICS:

Adult Career & Vocational; Art/Music; Audiology/Speech Pathology; Bilingual/E.S.L.; Counseling & Personnel Services; Curriculum Studies; Education Management/Administration; Educational Psychology; Educational Technology Systems; Elementary/Early Childhood; English Literature; Foreign Language; Gifted Children; Health & Physical Education; Higher Education; Languages & Linguistics; Library Science/Information Resources; Reading; Religious Education; Rural Education & Small Schools; School Law; Science Math & Environment; Secondary/Adolescent Studies; Social Studies/Social Science; Special Education; Teacher Education; Tests, Measurement & Evaluation; Urban Education, Cultural/Non-Traditional

MANUSCRIPT GUIDELINES/COMMENTS:

Essays in Education is a peer-reviewed electronic journal that seeks to explore the multitude of issues that impact and influence education.

In accord with its broad focus, the journal welcomes contributions that enhance the exchange of diverse theoretical and practical information among educators, practitioners, and researchers around the world.

Beyond publishing original articles, the journal's editorial board will consider reviews of educational software, books and pedagogical materials. However, reviews must describe the practitioner's actual experiences using such materials.

Submissions to the Journal

Authors submitting works to *Essays in Education* warrant that their works are not currently under consideration by any other publication and that any portion of the work is not subject to additional copyright regulations, unless prior required consents have been obtained.

Articles are to be submitted to the editor, preferably by electronic mail. Mail to:
tlinter@usca.edu

Articles (4 copies) may also be submitted by postal mail:
Editor
Essays in Education
University of South Carolina, Aiken
471 University Parkway
Aiken, SC 29801

Cover Sheet, Title, Author Information and Key Words

Please provide a cover sheet indicating the title of the article, the author's name and institutional affiliation, and both electronic and standard addresses.

The title of the manuscript should appear on the first page of the text. Leave blank a single line and then list the author's name and institutional affiliation. Continue this format for multiple authors.

Leave a blank line, then type "KEY WORDS" and list three to six key words or phrases (separated by semicolons) that may be used to index the manuscript.

Abstracts

Each manuscript should be accompanied by an abstract. Insert the abstract between the list of key words and the beginning of the text. Abstracts should not exceed 15 lines in length.

Guidelines

Although there is no established length, scholarly articles between 15-30 pages are preferred.

Though tables and graphs are welcome, these should be used sparingly within the body of the text.

Single space all copy. Insert a blank line between paragraphs, between references in the REFERENCE section, and before and after subheadings, etc.

Use the *American Psychological Association (APA)* format for all citations and references. Please contact the editors for any format questions that are not covered in the most recent edition of the *APA Publication Manual.*

312

All major headings and subheadings should be flush left.

Refereeing Process
Articles submitted for publication consideration to *Essays in Education* are peer-reviewed by three referees who are chosen from the *EIE* Editorial Board. The refereeing process is double-blind; authors and referees are anonymous to each other.

Before sending a submission to the referees, the author's name and affiliation are removed. Authors are responsible for removing any references or clues as to their identity or affiliation within the body of the paper.

Reprints of Articles
Articles included in *Essays in Education* may be reproduced for any medium for non-commercial purposes.

Essential Teacher

ADDRESS FOR SUBMISSION:

Kathy Weed, Editor
Essential Teacher
USA
Phone:
Fax: 703-836-6447
E-Mail: et@tesol.org
Web: www.tesol.org
Address May Change: 12/31/2007

CIRCULATION DATA:

Reader: Practicing Teachers,
   Administrators
Frequency of Issue: Quarterly
Copies per Issue: 10,001 - 25,000
Sponsor/Publisher: TESOL
Subscribe Price:
   Membership Only
   See www.tesol.org

PUBLICATION GUIDELINES:

Manuscript Length: 11-15
Copies Required: Electronic Submission
Computer Submission: Yes
Format: MS Word or WordPerfect
Fees to Review: 0.00 US$

Manuscript Style:
   American Psychological Association

REVIEW INFORMATION:

Type of Review: Editorial Review
No. of External Reviewers: 3
No. of In House Reviewers: 2
Acceptance Rate: 11-20%
Time to Review: 2 - 3 Months
Reviewers Comments: Yes
Invited Articles: 31-50%
Fees to Publish: 0.00 US$

MANUSCRIPT TOPICS:
Bilingual/E.S.L.; Curriculum Studies; Education Management/Administration; Educational Technology Systems; Elementary/Early Childhood; Higher Education; Languages & Linguistics; Reading; Teacher Education; Urban Education, Cultural/Non-Traditional

MANUSCRIPT GUIDELINES/COMMENTS:

About Essential Teacher
Essential Teacher offers teachers columns by practitioners in various communities of practice, practical articles that are theoretically sound, materials reviews, and association news. It also provides second and foreign language teachers of English with a forum for teaching practices, reflections, and perspectives.

Essential Teacher is primarily dedicated to language teachers and administrators in varied ESL and EFL workplaces, including pre-K-12, 2- and 4-year institutions of higher learning, and adult education. Each of these arenas has teachers with varied experience and expertise, making for a broad and diverse readership. *Essential Teacher* also offers guidance to mainstream teachers who work with students for whom English is an additional language.

Send your comments or letters to the editor to **et@tesol.org**.

Essential Teacher **Submission Guidelines**

Essential Teacher welcomes submissions that reflect the professional lives of educators working with students for whom English is an additional language. As professionals, you are interested in your work and curious about students, language, learning, and teaching. You have stories to tell, questions to pose, issues to ponder, and thoughts to express. *Essential Teacher* invites you to submit writing that inspires, informs, and situates the diverse practice of English language teaching within theoretically sound perspectives.

Essential Teacher offers

- short compositions about life as a TESOL educator in the various contexts in which you find yourselves
- essays that get you to think about practice
- creative, thinking-outside-the-box articles to change your perspective
- reviews of all means to professional development
- association news

In short, the magazine offers a variety of items for a variety of voices. Look through the descriptions of the magazine's sections and find the one that invites your voice and views.

General Information

Essential Teacher is published four times a year: winter, spring, summer, and autumn. Although you may submit as many pieces as you wish, no author's work will appear more than once in a given section in any volume year. Because *Essential Teacher* is a magazine for everyone in the field of TESOL, the editors seek an equal balance between ESL and EFL articles and between veteran and novice writers. *Essential Teacher* is committed to publishing diverse voices and new perspectives. Editors will respond to submissions within 6 weeks.

Essential Teacher asks all contributors to sign a release of their copyright to TESOL. Please do not submit work that has been published, that is under consideration elsewhere, or that is already under contract, and please do not submit work for which you wish to retain copyright.

Essential Teacher reserves the right to edit work that is accepted for publication. All submissions are collaboratively reviewed and edited.

Frequently Asked Questions about writing for *Essential Teacher* see website (420kb Adobe PDF document).

SECTIONS
Communities of Practice

Representing various TESOL constituencies, *Communities of Practice columnists* write from their experiences about the pleasures, challenges, surprises, and epiphanies that come from teaching English to speakers of other languages. Although this section does not accept articles, columnists welcome comments and questions. Be sure to identify the column or constituency you are addressing.

Portal

Portal looks at technology use in English language teaching settings around the world. What is working in your setting? What isn't? What do you recommend to your colleagues? What have you learned from your peers? Submit a short summary of your ideas to the Portal editor, Mercedes Rossetti (marossetti@prodigy.net.mx). Final articles should be written in a narrative, nonacademic style, and have 1,500-1,800 words, no foot or end notes, and a maximum of eight references.

Out of the Box

Are you forward-looking, creative, and imaginative? Are you writing an article in your head that you know is engaging and sound but that would not be at home in most traditional publications? Then consider Out of the Box. This section features thoughtful, innovative work from inside and outside the English language teaching world. Articles may take a perspective you may not usually associate with the field of TESOL. If writing an article for Out of the Box interests you, send a brief (maximum 250-word) description to the editor, Phil Quirke (phil.quirke@hct.ac.ae). Final articles should be written in a narrative, nonacademic style, and have 1,500-1,800 words, with a maximum of eight references.

Home and Other Pages

What kinds of materials--hard or soft, bound or floppy--have affected you and your teaching? How did a certain textbook inspire you? What connections have you found among texts, trade books, CDs, and software? Tell other teachers about them here. Home and Other Pages welcomes mixed-media reviews devoted to professional development. Consider reviewing Web sites, books, audiotapes, CDs, videos and films, or software. Send your review as an attachment via e-mail to Christine Meloni (meloni@gwu.edu). (Put "ET Review" on the subject line.) Web site and software reviews should be no longer than 440 words. Reviews of books, audiotapes, CDs, videos, or films should be no longer than 220 words.

Compleat Links

Compleat Links is an online complement to *Essential Teacher*. Items for this section, which are thematically linked to features in the printed magazine, appear only on TESOL's Web site. The Links expand on or give new perspectives on the themes and topics within the issue. When contributing to another section, you may include in your cover letter ideas that complement or augment your own or suggest people to interview regarding the content. The Compleat Links editor (Leslie Opp-Beckman, leslieob@darkwing.uoregon.edu) may opt to follow your leads if the submission is accepted for publication.

Exceptionality -- A Special Education Journal

ADDRESS FOR SUBMISSION:

Edward J. Sabornie, Editor
Exceptionality -- A Special Education
   Journal
NC State University
College of Education
Poe Hall
Campus Box 7801
Raleigh, NC 27695-7801
USA
Phone: 919-515-1777
Fax: 919-515-6978
E-Mail: edward_sabornie@ncsu.edu
Web: www.erlbaum.com
Address May Change:

PUBLICATION GUIDELINES:

Manuscript Length: 26-30
Copies Required: Five
Computer Submission: No
Format:
Fees to Review: 0.00 US$

Manuscript Style:
   American Psychological Association

CIRCULATION DATA:

Reader: Academics
Frequency of Issue: Quarterly
Copies per Issue: Less than 1,000
Sponsor/Publisher: Lawrence Erlbaum, Inc.
Subscribe Price: 45.00 US$ Individual

REVIEW INFORMATION:

Type of Review: Editorial Review
No. of External Reviewers: 3
No. of In House Reviewers: 1
Acceptance Rate: 11-20%
Time to Review: 1 - 2 Months
Reviewers Comments: Yes
Invited Articles: 21-30%
Fees to Publish: 0.00 US$

MANUSCRIPT TOPICS:
Adult Career & Vocational; Educational Psychology; Gifted Children; Reading; Science Math
& Environment; Secondary/Adolescent Studies; Special Education; Teacher Education; Tests,
Measurement & Evaluation

MANUSCRIPT GUIDELINES/COMMENTS:

Editorial Scope
The purpose of *Exceptionality* is to provide a forum for presentation of current research and
professional scholarship in special education. Areas of scholarship published in the journal
include quantitative, qualitative, and single-subject research designs examining students and
persons with exceptionalities, as well as reviews of the literature, discussion pieces, invited
works, position papers, theoretical papers, policy analyses, and research syntheses.
Appropriate data-based papers include basic, experimental, applied, naturalistic, ethnographic,
and historical investigations. Papers that describe assessment, diagnosis, placement, teacher
education, and service delivery practices will also be included. Manuscripts accepted for

publication will represent a cross section of all areas of special education and exceptionality and will attempt to further the knowledge base and improve services to individuals with disabilities and gifted and talented behavior.

Audience

Education researchers, education professionals interested in students at risk, developmental and school psychologists, neuropsychologists, medical personnel involved with students and persons with exceptionalities, social workers, teachers, and higher education students in education.

Instructions to Contributors

Manuscript Submission. Only manuscripts written in English will be considered. Submit five manuscript copies to the Editor, Dr. Edward J. Sabornie, North Carolina State University, College of Education and Psychology, Poe Hall, Campus Box 7801, Raleigh, NC 27695-7801. Prepare manuscripts according to the *Publication Manual of the American Psychological Association* (5th ed.). Type all components of the manuscript double-spaced, including the title page, abstract, text, quotes, acknowledgments, references, appendixes, tables, figure captions, and footnotes. An abstract of fewer than 200 words should be typed on a separate page. Authors should comply with the "Guidelines to Reduce Bias in Language," which appears on pages 46 to 53 of the *APA Manual*. Five photocopies of the illustrations and the original illustrations should accompany the manuscript. All manuscripts submitted will be acknowledged promptly. Authors should keep a copy of their manuscript to guard against loss.

Peer Review Policy. The editorial board evaluates manuscripts with regard to scientific rigor and importance of the implications for practice or policy. To accelerate the review process, reviewers only provide comments to authors whose manuscripts are found acceptable for publication. In this way, we are able to provide author feedback in approximately 6 weeks from the time of receipt of the manuscript. Authors who prefer that their identities and affiliations be masked are responsible for requesting blind review. Every effort should be made by the authors to see that the manuscript itself contains no clues to their identities.

Permissions. Authors are responsible for all statements made in their work and for obtaining permission from copyright owners to reprint or adapt a table or figure or to reprint a quotation of 500 words or more. Authors should write to the original author(s) and publisher to request nonexclusive world rights in all languages for use of the material in the article and in future editions. Provide copies of all permissions and credit lines obtained.

Regulations. In a cover letter, authors should state that the findings and ideas reported in the manuscript are original and have not been published previously and that the manuscript is not being simultaneously submitted elsewhere. Authors should also state that they have complied with American Psychological Association ethical standards in the treatment of their samples.

Production Notes. After a manuscript is accepted for publication, the author is asked to provide a computer disk containing the manuscript file. Files are copyedited and typeset into page proofs. Authors read proofs to correct errors and answer editors' queries. Authors may order reprints of their articles only when they return page proofs.

Family and Consumer Sciences Research Journal

ADDRESS FOR SUBMISSION:

Jane E. Workman, Editor
Family and Consumer Sciences Research
    Journal
Southern Illinois University
311 Quigley Hall
MC 4318
Carbondale, IL 62901
USA
Phone: 618-453-1981
Fax: 618-453-8190
E-Mail: jworkman@siu.edu
Web: www.sagepub.com
Address May Change:

PUBLICATION GUIDELINES:

Manuscript Length: 40 Max
Copies Required: Four
Computer Submission: Yes Disk or Email
Format: MS Word
Fees to Review: 40.00 US$

Manuscript Style:
    American Psychological Association

CIRCULATION DATA:

Reader: Academics, Extension Specialists
Frequency of Issue: Quarterly
Copies per Issue: 1,001 - 2,000
Sponsor/Publisher: American Association
    of Family and Consumer Sciences / Sage
    Publications
Subscribe Price: 86.00 US$
    30.00 US$ AAFCS Member

REVIEW INFORMATION:

Type of Review: Blind Review
No. of External Reviewers: 3
No. of In House Reviewers: 1
Acceptance Rate: 60%
Time to Review: 3 - 4 Months
Reviewers Comments: Yes
Invited Articles: 0-5%
Fees to Publish: 15.00 US$ Per Page

MANUSCRIPT TOPICS:
Education Management/Administration; Health & Physical Education; See Guidelines

MANUSCRIPT GUIDELINES/COMMENTS:

Manuscript Topics

Child and Family Studies
Clothing and Textiles
Food and Nutrition
Housing, Equipment, and Design

Hotel, Restaurant, and Institution Management
Consumer/Family Economics and Management
Family and Consumer Sciences

Manuscripts
Should be double-spaced in their entirety, should include line numbers and should not be right justified. Glossy prints and original drawings or figures should be submitted only after the final version of a manuscript is accepted. Send only photocopies of these with initial submission.

Family Relations: Interdisciplinary Journal of Applied Family Studies

ADDRESS FOR SUBMISSION:

Joyce A. Arditti, Editor
Family Relations: Interdisciplinary Journal
   of Applied Family Studies
Virgina Tech
Human Development
359 Wallace Hall
Blacksburg, VA 24061
USA
Phone: 540-231-1646
Fax: 540-231-7012
E-Mail: frjourn@vt.edu
Web: www.ncfr.com
Address May Change: 12/31/2008

CIRCULATION DATA:

Reader: Academics
Frequency of Issue: 5 Times/Year
Copies per Issue: 4,001 - 5,000
Sponsor/Publisher: National Council on
   Family Relations
Subscribe Price: 104.00 US$ Individual
   268.00 US$ Institution

PUBLICATION GUIDELINES:

Manuscript Length: 26-30
Copies Required: Five
Computer Submission: No
Format: N/A
Fees to Review: 15.00 US$

Manuscript Style:
   American Psychological Association

REVIEW INFORMATION:

Type of Review: Blind Review
No. of External Reviewers: 3
No. of In House Reviewers: 1
Acceptance Rate: 11-20%
Time to Review: 2 - 3 Months
Reviewers Comments: Yes
Invited Articles: 0-5%
Fees to Publish: 0.00 US$

MANUSCRIPT TOPICS:
Counseling & Personnel Services; Family Studies and Practice

MANUSCRIPT GUIDELINES/COMMENTS:

Family Relations publishes applied articles that are original, innovative and interdisciplinary and that focus on diverse families and family issues. Audiences include family life educators in academic and community settings, researchers with an applied or evaluation focus, family practitioners who utilize prevention or therapeutic models and techniques, and family policy specialists. Examples of appropriate articles include those dealing with applied research, educational philosophies or practices, syntheses of substantive areas, program evaluations, and curriculum development and assessment. Articles should be conceived and written with implications for practice and/or policy in mind.

320

General. **Manuscripts must be submitted online.** **For complete detailed instructions on uploading your manuscript, please visit the** *Family Relations* **online submission site (http://mc.manuscriptcentral.com/fr)** and log on. If you need assistance select "get help". Once logged on select author center, and then select "submit a new manuscript." If you do not have a user ID, click the "create an account" icon and follow the online instructions. Any major word processing software may be used, and both DOS-based and Macintosh operating systems are acceptable. Authors with no Internet connection should contact the Editorial Office. The author checklists must be completed during the submission process. Copyright assignment is a condition of publication, and papers will not be passed to the Publisher unless copyright has been assigned. A link to the appropriate copyright form can be found online during the submission process. However, authors should not submit a copyright form until their manuscript has been accepted for publication.

Complete instructions for preparing and submitting manuscripts online are provided at the submission site and at **http://www.ncfr.com/fr/authors/index.htm**. There also is an online tutorial available at **Scholar One Online Users Guide**.

If you need further assistance, please contact the editorial office by phone at 540-231-1646 or via e-mail at **frjourn@vt.edu**.

Please follow the appropriate *APA* 5th edition format when submitting manuscripts online. In addition, it is vital that manuscripts submitted online are prepared for blind review. A $15 processing fee also will be collected at the time of submission.

Tables. Formatting for tables must follow the guidelines listed at
http://oregonstate.edu/~acock/tables/

Feliciter

ADDRESS FOR SUBMISSION:

Peter Wilson, Communications Coordinator
Feliciter
Canadian Library Association
328 Frank Street
Ottawa, ON K2P 0X8
Canada
Phone: 613-232-9625 Ext. 322
Fax: 613-563-9895
E-Mail: publishing@cla.ca
Web: www.cla.ca
Address May Change:

PUBLICATION GUIDELINES:

Manuscript Length: 400-1,500 Words
Copies Required: One
Computer Submission: Yes
Format: MS Word for Macintosh
Fees to Review: 0.00 US$

Manuscript Style:
    Chicago Manual of Style

CIRCULATION DATA:

Reader: Academics, Library/Information
    Specialists
Frequency of Issue: 6 Times/Year
Copies per Issue: 3,000
Sponsor/Publisher: Canadian Library
    Association
Subscribe Price: 95.00 US$

REVIEW INFORMATION:

Type of Review:
No. of External Reviewers: 3+
No. of In House Reviewers: 0
Acceptance Rate: 95%
Time to Review: 2 Months
Reviewers Comments: Yes
Invited Articles: 10%
Fees to Publish: 0.00 US$

MANUSCRIPT TOPICS:
Library Science/Information Resources; Reading

MANUSCRIPT GUIDELINES/COMMENTS:

Feliciter is published by the Canadian Library Association as a service to members and is the only national magazine dedicated to serving the Canadian library and information services community. Each issue of *Feliciter* contains opinion pieces and feature articles on professional concerns and developments, along with news of the Canadian Library Association. Annual subscriptions are available at $95.00.

Style. Informal but informative. Conclusions should follow logically and statements should be supported. *Feliciter* uses the *Chicago Manual of Style*. Since *Feliciter* is not a scholarly journal, extensive footnoting is usually not required. References should follow *Chicago Manual of Style* Style A.

Format. Manuscripts may be submitted by mail to the attention of the Communications Coordinator at the CLA office, by fax to (613) 563-9895, or by e-mail to **publishing@cla.ca**.

Please include your daytime telephone number, fax number and mailing address. Manuscripts may be submitted in any standard word processing program for either IBM or Macintosh.

Length. 400 to 1,500 words.

Photographs/Illustrations. We welcome colour or black-and-white prints/slides as well as illustrations, charts and tables that support the text.

Acceptance. Manuscripts are accepted at the discretion of the Editor. If the submission is not in electronic format, an electronic copy will be requested upon acceptance.

Editing. CLA reserves the right to make revisions, deletions or additions that enhance the text or are required to meet length restrictions. All materials are copy-edited for consistency. Substantial revisions are discussed with the author.

Every effort is made to provide the author with an opportunity to review the edited text prior to publication.

Complimentary Copies. CLA provides the author with a reasonable number of complimentary copies of the issue in which published material appears.

Rights. Submissions to *Feliciter* must be original and not previously published. CLA retains world rights in all formats to all material published in *Feliciter* and acts as a clearinghouse for any subsequent use. Requests to make copies or otherwise use material must be made in writing to the Editor. Permission is usually granted for authors to reproduce their contributions as published in the magazine. The Editor clears any reprint or other requests to use material with the author.

Queries. CLA welcomes queries prior to submission.

Florida Reading Quarterly

ADDRESS FOR SUBMISSION:

Nile Stanley, Editor
Florida Reading Quarterly
University of North Florida
College of Education
4567 St. Johns Bluff Road, South
Jacksonville, FL 32224-2648
USA
Phone: 904-620-1849
Fax: 904-620-1025
E-Mail: nstanley@unf.edu
Web: www.flreads.org
Address May Change:

PUBLICATION GUIDELINES:

Manuscript Length: 16-20 Double spaced
Copies Required: Four
Computer Submission: Yes Email, Disk
Format: MS Word
Fees to Review: 0.00 US$

Manuscript Style:
    American Psychological Association

CIRCULATION DATA:

Reader: Practicing Teachers, Academics
Frequency of Issue: Quarterly
Copies per Issue: 4,001 - 5,000
Sponsor/Publisher: Florida Reading
    Association
Subscribe Price: 15.00 US$
    22.00 US$ Foreign

REVIEW INFORMATION:

Type of Review: Blind Review
No. of External Reviewers: 3
No. of In House Reviewers: 4
Acceptance Rate: 45%
Time to Review: 2 - 3 Months
Reviewers Comments: Yes
Invited Articles: 0-5%
Fees to Publish: 0.00 US$

MANUSCRIPT TOPICS:
Bilingual/E.S.L.; Creative Writing, Quality Works-All Genres; Curriculum Studies;
Elementary/Early Childhood; K-12; Language Arts; Reading; Secondary/Adolescent Studies

MANUSCRIPT GUIDELINES/COMMENTS:

1. *American Psychological Association Publication Manual* 5th Edition

2. *FRQ* publishes articles and features in a variety of formats and lengths. Contact editor for specific information.

The Florida Reading Quarterly is published for members of the Florida Reading Association and all others concerned with reading. Because *The Florida Reading Quarterly* serves as an open forum, its contents do not necessarily reflect or imply endorsement of the FRA, its officers, or its members.

The Florida Reading Quarterly invites teachers and graduate students to submit original articles related to all areas of reading and literacy education. *The Florida Reading Quarterly*

(*FRQ*) has a readership of approximately 3000 teachers and teacher educators. The editorial board encourages articles about classroom practice and current issues related to literacy education. *FRQ* also publishes research syntheses and reviews of professional materials, including technology related to literacy. Creative works including stories and poetry are accepted.

Online submissions are highly encouraged. Refer to the *FRQ* website:
   http://www.flreads.org/Publications/quarter.htm

Authors who prefer to use the mail are requested to submit only unpublished articles not under review by any other publication. A manuscript (8-14 pages) should be typed, double spaced, not right justified, not hyphenated, and should follow APA, 4th edition guidelines (*Publication Manual of the American Psychological Association*). Tables and graphs should be used only when absolutely necessary.

Submit four good copies with print the quality of an original (i.e., clear, dark letters on white paper with no extraneous marks). A cover page is needed on one copy giving the article title and the professional affiliation, complete address, email, and phone number of the author(s). A disk with the final copy of the article will be required when an article has been accepted for publication. The editors reserve the right to edit all copy. Contributors desiring more information may request the "Preparation of Manuscripts" guidelines by sending a stamped, self-addressed envelope to the editor.

Focus on Learning Problems in Mathematics

ADDRESS FOR SUBMISSION:

Jean Schmittau, Editor
Focus on Learning Problems in
   Mathematics
State University of New York
School of Education and
   Human Development
P O Box 6000
Binghamton, NY 13902-6000
USA
Phone: 607-777-4209
Fax: 607-777-3587
E-Mail: jschmitt@binghamton.edu
Web: www.unlv.edu/RCML
Address May Change:

PUBLICATION GUIDELINES:

Manuscript Length:
Copies Required: Five
Computer Submission: No
Format: MS Word
Fees to Review: 0.00 US$

Manuscript Style:
   American Psychological Association

CIRCULATION DATA:

Reader: Practicing Teachers, Researchers,
   Mathematic Educators, Academics,
   Administrators
Frequency of Issue: Quarterly
Copies per Issue: 2,001 - 3,000
Sponsor/Publisher: Professional Association
Subscribe Price: 45.00 US$ Institution
   30.00 US$ through CT/LM
   28.00 US$ through RCML

REVIEW INFORMATION:

Type of Review: Blind Review
No. of External Reviewers: 2
No. of In House Reviewers: 0
Acceptance Rate: 11-20%
Time to Review: 2 - 3 Months
Reviewers Comments: Yes
Invited Articles: 6-10%
Fees to Publish: 0.00 US$

MANUSCRIPT TOPICS:

Curriculum Studies; Educational Psychology; Educational Technology Systems;
Elementary/Early Childhood; Gifted Children; Higher Education; Learning Problems in Math;
Mathematics Learning and Teaching; Remedial Instruction; Science Math & Environment;
Secondary/Adolescent Studies; Special Education; Teacher Education; Tests, Measurement &
Evaluation

MANUSCRIPT GUIDELINES/COMMENTS:

FOCUS on Learning Problems in Mathematics is an inter-disciplinary journal, published
jointly by the Research Council on Mathematics Learning (RCML) and the Center for
Teaching/Learning o£ Mathematics (CT/LM). The objective of *FOCUS* is to disseminate
current research efforts designed to understand and/or influence factors that affect
mathematics learning. Contributions from the fields of education, psychology, mathematics
and medicine having the potential for impact on classroom or clinical practices are valued.
Specifically, the types of manuscripts sought for *FOCUS* include reports of research on

processes, techniques, tools and procedures useful for addressing problems in mathematics teaching and learning, descriptions of methodologies for conducting, and reporting and interpreting the results of various types of research,, research-based discussions of promising techniques or novel programs, and scholarly works such as literature reviews, philosophical statements or critiques.

For advertising and publication information, write to: Center For Teaching/Learning of Mathematics, PO Box 3149, Framingham, Massachusetts 01701. Phone 508-877-7895 or 617-0235-7200.

Foreign Language Annals

ADDRESS FOR SUBMISSION:

Emily Spinelli, Editor
Foreign Language Annals
c/o Sandy Cutshall, Managing Editor
 (sandy@printmanagementinc.com)
P O Box 391837
Mountain View, CA 94039-1837
USA
Phone:
Fax:
E-Mail: espinell@umich.edu
Web: www.actfl.org
Address May Change:

PUBLICATION GUIDELINES:

Manuscript Length: 25-35 pp.
Copies Required: Four + Disk or CD
Computer Submission: No
Format: N/A
Fees to Review: 0.00 US$

Manuscript Style:
 American Psychological Association

CIRCULATION DATA:

Reader: Academics, Administrators,
 Classroom Instructors, Researchers
Frequency of Issue: Quarterly
Copies per Issue: 8,500
Sponsor/Publisher: American Council on
 the Teaching of Foreign Languages
 (ACTFL)
Subscribe Price: 100.00 US$

REVIEW INFORMATION:

Type of Review: Blind Review
No. of External Reviewers: 2
No. of In House Reviewers: 1
Acceptance Rate: 20-25%
Time to Review: 4 - 6 Months
Reviewers Comments: Yes
Invited Articles: Occasionally
Fees to Publish: 0.00 US$

MANUSCRIPT TOPICS:

Assessment; Bilingual/E.S.L.; Evaluation; Foreign Language; Foreign Language Education;
Foreign Language Methodolgoy; Foreign Language Teaching; Languages & Linguistics;
Second Language Acquisition; Teacher Education; Tests, Measurement & Evaluation

MANUSCRIPT GUIDELINES/COMMENTS:

As the official journal of the American Council on the Teaching of Foreign Languages,
Foreign Language Annals is dedicated to the advancement of foreign language teaching and
learning. The journal seeks to serve the professional interests of classroom instructors,
researchers, and administrators concerned with the teaching of foreign languages at all levels
of instruction.

Foreign Language Annals is a refereed journal published quarterly (four issues per year).
Preference is given to articles that report educational research or experimentation, that
describe innovative and successful practice and methods, and/or that are relevant to the

concerns and issues of the profession. Special articles are occasionally commissioned but manuscripts on a wide variety of topics are welcomed.

APA style (the style set by the American Psychological Association) is used for text, references, and notes. Detailed style guidelines, including examples, are available in the *FLA Guidelines for Manuscript Preparation,* which may be requested from one of three sources: (1) the ACTFL website: **www.actfl.org**; (2) the Managing Editor Sandy Cuthall by e-mail: **sandy@printmanagementinc.com**; or (3) regular mail: ACTFL Headquarters, 700 South Washington Street, Suite 210 Alexandria, VA 22314.

Foreign Language Annals publishes only original works that have not been previously published elsewhere and that are not under consideration by any other publication. Each submission must contain the following five components: (1) a cover memo/letter with the consideration statement and contact information for the author(s); (2) title page; (3) abstract of the article; (4) manuscript of the article; (5) diskette or CD containing the entire manuscript in Microsoft Word.

To be considered for publication, manuscripts should be double-spaced throughout (including notes and references) with margins of at least one-and-one-half inches. Preference will be given to manuscripts that do not exceed 35 double-spaced pages. To assure anonymity the names of the authors and school affiliation should occur only within the cover letter and not within the title page, abstract, or article itself. Submit one copy of the cover letter, four paper copies of the article and one copy of the entire article on diskette or CD in Microsoft Word.

All properly submitted manuscripts will receive an acknowledgment of receipt from the Editorial Office. All properly submitted articles will be sent out for peer review shortly after receipt. Authors will be informed about the status of the article once the peer reviews have been received and processed. Reviewer comments will be shared with the contact author. Once an article has been accepted for publication, the contact author will receive further instructions regarding the submission of the final copy.

Gerontologist (The)

ADDRESS FOR SUBMISSION:

Linda S. Noelker, Editor-in-Chief
Gerontologist (The)
Benjamin Rose
Margaret Blenkner Research Institute
850 Euclid Avenue, Suite 1100
Cleveland, OH 44114
USA
Phone: 216-373-1686
Fax: 216-621-3505
E-Mail: tg@benrose.org
Web: tg.allentrack.net
Address May Change:

PUBLICATION GUIDELINES:

Manuscript Length: 6000 words
Copies Required: One
Computer Submission: Yes Email or Web
Format: MS Word
Fees to Review: 0.00 US$

Manuscript Style:
    American Psychological Association

CIRCULATION DATA:

Reader: Academics, Practitioners
Frequency of Issue: Bi-Monthly
Copies per Issue: 5,001 - 10,000
Sponsor/Publisher: The Gerontological
    Society of America
Subscribe Price: 225.00 US$ Institution
    235.00 US$ (Surface mail)
    285.00 US$ (Air mail) Foreign

REVIEW INFORMATION:

Type of Review: Blind Review
No. of External Reviewers: 2-3
No. of In House Reviewers: N/A
Acceptance Rate: 11-15%
Time to Review: 1 - 2 Months
Reviewers Comments: Yes
Invited Articles: 0-5%
Fees to Publish: 0.00 US$

MANUSCRIPT TOPICS:
Adult Career & Vocational; Aging; Policy; Practice

MANUSCRIPT GUIDELINES/COMMENTS:

1. Submission of Manuscripts
Authors are strongly encouraged to submit all manuscripts online at **http://tg.allentrack.net**.

Prior to submission, corresponding authors should gather the following information: (a) complete contact information for themselves and each contributing author; at a minimum, this should include mailing address, e-mail address and phone number; (b) a copy of the manuscript, in a Word-compatible format, including title page, key words, acknowledgements, abstract, text, and references; DO NOT BLIND the manuscript for online submissions. If the manuscript is selected for peer review, it will be blinded by TG staff; (c) a separate file for each table (in Word or Excel) and each figure (most common graphics formats are acceptable; figures also may be embedded in a Word-compatible file, though this is not recommended); (d) a cover letter (optional) explaining how the manuscript is innovative, provocative, timely, and of interest to a broad audience, and other information authors wish to share with editors. Note: The cover letter for new manuscripts will NOT be shared with reviewers.

For multi-author papers, the journal editors will assume that all the authors have been involved with the work and have approved the manuscript and agree to its submission. (If the manuscript is eventually accepted, all authors will be required to certify that this is the case).

Additional instructions regarding web-based submissions appear online.

If there is a compelling reason why the author cannot submit online, submissions will be accepted via e-mail to **tg@benrose.org**. If a manuscript is submitted through the mail (to Linda S. Noelker, Editor-in-Chief, The Gerontologist, Benjamin Rose,850 Euclid Avenue, Suite 1100,Cleveland,OH 44114-3301), the submission MUST include both a hard copy of the manuscript and an electronic version on disk.

2. **Acceptance of Manuscripts**
Submission of a manuscript to *The Gerontologist* implies that it has not been published or is not under consideration elsewhere. If accepted for this journal, it is not to be published elsewhere without permission. As a further condition of publication, the corresponding author will be responsible, where appropriate, for certifying that permission has been received to use copyrighted instruments or software employed in the research and that human or animal subjects approval has been obtained.

In the case of coauthored manuscripts, the corresponding author will also be responsible for submitting a letter, signed by all authors, indicating that they actively participated in the collaborative work leading to the publication and agree to be listed as an author on the paper. These assurances will be requested at the time a paper has been formally accepted for publication.

3. **Manuscript Preparation**
The Gerontologist uses APA style. General guidelines follow; for more detailed information, consult the *Publication Manual of the American Psychological Association* (5th ed.)

a. **Preparing the manuscript**. Manuscripts should be double-spaced (including references and tables) on 8 ½" x 11" paper using 1" margins. Number pages consecutively for the abstract, text, references, tables, and figures (in this order).

b. **Submitting the manuscript**. Manuscripts should be submitted online at http://tg.allentrack.net. (See above for details)

c. **Title page**. The page should include complete contact information for each author, including (at a minimum) affiliation, mailing address, e-mail address and phone number. Corresponding author should be clearly designated as such.

d. **Acknowledgement**. If the authors choose to include acknowledgements recognizing funders or other individuals, these should be placed on a separate page immediately following the title page. These will be removed from the manuscript when it is blinded for review.

e. **Abstract and key words**. On a separate page, each manuscript must include a brief abstract, double-spaced. Abstracts for research articles and Practice Concepts submissions should be approximately 200 words (the web-based system will not accept an abstract of more than 250 words), and must include the following headings: Purpose of the Study, Design and Methods, Results, and Implications. Forum manuscripts must also include an abstract of about 200 words, but the headings are not necessary. Brief reports should include a brief abstract (25 to 50 words). Below the abstract, authors must supply three to five key words that are not in the title (please avoid "elders," "older adults," or other key words that would apply to all manuscripts submitted to TG). Please note, you may not move forward in the online submission process until a minimum of three key words has been entered.

f. **Text references**. Refer to the *Publication Manual of the American Psychological Association* (5th ed.) for style. References in text are shown by citing in parentheses the author's surname and the year of publication. Example: "...a recent study (Jones, 1987) has shown...." If a reference has two authors, the citation includes the surnames of both authors each time the citation appears in the text (e.g., Jones & Smith, 1989). When a reference has more than two but fewer than six authors, cite all authors the first time the reference occurs (Jones, Smith, Simon, Medici, & Doe, 1991). In subsequent citations, and for all citations having six or more authors, include only the surname of the first author followed by "et al." (Jones et al., 1991). Multiple references cited at the same point in the text are in alphabetical order by author's surname.

g. **Reference list**. Type double-spaced and arrange alphabetically by author's surname; do not number. The reference list includes only references cited in the text and in most cases should not exceed 50 entries. Do not include references to private communications or submitted work. Consult the *Publication Manual of the American Psychological Association* (5th ed.) for correct form.

Examples:
Journals
Binstock, R. H. (1983). The aged as scapegoat. *The Gerontologist*, 23, 136-143.

Books
Quadagno, J. S. (1982). *Aging in early industrial societies*. New York: Academic Press.

h. **Tables**. Prepare tables, double-spaced, in separate files; number consecutively with Arabic numbers and supply a brief title for each. Place table footnotes immediately below the table, using superscript letters (a, b, c) as reference marks. Asterisks are used only for probability levels of tests of significance (*p ,.05). Indicate preferred placement for each table in the text.

i. **Illustrations**. Photographs must be black-and-white. Figures must be professionally lettered in a sans-serif type (e.g., Arial or Helvetica). Graphics must be submitted in a suitable, common graphic format.

4. Types of Manuscripts Considered for Publication

All manuscripts submitted to *The Gerontologist* should address practice and/or policy implications. The word limits listed below include abstract, text and references.

a. **Research Articles.** Most articles present the results of original research. These manuscripts may be no longer than 6,000 words. The text is usually divided into sections with the headings: Introduction, Design and Methods, Results, and Discussion. Subheads may also be needed to clarify content.

b. **The Forum.** Timely scholarly review articles or well-documented arguments presenting a viewpoint on a topical issue are published in this section. Total length should be no more than 5,000 words.

c. **Practice Concepts.** Practice Concepts are manuscripts of no more than 4,000 words that critically review the state-of-the-art in a major area of professional practice OR describe an innovative practice amenable to replication. Authors reporting on practice innovations should clearly specify the following information about the practice: uniqueness or innovativeness, theoretical or conceptual basis, essential components or features, lessons learned from implementation, and data concerning outcomes. An important goal is to provide enough information about the practice to allow its replication by readers.

d. **Letters to the Editor.** Letters related to content in recent issues are published as space permits. Letters should be no more than 900 words, double-spaced. Letters are subject to review, editing, and rebuttal.

e. **Book Reviews.** Book reviews are published in essay form. Reviews are prepared at the request of the Book Review Editor and are not guaranteed acceptance prior to submission. Unsolicited book review essays are not accepted. Books for review should be sent to Robert H. Binstock, PhD, Book Review Editor, Henry R. Luce Professor of Aging, Health and Society, School of Medicine, Case Western Reserve University, Cleveland, OH 44106.

f. **Audiovisual Reviews.** Audiovisual reviews are prepared at the invitation of the Audiovisual Review Editor. Unsolicited reviews are not accepted. Materials for review should be sent to Robert E. Yahnke, PhD, University of Minnesota, 254 Appleby Hall, 128 Pleasant St. S.E., Minneapolis, MN 55455.

g. **Guest Editorials.** The Editor-in-Chief occasionally will invite guest editorials. Unsolicited editorials are not accepted.

h. **Brief Reports.** Reports of research, descriptive data with broad implications, work in progress, or innovations in pedagogy or education are examples of articles published in this section. Manuscripts should be no more than 2,200 words.

i. *The Gerontologist* does not publish obituaries, speeches, poems, announcements of programs, or new product information.

5. Copyright

Authors of accepted manuscripts must transfer copyright to The Gerontological Society of America. However, authors have unlimited rights to republish their articles in volumes they write or edit and to duplicate the material for their own use in classroom activities. When articles are republished or duplicated under these circumstances, a citation to the previous publication in *The Gerontologist* and approval from the GSA Permissions Editor are required.

Gifted Child Quarterly

ADDRESS FOR SUBMISSION:

Paula Olszewski-Kubilius, Editor
Gifted Child Quarterly
Northwestern University
Center for Talent Development
617 Dartmouth
Evanston, IL 60208
USA
Phone: 847-491-3782
Fax: 847-467-4283
E-Mail: nagc@nagc.org
Web: www.nagc.org
Address May Change:

PUBLICATION GUIDELINES:

Manuscript Length: 15-40
Copies Required: Four
Computer Submission: Yes
Format: Must include hardcopy also
Fees to Review: 0.00 US$

Manuscript Style:
   American Psychological Association,
   (5th Edition)

CIRCULATION DATA:

Reader: Academics
Frequency of Issue: Quarterly
Copies per Issue: 5,001 - 10,000
Sponsor/Publisher: National Association for
   Gifted Children
Subscribe Price: 45.00 US$

REVIEW INFORMATION:

Type of Review: Blind Review
No. of External Reviewers: 3
No. of In House Reviewers: 1
Acceptance Rate: 16-26%
Time to Review: 2 - 3 Months
Reviewers Comments: Yes
Invited Articles: 6-10%
Fees to Publish: 0.00 US$

MANUSCRIPT TOPICS:
Gifted Children

MANUSCRIPT GUIDELINES/COMMENTS:

The *Gifted Child Quarterly* publishes manuscripts which offer new or creative insights about giftedness and talent development. Quality and technical competence are important criteria in the peer review process. In addition, the contribution of the manuscript to the advancement of the knowledge base is also considered. Manuscripts should be of interest and accessible to researchers, practitioners, policy makers and parents.

Prepare for Peer Review
All articles appearing in the *Gifted Child Quarterly* are peer reviewed. Authors are requested to prepare for blind review by submitting manuscripts accompanied by a cover sheet that lists the title of the manuscript, the names of the authors, the authors' institutional affiliations, the mailing address, and the date the manuscript is submitted. The first page of the manuscript should contain the title, but should omit the authors' names and any other identifying information.

Determine the Appropriateness of Submission
By submitting to the *Gifted Child Quarterly*, the authors are confirming that the manuscripts have not been published previously and are not under consideration for publication elsewhere. The *Gifted Child Quarterly* publishes scholarly reviews of the literature and quantitative or qualitative research studies. The journal occasionally publishes manuscripts which explore policy and policy implications. Authors interested in the policy format are requested to contact the editor prior to submission. Articles that are intended as program descriptions or practical guides without research documentation are inappropriate for the *Gifted Child Quarterly*.

Follow APA Style
Authors should follow the *Publication Manual of the American Psychological Association*, 5th Edition (2001). All manuscripts should be accompanied by an abstract of 100 to 150 words. Manuscript pages, including reference Lists, should be submitted double-spaced. Figures should be camera ready. Tables and figures should be used to present information which is also discussed in text.

Adhere to Copyright Laws and Professional Acknowledgments
Authors are responsible for obtaining and providing written permission for copyright material. Authors are also responsible for publication clearance if the article reports research presented at a professional meeting or developed through a project financed by a funding agency.

Submit Four Hard Copies and an Electronic Copy
Submit four copies of your manuscript to the Editor. Please also enclose a disk with an electronic copy of your entire manuscript (including abstract, tables, figures, etc.).

Gifted Child Today

ADDRESS FOR SUBMISSION:

Susan Johnsen, Editor
Gifted Child Today
Baylor University
School of Education
216 Burleson Hall
P.O. Box 97304
Waco, TX 76798-7304
USA
Phone: 254-710-6116
Fax: 254-710-3987
E-Mail: Susan_Johnsen@baylor.edu
Web: www.prufrock.com
Address May Change:

PUBLICATION GUIDELINES:

Manuscript Length: 1,500 - 4,000 Words
Copies Required: Four
Computer Submission: Yes
Format: Any Format / IBM or Macintosh
Fees to Review: 0.00 US$

Manuscript Style:
American Psychological Association

CIRCULATION DATA:

Reader: Practicing Teachers, and Parents
Frequency of Issue: Quarterly
Copies per Issue: 5,001 - 10,000
Sponsor/Publisher: Prufrock Press
Subscribe Price: 29.95 US$
36.00 US$ Canadian & Foreign

REVIEW INFORMATION:

Type of Review: Peer Review
No. of External Reviewers: 3
No. of In House Reviewers: 1
Acceptance Rate: 25%
Time to Review: 2 - 3 Months
Reviewers Comments: Yes
Invited Articles: 25%
Fees to Publish: 0.00 US$

MANUSCRIPT TOPICS:
Elementary/Early Childhood; Gifted Children; Gifted, Creative, or Talented Children and Youth; Secondary/Adolescent Studies

MANUSCRIPT GUIDELINES/COMMENTS:

Gifted Child Today is an award winning magazine designed to focus on the nurturing of talented, creative, and gifted learners.

Articles are based on classroom or home experiences and reflect the most current research in the field of gifted education. They include submissions by university professionals, classroom teachers, counselors, administrative professionals, and parents working with gifted, talented, and creative learners.

Gifted Child Today also features the following regular columns:
Advocacy by Sandra Kaplan, Ph. D.
International Perspectives by Tracy Riley, Ph. D.

Au Contraire by James Delisle, Ph. D.
Parenting the Gifted by Patricia Haensly, Ph. D.
Socia/Emotional Needs by Tracy Cross, Ph. D.
Exploring Options by Mary Ruth Coleman, Ph. D.

Each issue contains a news briefs section, upcoming state and national meetings, and new product announcements. Issues also contain professional biographical notes about all authors.

Guidelines for Authors
Manuscripts should be between 1,500 and 4,000 words long. Authors should send two copies of each manuscript. They should be typed, double-spaced on one side of the page only. Each page should be labeled with the page number and the author's name in the upper right-hand corner. They should be sent on Letterbond paper or heavier (no onion-skin or erasable-bond paper). Manuscripts should include at least a one-inch margin around the page. A cover page must be enclosed including the author's name, title, school and program affiliation, and home and work addresses and phone numbers.

Please enclose a brief (50-100 word) biography with each submission.

A complete list of works cited must accompany all manuscripts. Please use *American Psychological Association*, 4th edition, style for documentation and bibliographical information. References should be included on a separate sheet at the end of the manuscript.

Use non-sexist language whenever possible.

It is strongly encouraged that works be submitted on computer disk. Manuscripts may be sent on 3.5-inch computer disk in any word processing format, either IBM or Macintosh. The disk should be labeled with the author's name, address, and phone number, the title of the manuscript, and the word processing software used. Include two hard copies also, even when submitting a manuscript on disk.

Photographs may be submitted for consideration to accompany an article. They must be glossy prints, either black and white or color, or transparencies.

Graphs and illustrations must include complete attribution including author and publication. They should be as large as possible. All graphs will be reproduced by the *Gifted Child Today* staff prior to publication. Graphics designed on a computer in either TIFF, PICT, or EPS formats should be sent on disk (accompany the disk with a hard copy of the illustration). Illustrations must be in black ink on white paper.

Any submission of artwork, graphs, illustrations, or photographs must include reference as to the creator of the material and any copyright information available.

Address any questions you may have to the editorial offices of the journal: Attn.: Editors, Gifted Child Today, P.O. Box 8813, Waco, TX 76714-8813 or call 254-756-3337; 800-998-2208; fax: 800-240-0333. The website is **www.prufrock.com**

Harvard Educational Review

ADDRESS FOR SUBMISSION:

Manuscript Editor
Harvard Educational Review
Harvard Graduate School of Education
8 Story Street, 1st Floor
Cambridge, MA 02138
USA
Phone: 617-495-3432
Fax: 617-496-3584
E-Mail: hepg@harvard.edu
Web: gseweb.harvard.edu/~hepg/her.html
Address May Change:

CIRCULATION DATA:

Reader: Academics
Frequency of Issue: Quarterly
Copies per Issue: 10,001 - 25,000
Sponsor/Publisher: Harvard University
Subscribe Price: 59.00 US$ Individual
139.00 US$ Institution

PUBLICATION GUIDELINES:

Manuscript Length: 15,000 words
Copies Required: Three Print + electronic
Computer Submission: No
Format: N/A
Fees to Review: 0.00 US$

Manuscript Style:
Chicago Manual of Style, American
Psychological Association

REVIEW INFORMATION:

Type of Review: Blind Review
No. of External Reviewers: 0
No. of In House Reviewers: 3+
Acceptance Rate: 1-5%
Time to Review: Over 6 Months
Reviewers Comments: No
Invited Articles: 31-50%
Fees to Publish: 0.00 US$

MANUSCRIPT TOPICS:
Adult Career & Vocational; Art/Music; Bilingual/E.S.L.; Education Management/Administration; Higher Education; Languages & Linguistics; Teacher Education; Tests, Measurement & Evaluation; Urban Education, Cultural/Non-Traditional

MANUSCRIPT GUIDELINES/COMMENTS:

The *Harvard Educational Review* accepts contributions from teachers, practitioners, policymakers, scholars, and researchers in education arid related fields, as well as from informed observers. In addition to discussions and reviews of research and theory, *HER* welcomes articles that reflect on teaching and practice in educational settings in the United States and abroad. Authors can elect to indicate whether they are submitting their manuscript as an article, a Voices Inside Schools article, an essay review, or a book review. *HER* has a two stage review process. Manuscripts that pass the initial stage are then considered by the full Editorial Board and receive detailed written feedback. It is the policy of the *Review* to consider for publication only articles that are not simultaneously being considered elsewhere. Please follow our guidelines in preparing your manuscript for submission (**http://gseweb.harvard.edu/hepg/guidelines.html**).

1. Authors must submit **three copies** of the manuscript, including a one-page abstract. Manuscripts will be returned only if a stamped, self-addressed envelope is included at the time of submission. In addition, please include a clearly labeled 3.5-inch disk or cd-rom containing an electronic version of the manuscript in Microsoft Word format. If you do not have access to MS Word, please contact us to make other arrangements.

2. Manuscripts are considered **anonymously**. The author's name must appear *only* on the title page; any references that identify the author in the text must be deleted.

3. *HER* accepts manuscripts of **up to 15,000 words** and reserves the right to return any manuscript that exceeds that length.

4. All text must be **double-spaced**, and type size must be at least **12 point with 1" margins on both sides.**

5. Quoted material is extracted in the text when it is more than 45 words, unless the editors determine otherwise.

6. Authors should refer to *The Chicago Manual of Style* for general questions of style, grammar, punctuation, and form. Chicago should also be referred to for footnotes of theoretical, descriptive, or essay-like material.

7. For technical and research manuscripts, authors should use the *Publication Manual of the American Psychological Association* for reference and citations format.

8. *The Uniform System of Citation*, published by the *Harvard Law Review*, should be used for articles that rely heavily on legal documentation. Because this form is not easily adaptable to other sources, it is usually combined with *The Chicago Manual of Style* as necessary.

9. Authors should select the style most suitable for their manuscripts and adhere consistently to that style. The Editors reserve the right to request that authors use an alternative style if the one chosen seems inappropriate. Styles may not be combined, with the exception of legal citations.

10. **References must be in APA format.** We request that authors provide complete references, including page citations in book reviews. Authors should be certain that citations and footnotes in the text agree with those in the references.

11. As a generalist journal, *HER* discourages the use of technical jargon. We encourage authors to minimize the use of underlining, parentheses, italics, and quotation marks for emphasis in the text. Footnotes should be as few and as concise as possible. Tables and figures should be kept to a minimum.

Voices Inside Schools

The purpose of this section is to provide a forum devoted to the voices of teachers, students, and others committed to education within the school community broadly defined who interact with students and who have important knowledge and expertise about life inside schools gained through practice, reflection, and/or research. We value the writing of adults and students who have intimate and first-hand experience with teaching and learning.

Submissions for the Voices Inside Schools section are written by teachers and other professionals in the field of education about their own practice, and by students about their own educational experiences. In the past, *HER* has published articles by practitioners on a wide variety of issues: a Black educator's experiences teaching writing as a process to minority students, a literacy educator teaching women in a correctional facility, a university professor describing the content and pedagogy of her course on AIDS, and a school principal reflecting on school restructuring. Authors may choose to present their perspective through a range of formats, from data-driven to more reflective essays.

Please visit our Voices Inside Schools page for more information.

Book Reviews
HER also accepts reviews of recent publications (within the last 2 publication years) about education. Book reviews, in which the author reviews a book related to education, should be 8-12 double-spaced pages. *HER* also publishes essay reviews, in which one or more books in a particular field are analyzed and the implications for future research and practice are discussed. These essays should range from 15-20 pages. More detailed guidelines for book and essay reviews are available from the *HER* office or visit the website at **http://gseweb.harvard.edu/hepg/essay.htm**. Please call 617-495-3432, or write to the address below.

Health Education

ADDRESS FOR SUBMISSION:

Katherine Weare, Editor
Health Education
University of Southampton
School of Education
Head of Institutional and Professional
  Development Research Centre
Hampshire, SO17 1BJ
UK
Phone: 02380 593707
Fax:
E-Mail: skw@soton.ac.uk
Web: www.emeraldinsight.com/he.htm
Address May Change:

CIRCULATION DATA:

Reader: Academics
Frequency of Issue: Bi-Monthly
Copies per Issue:
Sponsor/Publisher: Emerald Group
  Publishing Limited
Subscribe Price: 2309.00 US$

PUBLICATION GUIDELINES:

Manuscript Length: 26-30
Copies Required: Two
Computer Submission: Yes Email
Format:
Fees to Review: 0.00 US$

Manuscript Style:

REVIEW INFORMATION:

Type of Review: Blind Review
No. of External Reviewers: 2
No. of In House Reviewers: 0
Acceptance Rate: 75%
Time to Review: 2 - 3 Months
Reviewers Comments: Yes
Invited Articles: 0-5%
Fees to Publish: 0.00 US$

MANUSCRIPT TOPICS:

Counseling & Personnel Services; Curriculum Studies; Educational Technology Systems; Elementary/Early Childhood; Health & Physical Education; Higher Education; Secondary/Adolescent Studies

MANUSCRIPT GUIDELINES/COMMENTS:

About the journal
Health Education plays a crucial role in the development of a healthy environment and society. The journal disseminates good practice in health education to enable you to build on the best ideas of others. Offering stimulating and incisive coverage of current concerns and campaign strategies, it provides a wealth of practical information that can be used to enhance the effectiveness of your own health campaigns.

NOTES FOR CONTRIBUTORS

Copyright
Articles submitted to the journal should be original contributions and should not be under consideration for any other publication at the same time. Authors submitting articles for publication warrant that the work is not an infringement of any existing copyright and will indemnify the publisher against any breach of such warranty. For ease of dissemination and to ensure proper policing of use, papers and contributions become the legal copyright of the publisher unless otherwise agreed. Submissions should be sent to:

The Editor
Professor Katherine Weare,
School of Education,
University of Southampton,
Hampshire, SO17 1BJ, UK
Tel: +44 (0) 23 8059 3707; Fax: +44 (0) 23 8059 2755
E-mail: **skw@soton.ac.uk**

Editorial objectives
This journal's main objective is to help disseminate good practice in health education. We aim to do this by publishing articles that will keep our readers informed about new developments and new approaches, and that will supply them with practical information which they can use in their day-to-day work. Each issue will contain material of specific interest to those involved in school health education.

Editorial scope
This covers all areas of health education. Our readers will include health promotion staff working for health authorities and education departments; teachers in schools who have responsibility for teaching health, personal and social education; school nurses; dieticians; police officers; academic staff involved in training health educators; those who run community drug and alcohol services; and those involved at all levels in encouraging the general public to follow healthier lifestyles.

The reviewing process
Each paper is reviewed by the editor and, if it is judged suitable for this publication, it is then sent to two referees for double blind peer review. Based on their recommendations, the editor then decides whether the paper should be accepted as it is, revised or rejected.

Emerald Literati Editing Service
The Literati Club can recommend the services of a number of freelance copy editors, all themselves experienced authors, to contributors who wish to improve the standard of English in their paper before submission. This is particularly useful for those whose first language is not English.   http://www.emeraldinsight.com/literaticlub/editingservice.htm

Manuscript requirements
Three copies of the manuscript should be submitted in double line spacing with wide margins. All authors should be shown and author's details must be printed on a separate sheet and the author should not be identified anywhere else in the article.

As a guide, articles should be between 4000 and 8000 words in length. A title of not more than eight words should be provided. A brief **autobiographical note** should be supplied including full name, affiliation, e-mail address and full international contact details. Authors must supply a structured abstract set out under 4-6 sub-headings: Purpose; Methodology/Approach; Findings; Research limitations/implications (if applicable); Practical implications (if applicable); and, the Originality/value of paper. Maximum is 250 words in total. In addition provide up to six keywords which encapsulate the principal topics of the paper and categorise your paper under one of these classifications: Research paper, Viewpoint, Technical paper, Conceptual paper, Case study, Literature review or General review. For more information and guidance on structured abstracts visit:

http://www.emeraldinsight.com/literaticlub/editors/editorialadmin/abstracts.htm

Where there is a **methodology**, it should be clearly described under a separate heading. **Headings** must be short, clearly defined and not numbered. **Notes** or **Endnotes** should be used only if absolutely necessary and must be identified in the text by consecutive numbers, enclosed in square brackets and listed at the end of the article.

Figures, charts and **diagrams** should be kept to a minimum. They should be provided both electronically and as good quality originals. They must be black and white with minimum shading and numbered consecutively using Arabic numerals.

Artwork should be either copied or pasted from the origination software into a blank Microsoft Word document, or saved and imported into a blank Microsoft Word document. Artwork created in MS PowerPoint is also acceptable. Artwork may be submitted in the following standard image formats: .eps - Postscript, .pdf - Adobe Acrobat portable document, .ai - Adobe Acrobat portable document, .wmf - Windows Metafile. If it is not possible to supply graphics in the formats listed above, authors should ensure that figures supplied as .tif, .gif, .jpeg, .bmp, .pcx, .pic, .pct are supplied as files of at least 300 dpi and at least 10cm wide.

In the text the position of a figure should be shown by typing on a separate line the words "take in Figure 2". Authors should supply succinct captions.

For photographic images good quality original **photographs** should be submitted. If submitted electronically they should be saved as tif files of at least 300dpi and at least 10cm wide. Their position in the text should be shown by typing on a separate line the words "take in Plate 2".

Tables should be kept to a minimum. They must be numbered consecutively with roman numerals and a brief title. In the text, the position of the table should be shown by typing on a separate line the words "take in Table IV".

Photos and **illustrations** must be supplied as good quality black and white original half tones with captions. Their position should be shown in the text by typing on a separate line the words "take in Plate 2".

References to other publications should be complete and in Harvard style. They should contain full bibliographical details and journal titles should not be abbreviated. For multiple citations in the same year use a, b, c immediately following the year of publication. References should be shown within the text by giving the author's last name followed by a comma and year of publication all in round brackets, e.g. (Fox, 1994). At the end of the article should be a reference list in alphabetical order as follows

(a) for books
surname, initials and year of publication, title, publisher, place of publication, e.g. Casson, M. (1979), Alternatives to the Multinational Enterprise, Macmillan, London.

(b) for chapter in edited book
surname, initials and year, "title", editor's surname, initials, title, publisher, place, pages, e.g. Bessley, M. and Wilson, P. (1984), "Public policy and small firms in Britain", in Levicki, C. (Ed.), Small Business Theory and Policy, Croom Helm, London, pp.111-26. Please note that the chapter title must be underlined.

(c) for articles
surname, initials, year "title", journal, volume, number, pages, e.g. Fox, S.(1994) "Empowerment as a catalyst for change: an example from the food industry", Supply Chain Management, Vol 2 No 3, pp. 29-33

If there is more than one author list surnames followed by initials. All authors should be shown.

Electronic sources should include the URL of the electronic site at which they may be found, as follows:
Neuman, B.C.(1995), "Security, payment, and privacy for network commerce", IEEE Journal on Selected Areas in Communications, Vol. 13 No.8, October,pp.1523-31. Available (IEEE SEPTEMBER) http://www.research.att.com/jsac/

Notes/Endnotes should be used only if absolutely necessary. They should, however, always be used for citing Web sites. They should be identified in the text by consecutive numbers enclosed in square brackets and listed at the end of the article. Please then provide full Web site addresses in the end list.

Final submission of the article
Once accepted for publication, the final version of the manuscript must be provided, accompanied by a 3.5" disk of the same version labelled with: disk format; author name(s); title of article; journal title; file name.

Each article must be accompanied by a completed and signed Journal Article Record Form available from the Editor or on http://www.emeraldinsight.com/literaticlub Authors should note that proofs are not supplied prior to publication.

The manuscript will be considered to be the definitive version of the article. The author must ensure that it is complete, grammatically correct and without spelling or typographical errors.

344

In preparing the disk, please use one of the following preferred formats: Word, Word Perfect, Rich text format or TeX/LaTeX.

Technical assistance is available from Emerald's Literati Club on http://www.emeraldinsight.com/literaticlub or by contacting Mike Massey at Emerald, e-mail mmassey@emeraldinsight.com.

A summary of submission requirements:
- Good quality hard copy manuscript
- A labelled disk
- A brief professional biography of each author
- An abstract and keywords
- Figures, photos and graphics electronically and as good quality originals
- Harvard style references where appropriate
- A completed Journal Article Record form

Health Education & Behavior

ADDRESS FOR SUBMISSION:

Marc A. Zimmerman, Editor
Health Education & Behavior
Unv of Michigan - Sch of Public Health
  ELECTRONIC SUBMISSION ONLY
Dept. of Health Behavior & Health Edu.
1420 Washington Heights
Ann Arbor, MI 48109-2029
USA
Phone: 734-764-9494
Fax: 734-763-7379
E-Mail: marcz@umich.edu
Web: www.sph.umich.edu/hbhe/heb/
Address May Change:

PUBLICATION GUIDELINES:

Manuscript Length: 21-25
Copies Required: Electronic Submission
Computer Submission: Yes
Format: N/A
Fees to Review: 0.00 US$

Manuscript Style:
  See Manuscript Guidelines

CIRCULATION DATA:

Reader: , Public Health Educators
Frequency of Issue: 6 Times/Year
Copies per Issue: 2,001 - 3,000
Sponsor/Publisher: Society of Public Health
  Education / Sage Publications
Subscribe Price: 134.00 US$ Individual
  853.00 US$ Institution

REVIEW INFORMATION:

Type of Review: Blind Review
No. of External Reviewers: 1-3
No. of In House Reviewers: 1-3
Acceptance Rate: 11-20%
Time to Review: 2 - 3 Months
Reviewers Comments: Yes
Invited Articles: 6-10%
Fees to Publish: 0.00 US$

MANUSCRIPT TOPICS:
Health & Physical Education; Program Evaluation

MANUSCRIPT GUIDELINES/COMMENTS:

Topics continued. Health Education; disease prevention and health promotion; health-related behavioral and social change; Program Evaluation; Quantitative and quantitative studies; theoretical & literature reviews.

About the Journal
Health Education & Behavior explores social and behavioural change as it affects health status and quality of life, as well as examining the processes of planning, implementing, managing, and assessing health education and social-behavioural interventions. *HEB* is a vital resource for practising health educators and researchers, as well as other health professionals and agencies. The journal offers material of interest to: administrators behavioural scientists businesses community organizers doctors government agencies health agencies health care

346

facilities HMO and managed care representatives hospitals insurance companies nurses public and community health planners social scientists and social workers.

Regular features include *Perspectives*, which offers thoughtful insights into complex subjects, and *Program Notes*, summarizing innovative programs in health education. Through articles, editorials, and special sections, each issue of *HEB* covers a wealth of information addressing such varied topics as: Theoretical and practical ways to implement change in health and social behaviour AIDS cardiovascular risk reduction cancer drug abuse violence chronic disease management stress social support the environment diverse populations of all ages and ethnic groups empowerment health care reform cultural factors ethics international health programme settings such as worksites, hospitals, clinics, communities and schools.

Instructions for Authors
Manuscripts should be electronically submitted. See **www.sph.umich.edu/heb** for instructions and the specific URL for submission.

Hard copies of manuscripts will only be accepted if electronic submission is not possible. One copy should be submitted with a diskette copy in MS Word or WordPerfect to Marc A. Zimmerman, Ph.D., Editor, Health Education & Behavior, Department of Health Behavior and Health Education, University of Michigan, School of Public Health, 1420 Washington Heights, Ann Arbor, MI, 48109-2029. Hard copies should be submitted in English on standard 8 1/2"x 11" (21 cm x 28 cm) paper with 1 1/2" (3.8 cm) margins.

Health Education & Behavior is interested in articles directed toward researchers and/or practitioners in health behavior and health education. Empirical research, case studies, program evaluation, literature reviews, and articles discussing theories are regularly published in the journal. Each manuscript submitted is expected to include a section discussing implications for practitioners in the reported work. If a study assesses an intervention, a description of the intervention should be included in the paper.

Manuscripts should be including captions, footnotes, tables, and references, must be typed double-spaced, font size 12 point, and on one side of the sheet only. Footnotes to the text should be avoided where possible.

Authors are asked not to use the term *subjects* when referring to research participants. Alternative terms such as respondents, (research) participants, or some other more specific designation (e.g., females, adolescents, residents) should be used.

The original should have a title page that contains the names of all authors, their affiliations, and a complete, current address and telephone number for each author. Include fax and e-mail numbers if possible. A footnote to the title page may contain simple statements of affiliation, credit, and research support. The names of the authors should not appear on the rest of the paper. Rather, a descriptive running head of no more than four words should appear at the top of each page of the manuscript.

An abstract of 100-150 words must accompany each submission. It should be placed on a page by itself after the title page in the manuscript. It should also include 3 keywords.

American Psychological Association reference and citation style should be used.

All figures must be cited in the text, numbered, and supplied with a caption. All captions should appear together on a separate sheet after the reference listing.

All artwork must be submitted in camera-ready form. Photographs to be used as illustrations must be supplied as fulltone original prints. Screened prints are unacceptable. Line art may be submitted either as original artwork or as matte photoprints, provided all linework and lettering is black and of a lineweight suitable for reduction. Line art is frequently reduced so that it will fit in the journal. The lettering should be done mechanically so that the lettering does not fill in or break up on reduction. Hand lettering and the use of typewriter labels are not acceptable. Clean, clear xerographic copies of artwork are acceptable for camera-ready use.

All tables should be cited sequentially in text, numbered, and supplied with explanatory captions. Table columns should have explanatory headings. Tables should be supplied typed on separate sheets and placed at the end of the manuscript following any figure captions. Tables should never be typed within the body of the manuscript.

Proofs will be supplied to authors to check the accuracy of typesetting and copyediting. Authors may be charged for excessive alterations to the proofs.

A reprint order form will be sent to the author after the issue containing his or her work is published, along with tearsheets of the article. Two complimentary copies of the entire issue will be sent to single authors; for articles with more than one author, each author will receive one copy.

Since a new U.S. copyright law became effective in January 1978, the transfer of copyright from author to publisher, heretofore implicit in the submission of a manuscript, must now be explicitly transferred to enable the publisher to assure maximum dissemination of the author's work. A copy of the agreement executed and signed by each author is now required with each manuscript submission. The agreement is sent to the author by the editor. (If the article is a "work for hire," the agreement must be signed by the employer.) No manuscript can be considered accepted unless a signed copyright transfer agreement exists. It is the author's responsibility to obtain written permission and defray all fees for the use of any quotes over 300 words from previously published academic material; non-original photographs, figures, or tables or any portion thereof, exclusive of data; quotes of any length from newspapers, magazines, poems, songs, and anything broadcast over radio or television. Without a copy of written permission on file with the publisher, the quote cannot be used. Original photographs require signed releases from those photographed.

For more information about the Journal, see our Web site: **www.sph.umich.edu/hbhe.heb**.

Health Education Journal

ADDRESS FOR SUBMISSION:

Anthony S. Blinkhorn, Editor
Health Education Journal
University Dental Hospital
Higher Cambridge Street
Manchester, M15 6FH
UK
Phone: 0161 275 6160
Fax: 0161 275 6299
E-Mail: anthony.blinkhorn@man.ac.uk
Web: www.hej.org.uk
Address May Change:

CIRCULATION DATA:

Reader: Academics, Health Professionals
Frequency of Issue: Quarterly
Copies per Issue: 1,001 - 2,000
Sponsor/Publisher:
Subscribe Price: 77.00 US$ Individual
   121.00 US$ Instition

PUBLICATION GUIDELINES:

Manuscript Length: 16-25
Copies Required: Three
Computer Submission: No Disk
Format: MS Word
Fees to Review: 0.00 US$

Manuscript Style:
, Index Medicus

REVIEW INFORMATION:

Type of Review: Blind Review
No. of External Reviewers: 2
No. of In House Reviewers: 1
Acceptance Rate: 50%
Time to Review: 2 - 3 Months
Reviewers Comments: Yes
Invited Articles: 11-20%
Fees to Publish: 0.00 US$

MANUSCRIPT TOPICS:
Counseling & Personnel Services; Health & Physical Education; Health Education;
Secondary/Adolescent Studies; Social Studies/Social Science

MANUSCRIPT GUIDELINES/COMMENTS:

Length of contributions. Papers should ideally be no longer than 3,000 words, although
we will publish longer papers following discussions with the Editor. Authors should keep
tables and illustrations to a minimum.

Presentation. Papers should be typed, with double spacing, on one side of A4 paper.
Authors should supply three copies of their submission, together with the text on disc.

Abstract. Research papers should have a structured abstract with the following headings:
Objective, Design, Setting, Method, Results, Conclusion. Clearly such a format may not be
appropriate for discussion papers, therefore the author/s should give a summary of no more
than 250 words.

Key words. Up to five key words should be included.

References. References should be numbered in the order in which they appear in the paper. They should give the full names and initials of all authors, unless there are more than six, when only the first three should be used followed by et al. Names should be followed by the titles of the article; the title of the journal; the year of publication; the volume number: and the first and large page numbers (see 1 below). Journal titles should be given in full, or abbreviated according to the style of Index Medicus. Titles of books should be followed by the place of publication; the publisher; and the year (see 2 below).

1. Aitken PP, Eadie DR. Reinforcing effects of cigarette advertising on under-age smoking. *British Journal of Addiction* 1990; 85: 399-412.

2. Reynolds M. *Gynaecological Nursing*. Oxford: Blackwell Science Publications, 1984.

Acknowledgements of submissions. All submissions are acknowledged immediately. Responses to further correspondence are made as appropriate.

Peer review. All papers submitted to the Health Education Journal undergo a peer review process. On the basis of the referees' response, papers will either be rejected, accepted subject to revision, or accepted unconditionally.

Acceptance of submissions. On acceptance, the Editor retains the right to make stylistic changes, decide on the date of publication (generally within three to six months of acceptance) and shorten material if necessary.

House style. Papers will be edited to confirm with house style with regard to spelling and presentation. Titles and acronyms should be given in full on first usage. Unnecessary capitalisation should be avoided. Where percentages are referred to in the text, the words 'per cent' should be used rather than the '%'.

Proofs. Authors are sent one copy of the proofs. Corrections should be confined to typographical errors or matters of accuracy. Extensive amendments are not acceptable. Authors should return proofs as soon as possible, preferably within two days of receipt, and not later than the date given in the covering letter.

Reprints. These are available if ordered well in advance. Please ask for details of current charges for bulk orders.

Copyright. All material received by the Health Education Journal is assumed to be submitted exclusively. It is understood that contributions have not and will not be published elsewhere, unless this has been expressly invited or agreed by the Editor.

The author bears the responsibility for checking whether material submitted is subject to copyright or ownership rights; for example, in the use of tables and figures. If a submission is finally published, the copyright becomes that of the Health Education Journal, and permission for any reproduction must be sought from the Editor.

Dual publication. If a submitted paper has been published elsewhere, or is being considered for another publication, the author(s) must inform the Editor.

Accuracy and liability. A contribution is accepted on the strict understanding that its author is responsible for the accuracy of all information contained in the contribution and that references to named people and/or organisations are both accurate and without libellous implications.

High School Journal

ADDRESS FOR SUBMISSION:

Howard Machtinger, Editor
High School Journal
University of North Carolina
c/o School of Education
CB 3500
212-D Peabody Hall
Chapel Hill, NC 27599-3500
USA
Phone: 919-962-2513
Fax: 919-962-1533
E-Mail: hmach@email.unc.edu
Web: http://uncpress.unc.edu
Address May Change:

CIRCULATION DATA:

Reader: Academics, Administrators,
    Practicing Teachers
Frequency of Issue: Bi-Monthly
Copies per Issue: 1,001 - 2,000
Sponsor/Publisher: University of North
    Carolina Press
Subscribe Price: 30.00 US$ Individual
    47.00 US$ Institution
    All others - see website

PUBLICATION GUIDELINES:

Manuscript Length: 10-25 pages
Copies Required: Three
Computer Submission: No
Format: N/A
Fees to Review: 0.00 US$

Manuscript Style:
    Chicago Manual of Style

REVIEW INFORMATION:

Type of Review: Blind Review
No. of External Reviewers: 3
No. of In House Reviewers: 1
Acceptance Rate: 21-30%
Time to Review: 3-4 Months
Reviewers Comments: Yes
Invited Articles: 0-5%
Fees to Publish: 0.00 US$

MANUSCRIPT TOPICS:

Art/Music; Curriculum Studies; Education Management/Administration; Educational Psychology; Rural Education & Small Schools; Secondary/Adolescent Studies; Social Studies/Social Science; Teacher Education

MANUSCRIPT GUIDELINES/COMMENTS:

Submit three copies of the manuscript, typed double-spaced (including quotations and references) on 8.5" x 11" paper with ample margins. Manuscripts should run between 10 and 25 pages in typed length. Only the title page should carry the author's name and institutional address, and manuscripts should include an abstract. If the manuscript is co-authored, please indicate to whom the correspondence should be addressed. Please clarify in the cover letter that the particular work is not under consideration by any other publication sources.

Editorial review usually takes 3-4 months. Manuscripts will be returned only when a self-addressed, stamped envelope is provided. For the format of manuscript preparation, please consult recent issues of *The High School Journal*. Particular attention needs to be paid to the

352

style of referencing used. In most aspects, *The High School Journal* follows the format elaborated in *The Chicago Manual of Style* (13th ed., 1982). All figures must be camera-ready.

Address for Editorial Matters

All editorial correspondence, manuscripts and books for review should be sent to:

Editorial Office
The High School Journal
c/o School of Education
The University of North Carolina at Chapel Hill
CB #3500
Chapel Hill, North Carolina, 27599-3500.

Hispania

ADDRESS FOR SUBMISSION:

Janet Perez, Editor
Hispania
Texas Tech University
Classical & Modern Languages
Lubbock, TX 79409-2071
USA
Phone: 806-742-1558
Fax: 806-742-4288
E-Mail: janet.perez@ttu.edu
Web:
Address May Change:

PUBLICATION GUIDELINES:

Manuscript Length: 4,000 - 7,500 Words
Copies Required: One
Computer Submission: Yes
Format: IBM WordPerfect 6.0 or MSWord
Fees to Review: 0.00 US$

Manuscript Style:
, MLA

CIRCULATION DATA:

Reader: Academics, Practicing Teachers
Frequency of Issue: Quarterly
Copies per Issue: 14,000 - 16,000
Sponsor/Publisher: American Association
of Teachers of Spanish & Portuguese
Subscribe Price: 60.00 US$ Mbr w/Jrnl.
    30.00 US$ 1st yr. Mbr w/ Journal
    15.00 US$ Student Mbr with Journal

REVIEW INFORMATION:

Type of Review: Blind Review
No. of External Reviewers: 2+
No. of In House Reviewers: 2
Acceptance Rate: 11-20%
Time to Review: 2-5 Months
Reviewers Comments: Yes
Invited Articles: 0-5%
Fees to Publish: 0.00 US$

MANUSCRIPT TOPICS:
Languages & Linguistics; Spanish & Portuguese Literatures

MANUSCRIPT GUIDELINES/COMMENTS:

Articles
Hispania invites submission of original, unpublished articles on literature, language, linguistics, and pedagogy having to do with Spanish and Portuguese. Current membership in AATSP is a requirement for submission. Articles may be in Spanish, Portuguese, or English; however, we encourage authors to submit in Spanish and Portuguese. Articles may refer to but not repeat previously published content.

The first section includes scholarly articles on Hispanic and Luso-Brazilian literature and language that are judged to be of interest to specialists in the subject areas as well as to a diverse readership of teachers of Spanish and Portuguese. Articles for this section should display thorough and comprehensive knowledge of the subject and field. We prefer articles that are not narrow in scope or on single recent works. Further considerations in the evaluation of manuscripts are their contribution to the advancement of knowledge, originality of method or focus, organization, and clarity of expression, free from jargon. Lead articles should conform to *MLA* format, with length between 4,000 and 7,500 words, including endnotes and works cited. Bibliographical submissions may reach 20,000 words.

N.B. Please note that all articles accepted for publication in *Hispania* are subject to the terms of the contract that appears in Section 3.

Initial submissions of articles for all sections may be sent as file attachments by electronic mail, or on diskette with hard copy. Authors of accepted articles will receive a style sheet with instructions for final submission.

Send all articles, for the first section as well as for Departments, by first-class mail only to Dr. Janet Perez, Editor, Hispania, Classical and Modern Languages, Texas Tech University, Lubbock, Texas 79409-2071, or send via electronic mail. Please see "Hispania Departments and Features" for information on submission to those sections.

News, Notes, and Reviews
Send news and notes directly to the Preparers of the Hispanic and Luso-Brazilian World/Professional News, and Media/Computers, following their indications regarding types of submissions, length, and mailing. Requests to review software should go directly to the Preparer of the Media/Computers Department, at the address listed. Instructions for Book Reviews are found in that section.

See the relevant sections for instructions on submitting to Departments.

General Format for All Articles
On the first page, type your name, institutional affiliation, mailing address, telephone, fax number, e-mail address, and title of submission. Set a page division after this information (or begin a new page), **but do not separate from the article file if sending as e-mail attachment.**

In typing the article, be careful not to include your name in a page header or in evident self-reference; any references to your previous writings should be in the third person so your identity is not obvious. Center the title on one line and, at the margin below, type the word "Abstract:" followed by a concise summary of no more than 150 words. The abstract should provide a summary of the content rather than a self-referential description mentioning "this study." Below that, type "Key Words:" and list up to ten terms of importance, separated by commas, for a subject index. The abstract and key words should be in the same language as the essay.

The format must be strictly in accordance with the standard system of the *MLA Style Manual*, with parenthetical documentation and list of works cited. Please do not cite unpublished or "in press" works, except for Ph.D. dissertations listed in Dissertation Abstracts. The author-date system as described in the *MLA Style Manual* is acceptable for linguistics and pedagogy. If you include endnotes (maximum of 12 per article), they must be manually typed out or "pasted" at the end. *Hispania* does not use footnotes. **Do not** use automatic endnotes. Please follow the *MLA's* recommendation to avoid essay like "content notes" that detract from the primary text.

Please limit the use of charts, graphs, and tables containing vertical lines, and send them on paper only. Such material will have to be supplied as high-resolution, camera-ready printouts for publication.

Typing Conventions
You may use any one of the following fonts in 12 point size: Century Schoolbook, Courier, Palation, Times Roman, or Times New Roman. The page layout should have one-inch margins. Turn off any custom "style" settings including "first-paragraph" or "first-line indent" and **use no special formatting**.

Single space the entire article, except for double space above and below blocked quotes and subtitles. **Bring all text to the left margin** excepting a single "tab" to begin a paragraph or to separate columns in a table. Do not use "tabs" to format your text. End each paragraph with a carriage return (press "Enter"). **Use only one space after all punctuation and do not use the space bar to format text.**

Use only standard style quotes and apostrophes (no angular characters) and two hyphens for a dash. Do not divide words with hyphens.

Submissions by Electronic Mail
This preferred method of submission allows us to acknowledge receipt and route the article to evaluators more expeditiously. Sending your manuscript as an e-mail attachment allows retention of all diacritics, foreign-language characters, and italics. Do not use any other form of encoding. Please put your author information on a separate page, but do not separate your article from your author information and **always attach your manuscript to a cover message**. Use a descriptive identifying file label (names such as "art," "article," "articulo" and "artigo" do not identify the file or allow separating it from many others like it, especially if the computer automatically sends e-mail to a folder). A short title ("siempre/jamas" or "Calderon's Sources", etc.) will allow matching up files with reader evaluations. Send articles to: **janet.perez@ttu.edu**

Submissions on Disk
Authors may send PC-formatted diskettes, 3.5 in. only; Mac diskettes must be high density (with the initials HD on them and formatted for high density). Save all files in the principal document format for the word processor that you are using, .DOC for Microsoft Word for example. Identify the type of computer (PC or Mac) and the word processing program and version on the disk label. If submitting on diskette, follow instructions above for submitting by electronic mail.

Send the diskette in a protected envelope with hard copy to Dr. Janet Perez, Editor of Hispania, Classical and Modern Languages, Texas Tech University, Lubbock, TX 79409-2071. Disks will not be returned; all unused files are erased.

Instructions for **final version of accepted articles** will be sent at time of acceptance.

HISPANIA DEPARTMENTS/FEATURES

Articles

Send **Articles** for Departments on both disk and paper, or by e-mail alone to Dr. Perez as per instructions in the Guide for Authors. Do **not** send **articles** to Preparers. Please indicate the name of the Department to which you are submitting (e.g., Pedagogy, Literature, etc.). See instructions below for requirements regarding length and type of submissions. Not all Departments will publish in all issues, since publication of articles depends on approval by peer review.

News, Notes, and Reports

Send this type of submission directly to the **Preparers** of The Hispanic and Luso-Brazitian World/Professional News and Media/Computers. See addresses and instructions below. Deadlines are four months before the month of publication.

Applied Linguistics
Dr. Joseph Collentine
Northern Arizona University
Flatstaff, AZ 86011

Articles

(3,000-6,250) words on analytical approaches to language learning: field and classroom research that expands our knowledge of the nature of the language as related to such topics as language acquisition, assessment, proficiency, and collaborative learning. Articles must be research oriented; focus should not be anecdotal.

Chapter News

Chapter secretaries/treasurers may send **Reports** of the proceedings of chapter meetings or announcements for posting on the AATSP website. Summaries of up to 300 words may be written in English, Spanish, or Portuguese. There is no limit to the number of times chapter may submit materials. Please send chapter items to **corporate@aatsp.org** and visit **http://www.aatsp.org**.

The Hispanic and Luso-Brazilian World/Professional News
Prof. Raquel Oxford
University of Wisconsin
Milwaukee, WI 53201

Research Articles

(3,000-7,500 words) on contemporary culture in Hispanic and Luso-Brazilian countries.

Notes, Reports, and News

(50-1,000 words; limit for quoted material 150 words) about literary prizes, cultural happenings, necrologies, and short bibliographies. No travel accounts, interviews, book notices, or editorials, please. Contributors should prepare **News** in essay format and submit directly to Prof. Oxford, preferably on double-density IBM disks in Microsoft Word 5 or 6, or by e-mail. All submissions are subject to selection and editing. **Articles** for this section must be submitted to the Hispania Editorial Office.

Professional News
Desurabke **Professional News** items comprise BRIEF ITEMS (to 1,000 words) relating to the professions of teaching Spanish and Portuguese in the following categories: News Items, Awards and Honors (AATSP members only), Recent Releases, Forthcoming Events, and Obituaries. Send news (in Spanish, Portuguese or English) to Professor Oxford. **Please note**: we do not publish news items about programs or activities of individual universities or items of a commercial nature. All submissions are subject to selection and editing.

Media/Computers
Dr. Mark Darhower
Foreign Languages and Literatures
North Carolina State University
Raleigh, NC 27695

Articles
(3,500 to 7,500 words) on the use of visual and audio media of all types, such as cinema and video, computers and computer software, multimedia, visual art, networks, videodiscs, videotapes, audiotapes, satellite TV, laboratories, and electronic databases in teaching and research. Articles may relate these media to literary, linguistic, or methodological topics (send all **Articles** to the *Hispania* Editorial Office). Send **Notes and Reports** (2,000 words) on disk or paper with self-addressed envelope or by electronic mail to Dr. Darhower. To write a **Review**, please contact the Preparer first.

Pedagogy
Pedagogical submissions can combine levels or focus on K-8, Secondary, Community Colleges, Jr. Colleges, and Colleges and Universities. All submissions must refer explicitly and substantially to Spanish or Portuguese.

Formats: K-8, Secondary Schools, Community and Junior Colleges: ideas (750-1,500 words), round tables and perspectives (several short essays) on a particular theme, temas (discussion), and full-length articles.

Colleges and Universities: Full-length articles only.

Some Possible Themes: adult education, articulation/collaboration, assessment, bilingualism, block schedule, career education, community resources, relations; and support; content-based instruction, cooperative learning, curriculum, distance learning, exceptional and special needs, implementing National Standards, interdisciplinary links, learning styles, lesson development, materials development, methodology, models, multiple intelligences, proficiency-based instruction, program models of FLES*: Sequential FLES, FLEX, Immersion; research procedures, restructuring, scheduling, service learning, Spanish for native speakers, Spanish for special purposes, standards, study abroad, teacher training, teaching culture, teaching literature, textbooks, tools, translating into Spanish, unusual programs, whole language learning, working with limited funds, writing.

Please define all technical terms and avoid jargon and acronyms.

Descriptions should be of models that others might follow rather than descriptions of your own programs or "success stories."

Please send submissions to the Editorial Office on computer disk with a paper printout or by electronic mail alone, in ASCII text format only. Manuscripts for K-8 may be on paper only if they are under 2,000 words. See Guide for Authors for preparation of disk files.

Theoretical Linguistics
Dr. Richard V. Teschner
University of Texas at El Paso
El Paso, TX 79968

Articles (3,000-7,500 words) should either use an accepted theoretical framework to enhance our understanding of Spanish and Portuguese, or use data from the latter to extend linguistic theory. Please submit manuscript electronically in **MS Word** to *Hispania's* editorial office.

History of Education

ADDRESS FOR SUBMISSION:

Joyce Goodman, Jane Martin, Co-Editors
History of Education
University College Winchester
Sparkford Road
Winchester, SO22 4NR
UK
Phone: 0 1962 827392
Fax: 0 1962 827479
E-Mail: joyce.goodman@winchester.ac.uk
Web: www.tandf.co.uk/journals
Address May Change:

PUBLICATION GUIDELINES:

Manuscript Length: 30+
Copies Required: Three
Computer Submission: Yes Disk, Email
Format: English, MS Word
Fees to Review: 0.00 US$

Manuscript Style:
    See Manuscript Guidelines

CIRCULATION DATA:

Reader: Academics, Administrators,
    Practicing Teachers
Frequency of Issue: 6 Times/Year
Copies per Issue:
Sponsor/Publisher: Taylor & Francis
Subscribe Price: 357.00 US$ Individual
    1097.00 US$ Institution

REVIEW INFORMATION:

Type of Review: Blind Review
No. of External Reviewers: 2
No. of In House Reviewers: 0
Acceptance Rate: 21-30%
Time to Review: 1 - 2 Months
Reviewers Comments: Yes
Invited Articles: 0-5%
Fees to Publish: 0.00 US$

MANUSCRIPT TOPICS:
Curriculum Studies; Education; Education Management/Administration; Elementary/Early Childhood; Gender; Health & Physical Education; Higher Education; Religious Education; Rural Education & Small Schools; School Law; Secondary/Adolescent Studies; Social Studies/Social Science; Special Education; Teacher Education; Urban Education, Cultural/Non-Traditional

MANUSCRIPT GUIDELINES/COMMENTS:

Aims and Scope
History of Education has established itself as a leading, international, peer-reviewed journal, focusing on the history of education in all parts of the world. The journal is recognised as a key resource for both educationists and social historians alike.

The journal publishes original research and major reviews of books in the history of education. Papers dealing with both formal and informal education systems, comparative education, policy-making, the politics and experience of education and pedagogy are welcomed.

The journal also includes a section entitled **Sources and Interpretations**, which examines historical sources and debates around their interpretation in research and practice.

Special Issues have focused on:

- Feminism, femininity and feminization
- The Second World War
- Education and economic performance
- Education and national identity
- Education in Wales and Scandinavia
- Ways of seeing education and schooling: emerging historiographies
- Reforming Lives? Progressivism, Leadership and Educational Change

History of Education is published on behalf of the *History of Education Society (UK)*.

Readership
Historians of education, policy researchers, administrative researchers and sociologists of education.

Instructions for Authors
Note to Authors: please make sure your contact address information is clearly visible on the **outside** of <u>all</u> packages you are sending to Editors.

Submitting a paper to *History of Education*
Please read these Guidelines with care and attention: failure to follow them may result in your paper being delayed. Note especially the referencing conventions used by *History of Education* and for all manuscripts, non-discriminatory language is mandatory. Sexist or racist terms should not be used.

History of Education considers all manuscripts on condition they are the property (copyright) of the submitting author(s) and that copyright will be transferred to *History of Education* and Taylor & Francis Ltd if the paper is accepted.

History of Education considers all manuscripts on the strict condition that they have been submitted only to *History of Education*, that they have not been published already, nor are they under consideration for publication, nor in press elsewhere. Authors who fail to adhere to this condition will be charged all costs which *History of Education* incurs, and their papers will not be published.

- Please write clearly and concisely, stating your objectives clearly and defining your terms. Your arguments should be substantiated with well-reasoned supporting evidence.
- For all manuscripts, non-discriminatory language is mandatory. Sexist or racist terms should not be used.
- In writing your paper, you are encouraged to review articles in the area you are addressing which have been previously published in the journal, and where you feel appropriate, to reference them. This will enhance context, coherence, and continuity for our readers.

- Introductions of around 100 - 200 words are required for all papers submitted and should precede the text of a paper.
- Manuscripts should be typed on one single side of A4 or 8 x 11 inch white good quality paper, double-spaced throughout, including the reference section.
- Three copies of the manuscript for consideration should be submitted to the Editor.
- A disk with a version of the manuscript in Microsoft Word should also be submitted to the Editor.
- Authors should include telephone and fax numbers as well as e-mail addresses on the cover page of manuscripts.
- Bionotes should be contained on a separate sheet and be located at the beginning of a paper.
- **Accepted** manuscripts in their **final, revised versions**, should also be submitted as electronic word processing files on disk - see 'Electronic Processing'.
- Articles for consideration should be sent to the Editors at the below address:

Editor
Professor Joyce Goodman
School of Education
University College Winchester
Hampshire SO22 4NR

Reviews Editor
William Richardson
School of Education
University of Exeter
Heavitree Road, Exeter EX1 1SL, UK

Sources and Interpretations Feature Editor
Dr Peter Cunningham
University of Cambridge, Faculty of Education
Homerton Site, Hills Road, Cambridge, CB23 2PH

Copyright Material
Contributors are required to secure permission for the reproduction of any figure, table, or extensive (more than fifty word) extract from the text, from a source which is copyrighted - or owned - by a party other than Taylor& Francis or the contributor.

This applies both to direct reproduction or 'derivative reproduction' - when the contributor has created a new figure or table which derives **substantially** from a copyrighted source.

The following form of words can be used in seeking permission:

Dear [COPYRIGHT HOLDER]

I/we are preparing for publication an article entitled

[STATE TITLE]

to be published by Taylor & Francis Ltd in *History of Education.*

I/we should be grateful if you would grant us permission to include the following materials:

[STATE FIGURE NUMBER AND ORIGINAL SOURCE]

We are requesting non-exclusive rights in this edition and in all forms. It is understood, of course, that full acknowledgement will be given to the source.

Please note that Taylor & Francis are signatories of and respect the spirit of the STM Agreement regarding the free sharing and dissemination of scholarly information.

Your prompt consideration of this request would be greatly appreciated.

Yours faithfully

Notes on style
All authors are asked to take account of the diverse audience of *History of Education*. Clearly explain or avoid the use of terms that might be meaningful only to a local or national audience. However, note also that the *History of Education* does not aspire to be international in the ways that McDonald's restaurants or Hilton Hotels are 'international'; we much prefer papers that, where appropriate, reflect the particularities of each higher education system.

Some specific points of style for the text of articles, research reports, case studies, reports, essay reviews, and reviews follow:

1. *History of Education* prefers US to 'American', USA to 'United States', and UK to 'United Kingdom'.

2. *History of Education* uses conservative British, not US, spelling, i.e. colour not color; behaviour (behavioural) not behavior; [school] programme not program; [he] practises not practices; centre not center; organization not organisation; analyse not analyze, etc.

3. Single 'quotes' are used for quotations rather than double "quotes", unless the 'quote is "within" another quote'.

4. Punctuation should follow the British style, e.g. 'quotes precede punctuation'.

5. Punctuation of common abbreviations should follow the following conventions: e.g. i.e. cf. Note that such abbreviations are not followed by a comma or a (double) point/period.

6. Dashes; em-dash should be clearly indicated in manuscripts by way of either a clear dash (—) or a triple hyphen (---) the en-dash should be indicated by a clear dash (–) or a double hyphen (--).

7. *History of Education* is sparing in its use of the upper case in headings and references, e.g. only the first letter of the first word in paper titles and all subheads is in upper case; titles of papers from journals in the references and other places are not in upper case.

8. Apostrophes should be used sparingly. Thus, decades should be referred to as follows: 'The 1980s [not the 1980's] saw ...'. Possessives associated with acronyms (e.g. APU), should be written as follows: 'The APU's findings that ...', but, NB, the plural is APUs.

9. All acronyms for national agencies, examinations, etc., should be spelled out the first time they are introduced in text or references. Thereafter the acronym can be used if appropriate, e.g. 'The work of the Assessment of Performance Unit (APU) in the early 1980s ...'. Subsequently, 'The APU studies of achievement ...', in a reference ... (Department of Education and Science [DES] 1989a).

10. Brief biographical details of significant national figures should be outlined in the text unless it is quite clear that the person concerned would be known internationally. Some suggested editorial emendations to a typical text are indicated in the following with square brackets: 'From the time of H. E. Armstrong [in the 19th century] to the curriculum development work associated with the Nuffield Foundation [in the 1960s], there has been a shift from heurism to constructivism in the design of [British] science courses'.

11. The preferred local (national) usage for ethnic and other minorities should be used in all papers. For the USA, African-American, Hispanic, and Native American are used, e.g. 'The African American presidential candidate, Jesse Jackson...' For the UK, African-Caribbean (not 'West Indian'), etc.

12. Material to be emphasized (italicized in the printed version) should be underlined in the typescript rather than italicized. Please use such emphasis sparingly.

13. n (not N), % (not per cent) should be used in typescripts.

14. Numbers in text should take the following forms: 300, 3000, 30 000. Spell out numbers under 10 unless used with a unit of measure, e.g. nine pupils but 9 mm (do not introduce periods with measure). For decimals, use the form 0.05 (not .05).

15. When using a word which is or is asserted to be a proprietary term or trade mark authors' must use the symbol ® or TM or alternatively a footnote can be inserted using the wording below:

This article includes a word which is or is asserted to be a proprietary term or trade mark. Its inclusion does not imply it has acquired for legal purposes a non-proprietary or general significance, nor is any other judgement implied concerning its legal status.

Notes on tables and figures
Artwork submitted for publication will not be returned and will be destroyed after publication, unless you request otherwise. Whilst every care is taken of artwork, neither the Editor nor Taylor & Francis shall bear any responsibility or liability for non-return, loss, or damage of artwork, nor for any associated costs or compensation. You are strongly advised to insure appropriately.

1. Tables and figures should be valuable, relevant, and visually attractive. Tables and figures must be referred to in the text and numbered in order of their appearance. Each table and figure should have a complete, descriptive title; and each table column an appropriate heading.

Tables and figures should be referred to in text as follows: figure 1, table 1, i.e. lower case. 'As seen in table [or figure] 1 ...' (not Tab., fig. or Fig).

2. The place at which a table or figure is to be inserted in the printed text should be indicated clearly on a manuscript:

[Insert table 2 about here]

3. Each table and/or figure must have a title that explains its purpose without reference to the text.

4. All figures and tables must be on separate sheets and not embedded in the text. Original copies of figures should be supplied. All figures should allow for reduction to page width (126mm). Please avoid figures that would require landscape reproduction, i.e., reading from bottom to top of the page. Photographs may be sent as glossy prints or negatives. All artwork will be reproduced in black and white.

Please number each figure on the reverse in pencil.

Do not type the caption to a figure on that figure; the legends to any illustrations must be typed separately following the main text and should be grouped together.

Acknowledgements
Any acknowledgements authors wish to make should be included in a separate headed section at the end of the manuscript. Please do not incorporate these into the bionote or notes.

Book reviews
1. The following header material should appear in all reviews in the following order (note also the punctuation):

School Leadership: Beyond Education Management. An Essay in Policy Scholarship, by Gerard Grace, Falmer, 1995, pp. 370 £38.00(hardback), £13.95 (paperback).

2. Page references within reviews should be given as follows: (p. 337) or (pp. 36-37).

Citations in text
References should be cited using the numerical system with superscripts (e.g. Scholarships provided free instruction 23. They should be listed separately at the end of the paper in the order in which they appear in the text.

References
History of Education uses the following conventions for references:

1. **Reference to a book:**
   C. Lacey, *The Socialization of Teachers* (London: Methuen, 1977).

2. **Reference to a chapter in a book:**
   M. Crozier, 'The vicious circle of bureaucracy', in T. Burns (ed.), *Industrial Man* (Harmondsworth: Penguin, 1969), 250–262.

3. **Reference to an article in a journal:**
   C. Buswell, 'Pedagogic change and social change', *British Journal of Sociology of Education*. 10 (1982), 167–70.

4. **Proceedings, reports and unpublished literature**
   R.J. M. Smith, Accountability to the state: an exploration of the educational market and parental choice literature. Paper presented to the Annual Conference of the New Zealand Association for Research in Education, Massey University, Palmerston North, 7–10 December, 1995.

   C.A. Burnham and T. H. Anderson, Learning to sew on a button by reading a procedural text. CSR Technical Report, No. 543, Center for the Study of Reading, University of Illinois at Urbana-Champaign, 1991. ERIC ED 332 157.

   D.K. Cohen, and D. L. Ball, Policy, Cognition, and Instruction. Unpublished manuscript, 1997.

   D.Macleod 'Miners, Mining Men and Mining Reform.' PhD thesis, Toronto, 1981.

   Hertfordshire Record Office [HRO] Hertfordshire County Council [HCC] 2/11 3, County Paper [CP] 45 Hertfordshire Education Committee [HEC] 29 March 1926.

5. **Parliamentary Papers**
   Royal Commission on the Civil Service, First Appendix to Fourth Report, *Parliamentary Papers*, xVI, 1914 [Cd. 7339], Appendix 6, 'Statement submitted on behalf of the Clerical Establishment of the Board of Education', 27.

6. **Reference to a newspaper or magazine**
   H.Richards, 1996, Republican lite? *The Times Higher Education Supplement*, 1 November, 16.

7. **Reference to an Internet source**
   Give the universal resource locator in full: http://acsinfo.acs.org/instruct/instruct.html

8. **Reference to a personal communication**
   J. Brannen, 1996, Personal communication.

9. **Reference to a case in law**
   In text, italicize names of plaintiffs and defendants: *Miranda* v. *Arizona* 1974

10. **Reference to government legislation**
    US Congress, Senate Committee on Foreign Relations, 1956, *The Mutual Security Act of 1956*, 84th Congress, second session, report 2273.

    United Kingdom Parliament, Committee on the Working of the Monetary System [Radcliffe Committee] 1960, *Principal Memoranda of Evidence*, vol. 2, Cmd 1958.

Electronic Processing
We strongly encourage you to send us the final, revised version of your article in both hard (paper) and electronic (disk) forms. This Guide sets out the procedures which will assure we can process your article efficiently. It is divided into three sections:

1. a guide for authors using standard word-processing software packages
2. a guide for authors using LaTeX mathematical software packages
3. a guide for authors using graphics software packages

There are some general rules which apply to all three options.

- these guides do not apply to authors who are submitting an article for consideration and peer review; they apply only to authors whose articles have been reviewed, revised, and accepted for publication
- print out your hard (paper) copy from the disk you are sending; it is essential that the hard-copy printout is identical to the material on the disk; where versions differ, the hard copy will take precedence. We advise that you maintain back-ups of your files
- save and send your files on a standard 3.5 inch high density disk (Mac or PC); please do not attempt to send the article via file transfer protocol or email
- when saving your article onto a disk, please make sure that the files do not exceed a manageable size. Please ensure that figures are saved on a separate disk
- ensure that the files are **not** saved as read only
- virus-check your disk before sending it to the Editor
- label your disk
- package disks in such a way as to avoid damage in the post
- disks are not returnable after publication

1. A guide for authors using standard word-processing software packages
For the main text of your article, most standard PC or Mac word-processing software packages are acceptable, although we prefer Microsoft Word in a PC format.

Word-processed files should be prepared according to the journal style.

Avoid the use of embedded footnotes. For numbered tables, use the table function provided with the word-processing package.

All text should be saved in one file with the complete text (including the title page, abstract, all sections of the body of the paper, references), followed by numbered tables and the figure captions.

You should send the following to the Editor:

- a 3.5-inch disk containing the final, accepted version of the paper
- include an ASCII/text only version on the disk as well as the word processed version if possible
- two hard copy printouts

Disks should be clearly labelled with the following information:
1. Journal title
2. Name of author
3. File names contained on disk
4. Hardware used (PC or Mac)
5. Software used (name and version)

Sample disk label: text

Journal title
A.N. Author
article.doc
IBM PC
MS Word for Windows 7.0

2. A guide for authors using LaTeX mathematical software packages

Authors who wish to prepare their articles using the LaTeX document preparation system are advised to use article.sty (for LaTex 2.09) or article.cls (for LaTex2e).

The use of macros should be kept to an absolute minimum but if any are used they should be gathered together in the file, just before the \begin{document} command

You should send the following to the Editor:
- a 3.5-inch disk containing the final, accepted version of the paper
- the files you send must be text-only (often called an ASCII file), with no system-dependent control codes
- two hard copy printouts

Disks should be clearly labelled with the following information:
1. Journal title
2. Name of author
3. File names contained on disk
4. Hardware used (PC or Mac)
5. Software used (name and version)

Sample disk label: LaTeX

Journal title
A.N. Author
article.tex article.sty
IBM PC
PCLaTeX v2.09

3. A guide for authors using graphics software packages

We welcome figures on disk, but care and attention to these guidelines is essential, as importing graphics packages can often be problematic.

1. Figures must be saved on a separate disk from the text.
2. Avoid the use of colour and tints for aesthetic reasons. Figures should be produced as near to the finished size as possible.
3. High quality reproducible hard copy for all line figures (printed out from your electronic files at a minimum of 600 dpi) must be supplied in case the disks are unusable; photographs and transparencies can be accepted as hard copy only. **Photocopies will not be accepted**.
4. All figures must be numbered in the order in which they occur (e.g. figure 1, figure 2 etc.). In multi-part figures, each part should be labelled (e.g. figure 1 (a), figure 1 (b) etc.)
5. The figure captions must be saved as a separate file with the text and numbered correspondingly.
6. The filename for the graphic should be descriptive of the graphic e.g. Figure1, Figure2a.
7. Files should be saved as TIFF (tagged image file format), PostScript or EPS (encapsulated PostScript), containing all the necessary font information and the source file of the application (e.g., CorelDraw/Mac, CorelDraw/PC).

Disks should be clearly labelled with the following information:
1. Journal title
2. Name of author
3. Figures contained on disk
4. Hardware used (PC or Mac)
5. Software used (name and version)

Sample disk label: figures

Journal title
A.N. Author
Figures 1-10
Macintosh
Adobe Illustrator 5.5

4. Early Electronic Offprints

Corresponding authors can now receive their article by e-mail as a complete PDF. This allows the author to print up to 50 copies, free of charge, and disseminate them to colleagues. In many cases this facility will be available up to two weeks prior to publication. Or, alternatively, corresponding authors will receive the traditional 50 offprints. A copy of the journal will be sent by post to all corresponding authors after publication. Additional copies of the journal can be purchased at the author's preferential rate of £15.00/$25.00 per copy.

Copyright

It is a condition of publication that authors vest or license copyright in their articles, including abstracts, in **Taylor & Francis Ltd**. This enables us to ensure full copyright protection and to disseminate the article, and the journal, to the widest possible readership in print and electronic formats as appropriate. Authors may, of course, use the article elsewhere after publication, providing that prior permission is obtained from Taylor & Francis Ltd. Authors themselves are responsible for obtaining permission to reproduce copyright material from other sources.

History of Education Quarterly

ADDRESS FOR SUBMISSION:

Richard Altenbaugh, Editor
History of Education Quarterly
Slippery Rock University
School of Education
220 McKay Education Building
Slippery Rock, PA 16057-1326
USA
Phone: 724-738-4556
Fax: 724-738-4548
E-Mail: richard.altenbaugh@sru.edu
Web: www.sru.edu/depts/scc/hes/hes.htm
Address May Change:

PUBLICATION GUIDELINES:

Manuscript Length: 35 Max
Copies Required: Four
Computer Submission: No
Format: N/A
Fees to Review: 0.00 US$

Manuscript Style:
      Chicago Manual of Style

CIRCULATION DATA:

Reader: Academics
Frequency of Issue: Quarterly
Copies per Issue: 1,001 - 2,000
Sponsor/Publisher: History of Education
   Association
Subscribe Price:

REVIEW INFORMATION:

Type of Review: Blind Review
No. of External Reviewers: 3
No. of In House Reviewers: 1
Acceptance Rate: 6-10%
Time to Review: 2 - 3 Months
Reviewers Comments: Yes
Invited Articles: 0-5%
Fees to Publish: 0.00 US$

MANUSCRIPT TOPICS:
Higher Education; History of Education and the Family; Religious Education; Rural
Education & Small Schools; Social Studies/Social Science; Urban Education, Cultural/Non-
Traditional

MANUSCRIPT GUIDELINES/COMMENTS:

The *History of Education Quarterly* publishes
- Articles
- Documents
- Debates on important issues in the history of education
- Retrospectives
- Research Notes
- Book Reviews
- Film Reviews

Topics span the history of education, both formal and nonformal, including the history of childhood, youth, and the family. The subjects are not limited to any time period and are universal in scope. The *Quarterly* is published in cooperation with the College of Education, Slippery Rock University of Pennsylvania.

Guidelines for Manuscripts

1. All copy should be typed double-spaced, including between and within endnotes. Allow approximately a one-inch margin on all four sides of the page.

2. Articles should be no longer than 35 pages *including* endnotes; that works out to about 9,000 words.

3. Type font should be 10 or 12 characters per inch.

4. FOUR copies of the manuscript should be submitted on white paper, addressed to:
   History of Education Quarterly
   College of Education
   Slippery Rock University
   Slippery Rock, PA 16057-1326

Manuscripts are not returned unless the article is accompanied by a self-addressed envelope with sufficient postage.

5. The author's name should appear *only* on the title page of the article.

6. Endnotes should appear in a separate section at the end of the article.

The following formats should be used for references:

Book
1. Lawrence A. Cremin, *Transformation of the School: Progressivism in American Education, 1876-1957* (New York: Vintage Books, 1964), 25.

Edited Book
2. Linda M. Perkins, "The History of Blacks in Teaching: Growth and Decline Within the Profession," in *American Teachers: Histories of a Profession at Work* ed. Donald Warren (New York: MacMillan Publishing Co., 1989), 351.

Journal Article
3. Guadalupe San Miguel, Jr., "The Struggle Against Separate and Unequal Schools: Middle-Class Mexican Americans and the Desegregation Campaign in Texas, 1929-1956," *History of Education Quarterly* 23 (Fall 1983): 343-359.

Popular Magazine Article
4. Caspari and R. E. Marshak, "The Rise and Fall of Lysenko," *Science*, 16 Aug. 1965, 275-78.

372

Unpublished Work
5. *Marjorie Murphy, "From Artisan to Semi-Professional: White-Collar Unionism among Chicago Public School Teachers, 1870-1930" (Ph.D. diss., University of California-Davis, 1981), 106.*

Manuscript
6. Hiram Johnson to John Callan O'Laughlin, 16 July 1916, file 6, box 20, O'Laughlin Papers, Roosevelt Memorial Collection, Harvard College Library.

Second and subsequent references
7. Cremin, *Transformation of the School*, 320.

8. San Miguel, Jr., "Struggle Against Separate and Unequal Schools," 350.

The style of the *History of Education Quarterly* conforms very closely to *The Chicago Manual of Style*, 14th ed. (Chicago 1993). Authors should consult this manual if they have further question.

History Teacher (The)

ADDRESS FOR SUBMISSION:

Nancy Quam-Wickham, Editor
History Teacher (The)
California State University - Long Beach
History Department
Long Beach, CA 90840
USA
Phone: 562-985-4449
Fax: 562-985-5431
E-Mail: quamwick@csulb.edu
Web: www.csulb.edu/~histeach/htm
Address May Change:

PUBLICATION GUIDELINES:

Manuscript Length: 21-25
Copies Required: Three
Computer Submission: Yes
Format: MS Word or WordPerfect 5.1 or 6
Fees to Review: 0.00 US$

Manuscript Style:
    Chicago Manual of Style, Turabian

CIRCULATION DATA:

Reader: Academics, Practicing Teachers
Frequency of Issue: Quarterly
Copies per Issue: 2000
Sponsor/Publisher: California State
    University - Long Beach
Subscribe Price: 30.00 US$ Indv. Dues
    60.00 US$ Institute Soc. Member Dues
    20.00 US$ Student/Retired Mem. Dues

REVIEW INFORMATION:

Type of Review: Blind Review
No. of External Reviewers: 3
No. of In House Reviewers: 3+
Acceptance Rate: 21-30%
Time to Review: 2 - 3 Months
Reviewers Comments: Yes
Invited Articles: 0-5%
Fees to Publish: 0.00 US$

MANUSCRIPT TOPICS:
Curriculum Studies; Higher Education; Social Studies/Social Science; Teacher Education;
Urban Education, Cultural/Non-Traditional

MANUSCRIPT GUIDELINES/COMMENTS:

The History Teacher is the most widely recognized journal in the United States devoted to the teaching of history in the secondary and higher education classroom. Published quarterly, it features practical and insightful professional analyses of traditional and innovative teaching techniques.

Membership in the the Society for History Education means you will become one of the thousands of faculty, administrators and student teachers who benefit from SHE 's special resources, including *The History Teacher!*

Members receive *The History Teacher* in November, February, May and August, as well as periodic mailings announcing new activities and resources, such as upcoming SHE conferences and special publications.

ICA Journal (Illinois Counseling Association)

ADDRESS FOR SUBMISSION:

Jobie Skaggs, Robert Davison-Aviles, Eds
ICA Journal (Illinois Counseling
  Association)
Bradley University
Education Leadership & Human
  Development
1501 West Bradley Avenue
Peoria, IL 61625
USA
Phone:
Fax: 309-677-3193
E-Mail: aviles@bradley.edu
Web: N/A
Address May Change:

PUBLICATION GUIDELINES:

Manuscript Length: 16-20
Copies Required: Four
Computer Submission: Yes Disk
Format: MS Word
Fees to Review: 0.00 US$

Manuscript Style:
    American Psychological Association,
    5th Edition Manual

CIRCULATION DATA:

Reader: Counselors, Counselor Educators
Frequency of Issue: 2 Times/Year
Copies per Issue: More than 2000
Sponsor/Publisher: Illinois Counseling
  Association
Subscribe Price:

REVIEW INFORMATION:

Type of Review: Blind Review
No. of External Reviewers: 3
No. of In House Reviewers: 2
Acceptance Rate: 60%
Time to Review: 2 - 3 Months
Reviewers Comments: Yes
Invited Articles: 0-5%
Fees to Publish: 0.00 US$

MANUSCRIPT TOPICS:
Counseling & Personnel Services

MANUSCRIPT GUIDELINES/COMMENTS:

ICA Journal is a publication of the Illinois Counseling Association. We invite contributions that are of interest to Illinois counselors at all levels. Please use the following guidelines:

1. Send four copies of all materials. Generally, manuscripts should not exceed 3,500 words (approximately 15 pages typewritten and double-spaced).

2. Article titles are not to exceed 50 letters and spaces.

3 Be sure to include an abstract (150 words maximum) of the manuscript. The abstract should be a brief, informative summary.

4. Materials are to be well organized, concise, and logical. Aim to communicate clearly.

5. Avoid footnotes.

6. Double-space all materials, including references.

7. Authors' names with position, title, and place of employment are to appear only on the cover page.

8. All aspects of manuscript preparation (references, tables, margins, abstract, etc.) are to follow the style described in the *Publication Manual of the American Psychological Association* (5th ed.). The manual may be purchased from APA; APA Order Dept., P.O. Box 2710, Hyattsville, Maryland 20784; 1-800-374-2721.

9. Never submit material that is under consideration by another periodical.

10. Avoid the use of generic masculine pronoun and sexist and/or racist terminology.

11. Ethical principles are to be followed in work with human and animals.

12. Submit materials to the Editor.

Usually, manuscripts are reviewed by three Editorial Board members. These are blind reviews, which means the reviewers and authors are not identified to each other. Allow two months for manuscripts to be returned after being submitted. Manuscripts are also reviewed and evaluated by the *ICA Journal* Editorial Board members.

The author is responsible for obtaining permission to use copyrighted materials used in the submitted manuscript. The *ICA Journal* assumes the copyrights to all materials published in the *ICA Journal*.

Illinois Schools Journal

ADDRESS FOR SUBMISSION:

Beverly J. Anderson, Editor
Illinois Schools Journal
Chicago State University
ADM 306
9501 South King Drive
Chicago, IL 60628
USA
Phone: 773-995-2411
Fax: 773-995-3584
E-Mail: b-anderson1@csu.edu
Web: www.illinoisschooljournal.org
Address May Change:

CIRCULATION DATA:

Reader: , Educational Practitioners and
Academicians
Frequency of Issue: 2 Times/Year
Copies per Issue: 4,001 - 5,000
Sponsor/Publisher: University
Subscribe Price:

PUBLICATION GUIDELINES:

Manuscript Length: 11-15
Copies Required: Two
Computer Submission: No
Format: N/A
Fees to Review: 0.00 US$

Manuscript Style:
    American Psychological Association

REVIEW INFORMATION:

Type of Review: Blind Review
No. of External Reviewers: 0
No. of In House Reviewers: 3+
Acceptance Rate: 11-20%
Time to Review: 1 - 2 Months
Reviewers Comments: Yes
Invited Articles: 21-30%
Fees to Publish: 0.00 US$

MANUSCRIPT TOPICS:

Adult Career & Vocational; Bilingual/E.S.L.; Curriculum Studies; Education
Management/Administration; Educational Technology Systems; Elementary/Early Childhood;
Gifted Children; Health & Physical Education; Higher Education; Reading; School Law;
Teacher Education

MANUSCRIPT GUIDELINES/COMMENTS:

Topics. Distance Learning, Diversity, Urban Issues in Higher Education and other topics
appropriate to all levels of education.

Articles
The *Illinois Schools Journal* is a professional journal for educators. Articles should be
directed toward issues attendant to education. The Journal aims to strike a balance between
educational theory and practice. Articles are usually about three thousand words. Both longer
and shorter articles are welcome.

Manuscript Form

Manuscripts should be styled according to the *Publication Manual of the American Psychological Association*. Avoid footnotes if at all possible; include pertinent information in the text.

Submit manuscripts in duplicate on 8½ by 11 inch bond paper. Send manuscripts first class and include a self-addressed envelope.

Infant Mental Health Journal

ADDRESS FOR SUBMISSION:

Joy Osofsky, Editor
Infant Mental Health Journal
Louisiana State University
Health Science Center
Department of Psychiatry
1542 Tulane Avenue
New Orleans, LA 70112
USA
Phone: 504-568-6004
Fax: 504-568-6246
E-Mail: imhj@lsuhsc.edu
Web:
Address May Change:

PUBLICATION GUIDELINES:

Manuscript Length: 20-25
Copies Required: Three
Computer Submission: No
Format: N/A
Fees to Review: 0.00 US$

Manuscript Style:
American Psychological Association

CIRCULATION DATA:

Reader: Academics, Counselors, Social
Workers
Frequency of Issue: 6 Times/Year
Copies per Issue: Less than 1,000
Sponsor/Publisher:
Subscribe Price: 95.00 US$
107.00 US$ Outside North America

REVIEW INFORMATION:

Type of Review: Blind Review
No. of External Reviewers: 2
No. of In House Reviewers: 0
Acceptance Rate: 50%
Time to Review: 4 - 6 Months
Reviewers Comments: Yes
Invited Articles: No Reply
Fees to Publish: 0.00 US$

MANUSCRIPT TOPICS:
Educational Psychology; Elementary/Early Childhood

MANUSCRIPT GUIDELINES/COMMENTS:

Reader: Counselors, Early Childhood Education Specialists, Nurses, Physicians, Psychologists, and Public Health Workers

The *IMHJ* publishes research articles, literature reviews, program descriptions/evaluations, clinical studies, and book reviews that focus on infant social-emotional development, care giver-infant interactions, contextual and cultural influences on infant and family development, and all conditions that place infants and/or their families at-risk for less than optimal development. The *IMHJ* is dedicated to an interdisciplinary approach to the optimal development of infants and their families, and, therefore, welcomes submissions from all disciplinary perspectives.

Manuscripts (An original and three copies) should be submitted to the Editor typed, with double spacing throughout and ample margins. Blind reviewing will be used. Each copy of the paper should include a cover sheet with the following information: Title of manuscript, name of author(s), and author(s) affiliation. The title should appear on the abstract and on the first page of text. Information about the identity of the author(s) contained in footnotes should appear on the title page only. The title page is not included when the manuscript is sent out for review. A cover letter to the Editor should accompany the paper: it should request a review and indicate that the manuscript has not been published previously or submitted elsewhere.

An abstract of approximately 150 words must be included. Tables and figures must be sufficiently clear so that they can be photographed directly. (Black and white glossy prints are acceptable.) Letter quality or near letter-quality print must be used for computer-prepared manuscripts.

Style must conform to that described by the *American Psychological Association Publication Manual*, Fourth Edition, 1994 revision (American Psychological Association, 1200 Seventeenth Street, N.W., Washington, D.C. 20036). Authors are responsible for final preparation of manuscripts to conform to the *APA* style.

Manuscripts are reviewed by the Editor, Associate Editor(s), members of the Editorial Board, and invited reviewers with special knowledge of the topic addressed in the manuscript. The Editor retains the right to reject articles that do not conform to conventional clinical or scientific ethical standards. Normally, the review process is completed in 3 months. Nearly all manuscripts accepted for publication require some degree of revision. There is no charge for publication of papers in the *Infant Mental Health Journal*. The publisher may levy additional charges for changes in proof other than correction of printers errors. Proof will be sent to the corresponding author and must be read carefully because final responsibility for accuracy rests with the author(s). Author(s) must return corrected proof to the publisher in a timely manner. If the publisher does not receive corrected proof from the author(s), publication will still proceed as scheduled.

Additional questions with regard to style and submission of manuscripts should be directed to the Editor.

Information Technology & Libraries

ADDRESS FOR SUBMISSION:

John Webb, Editor
Information Technology & Libraries
Washington State University Libraries
Asst. Director for Digital
   Services/Collections
Pullman, WA 99164-5610
USA
Phone: 509-335-9133
Fax: 509-335-6721
E-Mail: jwebb@wsu.edu
Web: www.ala.org/ala/lita
Address May Change: 12/31/2007

PUBLICATION GUIDELINES:

Manuscript Length: 21-25
Copies Required: Two
Computer Submission: Yes
Format: MS Word
Fees to Review: 0.00 US$

Manuscript Style:
   Chicago Manual of Style

CIRCULATION DATA:

Reader: Academics
Frequency of Issue: Quarterly
Copies per Issue: 5,001 - 10,000
Sponsor/Publisher: Library & Info.
   Technology Association (LITA) of the
   American Library Association
Subscribe Price: 55.00 US$

   Free to LITA members

REVIEW INFORMATION:

Type of Review: Blind Review
No. of External Reviewers: 1
No. of In House Reviewers: 1
Acceptance Rate: 50%
Time to Review: 1 - 2 Months
Reviewers Comments: Yes
Invited Articles: 11-20%
Fees to Publish: 0.00 US$

MANUSCRIPT TOPICS:
Educational Technology Systems; Library and Information Technology; Library
Science/Information Resources

MANUSCRIPT GUIDELINES/COMMENTS:

Subject Content
Information Technology and Libraries publishes material related to all aspects of libraries and information technology, including digital libraries, metadata, authorization and authentication, electronic journals and electronic publishing, telecommunications, distributed systems and networks, computer security and intellectual property rights, technical standards, geographic information systems, desktop applications, online catalogs and bibliographic systems, optical information systems, software engineering, universal access to technology, futuristic forecasting, library consortia, vendor relations, and technology and the arts.

Types of Contributions
ITAL includes feature articles, communications, tutorials, reviews, and letters to the editor.

Feature articles consist of original research or comprehensive and in-depth analyses. Although longer works may be considered, manuscripts of 3000 to 5000 words are most common. An abstract of 100 words or less should accompany article on a separate sheet.

Communications consist of brief research reports, technical findings, and application notes. Generally communications are 1000 to 3000 words in length. An abstract should be included, but is not absolutely required.

Book and Software Reviews Book reviews and software reviews are assigned by the respective editors. Contact the Book Review editor, Tom Zillner at tzillner@wils.wisc.edu. Readers wishing to review library-related software for the journal are invited to contact the software review editor, Andy Boze at Boze.1@nd.edu indicating their special areas of interest and expertise.

Tutorials are brief, instructional pieces on topics or issues of relevance.

Letters to the Editor may be submitted to the Editor for possible inclusion in the journal.

Instruction for Submissions

1. Submit original, unpublished manuscripts only. Do not submit manuscript being considered for publication elsewhere. Authors are responsible for the accuracy of the information in the manuscript, including references, statistics and URLs.

2. Manuscripts should be machine-printed and double-spaced. Two copies should be provided. It is not necessary to provide the manuscript in electronic format until it has been accepted for publication. Author name, title, and affiliation should appear on a separate cover page only. This information should not be repeated in the text of manuscript, or in the abstract. Pages should be numbered. An abstract of 100 words or less should be provided on a separate sheet.

3. *ITAL* follows *The Chicago Manual of Style*, 14th edition for capitalization, punctuation, quotations, tables, captions, and elements of bibliographic style, including references. Spelling will follow *Webster's Collegiate Dictionary*, 10th edition.

4. Information on submission of electronic copy, tables and illustrations, copyright forms, and other aspects of a final copy will be provided when a manuscript has been accepted for publication.

Review of Manuscripts

ITAL is a refereed journal using double-blind reviewing. The editor assigns manuscripts to reviewers who receive the manuscript with no direct information on the author or author's affiliation. Reviewers examine the manuscript considering the following:

- Is the topic within scope of *ITAL*?
- Is it meaningful and relevant to *ITAL* readers?
- Does it offer something to the literature?
- Is it timely?
- Is the presentation that of an article or merely the text of an oral presentation?

- Is it organized well? Does it have a point?
- Are the citations complete and accurate?

Upon completing the review, a recommendation is presented to the editor as to the suitability of the manuscript for publication in *ITAL*. Recommendations fall into one of the following categories:

- publishable in its current condition
- significant and sound and should be published with only minor editorial revisions.
- basically significant and sound but requires some rewriting to make it a solid publishable contribution.
- requires major rewriting, and it should be reviewed again after a revised draft has been received.
- does not warrant publication as a full article but might be published as a Communication.
- does not warrant further consideration by *ITAL*.

The author is informed of the recommendation and any comments made by the reviewers. The review process takes six to eight weeks.

Editor for ITAL v. 24- (2004-2007):
John Webb
Assistant Director for Digital Services/Collections
Washington State University Libraries

Submit manuscripts to:
John Webb
ITAL Editor
Washington State University Libraries
Pullman, WA 99164-5610
E-mail: **jwebb@wsu.edu**

Managing Editor:
Marc Truitt
Assistant Dean for Systems
University of Houston Libraries
114 University Libraries
Houston, TX 77204-2000
Phone: 713-743-8979, Fax: 713-743-9811
Email: **mtruitt@uh.edu**

Advertising Editor:
William Coffee
Benson, Coffee & Assoc.
1411 Peterson Avenue
Park Ridge, IL 60068
Phone:(847) 692-4695, Fax:(847) 692-3877
E-mail: **bencof@aol.com**

In all correspondence please indicate your name, institutional affiliation, mailing address, phone number, fax number and e-mail address.
- Copyright release form (Limited License)
- Copyright release form (All Rights)

Information Technology, Learning and Performance Journal

ADDRESS FOR SUBMISSION:

Susan Feather-Gannon, Editor
Information Technology, Learning and
    Performance Journal
826 Van Wagner Road
Poughkeepsie, NY 12601-6504
USA
Phone: 845-485-6450
Fax: 914-989-8633
E-Mail: sfeathergannon@fsmail.pace.edu
Web: www.osra.org
Address May Change:

PUBLICATION GUIDELINES:

Manuscript Length: 21-25
Copies Required: Four
Computer Submission: Yes
Format: MS Word, pdf
Fees to Review: 0.00 US$

Manuscript Style:
    American Psychological Association

CIRCULATION DATA:

Reader: Academics
Frequency of Issue: 2 Times/Year
Copies per Issue: Less than 1,000
Sponsor/Publisher: Organizational Systems
    Research Association
Subscribe Price: 35.00 US$

REVIEW INFORMATION:

Type of Review: Blind Review
No. of External Reviewers: 3
No. of In House Reviewers: 0
Acceptance Rate: 21-30%
Time to Review: 1 - 2 Months
Reviewers Comments: Yes
Invited Articles: 0-5%
Fees to Publish: 0.00 US$

MANUSCRIPT TOPICS:

Business Education; Educational Technology Systems; Library Science/Information Resources

MANUSCRIPT GUIDELINES/COMMENTS:

Manuscript Topics

Computers and information systems, end-user computing, organizational computing, information systems implementation and evaluation, human factors/ergonomics, teaching and learning computing skills, information systems curriculum development.

The *Information Technology, Learning, and Performance Journal* publishes manuscripts in the field of end-user and organizational information systems. Manuscripts may present the results of research in the discipline, deal with research methodologies and data treatment techniques, or describe research or experiences related to instruction in the discipline. Manuscripts that describe an innovative policy, procedure, method, technique, or practice that has potential benefit for systems professionals and/or educators and technology trainers are also welcomed.

The *Journal* is indexed in the *Business Education Index,* the *Current Index to Journals in Education,* and the *Computer Literature Index.* Articles are available from Bell & Howell in digital media (CD-ROM, online). For B&H information, call 800-524-0600, ext. 2888, or write: B&H, 300 North Zeeb Road, Box 1346, Ann Arbor, MI 48106-1346.

Manuscript Submission Guidelines
Authors should follow the style described for manuscripts and bibliographies in the Fifth Edition (2001) of the *Publication Manual of the American Psychological Association*; however, tables should be single-spaced. Authors should not be identified anywhere in the manuscript. Submit four copies of the manuscript. On the original copy, include a cover page with author name, title, organizational affiliation, telephone number, and email address. A 100-150 word abstract of the manuscript should be included with the manuscript.

Manuscripts should be submitted exclusively to the *Information Technology, Learning, and Performance Journal.* Previously published manuscripts are not acceptable. Manuscripts are selected through a blind review process involving the editors and referees selected from the membership of the Organizational Systems Research Association.

Authors of accepted manuscripts will be asked to submit their manuscript electronically in Word format.

Informing Science: The International Journal of an Emerging Transdiscipline

ADDRESS FOR SUBMISSION:

Eli Cohen, Editor
Informing Science: The International
  Journal of an Emerging Transdiscipline
131 Brookhill Court
Santa Rosa, CA 95409
USA
Phone: 707-537-2211
Fax: 815-352-9100
E-Mail: editor@inform.nu
Web: inform.nu
Address May Change:

PUBLICATION GUIDELINES:

Manuscript Length: 16-30+
Copies Required: Email and Online Only
Computer Submission: Yes Email, Online
Format: MS Word or RTF Format
Fees to Review: 0.00 US$

Manuscript Style:
  American Psychological Association

CIRCULATION DATA:

Reader: Academics
Frequency of Issue: Yearly
Copies per Issue: 4,001 - 5,000
Sponsor/Publisher: Informing Science
  Institute
Subscribe Price: 0.00 US$ Online
  50.00 US$ + S & H Print

REVIEW INFORMATION:

Type of Review: Blind Review
No. of External Reviewers: 3+
No. of In House Reviewers: 0
Acceptance Rate: 11-20%
Time to Review: 1-3 Months
Reviewers Comments: Yes
Invited Articles: 0-5%
Fees to Publish: 0.00 US$

MANUSCRIPT TOPICS:

Counseling & Personnel Services; Curriculum Studies; Educational Psychology; Educational Technology Systems; Higher Education; Information Technology; Library Science/Information Resources; Rural Education & Small Schools; Teacher Education; Tests, Measurement & Evaluation

MANUSCRIPT GUIDELINES/COMMENTS:

Editorial Guidelines

The academically refereed journal *Informing Science* endeavors to provide an understanding of the complexities in informing clientele. Fields from information systems, library science, journalism in all its forms to education all contribute to this science. These fields, which developed independently and have been researched in separate disciplines, are evolving to form a new transdiscipline, Informing Science. *Informing Science* publishes articles that provide insight into how best to inform clients using information technology. Authors may use epistemologies from engineering, computer science, education, psychology, business, anthropology, and such. The ideal paper will service to inform fellow researchers, perhaps from other fields, of contributions to this problem.

Guidelines for Authors
1. Follow the guidelines shown at **http://inform.nu/guidelines.htm**.

2. Authors submit their manuscripts electronically. Manuscripts must be "blinded" before submission.

3. All manuscripts must represent the authors' original, unpublished work. The manuscript must not be under consideration for publication elsewhere. Note the copyright policy shown at **http://inform.nu/copyrigh.htm**.

4. Submissions are to follow the *APA* style guidelines for citations, references, and headings.

5. The entire manuscript including artwork may not exceed 1,000 kilobytes of space. [This limit is set for reasons of economics and may be lifted if the author can provide resources for publishing. For example, on-line video might be housed on the authors' web server.]

6. The manuscript is to be submitted in MS Word or RTF format.

7. After a section editor determines that the topic of the manuscript fits within the section purview, the editor will have it reviewed by three referees. Most commonly, these reviewers shall be selected from the journal's Board of Reviewers, and will be dispersed geographically around the globe.

8. This process is designed to allow a manuscript of exceptional quality to be accepted and placed online within one month of submission. More commonly, an associate editor will provide the author with information regarding acceptance, provisional acceptance, or rejection of a manuscript within six weeks of submission.

9. The publisher will notify authors of accepted papers regarding additional formatting requirements. Articles appear on-line as soon as accepted and in print annually.

Innovations in Education and Teaching International

ADDRESS FOR SUBMISSION:

Philip Barker, Gina Wisker, Co-Editors
Innovations in Education and Teaching
   International
University of Teesside
School of Computing and Mathematics
Borough Road
Middlesbrough, TS1 3BA
UK
Phone: 01642 342660/1
Fax: 01642 342067
E-Mail: Philip.Barker@tees.ac.uk
Web: www.tandf.co.uk/journals
Address May Change:

PUBLICATION GUIDELINES:

Manuscript Length: 21-25
Copies Required: Three
Computer Submission: No
Format:
Fees to Review: 0.00 US$

Manuscript Style:
    See Manuscript Guidelines

CIRCULATION DATA:

Reader: Practicing Teachers, Academics,
   Administrators
Frequency of Issue: Quarterly
Copies per Issue:
Sponsor/Publisher: Staff and Educational
   Development Association / Taylor &
   Francis
Subscribe Price: 96.00 US$ Individual
   343.00 US$ Institution

REVIEW INFORMATION:

Type of Review: Editorial Review
No. of External Reviewers: 3
No. of In House Reviewers: 0
Acceptance Rate: 21-30%
Time to Review: 1 - 2 Months
Reviewers Comments: Yes
Invited Articles: 0-5%
Fees to Publish: 0.00 US$

MANUSCRIPT TOPICS:

Adult Career & Vocational; Education Management/Administration; Educational Technology Systems; Higher Education

MANUSCRIPT GUIDELINES/COMMENTS:

Gina Wisker, Co-Editor
Anglia Polytechnic University
East Road, Cambridge CB1 1PT, UK
Phone: 01223 363271; Fax: 01223 352973
Email: **g.wisker@apu.ac.uk**

Aims and Scope
IETI is essential reading for all practitioners and decision makers who want to stay informed about the developments in education and training.

388

It is the official journal of the Staff and Educational Development Association (**www.seda.ac.uk**).

The content includes a range of perspectives, and important contributions on new developments in educational technology.

IETI is a valuable resource for teaching staff, staff developers and managers in higher and further education, continuing education, and training organisations.

Instructions for Authors
Note to Authors: please make sure your contact address information is clearly visible on the **outside** of all packages you are sending to Editors.

The Editors are pleased to receive for consideration contributions on any aspects of education and training likely to be of interest to readers. The main criterion of acceptance is that the material should make a contribution to knowledge in this field. The aim is to publish clear and concise papers, case studies and opinions ranging from the theoretical to the applied. All contributions, with the exception of opinions, are refereed.

1. **Papers** should include one or more of the following: original work of a research or developmental nature; surveys of current or recent work; proposed new methods or ideas which are well elaborated and argued.

    Case Studies should be about work carried out on a national, regional or local basis. They are likely to include the following: a background scenario; a clear statement of the purpose of the work; a relationship to past or current work; who was involved; what happened; what happened; what deductions can be made; a critical review of the work; how the case study has implications for others.

    Opinions are likely to include one or more of the following: research or development work which is at an early stage (the contribution is really signalling that the work is in progress); unsubstantiated personal opinions which will be of interest to the readers of *IETI*; articles of a speculative nature; proposed new methods of working.

2. Contributions are accepted for publication on condition that the copyright in all original materials vests in the Staff and Educational Development Association and that the contributor has obtained any necessary permission and paid any fees for the use of other materials already subject to copyright. Contributors therefore undertake that their material is not a violation of any copyright and undertake to indemnify the Association for any loss occasioned to the Association in consequence of any breech of this undertaking.

3. Three copies should be sent to one of the Editors at the below addresses:

    Papers of a technical nature, relating to the uses of technology in teaching and learning, should be sent to: Philip Barker, School of Computing and Mathematics, University of Teesside, Borough Road, Middlesbrough TS1 3BA, UK, while papers dealing with non-technical, softer issues of teaching and learning should be addressed to: Gina Wisker, Anglia Polytechnic University, East Road, Cambridge CB1 1PT, UK.

The manuscript should be on A4 paper, typed double spaced with adequate margins. A disk copy (PC compatible) should also be provided as a Word or ASCII file.

4. Manuscripts must be in English. Straightforward language is preferred to the obscure or complex.

5. A summary of between 100 and 150 words should be enclosed. Authors are invited to supply summaries in French and/or German, and these will be printed with accepted papers.

6. Brief biographical notes, containing an address for correspondence, should be enclosed.

7. Footnotes should be avoided.

8. Main headings should by typed in capitals (INTRODUCTION, RESULTS, ETC.). Secondary headings should be in lower case.

9. Each table and figure should be on a separate sheet, clearly labelled. Material that contains numbers should be referred to as TABLES; materials containing diagrams or mostly words should be referred to as FIGURES. Each table and figure should have an explanatory legend, which should be typed at the bottom of the page. The approximate position of each table or figure in the text should be indicated thus:

TABLE 1 about here

10. All illustrations (i.e. charts, graphs, diagrams and photographs) must be of sufficiently high quality to permit immediate reproduction. Line diagrams should be drawn in black ink, with neat lettering. Coloured lettering is not acceptable. Photocopies of line diagrams are unsuitable for reproduction unless they are of the highest standard. Photographs should be glossy prints, unmarked and uncreased, with good contrast. Contributions which are otherwise acceptable may be rejected on the grounds that illustrations are of unsatisfactory quality.

11. References in the text should be made quoting the author's name, followed by the year of publication in brackets. Where reference has been made to a number of publications by an author in one year, these should be distinguished by using suffixes: 1974a, 1974b, etc. References should be listed alphabetically at the end of the paper, in the following way:

For articles: Connors, B. (1972) Testing innovations in course design, *British Journal of Educational Technology*, 3, 48-52.

For chapters: Lawless, C. J. & Kirkwood, A. (1976) *Individualising instructions for educational technology IX* (London, Kogan Page).

For books: Tyler, R. W. (1949) *Basic principles of curriculum and instruction* (Chigago, IL, University of Chicago Press).

Notice that the titles of journals are not abbreviated, and that pagination is always given.

If you have any further questions about the style for this journal, please submit your questions using the Style Queries form.

12. Authors are required to check proofs of their articles. However, alterations are expensive and authors may be required to bear any extra charges made by the printer where more than minor corrections are involved. It is important that proofs are returned promptly, certainly within a week of receipt. Any special instructions about the address to which proofs should be sent, or the author who will be responsible for proof-reading in the case of papers with more than one author, should be attached to the manuscript. Otherwise, proofs will be sent to the author named, at the address given in the biographical notes. An overseas author can nominate someone in Britain to proof-read on his or her behalf. Where proofs are not returned on time, papers may be printed in their uncorrected form, or held over. The author is asked to consult the Editor before submitting a paper if in any doubt.

13. Early Electronic Offprints Corresponding authors can now receive their article by e-mail as a complete PDF. This allows the author to print up to 50 copies, free of charge, and disseminate them to colleagues. In many cases this facility will be available up to two weeks prior to publication. Or, alternatively, corresponding authors will receive the traditional 50 offprints. A copy of the journal will be sent by post to all corresponding authors after publication. Additional copies of the journal can be purchased at the author's preferential rate of £15.00/$25.00 per copy.

International Education

ADDRESS FOR SUBMISSION:

Sue Carey, Managing Editor
International Education
University of Tennessee
College of Education, Health and
 Human Sciences
Knoxville, TN 37996-3400
USA
Phone: 865-974-5252
Fax: 865-974-8718
E-Mail: scarey@utk.edu
Web:
Address May Change:

PUBLICATION GUIDELINES:

Manuscript Length: 6-20
Copies Required: Two
Computer Submission: Yes 3.5 Disk
Format: IBM or Macintosh
Fees to Review: 0.00 US$

Manuscript Style:
 American Psychological Association,
 5th Edition

CIRCULATION DATA:

Reader: Academics
Frequency of Issue: 2 Times/Year
Copies per Issue: Less than 1,000
Sponsor/Publisher: The University of
 Tennessee
Subscribe Price: 16.00 US$
 22.00 US$

REVIEW INFORMATION:

Type of Review: Blind Review
No. of External Reviewers: 3
No. of In House Reviewers: 2
Acceptance Rate: 65%
Time to Review: 2 - 3 Months
Reviewers Comments: Yes
Invited Articles: 0-5%
Fees to Publish: 0.00 US$

MANUSCRIPT TOPICS:

Bilingual/E.S.L.; Elementary/Early Childhood; Foreign Language; Higher Education; Teacher Education; Tests, Measurement & Evaluation

MANUSCRIPT GUIDELINES/COMMENTS:

Articles should be typewritten and double-spaced and be six to twenty pages in length. The original and one copy should be submitted. You may also send your manuscript on a 3.5-inch, IBM or Macintosh-formatted disk with a self-addressed, stamped envelope and one hard copy.

Your submission of a manuscript requires assurance that it is an original work, that it has not been published previously, and that it is not currently being considered for publication elsewhere.

It is preferred that the references be noted according to the fifth edition of the *Publication Manual of the American Psychological Association*.

International Education Journal

ADDRESS FOR SUBMISSION:

Katherine Dix, Editor
International Education Journal
39 Dorrien Avenue
Woodcroft, SA 5162
Phone: 0414 858 959
Fax: 8201 3184
E-Mail: katherine.dix@flinders.edu.au
Web: http://iej.cjb.net
Address May Change:

PUBLICATION GUIDELINES:

Manuscript Length: 21-25
Copies Required:
Computer Submission: Yes Disk, Email
Format: MS Word, English
Fees to Review: 0.00 US$

Manuscript Style:
    American Psychological Association

CIRCULATION DATA:

Reader: Academics
Frequency of Issue: Quarterly
Copies per Issue: 4,001 - 5,000
Sponsor/Publisher: Shannon Research
    Press, Flinders Institute of International
    Education
Subscribe Price: 0.00 US$

REVIEW INFORMATION:

Type of Review: Blind Review
No. of External Reviewers: 2
No. of In House Reviewers: 3
Acceptance Rate: 60%
Time to Review: 4 - 6 Months
Reviewers Comments: Yes
Invited Articles: 0-5%
Fees to Publish: 0.00 US$

MANUSCRIPT TOPICS:
Bilingual/E.S.L.; Curriculum Studies; Education Management/Administration; Educational Psychology; Educational Technology Systems; Elementary/Early Childhood; Foreign Language; Gifted Children; Health & Physical Education; Higher Education; International Education; Languages & Linguistics; Reading; Religious Education; Rural Education & Small Schools; Science Math & Environment; Secondary/Adolescent Studies; Social Studies/Social Science; Special Education; Teacher Education; Tests, Measurement & Evaluation; Urban Education, Cultural/Non-Traditional

MANUSCRIPT GUIDELINES/COMMENTS:

IEJ is a broadly based, free online journal encompassing research and review articles. Education is interpreted in a wide manner and includes human development, learning, school education, formal and informal education, tertiary and vocational education, industry training and lifelong learning.

About *IEJ*
Welcome to the *International Education Journal*. *IEJ* is a freely accessible, full-text, peer reviewed, international online journal that seeks clear and significant contributions that further debate on educational issues. Education is interpreted in a wide manner and includes human development, learning, school education, formal and informal education, tertiary and

vocational education, industry training and lifelong learning. We publish articles from teachers, administrators, professors, graduate students, policy-makers, and education specialists from governmental and non-governmental organisations.

While a small number of hard copy versions of the journal are produced for archival and administrative purposes, it is intended that the Journal will be accessed in almost all instances in electronic format via the web.

The publishers have arranged for the Flinders Institute for International Education to produce an electronic mirror site containing all the material in the Journal. All material can be accessed in electronic format free of charge. There are no restrictions on downloading or printing single copies. The electronic version also provides readers with a search tool capable of searching by individual article, author or descriptor.

Copyright
Copyright of material produced in this journal rests with individual contributors. Apart from fair use such as brief quotation for scholarly purposes, permission to use material in this journal should be obtained from the authors concerned.

Peer Review
Material submitted for publication will be subjected to a rigorous referee process by one of the *IEJ* editors and at least one independent specialist in the field.

DEST Register of Refereed Journals
IEJ has been assessed by the Australian Department of Education, Science and Training (DEST) as satisfying the refereeing requirements for the Higher Education Research Data Collection (HERDC). Accordingly, articles published by authors from Australian Universities will be counted towards the allocation of research funding.

Publication Frequency
It is intended that the journal be published three times per year. However given the electronic characteristics of online publishing it is not necessary to wait until a full journal is assembled prior to publishing. Articles, once accepted in appropriate form, may be published without delay. Journal articles can be downloaded in PDF format, and require Acrobat Reader or equivalent to view.

Special Issues
In addition to the three standard issues of the journal published each year, *IEJ* undertakes to publish Special issues, at the discretion of the Editorial Board. Generally these Special issues take the form of selected articles from educational conferences where there isn't a Conference Proceedings. Through the publication of Special issues, *IEJ* has proudly supported the following conferences:
- The Educational Research Conference
- The Eleventh World Congress of Comparative Education Societies (WCCES)

394

JOURNAL ARTICLES
Invitation to Contributors
Authors are invited to submit material to this journal. It is expected that authors are affiliated with a Higher Education institution. As a general guide articles should be not more than 5000 words. The journal may publish longer works such as theses or dissertations as occasional monographs. In every instance material must be received in publisher ready format. Full details of publication style and other requirements are set out in Author Information.

BOOK REVIEWS
Invitation to Publishers
If you wish to have books or educational software reviewed and published in the *International Education Journal* please contact the editors.

Invitation to Reviewers
If you are interested in contributing to the journal by writing a review article (1500 words) please contact the authors indicating your areas of interest. We look forward to hearing from you.

OCCASIONAL PAPERS
Invitation to Contributors
Occasional Papers include larger documents such as Theses and Reports, among others. Such works, unless commercially published as a book, are generally only accessible to a small number of specialised readers. In accordance with the aims of *IEJ*, authors are invited to take advantage of this opportunity to reach a wider audience.

Aims of *IEJ*
The aim of the *International Education Journal* is to publish articles that possess one or more of the following characteristics or qualities.
1. The presentation of substantive findings which are of importance for policy and practice beyond the country in which the research was conducted.
2. The integration of education with academic disciplines such as anthropology, demography, economics, history, law, linguistics, philosophy, political science, psychology and sociology, or examines educational issues from the perspective of the disciplines or investigates issues at the interface between education and one or more of these disciplines.
3. The examination of educational issues from a cross-cultural or indigenous people's perspective.
4. The evaluation of educational policy or programs or the use of information technology of cross- national interest and significance.
5. The employment of advanced research methods and measurement procedures which are clearly explained.
6. The presentation of empirically or analytically based investigations of theory, models or conceptual frame works in the field of education.
7. The syntheses of research findings from comparative and cross-national studies in education.

The views and styles expressed in the articles in this publication are those of the individual authors and are not necessarily shared by the reviewers, the editors or the editorial advisory board.

Published by: Shannon Research Press, Adelaide, South Australia; ISSN 1443-1475

Designed by Katherine Dix; For cataloging purposes 10 Hard copies are produced. Printed in Adelaide, South Australia.

INFORMATION FOR AUTHORS
Article Content
IEJ welcomes practical and research manuscripts that focus on educational issues, provide a clear purpose and depth of discussion, and are presented in a straightforward style accessible to an international audience.

The issue of Bias
Avoid stereotyping on the basis of gender, race, or age.
Accordingly,
- choose gender-neutral terms, such as sports person rather than sportsman
- describe the person, not the disability: for example a person with visual impairment rather than a visually impaired person
- use people of both sexes and vary the ethnicity of names
- avoid using the third-person singular pronouns he, his, and him by rewording the sentence with alternatives such as they or their, he or she, his or her, or him or her.

Copyright and Permission
Copyrighted material allows the author to quote briefly (up to 100 words) for scholarly purposes from most published materials, providing the source is correctly cited within the manuscript. However, if the author wishes to use figures, tables, poems, or longer quotations, written permission must be obtained from the writer or publisher to reprint the material. Under such circumstances, the author needs to provide a permission summary with their manuscript submission. Written permissions must also be provided by subjects in any photographs or audio or video segments. If the subjects are children, a signed release from a parent or guardian must be provided for each child visible in the photograph or video segment, or heard on an audio clip.

In addition, although linking to another site does not require permission, replication (such as "screen shots") or description of a site within the manuscript requires permission to be sought from originator of web site, including those created by students, teachers, or schools.

Submission Criteria
The initial submission:
- should be prepared using the downloadable (for Mac or PC) WORD6/95 template document (iejbase.doc), complete with layout styles, images and tables correctly positioned in the text. Please refer to the WORD6/95 model for examples of correct layout.

- images that are imported or inserted into the text from an external source as figures should be included as separate graphic files (either GIF or JPG format) should be forwarded electronically, either by:
  - e-mail (preferably) to: **onlineeditor@iej.cjb.net or**,
  - on a 1.4MB 3.5 inch floppy diskette to:
  IEJ Online Editor,
  Shannon Research Press,
  39 Dorrien Avenue,
  Woodcroft, SA 5162.

The editors reserve the right to return poorly edited or improperly formatted manuscripts. Hard-copy only submissions cannot be accepted or returned.

Manuscript Style
The manuscript should:

- show the article's title, authors' names, affiliation, and email addresses (these will be included on the online page), and postal address and telephone numbers (these will be removed from the final online page)
- not exceed 5,000 words in length (20,000 for occasional papers)
- include an abstract of approximately 150 words
- include 5 keywords describing the article to assist searching
- be in final form ready for immediate reviewing
- comply with the document template and modified APA referencing system, both described in detail below

LAYOUT
General Principles

- Papers should be prepared using the template *iejbase.doc* with Microsoft WORD on either a Macintosh or a Windows system.
- Format paragraph text using the 'Normal' style in the styles menu. This puts a space before each paragraph so that a blank line is not required to separate paragraphs and automatically sets the text to single line, full justified, 12 pt layout.
- Format the Title of the paper using the 'Title' style in the styles menu, use the 'Abstract' style for the abstract and the 'Quotation' style for paragraph quotes.
- Use foot-notes, with one set of numbers running through the whole article.
- Do not create additional headers and footers in the template document *iejbase.doc*, just modify them appropriately. By double clicking on the header it should become active, allowing you to change the Author(s) name and Title of the article.

Figures

- Diagrams should be placed in the text where they are to appear.
- Diagrams should have a caption appearing beneath the figure on the same page, be numbered successively, and must be referred to in the text before their appearance, as shown in Figure 1.

Figure 1. Example of a figure

Tables

- Use the 'Table' commands to produce tables. Do not use the space bar or the Tab command to align numbers and text.
- Tables should have a caption appearing **above** the table, be numbered successively, and be referred to in the text.
- Use the 'Tabletext' style to format the text and numbers in the table.
- An example of how to format a table is given in Table 1.

Quotations

- Quotations less than three lines long should be incorporated into the text using double quotation marks
- For longer quotations (more than three lines or two sentences), use 'Quotation' style in the styles menu

References

- Insert 6 pts using the Paragraph command for the first reference in order to provide a gap between the references and the heading
- Format the reference list using the 'Reference' style in the styles menu.

Common Mistakes

- Use foot-notes, with one set of numbers running through the whole article.
- Use **bold** rather than underlining for emphasis.
- Use *italics* to emphasize book titles and foreign words or phrases (for example, via, however it is simpler and preferable to use 'through').
- Avoid using the slash /. Say his or her, rather than his/her, and never use and/or.
- Avoid writing in the first person. For example, use "This paper discusses...", rather than, "In this paper I will discuss...".
- Use single quote marks for words or phrases that have a new meaning, for example, so called 'in your face', because it is not standard or commonly accepted English or is an unknown phrase.
- Use 'in order to' rather than the infinitive 'for'.
- Tenses in sentences in a given paragraph MUST agree.
- Short quotes and short spoken quotes use double quotation marks. Italicize spoken quotes.
- Long quotes (over three lines), start a new line and use the 'Quotation' style.
- All written quotes should have a page number included in the reference. For example, "Work is love made visible" (Gibran, 1923, p.15). Use p. as the abbreviation for page, not pg.
- In-text references, when there are more than one, should be in alphabetical order. For example (Arnold, 1994; Jones and Demp, 1990; Lee, 2001; Smith and Yuan, 1983).

- Take care to avoid split infinitives.
- The word 'program' is not spelt the French way (programme).
- Avoid confusing the words 'methodology' and 'method'. Methodology it is the study of methods, not the methods themselves.
- Never abbreviate words. Always use United States (not US), United Kingdom (not UK), for example (not eg), and (not &).
- Always use per cent, and not %, unless it is in brackets or in a table. For example, 5 per cent or (5%), is fine.
- Numbers up to ten should be written in full (for example, three students were interviewed), unless it is a label, such as, Grade 3, or Year 5, or a statistical number, such as 7 per cent.
- Numbers above ten should be written as a numeral unless it is at the beginning of a sentence.
- Avoid using etc. at the end of a list of examples.
- Lists of items within a sentence should use letters (a), (b), and (c).
- Lists of that are complete sentences should start each item on a new line and use dotpoints or numbers 1. 2. 3. ...

Referencing

To reference in the body of the manuscript, cite authors' last names and the year of publication in parentheses: for example, (Baker, Robertson and Sloan, 1993). When citing several authors within the same set of parentheses, use alphabetical order separated by a semicolon (Anderson, 1997; Hart, 1990). Include only items cited in the text in the list of references. References should be listed at the end of the paper and conform to the modified APA system, as provided in Table 1. Note that Table 1 is also an example of how a table and the caption should appear in your paper.

Table 1. Example of the Modified APA System

Book	Baker, M., Robertson, F. and Sloan, J. (1993) *The Role of Immigration in the Australian Higher Education Market.* Canberra: Australian Government Publishing Service.
Journal Article	Hart, G. (1990) Peer consultation in review. *Australian Journal of Advanced Nursing,* 5 (4), 22-27.
Articles in Edited Works	Slee, R. (1991) Institutional approaches to discipline. In M. Lovegrove and R. Lewis, (eds) *Classroom Discipline,* Melbourne: Longman Cheshire.
Theses	Birkeland, J. (1992) *Planning for a sustainable society.* Unpublished doctoral thesis, University of Tasmania.
Unpublished Works	McGaw, B. (1993) *Improving education and training research.* Unpublished manuscript, Melbourne: Australian Council for Educational Research.

Online   Anderson, J. (1997) Australian College of Education
Sources   Review: 1996 in retrospect. Unicorn, 23 (1), 3-13. [Online]
        http://www.flinders.edu.au/education/Readings/Unicorn.html   [1997,
        August 4]

Recommended Reading

HOW TO WRITE PUBLISHABLE PAPERS

by Abby Day

Abby Day has now completed her three part special guide to how to write publishable papers and how to choose the right publishers:

The postings follow a logical, systematic structure which I originally developed for my book *How to Get Research Published in Journals.*

Much of the material derived from my long association with Emerald, publisher of the world's widest range of journals in management, including HR and marketing, and library and information services. In particular, Emerald sponsored original research I conducted on quality variables in academic journals, which led to me conducting further independent research to test the findings more widely. Day, A. and Peters, J. *Quality indicators in academic publishing*, Library Review, 45, (3/4).

Now, under the aegis of Emerald's Literati Club - the exclusive network for authors and editors you can read nine separate guidance notes offered in three installments:

Part 1: A purpose to publish - *March 2001*
    1.1 Four good reasons to publish your work
    1.2 Four even better reasons not to publish your work
    1.3 Answering the question: so what?

Part 2: Relationship publishing - April 2001
    2.1 When quality doesn't matter
    2.2 Who cares about your work?
    2.3 Guaranteeing acceptance

Part 3: Seven days to a perfect paper - *May 2001*
    3.1 The first draft
    3.2 The finishing touch
    3.3 Managing the review process

Tracking your article

IEJ have a tracking system so that authors, and reviewers for that matter, can monitor the progress of the article through the review process.

You can access this online facility at:
    http://ehlt.flinders.edu.au/education/iej/articles/tracking.htm

400

This process usually takes about six to nine months, depending on the celerity of the reviewer and the imminence of the next issue.

Once you send in your article to the online editor as an attached word document, you should receive within two weeks, a return email that provides the tracking code, consisting of the main author's initials, the date of receipt and a key word from the title. For purposes of confidentiality, each article is coded so that only the author and IEJ Editors know whose article it is.

Need Help?
If you have any questions regarding layout and presentation, please contact the *IEJ* Online Editor: Katherine Dix at **katherine.dix@flinders.edu.au**

International Journal of Applied Linguistics

ADDRESS FOR SUBMISSION:

Jean Hannah, Editorial Secretary
International Journal of Applied Linguistics
Fau-Blanc 20E
1009 Pully
Switzerland
Phone:
Fax:
E-Mail: jeanhannah@compuserve.com
Web: www.blackwellpublishing.com
Address May Change: 10/1/2005

CIRCULATION DATA:

Reader: Academics, Applied Linguists
Frequency of Issue: 3 Times/Year
Copies per Issue: 1,000 Includ'g On-line
Sponsor/Publisher: Blackwell Publishers,
   Inc.
Subscribe Price: 45.00 US$ Individual
   204.00 US$ Institution
      including on-line access

PUBLICATION GUIDELINES:

Manuscript Length: 10,000 words
   maximum
Copies Required: Four or 1 hardcopy + disk
Computer Submission: Yes
Format: MS Word
Fees to Review: 0.00 US$

Manuscript Style:
   See Manuscript Guidelines

REVIEW INFORMATION:

Type of Review: Editorial Review
No. of External Reviewers: 2
No. of In House Reviewers: 2
Acceptance Rate: 35%
Time to Review: 4-5 Months
Reviewers Comments: Yes
Invited Articles: 0-5%
Fees to Publish: 0.00 US$

MANUSCRIPT TOPICS:

Bilingual/E.S.L.; Foreign Language; Languages & Linguistics; Tests, Measurement &
Evaluation

MANUSCRIPT GUIDELINES/COMMENTS:

Topics. Articles that explore the relationship between expertise in linguistics, broadly defined, and the everyday experience of language; articles which show explicitly how local issues of language use or leaning exemplify more global concerns.

Guidelines
The working language of the journal is English. *InJAL* publishes original articles and reviews of current books, as well as notes and comments on points arising out of recently-published articles.

Style Sheet
Typescript. Manuscripts should be typed double-spaced throughout on one side only of standard-sized paper with at least 3cm-wide (1.25") margins. Indent the beginning of each paragraph. Use a clear system of headings (without numbers), preferably with not more than three levels of heading. Each table or figure should appear on a separate page, with an

indication of where it belongs in the text; keep to the margin width above and use minimal borders.

Title page. Include the name(s) and institutional affiliation(s) of the author(s) and the full postal address of the author to whom proofs and other correspondence should be sent, including an e-mail address or fax number.

Abstract. The abstract should consist of one paragraph, maximum 15 lines. It should be written in the third person and contain an informative summary of the main points, including, where relevant, the purpose, methodology (including specific names of scales/tests and types of questionnaire), type of data, special characteristics of subjects used, and conclusions. Please include 5 key words after the abstract.

Cited words and quotations. Put cited words or phrases in *italics* (or underline). Use single quotation marks for glosses, double for quoted material. Any quotation that runs for more than three lines should be set off from the main paragraph and does not need quotation marks.

In-text references. References should appear in the text, not in footnotes, using the author–year system and including the page number where relevant: e.g. (Bloomeld 1933: 45–6). If the author's name is part of the text, use the following form: "Bloomeld (1933: 45–6) maintained that . . .". A work by three authors should include all names in the first reference, with only the first author's name followed by et al. in subsequent citations; work by four or more authors should use et al. in all citations. Only use authors' first initials if two or more authors with the same surname are referred to in the article. When citing from a reprinting, give the original date first in brackets: e.g. (Sapir [1929] 1949: 166). All and only works referred to in the text should be listed at the end in the References.

Notes. These should be kept to an absolute minimum; they should be placed at the end of the main text. Do NOT use automatic footnote programs.

References. Full citations of the literature referred to should be arranged alphabetically by surname, with initials for first names. The format should be consistent with the following examples. Please make sure that only the first word and proper nouns are capitalized in titles of articles and books; journal titles should have all main words capitalized.

Hymes, D. (ed.) (1971) *Pidginization and creolization of languages* (2nd edition). Cambridge University Press.

Trudgill, P. (1992a) Ausbau sociolinguistics and the perception of language status in contemporary Europe. *International Journal of Applied Linguistics* 2.2: 167–77.

—— (1992b) *Introducing language and society*. London: Penguin.

Weinreich, U., W. Labov & M.I. Herzog (1968) Empirical foundations for a theory of language change. In W.P. Lehman & Y. Malkiel (eds.), *Directions for historical linguistics: a symposium*. Austin: University of Texas Press. 97–195.

International Journal of Bilingual Education and Bilingualism

ADDRESS FOR SUBMISSION:

Colin Baker, Editor
International Journal of Bilingual Education
   and Bilingualism
Multilingual Matters
Frankfurt Lodge, Clevedon Hall
Victoria Road
Clevedon, BS21 7HH
UK
Phone: +44-0-1275-876519
Fax: +44-0-1275-871673
E-Mail: See Guidelines
Web: www.multilingual-matters.com
Address May Change:

PUBLICATION GUIDELINES:

Manuscript Length: 7000 words
Copies Required: Four
Computer Submission: Yes
Format: N/A
Fees to Review: 0.00 US$

Manuscript Style:
   American Psychological Association

CIRCULATION DATA:

Reader: Academics
Frequency of Issue: Bi-Monthly
Copies per Issue: Less than 1,000
Sponsor/Publisher: Multilingual Matters
   Ltd.
Subscribe Price: 95.00 US$ Individual
   555.00 US$ Library

REVIEW INFORMATION:

Type of Review: Blind Review
No. of External Reviewers: 2
No. of In House Reviewers: 1
Acceptance Rate: 50%
Time to Review: 2 - 3 Months
Reviewers Comments: Yes
Invited Articles: 0-5%
Fees to Publish: 0.00 US$

MANUSCRIPT TOPICS:

Bilingual/E.S.L.; Curriculum Studies; Educational Psychology; Languages & Linguistics;
Teacher Education

MANUSCRIPT GUIDELINES/COMMENTS:

Aims of the Journal

As international communication increases, few topics have become so internationally
important as bilingualism, multilingualism, bilingual education and the acquisition of new
languages. At the same time, there is increasing concern and interest about language
minorities and survival of indigenous and immigrant languages. Aims of this new journal,
International Journal of Bilingual Education and Bilingualism are to:

1.   promote applied research into bilingual education and bilingualism;
2.   to provide a truly international exchange, and to encourage; international debates and
     discussions on problematic issues and areas of controversy in bilingual education and
     bilingualism;
3.   to disseminate internationally good practice in many areas;

4. to provide updates and reviews of latest ideas and research on topics that are of a general interest to a wider audience;
5. to provide periodically major thematic reviews of topics that are widely taught in courses for students and teachers;
6. to publicize new ideas, new approaches, interventions, initiatives in policy and practice at regional, community and institutional levels, including schools and classrooms;
7. to provide interdisciplinary perspectives in a manner that is clearly understandable by a international audience
8. to create new international networks of people working in different institutions: academics, professional workers, students and practitioners.

Guidelines

Articles should not normally exceed 7000 words. Note that it is our policy not to review papers that are currently under consideration by other journals. They should be typed, double-spaced on A4 (or similar) paper, with ample left and right-hand margins, on one side of the paper only, and every page should be numbered consecutively. A cover page should contain only the title, thereby facilitating anonymous reviewing by two independent assessors. Authors may also wish to take precautions to avoid textual references which would identify themselves to the referees. In such cases the authors of accepted papers will have the opportunity to include any such omitted material before the paper is published.

Submissions for Work in Progress/ Readers' Response /Letters to the Editor sections should be approximately 500 words in length.

Main contact author should also appear in a separate paragraph on the title page.

An abstract should be included. This should not exceed 200 words (longer abstracts are rejected by many abstracting services).

A short version of the title (maximum 45 characters) should also be supplied for the journal's running headline.

To facilitate the production of the annual subject index, a list of keywords (not more than six) should be provided, under which the paper may be indexed.

Four hard copies of the article and a disc must be submitted, or the article should be sent as an email attachment to **submissions@multilingual-matters.com**.

Footnotes should be avoided. Essential notes should be numbered in the text and grouped together at the end of the article. Diagrams and Figures, if they are considered essential, should be clearly related to the section of the text to which they refer. The original diagrams and figures should be submitted with the top copy.

References should be set out in alphabetical order of the author's name in a list at the end of the article. They should be given in standard form, as in the Appendix below.

References in the text of an article should be by the author's name and year of publication, as in these examples: Jones (1997) in a paper on ...(commonest version); Jones and Evans (1997c:22) state that ...(where page number is required); Evidence is given by Smith et al. (1994)...(for three or more authors). Further exploration of this aspect may be found in many sources (e.g. Brown & Green, 1992; Jackson, 1993; White, 1991a) (note alphabetical order, use of & and semicolons).

Once the refereeing procedures are completed, authors should, if possible, supply a word-processor disc containing their manuscript file(s). If presented on disc, we require files to be saved:

- on an IBM-PC compatible 3.5 inch disc (or CD-ROM) or on an Apple Mac high-density 3,5 inch disc.
- Text should be saved in the author's normal word-processor format. The name of the word-processor program should also be supplied. Tables and Figures should be saved in separate files.

The author of an article accepted for publication will receive page proofs for correction, if there is sufficient time to do so. This stage must not be used as an opportunity to revise the paper, because alterations are extremely costly; extensive changes will be charged to the author and will probably result in the article being delayed to a later issue. Speedy return of corrected proofs is important.

Contributions and queries should be sent to the Editors, Multilingual Matters Ltd., Frankfurt Lodge, Clevedon Hall, Victoria Road, Clevedon, BS21 7HH, England. A very large majority of authors' proof-corrections are caused by errors in references. Authors are therefore requested to check the following points particularly carefully when submitting manuscripts:

- Are all the references in the reference list cited in the text?
- Do all the citations in the text appear in the reference list?
- Do the dates in the text and the reference list correspond?
- Do the spellings of authors' names in text and reference list correspond, and do all authors have the correct initials?
- Are journal references complete with volume and pages numbers?
- Are references to books complete with place of publication and the name of the publisher?

It is extremely helpful if references are presented as far as possible in accordance with our house style. A few more typical examples are shown below. Note, especially, use of upper &lower case in paper titles, use of capital letters and italic (underlining can be used as an alternative if italic is not available) in book and journal titles, punctuation (or lack of it) after dates, journal titles, and book titles. The inclusion of issue numbers of journals, or page numbers in books is optional but if included should be as per the examples below.

Department of Education and Science (DES) (1985) *Education for All* (The Swann Report). London: HMSO

Evans, N.J. and Ilbery, B.W. (1989) A conceptual framework for investigating farm-based accommodation and tourism in Britain. *Journal of Rural Studies* 5 (3), 257-266.

Evans, N.J. and Ilbery, B.W. (1992) Advertising and farm-based accommodation: A British case-study. *Tourism Management* 13 (4), 415-422.

Laufer, B (2000) Vocabulary acquisition in a second language: The hypothesis of 'synforms'. PhD thesis, University of Edinburgh.

Mackey, W.F. (1998) The ecology of language shift. In P.H. Nelde (ed.) *Languages in Contact and in Conflict* (pp. 35-41). Wiesbaden: Steiner.

Marien, C. and Pizam, A. (1997) Implementing sustainable tourism development through citizen participation in the planning process. In S. Wahab and J. Pigram (eds) *Tourism, Development and Growth* (pp. 164-78). London: Routledge.

Morrison, D. (1999) Small group discussion project questionnaire. University of Hong Kong Language Centre (mimeo).

U.S. Census Bureau (1998) State profile: California. Online document: http/www.census.gov/statab/www/states/ca.txt.

Zahn, C.J. and Hopper, R (2000) The speech evaluation instrument: A user's manual (version 1.0a). Unpublished manuscript, Cleveland State University.

Zigler, E. and Balla, D. (eds) *Mental Retardation: The Developmental-Difference Controversy.* Hillsdale, N.J: Lawrence Erlbaum.

For more details, please e-mail us on **info@multilingual-matters com**

International Journal of Disability, Development and Education

ADDRESS FOR SUBMISSION:

Christa van Kraayenoord, Editor
International Journal of Disability,
  Development and Education
University of Queensland
Fred and Eleanor Schonell Special
  Education Research Centre
Brisbane, Queensland, 4072
Australia
Phone: +61 7 3365-6472
Fax: +61 7 3365-8553
E-Mail: See Guidelines
Web: www.tandf.co.uk/journals
Address May Change:

PUBLICATION GUIDELINES:

Manuscript Length: 16-25
Copies Required: Two
Computer Submission: Yes
Format: rtf
Fees to Review: 0.00 US$

Manuscript Style:
  American Psychological Association

CIRCULATION DATA:

Reader: Academics
Frequency of Issue: Quarterly
Copies per Issue:
Sponsor/Publisher: Taylor & Francis Ltd
Subscribe Price: 157.00 US$ Individual
  432.00 US$ Institution

REVIEW INFORMATION:

Type of Review: Blind Review
No. of External Reviewers: 3
No. of In House Reviewers: 0
Acceptance Rate: 50%
Time to Review: 2 - 3 Months
Reviewers Comments: Yes
Invited Articles: 0-5%
Fees to Publish: 0.00 US$

MANUSCRIPT TOPICS:
Disability; Educational Psychology; Special Education

MANUSCRIPT GUIDELINES/COMMENTS:

Aims and Scope
Founded in 1954, the *International Journal of Disability, Development and Education*
(*IJDDE*) is a multi-disciplinary peer-reviewed journal with an international focus. It provides
a single source of information on the education and development of persons with disabilities.
IJDDE aims to publish the very best research and review articles concerned with all aspects of
education, human development, special education and rehabilitation.

The content of *IJDDE* reflects a variety of topics, disciplines, research methods and cultural
perspectives. Various orientations are represented, including education and special education,
psychology, allied health, social work and psychiatry. Contributions from developed and
developing countries ensure a truly international perspective.

Instructions for Authors

Note to Authors: please make sure your contact address information is clearly visible on the **outside** of <u>all</u> packages you are sending to Editors.

Publication. *The International Journal of Disability, Development and Education* is published four times per year for the Fred and Eleanor Schonell Special Education Research Centre by Carfax, Taylor & Francis Ltd. Manuscripts should be forwarded to the Editor, Christa van Kraayenoord, Fred and Eleanor Schonell Special Education Research Centre, The University of Queensland, Brisbane Qld 072, Australia.

Articles. The Editor invites articles for consideration concerned with all aspects of theory, research, and practice in the areas of disability, human development, and education. Research, review, and issues oriented articles will be considered as will descriptions or cross-cultural comparisons of education, special education, and rehabilitation in developed and developing countries. Articles of 5,000 to 7,000 words would be considered a typical length. Brief reports (3-4,000 words) will also be considered for inclusion in the Journal.

Submissions. Submissions should be original and unpublished work suitable for an international audience and not currently under review by any other journal or publisher. Authors should forward two copies of their manuscript and a rtf version on disk or email to the Editor (**c.vankraayenoord@uq.edu.au**). Manuscripts should be typewritten in double line spacing, using the format and reference standard set out in the *Publication Manual of the American Psychological Association* (2001, 5th edition). A transmittal letter signed by the author should be included. This letter should request review of the manuscript and indicate that the manuscript has not been published nor submitted for publication elsewhere. The first page of the manuscript should be a cover page detailing the title of the article, running head, name(s) of author(s), affiliation(s), and postal and E-mail addresses for correspondence. Telephone and fax numbers should also be included.

Manuscripts that are selected and verbatim parts of documents available from websites will NOT be accepted for republication. Articles that refer to already published reports available on websites will be published under the following circumstances:

- The manuscript needs to make a unique contribution over and above that contained in the original report. This would generally imply that reflective analysis or critical review of the issues has been included and that the material presented has been contextualized appropriately, in addition to other material.
- In those instances where such a manuscript is submitted for review, the web address of the original document will need to be included in the manuscript so that reviewers (and potential readers) can access the full document and thereby make a judgement about the additional contribution being made by the manuscript under consideration.

If you have any further questions about the style for this journal, please submit your questions using the Style Queries form.

Review. Manuscripts are sent for blind peer-review to members of the Editorial Board and Guest Reviewers. The review process generally requires three months. The receipt of submitted manuscripts will be acknowledged by the Editor, from whom a decision and reviewers' comments will be received when the peer-review has been completed.

Final Copy. The final version of manuscripts accepted for publication should be submitted in rtf format on a disk or by email to the Editor (**c.vankraayenoord@mailbox.uq.edu.au**).

Early Electronic Offprints. Corresponding authors can now receive their article by e-mail as a complete PDF. This allows the author to print up to 50 copies, free of charge, and disseminate them to colleagues. In many cases this facility will be available up to two weeks prior to publication. Or, alternatively, corresponding authors will receive the traditional 50 offprints. A copy of the journal will be sent by post to all corresponding authors after publication. Additional copies of the journal can be purchased at the author's preferential rate of £15.00/$25.00 per copy.

Copyright. It is condition of publication that authors vest copyright in their articles, including abstracts, in Taylor & Francis Ltd. This enables us to ensure full copyright protection and disseminate the article, and the journal, to the widest possible readership in print and electronic formats as appropriate. Authors may, of course, use the article elsewhere after publication without prior permission from Carfax Publishing, Taylor & Francis Ltd, provided that acknowledgement is given to the Journal as the original source of publication, and that Carfax Publishing, Taylor & Francis Ltd is notified so that our records show that its use is properly authorised. Authors are themselves responsible for obtaining permission to reproduce copyright material from other sources.

Correspondence
Address correspondence to:
Christa van Kraayenoord, Fred and Eleanor Schonell Special Education Research Centre, The University of Queensland, Brisbane Qld 4072, Australia.
Telephone: (07) 3365 6521; Fax: (07) 3365 8553
International: +617 3365 6521
International: +617 3365 8553
E-mail address: **c.vankraayenoord@mailbox.uq.edu.au**

410

International Journal of Distance Education Technologies

ADDRESS FOR SUBMISSION:

Timothy K. Shih, Shi Kuo Chang, Editors
International Journal of Distance Education
   Technologies
Tamkang University
Department of Computer Science
   and Information Engineering
151, Ying-Chuan Road
Tamsui, Taipei Hsien, 25137
Taiwan
Phone:
Fax:
E-Mail: tshih@cs.tku.edu.tw
Web: www.idea-group.com/journals
Address May Change:

PUBLICATION GUIDELINES:

Manuscript Length: 16-20
Copies Required: One
Computer Submission: Yes Disk or Email
Format: MS Word or PDF Format
Fees to Review: 0.00 US$

Manuscript Style:
   American Psychological Association

CIRCULATION DATA:

Reader: Academics
Frequency of Issue: Quarterly
Copies per Issue: Less than 1,000
Sponsor/Publisher: IRMA (Information
   Resource Management Association) /
   Ideal-Group Publishing
Subscribe Price: 85.00 US$ Individual
   265.00 US$ Institution

REVIEW INFORMATION:

Type of Review: Blind Review
No. of External Reviewers: 3+
No. of In House Reviewers: 0
Acceptance Rate: 0-5%
Time to Review: 2 - 3 Months
Reviewers Comments: Yes
Invited Articles: 0-5%
Fees to Publish: 0.00 US$

MANUSCRIPT TOPICS:
Automatic assessment methods; Automatic FAQ reply methods; Broadband & wireless communication tools; Copyright protection & authentification mechanisms; Distance Education; Distributed systems; Effective & efficient authoring systems; Individualized distance learning; Intelligent tutoring; Mobile systems; Multimedia streamng technology; Multimedia synchronization controls; Neural network; New network infrastructures; Practical & new learning models; Quality-of Services issues; Real-time protocols; Statistical approache to behavior analysis; Urban Education, Cultural/Non-Traditional

MANUSCRIPT GUIDELINES/COMMENTS:

Description
The *International Journal of Distance Education Technologies* (*JDET*) is a forum for researchers and practitioners to disseminate practical solutions to the automation of open and distance learning. Targeted to academic researchers and engineers who work with distance learning programs and software systems, as well as general users of distance education

technologies and methods, *JDET* discusses computational methods, algorithms, implemented prototype systems, and applications of open and distance learning.

GUIDELINES FOR MANUSCRIPT SUBMISSIONS

Mission

The *International Journal of Distance Education Technologies* (*JDET*) publishes original research articles of distance education four issues per year. *JDET* is a primary forum for researchers and practitioners to disseminate practical solutions to the automation of open and distance learning. The journal is targeted to academic researchers and engineers who work with distance learning programs and software systems, as well as general participants of distance education.

Coverage. Discussions of computational methods, algorithms, implemented prototype systems, and applications of open and distance learning are the focuses of this publication. Practical experiences and surveys of using distance learning systems are also welcome. Distance education technologies published in *JDET* will be divided into three categories, Communication Technologies, Intelligent Technologies, and Educational Technologies: New network infrastructures, real-time protocols, broadband and wireless communication tools, Quality-of Services issues, multimedia streaming technology, distributed systems, mobile systems, multimedia synchronization controls, intelligent tutoring, individualized distance learning, neural network or statistical approaches to behavior analysis, automatic FAQ reply methods, copyright protection and authentification mechanisms, practical and new learning models, automatic assessment methods, effective and efficient authoring systems, and other issues of distance education.

Originality

Prospective authors should note that only original and previously unpublished manuscripts will be considered. Furthermore, simultaneous submissions are not acceptable. Submission of a manuscript is interpreted as a statement of certification that no part of the manuscript is copyrighted by any other publication nor is under review by any other formal publication. It is the primary responsibility of the author to obtain proper permission for the use of any copyrighted materials in the manuscript, prior to the submission of the manuscript.

Style

Submitted manuscripts must be written in the APA (*American Psychological Association*) editorial style. References should relate only to material cited within the manuscript and be listed in alphabetical order, including the author's name, complete title of the cited work, title of the source, volume, issue, year of publication, and pages cited. Please do not include any abbreviations. See the following examples:

- **Example 1**: Single author periodical publication. Smith, A.J. (2001). Information and organizations. Management Ideology Review. 16(2), 1-15.
- **Example 2**: Multiple authors periodical publication. Smith, A.J., & Brown, CJ. (2001). Organizations and information processing. Management Source, 10(4), J1-88.
- **Example 3**: Books.

State author's name and year of publication where you use the source in the text. See the following examples:

- **Example 1**: In most organizations, information resources are considered to be a major resource (Brown, 2001; Smith, 2000).
- **Example 2**: Brown (2002) states that the value of information is recognized by most organizations.

Direct quotations of another author's work should be followed by the author's name, date of publication, and the page(s) on which the quotation appears in the original text.

- **Example 1**: Brown (2001) states that "the value of information is realized by most organizations" (p. 45).
- **Example 2**: In most organizations, information resources are considered to be a major organization asset" (Smith, 2001, pp. 35-36) and must be carefully monitored by the senior management. For more information please consult the *APA Manual* or review previous issues of the *Information Resources Management Journal*.

Review process
To ensure the high quality of published material, *JDET* utilizes a group of experts to review submitted manuscripts. Each submission is reviewed on a blind basis by at least four members of the International Editorial review Board of the Journal. Revised manuscripts will be reviewed again by the original review panel with the addition of one new reviewer. Return of a manuscript to the author(s) for revision does not guarantee acceptance of the manuscript for publication. The final decision will be based upon the comments of the reviewers and associate editors, upon their final review of the revised manuscript.

Copyright
Authors are asked to sign a warranty and copyright agreement upon acceptance of their manuscript, before the manuscript can be published. All copyrights, including translation of the published material into other languages are reserved by the publisher, Idea Group Inc. Upon transfer of the copyright to the publisher, no part of the manuscript may be reproduced in any form without written permission of the publisher, except for noncommercial, educational use such as for classroom teaching purposes.

Submission
Interested authors are asked to submit their manuscript as an attachment to an email. The manuscript must be in Word or PDF format. The cover page should contain the paper title, and the name, affiliation, address, phone number, fax number, and email address of each author. The second page should start with the paper title at the top and be immediately followed by the abstract. Except on the cover page, the authors' names and affiliations must NOT appear in the manuscript. The abstract of 100-150 words should clearly summarize the objectives and content of the manuscript. For additional information, please consult the journal website at http://www.idea-group.com/journals/

Length
The length of the submitted manuscript is not specifically limited, however, the length should be reasonable in light of the chosen topic. Discussion and analysis should be complete, but not unnecessarily long or repetitive.

Correspondence

The acknowledgment e-mail regarding the receipt of the manuscript will be promptly sent. The review process will take approximately 8-16 weeks, and the author will be notified concerning the possibility of publication of the manuscript as soon as the review process is completed. All correspondence will be directed to the first author of multi-authored manuscripts. It is the responsibility of the first author to communicate with the other author(s). Authors of accepted manuscript will be asked to provide a final copy of their manuscript in Word format (IBM) or Apple Macintosh format stored on a 3/4" disk, accompanied by a hard copy of the manuscript and the signed copy of the Warranty and Copyright Agreement The accepted manuscript will be edited by the Journal copy editor for format and style.

Book Review

JDET invites prospective book reviewers to submit their review of either textbooks or professional books for possible inclusion in the Journal. Reviewers should focus on the following guidelines when developing the book review: Book reviews must not exceed 1500 words. Reviews should summarize the book and indicate the highlights, strengths, and weaknesses of the book. Reviews should evaluate the organizational and managerial applications of the material discussed in the book relevant to information resources and technology management. Reviews should critique and constructively evaluate the author's work and not merely list the chapters' contents. The writing style, accuracy, relevance, and the need for such a work in the discipline should be analyzed. The review must include the title of the book, author, publishing company, publication date, number of pages, cost (if listed), and ISBN number. Each submission must be accompanied by a short biography of the reviewer. biography of the reviewer.

Case studies

JDET also encourages submission of case studies based on actual cases related to different issues and aspects of electronic commerce in organizations. Case studies must provide adequate information regarding the organization upon which the case is based, discussion of the issues involved, coverage of any experiments or trials of techniques or managerial approaches, and finally, discussion of any lessons learned or conclusions drawn from this study. All submissions should be submitted to: All inquiries and submissions should be sent to:

Timothy K. Shih, Professor
Dept of Computer Science & Information Engineering
Tamkang University
Suite 200
151, Ying-Chuan Road, Tamsui, Taipei Hsien
Taiwan 25137, R.O.C.
Tel: + 886 2 26215656 x2743, x2616, Fax:+ 886 2 26209749
E-Mail: **tshih@cs.tku.edu.tw**

International Journal of e-Collaboration

ADDRESS FOR SUBMISSION:

Ned Kock, Editor
International Journal of e-Collaboration
Teaxas A&M International University
Dept. of MIS & Decision Science
5201 University Boulevard
Laredo, TX 78041
USA
Phone: 956-326-2521
Fax: 956-326-2494
E-Mail: nedkock@tamiu.edu
Web: www.tamiu.edu/~nedkock/
Address May Change: 1/1/2008

CIRCULATION DATA:

Reader: Academics
Frequency of Issue: Quarterly
Copies per Issue: 2,001 - 3,000
Sponsor/Publisher: International Resources
    Management Association
Subscribe Price: 85.00 US$ Individual
    195.00 US$ Institution

PUBLICATION GUIDELINES:

Manuscript Length: 30+
Copies Required: One
Computer Submission: Yes Preferred
    (email)
Format: MS Word or RTF formats
Fees to Review: 0.00 US$

Manuscript Style:
    American Psychological Association

REVIEW INFORMATION:

Type of Review: Blind Review
No. of External Reviewers: 2
No. of In House Reviewers: 2
Acceptance Rate: 6-10%
Time to Review: 2 - 3 Months
Reviewers Comments: Yes
Invited Articles: 0-5%
Fees to Publish: 0.00 US$

MANUSCRIPT TOPICS:
Educational Technology Systems; Electronic Collaboration

MANUSCRIPT GUIDELINES/COMMENTS:

Mission
E-collaboration technologies are broadly defined as electronic technologies that enable collaboration among individuals engaged in a common task. The mission of the *International Journal of e-Collaboration* is to publish papers that address the design and implementation of e-collaboration technologies, assess the behavioral impacts of e-collaboration technologies on individuals and groups, and present theoretical considerations on links between the use of e-collaboration technologies and behavioral patterns. Examples of such technologies are web-based chat tools, web-based asynchronous conferencing tools, e-mail, listservs, collaborative writing tools, group decision support systems, teleconferencing suites, workflow automation systems, and document management technologies.

Coverage

The *International Journal of e-Collaboration* invites authors to submit their research dealing with (but not limited to) the following topics:

- Comprehensive reviews of previous studies on e-collaboration technologies in organizations
- Analysis of different research methods and their impact on the study of e-collaboration technologies in organizations
- Design, implementation, and assessment of e-business solutions that include e-collaboration features
- E-collaboration technologies impact on knowledge management and organizational learning
- E-collaboration technologies support for quality certification programs
- E-collaboration technologies support for distributed process reengineering and process improvement
- Design and evaluation of intelligent e-collaboration technologies in organizational settings
- E-collaboration technologies impact on individuals and society
- Design and evaluation of asynchronous learning networks (ALNs) in organizational setting
- Organizational and national culture as moderating factors in the adoption and use of e-collaboration technologies in organizations
- E-collaboration technologies support for the creation of virtual teams and virtual organizations
- Web-based chat tools
- Web-based asynchronous conferencing tools
- E-mail
- Listservs
- Collaborative writing tools

Originality

Prospective authors should note that only original and previously unpublished manuscripts will be considered. Furthermore, simultaneous submissions are not acceptable. Submission of a manuscript is interpreted as a statement of certification that no part of the manuscript is copyrighted by any other publication nor is under review by any other formal publication. It is the primary responsibility of the author to obtain proper permission for the use of any copyrighted materials in the manuscript, prior to the submission of the manuscript.

Style

Submitted manuscripts must be written in the APA (American Psychological Association) editorial style. References should relate only to material cited within the manuscript and be listed in alphabetical order, including the author's name, complete title of the cited work, title of the source, volume, issue, year of publication, and pages cited. Please do not include any abbreviations. See the following examples:

- Example 1: Single author periodical publication.

Smith, A.J. (2001). Databases and organizations. Database Ideology Review. 16(2), 1-15.

416

- Example 2: Multiple authors periodical publication.
Smith, A.J., Caron, R.W. & Brown, CJ. (1999). Organizations and database management. Data Source, 10(4), 77-88.

- Example 3: Book.
Smith, A.J. (2001). Database Booklet. New York, NY: J.J. Press.

- Example 4: Book Chapter.
Hart, S.G. & Staveland, L.E. (1988). Development of the NASA-TLX index: Results of empirical and theoretical research. P. A. Hancock & N. Meshkati, eds. Human Mental Workload. Amsterdam, The Netherlands: North-Holland, 139-183.

- Example 5: Research Report.
Dennis, A. R., & Valacich, J. S. 1999. Rethinking media richness: Towards a theory of media synchronicity. Research report. Athens, GA: Terry College of Business, University of Georgia.

- Example 6: Conference proceedings paper.
Kinney, S. T., A. R. Dennis. 1994. Re-evaluating media richness: Cues, feedback, and task. J.F. Nunamaker & R.H. Sprague, eds. Proceedings of the Hawaii International Conference on System Sciences. Washington, DC: IEEE Computer Society Press, 21-30.

See the following examples:
- Example 1: In most organizations, information resources are considered to be a major resource (Brown, 2000; Smith, 2000).
- Example 2: Brown (2002) states that the value of information is recognized by most organizations.

Direct quotations of another author's work should be followed by the author's name, date of publication, and the page(s) on which the quotation appears in the original text.

- Example 1: Brown (2001) states that "the value of information is realized by most organizations" (p. 45).
- Example 2: In most organizations, information resources are considered to be a major organization asset" (Smith, 2002 pp. 35-36) and must be carefully monitored by the senior management.

For more information please consult the *APA* manual.

Review process
To ensure the high quality of published material, *IJeC* utilizes a group of experts to review submitted manuscripts. Upon receipt of the manuscript, two reviewers are selected from the Editorial Review Board of the Journal. The selection is based upon the particular area of expertise of the reviewers, matched to the subject matter of the submission. An additional ad-hoc reviewer is also selected to review the manuscript. Therefore, each submission is accordingly blind reviewed by at least three reviewers. Revised manuscripts will be reviewed

again by the original review panel with the addition of one new reviewer. Return of a manuscript to the author(s) for revision does not guarantee acceptance of the manuscript for publication. The final decision will be based upon the comments of the reviewers, upon their second review of the revised manuscript.

Copyright

Authors are asked to sign a warranty and copyright agreement upon acceptance of their manuscript, before the manuscript can be published. All copyrights, including translation of the published material into other languages are reserved by the publisher, Idea Group Inc. Upon transfer of the copyright to the publisher, no part of the manuscript may be reproduced in any form without written permission of the publisher, except for noncommercial, educational use such as for classroom teaching purposes.

Submission

Authors are asked to submit their manuscripts for possible publication by e-mail as a file attachment in Microsoft Word or RTF. The main body of the e-mail message should contain the title of the paper and the names and addresses of all authors. Manuscripts must be in English. The author's name should not be included anywhere in the manuscript, except on the cover page. Manuscripts must also be accompanied by an abstract of 100-150 words, precisely summarizing the mission and object of the manuscript.

Length

The length of the submitted manuscript must not exceed 20-25 double-spaced, typed pages. Discussion and analysis should be complete but not unnecessarily long or repetitive.

Correspondence

The acknowledgment letter regarding the receipt of the manuscript will be promptly sent. The review process will take approximately 8-16 weeks, and the author will be notified concerning the possibility of publication of the manuscript as soon as the review process is completed. All correspondence will be directed to the first author of multi-authored manuscripts. It is the responsibility of the first author to communicate with the other author(s). Authors of accepted manuscript will be asked to provide a final copy of their manuscript in either Word or RTF text format stored on a 3 1/2" disk, zip disk or CD-ROM, accompanied by a hardcopy of the manuscript and the original signed copy of the Warranty and Copyright Agreement. The accepted manuscript will be edited by the Journal copyeditor for format and style.

Book Reviews

IJeC invites prospective book reviewers to submit their review of either textbooks or professional books for possible inclusion in the Journal. Reviewers should focus on the following guidelines when developing the book review:

- Book reviews must not exceed 1500 words
- Reviews should summarize the book and indicate the highlights, strengths, and weaknesses of the book.
- Reviews should evaluate the organizational and managerial applications of the material discussed in the book relevant to information resources and technology management.
- Reviews should critique and constructively evaluate the author's work and not merely list the chapters' contents.

- The writing style, accuracy, relevance, and the need for such a work in the discipline should be analyzed.
- The review must include the title of the book, author, publishing company, publication date, number of pages, cost (if listed), and ISBN number.
- Each submission must be accompanied by a short biography of the reviewer.

Case Studies

IJeC also encourages submission of case studies based on actual cases related to the main areas of coverage of the journal. Case studies must provide adequate information regarding the organization upon which the case is based, discussion of the issues involved, coverage of any experiments or trials of techniques or managerial approaches, and finally, discussion of any lessons learned or conclusions drawn from this study.

All submissions and inquiries should be directed to the attention of
Ned Kock, Editor-in-Chief; International Journal of e-Collaboration;
Email: **nedkock@tamiu.edu**

International Journal of Education & the Arts

ADDRESS FOR SUBMISSION:

Liora Bresler & Thomas Barone, Co-Eds
International Journal of Education & the
    Arts
University of Illinois, Urbana-Champaign
Department of Curriculum and Instruction
393 Education Building
Champaign, IL 61820
USA
Phone: 480-965-3924 Barone
Fax: 480-727-7991 Barone
E-Mail: barone@asu.edu; liora@uniuc.edu
Web: ijea.asu.edu
Address May Change:

PUBLICATION GUIDELINES:

Manuscript Length: Approx. 25-30 pp
Copies Required: None
Computer Submission: Yes Email, Disk
Format: Rich Text, JPEG, Real Audio
Fees to Review: 0.00 US$

Manuscript Style:
    American Psychological Association,
    (5th Edition)

CIRCULATION DATA:

Reader: Academics
Frequency of Issue: 15/Ongoing
Copies per Issue: Online
Sponsor/Publisher: College Education,
    Arizona State University
Subscribe Price: 0.00 US$

REVIEW INFORMATION:

Type of Review: Blind Review
No. of External Reviewers: 3
No. of In House Reviewers: 2
Acceptance Rate: 21-50%
Time to Review: 2 - 3 Months
Reviewers Comments: Yes
Invited Articles: 0-5%
Fees to Publish: 0.00 US$

MANUSCRIPT TOPICS:
Art/Music; Arts - based pedagogy; Arts - based research; Dance; Drama; Education and the Arts; Film; Literature; Theater

MANUSCRIPT GUIDELINES/COMMENTS:

How to Submit an Article to *IJEA*
IJEA welcomes submitted articles for consideration for publication. Articles should pertain to issues in any of the various fields of aesthetics and arts education. These fields include, among others, aethetics, art theory, music education, visual arts education, drama education, dance education, education in literature and narrative. Holistic, integrated studies that cross or transcend these fields are also welcomed. A Book Review section contains thoughtful essays on current, recent, and classic works in arts education.

Because *IJEA* is published electronically, a wider array of representational forms and formats are possible than in print journals. These include musical, pictorial, and videographic, as well as verbal/print. Multi-media formats are especially welcome. Whatever the mode employed, articles (as examples of good art) should provide important insights into, or suggest provocative questions about, the phenomena of arts education. The originality, educational significance, and technical quality of submissions are important criteria in the review and selection processes. Manuscripts employing a verbal/print format may use interpretive, narrative, arts-based, contextualized quantitative, and critical approaches to studying education in the arts.

Written manuscripts should be in English and prepared in accordance with the format recommended in the *Publication Manual of the American Psychological Association*. Articles may be of any length.

Articles may be either included as text in email letters to the Editor, or word processor files attached to email letters addressed to **barone@asu.edu**. Rich Text Format is the preferred word processor format, but Microsoft WORD or Word Perfect is acceptable. Files sent through regular postal mail on floppy diskettes are also acceptable.

- Email articles to **liora@uiuc.edu**
- Or mail articles on floppy diskettes via regular mail to

Liora Bresler, Editor
Curriculum and Instruction
University of Illinois, Urbana-Champaign
393 Education Building.
1310 S. 6th St. MC708
Champaign IL 61820
Phone: 244-0734

Authors are normally informed of the publication decision within four to five weeks.

International Journal of Inclusive Education

ADDRESS FOR SUBMISSION:

Roger Slee, Editor
International Journal of Inclusive Education
McGill University
Faculty of Education
3700 McTavish Street
Montreal, Quebec, H3A 1Y2
Canada
Phone: +1 514-398-7037
Fax: +1 514-398-1527
E-Mail: roger.slee@mcgill.ca
Web: www.tandf.co.uk/journals
Address May Change:

PUBLICATION GUIDELINES:

Manuscript Length: 26-30
Copies Required: Three
Computer Submission: Yes Email
Format: MS Word
Fees to Review: 0.00 US$

Manuscript Style:
　　See Manuscript Guidelines

CIRCULATION DATA:

Reader: Practicing Teachers, Academics,
　　Administrators
Frequency of Issue: Quarterly
Copies per Issue:
Sponsor/Publisher: Taylor & Francis
Subscribe Price: 187.00 US$ Individual
　　378.00 US$ Institution

REVIEW INFORMATION:

Type of Review: Blind Review
No. of External Reviewers: 2
No. of In House Reviewers: 0
Acceptance Rate: 75%
Time to Review: 1 - 2 Months
Reviewers Comments: Yes
Invited Articles: 0-5%
Fees to Publish: 0.00 US$

MANUSCRIPT TOPICS:

Adult Career & Vocational; Bilingual/E.S.L.; Education Management/Administration; Educational Psychology; Special Education; Urban Education, Cultural/Non-Traditional

MANUSCRIPT GUIDELINES/COMMENTS:

Aims and Scope

The *International Journal of Inclusive Education* provides a strategic forum for international and multi-disciplinary dialogue on inclusive education for all educators and educational policy-makers concerned with the form and nature of schools, universities and technical colleges.

Papers published are original, refereed, multi-disciplinary research into pedagogies, curricula, organizational structures, policy-making, administration and cultures to include all students in education.

The journal extends beyond enrollment to successful participation which generates greater options for all people in education and beyond.

Readership
The journal is essential reading for those working in the following areas:
- intra-cultural studies
- special needs
- racism
- behavior and discipline
- bilingualism
- gender and sexuality
- educational psychology
- socio-economic disadvantage
- policy and administration/supervision in the early childhood, primary/elementary, secondary, further/higher/tertiary, and vocational educational sectors.

Instructions for Authors
Note to Authors: please make sure your contact address information is clearly visible on the **outside** of all packages you are sending to Editors.

International Journal of Inclusive Education is a quarterly refereed journal which focuses upon multi-disciplinary research into pedagogies, curricula, organizational structures, policy-making, administration and cultures to include all students in education. 'Inclusive' education extends beyond enrolment to successful participation which generates greater options for all people in education and beyond. *International Journal of Inclusive Education* therefore speaks to all, particularly those marginalized, placed 'at risk' by, or excluded from early childhood education, primary and secondary schooling, higher education or technical and further education colleges. *International Journal of Inclusive Education* aims to:
- provide an international medium for the publication of discussions of conceptual and methodological issues concerned with inclusive education across all school, higher education, technical and further education settings;
- provide a forum which brings together, rather than fragments, the consideration of the interactions of pedagogies, educational policy-making and administration, curricula and school organizational culture with race, ethnicity, class, gender and disabilities;
- provide a forum for international reporting on inclusive educational practices and research reports across a range of educational settings which promote equity and social justice for those groups and individuals 'at risk' of being marginalized on the basis of their gender, race, class, ethnicity or disability.

Papers for consideration should be sent to the Editor, at the editorial office, address given below. Please send four copies, three of which may be photocopies.

Contacting the Editor
Dean, Faculty of Education, McGill University, 3700 McTavish Street, Montreal, Quebec, Canada H3A 1Y2, email: **roger.slee@mcgill.ca**.

Contacting Taylor & Francis
4 Park Square, Milton Park, Abingdon, Oxon, OX14 4RN

Submitting a paper to *International Journal of Inclusive Education*
Please read these Guidelines with care and attention: failure to follow them may result in your paper being delayed. Note especially the referencing conventions used by *International Journal of Inclusive Education* and for all manuscripts, non-discriminatory language is mandatory. Sexist or racist terms should not be used.

International Journal of Inclusive Education considers all manuscripts on condition they are the property (copyright) of the submitting author(s) and that copyright will be transferred to *International Journal of Inclusive Education* and Taylor & Francis Ltd if the paper is accepted.

International Journal of Inclusive Education considers all manuscripts on the strict condition that they have been submitted only to *International Journal of Inclusive Education*, that they have not been published already, nor are they under consideration for publication, nor in press elsewhere. Authors who fail to adhere to this condition will be charged all costs which *International Journal of Inclusive Education* incurs, and their papers will not be published.

- Please write clearly and concisely, stating your objectives clearly and defining your terms. Your arguments should be substantiated with well-reasoned supporting evidence.
- For all manuscripts, non-discriminatory language is mandatory. Sexist or racist terms should not be used.
- In writing your paper, you are encouraged to review articles in the area you are addressing which have been previously published in the journal, and where you feel appropriate, to reference them. This will enhance context, coherence, and continuity for our readers.
- Introductions of around 100 - 200 words are required for all papers submitted and should precede the text of a paper.
- Manuscripts should be typed on one single side of A4 or 8 x 11 inch white good quality paper, double-spaced throughout, including the reference section.
- Three copies of the manuscript for consideration should be submitted.
- Authors should include telephone and fax numbers as well as e-mail addresses on the cover page of manuscripts.
- Bionotes should be contained on a separate sheet and be located at the beginning of a paper.
- Accepted manuscripts in their final, revised versions, should also be submitted as electronic word processing files on disk - see 'Electronic Processing'.
- Articles for consideration should be sent to the Editor (address on first page).

Copyright permission
Contributors are required to secure permission for the reproduction of any figure, table, or extensive (more than fifty word) extract from the text, from a source which is copyrighted - or owned - by a party other than Taylor & Francis or the contributor.

This applies both to direct reproduction or 'derivative reproduction' - when the contributor has created a new figure or table which derives substantially from a copyrighted source.

The following form of words can be used in seeking permission:

Dear [COPYRIGHT HOLDER]

I/we are preparing for publication an article entitled[STATE TITLE]

to be published by Taylor & Francis Ltd in *International Journal of Inclusive Education.*

I/we should be grateful if you would grant us permission to include the following materials:
[STATE FIGURE NUMBER AND ORIGINAL SOURCE]

We are requesting non-exclusive rights in this edition and in all forms. It is understood, of course, that full acknowledgement will be given to the source. Please note that Taylor & Francis are signatories of and respect the spirit of the STM Agreement regarding the free sharing and dissemination of scholarly information.

Your prompt consideration of this request would be greatly appreciated.

Yours faithfully

Notes on style
All authors are asked to take account of the diverse audience of *International Journal of Inclusive Education*. Clearly explain or avoid the use of terms that might be meaningful only to a local or national audience. However, note also that the *International Journal of Inclusive Education* does not aspire to be international in the ways that McDonald's restaurants or Hilton Hotels are 'international'; we much prefer papers that, where appropriate, reflect the particularities of each higher education system. Some specific points of style for the text of articles, research reports, case studies, reports, essay reviews, and reviews follow:
1. *International Journal of Inclusive Education* prefers US to 'American', USA to 'United States', and UK to 'United Kingdom'.
2. *International Journal of Inclusive Education* uses conservative British, not US, spelling, i.e. colour not color; behaviour (behavioural) not behavior; [school] programme not program; [he] practises not practices; centre not center; organization not organisation; analyse not analyze, etc.
3. Single 'quotes' are used for quotations rather than double "quotes", unless the 'quote is "within" another quote'.
4. Punctuation should follow the British style, e.g. 'quotes precede punctuation'.
5. Punctuation of common abbreviations should follow the following conventions: e.g. i.e. cf. Note that such abbreviations are not followed by a comma or a (double) point/period.
6. Dashes; em-dash should be clearly indicated in manuscripts by way of either a clear dash (-) or a triple hyphen (---) the en-dash should be indicated by a clear dash (-) or a double hyphen (--).
7. *International Journal of Inclusive Education* is sparing in its use of the upper case in headings and references, e.g. only the first letter of the first word in paper titles and all subheads is in upper case; titles of papers from journals in the references and other places are not in upper case.

8. Apostrophes should be used sparingly. Thus, decades should be referred to as follows: 'The 1980s [not the 1980's] saw ...'. Possessives associated with acronyms (e.g. APU), should be written as follows: 'The APU's findings that ...', but, NB, the plural is APUs.

9. All acronyms for national agencies, examinations, etc., should be spelled out the first time they are introduced in text or references. Thereafter the acronym can be used if appropriate, e.g. 'The work of the Assessment of Performance Unit (APU) in the early 1980s ...'. Subsequently, 'The APU studies of achievement ...', in a reference ... (Department of Education and Science [DES] 1989a).

10. Brief biographical details of significant national figures should be outlined in the text unless it is quite clear that the person concerned would be known internationally. Some suggested editorial emendations to a typical text are indicated in the following with square brackets: 'From the time of H. E. Armstrong [in the 19th century] to the curriculum development work associated with the Nuffield Foundation [in the 1960s], there has been a shift from heurism to constructivism in the design of [British] science courses'.

11. The preferred local (national) usage for ethnic and other minorities should be used in all papers. For the USA, African-American, Hispanic, and Native American are used, e.g. 'The African American presidential candidate, Jesse Jackson...' For the UK, African-Caribbean (not 'West Indian'), etc.

12. Material to be emphasized (italicized in the printed version) should be underlined in the typescript rather than italicized. Please use such emphasis sparingly.

13. n (not N), % (not per cent) should be used in typescripts.

14. Numbers in text should take the following forms: 300, 3000, 30 000. Spell out numbers under 10 unless used with a unit of measure, e.g. nine pupils but 9 mm (do not introduce periods with measure). For decimals, use the form 0.05 (not .05).

15. When using a word which is or is asserted to be a proprietary term or trade mark authors' must use the symbol ® or TM or alternatively a footnote can be inserted using the wording below: This article includes a word which is or is asserted to be a proprietary term or trade mark. Its inclusion does not imply it has acquired for legal purposes a non-proprietary or general significance, nor is any other judgment implied concerning its legal status.

Notes on tables and figures

Artwork submitted for publication will not be returned and will be destroyed after publication, unless you request otherwise. Whilst every care is taken of artwork, neither the Editor nor Taylor & Francis shall bear any responsibility or liability for non-return, loss, or damage of artwork, nor for any associated costs or compensation. You are strongly advised to insure appropriately.

1. Tables and figures should be valuable, relevant, and visually attractive. Tables and figures must be referred to in the text and numbered in order of their appearance. Each table and figure should have a complete, descriptive title; and each table column an appropriate heading. Tables and figures should be referred to in text as follows: figure 1, table 1, i.e. lower case. 'As seen in table [or figure] 1 ...' (not Tab., fig. or Fig).

2. The place at which a table or figure is to be inserted in the printed text should be indicated clearly on a manuscript: [Insert table 2 about here]

3. Each table and/or figure must have a title that explains its purpose without reference to the text.

426

4. All figures and tables must be on separate sheets and not embedded in the text. Original copies of figures should be supplied. All figures should allow for reduction to page width (126mm). Please avoid figures that would require landscape reproduction, i.e., reading from bottom to top of the page. Photographs may be sent as glossy prints or negatives. All artwork will be reproduced in black and white. Please number each figure on the reverse in pencil. Do not type the caption to a figure on that figure; the legends to any illustrations must be typed separately following the main text and should be grouped together.

Acknowledgements

Any acknowledgements authors wish to make should be included in a separate headed section at the end of the manuscript. Please do not incorporate these into the bionote or notes.

Book reviews

1. The following header material should appear in all reviews in the following order (note also the punctuation): School Leadership: Beyond Education Management. An Essay in Policy Scholarship, by Gerard Grace, Falmer, 1995, pp. 370 £38.00(hardback), £13.95 (paperback).
2. Page references within reviews should be given as follows: (p. 337) or (pp. 36-37).

Citations in text

References should be cited using the numerical system with superscripts (e.g. Scholarships provided free instruction 23. They should be listed separately at the end of the paper in the order in which they appear in the text.

References

International Journal of Inclusive Education uses the following conventions for references:
1. Reference to a book:
   C. Lacey, The Socialization of Teachers (London: Methuen, 1977).
2. Reference to a chapter in a book:
   M. Crozier, 'The vicious circle of bureaucracy', in T. Burns (ed.), Industrial Man (Harmondsworth: Penguin, 1969), 250-262.
3. Reference to an article in a journal:
   C. Buswell, 'Pedagogic change and social change', British Journal of Sociology of Education. 10 (1982), 167-70.
4. Proceedings, reports and unpublished literature
   R. J. M. Smith, Accountability to the state: an exploration of the educational market and parental choice literature. Paper presented to the Annual Conference of the New Zealand Association for Research in Education, Massey University, Palmerston North, 7-10 December, 1995.
   C. A. Burnham and T. H. Anderson, Learning to sew on a button by reading a procedural text. CSR Technical Report, No. 543, Center for the Study of Reading, University of Illinois at Urbana-Champaign, 1991. ERIC ED 332 157.D. K. Cohen, and D. L. Ball, Policy, Cognition, and Instruction. Unpublished manuscript, 1997.
   D. Macleod 'Miners, Mining Men and Mining Reform,' PhD thesis, Toronto, 1981.Hertfordshire Record Office [HRO] Hertfordshire County Council [HCC] 2/11 3, County Paper [CP] 45 Hertfordshire Education Committee [HEC] 29 March 1926.

5. Parliamentary Papers
   Royal Commission on the Civil Service, First Appendix to Fourth Report, Parliamentary Papers, xVI, 1914 [Cd. 7339], Appendix 6, 'Statement submitted on behalf of the Clerical Establishment of the Board of Education', 27.
6. Reference to a newspaper or magazine
   H. Richards, 1996, Republican lite? The Times Higher Education Supplement, 1 November, 16.
7. Reference to an Internet source
   Give the universal resource locator in full:http://acsinfo.acs.org/instruct/instruct.html
8. Reference to a personal communication
   J. Brannen, 1996, Personal communication.
9. Reference to a case in law
   In text, italicize names of plaintiffs and defendants:Miranda v. Arizona 1974
10. Reference to government legislation
    US Congress, Senate Committee on Foreign Relations, 1956, The Mutual Security Act of 1956, 84th Congress, second session, report 2273.United Kingdom Parliament, Committee on the Working of the Monetary System [Radcliffe Committee] 1960, Principal Memoranda of Evidence, vol. 2, Cmd 1958.

Early Electronic Offprints

Corresponding authors can now receive their article by e-mail as a complete PDF. This allows the author to print up to 50 copies, free of charge, and disseminate them to colleagues. In many cases this facility will be available up to two weeks prior to publication. Or, alternatively, corresponding authors will receive the traditional 50 offprints. A copy of the journal will be sent by post to all corresponding authors after publication. Additional copies of the journal can be purchased at the author's preferential rate of £15.00/$25.00 per copy.

Electronic Processing

We strongly encourage you to send us the final, revised version of your article in both hard (paper) and electronic (disk) forms. This Guide sets out the procedures which will assure we can process your article efficiently. It is divided into three sections:

1. a guide for authors using standard word-processing software packages
2. a guide for authors using LaTeX mathematical software packages
3. a guide for authors using graphics software packages

There are some general rules which apply to all three options.

- these guides do not apply to authors who are submitting an article for consideration and peer review; they apply only to authors whose articles have been reviewed, revised, and accepted for publication
- print out your hard (paper) copy from the disk you are sending; it is essential that the hard-copy printout is identical to the material on the disk; where versions differ, the hard copy will take precedence. We advise that you maintain back-ups of your files
- save and send your files on a standard 3.5 inch high density disk (Mac or PC); please do not attempt to send the article via file transfer protocol or email
- when saving your article onto a disk, please make sure that the files do not exceed a manageable size. Please ensure that figures are saved on a separate disk
- ensure that the files are not saved as read only

428

- virus-check your disk before sending it to the Editor
- label your disk
- package disks in such a way as to avoid damage in the post
- disks are not returnable after publication

1. A guide for authors using standard word-processing software packages

For the main text of your article, most standard PC or Mac word-processing software packages are acceptable, although we prefer Microsoft Word in a PC format. Word-processed files should be prepared according to the journal style. Avoid the use of embedded footnotes. For numbered tables, use the table function provided with the word-processing package. All text should be saved in one file with the complete text (including the title page, abstract, all sections of the body of the paper, references), followed by numbered tables and the figure captions. You should send the following to the Editor:

- a 3.5-inch disk containing the final, accepted version of the paper
- include an ASCII/text only version on the disk as well as the word processed version if possible
- two hard copy printouts

Disks should be clearly labelled with the following information:
1. Journal title
2. Name of author
3. File names contained on disk
4. Hardware used (PC or Mac)
5. Software used (name and version)

Sample disk label:
Journal title
A.N. Author
article.doc
IBM PC MS Word for Windows 7.0

2. A guide for authors using LaTeX mathematical software packages

Authors who wish to prepare their articles using the LaTeX document preparation system are advised to use article.sty (for LaTex 2.09) or article.cls (for LaTex2e).The use of macros should be kept to an absolute minimum but if any are used they should be gathered together in the file, just before the \begin{document} commandYou should send the following to the Editor:

- a 3.5-inch disk containing the final, accepted version of the paper
- the files you send must be text-only (often called an ASCII file), with no system-dependent control codes
- two hard copy printouts

Disks should be clearly labelled with the following information:
1. Journal title
2. Name of author
3. File names contained on disk

4. Hardware used (PC or Mac)
5. Software used (name and version)

Sample disk label: LaTeX
    Journal title
    A.N. Author
    article.tex
    article.sty
    IBM PC
    PCLaTeX v2.09

3. A guide for authors using graphics software packages

We welcome figures on disk, but care and attention to these guidelines is essential, as importing graphics packages can often be problematic.

1. Figures must be saved on a separate disk from the text.
2. Avoid the use of colour and tints for aesthetic reasons. Figures should be produced as near to the finished size as possible.
3. High quality reproducible hard copy for all line figures (printed out from your electronic files at a minimum of 600 dpi) must be supplied in case the disks are unusable; photographs and transparencies can be accepted as hard copy only. Photocopies will not be accepted.
4. All figures must be numbered in the order in which they occur (e.g. figure 1, figure 2 etc.). In multi-part figures, each part should be labelled (e.g. figure 1 (a), figure 1 (b) etc.)
5. The figure captions must be saved as a separate file with the text and numbered correspondingly.
6. The filename for the graphic should be descriptive of the graphic e.g. Figure1, Figure2a.
7. Files should be saved as TIFF (tagged image file format), PostScript or EPS (encapsulated PostScript), containing all the necessary font information and the source file of the application (e.g., CorelDraw/Mac, CorelDraw/PC).

Disks should be clearly labelled with the following information:
1. Journal title
2. Name of author
3. Figures contained on disk
4. Hardware used (PC or Mac)
5. Software used (name and version)

Sample disk label: figures
    Journal title
    A.N. Author
    Figures 1-10
    Macintosh
    Adobe Illustrator 5.5

International Journal of Information and Communication Technology Education

ADDRESS FOR SUBMISSION:

Lawrence Tomei, Editor-in-Chief
International Journal of Information and
    Communication Technology Education
Robert Morris University
Acad Services - PH Room 214
6001 University Blvd.
Moon Twp, PA 15108
USA
Phone: 412-269-3696
Fax: 412-269-3851
E-Mail: tomei@rmu.edu
Web: www.idea-group.com/journals
Address May Change:

PUBLICATION GUIDELINES:

Manuscript Length: 21-25
Copies Required: One
Computer Submission: Yes Email
Format: No Latex
Fees to Review: 0.00 US$

Manuscript Style:
    American Psychological Association

CIRCULATION DATA:

Reader: Academics
Frequency of Issue: Quarterly
Copies per Issue: Less than 1,000
Sponsor/Publisher: Idea Group, Inc.
Subscribe Price: 85.00 US$ Individual
    195.00 US$ Institution

REVIEW INFORMATION:

Type of Review: Blind Review
No. of External Reviewers: 3
No. of In House Reviewers: 0
Acceptance Rate:
Time to Review: 2 - 3 Months
Reviewers Comments: Yes
Invited Articles: 0-5%
Fees to Publish: 0.00 US$

MANUSCRIPT TOPICS:
Educational Technology Systems; Information Technology

MANUSCRIPT GUIDELINES/COMMENTS:

Mission
The *International Journal of Information and Communication Technology Education*
(*IJICTE*) publishes original materials concerned with the theoretical underpinnings, successful
application, and potential for advancing technology education within formal education,
corporate training, higher education, professional development, and proprietary education.
The primary mission of the *IJICTE* is to explore multiple perspectives of technology
education and promote research, positions, and practices that advance the state-of-the-art
application of technology for teaching and learning.

Coverage

The *IJICTE* will publish contributions from all disciplines of business, computer, and information technology education, educational technology, instructional systems design, teaching and learning with technology, computer science, corporate training science, and distance learning education. In particular, the journal supports multidisciplinary research in the:

- Pedagogy and androgogy of teaching with technology, technology as a teaching strategy, technology as a learning style, making technology work in schools, early childhood technology literacy, adult learners and technology education, impact of technology on student achievement, dimensions of technological learning
- Impact of technology in society, equity issues, technology education and copyright laws, censorship, acceptable use and fair use laws, community education and public outreach using technology
- Effective planning for technology education, marketing technology education, managing classroom technology education, developing successful information technology education leadership, teacher/trainer preparation and retention
- Impact of multicultural differences on technology education, special technology education for diversity and at-risk learners
- Information technology training tools, educational/ training software evaluation, writing technology training materials, models of instructional systems design, instructional design theories
- Corporate information technology training, administrative applications of information technology education
- Assessment of technology education, technology-based learning and training outcomes, assessment of technology-based curricular objectives
- School improvement and reform, developing standards-based technology education programs, data-driven decision making, strategic technology education planning, technology education standards development.

And, all other related issues that impact the research, position, and practice of information technology education on schools, corporate entities, and society.

Originality

Prospective authors should note that only original and previously unpublished manuscripts will be considered. Submission of a manuscript implies a certification that not part of the manuscript is neither copyrighted or under review by any other publication. It is the primary responsibility of the author to see and obtain proper permission for the use of any copyrighted materials in the manuscript prior to submission.

Style

Submitted manuscripts must be prepared in the *American Psychological Association* (APA) editorial style. References should relate only to material cited within the manuscript and be listed in alphabetical order by author(s)' name, complete title of the cited work, title of the source, volume, issue, year of publication, and pages cited. Please do not include any abbreviations. See the following examples:

432

- Single author periodical publication.
  Example 1: Smith, A.J. (2002). Information and organizations. Management Ideology Review. 16(2), 1-15.
  Multiple authors periodical publication.
- **Example 2**: Smith, A.J., & Brown, CJ. (2001). Organizations and information processing. Management Source, 10(4), J1-88.
  Single author text (book) publication.
- **Example 3**: Brown (2002) states that the value of information is recognized by most organizations.
  Multiple authors text (book) publication.
- **Example 4**: In most organizations, information resources are considered to be a major resource (Brown, 2001; Smith, 2000).

Direct quotations of another author's work should be followed by the author's name, date of publication, and the page(s) on which the quotation appears in the original text.

- **Example 5**: Brown(2001) states that "the value of information is realized by most organizations" (p. 45).
- **Example 6**: In most organizations, information resources are considered to be a major organization asset" (Smith, 2001, pp. 35-36) and must be carefully monitored by the senior management.

For more information please consult the *APA Manual* or review previous issues of the *Information Resources Management Journal*.

Review process
To ensure the high quality of published material, the *IJICTE* provides a cadre of technology content and writing experts to review submitted manuscripts. Upon receipt of a manuscript, it is judged by the editor-in-chief for focus and format. Suitable submissions are assigned at least three reviewers selected from the Editorial Review Board based upon the particular content involved. Both the original manuscript and the editorial reviews are sent to an associate editor for final recommendation. Final selections of manuscripts for publication is the responsibility of the editor-in-chief.

Manuscripts with potential for publication will be returned to the author for revision; requests for re-writes do not guarantee acceptance of the manuscript for final publication. Revised manuscripts will be reviewed again by the original review panel and one additional reviewer. Final recommendations will be based upon the quality of the revision and comments of reviewers and associate editors. Final selections of manuscripts for publication remains the responsibility of the editor-in-chief.

Copyright
Authors are asked to sign a warranty and copyright agreement upon acceptance of their manuscript, before the manuscript can be published. All copyrights, including translation of the published material into other languages are reserved by the publisher, Idea Group Inc.

Upon transfer of the copyright to the publisher, no part of the manuscript may be reproduced in any form without written permission of the publisher, except for noncommercial, educational uses such as for classroom teaching.

Submission

Prospective authors are invited to submit manuscripts for consideration for publication in the *International Journal of Information and Communication Technology Education* (*IJICTE*). Accepted manuscripts will comply with the following submission guidelines.

1. Authors are requested to submit their manuscripts electronically for consideration to the editor-in-chief at **tomei@rmu.edu** as an email attachment in Microsoft Word, RTF, or Plain Text format. Hard copy submissions may be sent via surface to: Dr. Lawrence Tomei, Robert Morris University, Acad Services - PH Room 214; 6001 University Blvd., Moon Twp PA 15108, and must include a disk containing the digital version of the manuscript.

2. Submissions must be double-spaced, prepared in English and include at least a 1" margin on all sides. The cover page should contain the paper title and the name, affiliation, address, phone number, fax number, and email address of each contributing author. The cover page must also specify the focus and format of the paper (e.g., Focus: Educational Technology, Format: Practice-based Abstract). Acceptable foci for the paper include: business, computer science, and information technology education; educational technology; instructional systems design; teaching and learning with technology; corporate training science; or, distance learning education. Acceptable formats for the journal include: research synopsis, position papers, and practice-based abstracts.

3. The second page of the submission should provide the title at the top followed immediately by the focus and format and an abstract of 100-150 words (maximum) clearly summarizing the target audience, objectives, nature of the paper, and key findings/recommendations of the manuscript. Except for the cover page, the author's name and affiliations must NOT appear anywhere in the abstract or manuscript to ensure anonymity during the refereed review process.

4. Submitted manuscripts (apart from the abstract) should normally not exceed 5000 words for position and practice manuscripts; longer research manuscripts (not to exceed 6000 words) may be considered subject to editorial revision prior to publication. Word count includes all appendices and references.

5. Submission of papers implies original content previously unpublished, free from copyright violations, and not currently under review elsewhere. Significantly extended papers previously presented at conferences and symposia may be considered. It remains the responsibility of the author to secure the proper permissions for use of any copyrighted materials in the manuscript prior to submission for consideration.

Correspondence/Communication of Review Status

An email acknowledging receipt of the manuscript will be promptly forwarded by the editor-in-chief. The review process is expected to take approximately 8-10 weeks and the author will be notified of the status of the review as soon as the review process is complete. All

434

correspondence will be directed to the lead author of multi-authored manuscripts. It is the responsibility of the lead author to communicate the status of the review process and editorial recommendations to other contributing author(s). Authors of accepts manuscripts will be asked to provide a final copy of their manuscript in Word format on floppy or zip disk or CDROM, accompanied by a hard copy of the manuscript and signed copy of the Warranty and Copyright Agreement. Digital signatures will are not acceptable. Final manuscripts may be edited by the Journal copy editor for format and style.

Book Reviews (Research-based)
The *IJICTE* invites prospective book reviewers to submit their review of either textbooks or professional books pertaining to technology education for possible inclusion in the Journal. Reviewers should focus on the following guidelines when developing the review. Book reviews must not exceed 1500 words. Reviews should summarize the book and point out the highlights, strengths, and weaknesses of its content. Reviews should concentrate on the educational research and practical applications of the material discussed in the book as they pertain to information technology education. Reviews should critique and constructively evaluate the research base offered by the author and not merely list the contents of the chapters. The accuracy and relevance of the book to technology education, along with the quality and importance of its findings and impact on furthering the discipline should be analyzed. The review must include the title of the book, author, publisher and publication date, number of pages, cost, and ISBN number. Each submission must be accompanied by a short biography of the reviewer.

Case Studies (Practice-based)
The *IJICTE* encourages submissions of case studies based on actual scenarios related to practice-based issues and practical applications of information technology education. Case studies must not exceed 2000 words and must provide adequate information regarding the educational environment upon which the study is based, presentation of the issues involved, coverage of any experiments or techniques involved, and elaborations of the lessons learned or conclusions drawn from the study.

Position Papers (Position-based)
Finally, the *IJICTE* solicits controversial opinions, viewpoints, and personal judgments focusing on all aspects of information technology education. Papers must not exceed 1000 words and only those papers backed by research, literature, or citations of practical application will be considered.

All inquiries and submissions should be sent to:
    Editor-in-Chief: Lawrence A. Tomei, EdD
    International Journal of Information and Communication Technology Education
    Robert Morris University
    Acad Services - PH Room 214
    6001 University Blvd
    Moon Twp PA 15108
    Phone: 412-269-3696; Fax: 412-269-3851
    Email: **tomei@rmu.edu**

International Journal of Instructional Media

ADDRESS FOR SUBMISSION:

Phillip J. Sleeman, Editor
International Journal of Instructional Media
149 Goose Lane
Tolland, CT 06084
USA
Phone: 860-875-5484 or 802-273-3185
Fax:
E-Mail: PLSleeman@aol.com
Web: www.adprima.com/ijim.htm
Address May Change:

PUBLICATION GUIDELINES:

Manuscript Length: 11-15
Copies Required: Three
Computer Submission: No
Format: IBM/MAC with Hardcopy
Fees to Review: 0.00 US$

Manuscript Style:
, See Website

CIRCULATION DATA:

Reader: Academics, Practicing Teachers,
    Administrative/Business/Industry
Frequency of Issue: Quarterly
Copies per Issue: 1,001 - 2,000
Sponsor/Publisher: Westwood Press, Inc.
Subscribe Price: 176.00 US$
    16.00 US$ In USA add Postage
    30.00 US$ Elsewhere add Postage

REVIEW INFORMATION:

Type of Review: Editorial Review
No. of External Reviewers: 3+
No. of In House Reviewers: 2
Acceptance Rate: 40%
Time to Review: 1 Month or Less
Reviewers Comments: No
Invited Articles: 11-20%
Fees to Publish: 0.00 US$

MANUSCRIPT TOPICS:

Adult Career & Vocational; Distance Education; Education Management/Administration; Educational Technology Systems; Higher Education; Internet; Library Science/Information Resources; School Law; Teacher Education; Tests, Measurement & Evaluation; Urban Education, Cultural/Non-Traditional

MANUSCRIPT GUIDELINES/COMMENTS:

IJIM, International Journal of Instructional Media, is a professional refereed journal directly responsive to the need for precise information on the application of media to your instructional and training needs.

About *IJIM*

The *International Journal of Instructional Media* (*IJIM*) is the source of cutting edge research and commentary on all forms of instructional media used in instruction and training today. *IJIM* bridges the gap between theory and practice. The present growth in educational technology confronts you, the instructor, with a vast array of instructional media without clearly defined guidelines as to their optimal use.

436

To help bridge the gap, *IJIM* focuses on quality research and presents articles about ongoing programs in instructional media and education. *IJIM* investigates and explains:

- Computer technology
- Computer mediated communications including the Internet
- Distance education including the Internet, ITV, video and audio conferencing
- Instructional media and technology
- Telecommunications
- Interactive video, videodisc, and software applications
- Instructional media management
- Instructional development and systems
- Media research and evaluation
- Media research and communications

Primarily, *IJIM* is concerned with the problem of applying the various distant learning strategies and instructional media to the learning process. Articles discuss specific applications and techniques for bringing the advantages of a particular instructional medium to bear on a complete curriculum system or program.

Most importantly, *IJIM* is not hardware oriented - it is instruction and systems oriented. It is concerned with hardware only to the extent that hardware forms part of an educational system called "instructional media," involving student, hardware, software, curriculum and instructor.

Manuscripts are to be submitted in triplicate. Retain one copy, as the manuscript will not be returned unless accompanied by a self-addressed, stamped envelope. Manuscripts must be typewritten on 8½" x 11' white paper, one side only, double-spaced, with wide margins. Paginate consecutively starting with the title page. The organization of your paper should be indicated by appropriate headings and sub-headings.

Originality. Authors should note that only original articles are accepted for publication. Submission of a manuscript represents certification on the part of the author(s) that neither the article submitted nor a version of it has been published, nor is being considered for publication elsewhere.

Abstracts of 100 to 150 words are required to introduce each article.

References should relate only to material cited within the text and be listed in numerical order according to their appearance within the text. State author's name, title of referenced work, editor's name, title of book or periodical, volume, issue, pages cited, and year of publication. Do not abbreviate titles. Please do not use ibid., op. cit., loc., etc. in case of multiple citations; simply repeat the original numeral. Detailed specifications are available from the editors upon request.

Footnotes should be placed at the end of the article under works cited. Footnotes should be brief with an average length of three lines.

Figures should be referenced in the text to appear in numerical sequence starting with Figure 1. Line art must be original drawings in black in proportion to out page size, and suitable for photographing. Indicate top and bottom of figure where confusion may exist. Labeling should be 8 point type. Clearly identify all figures. Figures should be drawn on separate pages and their placement in the text indicated by:

– Insert Figure 1 here –

Tables must be cited in text with numerical sequence starting with Table 1. Each table must have a descriptive title. Any footnotes to tables are indicated by superior lower case letters. Tables should be typed on separate pages and their approximate locations indicated within text by inserting:

– Insert Table 1 here –

Authors will receive ten complimentary reprints of their published article. Additional reprints may be ordered.

Remember To Include With Your Manuscript
- Your full name and title
- Your mailing address
- Your Phone number/fax number/E-mail address

International Journal of Learning

ADDRESS FOR SUBMISSION:

Bill Cope & Mary Kalantzis, Editors
International Journal of Learning
ELECTRONIC SUBMISSION ONLY
http://105.cgpublisher.com/welcome.html
Phone: +613 9398 80
Fax: +613 9398 8088
E-Mail: See Guidelines
Web: http://L05.cgpublisher.com/welcom
Address May Change:

CIRCULATION DATA:

Reader: Academics
Frequency of Issue: Yearly
Copies per Issue: 1,001 - 2,000
Sponsor/Publisher: Globalism Institute,
    RMIT University, Melbourne, Australia
Subscribe Price: AUD300.CD

PUBLICATION GUIDELINES:

Manuscript Length: 21-30
Copies Required:
Computer Submission: Yes Email
Format: MS Word
Fees to Review:
    Virtual Registration Fee

Manuscript Style:
    See Manuscript Guidelines

REVIEW INFORMATION:

Type of Review: Blind Review
No. of External Reviewers: 2
No. of In House Reviewers: 0
Acceptance Rate: 50%
Time to Review: 2 - 3 Months
Reviewers Comments: Yes
Invited Articles: 0-5%
Fees to Publish:
    Virtual Registration Fee

MANUSCRIPT TOPICS:
Adult Career & Vocational; Art/Music; Audiology/Speech Pathology; Bilingual/E.S.L.;
Curriculum Studies; Education Management/Administration; Educational Technology
Systems; Elementary/Early Childhood; English Literature; Higher Education; Languages &
Linguistics; Social Studies/Social Science; Special Education; Teacher Education; Tests,
Measurement & Evaluation; Urban Education, Cultural/Non-Traditional

MANUSCRIPT GUIDELINES/COMMENTS:

Email. **Bill.Cope@commongroundpublishing.com**

Submission Guidelines
Papers should be approximately 2,000-5,000 words in length. They should be written as
continuous expository narrative in a chapter or article style - not as lists of points or a
PowerPoint presentation.

Please remember that the papers are to be published in a fully refereed academic journal. This
means that the style and structure of your text should be relatively formal. For instance, you
should not submit a verbatim transcript of your oral presentation, such as 'Today I want to
speak to you about ...'.

You may use any referencing style you choose, as long as you use it consistently and to the appropriate standards. Spelling can vary according to national useage, but should be internally consistent. Papers should be thoroughly checked and proof-read before submission, both by the author and a critical editorial friend.

Papers will be assessed by referees against ten criteria - or fewer if some criteria do not apply to a particular kind of paper.

We require presenters to use Common Ground's Microsoft Word. We are not able to accept papers that have not used the template.

The Submission Process
Completed papers should be emailed as an attachment to:
papers@commongroundpublishing.com.

The deadline for submission is 14 August 2005, one calendar month after the closing date of the conference.

Once your paper has been received and checked to ensure that corresponding files open you will be sent an official receipt notice via email. This receipt notice will include the administration number allocated to your paper. If you do not receive an official receipt confirmation within five working days of submission please contact the conference secretariat immediately.

The publication process is as follows:
1. Submit a presentation proposal (in-person or virtual) at **www.LearningConference.com** before the next call for papers deadline.
2. If your proposal is accepted, you may then register for in-person or virtual presentation. You may submit your paper any time between registration and one calendar month after the closing date of the conference (conference close: 14 July 2004; final submission date: 14 August 2004).
3. Once your paper is received, your identity and contact details are removed, the paper is matched to two appropriate referees and then sent for review (maximum two week turnaround requested). You will be notified via email when the paper is received and sent too referees.
4. When referee reports are returned, they are sent back to you with the referees' identities removed (maximum two week turnaround requested). If full refereeing of your final paper is required before the conference in order to attend in-person, papers should be submitted more than three calendar months before the opening date of the conference.
5. Papers are published in print and electronic formats in the *International Journal of Learning*.

Conference participants will be provided one printed copy of their own paper (spiral bound, with a colour cover) and free access to all papers in the electronic format (a this stage, a CD once all papers for a conference or volume of the Journal have been finalised). The papers will be made publicly available at the Journal bookstore.

International Journal of Learning Technology

ADDRESS FOR SUBMISSION:

M. A. Dorgham, Editor
International Journal of Learning
   Technology
IEL Editorial Office
P O Box 735
Olney, Buckinghamshire, UK
MK46 5WB
Phone: 44 1234 240 519
Fax: 44 1234 240 515
E-Mail: m.dorgham@inderscience.com
Web: www.inderscience.com
Address May Change:

PUBLICATION GUIDELINES:

Manuscript Length: 21-25
Copies Required: Three
Computer Submission: Yes Disk, Email
Format: MS Word
Fees to Review: 0.00 US$

Manuscript Style:

CIRCULATION DATA:

Reader: Practicing Teachers, Academics,
   Administrators, Counselors
Frequency of Issue: Quarterly
Copies per Issue: 2,001 - 3,000
Sponsor/Publisher: Inderscience Publishers
Subscribe Price: 450.00 US$

REVIEW INFORMATION:

Type of Review: Blind Review
No. of External Reviewers: 3
No. of In House Reviewers: 0
Acceptance Rate: 21-30%
Time to Review: 2 - 3 Months
Reviewers Comments:
Invited Articles: 0-5%
Fees to Publish: 0.00 US$

MANUSCRIPT TOPICS:
Adult Career & Vocational; Counseling & Personnel Services; Curriculum Studies; Education Management/Administration; Educational Psychology; Educational Technology Systems; Health & Physical Education; Higher Education; Library Science/Information Resources; Science Math & Environment; Secondary/Adolescent Studies; Social Studies/Social Science; Special Education; Teacher Education; Tests, Measurement & Evaluation; Urban Education, Cultural/Non-Traditional

MANUSCRIPT GUIDELINES/COMMENTS:

Topics continued. Communities of Learners, Multimedia and Interactive Learning Systems, Virtual Reality Environment, Intelligent Agents, Distributed Learning Environment, Distance Learning.

Guide for authors
For papers submission are available on web site: **www.inderscience.com**.
• Focus and Scope
• Formal conditions of acceptance

- Author Guidelines (PDF Version)
- Copyright Notice
- Privacy Statement
- Peer Review Process
- Appendix 1: Sample Cover Letter/E-mail [the example used is the IJEB] (PDF Version)
- Appendix 2: Author Agreement (PDF Version)
- AUTHOR AGREEMENT: EXPLANATORY NOTES
- About this Publishing System

IJLT is an international, refereed, scholarly journal providing an interdisciplinary forum for the presentation and discussion of important ideas, concepts, and exemplars that can deeply influence the role of learning technologies in learning and instruction. This unique and dynamic journal focuses on the epistemological thrust of learning vis-à-vis instruction and the technologies and tools that support the process. *IJLT* publishes papers related to theoretical foundations, design and implementation, and effectiveness and impact issues related to learning technologies.

Objectives
IJLT aims:

- to act as an international forum for discussion of the use and design of technology in learning and instruction
- to foster communication between academics and practitioners
- to promote research on the use of learning technologies
- to encourage a multidisciplinary approach to the advancement of the use and design of technologies in teaching and learning
- to provide a deeper understanding of the nature, theory and practice of learning and instruction

Readership
Researchers and theorists, cognitive scientists, learning technologists, teachers and learners, instructional designers, designers and developers, implementers and evaluators, managers and administrators.

Contents
Papers are invited for IJLT on any of the topics listed below. Suggestions are also welcome for special issues.

Subject Coverage
- Communities of learners (practice)
- Constructivism and social constructivism
- Computer-supported collaborative learning
- Activity theory and social cultural perspectives
- Cognitive tools
- Distributed learning environments
- Virtual reality environments
- Intelligent agents

- Human-computer interface (HCI) issues
- Intelligent learning/tutoring environments
- Interactive learning environments
- Web-based instruction/learning
- Computer-mediated communication
- E-learning
- Learning objects for personalised learning
- Building learning communities
- Technology-facilitated learning in complex domains
- Evaluation of learning technology systems
- Simulation-supported learning and instruction
- Mobile learning applications
- Semantic web
- Learning technology in education and in commerce
- Technology-driven learning models and strategies
- Multimedia and interactive learning systems
- Technological standardisation in learning
- Knowledge creation and management in the internet age
- Disciplinary-related inquiry, e.g., learning technologies for science inquiry

Specific Notes for Authors
All papers are refereed through a double blind process. A guide for authors, sample copies and other relevant information for submitting papers are available on the Papers Submission section under Author Guidelines.

To submit a paper, please go to Submission of Papers
This is our preferred route for submitting papers; please use it if at all possible. However, if you experience any problems submitting papers in this way, an alternative route is suggested below.

Submitted papers should not have been previously published nor be currently under consideration for publication elsewhere.

As an alternative to using the Submission of Papers site, you may send THREE copies of each manuscript (in hard copy) or one copy in the form of an MS Word file attached to an e-mail (details of both formats in Author Guidelines) to Dr. Lorna Uden, below, with a copy to:
Editor-in-Chief
IEL Editorial Office
PO Box 735
Olney, Bucks MK46 5WB
UK
Fax: +44 1234-240515; E-mail: **ijlt@inderscience.com**

Please include in your submission the title of the Journal.

International Journal of Qualitative Studies in Education

ADDRESS FOR SUBMISSION:

James Scheurich & Christine Stanley, Eds
International Journal of Qualitative Studies
   in Education
Texas A & M University
511 Harrington Tower
4226 TAMU
College Station, TX 77843-4226
USA
Phone: 979-845-6456
Fax: 979-862-4347
E-Mail: qse@coe.tamu.edu
Web: www.tandf.co.uk/journals
Address May Change:

PUBLICATION GUIDELINES:

Manuscript Length: 15-35
Copies Required: Five
Computer Submission: Yes Email
   Attachment
Format: MS Word
Fees to Review: 0.00 US$

Manuscript Style:
   American Psychological Association

CIRCULATION DATA:

Reader: Academics
Frequency of Issue: 6 Times/Year
Copies per Issue:
Sponsor/Publisher: Taylor & Francis
Subscribe Price: 227.00 US$ Individual
   665.00 US$ Institution

REVIEW INFORMATION:

Type of Review: Blind Review
No. of External Reviewers: 3-6
No. of In House Reviewers: 3-5
Acceptance Rate: 15-20%
Time to Review: 4 - 6 Months
Reviewers Comments: Yes
Invited Articles: 0-5%
Fees to Publish: 0.00 US$

MANUSCRIPT TOPICS:
Curriculum Studies; Qualitative Methods; Qualitative Studies in All Areas of Education; Studies in Education; Urban Education, Cultural/Non-Traditional

MANUSCRIPT GUIDELINES/COMMENTS:

1. **Statement of General Policy**. The aim of this journal is to enhance the practice of qualitative research in education. *QSE* appears six times yearly and publishes research employing a variety of qualitative methods and approaches, including (but not limited to) ethnographic observation and interviewing, grounded theory, life history, case study, curriculum criticism, policy studies, ethnomethodology, social and educational critique, phenomenology, deconstruction, and genealogy. Discussions of epistemology, methodology, or ethics from a range of perspectives, including (but not limited) postpositivism, interpretivism, constructivism, critical theory, feminism, race-based, lesbian/gay, and poststructural ones are also considered. In addition, innovative or provocative approaches to qualitative research in general or to the way research is reported are encouraged.

2. **Papers**, written in English, are invited for consideration from all countries, provided they have not been published, nor are currently under consideration, elsewhere. Minimal variations of manuscripts published elsewhere or under consideration elsewhere are discouraged. **Five copies** of the manuscript and a version on disc using preferably Microsoft Word for Macintosh version 5.1 should be submitted to the Editor for the Region in which the author(s) is(are) located. Editors for the different Regions are listed on the inside front cover of the journal. [See Regional Editors below.]

3. **Manuscripts** should conform to the style set forth in the *Publication Manual of the American Psychological Association* (5th ed.) and be well edited. Manuscripts should appear as typewritten, double-spaced throughout (including indented quotes, endnotes, and the reference list), on 8½" x 11" white bond paper with 1½" margins all round. All figures must be camera ready. Manuscripts must be no longer than 35 pages or 12,000 words, including endnotes and the reference list. Although longer manuscripts will occasionally be accepted (only if they are particularly outstanding or significant and the length is necessary), manuscripts exceeding the 35 pages/12,000 word length will typically be returned to the authors. (Those seeking a longer limit should provide in a letter a substantive argument for the additional length.)

Artwork submitted for publication will not be returned and will be destroyed after publication. While every care will be taken of artwork, neither the Editor nor Taylor & Francis Ltd shall bear any responsibility or liability for nonreturn, toss or damage of artwork, nor for any associated costs or compensation. Authors are strongly advised to insure appropriately.

4. **An Abstract** of no more than 150 words and an academic biography, for each author, with the same word limit should be in each submission.

5. **The Name(s) of the Author(s), Title(s), and Affiliation(s)**, with complete mailing address(es), and telephone number(s), should appear on a separate cover page, and only on this page. The email address(es) should also appear on this page, but only if email is a reliable way to contact the author(s).

6. **Communication with the Editors**. If at all possible, communication by email is to be emphasized over telephone or mail.

7. **Manuscripts that do not conform to these specifications will be returned**.

8. **The Review Process** normally takes four months so please do not contact the editors prior to the completion of this time period.

9. **Fifty Free Offprints** of the published article will be supplied to the lead author(s).

10. **Book Reviews** are assigned by the Book review Editors:

Maricela Oliva, The University of Texas Pan American, Department of Educational Leadership, 1201 W. University Drive, Edinburg TX 78539, USA

Linda Skrla, Department of Educational Administration, 511 Harrington Tower, Texas A&M University, College Station, TX 77843-4226, USA

Linda Tillman, 348 Education Building, University of New Orleans, New Orleans, LA 70148, USA

Normally, *QSE* will not consider reviews more than two years after a book's publication date.

For information not discussed above, contact the Editors, James Scheurich and Christine Stanley, Texas A & M University, 511 Harrington Tower, 4226 TAMU, College Station, Texas 77843-4226, USA Tel: +1 979-845-6456; Fax: +1 979-862-4347; Communication by email is preferred: **qse@coe.tamu.edu**

Regional Editors

Canada
CELIA HAIG-BROWN, Faculty of Education, York University, North York, Ontario, Canada M3J IP3

Continental Europe
ROLAND VANDENBERGHE, Center for Educational Policy and Innovation, University of Leuven, Vesaliustraat 2, B-3000 Leuven, Belgium

Great Britain and Ireland
ELIZABETH ATKINSON, University of Sunderland, school of Education, Hammerton Hall, Grey Road, Sunderland, SR2 8JB, UK.

Scandinavia
ROGER SALJO, Department of Communication Studies, University of Linkoping, Linkoping, Sweden

Australia and New Zealand
BRONWYN DAVIES, School of Education, James Cook University of New Zealand Townsville, Queensland 4811, Australia

Mediterranean
RONALD G. SULTANA, Faculty of Education, University of Malta, Msida MSD 06, Malta

Mexico
ELSIE ROCKWELL, DIE, Apartado Postal 19-197, Mexico D.F., C.P. 03 100, Mexico

Central America
CLAUDIA TORRES, UNAH, Apartado Postal U-8956, Tegucigalpa, Honduras

South America
MARILDA CAVALCANTI, Departamento de Linguistica Aplicada/IEI, Campinas, Sao Paulo, Brazil
JOAO A. TELLES, UNESP-Assis, Depto, de Letras Modernas, Av. Dom Antonio, 2100, 19800-00 Assis, SP, Brazil

Asia
YOUNG CHUN KIM, Department of Education, Chinju National University of Education, 380, Shinan Dong, Chinju, Kyungsangnam Do, South Korea

International Journal of Research & Method in Education

ADDRESS FOR SUBMISSION:

Birgit Pepin, Lead Editor
International Journal of Research & Method
  in Education
Oxford Brookes University
Westminster Institute of Education
Harcourt Hill Campus
Oxford, OX2 9AT
UK
Phone:
Fax:
E-Mail: bpepin@brookes.ac.uk
Web: www.tandf.co.uk/journals
Address May Change:

PUBLICATION GUIDELINES:

Manuscript Length: 16-20
Copies Required: Three
Computer Submission: Yes Email
Format: MS Word
Fees to Review: 0.00 US$

Manuscript Style:
  See Manuscript Guidelines

CIRCULATION DATA:

Reader: Academics, Administrators
Frequency of Issue: 2 Times/Year
Copies per Issue:
Sponsor/Publisher: Taylor & Francis
Subscribe Price: 148.00 US$ Individual
  1051.00 US$ Institution

REVIEW INFORMATION:

Type of Review: Blind Review
No. of External Reviewers: 2
No. of In House Reviewers: 2
Acceptance Rate: New J
Time to Review: 1 - 2 Months
Reviewers Comments: Yes
Invited Articles:
Fees to Publish: 0.00 US$

MANUSCRIPT TOPICS:
Comparative Education, Non-Formal Education; Comparative Studies; Research Methods in Education; Tests, Measurement & Evaluation

MANUSCRIPT GUIDELINES/COMMENTS:

Aims and Scope
The *International Journal of Research & Method in Education* is an interdisciplinary and refereed journal, which draws its contributions from a wide community of researchers. The principal aim of the journal is to further international discourse in education with a particular focus on method. It achieves this aim by publishing empirical studies and scholarly discussions related to all aspects of education.

The journal particularly encourages contributions which:
- provide evidence of unusual or new methods of educational research
- discuss conceptual, theoretical and methodological issues in educational research

448

- have an international and/or comparative dimension
- contest or dissent from the orthodox or examine the innovative and the unusual.

The *International Journal of Research & Method in Education* encourages authors to write in a lucid and accessible style. Contributors should take care to communicate to an international readership of researchers, policy-makers and practitioners from a range of disciplines including philosophy, sociology, economics, psychology, and history of education.

Instructions for Authors
Papers should be original, but if there is overlap with material published elsewhere, details should be given. Manuscripts should be sent to:
> Dr Birgit Pepin, Westminster Institute of Education, Oxford Brookes University, Harcourt Hill Campus, Oxford OX2 9AT, UK. Email: **bpepin@brookes.ac.uk**

Papers should normally be around 5000 words in length, but longer or shorter articles will be considered.

Manuscripts should be typed on one side of A4 paper with double spacing and a wide margin to the left. **Three** copies should be submitted, and a copy in Word format sent to the Lead Editor by e-mail. In addition, a copy should be retained by the authors. All pages should be numbered. To allow anonymous refereeing, all submissions must be properly formatted for blind reviewing (see *Publication Manual of the American Psychological Association*, 5th edition, 2001, for instructions). Authors' names and institutions should be typed on a separate sheet and submitted with the manuscript. The full postal and email address of the author who will check proofs and receive correspondence and offprints should also be included.

Each paper should be accompanied on separate sheets by a summary of 100 to 150 words, and short note of biographical details for 'Notes on Contributors'.

Electronic Submission. Authors should send the final, revised version of their articles in both hard copy paper and electronic forms. It is essential that the hard copy (paper) version *exactly* matches the material on electronic file. Please print out the hard copy from the electronic version you are sending. Submit three printed copies of the final version, together with the electronic version, to the Lead Editor. Electronic material should be in PC compatible MS Word format.

Tables and captions to illustrations. Tables must be typed out on separate sheets and not included as part of the text. The captions to illustrations should be gathered together and also typed out on a separate sheet. Tables **and** Figures should be numbered consecutively by Arabic numerals. The approximate position of tables and figures should be indicated in the manuscript. Captions should include keys to any symbols used.

Figures. Please supply one set of artwork in a finished form, suitable for reproduction. Figures will not normally be redrawn by the publisher.

Citations of other work should be limited to those strictly necessary for the argument. Any quotations should be brief, and accompanied by precise references.

References should be indicated in the typescript by giving the author's name, with the year of publication in parentheses. If several papers by the same author and from the same year are cited, a, b, c, etc. should be put after the year of publication. The references should be listed in full, including pages, at the end of the paper in the following standard form:

> **For books**: Wertsch, J.V. (1991) *Voices of the mind* (Cambridge MA, Harvard University Press).

> **For articles**: Paul, J.L. & Marfo, K. (2001) Preparation of educational researchers in philosophical foundations of inquiry, *Review of Educational Research*, 71 (4), 525-547.

> **For chapters within books**: Denzin, N. & Lincoln, Y. (2000) Introduction: the discipline and practice of qualitative research, in: N. Denzin & Y. Lincoln (Eds) *Handbook of qualitative research* (2nd Edn) (Thousand Oaks CA, Sage), 1-23.

Titles of journals and names of publishers, etc. should **not** be abbreviated. Acronyms for the names of organisations, examinations, etc. should be preceded by the title in full.

If you have any further questions about the style for this journal, please submit your questions using the Style Queries form.

Proofs will be sent to authors by email if there is sufficient time to do so. They should be corrected and returned to the Publisher within three days. Major alterations to the text cannot be accepted.

Early Electronic Offprints. Corresponding authors can now receive their article by e-mail as a complete PDF. This allows the author to print up to 50 copies, free of charge, and disseminate them to colleagues. In many cases this facility will be available up to two weeks prior to publication. Or, alternatively, corresponding authors will receive the traditional 50 offprints. A copy of the journal will be sent by post to all corresponding authors after publication. Additional copies of the journal can be purchased at the author's preferential rate of £15.00/$25.00 per copy.

Copyright. It is a condition of publication that authors vest or license copyright in their articles, including abstracts, in Taylor & Francis Ltd. This enables us to ensure full copyright protection and to disseminate the article, and the journal, to the widest possible readership in print and electronic formats as appropriate. Authors may, of course, use the article elsewhere after publication providing that prior permission is obtained from Taylor & Francis, provided that acknowledgement is given to the Journal as the original source of publication, and that Taylor & Francis is notified so that our records show that its use is properly authorised. Authors are themselves responsible for obtaining permission to reproduce copyright material from other sources.

International Journal of Scholarly Academic Intellectual Diversity

ADDRESS FOR SUBMISSION:

William Kritsonis, Editor
International Journal of Scholarly Academic
 Intellectual Diversity
P.O. Box 7400
Lake Charles, LA 70605-7400
USA
Phone: 337-477-0008
Fax: 337-480-3663
E-Mail: wakritsonis@aol.com
Web: www.nationalforum.com
Address May Change:

PUBLICATION GUIDELINES:

Manuscript Length: 10-50
Copies Required: Five
Computer Submission: Yes
Format: IBM - MS Word 6.0
Fees to Review: 30.00 US$

Manuscript Style:
 American Psychological Association

CIRCULATION DATA:

Reader: Administrators, Professors,
 Scholars world-wide, Higher Education
Frequency of Issue: Monthly
Copies per Issue: World-wide
Sponsor/Publisher: National Forum
 Journals
Subscribe Price: 120.00 US$ Individual
 240.00 US$ Institution
 480.00 US$ International

REVIEW INFORMATION:

Type of Review: Blind Review
No. of External Reviewers: 3
No. of In House Reviewers: 2
Acceptance Rate: 21-30%
Time to Review: 1 Month or Less
Reviewers Comments: Yes
Invited Articles: 50% +
Fees to Publish:
 See Guidelines

MANUSCRIPT TOPICS:
Adult Career & Vocational; Curriculum Studies; Education Management/Administration;
Educational Psychology; Elementary/Early Childhood; Gifted Children; Health & Physical
Education; Higher Education; Higher Education Administrators; Professors; Reading;
Scholars World-wide; School Law; Science Math & Environment; Secondary/Adolescent
Studies; Social Studies/Social Science; Special Education; Teacher Education; Tests,
Measurement & Evaluation

MANUSCRIPT GUIDELINES/COMMENTS:

Sponsorship. National Forum Society of Educators.

The *International Journal of Scholarly Academic Intellectual Diversity* is a scholarly,
refereed, peer-reviewed, juried professional journal intended for national and international
dissemination. Readers from around the world will have access to your published article(s) by
contacting our website at: www.nationalforum.com.

Professors, scholars, academicians, intellectuals, researchers, theoreticians, practitioners,
administrators, and many others in higher education in colleges and universities publish in the

IJ SAID. The journal seeks to maintain a healthy respect for scholarship, academics, intellectualism, and diversity in higher education.

The *IJ SAID* is an electronic journal with an efficient review and publication process. Manuscripts are published within 30 days after formal acceptance by the International Board of Invited Distinguished Jurors representing the *IJ SAID*.

Writing for Publication

The *International Journal of Scholarly Academic Intellectual Diversity (IJ SAID)* is an electronic scholarly journal. Manuscripts are rigorously evaluated and recommended for international publication by members of the *International Board of Invited Distinguished Jurors*. Any manuscript published in the *IJ SAID* shall receive five affirmative votes from the editorial review board. It is absolutely imperative the scholarly, academic, intellectual, diversity, and ethic integrity of the *IJ SAID* be safely ensured.

Manuscripts

All of the family of National Forum Journals require that writers who submit manuscripts follow the latest technical specifications set in the *Publication Manual of the American Psychological Association*, 4th Edition.

The *International Journal of Scholarly Academic Intellectual Diversity* requires that manuscripts be typed double-spaced in a fixed-pitch font (Ex: Courier) and typically be 5 to 50 pages. Please **do not** use italics. *IJ SAID* requires that manuscripts be submitted on a 3.5 diskette, using IBM-format Microsoft Word 6.0 word processing software. **Manuscript will not be processed if submitted in format other than IBM-compatible**.

IJ SAID requires that five hard copies of the manuscript also must be submitted. Writers must include an abstract of 100-150 words. The writer's name, title, affiliation, telephone number, complete address and the date of submission should be on a separate cover page, and only on this page to ensure anonymity in the reviewing process. Authors should include on a separate page a brief biographical summary of 50-75 words.

The IJ SAID requires writers to submit manuscripts following the technical specifications set forth in their respective field of endeavor. Manuscripts should be addressed to: International Journal of Scholarly Academic Intellectual Diversity, Dr. William Kritsonis, Editor, P O Box 7400, Lake Charles, LA 70605-7400. Phone: (337) 477-0008/Fax: (337) 480-3663.

Processing Fee

At the time a manuscript is submitted for consideration for international publication in the *International Journal of Scholarly Academic Intellectual Diversity*, the writer, institution, or agency must include a non-refundable processing fee of $30. This fee covers the initial screening and evaluation of the manuscript by the editorial staff.

Professional Service Fee

Many professional journals are financed by associations as part of their dues structure. The *IJ SAID* has no such luxury. *IJ SAID* is a self-supported journal. This enables the journal to remain completely independent, non-biased, and diverse in the refereeing, review, assessment,

452

evaluation, and publication process. When a manuscript is recommended for publication by members of *The International Board of Invited Distinguished Jurors* representing the *IJ SAID*, the author(s), associated institution, school, or agency is expected to submit a pre-specified nominal professional service fee. The fee simply helps cover expenses relative to expediting the review process, evaluating, examining, and communicating about the manuscript, along with other constant escalating costs of advertising, marketing, and promoting the particular issue at the international, world-wide, and national levels.

How to Determine Your Professional Service Fee

The professional service fee is simple to calculate. It is determined by the number of authors and the length of manuscript. The number of authors and the length of manuscript determine it. The first author is assessed $100, second author $90, third author $80, fourth author $70, and fifth author $60. Also, $25.00 per double-spaced page, typed in a fixed-pitch font (ex: Courier), is assessed each manuscript. Each table or figure is assessed $50.00. Each reference is assessed $10.00. There is a $150.00 administrative manuscript fee. For example, a co-authored 10-page manuscript with two tables and five references would cost $740.00 ($190.00 authors + $250.00 page fee + $100.00 two tables/figures + $50.00 references + $150.00 administrative manuscript fee = $740.00).

Copies to Authors

Each author receives a 3.5 diskette with the MS Word formatted contents of the entire journal will also be provided to each author. Authors have permission to reproduce their articles and contents of the entire journal for instructional purposes without prior written permission as long as proper credit is given to the *International Journal of Scholarly Academic Intellectual Diversity*. Writers may supply labels for six persons they wish to receive complimentary copies of their articles.

International Journal of Science Education

ADDRESS FOR SUBMISSION:

John Gilbert, Editor
International Journal of Science Education
University of Reading
Bulmershe Court
Earley
Reading, RG6 1HY
UK
Phone: 0118 931 8869
Fax: 0118 931 8650
E-Mail: j.k.gilbert@reading.ac.uk
Web: www.tandf.co.uk/journals
Address May Change:

PUBLICATION GUIDELINES:

Manuscript Length: 26-30
Copies Required: Four
Computer Submission: No
Format:
Fees to Review: 0.00 US$

Manuscript Style:
See Manuscript Guidelines

CIRCULATION DATA:

Reader: Practicing Teachers, Academics
Frequency of Issue: 15 Times/Year
Copies per Issue:
Sponsor/Publisher: Taylor & Francis
Subscribe Price: 590.00 US$ Individual
1697.00 US$ Institution

REVIEW INFORMATION:

Type of Review: Blind Review
No. of External Reviewers: 2
No. of In House Reviewers: 0
Acceptance Rate: 32%
Time to Review: 3-4 Months
Reviewers Comments: Yes
Invited Articles: 0-5%
Fees to Publish: 0.00 US$

MANUSCRIPT TOPICS:
Earth Science; Science Math & Environment; Technology

MANUSCRIPT GUIDELINES/COMMENTS:

Aims and Scope
The *International Journal of Science Education* is firmly established as the authoritative voice in the world of science education. It bridges the gap between research and practice, providing information, ideas and opinion. It serves as a medium for the publication of definitive research findings. Special emphasis is placed on applicable research relevant to educational practice, guided by educational realities in systems, schools, colleges and universities.

The journal comprises peer-reviewed general articles, papers on innovations and developments, research reports and book reviews. Each volume contains a Special Issue devoted to a topic of major interest and importance, guest-edited by an acknowledged expert. Recent Special Issues have featured environmental education and policy and practice in science education.

Readership
Science education researchers and science educators worldwide.

Instructions for Authors
Note to Authors: please make sure your contact address information is clearly visible on the **outside** of all packages you are sending to Editors.

Publication
International Journal of Science Education (*IJSE*) is published 15 times per year by Taylor & Francis Ltd.

Authors based in North America or Australasia are invited to submit papers to the appropriate Regional Editor, whilst papers from Europe, Africa, Asia, and South America should be sent to the Editor-in-Chief. *IJSE* considers all manuscripts on condition they are the property (copyright) of the submitting author(s) and that copyright will be transferred to *IJSE* and Taylor & Francis Ltd if the paper is accepted.

Book reviews and books for review should be sent to
Jan Driel, ICLON, Universiteit Leiden, Wassenaarseweg 52,
PO Box 9555, NL-2300 RB Leiden, Netherlands

Editor-in-Chief
Professor John K.Gilbert, Institute of Education, The University of Reading, Bulmershe Court, Earley, Reading RG6 1HY, UK; Email: **j.k.gilbert@reading.ac.uk**

Regional Editor for Australasia
Professor David Treagust, Science and Mathematics Education Centre, Curtin University of Technology, GPO Box U1987, Perth, Western Australia 6845.
Email: **D.Treagust@smec.curtin.edu.au**

Regional Editor for North America
Dr Janice Gobert, c/o The Concord Consortium, 10 Concord Crossing, Suite 300, Concord, MA 01742, USA; Email: **jgobert@concord.org**

The *International Journal of Science Education* attaches importance to applicable research, that is, research that is capable of being used in real educational settings. Studies in all settings for science education, i.e. informal, primary, secondary, higher, adult and continuing, and vocational, are regarded as of equal importance. All papers which appear in *IJSE* have been thoroughly peer-reviewed.

The Journal carries four types of article
1. General articles These are theoretically-based papers (around 5000-8000 words in length) debating and exploring existing research, methodologies, and new perspectives.

2. Innovations and developments
    These are accounts of the nature of an innovation or a development, of how it was produced, and include an evaluation of its use in practice.

3. Research reports
   These are accounts of qualitative or quantitative enquiries that present conclusions and implications for future research and practice in the context of a critical review of relevant literature and an account of the methods and procedures used.

4. Book reviews
   These are concise critical reviews of books that address research into science education. Book reviews are prepared at the invitation of the editors. However, suggestions are welcomed.

Submissions

Submissions should be original and unpublished work not currently under review by another journal or publisher. Authors should forward four copies of their manuscript, typewritten in double line spacing using the format and reference standard set out in the *Publication Manual of the American Psychological Association* (2001, 5th edition). A transmittal letter signed by the author should be included. This letter should request review of the manuscript and indicate that the manuscript has not been published nor submitted for publication elsewhere. The first page of the manuscript should be a cover page detailing the title of the article, running head, name(s) of author(s), affiliation(s), and postal and E-mail addresses for correspondence. Telephone and fax numbers should also be included.

Review

Manuscripts are sent for blind peer-review to members of the Editorial Board and/or Guest Reviewers. The review process generally requires three months. The receipt of submitted manuscripts will be acknowledged by each Editor, from whom a decision and reviewers' comments will be received when the peer-review has been completed.

Final copy and Disks

Authors should send the final, accepted version of their articles in both hard copy paper and electronic disk forms. It is essential that the hard copy (paper) version **exactly** matches the material on disk. Please print out the hard copy from the disk you are sending. Submit three printed copies of the final version with the disk to the journal's editorial office. Save all files on a standard 3.5 inch high-density disk. We prefer to receive disks in Microsoft Word™ in a PC format, but can translate from most other common word processing programs as well as Macs. Please specify which program you have used. Do not save your files as "text only" or "read only".

Authors' Alterations

A copy of the final revised manuscript should be retained by the author for proof-reading purposes. Page proofs for correcting will be sent to authors by Taylor & Francis prior to the manuscript going to press. Every effort is made to publish accepted papers within twelve months of return of proofs.

Early Electronic Offprints. Corresponding authors can now receive their article by e-mail as a complete PDF. This allows the author to print up to 50 copies, free of charge, and disseminate them to colleagues. In many cases this facility will be available up to two weeks prior to publication. Or, alternatively, corresponding authors will receive the traditional 50 offprints. A copy of the journal will be sent by post to all corresponding authors after publication. Additional copies of the journal can be purchased at the author's preferential rate of £15.00/$25.00 per copy.

Copyright

It is a condition of publication that authors vest or license copyright in their articles, including abstracts, in Taylor & Francis Ltd. This enables us to ensure full copyright protection and to disseminate the article, and the journal, to the widest possible readership in print and electronic formats as appropriate. Authors may, of course, use the article elsewhere after publication without prior permission from Taylor & Francis, provided that acknowledgement is given to the Journal as the original source of publication, and that Taylor & Francis is notified so that its records show that its use is properly authorised. Authors are themselves responsible for obtaining permission to reproduce copyright material from other sources.

FORMAT OF MANUSCRIPTS

Number of copies

Four copies of the manuscript should be submitted, together with a disk version, to the appropriate editor (see above). Manuscripts should be typed on one side of A4 or 8½ x 11 inch good quality white paper, in 12-point font, double spaced throughout (including the reference section).

Cover Page

The first page of the manuscript should consist only of the running head, the title of the paper (in bold) , the author(s) name(s) and institutional affiliation(s) (in italics), and full details (mailing address, telephone, fax, email address) for correspondence with the main author. Only the first letter in each word of the title and author(s) name etc should be in upper case, the rest in lower case. To facilitate blind reviewing, this page will be removed from copies sent to reviewers.

Abstract

The second page of the manuscript should begin with the title of the paper and an abstract which should not exceed 150 words. The name(s) of the author(s) should not appear on this page. For papers reporting original research, state in brief: the primary objective (the research questions addressed or any hypothesis tested); the research design; the methods and procedures employed; the number of subjects; the main outcomes and results; the conclusions drawn from these data and results, including their implications for further research or application/practice.

Notes on style

For all manuscripts, gender-, race-, and creed-inclusive language is mandatory. The preferred local (national) usage for ethnic and other minorities should be used in all papers. For the USA, 'African-American', 'Hispanic', and 'Native American' are used. For the UK, 'Afro-Caribbean' is used.

Writing should be clear and concise, with objectives stated and terms defined. Arguments should be substantiated with well-reasoned supportive evidence. Relevant articles in the area being addressed should be reviewed. Such articles must be referenced accurately.

Authors are asked to take account of the diverse audience of the *IJSE*. Explain clearly-or avoid the use of - terms that might be meaningful only to a local or national audience. At the same time, where appropriate, preference is given to papers which reflect the particularities of each social and cultural system. In some cases it may be helpful if those particularities are contrasted with well-informed accounts of comparable situations elsewhere.

Brief biographical details of significant national figures or institutions should be outlined in the text unless it is quite clear that they would be known internationally. For example, some suggested editorial recommendations to a 'typical' text are indicated in the following by square brackets: 'From the time of H.E. Armstrong [in the 19th century] to the curriculum development work associated with the Nuffield Foundation [in the 1960s], there has been a shift from heurism to constructivism in the design of [British] science courses'.

Material to be emphasized (italicized in the printed version) should be underlined in the typescript rather than italicized. Please use such emphasis sparingly.

Spelling and Punctuation
UK and not USA spelling is used i.e. colour not color; behaviour not behavior; [school] programme not program; [he] practises not practices; centre not center; organization not organisation; analyse not analyze, etc.

Single 'quotes' are used for quotations rather than double "quotes", unless the 'quote is "within" another quote'.

Punctuation should follow the UK style, e.g. 'quotes precede punctuation'. Punctuation of common abbreviations should follow the following conventions: e.g. i.e. cf.

Note that such abbreviations are not followed by a comma or a (double) point/period. Dashes (M-dash) should be clearly indicated in manuscripts by way of either a clear dash (-) or a double hyphen (--).

Apostrophes should be used sparingly. Thus, decades should be referred to as follows: 'The 1980s [not the 1980's] saw ...'. Possessives associated with acronyms (e.g. PA), should be written as follows: 'The APU's findings that ...', but; NB, the plural is APUs.

Abbreviations and acronyms
'US' is preferred to 'American', USA to 'United States', and UK to 'United Kingdom'. All acronyms for national agencies, examinations, etc. should be spelled out the first time they are introduced in text or references. Thereafter the acronym can be used if appropriate, e.g. 'The work of the Assessment of Performance Unit (APU) in the early 1980s ...'. Subsequently, 'The APU studies of achievement ...', in a reference ... (Department of Education and Science [DES] 1989a).

458

Numbers
n (not N), % (not per cent) should be used in typescripts. Numbers in text should take the following forms: 300, 3000, 30 000. Spell out numbers under 10 unless used with a unit of measure, e.g. nine pupils but 9 mm (do not introduce periods with measure). For decimals, use the form 0.05 (not .05).

Tables and Figures
Artwork submitted for publication will not be returned and will be destroyed after publication, unless you request otherwise. Whilst every care is taken of artwork, neither the Editor nor Taylor & Francis shall bear any responsibility or liability for non-return, loss, or damage of artwork, nor for any associated costs or compensation. You are strongly advised to insure appropriately.

Tables and figures should be valuable, relevant, and visually attractive. Tables and figures must be referred to in the text and numbered in order of their appearance. Each table and figure should have a complete, descriptive title; and each table column an appropriate heading.

Tables and figures should be referred to in text as follows: figure 1, table 1, i.e. lower case. 'As seen in table [or figure] 1 ...' (not Tab., fig. or Fig).

The place at which a table or figure is to be inserted in the printed text should be indicated clearly on a manuscript:

[Insert table 2 about here]

Each table and/or figure must have a title that explains its purpose without reference to the text.

All figures and tables must be on separate sheets and not embedded in the text. Original copies of figures should be supplied. All figures should allow for reduction to column width (130 mm) or page width (160 mm). Please avoid figures that would require landscape reproduction, i.e. reading from bottom to top of the page. Photographs may be sent as glossy prints or negatives.

Please number each figure on the reverse in pencil.

Do not type the caption to a figure on that figure; the legends to any illustrations must be typed separately following the main text and should be grouped together. Tables should not contain vertical lines.

Acknowledgements
Any acknowledgements that authors wish to make should be included in a separate headed section at the end of the manuscript.

Citations in text
References should be cited in the text first by date, then alphabetically, thus: (Burbidge 1989, Higins and Browne 1989, Sherali et al. 1989); and listed in alphabetical order in the reference section at the end of the paper.

International Journal of Social Education

ADDRESS FOR SUBMISSION:

D. Antonio Cantu, Editor
International Journal of Social Education
Ball State University
Department of History - BB209
Muncie, IN 47306
USA
Phone: 765-285-8621
Fax: 765-285-5612
E-Mail: dcantu@bsu.edu
Web: www.bsu.edu/web/dcantu
Address May Change:

PUBLICATION GUIDELINES:

Manuscript Length:
Copies Required: Three
Computer Submission: Yes Disk, Email
Format: PC - MS Word
Fees to Review: 0.00 US$

Manuscript Style:
    Chicago Manual of Style

CIRCULATION DATA:

Reader: Practicing Teachers, Academics
Frequency of Issue: 2 Times/Year
Copies per Issue: 1,001 - 2,000
Sponsor/Publisher: Ball State University
    and the Indiana Council for the Social
    Studies
Subscribe Price: 10.00 US$

REVIEW INFORMATION:

Type of Review: Blind Review
No. of External Reviewers: 2
No. of In House Reviewers:
Acceptance Rate: 21-30%
Time to Review: 2 - 3 Months
Reviewers Comments: Yes
Invited Articles: 31-50%
Fees to Publish: 0.00 US$

MANUSCRIPT TOPICS:

Curriculum Studies; Elementary/Early Childhood; Secondary/Adolescent Studies; Social
Studies/Social Science; Teacher Education

MANUSCRIPT GUIDELINES/COMMENTS:

On behalf of the editorial board of the *International Journal of Social Education*, I want to
thank you for your interest in submitting a manuscript for consideration. Please forward two
paper copies of the manuscript along with the document file (PC – Microsoft Word format on
a 3.5" floppy disk or as an e-mail attachment) to the *IJSE* Editor at the address above.

Remember that all manuscripts submitted to the *IJSE* should conform to the guidelines in *The
Chicago Manual of Style* (14th edition). A copy of the *IJSE* Style Sheet is available at the
following URL: **http://www.bsu.edu/classes/cantu/ijsestylesheet.html**. Please note that you
should not use the automatic reference or endnote numbering function/option in Microsoft
Word. In addition, please include a contributor's biographical entry (a brief one paragraph
summary of your current position and major publications) with your submission.

Upon receipt of these items, your manuscript will be sent to two reviewers in the field most familiar with the material addressed in your article, in adherence with the double-blind review protocol. Should you have any questions or require further information please contact Professor Cantu or Kris Miller at the email and/or phone numbers listed below. Again, we appreciate your interest in the *IJSE* and look forward to working with you.

IJSE Style Sheet

All manuscripts submitted to the *IJSE* should conform to the guidelines in *The Chicago Manual of Style* (14th edition). The following points should be kept in mind in preparing copy for submission to the *IJSE*:

All copy must be double spaced with 1& ½ inch left and 1 inch top, bottom, and right margins (or whatever the default settings are on the word processing that you are using). Quotations, extracts, charts, tables, notes, bibliographies, references, titles, and all other material must be double spaced. Submit three printed copies of the manuscript. If accepted for publication, you will be asked to submit a disk (identifying the word processing program), together with a brief paragraph about your professional background and activities.

Make sure that you have the proper page numbers for all quotations. If you have used certain sections of a book or article, cite the proper pages.

Do not type anything in all capital letters.

If you must use subheads, avoid using more than two levels. Primary subheads are run in with the text, underscored, and typed flush left in upper-and lowercase letters, followed by a period. There is an extra line space above a primary head. Secondary heads have no extra space above them. They are run in with the text, underscored, indented, and typed in upper-and lowercase followed by a period.

Notes should be placed at the end of the text. Use the "documentary-note or humanities style," Do not use the author-date system. See *The Chicago Manual of Style* for samples of the "humanities style." Notes in the *IJSE* can be used as samples also. Use full references the first time you mention a source, and then shortened when you cite it subsequently. **Do not use** *op. Cit.* and *loc. Cit.*

For a dash (em dash), type two hyphens; do not space before or after a dash.

Use a comma before *and* or *or* in a series of three or more parallel elements. Make sure that the elements in your series are parallel.

When using ellipsis points, space before, between, and after the three dots. When using ellipsis points with a period, a fourth dot is required. If ellipsis indicates that the remaining part of a sentence has been omitted, the period follows the ellipsis with spaces before and after it; if the ellipsis follows a complete sentence, the period comes before the ellipsis with no space before the period.

Decades should be written as follows: "the 1920s" (no apostrophe) or "the twenties" (lowercase). Do not write "20s" or "20's" Webster's dictionaries are the *IJSE*'s reference for spelling.

Words referred to as words are underscored, e. g., "the term style."

In quotations, periods and commas are placed inside the closing quotation marks, colons and semicolons outside. Question marks and exclamation points are inside if they are part of the quotations, outside if not.

Inclusive page numbers in references (in the Notes at the end) follow the style outlined in *The Chicago Manual*. Please avoid jargon.

International Journal of Sport Management

ADDRESS FOR SUBMISSION:

William F. Stier, Jr., Editor
International Journal of Sport Management
Suny College at Brockport
Dept. of Physical Education and Sport
350 New Campus Drive
Brockport, NY 14420-2914
USA
Phone: 716-395-5331
Fax: 716-395-2771
E-Mail: bstier@brockport.edu
Web:
Address May Change:

PUBLICATION GUIDELINES:

Manuscript Length: 15-25
Copies Required: Four
Computer Submission: No
Format: N/A
Fees to Review: 0.00 US$

Manuscript Style:
   American Psychological Association

CIRCULATION DATA:

Reader: Academics, Practicing Teachers,
   Administrators
Frequency of Issue: Quarterly
Copies per Issue: Less than 1,000
Sponsor/Publisher: American Press -
   Boston, MA
Subscribe Price: 62.00 US$ U.S.
   102.00 US$ International

REVIEW INFORMATION:

Type of Review: Blind Review
No. of External Reviewers: 3
No. of In House Reviewers: 1
Acceptance Rate: 29-34%
Time to Review: 2 - 3 Months
Reviewers Comments: Yes
Invited Articles: 0-5%
Fees to Publish: 0.00 US$

MANUSCRIPT TOPICS:

Athletic Administration; Education Management/Administration; Educational Technology
Systems; Health & Physical Education; Higher Education; School Law; Sport Management;
Teacher Education

MANUSCRIPT GUIDELINES/COMMENTS:

Manuscripts should be prepared in accordance with the latest edition of the *Publication
Manual of the American Psychological Association.* A stamped, self-addressed return
envelope must be provided along with the four copies of the manuscript.

International Journal on E-Learning

ADDRESS FOR SUBMISSION:

Gary Marks, Editor
International Journal on E-Learning
ONLINE SUBMISSIONS ONLY
AACE
PO Box 3728
Norfolk, VA 23514-3728
USA
Phone: 757-623-7588
Fax: 703-997-8760
E-Mail: pubs@aace.org
Web: www.aace.org
Address May Change:

PUBLICATION GUIDELINES:

Manuscript Length: Max/30 pages
Copies Required: No Paper Copy Required
Computer Submission: Yes Online Subm.
  Only
Format: MSWord, html, rtf
Fees to Review: 0.00 US$

Manuscript Style:
  American Psychological Association

CIRCULATION DATA:

Reader: , See Guidelines
Frequency of Issue: Quarterly
Copies per Issue: 1,000-1,800
Sponsor/Publisher: AACE-Assn. for the
  Advancement of Computers in Education
Subscribe Price: 85.00 US$ Individual
  120.00 US$ Institution

REVIEW INFORMATION:

Type of Review: Blind Review
No. of External Reviewers: 2-4
No. of In House Reviewers: 2
Acceptance Rate: 11-20%
Time to Review: 2-4 Months
Reviewers Comments: Yes
Invited Articles: 15-25%
Fees to Publish: 0.00 US$

MANUSCRIPT TOPICS:
Distance Education; Educational Technology Systems; Higher Education; Knowledge
Management; On-line Learning; Science Math & Environment

MANUSCRIPT GUIDELINES/COMMENTS:

Reader. Researchers, Developers and Practitioners in Corporate, Government, Healthcare and
Higher Education.

Advances in technology and the growth of e-learning to provide educators and trainers with
unique opportunities to enhance learning and teaching in corporate, government, healthcare,
and higher education. IJEL serves as a forum to facilitate the international exchange of
information on the current research, development, and practice of e-learning in these sectors.

Please read through the guidelines below before submitting your paper.

Journal Content
Contributions for all journals may include research papers, case studies, tutorials, courseware experiences, evaluations, review papers, and viewpoints.

General Guidelines
Material must be original, scientifically accurate, and in good form editorially. The manuscript should be informative, summarizing the basic facts and conclusions, and maintaining a coherence and unity of thought.

Tutorial or how-to-do-it articles should preferably include a section on evaluation. Controversial topics should be treated in a factually sound and reasonably unbiased manner.

The format of headings, tables, figures, citations, references, and other details should follow the (APA) style as described in the *Publication Manual of the American Psychological Association*, 5th edition, available from APA, 750 1st St., NE, Washington, DC 20002 USA.

Preview
Manuscripts sent to the Editor for review are accepted on a voluntary basis from authors. Before submitting an article, please review the following suggestions. Manuscripts received in correct form serve to expedite the processing and prompt reviewing for early publication.

Spelling, punctuation, sentence structure, and the mechanical elements of arrangements, spacing, length, and consistency of usage in form and descriptions should be studied before submission. Due to the academic focus of AACE publications, the use of personal pronoun (I, we, etc.) and present tense is strongly discouraged.

Pre-publication
No manuscript will be considered which has already been published or is being considered by another journal.

Copyright
These journals are copyrighted by the Association for the Advancement of Computing in Education. Material published and so copyrighted may not be published elsewhere without the written permission of AACE.

Author Note(s)
Financial support for work reported or a grant under which a study was made should be noted just prior to the Acknowledgments. Acknowledgments or appreciation to individuals for assistance with the manuscript or with the material reported should be included as a note to appear at the end of the article prior to the References.

Handling of Manuscripts
All manuscripts are acknowledged upon receipt. Review is carried out as promptly as possible. The manuscript will be reviewed by at least two members of the Editorial Review Board, which takes approximately five months. When a decision for publication or rejection is made, the senior author or author designated to receive correspondence is notified. At the time

of notification, the author may be asked to make certain revisions in the manuscript, or the Editor may submit suggested revisions to the author for approval.

Presentation

Accepted Submission File Formats. All submissions must be sent in electronic form using the Article Submission Form. **No hard copy submission papers will be accepted.** Do NOT submit compressed files. Do not use any word processing options/tools, such as--strike through, hidden text, comments, merges, and so forth.

Submit your manuscript in either of the following formats:

- **DOC**- Microsoft Word (preferred)
- RTF - Rich Text Format

Manuscripts should be double-spaced and a font size of 12 is preferred.

Length. In general, articles should not exceed 30 double-spaced pages. Long articles or articles containing complex material should be broken up by short, meaningful subheads.

Title sheet. Do NOT include a title sheet. Manuscripts are blind reviewed so there should be no indication of the author(s) name on the pages.

Abstract. An informative, comprehensive abstract of 75 to 200 words must accompany the manuscript. This abstract should succinctly summarize the major points of the paper, and the author's summary and/or conclusions.

Tables, Figures & Graphics

All tables and figure graphics must be embedded within the file and of such quality that when printed be in camera-ready form (publication quality). Within the submitted file, number and type captions centered at the top of each table. Figures are labeled at the bottom of the figure, left justified, and numbered in sequence.

Any graphics that go in the article must be submitted as separate files. The highest quality master (e.g. TIF) is preferred. Additionally, the graphics must also be embedded in the correct locations within the document so the copyeditors know the proper placement. Please note that any graphics created in Microsoft Word must also be submitted as separate files.

Graphics, tables, figures, photos, and so forth, must be sized to fit a 6" x 9" publication with margins of: top, 1" inside 1" outside, .75" and bottom, 1" an overall measurement of 4.5 X 6.75 is the absolute limit in size. A table or figure sized on a full size 8.5 by 11 piece of paper does not always reduce and remain legible. Please adhere to the size stipulation or your manuscript will be returned for graphics/figures or tables to be re-done.

Quotations

Copy all quoted material exactly as it appears in the original, indicating any omissions by three spaced periods. At the close of the quotation, give the complete source including page numbers. A block quote must be a minimum of 40 words or four lines, single spaced.

Terminology and Abbreviations

Define any words or phrases that cannot be found in Webster's Unabridged Dictionary. Define or explain new or highly technical terminology. Write out the first use of a term that you expect to use subsequently in abbreviated form. Abbreviations (i.e., e.g., etc.) are only acceptable in parenthesis, otherwise they must be spelled out, that is, for example, and so forth, respectively. Please avoid other foreign phrases and words such as via.

Program Listings

Program listings will appear with the published article if space permits. Listings should be publication quality. The brand of computer required should be included. Lengthy program listings (more than four 6 x 9 pages) can not be published, but may be made available from the author; a note to that effect should be included in the article.

Citations

Citations should strictly follow *American Psychological Association* (APA) style guide. Examples of references cited within the texts of articles are as follows: (Williams, Allen, & Jones, 1978) or (Moore, 1990; Smith, 1991) or Terrell (1977). In citations, "et al." can only be used after all authors have been cited or referenced with the exception of six or more authors. As per APA all citations must match the reference list and vice versa. Over use of references is discouraged.

References

Authors are responsible for checking the accuracy of all references and that all references cited in the text also appear in the Reference section. All references should be in alphabetical order by author (unnumbered) *American Psychological Association* (APA), 5th edition, style. Citation examples (1) book and (2) periodical:

Knowles, M. (1975). *Self-directed learning: A guide for learners and teachers*. New York: Association Press.

Raybould, B. (1995). Performance support engineering: An emerging development methodology for enabling organizational learning. *Performance Improvement Quarterly*, 8(1), 7-22.

Citing Electronic Media

The following forms for citing on-line sources are taken from the APA Publication Guidelines, Appendix 3-A, Section I (pp. 218-222). Please see the APA manual for additional information on formatting electronic media. A block quote must be a minimum of 40 words or four lines, single spaced (not 20 and double spaced as is presently noted). In citations, et al., can only be used after all authors have been cited or referenced. As per APA all citations must match the reference list and vice versa.

Elements of references to on-line information

Author, I. (date). Title of article. <u>Name of Periodical</u> [On-line], xx. Available: Specify path

468

Author, I., & Author, I. (date). Title of chapter. In <u>Title of full work</u> [On-line]. Available: Specify path

Author, I., Author, I., & Author, I. (date). <u>Title of full work</u> [On-line]. Available: Specify path

The date element should indicate the year of publication or, if the source undergoes regular revision, the most recent update; if a date cannot be determined, provide an exact date of your search. (p. 219)

An availability statement replaces the location and name of a publisher typically provided for text references. Provide information sufficient to retrieve the material. For example, for material that is widely available on networks, specify the method used to find the material, such as the protocol (Telnet, FTP, Internet, etc.), the directory, and the file name. (p. 219)

Other Electronic Media
Author, I. (Version number) [CD-ROM]. (date). Location of producer/distributor: Name of producer/distributor.

Author, I. (date). Title of article [CD-ROM]. <u>Title of Journal, xx,</u> xxx-xxx. Abstract from: Source and retrieval number

Author, I. (date). Name of Software (Version number) [Computer software]. Location of Location of producer/distributor: Name of producer/distributor.

After the title of the work, insert in brackets as part of the title element (i.e., before the period) the type of medium for the material (current examples include CD-ROM, Electronic data tape, cartridge tape, and computer program). (p. 220)

Include the location and name of the producer and distributor if citing an entire bibliographic database. (p. 220)

Post-publication
Upon publication, the contact author will receive complimentary copies of the journal issue in which the article appears for distribution to all of the co-authors.

Please carefully read and adhere to these guidelines. Manuscripts not submitted according to the guidelines will be rejected and returned to the author.

International Research in Geographical and Environmental Education

ADDRESS FOR SUBMISSION:

John Lidstone, Editor
International Research in Geographical and
    Environmental Education
Queensland University of Technology
Kelvin Grove Campus
Victoria Park Road
Red Hill, Qld 4059
Australia
Phone: +61-7-3864-3289
Fax: +61-7-3864-3981
E-Mail: j.lidstone@qut.edu.au
Web: www.multilingual-matters.com/
Address May Change:

PUBLICATION GUIDELINES:

Manuscript Length: 7,000 words
Copies Required: Four
Computer Submission: Yes
Format: MS Word
Fees to Review: 0.00 US$

Manuscript Style:
    American Psychological Association

CIRCULATION DATA:

Reader: Academics, Practicing Teachers
Frequency of Issue: Quarterly
Copies per Issue: Less than 1,000
Sponsor/Publisher: International
    Geographical Union, Commission on
    Geographical Education, Multilingual
    Matters Ltd
Subscribe Price: 95.00 US$ Individual
    320.00 US$ Institution

REVIEW INFORMATION:

Type of Review: Blind Review
No. of External Reviewers: 3
No. of In House Reviewers: 1
Acceptance Rate: 21-30%
Time to Review: 2 - 3 Months
Reviewers Comments: Yes
Invited Articles: 6-10%
Fees to Publish: 0.00 US$

MANUSCRIPT TOPICS:
Curriculum Studies; Education; Environmental Education; Geographical Education; Higher
Education; Science Math & Environment; Secondary/Adolescent Studies; Social
Studies/Social Science; Teacher Education

MANUSCRIPT GUIDELINES/COMMENTS:

Email. j.lidstone@qut.edu.au and irgee@office-logistics.com

International Research in Geographical & Environmental Education is a quarterly
publication. The journal aims to publish quality research studies in geographical and
environmental education; promote an expanded international interest in research in
geographical and environmental education; provide a forum for the critique of research studies
and the discussion of relevant research issues in geographical and environmental education;
encourage the international dissemination of research in geographical and environmental

education, and demonstrate the relevance of research studies to good professional practice in geographical and environmental education. Each issue includes editorial comment, refereed research papers, a Forum section of debate on matters of current concern, and book reviews.

Guidelines

Articles should not normally exceed 7000 words. Note that it is our policy not to review papers that are currently under consideration by other journals. They should be typed, double-spaced on A4 (or similar) paper, with ample left and right-hand margins, on one side of the paper only, and every page should be numbered consecutively. A cover page should contain only the title, thereby facilitating anonymous reviewing by three independent assessors. As far as possible it is *IRGEE* Editorial policy that all papers be reviewed by one reviewer from the country of origin of the author plus two other reviewers from two other continents. Authors may also wish to take precautions to avoid textual references which would identify themselves to the referees. In such cases the authors of accepted papers will have the opportunity to include any such omitted material before the paper is published.

Submissions for Work in Progress/ Readers' Response /Letters to the Editor sections should be approximately 500 words in length.

Main contact author should also appear in a separate paragraph on the title page which will be removed before refereeing.

An abstract should be included. This should not exceed 200 words (longer abstracts are rejected by many abstracting services).

A short version of the title (maximum 45 characters) should also be supplied for the journal's running headline.

To facilitate the production of the annual subject index, a list of keywords (not more than six) should be provided, under which the paper may be indexed.

If submitted in hard copy, four copies of the articles must be submitted. However, articles may also be submitted to the editors by email attachment. Electronically submitted articles should conform to the guidelines above and any graphics should be included as separate files at a sufficiently high resolution to permit reduction and printing. Such graphics should be presented in monochrome format (no colour).

Footnotes should be avoided. Essential notes should be numbered in the text and grouped together at the end of the article. Diagrams and Figures, if they are considered essential, should be clearly related to the section of the text to which they refer. The original diagrams and figures should be submitted with the top copy.

References should be set out in alphabetical order of the author's name in a list at the end of the article. They should be given in standard form, as in the Appendix below.

References in the text to an article should be by the author's name and year of publication, as in these examples: Jones (1997) in a paper on ...(commonest version); Jones and Evans

(1997c:22) state that ...(where page number is required); Evidence is given by Smith et al. (1994)...(for three or more authors). Further exploration of this aspect may be found in many sources (e.g. Brown & Green, 1992; Jackson, 1993; White, 1991a) (note alphabetical order, use of & and semicolons).

Once the refereeing procedures are completed, and any amendments recommended by reviewers attended to, authors should, if possible, supply revised electronic copy either as a word-processor disc containing their manuscript file(s) or as an email attachment. If presented on disc, we require files to be saved:

- on an IBM-PC compatible 3.5 inch disc (or CD-ROM) or on an Apple Mac high-density 3,5 inch disc.
- Text should be saved in the author's normal word-processor format. The name of the word-processor program should also be supplied if other than MSWord. Tables and Figures should be saved in separate files.

The author of an article accepted for publication will receive page proofs for correction if there is sufficient time to do so. This stage must not be used as an opportunity to revise the paper, because alterations are extremely costly; extensive changes will be charged to the author and will probably result in the article being delayed to a later issue. Speedy return of corrected proofs is important.

Contributions and queries should be sent to the Editors, Multilingual Matters Ltd., Frankfurt Lodge, Clevedon Hall, Victoria Road, Clevedon, BS21 7HH, England. A very large majority of authors' proof-corrections are caused by errors in references. Authors are therefore requested to check the following points particularly carefully when submitting manuscripts:

- Are all the references in the reference list cited in the text?
- Do all the citations in the text appear in the reference list?
- Do the dates in the text and the reference list correspond?
- Do the spellings of authors' names in text and reference list correspond, and do all authors have the correct initials?
- Are journal references complete with volume and pages numbers?
- Are references to books complete with place of publication and the name of the publisher?

It is extremely helpful if references are presented as far as possible in accordance with our house style. A few more typical examples are shown below. Note, especially, use of upper &lower case in paper titles, use of capital letters and italic (underlining can be used as an alternative if italic is not available) in book and journal titles, punctuation (or lack of it) after dates, journal titles, and book titles. The inclusion of issue numbers of journals, or page numbers in books is optional but if included should be as per the examples below.

Department of Education and Science (DES) (1985) *Education for All* (The Swann Report). London: HMSO

Evans, N.J. and Ilbery, B.W. (1989) A conceptual framework for investigating farm-based accommodation and tourism in Britain. *Journal of Rural Studies* 5 (3), 257-266.

472

Evans, N.J. and Ilbery, B.W. (1992) Advertising and farm-based accommodation: A British case-study. *Tourism Management* 13 (4), 415-422.

Laufer, B (2000) Vocabulary acquisition in a second language: The hypothesis of ' synforms'. PhD thesis, University of Edinburgh.

Mackey, W.F. (1998) The ecology of language shift. In P.H. Nelde (ed.) *Languages in Contact and in Conflict* (pp. 35-41). Wiesbaden: Steiner.

Marien, C. and Pizam, A. (1997) Implementing sustainable tourism development through citizen participation in the planning process. In S. Wahab and J. Pigram (eds) *Tourism, Development and Growth* (pp. 164-78). London: Routledge.

Morrison, D. (1999) Small group discussion project questionnaire. University of Hong Kong Language Centre (mimeo).

U.S. Census Bureau (1998) State profile: California. Online document: http/www.census.gov/statab/www/states/ca.txt.

Zahn, C.J. and Hopper, R (2000) The speech evaluation instrument: A user's manual (version 1.0a). Unpublished manuscript, Cleveland State University.

Zigler, E. and Balla, D. (eds) *Mental Retardation: The Developmental-Difference Controversy.* Hillsdale, N.J: Lawrence Erlbaum.

For more details, please e-mail the editors, A/Prof John Lidstone **j.lidstone@qut.edu.au** or Professor Joe Stoltman **stoltman@wmich.edu**.

For general enquiries, email **irgee@office-logistics.com**.

International Review of Education

ADDRESS FOR SUBMISSION:

Orrin F. Summerell, Executive Editor
International Review of Education
UNESCO Institute for Education
Publications and Information Unit
Feldbrunnenstrasse 58
20148 Hamburg,
Germany
Phone: +49-40 4480410
Fax: +49-40 4107723
E-Mail: uie@unesco.org
Web: www.unesco.org/education/uie
Address May Change:

PUBLICATION GUIDELINES:

Manuscript Length: 8-20 Pages
Copies Required: Four
Computer Submission: Yes Required
Format: MS Word, WordPerfect
Fees to Review: 0.00 US$

Manuscript Style:
    See Manuscript Guidelines

CIRCULATION DATA:

Reader: Academics, Policy Makers
Frequency of Issue: Bi-Monthly
Copies per Issue: 1,001 - 2,000
Sponsor/Publisher: UNESCO / Kluwer
    Academic Publishers
Subscribe Price: 108.00 US$ Individual
    351.60 US$ Institution
    98.00 US$ Developing Countries

REVIEW INFORMATION:

Type of Review: Blind Review
No. of External Reviewers: 2
No. of In House Reviewers: 1
Acceptance Rate: 35%
Time to Review: 2-6 Months
Reviewers Comments: Yes
Invited Articles: 35%
Fees to Publish: 0.00 US$

MANUSCRIPT TOPICS:

Administration; Adult Career & Vocational; All levels of Education; Comparative Education, Non-Formal Education; Curriculum Studies; Educational Theory & Research Studies; Foreign Language; International Education; Lifelong Learning; Management; Policy of Interest to a Worldwide Readership

MANUSCRIPT GUIDELINES/COMMENTS:

General
Material submitted for publication and all related correspondence should be sent to

    The Journals Editorial Office of the International Review of Education
    Kluwer Academic Publishers, Van Godewijkstraat 30
    3311 GX Dordrecht, The Netherlands

The copyright for any submission published in the *International Review of Education* is owned by *Kluwer Academic Publishers*.

474

Permission to reprint is normally granted, provided that credit, including details as to volume and issue of the journal in which the original appeared, is given. No honorarium is paid to contributors.

Rejected material is not normally returned. If the author wishes to have his submission returned, he should specify that this is the case and accompany it with an International Postal Order to cover postage.

Character of publications
The *International Review of Education* publishes original essays, studies and reports of research in the areas of comparative and international education, including lifelong learning, as well as more general discussions of educational theory and practice of interest to a worldwide readership.

Usually only original contributions are welcomed, although in exceptional cases essays that have previously been published in journals with a purely national circulation may be accepted.

Contributions are published in English, French or German. The Editorial Office is prepared to consider submissions in other languages on condition that a short summary in one of the above three languages is attached. In the case of the acceptance of such a work, the author must arrange for its competent translation.

Three types of contributions are accepted: essays and studies, notes and book reviews. Essays and studies consist of a well-rounded discussion of a topic chosen for its international significance. They should normally not exceed 6,000 words in length (10-20 pages, 12-point type, double-spaced).

Notes are short, descriptive accounts of educational innovations, research results etc. Their length should normally not exceed 2,000 words (approximately 8 double-spaced pages). See the guidelines for book reviews at the end of these instructions.

Presentation of the manuscript
All submissions should be grammatically correct and stylistically consistent in a manner reflecting the propriety and facility of a native speaker of the language in which they are composed. They should be submitted both on paper (in four copies) and on diskette (preferably in Word or WordPerfect). The text should be double-spaced throughout with wide margins on both sides and the pages numbered consecutively. The author should retain an exact copy of the material submitted so that if questions arise the Editorial Office can refer to specific pages, paragraphs or lines for clarification. Inadequately prepared texts may be returned without comment.

All material should be arranged in the following order except as otherwise noted:

Title page (page 1)

The title should be as short as possible and capitalized. A subtitle may be used if necessary to supply greater information on the contents. The authors full name should be given below the title.

Abstract and/or Key words (page 2)

If the submission is an essay, it must be accompanied by an abstract: a short summary (approx. 150 words) typed double-spaced on a separate sheet. Both essays and notes should be attended by a list of five key words defining the content of the text. These will help in its evaluation. In the case of acceptance the abstract will be translated by the Editorial Office into the four other languages for inclusion at the beginning of the essay.

Biographical note (page 3)

If the submission is an essay or study, a brief biographical note of some 5-8 typewritten lines should also be included. It should give: full name, major professional qualifications, relevant past positions and present position (with dates), main field(s) of research. It must also include the authors full address and, if available, e-mail address.

Main text

- The title of the essay or note should appear once more at the beginning of the main text. The authors name should not appear.
- The main text should be prepared for blind review. There should be no references identifying the author in any way at all.
- The relative importance of headings and subheadings in essays should be clear.

Use of the term **Introduction** should be avoided. Four types of heading can be used:
- Main Heading (H1) **bold**, with two lines of extra spacing above and one below.
- Second-order Heading (H2) italicized, with extra spacing above and below.
- Third-order Heading (H3) italicized, with extra spacing above and no spacing below.
- Fourth-order Heading (H4) italicized, ending with a full stop and with text following on the same line.

In addition,
- The location of figures and tables should be indicated in the text.
- New paragraphs should be indicated by clear indentation.
- Quoted passages longer than 3 lines should be indented throughout.
- The use of endnotes should be avoided; footnotes are not acceptable. However, if essential, endnotes should be designated by superscript numbers consecutively throughout the manuscript and placed in **Notes** after the main text. The endnote function of the word-processing system must be employed for this purpose.
- Italicization. Single foreign words and phrases are italicized, although authors are requested to substitute the native term for the foreign one whenever possible. A definition of the foreign term should be supplied the first time it is used.
- No other formatting should be employed.

Following the main text

- **Notes** (if any) should be listed in numerical order and placed after the main text.
- **Appendix** (if any) should follow the **Notes**.

476

References
The **References** should be arranged alphabetically. They should be typed double-spaced and given in the text as: author and year of publication, for example: (Wilson 1966; Olsen 1966a, b; Stodolsky and Lesser 1993: 580). For the list of References follow the style shown below:

Essays and studies in journals:
Roberts, Peter. 1999. The Future of the University. *International Review of Education* 45(1): 65-85.
Forrester, Keith, Nick Frost, and Keven Ward. 2000. Researching Work and Learning: A Birds Eye View. *International Review of Education* 46(6): 483-489.

Books:
Bernardo, Allan B. I. 1998. *Literacy and the Mind. The Contexts and Cognitive Consequences of Literacy Practice.* Hamburg: UNESCO Institute for Education.

Hill, Dave, and Mike Cole (eds.). 2001. *Schooling and Equality. Fact, Concept and Policy.* London: Kogan Page.

Essays in books:
Jewett, Alfred E. 1987. Participant Purposes for Engaging in Physical Activity. In: *Myths, Models, and Methods in Sport Pedagogy*, ed. by George T. Barrette, 87-100. Champaign, IL: Human Kinetics

Dunn, Judy, and Jane Brown. 1991. Becoming American or English? Talking about the Social World in England and the United States. In: *Cultural Approaches to Parenting*, ed. by Marc H. Bornstein, 155-172. Hillsdale, NJ: Lawrence Erlbaum Associates.

Citations in languages other than English, French and German should include a translation of the title in parentheses, thus:

Esipov, Boris P. (ed.). 1967. *Osnovy didaktiki* [Bases of Didactics]. Moscow: Prosveshchenie.

Websites should be cited as follows:
http://www.unesco.org/education/uie/publications/uiestud8.shtml, accessed August 4, 2004.

Note that first names of authors must be included along with date and place of publication and publisher for books as well as the pagination of the essay and the full name of the editor for anthologies.

Titles, including those of journals, should not be abbreviated; subtitles should be included.

All other cases should be treated in accordance with these examples.

If there is both a list of **Notes** and a list of **References**, all bibliographical details should be included in the **References** and not repeated in the **Notes**.

Book reviews
The same rules of style and presentation apply to book reviews. Each review should be headed by the details of the book, as follows:

NASH, GARY B. 1997. *History on Trial*. New York: Alfred A. Knopf. 318 pp. ISBN 0-679-44687-7.

In length, book reviews should not exceed 800 words.

Where two or more books are reviewed together the review can be commensurately longer.

Book reviews can be in English, French or German. The books reviewed are normally in one of those languages, but books in other languages can also be considered for review on a case-by-case basis.

Offprints
Authors of essays, studies and notes will receive 50 complimentary offprints of their publication in addition to a copy of the issue of the journal in which their contribution is published. Authors of book reviews will receive a complimentary copy of the issue in which their review appears.

Intervention in School & Clinic

ADDRESS FOR SUBMISSION:

Brenda Smith Myles, Editor
Intervention in School & Clinic
University of Kansas
KU Edward Campus
Department of Education
12600 Quivira Road
Overland Park, KS 66213
USA
Phone: 913-588-5946
Fax: 913-588-5942
E-Mail: bmyles@ku.edu
Web:
Address May Change:

PUBLICATION GUIDELINES:

Manuscript Length: 11-15
Copies Required: Four
Computer Submission: N/A
Format: N/A
Fees to Review: 0.00 US$

Manuscript Style:
American Psychological Association

CIRCULATION DATA:

Reader: Academics, Practicing Teachers,
 Administrators
Frequency of Issue: 5 Times/Year
Copies per Issue: 3,001 - 4,000
Sponsor/Publisher: PRO-ED, Inc.
Subscribe Price: 39.00 US$ Individual
 114.00 US$ Institution

REVIEW INFORMATION:

Type of Review: Editorial Review
No. of External Reviewers: 3
No. of In House Reviewers: 1
Acceptance Rate: 40%
Time to Review: 2 - 3 Months
Reviewers Comments: Yes
Invited Articles: 0-5%
Fees to Publish: 0.00 US$

MANUSCRIPT TOPICS:
Behavior Disorders; Gifted Children; Learning Disabilities; Special Education

MANUSCRIPT GUIDELINES/COMMENTS:

Intervention in School and Clinic is a practitioner-oriented journal designed to provide practical, research-based ideas to those who work with students with severe learning disabilities and emotional/behavioral problems for whom typical classroom instruction is not effective. Emphasis is placed on providing information that can be easily implemented in school or clinic settings. Appropriate topics include, but are not limited to, assessment, curriculum, instructional techniques/strategies, management, social interventions, and vocational issues.

In accordance with the editorial policy of *Intervention in School and Clinic*, authors are asked to emphasize individuals and realize that exceptionality is only one attribute of the individual. Therefore, authors should "write with dignity" and use phrasing that emphasizes this relationship. References should be made to, for example, children with behavioral problems or students with learning disabilities rather than to emotionally disturbed persons or dyslexic students. Those without disabilities should be referred to as normally achieving or nondisabled rather than normal. In addition, the term general education rather than regular education should be used.

Types of Articles
Articles sought for *Intervention in School and Clinic* the following:

Feature Articles, which can vary in length from 9 to 18 manuscript pages, should discuss one technique/strategy that can be implemented in school or clinic settings. They should be written in such a manner that educators can read and apply presented information. Authors are encouraged not to write an extensive review of literature on the topic, but to overview in one to two paragraphs: (a) the need for the technique/ strategy, and (b) types of students who would benefit from the technique/strategy. The articles should include a thorough description of the topic as well as a brief overview of how to evaluate its effectiveness. Authors who wish to include references of data-based materials can list them at the end of the article. The use of reproducible items, photographs, and tables that easily illustrate article content are encouraged.

Current Topics in Review provides a brief overview of research-based topics and position papers for teachers and other educational professionals. These brief reviews are designed to encourage professionals to seek out distinct or varied ways of planning and implementing instructional programs.

An Interview With . . . provides readers with perspectives from a leader in the field of special education. The authors will discuss research, professional opinion, and other topics related to current issues and trends.

Technology Tips reviews recent software or innovative uses of technology with students with severe learning disabilities and emotional/behavioral problems. Tips typically varies in length from 3 to 5 manuscript pages.

New Products includes descriptions of recently published teaching materials or tests. These pieces are often written by field-based practitioners or authors of the products and are 3 to 5 manuscript pages in length.

Book Notes contains reviews of current books of interest to field based practitioners. Length is 3 manuscript pages.

20 Ways To. . . column is a brief listing of a number of techniques related to a specific theme. Examples of this type of column include 20 Ways to Modify a Test, 20 Ways to Do Graphic Organizers, 20 Ways to Encourage Students to Read. Each of the 20 methods should be 2 to 3 sentences in length.

Manuscript Requirements
Manuscripts must be in English (with American spelling and punctuation), and typed single-sided, double-spaced, with 1-inch margins. The manuscript must be a good final version, with

480

no handwritten changes. Hand-number pages consecutively, starting with the title page as page 1, and continuing through the last figure. The following is the appropriate order for the elements of the manuscript:

Title Page. Title of the article, complete names and affiliations of all of the authors. Short title (running head) not to exceed 50 characters. Mailing address and telephone number of the corresponding author.

Abstract. The second manuscript page should be an abstract of 100 to 125 words for empirical research and 75 to 100 words for reviews or theoretical articles.

Text. The text begins on page 3 of the Manuscript. Use headings and subheadings to organize the text clearly. Authors should not write a typical review of literature to introduce the topic; rather, in one or two brief paragraphs the authors should outline the need for the technique or strategy and types of students/teachers who would benefit from the strategy. A final summary section entitled Relevant Research may be included to list empirically based articles that have been written on the subject. Authors including copyrighted material must follow *APA* guidelines.

Biographical Statements. Names, degrees/from, current position, and brief description of scholarly interests for all authors; follow with name and address of senior author.

Author's Notes. Acknowledgments should appear on a separate page if they are included.

References. All sources cited in text must be in the reference list, and all items in the reference list must be cited in the text. Personal communication references should be cited in the text only.

Tables. Number tables with Arabic numerals. All tables must be cited in the text.

Figures. Authors are encouraged to include items that can be readily reproduced by readers. Type figure captions on a separate sheet. Photocopies of all the figures follow the figure captions. The author is responsible for supplying camera-ready art. High quality laser prints are acceptable. Photocopies are not.

Photographs. Photographs can often enhance ideas presented in articles. Only black-and-white illustrations will be considered for publication. The author is responsible for obtaining releases to publish photographs.

Manuscript Preparation
All manuscripts must be prepared according to the guidelines of the *Publication Manual of the American Psychological Association* (5th ed., 2001). Authors are now requested to send a computer disk containing the article with their manuscript after the manuscript has been accepted for publication. Certain word-processing programs are preferable: WordPerfect for PC (up to and including version 6.0) or Microsoft Word for Macintosh (up to and including version 6.0). The following are guidelines for preparing a manuscript on disk:

1. Please type all copy upper and lowercase--do not use all capitals or small capitals. You may use boldface and italics, but please use the word-processing software's italic function, not the underline key.

2. Do not put 2 spaces after any element, such as periods (e.g., only 1 space after closing punctuation for a sentence or after a colon, not 2).

3. Do not use an auto-hyphenation (machine-generated) program--allow words to wrap to the next line rather than break them.

4. Do not use lowercase "l" (el) in the place of the numeral 1 and vice versa. Do not use capital letter "O" (oh) for zero and vice versa.

5. Use a hard return at the end of paragraphs and after each element, such as title, author names), heads, etc. No hard returns at the end of lines. Never use double hard returns.

6. Indicate correct location of tables and figures in text in boldface, enclosed in angle brackets. Example: <Fig. 1 here>

7. Please use your tab key and centering function to do head alignment, paragraph indents, etc. **Do not use the space bar.** This is very important.

8. Please make manuscript printouts of this word-processing version, single-sided, and double-spaced (including references, bios, tables, etc.) to send to the editor.

Call PRO-ED Journals if you have any questions regarding disk preparations.

Permissions
Obtaining **written permissions** for material such as figures, tables, extensive quotes, clip art, screen captures, and other material taken directly—or adapted in minor ways—from another source **is the author's responsibility, as is payment of any fees the copyright holder may require**. Please be aware that material downloaded from the Internet may be copyrighted. Authors should read the entire policy on permissions. Authors should begin the request process as early as possible, because obtaining permissions may often take weeks or months.

Submission Procedures
It is understood that when an author submits a manuscript for review in *Intervention*, the author: (a) assures that the manuscript is not being considered concurrently by another journal; (b) has not published a substantial part of the article; (c) is responsible for the accuracy of all statements; (d) agrees that the editor has the right to edit the manuscript as necessary for publication; (e) will obtain permission, if appropriate, to quote and reproduce material owned by someone else; and (f) assigns all rights for the publication of the manuscript, if accepted for publication, to *Intervention in School and Clinic*.

Authors should retain one copy of the manuscript for their files. If it contains figures, the authors should submit only copies of the figures; the original figures will be requested upon publication acceptance.

Receipt of the manuscript will be acknowledged by mail. Each manuscript is initially screened by the editor for appropriateness of content and readability, as well as adherence to publication guidelines. A manuscript that meets these criteria may be sent to consulting or guest editors who are experts in the content area. When reviews are returned, the editor considers reviewers' comments and makes an editorial decision to: (a) accept as is, (b) request a revision that will be reviewed by the editor, (c) request a revision that will receive further review, or (d) reject. The author is usually notified about the status of the article within 8 to 10 weeks following submission.

The author should send four clear, easily readable copies of the manuscript to the Editor.

Issues in Teacher Education

ADDRESS FOR SUBMISSION:

Margaret Olebe, Editor
Issues in Teacher Education
California State University
  Dominguez Hills
Institute for Urban Literacy Research
1000 East Victoria Street
Carson, CA 90747
USA
Phone: 310-243-1032
Fax: 310-243-3518
E-Mail: molebe@csudh.edu
Web:
Address May Change:

PUBLICATION GUIDELINES:

Manuscript Length: 16-20
Copies Required: Four
Computer Submission: No
Format:
Fees to Review: 0.00 US$

Manuscript Style:
  American Psychological Association

CIRCULATION DATA:

Reader: Academics
Frequency of Issue: 2 Times/Year
Copies per Issue: Less than 1,000
Sponsor/Publisher: California Council on
  Teacher Education
Subscribe Price: 40.00 US$ Institution
  25.00 US$ Other
  Free to Organization Member

REVIEW INFORMATION:

Type of Review: Blind Review
No. of External Reviewers: 3
No. of In House Reviewers: 1
Acceptance Rate: 40%
Time to Review: 2 - 3 Months
Reviewers Comments: Yes
Invited Articles: 31-50%
Fees to Publish: 0.00 US$

MANUSCRIPT TOPICS:
Teacher Education

MANUSCRIPT GUIDELINES/COMMENTS:

Issues in Teacher Education is a peer-reviewed scholarly journal published twice yearly by the California Council on Teacher Education (CCTE). *ITE* publishes original manuscripts focusing on topics, concerns, and methodologies for improving the quality of teacher education broadly defined to include preservice preparation, the induction years, and the professional development of career teachers. *ITE* welcomes submissions in a variety of formats: research studies, essays, opinion papers, descriptions of exemplary programs, reports of innovations in the clinical aspects of teaching, legislative summaries, book reviews, etc. Submissions range from 500 to 5,000 words, with the average printed article around 3,000 words.

Manuscripts are received and reviewed year-round. To have a manuscript considered for publication, submit four double-spaced copies to the Editor along with one self-addressed,

484

stamped, business envelope. Manuscripts should follow style guidelines set in the most recent edition of the *Publication Manual of the American Psychological Association*. *ITE* will return manuscripts, unread, that do not meet acceptable style standards. Provide a separate cover page that includes author's name, title, institution, mail and e-mail addresses, voice and FAX numbers, a brief professional sketch (3 - 5 sentences), and a statement that the manuscript is not under consideration for publication elsewhere. Upon acceptance of a manuscript, authors will be required to submit a (revised) hard copy manuscript, an email attachment version, and/or a disk version in MS Word 6.0.1 or later for Macintosh operating system. Any graphic material should be submitted camera ready.

Send manuscripts and other editorial correspondence to:
Margaret Olebe, Editor
Issues in Teacher Education
California State University, Dominguez Hills
Institute for Urban Literacy Research
1000 East Victoria Street
Carson, CA 90747, USA
Phone: 310-243-1032; Fax: 310-243-3518; E-Mail: **molebe@csudh.edu**

Issues in Undergraduate Mathematics Preparation of School Teachers:The Journal

ADDRESS FOR SUBMISSION:

Gary A. Harris, Editor
Issues in Undergraduate Mathematics
   Preparation of School Teachers:The
   Journal
Texas Tech University
College of Arts and Sciences
Department of Mathematics
Lubbock, TX 79409
USA
Phone: 806-742-2566
Fax: 806-742-1112
E-Mail: gary.harris@ttu.edu
Web: www.k-12prep.math.ttu.edu
Address May Change:

PUBLICATION GUIDELINES:

Manuscript Length: Open
Copies Required: One
Computer Submission: Yes Email, Disk
Format: MS Word
Fees to Review: 0.00 US$

Manuscript Style:
   See Manuscript Guidelines

CIRCULATION DATA:

Reader: Academics
Frequency of Issue: Continuously
Copies per Issue: Online
Sponsor/Publisher: Department of
   Mathematics and Statistics, Texas Tech
   University
Subscribe Price:

REVIEW INFORMATION:

Type of Review: Blind Review
No. of External Reviewers: 2
No. of In House Reviewers: 0
Acceptance Rate: 50%
Time to Review: 4 - 6 Months
Reviewers Comments: Yes
Invited Articles: 0-5%
Fees to Publish: 0.00 US$

MANUSCRIPT TOPICS:
Educational Technology Systems; Higher Education; Math Preperation of Teachers; Teacher Education

MANUSCRIPT GUIDELINES/COMMENTS:

TITLE OF PAPER CENTERED
AT THE TOP
BOLD FACE, ALL CAPS, 12 PT

First Author's Name   Second Author's Name (if needed) Third Author's Name(if needed)
   Affiliation   Affiliation   Affiliation
   Address   Address   Address
E-mail Address   E-mail Address   E-mail Address

Abstract
The abstract should be single spaced, in italics, with 12 point type and should be fully justified. The abstract should contain between 50 and 100 words. It should contain key words sufficient to describe the contents of the article and attract search engines, and the abstract should be devoid of symbols if possible.

Introduction
The body of the article should be single spaced with 12 point type. As mentioned in the abstract, the article should be fully justified. Page numbers should be centered at the bottom, beginning with this page as page 1. Section headings should be centered in bold face.

The particular method of referencing bibliographical entries in the body of the article is left to the discretion of author. Two common methods are by name and date (Doe, 1997) or by name and number of the entry in the references (Doe, [3]). Whatever method used should be clear, concise, and consistent. Footnotes should not be used in the text of the paper.

Summary
These guidelines are intended to aid authors in the preparation of the final versions of the electronic manuscripts to be published in *IUMPST: The Journal*. Authors submitting manuscripts are encouraged to follow them as well.

References
(List all works sited in the article in alphabetical order according to last name of first author, or name of organization. Number each entry on the left and do not space between entries, and follow the *Chicago Style* or the *APA Style* whenever possible.)

Biographical Sketch(es)
A short biographical sketch of each author will appear at the end of each article published in *IUMPST: The Journal*. Included in these sketches should be information on the academic background, research interests, and current professional positions of each author; as well as, any other personal information the authors wish to convey.

Appropriate Submissions
IUMPST: The Journal is intended to provide a formal forum for the dissemination of the research results, insights, and ideas of professional educators and mathematicians on the wide variety of issues that pertain to the college level mathematics preparation of future K-12 teachers. To this end *IUMPST* encourages submissions in the form of high quality manuscripts. These can include research and expository articles, essays and thought pieces, or professional observations and discussions which focus specifically on issues of content and pedagogy, philosophical and practical, related to the college level mathematical preparation of future K-12 teachers.

Submission Process
To submit an article for consideration by *IUMPST: The Journal* send (preferably via e-mail) one copy of the manuscript to the journal editor:

Gary A. Harris
Department of Mathematics
College of Arts and Sciences
Texas Tech University
Lubbock, TX 79409
harris@math.ttu.edu

Include the names and affiliations of all authors, along with a 50 to 100 word abstract of the article on a separate cover page. This will contribute to the anonymity of the refereeing process.

Submission Deadlines
Manuscripts will be accepted anytime.

Refereeing Process
Submissions will be reviewed (in a blind referee format) by professional educators and mathematicians (chosen by the editors according to areas of specialization) for appropriateness of the topic, validity of the results or conclusions, general interest in the topic and adherence to generally accepted standards of good writing.

Publication Schedule
Journal articles will be published on-line as they are accepted by the editors.

Submission Formats
When an article is accepted for publication in *IUMPST: The Journal* the author(s) will be expected to provide it in final form to *The Journal* in one of the following electronic formats:
- WordPerfect® Document, Version 6.0 or later
- Microsoft® Word Document, Version 6.0 or later
- LaTeX, Version 2.09 or 2.0E (Standard style files only)
- AMS LaTeX, Version 1.2

Graphical images and photos which accompany a document need to be submitted in one of the following formats:
- Camera-ready Copy
- Encapsulated PostScript File
- Tagged Image File Format (TIF file)

Submission Style
When an article is accepted for publication in *IUMPST: The Journal* the author(s) will be expected to provide it to *The Journal* in the general style adopted by *The Journal*. While the general style for essays and book reviews is almost entirely at the discretion of the author(s); research articles, expository articles and descriptions of projects should follow the general guidelines established by *The Journal*. To aid the authors, a discussion (in the general style) of these guidelines is available.

488

Abstracts
When an article is accepted for publication in *IUMPST: The Journal* the author(s) will be expected to provide the abstract of it, in a separate file, to *The Journal* in one of the following electronic formats:
- WordPerfect® Document, Version 6.0 or later
- Microsoft® Word Document, Version 6.0 or later

Biographical Sketches
When an article is accepted for publication in *IUMPST: The Journal* the author(s) will be expected to provide brief biographical sketches of each author to *The Journal* in one of the following electronic formats:
- WordPerfect® Document, Version 6.0 or later
- Microsoft® Word Document, Version 6.0 or later

Copyright Information
The author(s) also will be expected to sign the copyright over to *IUMPST: The Journal*.

Journal for Research in Mathematics Education

ADDRESS FOR SUBMISSION:

Steven R. Williams, Editor
Journal for Research in Mathematics
    Education
Brigham Young University
Department of Mathematics Education
P.O. Box 26537
Provo, UT 84602-6537
USA
Phone: 801-422-3711
Fax: 801-422-0511
E-Mail: jrme@byu.edu
Web: www.nctm.org/jrme
Address May Change:

PUBLICATION GUIDELINES:

Manuscript Length: 30+
Copies Required: Six
Computer Submission: No
Format: N/A
Fees to Review: 0.00 US$

Manuscript Style:
    American Psychological Association

CIRCULATION DATA:

Reader: Academics, Researchers
Frequency of Issue: 5 Times/Year
Copies per Issue: 8,000
Sponsor/Publisher: National Council of
    Teachers of Mathematics
Subscribe Price:
    94.00 US$ JRME+ NCTM Membership

REVIEW INFORMATION:

Type of Review: Blind Review
No. of External Reviewers: 3+
No. of In House Reviewers: 1
Acceptance Rate: 6-10%
Time to Review: 4 - 6 Months
Reviewers Comments: Yes
Invited Articles: 0-5%
Fees to Publish: 0.00 US$

MANUSCRIPT TOPICS:

Curriculum Studies; Educational Technology Systems; Research in Mathematics Education;
Teacher Education

MANUSCRIPT GUIDELINES/COMMENTS:

The *Journal for Research in Mathematics Education*, an official journal of the National
Council of Teachers of Mathematics, is devoted to the interests of teachers of mathematics
and mathematics education at all levels—preschool through adult. The *JRME* is a forum for
disciplined inquiry into the teaching and learning of mathematics. The editors encourage the
submission of a variety of manuscripts: reports of research, including experiments, case
studies, surveys, philosophical studies, and historical studies; articles about research,
including literature reviews and theoretical analyses; brief reports of research; critiques of
articles and books; and brief commentaries on issues pertaining to research. An Index for each
volume appears in the November issue. The *JRME* is indexed in Contents Pages in Education,
Current Index to Journals in Education, Education Index, Psychological Abstracts, Social
Sciences Citation Index, and Zentralblatt für Didaktik der Mathematik.

490

Correspondence
JRME Manuscripts and editorial correspondence should be sent to Steven R. Williams, Journal for Research in Mathematics Education, Brigham Young University, Department of Mathematics Education, P.O. Box 26537, Provo, UT 84602-6537.

Review copies of books and other publications, and suggestions for books to be considered for review, should be directed to Norma C. Presmeg, Mathematics Department, 313 Stevenson Hall, Illinois State University, Normal, IL 61790-4520.

Manuscripts and inquiries regarding potential submissions to the *JRME* monograph series should be directed to Neil A. Pateman, Wist Annex 2-223, Dept. of Teacher Education and Curriculum Studies, University of Hawaii, 1776 University Ave., Honolulu, HI 96822.

Manuscripts and inquiries regarding potential submissions to the Research Commentary section of *JRME* should be directed to Jeremy Kilpatrick, 105 Aderhold Hall, University of Georgia, Athens, GA 30602-7124

All other correspondence should be addressed to the National Council of Teachers of Mathematics, 1906 Association Drive, Reston, VA 20191-9988.

Types of Manuscripts
A manuscript may be prepared as an article or for one of the *JRME* departments. A manuscript submitted to the *JRME* should not be under consideration for publication by another journal, nor should it have been published previously in a copyrighted publication, whether non-electronic or electronic.

Articles
Articles over 40 pages, not counting cover page, abstract, tables and figures will be sent out for review at the discretion of the editor. Longer manuscripts tend to have a greater publication lag.

Reports of research studies. Research reports should be tersely and clearly written. The importance and relevance of the research topic to mathematics education should be presented in the rationale or the discussion. Any analysis should be suited to the data and the research questions. Reports of many types of research are encouraged, including experiments, case studies, surveys, philosophical investigations, and historical studies.

Articles about research. The journal welcomes literature reviews and syntheses of research in an area, as well as theoretical analyses of research.

Departments
Brief reports. A brief report of a study is especially appropriate when a fuller report is available elsewhere or when a more comprehensive follow-up study is planned. A brief report of a first study on some topic might stress the rationale, hypotheses, and plans for further work. A brief report of a replication or extension of a previously reported study might contrast the results of the two studies, referring to the earlier study for methodological details. A brief

report of a monograph or other lengthy nonjournal publication might summarize the key findings and implications or might highlight an unusual observation or methodological approach. Under some circumstances brief reports may be recommended after a longer manuscript has been reviewed.

A brief report should not exceed six manuscript pages. If source materials are needed in order to evaluate a brief report manuscript, six copies of such material should be provided along with six copies of the manuscript. Brief reports have a shorter publication lag than articles.

Critiques of articles. Constructive critiques are invited that respond to articles that have appeared in the *JRME* or other research journals. Critiques should stimulate discussions and present ideas. They should initiate a potential dialogue in print through thoughtful criticism and a presentation of alternatives.

A critique should not exceed six manuscript pages. When a critique is accepted for publication, the editor will send a copy to the author of the original article along with an invitation to respond within a specified period of time. Whenever possible, the critique and the response will be published in the same issue.

Research commentary. The Editorial Board of the *JRME* is committed to the continual appraisal of the nature, scope, and function of research as it applies to the teaching and learning of mathematics, policy, and decision making. Accordingly, the board invites brief analyses, critiques, or proposals pertaining to the character of research in the field of mathematics education. Such papers will be considered for publication in the "Research Commentary" department of the journal.

To be considered for the Research Commentary department, a manuscript should provide a clear, logical presentation of a position developed from an explicit rationale. An argument should be substantiated by data or illustrations when they are appropriate. Topics for this section may include, but are not restricted to: commentaries on research; discussions of the connections between research, policy, and practice; scholarly analyses of policy trends related to mathematics education, (e.g. research funding, national policies); commentaries on the relationship between research and evaluation; extended reviews of books with critical commentary; and scholarly debates among proponents of differing views. Research commentary articles will be peer reviewed and should generally be 8-12 (not to exceed 20) manuscript pages in length.

Manuscripts and inquiries regarding potential submissions to the Research Commentary section of *JRME* should be directed to Jeremy Kilpatrick, 105 Aderhold Hall, University of Georgia, Athens, GA 30602-7124

Reviews. The review editor welcomes suggestions for material to be reviewed and for prospective reviewers. Analytic reviews of selected scholarly publications that have been received for review are solicited by the review editor, who also assembles telegraphic reviews. Review copies of books and other publications, and suggestions for books to be considered for review, should be directed to Norma C. Presmeg, Mathematics Department, 313 Stevenson Hall, Illinois State University, Normal, IL 61790-4520.

Letter to the editor. This department welcomes responsible comment on issues of potential interest to the readers of the journal. Letters to the editor are not evaluated by reviewers and are published at the discretion of the editor.

Preparation of Manuscripts

Except for reviews and letters to the editor, six copies of the manuscript should be submitted. One copy will be retained in the *JRME* files regardless of the action taken on the paper. Manuscripts should conform to the conventions specified in the *Publication Manual of the American Psychological Association* (5th ed., 2001). This publication is available from the American Psychological Association, 750 First Street, NE, Washington, DC 20002.

Manuscripts should be typed double-spaced on one side of plain paper, with wide margins to allow for editorial commentary. Use as a model the sample paper included on pages 306-320 of the *Publication Manual*. Give particular attention to the content and format illustrated on page 306 for the cover sheet, abstract, and first sheet of actual manuscript text. Also note the use of a running head on subsequent manuscript pages. If the manuscript is based on dissertation research, a funded research project, or a paper presented at the professional meeting, a footnote on the cover sheet should provide the relevant facts, including the director of the dissertation or the organization sponsoring the project. The numbered pages of a manuscript submitted as a feature article should begin with an abstract of about 100 words on a separate sheet. Manuscripts submitted as brief reports, critiques, forum articles and reviews do not require abstracts.

Prior to printing out the final copies for submission, authors should submit five blinded copies by (a) substituting "Author (date)" in place of all references in the text to their authored or coauthored publications related to the topic of the current paper and (b) deleting those same references from the reference list. Authors should also submit one unblinded copy together with the five-blinded copies.

Authors must accept sole responsibility for the factual accuracy of their contributions and for obtaining permission to quote lengthy excerpts from copyrighted sources. All figures submitted must be camera ready.

Processing of Manuscripts

When a manuscript arrives at the *JRME* editorial office, the editor checks to see if it falls within the journal's domain of interests and meets the journal's technical and stylistic requirements. If the manuscript is not appropriate for *JRME*, it is returned to the author without further consideration. If the manuscript falls within the journal's domain but does not meet its technical or stylistic requirements, the manuscript is returned to the author for revision before processing will continue. The reviewing process is greatly facilitated when manuscripts are submitted in proper form.

If a manuscript is deemed eligible for review and evaluation, the editor sends the author notification that the manuscript has been received and is being processed for review, and requests an evaluation from at least three reviewers (of whom at least one is a member of the

JRME Editorial Board). Reviewers are chosen for their scholarship and expertise relative to various aspects of the paper.

When the reviewers' evaluations have been received, the editor notifies the author of the decision--
1. to accept the manuscript for *JRME* publication, often pending some revision by the author or editor;
2. to reconsider the manuscript following substantial revision by the author and further evaluation by reviewers; or
3. to reject the manuscript.

The editor communicates the decision to the author, including suggestions for a revision or an indication of the reasons for a rejection. If the manuscript has been accepted, we request that a disk be submitted with the final revision.

The *JRME* editorial office attempts to process manuscripts expeditiously. The goal is to complete the reviewing process within three months. Occasionally a longer time is required.

After the manuscript has been accepted for publication, various factors contribute to determining the issue in which it will appear: manuscript backlog, lead time for production (copy editing and printing), manuscript length, and other considerations pertaining to the content and makeup of particular *JRME* issues. Manuscripts are not necessarily published in the order in which they are received or accepted.

Assignment of copyright for the article to the National Council of Teachers of Mathematics is required as a condition of publication. After acceptance by the *JRME*, a manuscript may not be published elsewhere without written permission from NCTM. Each author of a paper published in the *JRME* will receive five complimentary copies of the issue in which the paper appears.

Monograph Series
The *JRME* monograph series is published by the Editorial Board as a supplement to the journal for manuscripts in the range of about 200 pages. Each monograph has a single theme related to the learning or teaching of mathematics. To be considered for publication, a manuscript should be (a) a single treatise that examines a major research issue, (b) a report of a single research study that is too lengthy to be published as a journal article, (c) a report of a series of coordinated studies, or (d) a synthesis of a large body of research.

Procedure for Submission of Monograph Series Manuscripts
Any person(s) wishing to submit a manuscript for consideration as a monograph should send four copies of the complete manuscript to the monograph series editor. The name and affiliation of each contributing author should be included with the manuscript. Manuscripts may be sent at any time and should conform to the conventions specified in the *Publication Manual of the American Psychological Association* (5th ed. 2001). Any other information about the nature of the monograph that might assist the series editor with the review process is welcome.

494

Processing of Manuscripts
The procedures followed for processing and reviewing a manuscript submitted for consideration as a monograph are essentially the same as for the journal. Because of the length of monograph manuscripts, the reviewing process may take up to six months.

Manuscripts and inquiries regarding potential submissions to the *JRME* monograph series should be directed to Neil A. Pateman, Wist Annex 2-223, Dept. of Teacher Education and Curriculum Studies, University of Hawaii, 1776 University Ave., Honolulu, HI 96822.

References
American Psychological Association. (2001).
Publication Manual of the American Psychological Association (4th ed.). Washington, D.C.: Author.

JRME Editorial Board. (1970). Call for research manuscripts, including general guidelines, Journal for Research in Mathematics Education, 1, 61-62.

JRME Editorial Board. (1976). Revised information for contributors to the Journal for Research in Mathematics Education. Journal for Research in Mathematics Education, 3-7.

JRME Editorial Board. (1979). Information for contributors to the Journal for Research in Mathematics Education. Journal for Research in Mathematics Education, 10, 3-6.

Journal for the Education of the Gifted (The)

ADDRESS FOR SUBMISSION:

Laurence J. Coleman, Editor
Journal for the Education of the Gifted
(The)
University of Toledo
College of Education
Mail Stop 954
2801 W. Bancroft Steet
Toledo, OH 43606-3390
USA
Phone: 419-530-2626
Fax:
E-Mail: laurence.coleman@utoledo.edu
Web: www.prufrock.com/mag_jeg.html
Address May Change:

PUBLICATION GUIDELINES:

Manuscript Length: 26-30
Copies Required: Five
Computer Submission: No
Format: N/A
Fees to Review: 0.00 US$

Manuscript Style:
American Psychological Association

CIRCULATION DATA:

Reader: Academics
Frequency of Issue: Quarterly
Copies per Issue: 2,001 - 3,000
Sponsor/Publisher: Assn. for the Gifted,
Division of the Council for Exceptional
Children / Prufrock Press
Subscribe Price: 44.00 US$ Individual
60.00 US$ Institution
54.00 US$ & $70.00 Foreign

REVIEW INFORMATION:

Type of Review: Blind Review
No. of External Reviewers: 3
No. of In House Reviewers: 1
Acceptance Rate: 11-21%
Time to Review: 2 - 3 Months
Reviewers Comments: Yes
Invited Articles: 0-10%
Fees to Publish: 0.00 US$

MANUSCRIPT TOPICS:

Curriculum Studies; Educational Psychology; Gifted Children; Policy; Special Education;
Teaching

MANUSCRIPT GUIDELINES/COMMENTS:

Policy Statement

The Journal for the Education of the Gifted is the official journal of *The Association for the Gifted, a Division of the Council for Exceptional Children.* Its major purpose is communication of information about the needs of gifted and talented children. The *Journal* also serves as a forum for the exchange of diverse ideas and points of views on the education of the gifted arid talented.

Articles than demonstrate a high degree of critical analysis in their treatment of salient themes relating to gifted and talented individuals will be given *priority*. The publication includes

496

theoretical, descriptive, and research articles. The *Journal* solicits articles in the following categories.

- Original research with practical relevance to the education for gifted and talented individuals;
- Theoretical position papers;
- Descriptions of innovative programming and instructional practices for gifted and talented individuals based on existing or novel models of gifted education;
- Reviews of the literature in areas pertinent to the education of gifted and talented individuals; and
- Historical perspectives.

The Journal strives to reach parents as well as educators with a balanced presentation of theory and practice that addresses the unique psychological and educational needs of gifted, talented, and creative people.

Preparation of Copy
Manuscripts are evaluated by referees. To permit anonymity, attach a cover page giving authorship and institutional affiliation but provide only the title as a running head. Submit FIVE COPIES. To prepare a manuscript, type double-spaced on white standard bond paper; insert a location note of any tables at the appropriate place in the text; prepare Camera-ready figures and tables whenever possible. Include an abstract of 100-150 words. For information regarding citations, please sec the *Publication Manual, American Psychological Association,* Fifth Edition. Manuscripts arc accepted subject to editing. Upon final acceptance, submit a computer diskette containing the corrected manuscript and all tables.

The Journal of the Education of the Gifted welcomes manuscripts for consideration for publication. Please submit to:

Laurence J. Coleman, Editor
Journal for the Education of the Gifted
The University of Toledo
College of Education
Mail Stop 954
2801 W. Bancroft St.
Toledo, OH 43606-3390

Currently abstracted in: *The Psychological Abstracts, Current index to Journals in Education, Exceptional Child Education Resources, Educational Administration Abstracts, Child Development Abstracts and Bibliography, Social Sciences Citation Index® (SSCI ®),* and *Research Alert.*™

Journal of Academic Librarianship

ADDRESS FOR SUBMISSION:

David Kohl, Editor
Journal of Academic Librarianship
2929 Courtropes Lane
Cincinnati, OH 45244
USA
Phone:
Fax:
E-Mail: david.kohl@uc.edu
Web:
Address May Change:

PUBLICATION GUIDELINES:

Manuscript Length: 16-25
Copies Required: Four
Computer Submission: Yes
Format: N/A
Fees to Review: 0.00 US$

Manuscript Style:
    Chicago Manual of Style

CIRCULATION DATA:

Reader: , See 'Audience' in Guidelines
Frequency of Issue: Bi-Monthly
Copies per Issue:
Sponsor/Publisher: Elsevier Science
    Publishing Co
Subscribe Price: 105.00 US$ Individual
    266.00 US$ Institution

REVIEW INFORMATION:

Type of Review: Blind Review
No. of External Reviewers: 2
No. of In House Reviewers: 1
Acceptance Rate: 40-45%
Time to Review: 4 Weeks
Reviewers Comments: Yes
Invited Articles: 1% Maximum
Fees to Publish: 0.00 US$

MANUSCRIPT TOPICS:
Library Science/Information Resources; Management

MANUSCRIPT GUIDELINES/COMMENTS:

Description
The *Journal of Academic Librarianship*, an international and refereed journal, publishes articles that focus on problems and issues germane to college and university libraries. *JAL* provides a forum for authors to present research findings and, where applicable, their practical applications and significance; analyze policies, practices, issues, and trends; speculate about the future of academic librarianship; present analytical bibliographic essays and philosophical treatises. *JAL* also brings to the attention of its readers information about hundreds of new and recently published books in library and information science, management, scholarly communication, and higher education. *JAL*, in addition, covers management and discipline-based software and information policy developments.

Audience
College and University Librarians, Academic Administrators, Educators and Students in programs of library and information science, and others interested in academic librarianship.

498

GUIDE FOR AUTHORS

Correspondence
Although both print and electronic submissions are accepted, electronic submission as a Word attachment to an e-mail to the editor is preferred. E-mail submission should be sent to the editor at **david.kohl@uc.edu**.

If you would rather submit hard copies, please send four copies (three blind copies and one original) to:
David Kohl
2929 Courtropes Lane
Cincinnati, OH 45244, USA

Receipt of all manuscripts will be acknowledged. Unaccepted manuscripts will be returned; please enclose a self-addressed envelope with ample postage.

Papers must be neither previously published nor submitted elsewhere simultaneously. Manuscripts are evaluated using a **double blind-reviewing process**. On completion of this process, usually within 4-6 weeks, authors will be notified of the decision. To determine whether a manuscript fits within *JAL' s* scope of interest, consult recent issues for content. Write in a style that is clear and concise, and use references only when they are required. Copies of speeches are rarely accepted unless they are rewritten for publication.

Upon acceptance of an article, authors will be asked to transfer copyright (for more information on copyright, see http://authors.elsevier.com). This transfer will ensure the widest possible dissemination of information. A letter will be sent to the corresponding author confirming receipt of the manuscript. A form facilitating transfer of copyright will be provided after acceptance.

If material from other copyrighted works is included, the author(s) must obtain written permission from the copyright owners and credit the source(s) in the article. Elsevier has preprinted forms for use by authors in these cases: contact Elsevier Global Rights Department, P.O. Box 800, Oxford OX5 1DX, UK; phone: (+44) 1865 843830, fax: (+44) 1865 853333, e-mail: **permissions@elsevier.com**.

Preparation of Manuscripts
All manuscripts must be word processed (double-spaced) on one side only and numbered consecutively, including references at the end and an **abstract of no more than 50 words** (highlighting the scope, methodology, and conclusions of the paper) at the beginning. The author's full name, affiliation, and, when applicable, e-mail address should appear on the title page. Headings and subheadings should be included to make the paper more readable. Standard United States spelling will be used throughout. All acronyms and abbreviations should be spelled out when first used in the text.

Tables, figures, and illustrations should accompany the manuscript on separate sheets. Captions should clearly identify all separate matter. Each table, figure, illustration, and photograph should be numbered in sequence, using Arabic numerals in order of its mention.

All tables, etc., should be gathered together at the end of the manuscript. If, together with your accepted article, you submit usable color figures, then Elsevier will ensure, at no additional charge, that these figures will appear in color on the Web (e.g., ScienceDirect and other sites) regardless of whether these illustrations are reproduced in color in the printed version. For color reproduction in print, you will receive information regarding the costs from Elsevier after receipt of your accepted article. For further information on the preparation of electronic artwork, please see **http://authors.elsevier.com/artwork.**

Please note: Because of technical complications that can arise in converting color figures to "gray scale" (for the printed version should you not opt for color in print), please submit in addition usable black-and-white files corresponding to all the color illustrations.

References
References should be double-spaced at the end of the text. JAL follows the 15th edition of the Manual of Style, published by the University of Chicago Press. For journal articles, include the issue number only when issues within a journal volume are not consecutively numbered. Examples of the correct format for references are:

Article from a Journal. Paul Metz, "Thirteen Steps to Avoiding Bad Luck in a Serials Cancellation Project," *Journal of Academic Librarianship* 18 (May 1992): 76-82.

Ibid. Ibid., pp. 77-81.

Book. Charles T. Meadow, *Text Information Retrieval Systems* (San Diego, CA: Academic Press, 1992), p. 177.

Articles from a Book. Joe E. Hewitt, "The Role of the Library Administrator in Improving LIS Research," in *Library and Information Science Research*, edited by Charles R. McClure & Peter Hernon (Norwood, NJ: Ablex, 1991), pp. 163-178.

Web Sources. Thomas J. Pritzker, An Early Fragment from Central Nepal. Online. Ingress Communications. (N.D.) Available: http://www.ingress.com/~astanart/pritzker/pritzker.html (June 8, 1995). (For other examples, see Electronic Sources: MLA Style of Citation. Available: http://www.uvm.edu/~xli/reference/mla.html.)

Shortened Reference. Metz, "Thirteen Steps," p. 78.

Provision of Disks
Upon acceptance of the paper, authors should supply the editor with an electronic version of the paper, in an IBM-compatible format preferably in Word or WordPerfect 8 or under, with text files stripped of all embedded graphics. Use only required hyphenation: do not use discretionary hyphens, and do not break words at the end of lines. Save graphics as an .eps or .tiff file. Graphics include complex equations, graphs, and line drawings. Tables should be in separate files.

Publication
The lead author will receive PDF proofs for final inspection before publication. Changes on page proofs are expensive; aside from errors made during production, changes will be billed to the author. The lead author receives 25 free offprints.

Guidelines for Book Reviews
Our audience expects JAL book reviews to be based on a thorough, careful reading, and on informed judgment. There can be no single model for all reviews, but an ideal review should include the essential elements in a statement that reflects both the reviewer's way of thinking and the character of the book. The following guidelines are offered to help our reviewers and to inform our readers about editorial policy.

Basic Requirements
JAL book reviews should be addressed to library professionals--those interested in keeping abreast of the literature and/or involved in book selection. Within 250-300 (2 double-spaced pages), unless the editor authorizes a longer review, the reviewer should provide a brief description of the contents or statement of the thesis, critically appraise both the substance and the execution, indicate the book's value for a collection, and make a personal recommendation. The reviewer's full name, affiliation, and mailing and e-mail addresses should appear following the review. In addition to the paper copy, either a disk or an electronic submission (**david.kohl@uc.edu**) or (**ZLATOS@WSUVM1.CSC.WSU.EDU**) would be appreciated.

Reviews should be written within 2-4 weeks after receipt of the book. If reviewers do not receive the book shortly after having agreed to review it, they should contact either Book Review Editor.

Points to Remember
Because library budgets are tight, the review should compare the new title with one or two alternatives. If little else is available on the topic, that should also be noted. The importance of the topic itself and the level of its treatment should be noted, if it is not self-evident. If the book makes a significant contribution to the professional literature, that should be clearly noted. Objectivity is essential. Note any bias in an essentially nonpolemical work, but resist becoming embroiled in parochial academic debate.

Accuracy
Pay special attention to accuracy in the reviews. Quoted passages should be checked against the text; names and dates should be verified; in reference to other authors and titles, give the author's name in full and the title exactly, as well as the publisher and date.

Statements made about the book (e.g., that it is full of errors) should be supported by examples. We expect reviewers to check the "facts" from the publisher's blurb or the book jacket (e.g., that it is "the most comprehensive to date") before using them.

Editorial Policy
When necessary, reviews are condensed or reorganized and editorial changes are made to conform to house style, but the reviewer's essential opinion is preserved. We do reserve the right to reject a review, if necessary.

We ask that our contributors not review for any other publication the book they review for *JAL*. Reviewers should not send copies of reviews to publishers or authors.

Format
The book's citation should include the full name of the work; author/editor; city of publication; publisher and year; pagination; price; and ISBN, ISSN (if available), and LC numbers. Please double-space citations.

Opportunity to Serve as a Reviewer
Anyone interested in serving as a book reviewer should send a letter of intent, a sample of his/her writing, and areas of interest to the Editor-in-Chief at 2929 Courtropes Lane, Cincinnati, OH 45244, USA; or Christy Zlatos, Washington State University, Holland Library, Pullman, WA 99164-5610, USA.

Journal of Access Services

ADDRESS FOR SUBMISSION:

Lori Driscoll, Editor
Journal of Access Services
University of Florida in Gainesville
George A Smathers Libraries
P O Box 117001
Gainesville, FL 32611-7001
USA
Phone: 352-392-4714
Fax: 352-392-4507
E-Mail: ldriscoll@uflib.ufl.edu
Web: www.haworthpressinc.com/web/JAS/
Address May Change:

PUBLICATION GUIDELINES:

Manuscript Length: 15-50
Copies Required: Four
Computer Submission: Yes Email, Disk
Format:
Fees to Review: 0.00 US$

Manuscript Style:
      Chicago Manual of Style

CIRCULATION DATA:

Reader: Academics, Librarians
Frequency of Issue: Quarterly
Copies per Issue: 1,001 - 2,000
Sponsor/Publisher: Haworth Press, Inc.
Subscribe Price: 45.00 US$ Individual
      150.00 US$ Institution

REVIEW INFORMATION:

Type of Review: Blind Review
No. of External Reviewers: 2
No. of In House Reviewers: 1
Acceptance Rate: No Reply
Time to Review: 2 - 3 Months
Reviewers Comments: Yes
Invited Articles: 31-50%
Fees to Publish: 0.00 US$

MANUSCRIPT TOPICS:
Information Science; Library Science/Information Resources

MANUSCRIPT GUIDELINES/COMMENTS:

About the Journal
"*Access*" is perhaps the most dynamic and powerful word in librarianship today. While it refers first to the policies and conditions that govern the use of library collections, services, and facilities, the access concept also describes how, through interlibrary loan and document delivery, library users can obtain materials from a broader universe of information resources. Over the last decade, collection management librarians have developed entirely new models based upon the primary goal of providing access to resources as a more cost-effective alternative to purchasing them. Technology has also affected the means by which access is gained. Many of these services are unmediated and customized. Administratively, these and many other concerns have increasingly resulted in the creation of an emerging organizational unit called "Access Services."

The literature on this aspect of librarianship has not yet caught up with current practice, so The Haworth Press is now launching the *Journal of Access Services*--the first to cover this field--to fill the gap.

An essential guide to the basic business of providing library users with access to information, the *Journal of Access Services* is a one-of-a-kind resource that helps librarians stay up to date on continuing education and professional development in this complex and evolving field. This peer-reviewed quarterly journal was the first to examine the policies and conditions that govern the use of library collections, services, and facilities. And as collection management librarians develop new models of providing access to materials as a more cost-effective alternative to purchasing them, the journal keeps pace with the changing theories and practices of interlibrary loan and document delivery. The journal includes substantive essays, articles, reviews, feature columns, conference reports, and research results that explore the dimensions of this expanding field of librarianship.

Topics addressed in the Journal of Access Services include:
- circulation and reserves services
- interlibrary loan, document delivery, and remote access
- technological frontiers of access services
- resource sharing and networking
- library building design, maintenance, renovation, and construction
- managing and operating library remote storage facilities
- statistical analyses and measurements of library effectiveness
- access/ownership and collection management
- organization and administration of access services departments
- training, education, and development of access services staff
- copyright, licensing, and legal aspects of electronic access
- cost analyses and the economics of access services

Instructions for Authors

1. **Original Articles Only**. Submission of a manuscript to this journal represents a certification on the part of the author(s) that it is an original work, and that neither this manuscript nor a version of it has been published elsewhere nor is being considered for publication elsewhere.

2. **Manuscript Length**. Your manuscript may be approximately **5–50** typed pages double-spaced (including references and abstract). Lengthier manuscripts may be considered, but only at the discretion of the editor. Sometimes, lengthier manuscripts may be considered if they can be divided up into sections for publication in successive journal issues.

3. **Manuscript Style**. References, citations, and general style of manuscripts for this Journal should follow the Chicago style (as outlined in the latest edition of the *Chicago Manual of Style*). References should be double-spaced and placed in alphabetical order. The use of footnotes within the text is discouraged. Words should be underlined only when it is intended that they be typeset in italics.

If an author wishes to submit a paper that has been already prepared in another style, he or she may do so. However, if the paper is accepted (with or without reviewer's alterations), the author is fully responsible for retyping the manuscript in the correct style as indicated above. Neither the editor nor the publisher is responsible for re-preparing manuscript copy to adhere to the journal's style.

4. Manuscript Preparation.
Margins. Leave at least a one-inch margin on all four sides.
Paper. Use clean, white 8-1/2" x 11" bond paper.
Number of copies. 4 (the original plus three photocopies).
Cover page. *Important*—staple a cover page to the manuscript, indicating only the article title (this is used for anonymous refereeing).
Second "title page". Enclose a regular title page but do not staple it to the manuscript. Include the title again, plus:

- full authorship
- an ABSTRACT of about 100 words. (Below the abstract provide 3–10 key words for index purposes).
- a header or footer on each page with abbreviated title and pg number of total (e.g., pg 2 of 7)
- an introductory footnote with authors' academic degrees, professional titles, affiliations, mailing and e-mail addresses, and any desired acknowledgment of research support or other credit.

5. Reference Linking.
The Haworth Press is participating in reference linking for journal articles. (For more information on reference linking initiatives, please consult the CrossRef Web site at www.crossref.org.) When citing a journal article include the article's Digital Object Identifier (DOI), when available, as the last item in the reference. A Digital Object Identifier is a persistent, authoritative, and unique identifier that a publisher assigns to each article. Because of its persistence, DOIs will enable The Haworth Press and other publishers to link to the article referenced, and the link will not break over time. This will be a great resource in scholarly research.

An example of a reference to a journal article which includes a DOI:
Vizine-Goetz, Diane (2002).
Classification Schemes for Internet Resources Revisited.
Journal of Internet Cataloging 5(4): 5:18. doi: 10.1300/J141v05n04_02

6. Return Envelopes.
When you submit your four manuscript copies, also include:

- a 9" x 12" envelope, self-addressed and stamped (with sufficient postage to ensure return of your manuscript);
- a regular envelope, stamped and self-addressed. This is for the Editor to send you an "acknowledgement of receipt" letter.

7. Spelling, Grammar, and Punctuation.
You are responsible for preparing manuscript copy which is clearly written in acceptable, scholarly English and which contains no errors of spelling, grammar, or punctuation. Neither the editor nor the publisher is responsible for

correcting errors of spelling and grammar. The manuscript, after acceptance by the editor, must be immediately ready for typesetting as it is finally submitted by the author(s). Check your paper for the following common errors:

- dangling modifiers
- misplaced modifiers
- unclear antecedents
- incorrect or inconsistent abbreviations

Also, check the accuracy of all arithmetic calculations, statistics, numerical data, text citations, and references.

8. **Inconsistencies Must Be Avoided.** Be sure you are consistent in your use of abbreviations, terminology, and in citing references, from one part of your paper to another.

9. **Preparation of Tables, Figures, and Illustrations.** Any material that is not textual is considered artwork. This includes tables, figures, diagrams, charts, graphs, illustrations, appendices, screen captures, and photos. Tables and figures (including legend, notes, and sources) should be no larger than 4 ½ x 6 ½ inches. Type styles should be Helvetica (or Helvetica narrow if necessary) and no smaller than 8 point. We request that computer-generated figures be in black and white and/or shades of gray (preferably no color, for it does not reproduce well). Camera-ready art must contain no grammatical, typographical, or format errors and must reproduce sharply and clearly in the dimensions of the final printed page (4 ½ x 6 ½ inches). Photos and screen captures must be on disk as a TIFF file, or other graphic file format such as JPEG or BMP. For rapid publication we must receive black-and-white glossy or matte positives (white background with black images and/or wording) in addition to files on disk. Tables should be created in the text document file using the software's Table feature.

10. **Submitting Art.** Both a printed hard copy and a disk copy of the art must be provided. We request that each piece of art be sent in its own file, on a disk separate from the disk containing the manuscript text file(s), and be clearly labeled. We reserve the right to (if necessary) request new art, alter art, or if all else has failed in achieving art that is presentable, delete art. If submitted art cannot be used, the publisher reserves the right to redo the art and to change the author for a fee of $55.00 per hour for this service. The Haworth Press, Inc. is not responsible for errors incurred in the preparation of new artwork. Camera-ready artwork must be prepared on separate sheets of paper. Always use black ink and professional drawing instruments. On the back of these items, write your article title and the journal title lightly in soft-lead pencil (please do not write on the face of art). In the text file, skip extra lines and indicate where these figures are placed. Photos are considered part of the acceptable manuscript and remain with the publisher for use in additional printings.

11. **Electronic Media.** Haworth's in-house typesetting unit is able to utilize your final manuscript material as prepared on most personal computers and word processors. This will minimize typographical errors and decrease overall production time. Please send the first draft and final draft copies of your manuscript to the journal editor in print format for his/her final review and approval. After approval of your final manuscript, please submit the final approved version both on printed format ("hard copy") and floppy diskette. On the outside of the diskette package write:

1) the brand name of your computer or word processor
2) the word processing program and version that you used
3) the title of your article, and
4) the file name.

Note: Disk and hard copy must agree. In case of discrepancies, it is The Haworth Press' policy to follow hard copy. Authors are advised that no revisions of the manuscript can be made after acceptance by the editor for publication. The benefits of this procedure are many with speed and accuracy being the most obvious. We look forward to working with your electronic submission which will allow us to serve you more efficiently.

12. **Alterations Required By Referees and Reviewers**. Many times a paper is accepted by the editor contingent upon changes that are mandated by anonymous specialist referees and members of the editorial board. If the editor returns your manuscript for revisions, you are responsible for retyping any sections of the paper to incorporate these revisions (if applicable, revisions should also be put on disk).

13. **Typesetting**. You will not be receiving galley proofs of your article. Editorial revisions, if any, must therefore be made while your article is still in manuscript. The final version of the manuscript will be the version you see published. Typesetter's errors will be corrected by the production staff of The Haworth Press. Authors are expected to submit manuscripts, disks, and art that are free from error.

14. **Reprints**. The senior author will receive two copies of the journal issue as well as complimentary reprints of his or her article. The junior author will receive two copies of the journal issue. These are sent several weeks after the journal issue is published and in circulation. An order form for the purchase of additional reprints will also be sent to all authors at this time. (Approximately 8 weeks is necessary for the preparation of reprints.) Please do not query the journal's editor about reprints. All such questions should be sent directly to The Haworth Press, Inc., Production Department, 37 West Broad Street, West Hazleton, PA 18202. To order additional reprints (minimum: 50 copies), please contact The Haworth Document Delivery Center, 10 Alice Street, Binghamton, NY 13904–1580; 1–800–342–9678 or Fax (607) 722–6362.

15. **Copyright**. Copyright ownership of your manuscript must be transferred officially to The Haworth Press, Inc. before we can begin the peer-review process. The editor's letter acknowledging receipt of the manuscript will be accompanied by a form fully explaining this. All authors must sign the form and return the original to the editor as soon as possible. Failure to return the copyright form in a timely fashion will result in a delay in review and subsequent publication.

Journal of Adolescent & Adult Literacy

ADDRESS FOR SUBMISSION:

F. Todd Goodson, Editor
Journal of Adolescent & Adult Literacy
International Reading Association
PO Box 8139
Newark, DE 19714
USA
Phone: 302-731-1600
Fax: 302-368-2449
E-Mail: tgoodson@ksu.edu
Web: www.reading.org
Address May Change:

PUBLICATION GUIDELINES:

Manuscript Length: 6-25 dbl-spaced
Copies Required: Two
Computer Submission: Yes
Format: No Reply
Fees to Review: 0.00 US$

Manuscript Style:
    American Psychological Association

CIRCULATION DATA:

Reader: Practicing Teachers, At Jr. High,
    High School or Above
Frequency of Issue: 8 Times/Year
Copies per Issue: 15,000+
Sponsor/Publisher: International Reading
    Association
Subscribe Price: 61.00 US$ Individual
    122.00 US$ Institution

REVIEW INFORMATION:

Type of Review: Blind Review
No. of External Reviewers: 3
No. of In House Reviewers: 0
Acceptance Rate: 11-20%
Time to Review: 3 Months
Reviewers Comments: Yes
Invited Articles: 0-5%
Fees to Publish: 0.00 US$

MANUSCRIPT TOPICS:

Adult Career & Vocational; Art/Music; Bilingual/E.S.L.; Curriculum Studies; English Literature; Foreign Language; Gifted Children; Health & Physical Education; Higher Education; Languages & Linguistics; Literacy Among Adolescents and Adults; Reading; Secondary/Adolescent Studies; Special Education; Teacher Education; Tests, Measurement & Evaluation

MANUSCRIPT GUIDELINES/COMMENTS:

About This Journal

The *Journal of Adolescent & Adult Literacy* is a peer reviewed (refereed) journal published 8 times a year; September through May with a December/January combined issue, as a service to members of the International Reading Association. It is intended as an open forum for the field of reading education, with the goal of encouraging effective instruction by interpreting the results of research and practice for a broad audience of reading professionals.

Authors should note that *JAAL* carries material pertaining to learners of middle school age and above (adolescents and adults) whether in or out of school. Articles may deal with theory, practice, research, or trends in the field, keeping in view the concerns of teachers and scholars whose interests include classroom instruction as well as reading outside the school.

Audience
JAAL goes to 15,000 IRA members in 90 countries, with roughly 95% located in Canada and the United States. About 75% of the individuals currently receiving the journal are school-based professionals (teachers, reading specialists, supervisors/coordinators, and other administrators); 20% are college or university faculty.

Most of these individuals have taught 10 or more years, hold at least one graduate degree (master's or above), and are educators interested in middle school through adult years. *JAAL* also reaches teachers and university students through institutional libraries.

Article and Format Style
JAAL welcomes practical, theoretical, and research articles of 1,000-6,000 words (6-25 double-spaced pages, including tables and reference list).

The ideal article has a clearly defined topic dealt with in some depth and is written in a straightforward style calculated to appeal to a wide audience in a variety of countries. Research studies should be treated as articles rather than as formal reports--avoid dissertation format, incorporate necessary statistics in the text, and include a minimum of tabular material.

Avoiding Bias
Avoid stereotyping on the basis of sex, race, age, etc. When providing examples, use students of both sexes and vary the ethnicity of names. Employ terms with no gender reference (such as mail carrier rather than mailman). As alternatives for the so called neutral pronouns he, his, him, pluralize the antecedent, recast the phrase to avoid use of pronouns, or use s/he and her/him.

Questions of Copyright
The concept of "fair use" or "fair dealing" in use of copyrighted material includes the right to quote briefly for scholarly purposes from most published materials. However, if you wish to include items from published tests or use longer quotations, especially parts of an original work like a poem or short story, you must obtain written permission from the author or publisher to reprint the material.

Style Manual
For specifics on style, especially citations and a list of References, follow the *Publication Manual of the American Psychological Association*, 5th edition (2001).

Note: *JAAL* uses no footnotes; weave all information into the text.

Include one or two tables or figures if they simplify and clarify the presentation. Type each table double spaced on a separate sheet and place it at the end of the manuscript.

Submitting the Manuscript

JAAL reviews only original articles that would be of interest to professionals in the field of reading. It does not review articles that have been published or are under consideration elsewhere. (No duplicate submissions, please.)

See our website **www.reading.org** for submission requirements.

Review Process

Material submitted to *JAAL* is reviewed anonymously (blind review) by two or more professionals in the field of reading unless the item is clearly inappropriate because of length, style, topic, or age of learner being discussed. Material that would be appropriate for a different IRA journal will be forwarded to the appropriate editor unless authors specify otherwise. Authors are generally notified of a decision within 3 months after receipt. Articles are judged primarily for their contribution to the field, usefulness to teachers or researchers, timeliness, freshness of approach, and clarity and cohesiveness of presentation. Selection also depends on editorial determination of overall balance of content in the journal.

Journal of Adult Education

ADDRESS FOR SUBMISSION:

Andy Shinkley, Pamela Dupin-Bryant,
   CoEd
Journal of Adult Education
Utah State University
265 West 1100 South
Brigham City, UT 84302
USA
Phone: 435-734-9958
Fax: 435-797-3943
E-Mail: a.shinkle@usu.edu
Web: www.mpaea.org
Address May Change:

PUBLICATION GUIDELINES:

Manuscript Length: 3,500
Copies Required: Three
Computer Submission: Yes
Format: MS Word
Fees to Review: 0.00 US$

Manuscript Style:
   American Psychological Association

CIRCULATION DATA:

Reader: Practicing Teachers
Frequency of Issue: 2 Times/Year
Copies per Issue: Less than 1,000
Sponsor/Publisher: Mountain Plains Adult
   Education Association
Subscribe Price: 30.00 US$ Individual
   55.00 US$ Institution

REVIEW INFORMATION:

Type of Review: Blind Review
No. of External Reviewers: 3
No. of In House Reviewers: 2
Acceptance Rate: 21-30%
Time to Review: 2 - 3 Months
Reviewers Comments: Yes
Invited Articles: 11-20%
Fees to Publish: 0.00 US$

MANUSCRIPT TOPICS:
Adult Career & Vocational; Education Management/Administration; Educational Psychology; Educational Technology Systems; Higher Education; Rural Education & Small Schools; Teacher Education; Tests, Measurement & Evaluation

MANUSCRIPT GUIDELINES/COMMENTS:

The *MPAEA Journal of Adult Education* is a refereed journal intended to serve as a voice for the translation of theory into practice for the membership of the Mountain Plains Adult Education Association (MPAEA). The Editors of the *MPAEA Journal of Adult Education* encourage the submission of clearly written research articles, technique manuscripts, and book reviews which have the potential of stimulating thought, discussion, and inquiry. The criteria for evaluating each manuscript will be based upon: (a) potential contribution to the improvement and/or understanding of practice, (b) clarity of purpose, (c) logical relationship to conceptual base, (d) writing style, (e) general scholarship, (f) strength of conclusions, (g) implications for practice, and (h) adherence to submission guidelines.

Article Categories
MPAEA Journal of Adult Education accepts submissions in the following categories:

Research Articles. Discuss concepts, theory, and research findings of particular interest and significance to adult education professionals. Maximum length: 3,500 words including abstract, figures, and references.

Technique Articles. Describe examples of innovative practice and procedures in relationship to recognized principles of adult education research and practice. Maximum length: 1,000 words including abstract, figures, and references.

Book Reviews. Describe the content of a book, evaluate the book's success in accomplishing the intended purpose, and give a recommendation based on the book's relevance and benefits to adult education professionals. Maximum length: 1,000 words. Do not include an abstract.

Letters to the Editors. Readers are invited to submit letters, rebuttals, and comments related to published articles or ideas reflected in the *MPAEA Journal of Adult Education*. Letters should be no longer than one typewritten page.

Submission Guidelines
Original manuscripts should be organized and submitted as follows:

1. **Title Page.** The title page should include the following: (a) the title of the manuscript, (b) the full names of authors, institutional affiliations, and positions of the authors, and (c) a typewritten, signed, and dated warrant statement as follows:

I hereby confirm the assignment of first publication rights only in and to the manuscript named above in all forms and media to MPAEA effective if and when it is accepted for publication by the *MPAEA Journal of Adult Education* editorial board. I warrant that my manuscript is original work and has not been accepted for publication by another periodical. I further warrant that my work (including tables, figures, photographs, and other illustrative material) does not infringe upon any copyright or statutory rights of others, does not contain libelous statements, and that editorial board members, staff, and officers of MPAEA are indemnified against all costs, expenses, and damages arriving from my breach of the foregoing in regard to this manuscript. I acknowledge that the *MPAEA Journal of Adult Education* is relying on this statement in any publishing of the manuscript's information. Finally, I acknowledge that articles printed in the *MPAEA Journal of Adult Education* become the property of the Mountain Plains Adult Education Association and that permission must be granted for reprinting articles.

2. **First Page of Text.** Do not include your name or affiliation on the first page of text or on any subsequent page.

a. **Research articles and technique manuscripts**. The first page of the text should (a) repeat the manuscript title and (b) include an abstract of no more than 100 words that summarizes the manuscripts purpose, methods, and conclusions.

b. **Book reviews**. The first page of the text should include the book's bibliographic information (i.e. title, author(s), publisher, place and date of publication, number of pages, and price) immediately followed by the book review.

3. **Formatting**. Manuscripts should be type-written, double-spaced with 1 inch margins and should be printed on 8 ½ x 11 inch plain white paper. All manuscripts must conform to the American Psychological Association (APA) style requirements. For rules governing references and style consult the American Psychological Association, *Publication Manual of the American Psychological Association* (Fifth Edition).

4. **Submission**. Mail four stapled copies to:

Dr. Andy Shinkle and Dr. Pam Dupin-Bryant
Editors, *MPAEA Journal of Adult Education*
Utah State University Brigham City
265 West 1100 South
Brigham City, UT 84302

Journal of Adventist Education

ADDRESS FOR SUBMISSION:

Beverly J. Robinson-Rumble, Editor
Journal of Adventist Education
12501 Old Columbia Pike
Silver Spring, MD 20904-6600
USA
Phone: 301-680-5075
Fax: 301-622-9627
E-Mail: rumbleb@gc.adventist.org
Web: http://education.gc.adventist.org
Address May Change:

PUBLICATION GUIDELINES:

Manuscript Length: 6-10 double spaced
Copies Required: One
Computer Submission: Yes Disk, Email
Format: English, MS Word or WordPerfect
Fees to Review: 0.00 US$

Manuscript Style:
Chicago Manual of Style

CIRCULATION DATA:

Reader: Practicing Teachers, Educational
Administrators
Frequency of Issue: 5 Times/Year
Copies per Issue: 10,001 - 25,000
Sponsor/Publisher: General Conference of
Seventh-day Adventists
Subscribe Price: 17.25 US$ US
18.25 US$ Outside US

REVIEW INFORMATION:

Type of Review: Blind Review
No. of External Reviewers: 2 or 3
No. of In House Reviewers: 2
Acceptance Rate: 11-20%
Time to Review: 1 - 2 Months
Reviewers Comments: Yes
Invited Articles: 50% +
Fees to Publish: 0.00 US$

MANUSCRIPT TOPICS:

Bilingual/E.S.L.; Counseling & Personnel Services; Education Management/Administration; Educational Psychology; Educational Technology Systems; Elementary/Early Childhood; Gifted Children; Health & Physical Education; Higher Education; Library Science/Information Resources; Reading; Religious Education; Rural Education & Small Schools; School Administration; School Law; Secondary/Adolescent Studies; Social Studies/Social Science; Special Education; Teacher Education; Tests, Measurement & Evaluation

MANUSCRIPT GUIDELINES/COMMENTS:

Website.   http://education.gc.adventist.org/jae/

Mission Statement
A professional journal for Seventh-day Adventist teachers from kindergarten through university level, as well as educational administrators at all levels. Published bimonthly, except one issue for June through September. Each issue features informational and practical articles on a variety of topics relating to Christian education and devotional items. Occasional theme issues also deal with practical applications of Christian education and the integration of faith and learning in the classroom.

Articles by freelance authors are welcome. Please submit an inquiry or summary of the article before sending a finished manuscript.

The *Journal of Adventist Education* purchases first North American rights for each article it prints. Articles may be translated and printed in the international edition of the Journal (French, Spanish, Portuguese)

Photos on all subjects relating to education are also welcome. Sharp, high-quality black-and-white or color photos are preferred, high-resolution scans or digital photos are also acceptable (at least 300 dpi). Payment varies, but may run as high as $250-300 for a photo used as a cover.

Authors are paid upon publication of their articles. Amount varies, depending on length and other factors. Authors also receive two copies of the finished magazine in which their article appears.

Writing for the Journal of Adventist Education

The *Journal of Adventist Education* is the professional publication of Seventh-day Adventist teachers and educational administrators, worldwide, and should address topics of interest to that group.

The target audience may be teachers: elementary, secondary, or college/university level; or educational administrators. The *Journal's* constituency is international, a fact writers should keep in mind as they explore the implications or applications of a given topic. Special attention, where applicable, should be given to the concerns of minorities and students with special needs. Writers should define their target group precisely and address its concerns in a specific manner.

Articles by free-lance authors are welcome. Please submit an inquiry or summary of the article before sending a finished manuscript. The *Journal of Adventist Education* purchases first North American rights for each article it prints. Authors are paid upon publication of their articles. Amount varies, depending on length and other factors. Authors also receive two copies of the finished magazine in which their article appears. Articles may be translated and printed in the international edition of the *Journal* (French, Spanish, and Portuguese), and/or posted on the *Journal's* Web site.

Articles may deal with educational theory or practice, although the *Journal* seeks to emphasize the practical. Articles dealing with the creative and effective use of methods to enhance teaching skills or learning in the classroom are especially welcome. Whether theoretical or practical, such essays should demonstrate the skillful integration of Seventh-day Adventist faith/values and learning.

Periodically, issues will deal extensively with a single topic or issue. Articles representing various approaches or the in-depth discussion of aspects of the issue will be welcome.

Topics Preferred for *Journal of Adventist Education*:

- A call for action on some problem (*drug use, need for physical activity, lack of computer access, minority graduation rates, violence, sexual harassment, teacher burnout and morale, hazards at school*); with suggestions about how to solve it
- Addressing the needs of students with special needs-learning disabilities, physical handicaps
- New methods and approaches; applying educational research in the classroom
- Church projects related to education
- Classroom climate, interpersonal skills; counseling; discipline
- New methods and approaches, such as cooperative learning, multiple intelligences, individualized instruction, thematic instruction, etc.
- Educational administration
- Extracurricular activities
- Ideas for professional enrichment, staff development, teacher training
- Ideas for worships, religious activities
- Inspirational articles related to the task of the teacher, goals of Adventist education
- Integration of faith and learning
- Issues relating to multigrade and multicultural classrooms
- Legal issues in schools
- Marketing, promoting Adventist education
- Personal experience or inspirational articles (*school-related*)
- Pro and con on a controversial topic
- Relations with boards, parents, administrators
- Reports on innovative programs and projects or research on Adventist education
- School libraries
- Service and outreach activities
- Teaching techniques, innovative and practical methods of presenting specific topics and subjects
- Testing and assessment
- Use of technology in the classroom

Clear, sharp, black-and-white photographs and appropriate charts and graphs are a welcome adjunct. Photos can be submitted as prints, slides, or in electronic format such as high-resolution scans or digital photos (300 dpi).

The *Journal of Adventist Education* is published five times yearly, with approximately eight articles appearing in each issue. Due to space limitations, many articles will not be published immediately. Articles should be submitted at least five months before publication date. The editorial staff reserves the right to edit all manuscripts as they deem necessary.

Please call, fax, or write the Editor before submitting an article, to be sure that the topic is usable and that the *Journal* has not printed anything recently on the same subject.

If the article has already been printed elsewhere, please include information regarding publisher, source, and date of issue.

When sending materials to the *Journal*, include the following: your name, employer, position as an educator or status if a student; Social Security number and home address if employed in the United States; and other contact information such as E-mail address and fax number. Please include a photo of yourself.

The following manuscript form is preferred:

- Articles should be six to eight pages long, with a maximum of ten pages in length, including references.
- Two-part articles will be considered.
- Material should be double-spaced, using a 70-character line and standard paragraph indention.
- Subheads should be inserted at appropriate intervals.
- Articles submitted on disk or by E-mail as attached files are welcome.
- Please store in IBM WordPerfect or Word format.
- If you submit a disk, be sure to include a printed copy of the article with the disk.

Quotations should be clearly indicated. Please follow the instructions in the Chicago Manual of Style for bibliography and endnotes. Endnotes, in numerical order, should include complete bibliographic information: full name of author, title of work, volume and number if applicable, city of publication, publisher, year of publication (include month if a periodical), and page number(s). *Please enclose photocopies pages to verify facts and quotations. The information to be photocopied is as follows: the page(s) on which the fact or quotation occurs, the title page of the book or journal, and copyright information.* Authors should obtain permission for reprints of charts, graphs, and photos.

Writers are paid upon publication of their articles. In addition to financial remuneration, they will receive two copies of the issue in which their article appears, and may purchase additional copies (a discount will be offered on orders of ten or more copies).

All of the magazine's articles are copyrighted, and may not be reproduced without permission of the editor.

The *Journal* purchases first North American rights to all articles published, unless other arrangements are made. Articles published in the English edition may be translated into French, Spanish, and Portuguese for the *Journal's* international edition, and may be featured on the *Journal's* Web site.

Submit completed manuscripts to
Journal of Adventist Education
12501 Old Columbia Pike
Silver Spring, MD 20904-6600; U.S.A.
Phone: (301) 680-5069, 5075; Fax: (301) 622-9627
E-mail: **rumbleb@gc.adventist.org** *OR* **goffc@gc.adventist.org**

Journal of Adventure Education and Outdoor Learning

ADDRESS FOR SUBMISSION:

Peter Allison, Editor
Journal of Adventure Education and
    Outdoor Learning
University of Edingurgh
School of Education
Outdoor Education Section
St. Leonard's Land, Holyrood Road
Edinburgh, EH8 8AQ
Scotland
Phone: +44 131 651 6001
Fax:
E-Mail: JAEOL@btinternet.com
Web: www.outdoor-learning.org/jaeol
Address May Change:

PUBLICATION GUIDELINES:

Manuscript Length: 21-25
Copies Required: Four
Computer Submission: No
Format:
Fees to Review: 0.00 US$

Manuscript Style:
    American Psychological Association

CIRCULATION DATA:

Reader: Academics
Frequency of Issue: 2 Times/Year
Copies per Issue: Less than 1,000
Sponsor/Publisher: Institute for Outdoor
    Leaning, UK
Subscribe Price: 50.00 US$

REVIEW INFORMATION:

Type of Review: Blind Review
No. of External Reviewers: 2
No. of In House Reviewers: 1
Acceptance Rate: 21-30%
Time to Review: 2 - 3 Months
Reviewers Comments: Yes
Invited Articles: 0-5%
Fees to Publish: 0.00 US$

MANUSCRIPT TOPICS:
Adult Career & Vocational; Higher Education; Social Studies/Social Science; Teacher Education

MANUSCRIPT GUIDELINES/COMMENTS:

The purpose of this international journal is to promote dialogue, research, thinking, understanding, teaching and practice in the field of adventure education and outdoor learning. *JAEOL* publishes original papers that encourage a wider appreciation of the interdisciplinary and multidisciplinary components of adventure education and outdoor learning. *JAEOL* will consider original papers, written in English, which have not been published or are simultaneously being submitted to another journal. Papers that report on research with a wide international interest will be welcomed. All submissions are peer reviewed and should be sent to the editor.

1. **Length**: Articles should generally range from 500 to 6000 words in length.

2. **Layout**. Four typed double spaced copies should be submitted, on A4 paper, with wide margins. Do not initially submit a computer disc — after acceptance authors will be asked to send a computer disc of their article. Only the first page of the paper should bear the title, the name(s) of the author(s) and the address (including fax, email and telephone numbers) to which correspondence should be sent. A brief biographical statement of the author(s) should also be included on a separate sheet. In order to enable 'blind' refereeing, after the title page, indications of the authors identity should be avoided as much as possible within the text.

3. **Abstract**. Each article should be accompanied by an abstract of about 150 words typed on a separate sheet. Abstracts should also include the title of the article. No references should appear in the abstract.

4. **Headings**. Where necessary, the structure of the article should be made clear by sub-headings. The author should indicate in the margin against each sub-heading its rank in the structure.

5. **Footnotes** to the text should be kept to an absolute minimum. They should be typed on a separate sheet at the end of the article, numbered 1, 2 etc. and the text reference indicated by the corresponding number in square brackets.

6. **Quotations** exceeding three lines from other works and other matter requiring separation from the text should be clearly indicated and typed as a hanging indent (no quotation marks). Always state authors, date and page number.

7. **Tables** should be numbered with Arabic numerals and should carry a descriptive title. Vertical rules should be avoided.

8. **Figures** should be 15x22cm, created at a minimum of 300dpi and stored as a TIFF image.

9. **Non-Discriminatory** Text. Be alert to all forms of bias (e.g., sexist, racist). Ensure that writing does not emphasise bias. Beware of treating groups as oddities, exceptional cases and of stereotyping.

10. **References**. should be indicated in the text by giving the author(s) name, with the year of publication in parentheses. When quoting state author(s), year and page number. Authors are responsible for obtaining and supplying with the manuscript written permission to quote or use material from copyright sources. The references should be listed in full at the end of the paper following fifth edition *American Psychological Association* (APA) guidelines. Examples are as follows, further information is available at www.apa.org.

Books
Wurdinger, S. (1997). *Philosophical issues in adventure education.* Dubuque, Iowa: Kendall Hunt.

Chapters in edited books
Ewert, A. & Smith, E. (1999). Should wildlands be made available to more people, as opposed to more restrictions and limitations? Yes. In S. D. Wurdinger & T. G. Potter (Eds.), *Controversial issues in adventure education: A critical examination* (pp. 211–221). Dubuque, Iowa: Kendall/Hunt Publishing.

Journal papers
Higgins, P. (2002). Outdoor education in Scotland. *Journal of Adventure Education and Outdoor Learning*, 2(2), 149–168.

Dissertations
Donnison, P. (2000). *Images of outdoor management development.* Unpublished doctoral thesis, Lancaster University, Department of Management Learning.

Conference proceedings
Potter, T. G., & Cuthbertson, B. (2002). Inclusive Recreation in the Outdoors: A Canadian Perspective. *Proceedings of The First Pacific Rim Conference on Leisure Education*, Hawaii Tokai International College, Honolulu, Hawaii, January 11th–14th, 2002, 176–184.

Electronic Source
Outward Bound Australia (1998) *What the Research Really Says.* Retrieved December 3, 2000, from http://www.outwardbound.com.au/featresearch.htm.

12. **Reviews**. Books and materials for review should be sent to the book reviews editor.

13. **Authors Copies**. Two complementary copies per article will be sent upon publication.

14. **Copyright**. No part of this publication may be reproduced, stored in a retrieval system or transmitted in any form or by any means, electronic, mechanical, photocopying, recording or otherwise without the written permission of the editor. Reproduction in whole or in part of the contents of this publication is forbidden without the express permission of the editor who is normally happy to grant requests for educational purposes.

15. **Originality**. Papers submitted for review should not appear in other journals or be submitted for consideration by other journals. The journal accepts original papers for review that have not been previously published elsewhere (such as conference proceedings, the internet, journals, magazines and book chapters). Authors must make a clear indication with regard to originality at the time of submission.

16. **Review process**. The review process normally follows the following sequence.
   i. Paper received and two reviewers are requested to comment
   ii. Reviewers comment
   iii. Comments returned to authors via editor who may also comment.
   iv. Paper is accepted, accepted with minor changes, revise and resubmit or reject.
   v. Depending on (iv) above authors may select to resubmit
   vi. Editor reviews the revised paper and may re-contact reviewers if necessary

520

vii.   Further edits may be required of the authors depending on the changes and edits required at different stages.

viii.   If accepted for publications authors receive a PDF file of print set copy for approval prior to printing.

Editorial Enquiries
Pete Allison; **jaeol@btinternet.com**

Submissions
Dr. P. Allison – JAEOL
Outdoor Education Section,
School of Education, University of Edinburgh
St. Leonard's Land, Holyrood Road,
Edinburgh. EH8 8AQ, Scotland.

Subscriptions
Melanie Bardgett, Institute for Outdoor Learning (IOL)
Plumpton Old Hall, Plumpton, Penrith,
Cumbria, CA11 7YE. UK
Tel: 01768 885800; Fax: 01768 885801
Email: subs@outdoor-learning; Website: org; www.outdoor-learning.org

Journal of Aesthetic Education

ADDRESS FOR SUBMISSION:

Pradeep A. Dhillon, Editor
Journal of Aesthetic Education
University of IL at Urbana-Champaign
Education Building
1310 S. 6th Street
Champaign, IL 61820
USA
Phone: 217-333-0787
Fax:
E-Mail: dhillon@uiuc.edu
Web:
Address May Change:

PUBLICATION GUIDELINES:

Manuscript Length: 11-20
Copies Required: Two
Computer Submission: Yes
Format: N/A
Fees to Review: 0.00 US$

Manuscript Style:
    Chicago Manual of Style

CIRCULATION DATA:

Reader: Academics, Practicing Teachers,
    Aesthetics Students
Frequency of Issue: Quarterly
Copies per Issue: 1,001 - 2,000
Sponsor/Publisher: University of Illinois
    Press at Urbana-Champaign Press
Subscribe Price: 30.00 US$ Individual
    45.00 US$ Institution

REVIEW INFORMATION:

Type of Review: Varies
No. of External Reviewers: Varies
No. of In House Reviewers: 2
Acceptance Rate: No Reply
Time to Review: 2 Months
Reviewers Comments: Usually
Invited Articles: Some
Fees to Publish: 0.00 US$

MANUSCRIPT TOPICS:

Art/Music; Educational Psychology; English Literature; Interdisciplinary Arts Education;
Theater; Urban Education, Cultural/Non-Traditional

MANUSCRIPT GUIDELINES/COMMENTS:

Type of Review: Refereed

No. of External Reviewers: Varies

Journal of Alcohol and Drug Education

ADDRESS FOR SUBMISSION:

Manoj Sharma, Editor
Journal of Alcohol and Drug Education
P O Box 31307
Omaha, NE 68131-0307
USA
Phone: 513-556-3878
Fax: 513-556-3898
E-Mail: manoj.sharma@uc.edu
Web: See Guidelines
Address May Change:

PUBLICATION GUIDELINES:

Manuscript Length: 11-20
Copies Required: Three
Computer Submission: Yes
Format: N/A
Fees to Review: 0.00 US$

Manuscript Style:
    American Psychological Association

CIRCULATION DATA:

Reader: Practicing Teachers, Academics,
    Adminstrators
Frequency of Issue: 3 Times/Year
Copies per Issue: 1,001 - 2,000
Sponsor/Publisher:
Subscribe Price: 40.00 US$

REVIEW INFORMATION:

Type of Review: Blind Review
No. of External Reviewers: 3
No. of In House Reviewers: 1
Acceptance Rate: 43%
Time to Review: 2 - 3 Months
Reviewers Comments: Yes
Invited Articles: Yes
Fees to Publish: 0.00 US$

MANUSCRIPT TOPICS:
Adult Career & Vocational; Alcohol & Drugs, Behavior, and Prevention; Elementary/Early Childhood; Health & Physical Education; Policy; Public Health; Secondary/Adolescent Studies

MANUSCRIPT GUIDELINES/COMMENTS:

Journal of Alcohol and Drug Education [Web: **www.unomaha.edu/~healthed/JADE.htm**] encourages submission of reports of empirical studies, review articles (including meta-analyses), theoretical articles, methodological articles, and case studies pertaining to alcohol, tobacco, and other drugs. Educational and ecological intervention studies are especially encouraged. Manuscripts submitted to the *Journal of Alcohol and Drug Education* must follow these guidelines:

1. Manuscripts must be prepared in accordance with the *Publication Manual of the American Psychological Association* (5th ed.) published in July 2001.

2. Manuscripts should not exceed twenty double spaced pages in length with one-inch margin on all sides. This page length includes the tables and references but excludes the title page and

the abstract page. The preferred font as suggested by *APA Manual* is *Sans* for the text and *Sans Serif* for the figures.

3. Tables and figures must be camera ready.

4. The abstract should not be more than 120 words.

5. *Journal of Alcohol and Drug Education* only accepts original articles. Simultaneous submissions to other journals are not permitted and a statement confirming this must be included in the accompanying letter. Submission and acceptance of manuscript implies transfer of copyright to the *Journal of Alcohol and Drug Education*.

6. Conflict of interest including financial support, any other colleagues' professional contributions, any earlier professional presentations, and any other relationships must be explicated in the author's note section.

7. The editor determines the manuscripts sent for blind review to three reviewers based on the criteria of:
   a. Originality statement
   b. Recent nature of work
   c. Level of interest to the readers
   d. Format, organization, and adherence to guidelines

8. The reviewers rate the manuscripts based on the criteria of:
   a. Contribution to the field
   b. Methodology
   c. Scientific accuracy
   d. Writing style

9. Reviewers recommend:
   a. Acceptance
   b. Acceptance with minor revisions
   c. Acceptance with major revisions
   d. Rejection
   e. Recommendation for submission to another journal

10. For the manuscript to be considered for publication two reviewers must recommend acceptance.

11. Manuscripts not accepted for review will not be returned to authors unless accompanied by a self-addressed, stamped envelope.

12. In the event of manuscript being accepted authors, must provide the word-processed manuscript, preferably as a Microsoft Word document.

Journal of American Indian Education

ADDRESS FOR SUBMISSION:

David Beaulieu, Editor
Journal of American Indian Education
Arizona State University
Center for Indian Education
PO Box 871311
Tempe, AZ 85287-1311
USA
Phone: 480-965-6292
Fax: 480-965-8115
E-Mail: david.beaulieu@asu.edu
Web: jaie.asu.edu/
Address May Change:

PUBLICATION GUIDELINES:

Manuscript Length: 26-30
Copies Required: Five
Computer Submission: No
Format: N/A
Fees to Review: 0.00 US$

Manuscript Style:
American Psychological Association

CIRCULATION DATA:

Reader: Academics, Practicing Teachers
Frequency of Issue: 3 Times/Year
Copies per Issue: Less than 1,000
Sponsor/Publisher: Center for Indian
Education, College of Education, Arizona
State University
Subscribe Price: 20.00 US$ Individual
45.00 US$ Institution

REVIEW INFORMATION:

Type of Review: Blind Review
No. of External Reviewers: 3
No. of In House Reviewers: 2
Acceptance Rate: 21-30%
Time to Review: 1 - 2 Months
Reviewers Comments: Yes
Invited Articles: 11-20%
Fees to Publish: 0.00 US$

MANUSCRIPT TOPICS:
American Indian Education; Bilingual/E.S.L.; Curriculum Studies; Elementary/Early
Childhood; Indigenous Peoples of the World; Languages & Linguistics

MANUSCRIPT GUIDELINES/COMMENTS:

About the Journal
The *Journal of American Indian Education* (*JAIE*) is a refereed journal that publishes papers
directly related to the education of American Indian/ Alaska Natives and also invites
scholarship on educational issues pertaining to Native Peoples of the world, including First
Nations (Aboriginal People of Canada), Native Hawaiians, Maori, indigenous peoples of Latin
America and others. *JAIE's* goal is to improve Native Education through knowledge
generation and transmission to classrooms and other educational settings. It encourages
dialogues between researchers and teachers through research-based scholar and practitioner
articles elucidating current innovations in the classroom. Essays that advance a point of view
about an educational question or issue if supported by cited research literature are acceptable
for consideration as well as manuscripts that present reviews of literature in areas that are
relatively unexplored. The *Journal* also seeks expository manuscripts that present an

explicative or interpretive perspective to an existing theory or issue. *JAIE* is particularly interested in publishing manuscripts that express the viewpoint of AI/AN and research that is initiated, conducted, and interpreted by natives.

JAIE was founded in 1961, and has been published continuously since. It is published three times yearly by the Center for Indian Education of the College of Education at Arizona State University.

The *Journal* is refereed by Native educators and experts in various academic disciplines. Please visit our current Review Panel at the *JAIE* website.

Manuscript Submission Procedure
Please refer to the 1994 *Publication Manual of the American Psychological Association* (4th ed.) when preparing manuscripts for submission. The term Indian/Alaska Native rather than Native American should be used in manuscripts referring to the native or indigenous peoples of the United States.

In submitting a manuscript the following procedures must be followed:

1. Articles may be up to 25 pages in length and must conform to the standards of the *Publication Manual of the American Psychological Association*, 4th Ed.

2. Five copies of the manuscript must be mailed to:
Journal of American Indian Education
Center for Indian Education
Arizona State University
P.O. Box 871311
Tempe, AZ 85287-1311

3. The manuscript must include a 100-150-word abstract describing the article and a 50 word biographical sketch of the author or authors.

4. Once the manuscript is accepted for publication, and all revisions have been completed, the author will be required to submit the final work on diskette (Microsoft Word) and in paper copy form.

Manuscripts will be accepted throughout the year and will be published in any of the three issues at the discretion of the editorial staff. There is no remuneration for *JAIE* contributors; authors will receive five copies of the issue in which their manuscript is published.

Journal of Athletic Training

ADDRESS FOR SUBMISSION:

Christopher Ingersoll, Editor
Journal of Athletic Training
Hughston Sports Medicine Foundation, Inc
6262 Veterans Parkway
Columbus, GA 31909
USA
Phone: 706-494-3345
Fax: 706-494-3348
E-Mail: jathtr@mindspring.com
Web: www.journalofathletictraining.org
Address May Change:

PUBLICATION GUIDELINES:

Manuscript Length: Any Length
Copies Required: Five
Computer Submission: Yes
Format: N/A
Fees to Review: 0.00 US$

Manuscript Style:
, AMA

CIRCULATION DATA:

Reader: Academics, Athletic Trainers /
   Administrators
Frequency of Issue: Quarterly
Copies per Issue: 27,000
Sponsor/Publisher: National Athletic
   Trainer's Association
Subscribe Price: 32.00 US$
   40.00 US$ Foreign

REVIEW INFORMATION:

Type of Review: Blind Review
No. of External Reviewers: 3
No. of In House Reviewers: 1
Acceptance Rate: 21-30%
Time to Review: 2 - 3 Months
Reviewers Comments: Yes
Invited Articles: 0-5%
Fees to Publish: 0.00 US$

MANUSCRIPT TOPICS:
Education Management/Administration; Educational Psychology; Educational Technology Systems; Health & Physical Education; Library Science/Information Resources; Teacher Education; Tests, Measurement & Evaluation

MANUSCRIPT GUIDELINES/COMMENTS:

The mission of the *Journal of Athletic Training* is to enhance communication among professionals interested in the quality of health care for the physically active through education and research in prevention, evaluation, management, and rehabilitation of injuries.

Submission Policies
1. Submit one original and five copies of the entire manuscript (including tables and figures) to: Journal of Athletic Training Submissions, Hughston Sports Medicine Foundation, Inc., 6262 Veterans Parkway, PO Box 9517, Columbus, GA 31908. The term figure refers to items that are not editable, either halftones (photographs) or line art (charts, graphs, tracings, schematic drawings), or combinations of the two. A table is an editable item that needs to be typeset.

2. All manuscripts must be accompanied by a letter signed by each author and must contain the following statements:

"This manuscript 1) contains original unpublished material that has been submitted solely to the *Journal of Athletic Training*, 2) is not under simultaneous review by any other publication, and 3) will not be submitted elsewhere until a decision has been made concerning its suitability for publication by the *Journal of Athletic Training*. In consideration of the NATA'S taking action in reviewing and editing my submission, I the undersigned author hereby transfer, assign, or otherwise convey all copyright ownership to the NATA in the event that such work is published by the NATA. Further, I verify that I have contributed substantially to this manuscript as outlined in item #3 of the current Authors' Guide."

By signing the letter, the authors agree to comply with all statements. Manuscripts that are not accompanied by such a letter will not be reviewed. Accepted manuscripts become the property of the NATA. Authors agree to accept any minor corrections of the manuscript made by the editors.

3. Each author must have contributed to the article. This means that all co-authors should have made some useful contribution to the study, should have had a hand in writing and revising it, and should be expected to be able to defend the study publicly against criticism.

4. Financial support or provision of supplies used in the study must be acknowledged. Grant or contract numbers should be included whenever possible. The complete name of the funding institution or agency should be given, along with the city and state in which it is located. If individual authors were the recipients of funds, their names should be listed parenthetically.

5. Authors must specify whether they have any commercial or proprietary interest in any device, equipment, instrument, or drug that is the subject of the article in question. Authors must also reveal if they have any financial interest (as a consultant, reviewer, or evaluator) in a drug or device described in the article.

6. For experimental investigations of human or animal subjects, state in the "Methods" section of the manuscript that an appropriate institutional review board approved the project. For those investigators who do not have formal ethics review committees (institutional or regional), the principles outlined in the Declaration of Helsinki should be followed (41st World Medical Assembly. Declaration of Helsinki: recommendations guiding physicians in biomedical research involving human subjects. Bull Pan Am Health organ. 1990; 24:606-609). For investigations of human subjects, state in the "Methods" section the manner in which informed consent was obtained from the subjects. (Reprinted with permission of JAMA 1997; 278:68, copyright 1997, American Medical Association.)

7. Signed releases are required to verify permission for the *Journal of Athletic Training* 1) to reproduce materials taken from other sources, including text, figures, or tables; 2) to reproduce photographs of individuals; and 3) to publish a Case Report. A Case Report cannot be reviewed without a release signed by the individual being discussed in the Case Report.

Release forms can be obtained from the Editorial Office and from the *JAT* web page, or authors may use their own forms.

8. The *Journal of Athletic Training* uses a double-blind review process. Authors should not be identified in any way except on the title page.

9. Manuscripts are edited to improve the effectiveness of communication between author and readers and to aid the author in presenting a work that is compatible with the style policies found in the *AMA Manual of Style*, 9th ED. (Williams & Wilkins), 1998. Page proofs are sent to the author for proofreading when the article is typeset for publication. It is important that they be returned within 48 hours. Important changes are permitted, but authors will be charged for excessive alterations.

10. Published manuscripts and accompanying work cannot be returned. Unused manuscripts will be returned if submitted with a stamped, self-addressed envelope.

Style Policies
11. Each page must be printed on one side of 8½ by 11-inch plain paper, double spaced, with one-inch margins. Do not right justify pages.

12. Manuscripts should contain the following, organized in the order listed below, with each section beginning on a separate page:
a. Title page
b. Acknowledgments
c. Abstract and Key Words (first numbered page)
d. Text (body of manuscript)
e. References
f. Tables (each on a separate page)
g. Legends to figures
h. Figures

13. Begin numbering the pages of your manuscript with the abstract page as #1; then, consecutively number all successive pages.

14. Units of measurement shall be recorded as SI units, as specified in the *AMA Manual of Style*, except for angular displacement, which should be measured in degrees rather than radians. Examples include mass in kilograms (kg), height in centimeters (cm), velocity in meters per second (m sec or m/sec), angular velocity in degrees per second (sec), force in Newtons (N), and complex rates (mL/kg per minute).

15. Titles should be brief within descriptive limits (a 16-word maximum is recommended). If a disability is the relevant factor in an article, the name of the disability should be included in the title. If a technique is the principal reason for the report, it should be in the title. Often both should appear.

16. The title page should also include the name, title, and affiliation of each author, and the name, address, phone number, fax number, and E-mail address of the author to whom correspondence is to be directed.

17. A structured abstract of 75 to 200 words must accompany all manuscripts. Type the complete title (but not the authors names) at the top, skip two lines, and begin the abstract. Items that are needed differ by type of article. **Literature Review**: Objective, Data Sources, Data Synthesis, Conclusions/Recommendations, and Key Words; **Original Research** articles: Objective, Design and Setting, Subjects, Measurements, Results, Conclusions, and Key Words; **Case Reports**: Objective, Background, Differential Diagnosis, Treatment, Uniqueness, Conclusions, and Key Words; **Clinical Techniques**: Objective, Background, Description, Clinical Advantages, and Key Words. For the Key Words entry, use three to five words that do not appear in the title.

18. Begin the text of the manuscript with an introductory paragraph or two in which the purpose or hypothesis of the article is clearly stated and developed. Tell why the study needed to be done or the article written and end with a statement of the problem (or controversy). Highlights of the most prominent works of others as related to your subject are often appropriate for the introduction, but a detailed review of the literature should be reserved for the discussion section. In a one- to two-paragraph review of the literature, identify and develop the magnitude and significance of the controversy, pointing out differences among others' results, conclusions, and/or opinions. The introduction is not the place for great detail; state the facts in brief specific statements and reference them. The detail belongs in the discussion. Also, an overview of the manuscript is part of the abstract, not the introduction. The active voice is preferred. For examples, consult the *AMA Manual of Style*.

19. The body or main part of the manuscript varies according to the type of article (examples follow); however, the body should include a discussion section in which the importance of the material presented is discussed and related to other pertinent Literature. Liberal use of headings and subheadings, charts, graphs, and figures is recommended.

a. The body of an **Original Research** article consists of a methods section, a presentation of the results, and a discussion of the results. The methods section should contain sufficient detail concerning the methods, procedures, and apparatus employed so that others can reproduce the results. The results should be summarized using descriptive and inferential statistics and a few well-planned and carefully constructed illustrations.

b. The body of a **Literature Review** article should be organized into subsections in which related thoughts of others are presented, summarized, and referenced. Each subsection should have a heading and brief summary, possibly one sentence. Sections must be arranged so that they progressively focus on the problem or question posed in the introduction.

c. The body of a **Case Report** should include the following components: personal data (age, sex, race, marital status, and occupation when relevant-but not name), chief complaint, history of present complaint (including symptoms), results of physical examination (example: "Physical findings relevant to the rehabilitation program were

530

...("), medical history (surgery, laboratory results, exam, etc), diagnosis, treatment and clinical course (rehabilitation until and after return to competition), criteria for return to competition, and deviation from expectations (what makes this case unique).

d. The body of a **Clinical Techniques** article should include both the how and why of the technique: a step-by-step explanation of how to perform the technique, supplemented by photographs or illustrations, and an explanation of why the technique should be used. The discussion concerning the why of the technique should review similar techniques, point out how the new technique differs, and explain the advantages and disadvantages of the technique in comparison with other techniques.

20. **Communications** articles, including official Position Statements and Policy Statements from the NATA Pronouncements Committee; technical notes on such topics as research design and statistics; and articles on other professional issues of interest to the readership are solicited by the Journal. An author who has a suggestion for such a paper is advised to contact the Editorial Office for instructions.

21. The manuscript should not have a separate summary section--the abstract serves as a summary. It is appropriate, however, to tie the article together with a summary paragraph or list of conclusions at the end of the discussion section.

22. References should be numbered consecutively, using superscripted Arabic numerals, in the order in which they are cited in the text. References should be used liberally. It is unethical to present others' ideas as your own. Also, use references so that readers who desire further information on the topic can benefit from your scholarship.

23. References to articles or books, published or accepted for publication, or to papers presented at professional meetings are listed in numerical order at the end of the manuscript. Journal title abbreviations conform, to *Index Medicus* style. Examples of references are illustrated below. See the *AMA Manual of Style* for other examples.

Journals
1. van Dyke JR 111, Von Trapp JT Jr., Smith BC Sr. Arthroscopic management of postoperative arthrofibrosis of the knee joint: indication, technique, and results. J Bone Joint Surg Br. 1995; 19:517-525.

2. Council on Scientific Affairs. Scientific issues in drug testing. JAMA. 1987; 257:3110-3114.

Books
1. Fischer DH, Jones RT. Growing Old in America. New York, NY: Oxford University Press Inc; 1977:210-216.

2. Spencer JT, Brown QC. Immunology of influenza. In: Kilbourne ED, Gray JB, eds. The Influenza Viruses and Influenza. 3rd ed. Orlando, FL: Academic Press Inc; 1975:373-393.

Presentations
1. Stone JA. Swiss ball rehabilitation exercises. Presented at the 47th Annual Meeting and Clinical Symposia of the National Athletic Trainers' Association; June 12, 1996; Orlando, FL.

24. Table Style: 1) Title is bold; body and column headings are roman type, 2) units are set above rules in parentheses; 3) numbers are aligned in columns by decimal; 4) footnotes are indicated by symbols (order of symbols: *, , , §,); 5) capitalize the first letter of each major word in titles; for each column or row entry, capitalize the first word only. See a current issue of the Journal for examples.

25. All black and white line art should be submitted in camera-ready form. Line art should be of good quality; should be clearly presented on white paper with black ink, sans serif typeface, and no box; and should be printed on a laser printer--no dot matrix. Figures that require reduction for publication must remain readable at their final size (either one column or two columns wide). Photographs should be glossy black and white prints. Do not use paper clips, write on photographs, or attach photographs to sheets of paper. On the reverse of each figure attach a write-on label with the figure number, name of the author, and an arrow indicating the top. (Note: Prepare the label before affixing it to the figure.) Authors should submit one original of each figure and five copies for review.

26. Authors must request color reproduction in a cover letter with the submitted manuscript. Authors will be notified of the additional cost of color reproduction and must confirm acceptance of the charges in writing.

27. Legends to figures are numbered with Arabic numerals in order of appearance in the text. Legends should be printed on separate pages at the end of the manuscript.

Journal of Autism and Developmental Disorders

ADDRESS FOR SUBMISSION:

Gary Mesibov, Editor
Journal of Autism and Developmental
    Disorders
University of North Carolina,Chapel Hill
Division TEACCH
Campus Box 7180
100 Renee Lynn Drive
Carrboro, NC 27510-7180
USA
Phone: 919-966-8189
Fax: 919-966-4127
E-Mail: gary_mesibov@unc.edu
Web: www.wkap.com
Address May Change:

PUBLICATION GUIDELINES:

Manuscript Length: 16-20
Copies Required: Three
Computer Submission: Yes
Format: N/A
Fees to Review: 0.00 US$

Manuscript Style:
    American Psychological Association,
    4th or 5th Edition

CIRCULATION DATA:

Reader: Academics, Professionals, Parents
Frequency of Issue: Bi-Monthly
Copies per Issue: 2,001 - 3,000
Sponsor/Publisher: Kluwer Academic
    Publishers
Subscribe Price: 93.00 US$ Individual
    93.00 Euro Individual
    For more info. See website

REVIEW INFORMATION:

Type of Review: Editorial Review
No. of External Reviewers: 4
No. of In House Reviewers: 1
Acceptance Rate: 35%
Time to Review: 2 - 3 Months
Reviewers Comments: Yes
Invited Articles: No Reply
Fees to Publish: 0.00 US$

MANUSCRIPT TOPICS:
Audiology/Speech Pathology; Children with Disabilities; Children with Emotional and
Behavioral Disorders; Communication; Health & Physical Education; Learning Disabilities;
Special Education; Tests, Measurement & Evaluation

MANUSCRIPT GUIDELINES/COMMENTS:

Topics. Subjects related to autism and other developmental disorders: Communication;
diagnosis-assessment/characteristics of disability, testing or screening instruments;
Epidemiology; Family/parents, siblings; Genetics; Medical/intervention or therapy/physical
conditions or attributes; Methodology; Neurobiology/brain function, face processing-eye
movement; Psychosocial-behavioral interventions, Social Development/joint attention, play,
imitation; Other.

Aims and Scope

Journal of Autism and Developmental Disorders covers all the severe psychopathologies in childhood, including autism and childhood schizophrenia. Original articles discuss experimental studies on the biochemical, neurological, and genetic aspects of a particular disorder; the implications of normal development for deviant processes; and interaction between disordered behavior of individuals and social or group factors. The *Journal* also features research and case studies involving the entire spectrum of interventions (including behavioral, biological, educational, and community aspects) and advances in the diagnosis and classification of disorders.

This journal is devoted to all severe psychopathologies in childhood and is not necessarily limited to autism and childhood schizophrenia. The following topics fall within its scope: (1) experimental studies on the biochemical, neurological, and genetic aspects of the disorder; (2) the implications of normal development for deviant processes; (3) interaction between disordered behavior of individuals and social or group factors; (4) research and case studies involving the entire spectrum of interventions, including behavioral, biological, educational, and community aspects; (5) diagnosis and classification of disorders reflecting new knowledge.

Topics may be explored in several forms: (1) experimental studies of original research; (2) theoretical papers based on scholarly review of relevant topics; (3) critical reviews of important research or treatment activity; (4) case studies in which new insights for the individual are demonstrated and implications for other children or research are discussed. Papers, or substantial parts of such papers, that have already been published or committed elsewhere will not be accepted for publication in this journal.

Guidelines for Submission

1. Manuscripts should be submitted to the Editor:

Gary B. Mesibov
Division of TEACCH
100 Renee Lynn Drive
Campus Box 7180
University of North Carolina
Carrboro, North Carolina 27510-7180

The Journal will operate a dual system until all paper manuscripts have been reviewed. The new electronic system will be activated in June 2004. Information regarding this can be found in Author Instructions at **http://www.kluweronline.com/issn/0162-3257**.

Please direct all inquiries concerning manuscripts to Kathie Barron at
Kathie barron@med.unc.edu (919) 966-8182.

2. Submission is a representation that the manuscript has not been published previously and is not currently under consideration for publication elsewhere. This statement should be included in the cover letter. Also, a statement transferring copyright from the authors (or their employers, if they hold the copyright) to Kluwer Academic Publishing Corporation will be required before the manuscript can be accepted for publication. The Editor will supply the

necessary forms for this transfer. Such a written transfer of copyright, which previously was assumed to be implicit in the act of submitting a manuscript, is necessary under the U.S. Copyright Law in order for the publisher to carry through the dissemination of research results and reviews as widely and effectively as possible. Note: The new electronic system requires this form at the time of submission.

3. Type double-spaced, and submit the original and three copies (including copies of all illustrations and tables). Academic affiliations of all authors and the full mailing address of the one author who will review the proofs should be included.

4. A 120-word abstract is to be provided for articles and brief reports. It is not needed for a letter to the editor.

5. Tables should be numbered and referred to by number in the text. Each table should be typed on a separate sheet of paper and should have a descriptive title. Tables appear after the Reference section. The manuscript text should contain "call outs" in brackets to indicate the placement of tables and figures. Example: [place Table 1 about here].

6. Figures must be preceded by a Figure Caption sheet listing all captions for figures. Figures (photographs, drawings, diagrams, and charts) are to be numbered in one consecutive series of Arabic numerals. Photographs should be large, glossy prints, showing high contrast. Drawings should be prepared with India ink. Either the original drawings or good-quality photographic prints are acceptable. Identify figures on the back with author's name and number of the illustration. Electronic artwork submitted on disk should be in the TIFF or EPS format (1200 dpi for line and 300 dpi for half-tones and gray-scale art). Color art should be in the CYMK color space. Artwork should be on a separate disk from the text, and hard copy **must** accompany the disk. The manuscript text should contain "call outs" in brackets to indicate the placement of tables and figures. Example: [place Table 1 about here].

7. The 1994 fourth edition of the *Publication Manual of the American Psychological Association* should be used as the style guide for the preparation of manuscripts, particularly with respect to such matters as the citing of references and the use of abbreviations, numbers, and symbols. Transition will be made to APA – Fifth Edition in 2005. At present, either 4th or 5th guidelines are acceptable.

8. Instructions will be provided by the electronic system to be activated in June 2004. For manuscript presented under the former print system: after all revisions have been incorporated, manuscripts should be submitted to the Editor's Office as hard copy accompanied by electronic files on disk. Label the disk with identifying information-- software, journal name, and first author's last name. **The disk must be the one from which the accompanying manuscript (finalized version) was printed out.** The Editor's Office cannot accept a disk without its accompanying, matching hard-copy manuscript.

9. The journal makes no page charges. Reprints are available to authors, and order forms with the current prices schedule are sent with proofs. Complementary copies are not provided to authors.

Journal of Basic Writing

ADDRESS FOR SUBMISSION:

Bonne August, Rebecca Mlynarczyk, Co-Ed
Journal of Basic Writing
Kingsborough Community College, CUNY
2001 Oriental Blvd.
Brooklyn, NY 11235
USA
Phone: 718-368-5849
Fax: 718-368-4786
E-Mail: baugust@kbcc.cuny.edu
Web:
Address May Change: 6/3/2002

PUBLICATION GUIDELINES:

Manuscript Length: 15-25
Copies Required: Five
Computer Submission: Yes (Preferred)
Format: RTF, Word, WordPerfect
Fees to Review: 0.00 US$

Manuscript Style:
, MLA

CIRCULATION DATA:

Reader: Practicing Teachers
Frequency of Issue: 2 Times/Year
Copies per Issue: 2,001 - 3,000
Sponsor/Publisher: The City University of
New York
Subscribe Price: 15.00 US$ Individual
20.00 US$ Institution
5.00 US$ Add for Foreign Postage

REVIEW INFORMATION:

Type of Review: Blind Review
No. of External Reviewers: 2
No. of In House Reviewers: 2
Acceptance Rate: 21-30%
Time to Review: 2 - 3 Months
Reviewers Comments: Yes
Invited Articles: 0-5%
Fees to Publish: 0.00 US$

MANUSCRIPT TOPICS:

Bilingual/E.S.L.; Curriculum Studies; Higher Education; Languages & Linguistics; Urban Education, Cultural/Non-Traditional

MANUSCRIPT GUIDELINES/COMMENTS:

We welcome manuscripts of 15-25 pages on topics related to basic writing, broadly interpreted.

Manuscripts will be refereed anonymously. We require five copies of a manuscript and an abstract of about 100 words. To assure impartial review, give author information and a short biographical note for publication on the cover page only. One copy of each manuscript not accepted for publication will be returned to the author, if we receive sufficient stamps (no meter strips) clipped to a self-addressed envelope. Submissions should follow current *MLA* guidelines.

All manuscripts must focus clearly on basic writing and must add substantively to the existing literature. We seek manuscripts that are original, stimulating, well grounded in theory, and clearly related to practice. Work that reiterates what is known or work previously published will not be considered.

We invite authors to write about such matters as classroom practices in relation to basic writing theory; cognitive and rhetorical theories and their relation to basic writing, social, psychological, and cultural implications of literacy: discourse theory, grammar, spelling, and error analysis; linguistics; computers and new technologies in basic writing; English as a second language; assessment and evaluation; writing center practices; teaching logs and the development of new methodologies; and cross-disciplinary studies combining basic writing with psychology, anthropology, journalism, and art. We publish observational studies as well as theoretical discussions on relationships between basic writing and reading, or the study of literature, or speech, or listening. The term "basic writer" is used with wide diversity today, sometimes referring to a student from a highly oral tradition with little experience in writing academic discourse, and sometimes referring to a student whose academic writing is fluent but otherwise deficient. To help readers therefore, authors should describe clearly the student population which they are discussing.

We particularly encourage a *variety* of manuscripts: speculative discussions which venture fresh interpretations; essays which draw heavily on student writing as supportive evidence for new observations; research reports, written in non-technical language which offer observations previously unknown or unsubstantiated; and collaborative writings which provocatively debate more than one side of a central controversy.

Journal of Business & Finance Librarianship

ADDRESS FOR SUBMISSION:

Charles Popovich, Editor
Journal of Business & Finance
   Librarianship
Ohio State University
Head Librarian, Business Library
Mason Hall
250 W. Woodruff Ave.
Columbus, OH 43210
USA
Phone: 614-292-2136
Fax: 614-292-5559
E-Mail: popovich.1@osu.edu
Web: www.haworthpressinc.com
Address May Change:

PUBLICATION GUIDELINES:

Manuscript Length: 30+
Copies Required: Three
Computer Submission: Yes 3 Disks
   aft.accpt.
Format: WordPerfect 7.0 / MS Word 2000
Fees to Review: 0.00 US$

Manuscript Style:
   American Psychological Association

CIRCULATION DATA:

Reader: Academics
Frequency of Issue: Quarterly
Copies per Issue: 1,001 - 2,000
Sponsor/Publisher: Haworth Press, Inc.
Subscribe Price: 36.00 US$ Individual
   75.00 US$ Institution
   75.00 US$ Libraries

REVIEW INFORMATION:

Type of Review: Blind Review
No. of External Reviewers: 2
No. of In House Reviewers: 1
Acceptance Rate: 50%
Time to Review: 2 - 3 Months
Reviewers Comments: Yes
Invited Articles: 21-30%
Fees to Publish: 0.00 US$

MANUSCRIPT TOPICS:
Education Management/Administration; Higher Education; Library Science/Information
Resources

MANUSCRIPT GUIDELINES/COMMENTS:

Editor's Note: All manuscript topics must discuss some relationship to libraries.

About the Journal
This quarterly journal is devoted entirely to providing useful articles to information
professionals who are involved with, or have an interest in, the creation, organization,
dissemination, retrieval, and use of business information. The journal covers the business
information needs of special libraries, academic libraries, and public libraries--as well as
information services and centers outside of the traditional library setting. The immediate focus
of the journal is practice-oriented articles, but it also provides an outlet for new empirical
studies on business librarianship, and business information. The *Journal of Business &*

Finance Librarianship is international in scope to reflect the multinational and international scope of the business community today.

Instructions for Authors

1. **Original Articles Only.** Submission of a manuscript to this journal represents a certification on the part of the author(s) that it is an original work, and that neither this manuscript nor a version of it has been published elsewhere nor is being considered for publication elsewhere.

2. **Manuscript Length.** Your manuscript may be approximately 10-35 typed pages double-spaced (including references and abstract). Lengthier manuscripts may be considered, but only at the discretion of the Editor. Sometimes, lengthier manuscripts may be considered if they can be divided up into sections for publication in successive Journal issues.

3. **Manuscript Style.** References, citations, and general style of manuscripts for this Journal should follow the APA style (as outlined in the latest edition of the *Publication Manual of the American Psychological Association*). References should be double-spaced and placed in alphabetical order.

If an author wishes to submit a paper that has been already prepared in another style, he or she may do so. However, if the paper is accepted (with or without reviewer's alterations), the author is fully responsible for retyping the manuscript in the correct style as indicated above. Neither the Editor nor the Publisher is responsible for re-preparing manuscript copy to adhere to the Journal's style.

4. **Manuscript Preparation**.
Margins. Leave at least a one-inch margin on all four sides.
Paper. Use clean, white, 8 1/2 " x 11" bond paper.
Number of Copies. 4 (the original plus three photocopies).
Cover Page. Important--staple a cover page to the manuscript, indicating only the article title (this is used for anonymous refereeing).
Second "Title Page". Enclose a regular title page but do not staple it to the manuscript. Include the title again, plus:
- full authorship
- an ABSTRACT of about 100 words. (Below the abstract provide 3-10 key words for index purposes)
- an introductory footnote with authors' academic degrees, professional titles, affiliations, mailing addresses, and any desired acknowledgment of research support or other credit.

5. **Return Envelopes.** When you submit your four manuscript copies, also include:
- a 9" x 12" envelope, self-addressed and stamped (with sufficient postage to ensure return of your manuscript);
- a regular envelope, stamped and self-addressed. This is for the Editor to send you an "acknowledgement of receipt" letter.

6. **Spelling, Grammar, and Punctuation**. You are responsible for preparing manuscript copy which is clearly written in acceptable scholarly English, and which contains no errors of

spelling, grammar, or punctuation. Neither the Editor nor the Publisher is responsible for correcting errors of spelling and grammar: the manuscript, after acceptance by the Editor, must be immediately ready for typesetting as it is finally submitted by the author(s). Check your paper for the following common errors:

- dangling modifiers
- misplaced modifiers
- unclear antecedents
- incorrect or inconsistent abbreviations

Also, check the accuracy of all arithmetic calculations, statistics, numerical data, text citations, and references.

7. **Inconsistencies Must Be Avoided**. Be sure you are consistent in your use of abbreviations, terminology, and in citing references, from one part of your paper to another.

8. **Preparation of Tables, Figures, and Illustrations**. All tables and figures, illustrations, etc. must be "camera-ready". That is, they must be cleanly typed or artistically prepared so that they can be used either exactly as they are or else used after a photographic reduction in size. Figures, tables, and illustrations must be prepared on separate sheets of paper. Always use black ink and professional drawing instruments. On the back of these items, write your article title and the journal title lightly in pencil, so they do not get misplaced. In text, skip extra lines and indicate where these figures and tables are to be placed (please **do not write** on the face of art). Photographs are considered part of the acceptable manuscript and remain with the publisher for use in additional printings. If submitted art cannot be used, the Publisher reserves the right to redo the art and to charge the author a fee of $35.00 per hour for this service.

9. **Alterations Required By Referees and Reviewers**. Many times a paper is accepted by the Editor contingent upon changes that are mandated by anonymous specialist referees and members of the Editorial Board. If the Editor returns your manuscript for revisions, you are responsible for retyping any sections of the paper to incorporate these revisions (if applicable, revisions should also be put on disk).

10. **Typesetting**. You will not be receiving galley proofs o your article. Editorial revisions, if any, must therefore be made while your article is still in manuscript. The final version of the manuscript will be the version you see published. Typesetter's errors will be corrected by the production staff of The Haworth Press. Authors are expected to submit manuscripts, disks, and art that are free from error.

11. **Electronic Media**. Haworth's in-house typesetting unit is able to utilize your final manuscript material as prepared on most personal computers and word processors. This will minimize typographical errors and decrease overall production timelag. Please send the first draft and final draft copies of you manuscript to the journal Editor in print format for his/her final review and approval.

After approval of your final manuscript, please submit the final approved version both on printed format ("hard copy") and floppy diskette. On the outside of the diskette package write:

540

A. The brand name of your computer or word processor
B. The word-processing program that you used
C. The title of your article, and
D. File name

Note: Disk and hard copy must agree. In case of discrepancies, it is The Haworth Press' policy to follow hard copy. Authors are advised that **No Revisions** of the manuscript can be made after acceptance by the Editor for publication. The benefits of this procedure are many with speed and accuracy being the most obvious. We look forward to working with you on this, knowing we will be able to serve you more efficiently in the future.

12. **Reprints**. The senior author will receive two copies of the journal issue and 25 complimentary reprints of his or her article. The junior author will receive two copies of the journal issue. These are sent several weeks after the journal issue is published and in circulation. An order form for the purchase of additional reprints will also be sent to all authors at this time. (Approximately 4-6 weeks is necessary for the preparation of reprints.) Please do not query the Journal's Editor about reprints. All such questions should be sent directly to The Haworth Press, Inc. Production Department, 21 East Broad Street, West Hazleton, PA 18201 USA. To order additional reprints (minimum: 50 copies), please contact The Haworth Document Delivery Center, 10 Alice Street, Binghamton, NY 13904-1580 USA; 1-800-342-9678 or Fax (607) 722-6362.

13. **Copyright**. Copyright ownership of your manuscript must be transferred officially to The Haworth Press, Inc. before we can begin the peer-review process. The Editor's letter acknowledging receipt of the manuscript will be accompanied by a form fully explaining this. All authors must sign the form and return the original to the Editor as soon as possible. Failure to return the copyright form in a timely fashion will result in delay in review and subsequent publication.

Manuscript Submission Form
This Copyright Transmittal Form--signed by all authors--must be included with any journal article submission to the Editor. Original signatures, not photocopies, must be received with submission.

Publication Agreement
1. **Copyright**. In consideration for publication of our Work, if accepted and published by the journal noted on the reverse side of the page, the Author(s) agree to transfer copyright of the Work to The Haworth Press, Inc., including full and exclusive rights to publication in all media now known or later developed, including but not limited to electronic databases and microfilm, and in anthologies of any kind. (**Note to U.S. Government Employees: See Your Exemption, Paragraph 5 Below.**)

2. **Author Re-Use of Work**. As a professional courtesy, the authors retain the right to reprint their article submitted again, after publication in the journal, in any work for which they are sole Author, or in any edited work for which the author is Senior Editor. No further permission is necessary in writing from The Haworth Press, Inc., nor will the Press require fees of any kind for the reprinting. This statement is intended to provide full copyright release

for the purposes listed above, and a photocopy of this page (front and back) may be used when another Publisher requires a written release.

3. **Author Warranties**. The author(s) represent(s) and warrant(s):
a) that the manuscript submitted is his/her (their) own work;
b) that the work has been submitted only to this journal and that it has not been submitted or published elsewhere;
c) that the article contains no libelous or unlawful statements and does not infringe upon the civil rights of others;
d) that the author(s) is(are) not infringing upon anyone else's copyright.

The authors agree that if there is a breach of any of the above representations and warranties that (s)he (they) will indemnify the Publisher, Editor, or Guest Editor and hold them harmless.

4. a) **Rights Retained by the Author**. This transmittal form conveys copyright to the Publisher, but patent rights are retained by the Author;
b) **Materials Retained by the Publisher**. Photographs and illustrative material are, considered part of the manuscript, and must be retained by the Publisher for use in additional printings in case the journal issue or reprint edition needs to be reprinted.

5. **Note for U.S. Government Employees**. If the article is single-authored by a U.S. government employee as part of his/her official duties, it is understood that the article is not copyrightable. It is called a "Work of the U.S. Government." However, if the article was not part of the employee's official duties, it may be copyrighted. If the article was jointly written, the authors understand that they are delegating the right of copyright to the nongovernment employee, who must sign this agreement.

6. **"Work for Hire" Authors**. If the article was written by an author who was hired by another person or company to do so, the article is called a "Work for Hire" manuscript. This agreement must then be signed by the "employer" who hired the author, as well as the author.

7. **No Amendments**. No amendments or modifications of the terms of this Agreement are permissible unless same shall be in writing and signed by a duly authorized officer of The Haworth Press, Inc. No Journal Editor, Guest Editor or Special Issue Editor is authorized to waive, amend or modify any of the procedures or other provisions of this Agreement. This form is not valid if the Author(s) add any additional constraints and/or amendments. Please submit the article elsewhere for publication if the Author(s) do not sign this agreement without alteration.

8. **Integration**. This Agreement embodies the entire agreement and understanding between the Authors and The Haworth Press, Inc. and supersedes all other agreements and understandings, whether oral or written, relating to the subject matter hereof.

COPYRIGHT TRANSFER FORM

Name of journal:
Journal of Business & Finance Librarianship

542

Name and **Exact** Mailing Address of Contributor:

Special note: **This will be used for mailing reprints**. You must include exact street address, name of your department if at a university, and ZIP CODE. The Haworth Press cannot be responsible for lost reprints if you do not provide us with your exact mailing address.

In Reference To Your Journal Article:

☐ **If this box is checked...**

Thank you for your article submission! Please allow 10-15 weeks for the review process. Before sending out your article for review, however, the Publisher requires us to obtain your signature(s) confirming that you have read the PUBLICATION AGREEMENT on the reverse side of this page.

All co-authors must sign and return the ORIGINAL signed copy.

IT IS CONFIRMED that I/we have read the PUBLICATION AGREEMENT on the reverse side of the page, and agree and accept all conditions:

author's signature	date
author's signature	date
author's signature	date

☐ **If this box is checked...**

Your article has been favorably reviewed. Our reviewers, however, require certain revisions which are indicated on the attached sheets. Please review and incorporate their suggestions, and return your manuscript/disk retyped within 14 days. A decision about publication will he made at that time. Thank you for your help and cooperation.

Please reply to '

Journal Editor:
Charles Popovich, MSLS, MBA
Head Librarian, Business Library
Mason Hall / W. Woodruff Ave.
The Ohio State University
Columbus, OH 43210

☐ **If this box is checked...**

We are pleased to inform you that your article has been accepted for publication in the journal noted above. In addition to the standard journal edition, at the editor's discretion, this issue may also be co-published in a hardcover monographic co-edition.

Please note the following:

1. **Publication**: Your article is currently scheduled to appear in

Volume: _____ Number: _____

2. **Typesetting**: Your article will be sent to the Production Department of The Haworth Press, Inc., 21 East Broad Street, West Hazleton, PA 18201-3809. They will typeset your article (preferably from your computer disk) exactly as submitted. Please note that you will not be receiving galley proofs. The production staff will proofread the galleys for typesetting errors against the final version of the manuscript as submitted. No revisions are allowed.

3. **Reprints**: Shortly after publication you will receive an order form for purchasing quantities of reprints. (About three weeks after publication, the senior author will receive two complimentary copies of the issue and ten copies of the article, and the junior author(s) will receive two complimentary copies of the issue.) Please note that preparation of reprints takes about eight weeks additional time after the actual issue is printed and in circulation.

☐ **If this box is checked...**

We are sorry, but the reviewers for this journal did not agree that your article was appropriate for publication in this periodical. If the reviewers consented in having their comments forwarded to you, their critiques are attached. Your submission is appreciated, and we hope that you will contribute again in the future.

Journal of Business and Training Education

ADDRESS FOR SUBMISSION:

Betty A. Kleen, Editor
Journal of Business and Training Education
Nicholls State University
Information Systems Department
P O Box 2042
Thibodaux, LA 70310
USA
Phone: 985-448-4191
Fax: 985-448-4922
E-Mail: Betty.Kleen@nicholls.edu
Web:
Address May Change:

PUBLICATION GUIDELINES:

Manuscript Length: 6-15 pg. Dbl spaced
Copies Required: Computer submission
Computer Submission: Yes
Format: MS Word
Fees to Review: 0.00 US$

Manuscript Style:
    American Psychological Association,
    5th Edition

CIRCULATION DATA:

Reader: Academics, Practicing Teachers,
    Trainers/Business & Industry
Frequency of Issue: 1-2 Times/Year
Copies per Issue: Less than 1,000
Sponsor/Publisher: Louisiana Association
    of Business Educators
Subscribe Price: 10.00 US$

REVIEW INFORMATION:

Type of Review: Blind Review
No. of External Reviewers: 3
No. of In House Reviewers: 0
Acceptance Rate: 21-30%
Time to Review: 2 - 3 Months
Reviewers Comments: Yes
Invited Articles: 0-5%
Fees to Publish: 0.00 US$

MANUSCRIPT TOPICS:
Adult Career & Vocational; Business Education

MANUSCRIPT GUIDELINES/COMMENTS:

Call for Papers
The Louisiana Association of Business Educators invites business educators and trainers to contribute articles for publication in the *Journal of Business and Training Education*, a national refereed publication. Manuscripts should deal with topics of interest to educators (at both the secondary and post-secondary levels) and to trainers in business and industry. Submission of manuscripts dealing with practical topics are encouraged, as are research based or theoretical papers. Book reviews are accepted. Occasionally, invited authors' papers will be published.

Manuscripts will be selected through a blind review process. Manuscripts should not have been published or be under current consideration for publication by another journal. The manuscripts should range from 6 to 15 double-spaced typed pages of 12 point type-size, including tables and references. Manuscripts must be prepared using the style format in the

Publication Manual of the American Psychological Association, Fifth Edition, 2001. Remove all personal and institutional identification from the body and title of the paper. The Title Page is to include the title of the manuscript, a 50 - 100 word abstract, and a running header. The following information needs to be included in the email message accompanying the manuscript: Title of manuscript; and for each author, full name, position title, place of employment, city, state, zip code, telephone numbers and e-mail address.

Journal of Chemical Education

ADDRESS FOR SUBMISSION:

John W. Moore, Editor
Journal of Chemical Education
University of Wisconsin, Madison
Department of Chemistry
209 North Brooks Street
Madison, WI 53715-1116
USA
Phone: 608-262-7146
Fax: 608-262-7145
E-Mail: jce@chem.wisc.edu
Web: jehemed.chem.wisc.edu
Address May Change:

PUBLICATION GUIDELINES:

Manuscript Length: 1-20
Copies Required: Four
Computer Submission: No
Format: N/A
Fees to Review: 0.00 US$

Manuscript Style:
   See Manuscript Guidelines

CIRCULATION DATA:

Reader: Academics
Frequency of Issue: Monthly
Copies per Issue: 10,001 - 25,000
Sponsor/Publisher: Division of Chemical
   Education, American Chemical Society
Subscribe Price:

REVIEW INFORMATION:

Type of Review: Editorial Review
No. of External Reviewers: 3
No. of In House Reviewers: 2
Acceptance Rate: 50%
Time to Review: 1 - 2 Months
Reviewers Comments: Yes
Invited Articles: 0-5%
Fees to Publish: 0.00 US$

MANUSCRIPT TOPICS:
Science Math & Environment

MANUSCRIPT GUIDELINES/COMMENTS:

Our Expectations
To be considered for publication by *JCE*, a manuscript must
- have pedagogical content
- be useful to a clearly defined audience of teachers
- be accurate and original
- include a complete list of literature cited

We expect that your manuscript has not been published or submitted for publication elsewhere and that you have done a thorough literature search to ensure that it does not duplicate previously published work, especially from *JCE*. (Use our online *JCE* Index to find *JCE* references.) The text should be in clear, concise, proper English and should begin with an overview of how the work presented is relevant to classroom, laboratory, or curriculum.

Whenever possible, incorporate materials by citing relevant publications. Do not repeat what has already been published. Make certain that tables and illustrations convey information effectively, and that graphs and figures are appropriately drawn. You can supply supplemental material that we can make available in *JCE Online* for downloading.

How to Submit

Letters to the Editor. Send to the Editorial Office or email to **jceletters@chem.wisc.edu**. Your letter should be brief (400 words or less) and to the point. It may be edited for style, consistency, clarity, or length. Include your complete address, daytime phone number, and signature.

News and Announcements. Send to Elizabeth A. Moore at the Editorial Office or email to **betmoore@chem.wisc.edu**. Announcements should be concise, to the point, and appropriate for the Journal's audience. They may be edited for clarity, timeliness, appropriateness, or length. We need to receive announcements about two months before you want them to appear in print. Some announcements will appear only online on the Chemical Education Happenings page at http://jchemed.chem.wisc.edu/ChemEd/Index.html.

All other submissions. Send print copies of all other submissions to the Journal's Editorial Office, Journal of Chemical Education, University of Wisconsin-Madison, 209 N. Brooks Street, Madison, WI 53715-1116. This includes those intended for feature columns and the Secondary School Chemistry section. Do not attach your submission to an email message. Submissions that do not conform to the *JCE* guidelines will be returned for revision. There are additional requirements, described separately, for laboratory experiments and for *JCE* Classroom Activities.

A complete submission includes...

1. **A cover letter** from the corresponding author that states that the manuscript is being submitted exclusively to *JCE* and indicates why it is appropriate for the *Journal*. Authors are invited to suggest reviewers (please include complete, current postal addresses) and to suggest graphics that could be used for cover illustrations.

2. **A cover sheet** that includes the title of the manuscript, the area (In the Classroom, etc.) in which the manuscript best fits, the number of words in the manuscript, the name of the corresponding author, and the names of all other authors. For each author give complete postal and email addresses and telephone and fax numbers. Indicate which method of communication the corresponding author prefers. If the manuscript is suitable for any of the *Journal's* feature columns, please indicate which one(s).

3. **An original plus three copies (four total) of the manuscript**. The manuscript must be printed, double-spaced (no more than one line per vertical centimeter), in a font no smaller than 10 point. Number each page at the bottom right corner. Use 1-in. (2.5-cm) margins on top and sides of the page, and adjust the bottom margin so that all text and page numbers are no more than 10.5 in. (26.5 cm) from the top of the page. Fasten the pages in the upper left corner (paper clip the original and staple the copies). Do not put them in binders, folders, report covers, or plastic page protectors. The manuscript should include, in this order:

548

- **Abstract**. Page 1 should contain the title of the manuscript, the authors' names and institutional addresses, the abstract, and the keywords, in that order. The abstract should be no more than 200 words long and should summarize the important points made in the manuscript. (Abstracts will appear in *JCE Online* and *JCE CD* but not in print.)
- **Keywords**. Page 1 should also contain at least three *keywords* selected from the *Journal's* list; Keywords help categorize your manuscript and aid in the preparation of the index.
- **Manuscript text**. Page 2 should begin with the title and the authors' names and institutional addresses, followed by the manuscript text. The text should follow ACS style guidelines (see *The ACS Style Guide*, 2nd ed.; Dodd, J. S., Ed.; American Chemical Society: Washington, DC, 1997.) Place tables, and figures with their captions, in the text where they will be most useful to the reader. Also print or copy all tables and figures, one per page, and collect them, with a separate list of captions, at the end of the manuscript text.
- **Literature Cited**. Place the bibliography at the end of the manuscript text, following the adopted style (see website) of the *Journal*. If you cite no references, include the results of a literature search that cites your own and others' work that has a bearing on the manuscript you are submitting and explain why no citations are needed. Include in this section only material that has been published in the literature or on the Internet. Additional comments may be placed in numbered endnotes, indicated by superscripts in the text.
- **Tables** (if any) should be collected on separate sheets as well as included in the manuscript at the point where they are referred to. Column headings for physical quantities should consist of quantity/units. (For a concentration of 2.47 μmol/L, the heading would be concentration/μmol L^{-1} or concentration/10^{-6} mol L^{-1}, and the number entered in the table would be 2.47.)
- **Figures** (if any) should be collected at the end of the manuscript, each on a separate page. Four copies of each color figure must be submitted in color. Four copies (not photocopies) of each photograph must be submitted. Axes of graphs should be labeled with quantity/units in the same way that table headings are done.

4. **An original plus three copies (four total) of any supplemental material**. Many manuscripts include supplemental material for publication via *JCE Online*, the *JCE* Web site. (The Lab Documentation section of a laboratory experiment is supplemental material.) When possible, prepare supplemental material in the same format as the manuscript text. Label it clearly as supplemental material for online publication.

Digital versions on disk are required only after a manuscript has been accepted. However, consulting our Instructions for Final Manuscript Preparation (see website) while you are preparing your manuscript may save you time later.

Journal of Child Language

ADDRESS FOR SUBMISSION:

Elena Lieven, Editor
Journal of Child Language
University of Manchester
Department of Psychology
Manchester, M13 9PL
UK
Phone: +44-0-161-275-2580
Fax: +44-0-161-275-2588
E-Mail: jcl@fs4.psy.man.ac.uk
Web: journals.cambridge.org
Address May Change:

PUBLICATION GUIDELINES:

Manuscript Length: 20-40
Copies Required: Four
Computer Submission: No
Format: N/A
Fees to Review: 0.00 US$

Manuscript Style:
    See Manuscript Guidelines

CIRCULATION DATA:

Reader: Academics
Frequency of Issue: 4 Times/Year
Copies per Issue: 1,001 - 2,000
Sponsor/Publisher: Cambridge University
    Press
Subscribe Price: 194.00 US$

REVIEW INFORMATION:

Type of Review: Blind Review
No. of External Reviewers: 2
No. of In House Reviewers: 1
Acceptance Rate: 20% -/+
Time to Review: 4 Months
Reviewers Comments: Yes
Invited Articles: 0-5%
Fees to Publish: 0.00 US$

MANUSCRIPT TOPICS:
Bilingual/E.S.L.; Elementary/Early Childhood; Only Bilingual & Early Childhood

MANUSCRIPT GUIDELINES/COMMENTS:

Topics. All aspects of the scientific study of language development in children; phonological development; semantics of child language; crosslinguistic development; morphological development; syntactic development; pragmatic development.

Articles, and papers for the Notes and Discussion section, should be sent to the Editor, Elena Lieven, Department of Psychology, University of Manchester, Manchester, M13 9PL UK, email: **jcl@fs4.psy.man.ac.uk**. All submissions are read by a member of the editorial team to check whether, with regard to readability and content, they are appropriate to send to referees. All eligible manuscripts are then sent, anonymously, to two referees. When the referees' reports are received, each manuscript is evaluated by the editorial team and the Editor informs the author of their decision. Articles should be written in English and should not normally exceed 24 printed pages (roughly 10,000 words). Typescripts that conform to the following guidelines help to speed the production process. (For a more detailed style sheet, please write to the Editor.)

1. **Four** copies should be submitted.

2. Submissions should be typed on A4 paper (or 21-6 cm), on one side of the paper only. The entire text should be double-spaced, with ample margins. Authors of accepted articles should send the final version on disk (Apple Macintosh or IBM compatible PC) together with the hard copy typescript, giving details of the word-processing software used. However, the publisher reserves the right to typeset by conventional means if an author's disk proves unsatisfactory.

3. Each copy should have a separate title page giving the title, the full names of the author(s) with their affiliations, any acknowledgements, a full address for correspondence and - at the top - a running headline of not more than 40 characters. Other pages in the typescript should **not** carry the author's name.

4. Each copy should have an abstract on a separate sheet (not more than 150 words long for articles and 100 words for notes). The abstract should give the aims of the study, the general method and the principal conclusions.

5. Articles should be clearly divided into appropriately - labeled but unnumbered sections: often, but not necessarily, Introduction, Method, Results, and Discussion, Side headings should be used within these sections, e.g. Subjects, Procedure, etc.

6. Footnotes should not be used unless absolutely necessary; they should not contain phonetic characters or other special symbols. They should be numbered and listed on a separate sheet at the end of the article.

7. Each table and figure should be on a separate sheet at the end of the article; their position in the text should be clearly indicated. They should have a title and should be numbered independently of any numbered examples in the text. Figures should, if possible, be camera-ready

8. Ages should be stated in years, months and - if necessary - days, like this: 1;10.22.

9. Phonetic transcriptions should, wherever possible, employ the IPA symbols.

10. Emphasis and technical terms should be marked by double underlining (small capitals). Standard linguistic abbreviations should be in large capitals, e.g. AUX, NP. Language examples in the body of the text should be underlined (italics). Translations and glosses should be given between single inverted commas.

11. References in the body of the text should be made like this: According to Snow (1990: 698); OR, In the sixties and seventies, several authors published important work on combinatorial speech (Braine, 1963; Miller & Ervin, 1964; Bloom, 1970; Schlesinger, 1974).

Note that such references are in DATE order, not alphabetical order, and that pairs of authors are joined by &.

12. All works referred to should be listed at the end of the article in alphabetical order, as in these examples:

Cruttenden, A. (1986). Intonation. Cambridge: Cambridge University Press.

Karmiloff-Smith, A'. (1986). Some fundamental aspects of language development after age five. In P. Fletcher & M. Garman (eds), Language acquisition: studies in first language development. Second edition. Cambridge, Cambridge University Press.

O'Grady, W., Peters, A. M. & Masterson, D. (1989). The transition from optional to required subjects. Journal of Child Language 16, 513-29.

Journal of Classroom Interaction

ADDRESS FOR SUBMISSION:

H. Jerome Freiberg, Editor
Journal of Classroom Interaction
University of Houston
College of Education
442 Farish Hall
Houston, TX 77204-5026
USA
Phone: 713-743-5919
Fax: 713-743-8586
E-Mail: louamyx@cmcdmail.coe.uh.edu
Web: http://cmcd.coe.uh.edu/coejc/
Address May Change:

PUBLICATION GUIDELINES:

Manuscript Length: 20-25
Copies Required: Three
Computer Submission: Yes
Format: N/A
Fees to Review: 0.00 US$

Manuscript Style:
American Psychological Association

CIRCULATION DATA:

Reader: Academics, Practicing Teachers
Frequency of Issue: 2 Times/Year
Copies per Issue: 1,001 - 2,000
Sponsor/Publisher: University of Houston
Subscribe Price: 40.00 US$ Individual
45.00 US$ Institution
35.00 US$ Indv. & $55 Inst. On-line

REVIEW INFORMATION:

Type of Review: Blind Review
No. of External Reviewers: 2
No. of In House Reviewers: 1
Acceptance Rate: 11-20%
Time to Review: 2 - 3 Months
Reviewers Comments: Yes
Invited Articles: 11-20%
Fees to Publish: 0.00 US$

MANUSCRIPT TOPICS:
Classroom Interaction PreK-H; Elementary/Early Childhood; Secondary/Adolescent Studies

MANUSCRIPT GUIDELINES/COMMENTS:

The *Journal of Classroom Interaction* was founded in 1965 to meet the need to share, discuss and disseminate new ideas on research methodology and variables in order to generate new knowledge about classroom interaction. The research interest, agenda and interest in classroom interaction studies has continued to expand to new audiences, including the public schools. The *Journal* remains a publication devoted to empirical investigations and theoretical papers dealing with observation techniques, research on student and teacher behavior, and other issues relevant to the domain of classroom interaction.

The *Journal of Classroom Interaction* is distributed in 50 countries and reported in the abstracts of the American Psychological Association - Psyclnfo, Institute of Scientific Information - Current Contents / Social and Behavioral Sciences and Social Sciences Citation Index, SEMBCS Information Center, Sciences de L'Education, and Sociology Abstracts. The publication is unaffiliated with any organization and receives its support from subscriptions and a grant from the office of the Provost and Vice Chancellor at the University of Houston, and does not accept paid advertising.

Manuscript Instructions

Authors are advised to follow the guidelines given in the *Publication Manual of the American Psychological Association* (4th Edition), 1200 Seventeenth Street, N.W., Washington, D.C. 20036. The entire manuscript should be double-spaced and should be limited to 20 pages including references and tables. The manuscript should contain the following sections: abstract of 75-100 words, introduction, methodology, results, and discussion.

The *Journal* has a 10-15% acceptance rate. Each manuscript is double blind reviewed by a least two standing review board members and/or guest reviewers. Review board members are listed in each issue of the *Journal*. The review process generally takes from 8-12 weeks and new researchers have the same opportunity to publish as the veteran researcher. All authors are encouraged to submit current research on classroom interaction. There are no fees to publish in the *Journal of Classroom Interaction*.

Journal of College Literacy and Learning

ADDRESS FOR SUBMISSION:

Shirley A. Biggs, Editor
Journal of College Literacy and Learning
University of Pittsburgh
School of Education
Office of the Dean
Pittsburg, PA 15260
USA
Phone: 412-648-1782
Fax: 412-648-1825
E-Mail: biggs@pitt.edu
Web:
Address May Change:

PUBLICATION GUIDELINES:

Manuscript Length: 10-15
Copies Required: Four
Computer Submission: Yes
Format:
Fees to Review: 0.00 US$

Manuscript Style:
American Psychological Association

CIRCULATION DATA:

Reader: Academics
Frequency of Issue: 1 Time/Year
Copies per Issue: Less than 1,000
Sponsor/Publisher: College Literacy and
   Learning Special Interest Group,
   International Reading Association
Subscribe Price:

REVIEW INFORMATION:

Type of Review: Blind Review
No. of External Reviewers: 2
No. of In House Reviewers: 0
Acceptance Rate: No Reply
Time to Review: 4 - 6 Months
Reviewers Comments: Yes
Invited Articles: 11-20%
Fees to Publish: 0.00 US$

MANUSCRIPT TOPICS:
College & Adult Literacy Developmental Education; Higher Education; Languages &
Linguistics; Reading; Tests, Measurement & Evaluation

MANUSCRIPT GUIDELINES/COMMENTS:

The Journal of College Literacy and Learning seeks articles which are related to any of the
many aspects of college/postsecondary reading and writing improvement. Authors wishing to
submit manuscripts are encouraged to review the following guidelines before submission.

Manuscripts should be word-processed in letter quality print, double-spaced, and
approximately 15 to 20 pages in length. Contributors must submit four clear copies and are
advised to keep a copy on disk. *The Journal of College Literacy and Learning* will not return
manuscripts unless the sender provides a large, self-addressed stamped envelop. Content,
organization and style of manuscripts should follow *APA*, Fifth Edition guidelines. Tables and
figures should be camera-ready for publication.

All manuscripts are evaluated by at least two reviewers. To insure an impartial review, the author should make every effort to avoid inclusion of clues to her/his identity. Each manuscript should include a cover sheet containing the author's name, affiliation, position, addresses (preferred location for correspondence, email), and the date that the manuscript is submitted. The pages of the manuscript should not contain the name of the author or her/his affiliation.

Upon receipt of a manuscript, an acknowledgment is sent. The manuscripts submitted should be unpublished and not under simultaneous consideration by any other publication. Manuscripts are evaluated in terms of interest, quality of writing, appropriate documentation of ideas, uniqueness and needs of the editor. Accepted manuscripts may be edited to promote clarity and improve organization. In the event that the manuscript is accepted for publication but cannot be used in the forthcoming issue, the editor reserves the right to accept the article for inclusion in a subsequent issue. Questions can be addressed via e-mail to: **biggs@pitt.edu**

Manuscript correspondence can be sent to either:

Dr. Shirley A. Biggs, Editor
The Journal of College
 Literacy and Learning
Office of the Dean
School of Education
University of Pittsburgh
Pittsburgh, PA 15260

Dr. Terry Bullock, Associate Editor
The Journal of College
 Literacy and Learning
P. O. Box 210047
University College
University of Cincinnati
Cincinnati, OH 45221-0047

Journal of Computer Science Education

ADDRESS FOR SUBMISSION:

J. Philip East, Editor
Journal of Computer Science Education
University of Northern Iowa
Computer Science Department
Cedar Falls, IA 50614-0507
USA
Phone: 319-273-2939
Fax: 319-273-7123
E-Mail: east@cs.uni.edu
Web: http://.iste.org/sigcs
Address May Change:

PUBLICATION GUIDELINES:

Manuscript Length: 1-20
Copies Required: One
Computer Submission: Yes Email
Format: RTF with separate graphic files
Fees to Review: 0.00 US$

Manuscript Style:
American Psychological Association

CIRCULATION DATA:

Reader: Practicing Teachers, Academics
Frequency of Issue: 4 Times/Year
Copies per Issue: 1,001 - 2,000
Sponsor/Publisher: ISTE and Special
Interest Group for Computer Science
(SIGCS)
Subscribe Price: 65.00 US$

REVIEW INFORMATION:

Type of Review: Blind Review
No. of External Reviewers: 0-2
No. of In House Reviewers: 1
Acceptance Rate: 65%
Time to Review: 2 - 3 Months
Reviewers Comments: Yes via editor
comments
Invited Articles: 31-50%
Fees to Publish: 0.00 US$

MANUSCRIPT TOPICS:
Computer Science Education; Curriculum Studies; Educational Technology Systems

MANUSCRIPT GUIDELINES/COMMENTS:

JCSE Online is a produced cooperatively by the International Society for Technology in Education (ISTE) and its Special Interest Group for Computer Science (SIGCS) with the mission to enhance precollege instruction in computer science. While we have previously focused on secondary instruction we wish to expand our audience and coverage to essentially all aspects of teaching about computers and computer science is PK-12 education. *JCSE Online* is published electronically during the academic year and a print compendium (*JCSE Annual*) is produced at the end of the academic year. Both editor-reviewed and peer-reviewed/refereed articles are accepted. We are interested in:

• Articles
• Well-reasoned opinion pieces
• Book, software, and site reviews
• Reports of/from conferences, programming contests, etc.

- Letters to the editor
- Advertisements for and announcements of appropriate instructional materials and professional conferences

We seek items addressing current issues in computer science education and policies, curriculum issues, instructional strategies, etc. about the following topics:

- Use of computers and systems-level software
- Use of general-purpose and special-purpose computer applications
- Functioning of computers and related systems
- Design, implementation, and testing and revision of computer-based systems (e.g., spreadsheets, Web sites, databases, etc. that require design, planning, and testing (algorithmic thinking and problem solving are required)
- History of computing
- Social impact of and issues involving computing
- Computer programming (at various school levels and at various depths of skill)
- Lifelong learning of computer applications and about computing and computing-related issues
- Other related skills and knowledge (e.g., advanced placement computer science, networking, system/Web administration)

Manuscript Submission

Please download the ISTE style guide at **www.iste.org/L&L/styleguide/ISTEstyle.pdf** for general information, and contact the editor for more specific information. For papers that are to be editor-reviewed, submit a single RTF file. For pieces that are to be refereed or peer-reviewed, we would like to receive two electronic versions--one should have complete author information while the other should be sanitized of author information. Sanitization involves substituting "name(s) omitted for review" for name(s) in citations and references, and "institution omitted for review" for your institution if it is indicated in the body or references. Files should be saved and submitted in rich text format (RTF).

Text-based tables and figures may be placed in the text where they are to be located on the final copy. Submit electronic copies of all graphic images in their original file formats (e.g., PICT screenshot). Please also send original Excel spreadsheets with data included and charts created for all Excel-based elements. Graphic elements may be placed in files to indicate placement, but the original files must also be submitted. Send electronic files as e-mail attachments to Philip East at the address below. We prefer e-mail submissions, but paper submissions with accompanying electronic files are also accepted at the mailing address below.

As we will be formatting for the Web, keep formatting as simple as possible.

- Generally, use a single type size (12) and typeface (Times or Times Roman).
- Represent code (in figures and in the body of paper) in the Courier typeface.
- Omit headers and footers.
- Avoid special paragraph spacing.

- Insert blank lines between paragraphs.
- Avoid full justification of prose (use left, center, and right alignment).
- Use bold and italic style sparingly and consistently. Do not underline text.
- Do not hyperlink URLs or e-mail addresses in the article. But, please include URLs where necessary, just don't automatically make them live links.
- Use bulleted and numbered lists when necessary.

Use numbered subheads, with each on a separate line (except level four, which should be a run-in subhead). Follow standard *APA* style. Proofread carefully. Editing does not routinely include major rewriting or stylistic correction. Authors are responsible for the correctness and consistency of their words- Double-check and update all references and URLs. Follow this format for citing Web sources:

Roland, J. (1999). JRTE submission guidelines [Online document]. Eugene, OR: International Society for Technology in Education. Available: www.iste.org/jrtelsubmissions.html.

Send all submissions and queries to:
J. Philip East
Computer Science Department
University of Northern Iowa
Cedar Falls, to 50614-0507
Phone: 319.273.2939; E-mail: **east@cs.uni.edu**

If your article is accepted, you will be asked to transfer copyright to ISTE.

Manuscript Review
Feature articles are reviewed by the editor and two referees selected from volunteers among the SIGCS membership. Reviewer comments are filtered through the editor. **Regular** articles are reviewed by the editor. The editors reserve the right to make editorial changes in manuscripts to achieve greater clarity. Major revisions will be made only after consultation with the author.

Journal of Computers in Mathematics and Science Teaching

ADDRESS FOR SUBMISSION:

Gary Marks, Editor
Journal of Computers in Mathematics and
Science Teaching
ONLINE SUBMISSION ONLY
AACE
P.O. Box 3728
Norfolk, VA 23514-3728
USA
Phone: 757-623-7588
Fax: 703-997-8760
E-Mail: pubs@aace.org
Web: www.aace.org/pubs
Address May Change:

PUBLICATION GUIDELINES:

Manuscript Length: Max. 30 pages
Copies Required: No Paper Copy
Computer Submission: Yes Online
Submission
Format: MS Word, html, RTF
Fees to Review: 0.00 US$

Manuscript Style:
See Manuscript Guidelines

CIRCULATION DATA:

Reader: Academics, Corporate Researchers
Frequency of Issue: Quarterly
Copies per Issue: 1,001 - 2,000
Sponsor/Publisher: AACE - Assn. For the
Advancement of Computers in Education
Subscribe Price: 95.00 US$ Individual
120.00 US$ Institution

REVIEW INFORMATION:

Type of Review: Blind Review
No. of External Reviewers: 2-4
No. of In House Reviewers: 2
Acceptance Rate: 11-20%
Time to Review: 2-4 Months
Reviewers Comments: Yes
Invited Articles: 15%
Fees to Publish: 0.00 US$

MANUSCRIPT TOPICS:
Computer Science Education; Science Math & Environment

MANUSCRIPT GUIDELINES/COMMENTS:

JCMST is a highly respected scholarly journal which offers an in-depth forum for the interchange of information in the fields of science, mathematics, and computer science. *JCMST* is the only periodical devoted specifically to using information technology in the teaching of mathematics and science.

Please read through the guidelines below before submitting your paper.

Journal Content
Contributions for all journals may include research papers, case studies, tutorials, courseware experiences, evaluations, review papers, and viewpoints.

General Guidelines

Material must be original, scientifically accurate, and in good form editorially. The manuscript should be informative, summarizing the basic facts and conclusions, and maintaining a coherence and unity of thought.

Tutorial or how-to-do-it articles should preferably include a section on evaluation. Controversial topics should be treated in a factually sound and reasonably unbiased manner.

The format of headings, tables, figures, citations, references, and other details should follow the (APA) style as described in the *Publication Manual of the American Psychological Association*, 5th Edition, available from APA, 750 1st St., NE, Washington, DC 20002 USA.

Preview

Manuscripts sent to the Editor for review are accepted on a voluntary basis from authors. Before submitting an article, please review the following suggestions. Manuscripts received in correct form serve to expedite the processing and prompt reviewing for early publication.

Spelling, punctuation, sentence structure, and the mechanical elements of arrangements, spacing, length, and consistency of usage in form and descriptions should be studied before submission. Due to the academic focus of AACE publications, the use of personal pronoun (I, we, etc.) and present tense is strongly discouraged.

Pre-publication

No manuscript will be considered which has already been published or is being considered by another journal.

Copyright

These journals are copyrighted by the Association for the Advancement of Computing in Education. Material published and so copyrighted may not be published elsewhere without the written permission of AACE.

Author Note(s)

Financial support for work reported or a grant under which a study was made should be noted just prior to the Acknowledgments. Acknowledgments or appreciation to individuals for assistance with the manuscript or with the material reported should be included as a note to appear at the end of the article prior to the References.

Handling of Manuscripts

All manuscripts are acknowledged upon receipt. Review is carried out as promptly as possible. The manuscript will be reviewed by at least two members of the Editorial Review Board, which takes approximately five months. When a decision for publication or rejection is made, the senior author or author designated to receive correspondence is notified. At the time of notification, the author may be asked to make certain revisions in the manuscript, or the Editor may submit suggested revisions to the author for approval.

Presentation

Accepted Submission File Formats - All submissions must be sent in electronic form using the Article Submission Form. No hard copy submission papers will be accepted. Do NOT submit compressed files. Do not use any word processing options/tools, such as--strike through, hidden text, comments, merges, and so forth.

Submit your manuscript in either of the following formats:
* **DOC**- Microsoft Word (preferred)
* RTF - Rich Text Format

Manuscripts should be double-spaced and a font size of 12 is preferred.

Length. In general, articles should not exceed 30 double-spaced pages. Long articles, or articles containing complex material should be broken up by short, meaningful subheads.

Title sheet. Do NOT include a title sheet. Manuscripts are blind reviewed so there should be no indication of the author(s) name on the pages.

Abstract. An informative, comprehensive abstract of 75 to 200 words must accompany the manuscript. This abstract should succinctly summarize the major points of the paper, and the author's summary and/or conclusions.

Tables, Figures & Graphics
All tables and figure graphics must be embedded within the file and of such quality that when printed be in camera-ready form (publication quality). Within the submitted file, number and type captions centered at the top of each table. Figures are labeled at the bottom of the figure, left justified, and numbered in sequence.

Any graphics that go in the article must be submitted as separate files. The highest quality master (e.g. TIF) is preferred. Additionally, the graphics must also be embedded in the correct locations within the document so the copyeditors know the proper placement. Please note that any graphics created in Microsoft Word must also be submitted as separate files.

Graphics, tables, figures, photos, and so forth, must be sized to fit a 6" x 9" publication with margins of: top, 1" inside 1" outside, .75" and bottom, 1" an overall measurement of 4.5 X 6.75 is the absolute limit in size. A table or figure sized on a full size 8.5 by 11 piece of paper does not always reduce and remain legible. Please adhere to the size stipulation or your manuscript will be returned for graphics/figures or tables to be re-done.

Quotations
Copy all quoted material exactly as it appears in the original, indicating any omissions by three spaced periods. At the close of the quotation, give the complete source including page numbers. A block quote must be a minimum of 40 words or four lines, single spaced.

Terminology and Abbreviations
Define any words or phrases that cannot be found in Webster's Unabridged Dictionary. Define or explain new or highly technical terminology. Write out the first use of a term that you

expect to use subsequently in abbreviated form. Abbreviations (i.e., e.g., etc.) are only acceptable in parenthesis, otherwise they must be spelled out, that is, for example, and so forth, respectively. Please avoid other foreign phrases and words such as via.

Program Listings
Program listings will appear with the published article if space permits. Listings should be publication quality. The brand of computer required should be included. Lengthy program listings (more than four 6 x 9 pages) can not be published, but may be made available from the author; a note to that effect should be included in the article.

Citations
Citations should strictly follow *American Psychological Association* (APA) style guide. Examples of references cited within the texts of articles are as follows: (Williams, Allen, & Jones, 1978) or (Moore, 1990; Smith, 1991) or Terrell (1977). In citations, "et al." can only be used after all authors have been cited or referenced with the exception of six or more authors. As per APA all citations must match the reference list and vice versa. Over use of references is discouraged.

References
Authors are responsible for checking the accuracy of all references and that all references cited in the text also appear in the Reference section. All references should be in alphabetical order by author (unnumbered) *American Psychological Association* (APA), 5th edition, style. Citation examples (1) book and (2) periodical:

> Knowles, M. (1975). *Self-directed learning: A guide for learners and teachers*. New York: Association Press.

> Raybould, B. (1995). Performance support engineering: An emerging development methodology for enabling organizational learning. *Performance Improvement Quarterly*, 8(1), 7-22.

Citing Electronic Media
The following forms for citing on-line sources are taken from the *APA Publication Guidelines*, Appendix 3-A, Section I (pp. 218-222). Please see the *APA Manual* for additional information on formatting electronic media. A block quote must be a minimum of 40 words or four lines, single spaced (not 20 and double spaced as is presently noted). In citations, et al., can only be used after all authors have been cited or referenced. As per APA all citations must match the reference list and vice versa.

Elements of references to on-line information
Author, I. (date). Title of article. Name of Periodical [On-line], xx. Available: Specify path

Author, I., & Author, I. (date). Title of chapter. In Title of full work [On-line]. Available: Specify path

Author, I., Author, I., & Author, I. (date). Title of full work [On-line]. Available: Specify path

The date element should indicate the year of publication or, if the source undergoes regular revision, the most recent update; if a date cannot be determined, provide an exact date of your search. (p. 219)

An availability statement replaces the location and name of a publisher typically provided for text references. Provide information sufficient to retrieve the material. For example, for material that is widely available on networks, specify the method used to find the material, such as the protocol (Telnet, FTP, Internet, etc.), the directory, and the file name. (p. 219)

Other Electronic Media
Author, I. (Version number) [CD-ROM]. (date). Location of producer/distributor: Name of producer/distributor.

Author, I. (date). Title of article [CD-ROM]. Title of Journal, xx, xxx-xxx. Abstract from: Source and retrieval number

Author, I. (date). Name of Software (Version number) [Computer software]. Location of Location of producer/distributor: Name of producer/distributor.

After the title of the work, insert in brackets as part of the title element (i.e., before the period) the type of medium for the material (current examples include CD-ROM, Electronic data tape, cartridge tape, and computer program). (p. 220)

Include the location and name of the producer and distributor if citing an entire bibliographic database. (p. 220)

Post-publication
Upon publication, the contact author will receive complimentary copies of the journal issue in which the article appears for distribution to all of the co-authors.

Please carefully read and adhere to these guidelines. Manuscripts not submitted according to the guidelines will be rejected and returned to the author.

Journal of Cooperative Education and Internships

ADDRESS FOR SUBMISSION:

ELECTRONIC SUBMISSION ONLY
Journal of Cooperative Education and
  Internships
Phil D. Gardner, Senior Editor
Michigan State University
CERI - 113SSB
East Lansing, MI 48824
USA
Phone: 517-355-2211
Fax:
E-Mail: gardnerp@msu.edu
Web: www.ceiainc.org/journal
Address May Change:

PUBLICATION GUIDELINES:

Manuscript Length: Maximum 30
Copies Required: On-line
Computer Submission: Final Copy
Format: MS Word
Fees to Review: 0.00 US$

Manuscript Style:
    American Psychological Association

CIRCULATION DATA:

Reader: Academics, Practitioners
Frequency of Issue: Continuous
Copies per Issue:
Sponsor/Publisher: Professional Association
Subscribe Price: 50.00 US$
    See website for information

REVIEW INFORMATION:

Type of Review: Blind Review
No. of External Reviewers: 2
No. of In House Reviewers: 1
Acceptance Rate: 50%
Time to Review: 2 - 3 Months
Reviewers Comments: Yes
Invited Articles: 30%
Fees to Publish: 0.00 US$

MANUSCRIPT TOPICS:
Adult Career & Vocational; Counseling & Personnel Services; Curriculum Studies; Education
Management/Administration; Educational Psychology; Educational Technology Systems;
Higher Education; Science Math & Environment; Tests, Measurement & Evaluation; Work
Intergrated Curriculum

MANUSCRIPT GUIDELINES/COMMENTS:

The *Journal of Cooperative Education* is dedicated to the advancement of work-integrated
education through the publication of thoughtful and timely articles. Manuscripts submitted for
consideration will be reviewed for their appropriateness, cogency, technical adequacy, and the
contribution they will be judged to make to the literature of cooperative education and work-
integrated education generally.

Two distinctive kinds of manuscripts are invited:

- *Reports of Empirical Research*, in which the author presents a detailed account of an empirical study (quantitative, qualitative, historical, literature review and analysis) of some problem germane to work integrated education, or
- *Descriptive Articles (Theory and Practice) which includes Essays*, in which the author presents a description of an innovative program practice or procedure, a unique program, or of a 'local' program assessment of study.

Review Criteria
The criteria for all manuscripts and those for each of the above kinds are as follows:

General Characteristics
1. The topic is appropriate for the *Journal of Cooperative Education and Internships*.
2. The article is of reasonable length. In general, manuscripts should not exceed 7,000 words or 30 double-spaced pages).
3. The article is written clearly and in an interesting manner.
4. There is a good use of headings in the article.

Essay
1. The point of the essay (the issue to be discussed, reviewed, examined, analyzed) is clear and is significant to the field.
2. There is a concise and well-focused review of the relevant literature to provide background to the reader, clarify the issue, and to substantiate the significance of the issue.
3. Technical or other potentially unfamiliar terms that are to be used are defined and/or explained.
4. The discussion, review, examination, or analysis is clear, logical, and coherent, and it flows from the issue or the problem presented is the introduction.
5. Appropriate references are used to document claims and to argue points.
6. Conclusions are clear and unambiguous.
7. Conclusions flow logically from the analysis presented and are not a reinstatement of previously presented information.

Research Report
1. The research problem is stated clearly and is significant to the field.
2. The review of the literature is comprehensive. Previous research relating to the problem is well-referenced.
3. Variables are clearly and succinctly defined.
4. Hypotheses and/or research questions are formulated clearly and succinctly.
5. Who the subjects are, how many of them thee are, and how and why they were selected is carefully explained.
6. Data collection instruments (questionnaires, tests, interview guides) are clearly described and, if published, referenced.
7. Research procedures are described clearly and completely so that the research could be replicated by someone else.
8. The research design, sampling procedures, and data collection procedures are sound.

9. Data analyses are appropriate to the research design and the data collected, and are presented clearly.
10. Tables of data, graphs, and figures are used appropriately and, if included, are clearly presented.
11. There is a clear statement of support or non-support for each hypothesis or a clear answer to each research question.
12. Speculation beyond specific results is logical and clear.
13. Conclusions are clear, specific, and not simply a restatement of results presented.

Description
1. The problem or situation giving rise to the innovation, procedure, or practice is clear.
2. The description of the innovation, procedure, or practice is clear and follows logically from the statement of the problem.
3. Some form of assessment is presented to indicate the success or failure of the innovation, procedure, or practice designed to solve the original problem.
4. The innovation, procedure, or practice described has applicability to cooperative education generally.
5. A concise and clear summary of the problem and the solution are presented.

Requirements
Submit the article on-line following the guides provided at **www.ceiainc.org/journal**

A cover page should be affixed only to the original and contain the title of the article, author, official title, and affiliation, and complete address, phone number, and e-mail address.

The title, *brief but descriptive,* should appear on the first page, but the name of the author and other indicators of authorship should be avoided in the text to permit anonymous review.

Double-space everything, including references, quotations, tables and figures.

Leave a generous margin (about an inch around) on each page. Each page should be numbered.

Standardize the editing of the following terminology and punctuation: *cooperative education; Capitalize only when referring to a specific program, title, or office, e.g., "Office of Cooperative Education, Rutgers University."* Co-ops: *As a noun, to abbreviate references to students, e.g., "35 co-ops and 36 non-co-ops."* Co-ops: *As an adjective, e.g., "the co-op coordinator," "co-op placement."*

Avoid use of the generic masculine pronoun and other sexist terminology.

Minimize discursive footnotes.

References should follow the predominant style of the journal (preferably following the style of the *American Psychological Association*). Check all references for completeness and give adequate information to allow the reader to retrieve the referenced material from the most available source. All references cited in the text must be listed in the reference section and vice versa.

Tables should be kept to a minimum. Include only essential data, and combine tables where possible. Refer to a recent issue of the journal for style of tabular presentations. Each table should be typed on a separate page following the reference section of the article. Note the approximate location of the table within the text.

Do not submit material that is under consideration by another periodical.

Journal of Curriculum and Supervision

ADDRESS FOR SUBMISSION:

Ozro L. Davis, Jr., Editor
Journal of Curriculum and Supervision
University of Texas at Austin
College of Education
Dept. of Curriculum & Instruction
SZB 406
Austin, TX 78712
USA
Phone: 512-471-4611
Fax: 512-471-8460
E-Mail: oldavisjr@mail.utexas.edu
Web: www.ascd.org
Address May Change:

PUBLICATION GUIDELINES:

Manuscript Length: Any
Copies Required: Four
Computer Submission: No
Format: N/A
Fees to Review: 0.00 US$

Manuscript Style:
    See Manuscript Guidelines

CIRCULATION DATA:

Reader: Academics, School Curriculum
    Leaders
Frequency of Issue: Quarterly
Copies per Issue: 5,001 - 10,000
Sponsor/Publisher: Association for
    Supervision and Curriculum
    Development (ASCD)
Subscribe Price: 49.00 US$ Non Member
    39.00 US$ ASCD Member
    12.00 US$ Individual Issue

REVIEW INFORMATION:

Type of Review: Blind Review
No. of External Reviewers: 3
No. of In House Reviewers: 2
Acceptance Rate: 11-20%
Time to Review: 2 - 3 Months
Reviewers Comments: Yes
Invited Articles: 0-5%
Fees to Publish: 0.00 US$

MANUSCRIPT TOPICS:
Curriculum Studies; Education Management/Administration; Supervision of Instruction;
Teacher Education

MANUSCRIPT GUIDELINES/COMMENTS:

The *Journal's* style uses footnotes rather than textual references. Format of references varies
slightly from *The Chicago Manual of Style*. Contributors should consult an issue of the
Journal for details.

Journal Description and Purpose
The *Journal of Curriculum and Supervision* is a refereed, scholarly journal published by the
Association for Supervision and Curriculum Development. It welcomes articles that
reflectively examine curriculum and supervision practices and related policy issues. A wide
variety of research methods are appropriate, including interpretive, empirical, historical,
critical, and analytical. Theoretical and speculative perspectives are encouraged as well as

rigorous studies of concrete practices. Highest priority is given manuscripts dealing with comprehensive, holistic, or interactive views of professional practices in curriculum and supervision.

Manuscript Submission and Review

Manuscripts must be original work, scholarly in style and intent, and should not be under consideration by any other journal. Four complete copies of a manuscript should be sent to the Editors. Thorough review of each manuscript will be conducted and decisions resulting from this review will be conveyed to authors as soon as possible. Authors of promising manuscripts may be asked to revise their manuscripts and submit them for additional review before a decision to publish is made.

Editorial Procedures

All manuscripts, once reviewed for appropriateness by the Editor, are submitted anonymously to the reviewers. The Editor relies on, but is not governed by, reviewers' recommendations. Manuscripts are accepted for publication subject to copyediting and transfer of copyright to ASCD. Authors will be required to sign a Transfer of Copyright form supplied by ASCD.

Copy Preparation

- All copy should be typed and double-spaced—including indented matter and footnotes (submitted as endnotes)—on one side of 8½ x 11 paper with uniform margins.

- The author's name, professional title and affiliation, mailing address, telephone number, fax number, and e-mail address should appear only on a separate title page to ensure anonymity in the reviewing process. If the article is based on dissertation research, a funded research project, or a paper presented at a professional meeting, a note on the title page should provide the relevant facts. The remaining pages should be numbered consecutively, and only the title of the article (not the author's name) should appear on page 1. No specific length of manuscript is preferred.

- Tables should be double-spaced on separate pages and numbered consecutively. Figures should be drawn on white paper with India ink; high-quality computer graphics also may be submitted. Tables and figures should be captioned and keyed to the text.

- Include an abstract (200 words or less) that summarizes the manuscript's major contribution.

- Submit four paper copies of the manuscript and abstract and one computer disc copy to:
  Editors
  Journal of Curriculum and Supervision
  Department of Curriculum and Instruction, SZB 406
  The University of Texas at Austin
  Austin, TX 78712-1294

Please identify on the disc the name of the word processing program used (e.g., WordPerfect), the version of the program (e.g., 6.0), and the name of the disk file. Manuscripts are not returned to authors.

570

All other correspondence should be addressed to:
ASCD
Journal of Curriculum and Supervision
1703 N. Beauregard Street
Alexandria, VA 22311-1714

Reference Format
Do not use APA style. Accuracy and completeness of references are the author's responsibility. Examples of common references are:

Jerome Bruner, *Actual Minds, Possible Worlds* (Cambridge, MA: Harvard University Press, 1986), 11.

Carl Glickman, ed. *Supervision in Transition* (Alexandria, VA: Association for Supervision and Curriculum Development, 1992).

Larry Cuban, "Curriculum Stability and Change," in *The Handbook of Research on Curriculum*, ed. Philip W. Jackson (New York: Macmillan, 1992), 216-247.

Arthur W. Foshay, "The Curriculum Matrix: Transcendence and Mathematics," *Journal of Curriculum and Supervision* 6 (Summer 1991): 277-293.

Stephen P. Gordon, "The Theory of Developmental Supervision: An Investigation of the Critical Aspects" (doctoral dissertation, The University of Georgia, 1989).

Journal of Curriculum Studies

ADDRESS FOR SUBMISSION:

Ian Westbury, Editor
Journal of Curriculum Studies
University of Illinois Urbana-Champaign
Department of Curriculum and Instruction
341 Armory Building
505 E. Armory Ave.
Champaign, IL 61820
USA
Phone: 217-244-5811
Fax: 217-244-4572
E-Mail: westbury@uiuc.edu
Web: www.tandf.co.uk/journals
Address May Change:

PUBLICATION GUIDELINES:

Manuscript Length: 30+
Copies Required: Three
Computer Submission: Yes Email
Format: MSWord preferred
Fees to Review: 0.00 US$

Manuscript Style:
    See Manuscript Guidelines

CIRCULATION DATA:

Reader: Academics
Frequency of Issue: Bi-Monthly
Copies per Issue:
Sponsor/Publisher: Taylor & Francis
Subscribe Price: 111.00 US$ Individual
    582.00 US$ Institution

REVIEW INFORMATION:

Type of Review: Blind Review
No. of External Reviewers: 3
No. of In House Reviewers: 2
Acceptance Rate: 11-20%
Time to Review: 2 - 3 Months
Reviewers Comments: Yes
Invited Articles: 0-5%
Fees to Publish: 0.00 US$

MANUSCRIPT TOPICS:
Curriculum Studies; Teacher Education

MANUSCRIPT GUIDELINES/COMMENTS:

Journal website. **faculty.ed.uiuc.edu/westbury/JCS**

The *Journal of Curriculum Studies* publishes original refereed contributions to the theory and practice of, and policy making for, curriculum, teaching, and the assessment of schooling. The primary focus is on schools and the curriculum of teacher education, but papers in any area where the curriculum is researched and debated are welcome. *JCS* publishes papers reporting research studies, critical essays, case studies, essays reviews and book reviews.

Notes for Contributors
Please read these Guidelines with care. Authors are also advised to refer to the Author's Checklist (see **http://www.ed.uiuc.edu/jcs**) as they complete a final review of their papers prior to submission. Failure to follow the instructions in this style sheet and in the checklist

may result in your paper being delayed in production. Note especially the referencing conventions used by *JCS* and the requirement for gender-, race-, and creed-inclusive language.

JCS considers all manuscripts on condition they are the property (copyright) of the submitting author(s) and that copyright will be transferred to the *Journal of Curriculum Studies* and the publishers, Taylor & Francis Ltd., if the paper is accepted. *JCS* considers all manuscripts on the strict condition that they have been submitted only to *JCS* that they have not been published already, nor are they under consideration for publication, nor in press elsewhere. Authors who fail to adhere to this condition will be charged all costs which the journal incurs, and their papers will not be published.

- For all manuscripts, gender-, race-, and creed-inclusive language is mandatory. Abstracts are required for all papers submitted and should precede the text of a paper. Length should be approximately 150 words.
- Authors should include a biographical note of approximately 50 words.
- Manuscripts should be printed single-sided on A4 or 8 x 11 inch white, good quality paper, double-spaced throughout, including the reference section. Six copies of the manuscript should be submitted.
- Accepted manuscripts in their final, revised versions, should also be submitted on disk; see 'Disk submission' below.
- Authors should include telephone and fax numbers as well as e-mail addresses on the cover page of manuscripts.

In preparing your paper, you are encouraged to review papers in the area you are addressing which have been previously published in *JCS*, and where you feel appropriate, to reference them. This will enhance context, coherence, and continuity for our readers. For listing of papers published in *JCS* since 1968, see the catalogue of papers (please see the website at http://www.ed.uiuc.edu/jcs).

Abstracts

Abstracts are required for all papers, and should follow the title and author's name and address, preceding the main text. Abstracts should **not** include references. Abstracts should be approximately 150 words.

Copyright Permission

Contributors are required to secure permission for the reproduction of any figure, table, or extensive (more than fifty words) extract from the text, from a source which is copyrighted---or owned---by a party other than Taylor & Francis or the contributor. This applies both to direct reproduction or 'derivative reproduction'---when the contributor has created a new figure or table which derives substantially from a copyrighted source.

The following form of words can be used in seeking permission.

Dear

I/we are preparing an academic work entitled *(Title, Author)* which will be published in *(Journal Name)* by Taylor and Francis Ltd.

I/we would like to ask your permission to enclose the work listed below. I/we request non-exclusive world rights in English for the following material, which may be published in print, electronic, or digital forms.

I/we hope that you will be able to grant us permission to use this material for which full acknowledgement will be made. If you do not control these rights, please let me know to whom I/we should apply.

I/we appreciate your co-operation in making this material available and would ask you kindly to return this complete form duly signed.

Yours faithfully,

Permissions Request

<Article Title and Author's Name>

<Paper, Figure, Photo, Table, you wish to reproduce>

I grant permission for the use of the work listed above for non-exclusive world rights in English, which may be published in print, electronic, or digital forms:

Signed: ....

Please print name: ....

Position: ....

Organization: ....

Notes on Style

All authors are asked to take account of the diverse audience of the *JCS*. Clearly explain or avoid the use of terms that might be meaningful only to a local or national audience. However, note also that *JCS* does not aspire to be international in the ways that McDonald's restaurants or Hilton Hotels are 'international'; we much prefer papers that, where appropriate, reflect the particularities of each country's education system.

Some specific points of style for the text of papers, research reports, case studies, reports, essay reviews, and reviews follow.
*   *JCS* prefers US to 'American', USA to 'United States', and UK to 'United Kingdom'.

- *JCS* uses conservative British, not US, spelling, i.e. colour, not color; behaviour (behavioural), not behavior, [school] programme, not program; [she] practises, not practices; centre, not center; organization, not organisation; but analyse, not analyze; etc.
- Single 'quotes' are used for quotations rather than double "quotes", unless the 'quote is "within" another quote'.
- Punctuation should follow the British style, e.g. 'quotes precede punctuation'.
- Punctuation of common abbreviations should follow the following conventions: e.g. i.e. cf. etc. Note that such abbreviations are **not** followed by a comma or a (double) point/period.
- Dashes in the text of manuscripts should be clearly indicated by way of either a closed M-dash dash or a triple hyphen (---), e.g. 'I tried to help Anita identify a topic---within the area'. Page and number ranges should be separated by a closed N-dash or a double hyphen, e.g. 345--356.
- *JCS* avoids the use of the upper case in headings and references, i.e. only the first word in paper titles and of all subheads are in upper case. Titles of papers from journals in the references and other places are not in upper case.
- Apostrophes should be used sparingly. Thus, decades should be referred to as follows: 'The 1980s [not the 1980's] saw . . .'. Possessives associated with acronyms (e.g. APU), should be written as follows: 'The APU's findings that . . .', but, NB, the plural is APUs.
- All acronyms for national agencies, examinations, etc., should be spelled out that first time they are introduced in text or references. Thereafter the acronym can be used if appropriate, e.g. 'The work of the Assessment of Performance Unit (APU) in the early 1980s . . .'. Subsequently, 'The APU studies of achievement . . .', (Department of Education and Science [DES] 1989a).
- Brief biographical details of significant national figures should be outlined in the text unless it is quite clear that the person concerned would be known internationally. Some suggested editorial emendations to a typical text are indicated in the following with square brackets:
    From the time of H. E. Armstrong [in the 19th century] to the curriculum development work associated with the Nuffield Foundation [in the 1960s], there has been a shift from heurism to constructivism in the design of [British] science courses.
- The preferred local (national) usage for ethnic and other minorities should he used in all papers. For the USA, African-American, Hispanic, and Native American are used., e.g. 'The African-American presidential candidate, Jesse Jackson . . .' For the UK, African-Caribbean (not 'West Indian'), for Canada, First Nations, etc.
- Material to be emphasized (italicized in the printed version) should be <u>underlined</u> in the typescript rather than italicized. Please use such emphasis sparingly.
- <u>n</u> (not <u>N</u>) should be used.
- Numbers in text should take the following forms: 300, 3000, 30 000. Spell out numbers under 10 unless used with a unit of measure, e.g. nine pupils but 9 mm. For decimals, use the form 0.05 (not .05).
- When using a word which is or is asserted to be a propriety term or trade mark authors must use the symbols ™ or ®.

575

Citations in Text
References should be cited using the author/date system and sequenced by date of publication of the cited work. Where a paper being cited is authored by three or more authors, the first author's name only should be specified followed by et al. All references should be referenced alphabetically at the end of the paper. 'Ibid.' (and the like) are **not** used when repeating citations.

Notes in Text
Notes to text should be included in a separate section of endnotes to the text of a manuscript preceding the reference listing. References for notes in text should be numbered sequentially. Do **not** use footnotes. **Do not use the note facility of a word-processing program to prepare the endnotes.**

Tables and Figures
Artwork submitted for publication will not be returned and will be destroyed after publication, unless you request otherwise. While every care is taken of artwork, neither the Editor nor Taylor & Francis Ltd. shall bear any responsibility or liability for non-return, loss, or damage of artwork, nor for any associated costs or compensation. You are strongly advised to insure appropriately.
1. Tables and figures should be referred to in text as follows: figure 17, table 1, i.e. lower case. 'As seen in table [or figure] 1 . . .' (not Tab., Table, fig., or Fig. or Figure).
2. The place at which a table or figure is to be inserted in the printed text should be indicated clearly on a manuscript: Insert table 2 about here
3. Each table and/or figure must have a title that explains its purpose without reference to the text.
4. All figures and tables must be on separate sheets and not embedded in the text.
5. Notes to a table should be included after the table, preceded by the heading Note or Notes. Do not incorporate notes to tables in the Notes section of the manuscript.

Tables and figures must be referred to in the text and numbered in order of appearance. Each table should have a descriptive title and each column in a table should have an appropriate heading.

For all figures, original copies should be supplied. All figures should allow for reduction to column width 12.5 cm. Photographs may be sent as glossy prints or negatives.

The legends to any illustrations must be typed separately following the text and should be grouped together.

Author's Bionote
This note should be brief (two or three sentences) and include the author's institutional position and affiliation and a full address for correspondence. For example:
Sirkka Ahonen is a senior lecturer in social studies education in the Department of Teacher Education, PB 38, 00014 University of Helsinki, Finland (e-mail: sirkka.ahonen@helsinki.fi). Her research has focused on post-communist history curricula in eastern Europe and the formation of historical identity among young adults in Finland.

576

Her ongoing research deals with the role of schooling in the making of a civic society in northern Europe.

Acknowledgements
Any acknowledgements authors wish to make should be included in a separate headed section at the end of the manuscript. Please do not incorporate these into the bionote or notes and do not include titles, e.g. Professor, Dr. Ms. etc., with names.

Essay reviews
References to the book being reviewed are included in a footnote at the bottom of the first page of the essay review using the following conventions, i.e. for an essay review entitled 'Power and Criticism: Poststructural Investigations in Education', the footnote should read:

The book reviewed here is Cleo H. Cherryholmes, <u>Power and Criticism: Poststructural Investigations in Education,</u> 2nd edn. (Teachers College Press, New York, 1989), 158 pp., $22.95 (hbk), ISBN 0-8077-2927-2.

A bionote on the reviewer(s) follows using the format outlined above.

References
JCS uses the following conventions for references. Note that references to multi-authored books and papers should be fully spelled out in the reference, i.e. <u>et al</u>. should not be used. The '&' should not be used except for publisher's names. Initials only, not given names, are used in references.

Book
Hare, W. (1993) <u>What Makes a Good Teacher: Reflections on Some Characteristics Central to the Educational Enterprise</u> (London, ON: The Althouse Press).

Ellerton, N. F. and Clements, M. A. (1994) <u>The National Curriculum Debacle</u> (West Perth, Australia: Meridian Press).

Jackson, P. W. (ed.), <u>Handbook of Research on Curriculum</u> (New York: Macmillan).
Dewey, J. (1956 [1902]) <u>The Child and the Curriculum</u> (Chicago: University of Chicago Press).

Note the following expansions of the above convention:

Foucault, M. (1992) <u>Nonsense,</u> trans W. Smith (London: Falmer).
Foucault, M. (1992) <u>Nonsense,</u> ed. W. Smith
Foucault, M. (1992) <u>Nonsense,</u> 3rd edn
Foucault, M. (1992) <u>Nonsense,</u> 3rd revised edn
Foucault, M. (1992) <u>Nonsense,</u> revised
Foucault, M. (1992) <u>Nonsense,</u> 3rd edn, ed. W. Smith
Foucault, M. (1992) <u>Nonsense,</u> 3rd edn, trans. W. Smith
Foucault, M. (1992) <u>Nonsense,</u> ed. and trans. W. Smith

Chapter in a book
Schrag, F. (1996) Conceptions of knowledge. In P. W. Jackson (ed.), <u>Handbook of Research on Curriculum</u> (New York: Macmillan), 268--300.

Stodolsky, S. (1989) Is teaching really by the book? In P. W. Jackson and S. Haroutunian-Gordon (eds), <u>From Socrates to Software: The Teacher as Text and the Text of the Teacher</u> 89th Yearbook, Part 1, of the National Society for the Study of Education (Chicago: NSSE), 159--184.

References to chapters in edited books **must** include the page references for any chapter being cited. Such references should include the full page span (e.g. 212--252, NOT 212--52). Note that a single editor is indicated by (ed.) --- with a point/period--- and multiple editors by (eds) ---without a point/period.

Paper in a journal
Hansén, S.-E. (1998) Preparing teachers for curriculum-making. <u>Journal of Curriculum Studies,</u> 30 (2), 165--179.

Technical reports and unpublished papers
Burnham, C. A. and Anderson, T. H. (1991) Learning to sew on a button by reading a procedural text. CSR Technical Report No. 543, Center for the Study of Reading, University of Illinois at Urbana-Champaign. ERIC ED 332 157.

Clark, C. M. and Lampert, M. (1985) What knowledge is of most worth to teachers? Insights from studies of teacher thinking. Paper presented at the annual meeting of the American Educational Research Association (East Lansing, MI: College of Education, Michigan State University). ERIC ED 266 109.

Wherever possible ERIC references should be included in all unpublished material, e.g. ERIC ED 332 157. The availability of ERIC numbers enormously simplifies the work of those who want to follow-up a reference.

Dissertations and theses
Gravemeijer, K. P. E. (1994) Developing Realistic Mathematics Education. Doctoral dissertation, Utrecht University, The Netherlands.

An electronic journal
Seidman, R. H. (1996) National Education 'Goals 2000': some disastrous unintended consequences. <u>Educational Policy Analysis Archives,</u> 4 (11). http://olam.ed.asu.edu/epaa/v4n11/ [visited March 12, 2000].

A newspaper or magazine
Richards, H. (1996) Republican lite? <u>Times Higher Education Supplement,</u> 1 November, 16.

Reference to an Internet source
Give the URL in full (including the date of the visit to the site):
http://acsinfo.acs.org/instruct/instruct. html [visited February 5, 2000].

Reference to a personal communication
Brannen, J. (1996) Personal communication.

Reference to a case in law
In text, underline names of plaintiffs and defendants: e.g. <u>Miranda</u> v <u>Arizona</u> 1974

Disk Submission
JCS strongly requires submission of the **final**, revised version of a paper in both paper and disk forms. This Guide sets out the procedures which will assure we can process your paper efficiently.

- These guides do not apply to authors who are submitting a paper for consideration and peer review; they apply **only** to authors whose papers have been reviewed, revised, and accepted for publication;
- Print out a hard (paper) copy from the disk you are sending; it is essential that the hard-copy printout is identical to the material on the disk; where versions differ, the hard copy will take precedence. We advise you to maintain back-ups of your files;
- Save and send files on a standard 3.5 inch high density disk (MAC or PC);
- When saving the paper onto a disk, please make sure that the files do not exceed a manageable size. Please save figures on a separate disk;
- Ensure that the files are not saved as read-only;
- Virus-check your disk before sending it to the Editor;
- Label your disk;
- Package disks in such a way as to avoid damage in the mail;
- Disks are not returnable after publication.

For the main text of a paper, most standard PC or MAC word-processing software packages are acceptable, although we prefer Microsoft Word in a PC or MAC format. Please save files in **both** RTF and WORD format.

Word-processed files should be prepared according to the journal style. **Do not use embedded footnotes.** For numbered tables, use the table function provided with the word-processing package All text should be saved in one file with the complete text (including the title page, abstract, all sections of the body of the paper, references), followed by numbered tables and the figure captions.

Disks should be clearly labeled with the following information:
Journal title, Name of author, File names contained on disk, Hardware used (PC or MAC), Software used (name and version).

Manuscripts for publication should be sent to the appropriate regional editor as follows:

Asia/Pacific Margery D. Osborne, Centre for Research in Pedagogy and Practice, National Institute of Education, Nanyang Technological Univversity, 1 Nanyang Walk, Blk 2, Level 2, Singapore 637616.

Canada Geoffrey Milburn, Faculty of Education, University of Western Ontario, 1137 Western Rd, London, Ontario N6G 1G7, Canada.

Europe Andrew Stables, Department of Education, University of Bath, Bath BA2 7AY, England, UK.

United States Robert Boostrom, Department of Teacher Education, University of Southern Indiana, 8600 University Blvd., Evansville, IN 47712, USA.

Authors from all other regions should submit manuscripts to: Ian Westbury, Department of Curriculum & Instruction, University of Illinois at Urbana-Champaign, 341 Armory, 505 E. Armory, Champaign, IL 61820, USA

Journal of Curriculum Theorizing

ADDRESS FOR SUBMISSION:

Marla Morris, Editor
Journal of Curriculum Theorizing
c/o Alan H. Jones
Caddo Gap Press
Publisher
3145 Geary Boulevard, PMB 275
San Francisco, CA 94118
USA
Phone: 912-790-8079
Fax:
E-Mail: mdoll4444@aol.com
Web:
Address May Change:

PUBLICATION GUIDELINES:

Manuscript Length: 21-25
Copies Required: Three
Computer Submission: No
Format: N/A
Fees to Review: 0.00 US$

Manuscript Style:
American Psychological Association, ,
Chicago Manual of Style

CIRCULATION DATA:

Reader: Academics
Frequency of Issue: Quarterly
Copies per Issue: Less than 1,000
Sponsor/Publisher: Academic Institutions,
    See Manuscript Guidelines
Subscribe Price:

REVIEW INFORMATION:

Type of Review: Blind Review
No. of External Reviewers: 2
No. of In House Reviewers: 1
Acceptance Rate: 21-30%
Time to Review: 2 - 3 Months
Reviewers Comments: Yes
Invited Articles: 0-5%
Fees to Publish: 0.00 US$

MANUSCRIPT TOPICS:

Art/Music; Curriculum Studies; English Literature; Higher Education; Languages & Linguistics; Reading; Religious Education; Rural Education & Small Schools; Science Math & Environment

MANUSCRIPT GUIDELINES/COMMENTS:

JCT: Journal of Curriculum Theorizing is an interdisciplinary journal of curriculum studies. It offers an academic forum for scholarly discussions of curriculum. Aligned with the "reconceptualist" movement in curriculum theorizing, and oriented toward informing and affecting classroom practice, *JCT* presents compelling pieces within forms that challenge disciplinary, genre, and textual boundaries.

Guidelines for Submitting Manuscripts

JCT: Journal of Curriculum Theorizing publishes original refereed articles on topics related to the study of curriculum. Specifically, *JCT* seeks contributions that challenge disciplinary, genre, and textual boundaries. Authors are therefore encouraged to submit papers that undertake scholarly, interdisciplinary discussions of curriculum within forms that are provocative. In addition, submissions are invited that are not limited to print media. A goal of the editors is to utilize emerging electronic technologies to present academic work in ways that complement conventional textual forms.

Manuscript Specifications
Allowing some latitude for experimental forms, to the extent possible, manuscripts submitted to *JCT* should conform to the guidelines specified in the most recent edition of the Chicago Manual of Style or the most recent edition of *The Publication Manual of the American Psychological Association*.

Manuscripts should be double spaced with 1-inch margins and numbered pages. Footnotes should be gathered together at the end of the paper. A 100-150 word abstract must be included as the first page of the manuscript. A submission must include: four copies of the manuscript which exclude all references to authorship, and one title page which includes the name(s) and institutional affiliation(s) of the author(s), and the address, telephone number, and e-mail address of the first author. Manuscripts (including notes and references) should not exceed 25 pages.

Manuscripts submitted for publication consideration to *JCT* should not be under review elsewhere.

Manuscripts submitted to *JCT* will undergo an initial internal review. Those judged suitable for publication will be externally reviewed. The editors rely heavily on the judgments of the reviewers, but are not bound by them. Manuscripts not accepted for publication will not be returned.

Manuscripts that do not conform to these specifications—or that are not accompanied by an explanatory note detailing why they do not conform—will not be considered for publication. Manuscripts accepted for publication are subject to non-substantive editing.

Section Guidelines and Editors' Addresses
Manuscripts should be submitted to the appropriate section editor. Please review the section descriptions below to determine where you would like your manuscript to receive an initial evaluation and consideration for external review.

Biblio-Revenance
Biblio-Revenance celebrates the "act of returning to a book" and embraces the bibliographic belief that Nothing Remains the Same (Lesser, 2002). The Biblio-Revenance section invites authors to return to previously published works and to reexamine ideas in relation to the passing of time and the "differing sense of self." As Wendy Lesser has noted, "you cannot reread a book from your youth without perceiving it as, among other things, a mirror. Wherever you look in that novel or poem or essay, you will find a little reflected face peering out at you—the face of your own youthful self, the original reader, the person you were when you first read the book" (2002, p. 4). During its introductory period, Biblio-Revenance will invite submissions. *Journal of Curriculum Theorizing* readers are encouraged to suggest

582

specific authors and publications for biblio-revenance. Send suggestions to Craig Kridel, Wardlaw Hall, University of South Carolina, Columbia, SC 29208.

Childhood and Cultural Studies

The Childhood and Cultural Studies section will focus on "childhood" as cultural construction, created through artistic and religious visions, historical accounts, cultural politics, the "science" of psychology, popular culture, economics, public policy, educational legislation, and court decisions, and the impact of these constructions on the lives and identities of those who are younger. Example topics include, but are not limited to: examination of the role of history, politics, philosophies of research, and context on beliefs about childhood; exploration of the concepts that have been linked to childhood in historical and contemporary global society(ies) that include care, schooling, language, culture, and life conditions (e.g. poverty, power); and the dichotomization of adult/child, and how problems such as violence and abuse are characterized to empower and disempower children. Mail manuscripts to Gaile Cannella, Department of Educational Psychology, College of Education, Texas A&M University, 704 Harrington Tower, College Station, TX; 77843-4225. Phone: 409-845-8050, **g-cannella@tamu.edu**

International Curriculum Discourses

The International Curriculum Discourses section is committed to developing international dialogue on curriculum issues. For example, 1. If the postcolonial critique of Western epistemology encourages ways of knowing that are more ecumenical (GK. oikoumenikos, "of the inhabited earth"), how can these be brought more clearly into the centre of curriculum of deliberation?; 2. If intellectual colonization continues, albeit in diffuse and hidden forms, how can we attempt to crucially interrogate the colonial present, so that we may move closer to a truly postcolonial state?; 3. Contemporary Euro-American power structures are attempting to make the entire enterprise of public education accountable to Market forces. What is the unique responsibility of Curriculum Theory in meeting the challenge of such pressure?; 3. What is the particular poverty of curriculum theorizing today, and what international/intercultural resources can be accessed to alleviate that poverty? This section invites papers on these or other themes that directly take up the task of broadening curriculum work in a "globalizing" world. Mail manuscripts to Yatta Kanu, Department of Curriculum, Humanities, and Social Sciences, Faculty of Education, University of Manitoba, Winnipeg, MB, Canada R3T 2N2, **kanuy@ms.umanitoba.ca**

Literacies

We interpret literacies broadly to include reading, writing, and interpreting texts in various forms: not only books, arts, and film, but also reading and writing the world and reading and writing oneself into the world. The following areas are of interest: *Literacy and the Self*—the relationship between reading texts in the context of lived experience, including psychic life: In what ways does reading poetry, fiction, drama provide a theoretical base for my work? What do I read *for*? What reading has changed my life? *Social and aesthetic literacies*—the construction, teaching, and development of literacy in the schools; student literacy; literacy and the standards movement. *Modes of expressing literacy*—creative work, including fiction and poetry and nontraditional forms. Manuscripts for this section should not exceed fifteen pages. Mail manuscripts to Mary Aswell Doll, 527 East 56th Street, Savannah, GA 31405, **mdoll4444@aol.com**

[Popular] Culture Matters

This section of *JCT* is committed to celebrating without colonizing [popular] culture matters. Manuscripts should bring youth cultures, generational cultures, gothic cultures, cultures of information technology and technoscience, academic cultures, music, television, film and other media into the discourses of curriculum theorizing; likewise, manuscripts should bring curriculum theorizing and educational practice to cultural studies movements, web-cultures, hypermedia analysis, alternative re-presentations, and alternative mass media. Advertising and other mind-altering experiences, vampires, school practices as commodities and cultural resources, digital entertainment industries, extreme sports, and their implications for new postmodern identities and curriculum work are particularly encouraged. The primary perspective of this section asks manuscripts to challenge the presumptions that telescope culture into "popular" or "consumer culture"—and to challenge the boundaries of traditional curriculum studies that fear the relevance of cultural studies movements for educational practice—by declaring that [popular] culture does matter. Mail manuscripts to Peter Appelbaum, Toby Daspit, & John Weaver, c/o Peter Appelbaum, Department of Education, Arcadia University, 450 S. Easton Rd., Glenside, PA 19038-3295 USA, **appelbaum@arcadia.edu**

Reading Between the Lines: Perspectives on Contemporary Cultural Texts

This section solicits manuscripts that explore perspectives on contemporary cultural texts. This may include any artifact or event—including books, movies, art installations, television shows, theater productions, performance art, arts-based research, computer software, home pages, and so on—that, in some manner, relates to *JCT*'s focuses on curriculum theory and classroom practice. Mail manuscripts to Denise Taliaferro, Education Department, Colgate University, 13 Oak Drive, Hamilton, NY 13346. 315-228-7291, Email: **dtaliaferro@mail.colgate.edu**

Post-structural Lines of Flight

This section provides a space for work in post-structural theorizing. Manuscripts are sought that challenge and question not only the central themes, organizing metaphors, and discursive strategies constituting Western [educational curriculum] thought and informing the Enlightenment project, but all that is modernism itself, including those perspectives and cultural structures associated with moderism. Work, as well, that is multidisciplinary, that deconstructs the bifurcations, strict disciplinarity, and entrenchment of much educational/curriculum research from various poststructural perspectives is sought. Send manuscripts to William M. Reynolds, Department of Curriculum, Foundations, and Research, Post Office Box 8144, Georgia Southern University, Statesboro, Georgia 30460-8144. Email **wrey@gasou.edu**.

Studies in Philosophy, Ethics, and Education

How does the engagement of philosophy and education within the field of social and cultural practices redefine the ethical bounds of pedagogy? How does this foregrounding of the relationship between philosophy, ethics, and education affect our responsibility to re-think and revolutionize what it means to teach, to learn, to know? Studies in Philosophy, Ethics, and Education focuses on and probes the articulation of the tensions among the discursive spaces and the real-world dimensions of an interdisciplinary nexus of theory and practice that informs and manifests the pedagogical application of ideas. Any critical engagement and identification

584

with a philosophical or theoretical position and its performative direction (e.g., a theorem, a system, a methodology, a "proof," an ideology, an argument) implies the pragmatic outworking of an academic responsibility we have to uphold an obligation owed to the search for truth at all costs. This is what *makes* theory practice and provides a justifying principle, a principle of reason for what we think, do, and write. Studies in Philosophy, Ethics, and Education converges upon specific interpretations of the obligation we have to respond responsibly to the alterity of those we teach, research, and write for beyond ourselves. It seeks to present texts that challenge us to reflect upon and to re-examine the ethics and logic of the boundaries of "thought" and "action," "theory" and "practice," and what comprises and displaces the opposition of these two entities in the name of pedagogy. The point of this section is to highlight work that complicates and radicalizes the normative limits of academic responsibility and its ethics in the hopes of making the relation between the philosophical and the pedagogical more responsive to the difference of another. Studies in Philosophy, Ethics, and Education makes the assumption that there is value to opening the empirico-conceptual and epistemic limits of one's work and oneself to the risk of less than canonical modes of thinking. It therefore solicits texts from theorists and educators whose practice has and is struggling to re-think the ethics and politics of dominant modes of knowledge and the pedagogical forms of expression that have operated within the institutional purview of a traditional system of education. One of its aims is to relocate the epistemic and performative parameters of the scene of teaching beyond a normative axis of response and responsibility. Studies in Philosophy, Ethics, and Education challenges the form and content of seemingly benign dimensions of what has been protected under the aegis of an existing codification of social infrastructures and their prevailing cultural conditions as the "knowledge worth knowing." Mail manuscripts to Peter Pericles Trifonas, Center for Social Justice and Cultural Studies in Education, Department of Curriculum, Teaching, and Learning, Ontario Institute for Studies in Education/University of Toronto, 252 Bloor Street West, Toronto, Ontario M5S 1V6, Canada. (416) 923-6641 ext. 2760, **ptrifonas@oise.utoronto.ca**.

Feature Articles and Artwork
Manuscripts that do not conform to the specifications of one of the sections above should be submitted to the *JCT* Editorial Office for consideration as a feature article. Be sure to follow all manuscript submission guidelines when submitting feature articles as well as special section articles to *JCT*. All manuscripts for feature articles, submissions of art work for the cover and other pages of the journal, and all general correspondence should be directed to:

Marla Morris, JCT Editor
Department of Curriculum, Foundations, and Research
Georgia Southern University
Post Office Box 8144, Statesboro, GA 30460-8144
E-mail: **mdoll4444@aol.com**

See the *Journal of Curriculum Theorizing* website at: **http://orgs.bloomu.edu/jct/**

Journal of Distance Learning (The)

ADDRESS FOR SUBMISSION:

Mary Simpson, Bill Anderson, Co-Editors
Journal of Distance Learning (The)
Massey University
College of Education
Private Bag 11 222
Palmerston North,
New Zealand
Phone: +64 6 356 9099 x 8839 or 8871
Fax: +64 6 351 3385
E-Mail: journaleditor2@deanz.org.nz
Web: www.deanz.org.nz
Address May Change:

CIRCULATION DATA:

Reader: Practicing Teachers, Academics,
    Administrators
Frequency of Issue: 2 Times/Year
Copies per Issue: Less than 1,000
Sponsor/Publisher: The Distance Education
    Association of New Zealand
Subscribe Price: 25.00 US$ Individual

PUBLICATION GUIDELINES:

Manuscript Length: 16-20
Copies Required:
Computer Submission: Yes Disk, Email
Format: MS Word or RTF (rich text format
Fees to Review: 0.00 US$

Manuscript Style:
    American Psychological Association

REVIEW INFORMATION:

Type of Review: Blind Review
No. of External Reviewers: 2
No. of In House Reviewers: 1
Acceptance Rate: 21-30%
Time to Review: 1 - 2 Months
Reviewers Comments: Yes
Invited Articles: 11-20%
Fees to Publish: 0.00 US$

MANUSCRIPT TOPICS:
Distance Education; Educational Technology Systems; E-Learning

MANUSCRIPT GUIDELINES/COMMENTS:

First published in 1995, *The Journal of Distance Learning* will appeal to readers with interests in:
- on-line or distance education
- e-learning
- flexible delivery systems
- application of technology in distance and open learning to education
- innovative teaching methods
- open learning
- developments in the Pacific.

The readership of the journal comes from both the private and public educational and training sectors. Readers include academics engaged in the study of distance education; distance education practitioners (teachers, administrators and policy makers); and, those with an interest in the use of learning technologies in education.

Annual Publication

The Journal of Distance Learning is a refereed journal published annually by DEANZ. It publishes both theoretical and empirically based research articles, research notes, reports and case studies of practice, and reviews by or of interest to those involved in distance education and open learning, which meet the journal's requirements and standards.

Advice to Contributors

Manuscripts should be sent to Dr Mary Simpson, Editor address above.

Submission using electronic mail is strongly encouraged. Articles submitted via e-mail should be sent as attachments in Microsoft Word or Rich Text Format. If submitting by post, authors should send a PC-readable floppy disk or CD containing their article in Microsoft Word or Rich Text Format. Once an article has been accepted for publication, the final version should be submitted electronically to the editors in a format agreed on with them. The language of publication is English.

Length. 3000-6000 words for an article, up to 4000 words for a research note or report, up to 1000 words for a book review.

Abstract. Each article should be summarised in an abstract of up to 100 words.

Author. Each author should provide their full name, title and affiliation, full details of postal address, telephone number, facsimile number and email address. Authors should also include brief biographical details for each named author (no more than 50 words per author).

Format and references. The format and references should follow the published guidelines of the *American Psychological Association* (5th Edition). Footnotes should be employed only when necessary. Tables and figures should be designed to fit into one column (70 mm) or two (145 mm).

Submission of a paper to *The Journal of Distance Learning* will be taken to imply that it represents original work not previously published, that is not being considered for publication elsewhere, and that the contributor has all obtained all necessary permission and paid any fees for the use of copyright materials. Contributors therefore undertake to indemnify the Distance Education Association of New Zealand for any loss occasioned in consequences of any breach of copyright. The Association is not responsible for opinions or statements of authors in this journal.

Contributors of articles accepted for publication will receive one free copy of the issue of *The Journal of Distance Learning* in which their paper is published.

Journal of Documentation

ADDRESS FOR SUBMISSION:

David Bawden, Editor
Journal of Documentation
Emerald Group Publishing Limited
60/62 Toller Lane
Bradford, BD8 9BY
UK
Phone: +44 (0) 1274 777700
Fax: +44 (0) 1274 785200
E-Mail: jdoc@emeraldinsight.com
Web: www.emeraldinsight.com/jd.htm
Address May Change:

CIRCULATION DATA:

Reader: Academics
Frequency of Issue: 6 Times/Year
Copies per Issue:
Sponsor/Publisher: Emerald Group
  Publishing Limited
Subscribe Price: 709.00 US$
  469.00 Pounds

PUBLICATION GUIDELINES:

Manuscript Length: Varies
Copies Required: One
Computer Submission: Yes preferred
Format: N/A
Fees to Review: 0.00 US$

Manuscript Style:
  See Manuscript Guidelines, at
  www.emeraldinsight.com/jd.htm

REVIEW INFORMATION:

Type of Review: Blind Review
No. of External Reviewers: 2
No. of In House Reviewers: 1
Acceptance Rate: No Reply
Time to Review: 2 Months
Reviewers Comments: Yes
Invited Articles:
Fees to Publish: 0.00 US$

MANUSCRIPT TOPICS:
Adult Career & Vocational; Documentation; Information Science; Library
Science/Information Resources

MANUSCRIPT GUIDELINES/COMMENTS:

Copyright
Articles submitted to the journal should be original contributions and should not be under
consideration for any other publication at the same time. Authors submitting articles for
publication warrant that the work is not an infringement of any existing **copyright** and will
indemnify the publisher against any breach of such warranty. For ease of dissemination and to
ensure proper policing of use, papers and contributions become the legal copyright of the
publisher unless otherwise agreed. Submissions should be sent **preferably by e-mail** to: E-
mail: **jdoc@emeraldinsight.com**. **Postal address**. Journal of Documentation, Emerald Group
Publishing Limited, 60/62 Toller Lane, Bradford, BD8 9BY, United Kingdom

Aims
The aim of the *Journal of Documentation* is to provide a forum for the dissemination of
scholarly articles, research reports and critical reviews in the information sciences. In doing

so, it provides a link between research and scholarship and reflective professional practice, so that both are informed and enhanced.

Perspective
The *Journal of Documentation* has the unique perspective of focusing on theories, concepts, models, frameworks, and philosophies in the information sciences. The *Journal* also publishes articles on the methodology of research, and the results of research projects, as well as on reflections on practice, historical articles, and items on education and training for information use. Critical reviews of the literature in subject areas of interest, and reviews of the evidence-base for professional practice, are welcome, as are articles dealing with analogies and comparisons between concepts of information and knowledge in different domains, for example between human information and information physics.

Scope
The scope of the *Journal of Documentation* is broadly 'information studies', encompassing all of the academic and professional disciplines which deal with recorded information. These include, but are certainly not limited to:
- information science and librarianship
- information and knowledge management, and information retrieval
- records management and archiving
- national and international information policy
- human information behaviour and the sociology of information
- information and digital literacies

The *Journal* is inclusive in its scope, and welcomes contributions from any subject area where the focus is on the concepts and frameworks for understanding, and helping to manage, knowledge and information.

Readership
The primary readership is:
- educators, researchers and advanced students in the information sciences
- reflective practitioners in the information professions
- policy makers and funders in information-related areas
- The Journal's content will also be of value to scholars and students in many related subject areas.

The Journal offers authors
- a high impact and very well-known and respected platform
- rigorous, but constructive, review and criticism by international experts
- effective dissemination and publicity
- support for self-archiving
- support for authors through Emerald's Literati Club

The reviewing process
All articles are subject to rigorous double blind peer review.

Manuscript requirements

The manuscript should be submitted as a Word or rtf document, formatted with double line spacing with wide margins. All authors should be shown and author's details must be printed on a separate sheet and the author should not be identified anywhere else in the article.

As a guide, articles should be between 3,000 and 10,000 words in length. A title of not more than eight words should be provided. A brief **autobiographical note** should be supplied including full name, affiliation, e-mail address and full international contact details. Authors must supply a structured abstract set out under 4-6 sub-headings: Purpose; Methodology/Approach; Findings; Research limitations/implications (if applicable); Practical implications (if applicable); and, the Originality/value of paper. Maximum is 250 words in total. In addition provide up to six keywords which encapsulate the principal topics of the paper and categorise your paper under one of these classifications: Research paper, Viewpoint, Technical paper, Conceptual paper, Case study, Literature review or General review. For more information and guidance on structured abstracts visit:

http://www.emeraldinsight.com/literaticlub/editors/editorialadmin/abstracts.htm

Where there is a **methodology**, it should be clearly described under a separate heading. **Headings** must be short, clearly defined and not numbered. **Notes** or **Endnotes** should be used only if absolutely necessary and must be identified in the text by consecutive numbers, enclosed in square brackets and listed at the end of the article.

Figures, charts and **diagrams** should be kept to a minimum. They should be provided both electronically and as good quality originals. They must be black and white with minimum shading and numbered consecutively using Arabic numerals.

Artwork should be either copied and pasted from the origination software into a blank Microsoft Word document, or saved and imported into a blank Microsoft Word document. Artwork created in MS PowerPoint is also acceptable. Artwork may be submitted in the following standard image formats: .eps - Postscript, .pdf - Adobe Acrobat portable document, .ai - Adobe Illustrator, .wmf - Windows Metafile. If it is not possible to supply graphics in the formats listed above, authors should ensure that figures supplied as .tif, .gif, .jpeg, .bmp, .pcx, .pic, .pct are supplied as files of at least 300dpi and at least 10cm wide.

In the text, the position of a figure should be shown by typing on a separate line the words "take in Figure 2". Supply succinct captions. For photographic images good quality original photographs should be submitted. If submitted electronically they should be saved as tif files of at least 300dpi, and at least 10cm wide. Their position in the text should be shown by typing on a separate line the words "take in Plate 2".

Tables should be kept to a minimum. They must be numbered consecutively with roman numerals and a brief title. In the text, the position of the table should be shown by typing on a separate line the words "take in Table IV".

References to other publications must be in Harvard style. That is, shown within the text as the first author's name followed by a comma and year of publication all in round brackets, e.g.

590

(Fox, 1994). At the end of the article a reference list in alphabetical order must be given as follows:

- *For books:* surname, initials, (year) *title*, publisher, place of publication, e.g. Casson, M. (1979), *Alternatives to the Multinational Enterprise*, Macmillan, London.
- *For journals:* surname, initials, (year) "title", journal, volume, number, pages, e.g. Fox, S. (1994), "Empowerment as a catalyst for change: an example from the food industry", *Supply Chain Management*, Vol. 2 No. 3, pp. 29-33.

Final submission of the article
Once accepted for publication, the final version of the manuscript must be provided, accompanied by a 3.5" disk, Zip disk or CD-ROM of the same version labelled with: disk format (Macintosh or PC); author name(s); title of article; journal title; file name.

Alternatively, the editor may request the final version as an attached file to an e-mail.

Each article must be accompanied by a completed and signed Journal Article Record Form available from the Editor or on **http://www.emeraldinsight.com/literaticlub**.

The manuscript will be considered to be the definitive version of the article. The author must ensure that it is complete, grammatically correct and without spelling or typographical errors.

In preparing the disk, please use one of the following preferred formats: Word, Word Perfect, Rich text format or TeX/LaTeX. Technical assistance is available from Emerald's Literati Club on http://www.emeraldinsight.com/literaticlub or by contacting Mike Massey at Emerald, e-mail **mmassey@emeraldinsight.com**.

Final submission requirements
Manuscripts must:
- be clean, good quality hard copy
- include an abstract and keywords
- have Harvard style references
- include any figures, photos and graphics electronically and as good quality originals
- be accompanied by a labelled disk
- be accompanied by a completed Journal Article Record Form

Journal of Drug Education

ADDRESS FOR SUBMISSION:

James Robinson III, Editor
Journal of Drug Education
Texas A & M Health Science Center
School of Rural Public Health
1103 University Drive, 200
College Station, TX 77840
USA
Phone: 979-862-1700
Fax: 979-458-4422
E-Mail: jrobinson@srph.tamuhsc.edu
Web: http://srph.tamushsc.edu/jde
Address May Change:

PUBLICATION GUIDELINES:

Manuscript Length: 11-15
Copies Required: Three
Computer Submission: Yes Disk, Email
Format: MS Word / English only
Fees to Review: 0.00 US$

Manuscript Style:
 American Psychological Association

CIRCULATION DATA:

Reader: Counselors, ATOD Prevention
Frequency of Issue: Quarterly
Copies per Issue: 5,001 - 10,000
Sponsor/Publisher: Baywood Publishing
Subscribe Price: 237.00 US$

REVIEW INFORMATION:

Type of Review: Blind Review
No. of External Reviewers: 2
No. of In House Reviewers: 1
Acceptance Rate: 40%
Time to Review: 2 - 3 Months
Reviewers Comments: Yes
Invited Articles: 6-10%
Fees to Publish: 0.00 US$

MANUSCRIPT TOPICS:

Adult Career & Vocational; Alcohol & Drugs, Behavior, and Prevention; Counseling & Personnel Services; Curriculum Studies; Drug Research; Educational Psychology; Teacher Education

MANUSCRIPT GUIDELINES/COMMENTS:

Manuscripts are to be submitted in triplicate (1 original, and 2 copies) to the Executive Editor along with a disk copy. E-mail electronic submissions are also acceptable. Retain one copy, as manuscript will not be returned. Manuscript must be typewritten on 8 1/2" X 11" white paper, one side only, double-spaced, with wide margins. Paginate consecutively starting with the title page. An abstract of 100 to 125 words is required. The organization of the paper should be clearly indicated by appropriate headings and subheadings (note the use of such headings throughout this manual).

Manuscripts

The receipt of all manuscript will be acknowledged by return mail. Authors should note that only original articles are accepted for publication. Submission of a manuscript represents

592

certification on the part of the author(s)'that neither the article submitted nor a version of it has been published or is being considered for publication elsewhere.

Copyright Agreement
The author's Warranty and Transfer of Copyright Agreement must be signed and received before an article is refereed and composition begins. Current laws state that publishers must receive signed agreements for all manuscripts, in order to protect the copyright.

The publisher grants permission to the author/s to use their articles in whole, or part, without further consent of the publisher. In reuse, state journal name, volume, issue and date of original appearance. The use of this copy written material, by other than the author, is prohibited without expressed written permission of the publisher.

Title Page and Affiliation
The title page should include the complete title of the article, the author's name(s), the academic or professional affiliation(s), and complete address(es). If the title contains fifty or more characters submit a shortened version to be used in the running head. When a source footnote is used for the article, indicate it by an asterisk placed after the title and type the footnote at the bottom of the title page. The complete name and address, including zip code, of the person to whom proofs and reprint requests are to be sent should be shown on the title page.

References
The journal follows the style of the *American Psychological Association* (6th ed.)

Footnotes
Footnotes are notes placed at the foot of the page where cited. They give information or commentary which, though related to the subject discussed, would interrupt the flow of the narrative or argument; or give additional evidence or illustration in support. Footnotes should be numbered red with superior Arabic numbers without parentheses or brackets. Table footnotes are indicated by lower case letters. Footnotes should be brief with an average length of three lines.

Display Material
Figures. All line figures submitted must be original drawings in black ink on a good quality paper done to professional standards. Two-color work will not be accepted. Photographs should be glossy prints with high contrast. Plan all figures to be proportionate to the 4 ½ " x 7 ½ final size image area. Figures larger than final size must remain easily readable with points and lines clearly distinguishable after reduction; 8 point is the standard callouts (labeling) size. All figures must be referenced in text and positioned as close to citation as possible. Identify all figures on front, outside image area, with author's name, article title, figure number, figure title, and figure top. If additional space is needed attach a paper to the bottom of the illustration. Please be accurate, as the position of this material will identify the correct reading position of the illustration. All figures appear in strict numerical sequence starting with Figure 1. Clearly indicate on manuscript page margin where each figure is to appear.

Tables. Tables must be cited in text in numerical sequence. Use Arabic numbers starting with Table 1. Place each table as close to citation as possible and indicate placement in margin on the manuscript. Keep in mind the 4 ½" x 7 ½," final size when planning tabular material. Tables larger than this size will have to be reduced and type must remain large enough to be easily read. Each table must have a descriptive title. Footnotes to tables are indicated by superior lower case letters. Each table will have one opening rule, a rule under column heads, and a closing rule. Avoid vertical ruling.

Scheduling. After editor's acceptance the manuscript is sent to the publisher for production editing and composition. On completion of these phases, proofs are sent to the editor and author for careful proofreading and checking. After author and editor review the proofs, corrections will be made as required, and the article is considered final.

It is mandatory that the author review proofs and mail them within 48 hours of receipt in order that the publisher may fulfill the rigorous scheduling requirements.

Authors may order reprints of their articles by completing the reprint order form enclosed with the proofs. All reprint orders must be prepaid.

Cabell's Directories
of Publishing Opportunities in Business

NINTH EDITION 2004-2005

Accounting
Economics & Finance
Management
Marketing

To order Hardcopy or On-line versions - visit
www.cabells.com